GLOSSAIRE DE DROIT ANGLAIS

MÉTHODE, TRADUCTION ET APPROCHE COMPARATIVE

MÉTHODES DU DROIT

Collection dirigée par Philippe Jestaz

GLOSSAIRE DE DROIT ANGLAIS

MÉTHODE, TRADUCTION ET APPROCHE COMPARATIVE

Sous la direction de

Géraldine Gadbin-George

Anne Brunon-Ernst
Armelle Sabatier
Suhasini Vincent
Justin Beplate

2014

DALLOZ

DALLOZ

31-35 rue Froidevaux, 75685 Paris cedex 14

ISBN : 978-2-247-13727-5
978-2-247-13857-9

Sommaire

English abbreviations XI

Abréviations françaises XV

Introduction 1

Biographies 5

PART 1
Presentation of the legal system of England and Wales

- ☐ 1 European union law in England and Wales 7
- ☐ 2 Presentation of the common law system 12
- ☐ 3 Court system 17
- ☐ 4 Legal professions 22
- ☐ 5 Academic background of the legal professions and organisation 24
- ☐ 6 Solicitors' and barristers' duties 29

PART 2
Non-contentious law

Chapitre 1. Contract law

- ☐ 7 Introduction 35
- ☐ 8 Agreements 38
- ☐ 9 Consideration and promissory estoppel 42
- ☐ 10 Intention and formalities of contract 45
- ☐ 11 Privity of contract, assignment and agency 48
- ☐ 12 Express and implied terms 51

Chapitre 2. Company law

- ☐ 13 Business structures 55
- ☐ 14 Capital 58
- ☐ 15 Pre-incorporation and incorporation 61
- ☐ 16 Directors, shareholders and members 64

Chapitre 3. Commercial law

☐ 17 Introduction 69
☐ 18 Commercial contracts 72
☐ 19 Agency 75
☐ 20 Sale and supply of goods and services 78
☐ 21 International shipping agreements 81
☐ 22 Bill of exchange 85
☐ 23 Other financial instruments 88
☐ 24 Commercial credit and security 90

Chapitre 4. Tax law

☐ 25 Individuals and employees 95
☐ 26 Companies, partnerships or self-employed people 98

Chapitre 5. Criminal law

☐ 27 Introduction 103
☐ 28 Offences against the person 106
☐ 29 Offences against property 109
☐ 30 Corporate crime 110
☐ 31 Military criminal law 112
☐ 32 The English police 114
☐ 33 Police powers 117
☐ 34 Investigating 121

Chapitre 6. Intellectual property law

☐ 35 Introduction 123
☐ 36 Copyright 126
☐ 37 Designs 130
☐ 38 Patents 133
☐ 39 Trademarks 136

Chapitre 7. Insurance law

☐ 40 Introduction 141
☐ 41 Insurance policies in general 143
☐ 42 Different types of insurance 146
☐ 43 Specific case : life and life-related insurance 148
☐ 44 Specific case : home insurance 150
☐ 45 Specific case : car insurance 153
☐ 46 Specific case : health or private medical insurance (PMI) 155

☐ 47 Specific case : industrial risks insurance 157
☐ 48 Specific case : contractors' all risks insurance and machinery breakdown insurance.................... 159

Chapitre **8.** Environmental law
☐ 49 Introduction.. 161
☐ 50 Environmental law sources.................................... 164
☐ 51 Environmental framework, standards and principles... 167
☐ 52 Sustainable development and green growth 172

Chapitre **9.** Employment law
☐ 53 Different types of status in the labour market 177
☐ 54 Contract of employment....................................... 180
☐ 55 Employer's rights and duties 184
☐ 56 Employees' rights and duties 187

Chapitre **10.** Human rights and immigration law
☐ 57 Human rights – general information...................... 191
☐ 58 Basic substantive rights... 194
☐ 59 Formal procedural rights....................................... 197
☐ 60 Human rights issues and debates 200
☐ 61 Immigration rights... 204

Chapitre **11.** Family law
☐ 62 Marriage and cohabitation.................................... 209
☐ 63 Children and parents... 212

Chapitre **12.** Probate/inheritance law
☐ 64 What is inheritance law ?...................................... 217
☐ 65 Administering an estate.. 220

Chapitre **13.** Property law
☐ 66 Introduction.. 223
☐ 67 Legal interests in land... 225
☐ 68 Equitable interests in land 228
☐ 69 Specific case of house conveyancing 230
☐ 70 Specific case : tenancy agreements 235
☐ 71 Landlord's and tenant's responsibilities 238
☐ 72 Termination of a tenancy agreement 240

PART 3
Litigation

Chapitre 1. Presentation of litigation

☐ 73 Civil litigation and scope 245
☐ 74 Alternatives to civil litigation 247
☐ 75 Various stages of civil litigation 251
☐ 76 Other form of litigation : judicial review 258

Chapitre 2. Contract law and litigation

☐ 77 Discharge of contract 263
☐ 78 Mistake 266
☐ 79 Misrepresentation 269
☐ 80 Duress and undue influence 271
☐ 81 Illegality and unfairness 274
☐ 82 Frustration 277
☐ 83 Termination for breach 280
☐ 84 Remedies 282

Chapitre 3. Tort litigation

☐ 85 Introduction 287
☐ 86 Negligence 289
☐ 87 Special cases of negligence 292
☐ 88 Defences 295
☐ 89 Defamation 298
☐ 90 Nuisance 300
☐ 91 Trespass 302
☐ 92 Statutory torts 305
☐ 93 Remedies 307

Chapitre 4. Insolvency procedures and company law remedies

☐ 94 Introduction 313
☐ 95 Bankruptcy and compulsory liquidation 316
☐ 96 Procedure and payment of creditors 319
☐ 97 Voluntary arrangement 321
☐ 98 Administration and administrative receivership 323
☐ 99 Voluntary procedures : specific case of voluntary bankruptcy and liquidation 324
☐ 100 Business structures & shareholder's remedies 327

Chapitre **5.** Tax litigation

☐ 101 General rules 329

Chapitre **6.** Criminal litigation

☐ 102 Introduction 333
☐ 103 Criminal jurisdiction and personnel 335
☐ 104 Parties to the trial 339
☐ 105 Jury 343
☐ 106 Criminal trial 346
☐ 107 Military trial 349
☐ 108 Convicting and sentencing 351
☐ 109 Appeal and review 354

Chapitre **7.** Intellectual property litigation

☐ 110 Introduction 359
☐ 111 Copyright infringement and defences 361
☐ 112 Design infringement and defences 364
☐ 113 Patent infringement and defences 365
☐ 114 Trademark infringement defences 367

Chapitre **8.** Insurance litigation

☐ 115 General rules 371

Chapitre **9.** Environmental litigation

☐ 116 Introduction 373
☐ 117 Regulatory strategies and jurisdiction 375
☐ 118 Sanctions and enforcement 377

Chapitre **10.** Employment litigation

☐ 119 Termination of employment 381
☐ 120 Disputes 384
☐ 121 Trade union 387

Chapitre **11.** Immigration litigation

☐ 122 Immigration law and related human rights 391
☐ 123 Asylum process and appeals 394
☐ 124 Border controls 396
☐ 125 Deprivation of nationality 399
☐ 126 Immigration enforcement 401

Chapitre **12.** Family litigation

☐ 127 Divorce and dissolution 403
☐ 128 Divorce and children 407
☐ 129 Divorce and financial issues 409

☐ 130 Guardianship 412
☐ 131 Protecting children 414

Chapitre 13. Probate litigation

☐ 132 General rules 417

Chapitre 14. Property litigation

☐ 133 Introduction 419
☐ 134 Disputes concerning leases 422
☐ 135 Disputes concerning freehold land 423
☐ 136 Specific case : landlord's eviction of a tenant 425

Index 431

English abbreviations

ABS	Alternative Business Structures
ACAS	Advisory, Conciliation and Arbitration Service
ADR	Alternative Dispute Resolution
AEI	after the event insurance
AGM	Annual General Meeting
ADR	alternative dispute resolution
ART	Article
ASBO	anti-social behaviour order
AST	Assured shorthold tenancy
ATED	annual tax on enveloped dwellings
B/L & BOL	bill of lading
BoEA	Bill of Exchange Act 1882
BPTC	Bar Professional Training Course
Cafcass	Children and Family Court Advisory and Support Service
CDC	Crime and Disorder Committee
CDPA	Copyright, Designs and Patent Act
CFE	conditional fee agreement
CID	Criminal Investigation Department
CO	Commanding Officer
CPA	Consumer Protection Act 1987
CPC	Cooperative Patent Classification
CPE	Common Professional Examination
CPR	Civil Procedure Rules
CPS	Crown Prosecution Service
CTA	Common Travel Area
CVA	company voluntary arrangements
CVL	creditors' voluntary liquidation
DEFRA	Department for Environment, Food and Rural Affairs
DGFT	Director General of Fair Trading
DNA	Deoxyribonucleic acid
DPP	Director of Public Prosecutions

EA	Environmental Agency
EAT	Employment Appeal Tribunal
ECHR	European Convention on Human Rights
ECLA	European Classification System
ECtHR	European Court of Human Rights
EEA	European Economic Area
EPA	Environment Protection Act
EPO	European Patent Office
EPR	Extended Producer Responsibility
ET	Employment Tribunal
EU	European Union
FOS	Financial Ombudsman Services
FTVA	fast-track voluntary arrangement
GBH	grievous bodily harm
GDL	Graduate Diploma in Law
GLO	Group Litigation Order
GM	genetically modified
GMOs	genetically modified organisms
GP	general practitioner
HHSRS	Housing Health and Safety Rating System
HM	Her Majesty
HMCS	Her Majesty's Court Service
HMCTS	Her Majesty's Courts and Tribunals Service
HMRC	Her Majesty's Revenue and Customs
HRA	Human Rights Act
ICC	International Chamber of Commerce
ICJ	International Court of Justice
IIR	Individual Insolvency Register
INCOTERMS	International Chamber of Commerce terms
IP	insolvency practitioner
IPA	International Patent Classification
IPO	Intellectual Property Office
ISO	International Standard Organisation
IVA	individual voluntary arrangements
JAC	Judicial Appointments Commission
JSA	Jobseeker Allowance

LASPO	Legal Aid, Sentencing and Punishment of Offenders Act 2012
LEI	legal expenses insurance
LLB	undergraduate law degree
LLP	Limited Liability Partnership
LPA	Lasting Power of Attorney
LPC	Legal Practice Course
LSSA	Local Social Services Authority
MDP	Ministry of Defense Police
MVL	members' voluntary liquidation
NCB	no-claims bonus
NGOs	non-governmental organisations
NHS	National Health Service
NIC	national insurance contributions
NMW	National Minimum Wages
OECD	Organisation for Economic Co-operation and Development
OFT	office of fair trading
OML	ordinary maternity leave
OR	Official receiver
PACE	Police and Criminal Evidence Act 1984
PAYE	Pay As You Earn
PCC(S)A	Powers of Criminal Courts (Sentencing) Act
PCSO	Police Community Support Officers
PDO	Protected Designation of Origin
PDs	prescribed disease
PGI	Protected Geographical Indication
PMI	private medical insurance
PPO	periodical payment order
PR	personal representative
PSC	Professional Skills Course
QBD	Queen's Bench Division
QC	Queen's Counsel
RPB	recognised professional body
SCC	Service Civilian Court
SDC	Sustainable Development Commission
SDLT	stamp duty land tax

SDRT	stamp duty reserve tax
SFO	Serious Fraud Office
SGSA	Supply of Goods and Services Act 1982
SJE	single joint expert
SMP	Statutory Maternity Pay
SoGA	Sale of Goods Act 1979
SPP	Statutory Paternity Pay
SRA	Solicitors Regulations Authority
SSP	statutory sick pay
TDP	tenancy deposit protection
TICs	Offences to be Taken Into Consideration
TMA 1994	Trade Marks Act
TRIPS	Trade Related Aspects of Intellectual Property Rights
TSG	Traditional Speciality Guaranteed
UCTA	Unfair Contract Terms Act 1977
UDHR	Universal Declaration of Human Rights
UK	United Kingdom
UKEOF	UK Environmental Observation Framework
UKSC	Supreme Court of the United Kingdom
UNEP	United Nations Environment Programme
UTCCR	Unfair Terms in Consumer Contracts Regulations
UTPR	Consumer Protection from Unfair Trading Practices Regulations 2009
VAT	Value Added Tax
WIPO	World Intellectual Property Organisation
WTC	working tax credit

Abréviations françaises

CDD	contrat à durée déterminée
CDI	contrat à durée indéterminée
CEDH	Convention européenne des droits de l'Homme
CFE	taxe d'habitation & cotisation foncière des entreprises
CIDD	comité interministériel pour le développement durable
CJA	Code de justice administative
CMU	Couverture Maladie Universelle
CNDD	conseil national du développement durable
CPAM	Caisse Primaire d'Assurance Maladie
CPC	Code de procédure civile
CRPC	comparution sur reconnaissance préalable de culpabilité
DDCS	direction départementale de la cohésion sociale
DDT	direction départementale des territoires
DDTM	direction départementale des territoires et de la mer
DREAL	direction régionale de l'environnement, de l'aménagement et du logement
DUDH	Déclaration universelle des droits de l'Homme
ENA	École Nationale d'Administration
ENM	École Nationale de la Magistrature
FCDDV	Fichier central des dispositions de dernières volontés
GPA	gestation pour autrui
HLM	habitation à loyer modéré
IGAS	Inspection générale des affaires sociales
INPI	Institut national de la propriété intellectuelle
ISF	impôt de solidarité sur la fortune
Pacs	pacte civil de solidarité
PMA	procréation médicalement assistée
SARL	société à responsabilité limitée
SMIC	salaire minimum interprofessionnel de croissance
SoeS	Service de l'observation et des statistiques

TASS	Tribunaux des affaires de sécurité sociale
TGAP	taxe générale sur les activités polluantes
TGI	Tribunal de grande instance
UE	Union européenne

Introduction

Cet ouvrage s'adresse aux étudiants en droit (Licence, Master) et à tous ceux, notamment aux professionnels du droit, qui souhaitent acquérir une connaissance approfondie de l'anglais juridique utilisé en Grande-Bretagne et plus particulièrement, dans le système applicable en Angleterre et au Pays de Galles. Son objectif principal est de fournir aux lecteurs un glossaire anglais des termes ou expressions usités dans une multitude de domaines du droit. Ces termes sont présentés en contexte, dans une introduction abordant un point de droit précis, et sont ensuite systématiquement accompagnés d'une traduction française.

L'originalité de cet ouvrage est triple.

Tout d'abord, outre les domaines traditionnellement traités (droit des contrats, de la responsabilité, droit pénal, etc.), l'ouvrage aborde en détail le droit fiscal, des sociétés, de l'environnement, des assurances, des procédures collectives, de la propriété intellectuelle, de l'immigration, de la famille, du travail, de la propriété, des successions et des droits de l'Homme. S'il n'existe pas, en Angleterre et au Pays de Galles, une distinction entre droit privé et droit public telle qu'on la conçoit en France, le lecteur trouvera cependant dans cet ouvrage de nombreux chapitres correspondant à ce qui relève, en France, du droit public.

Ensuite, l'approche de la langue et du droit dans cet ouvrage est novatrice. Si la partie introductive et le glossaire dressent un état du droit en Angleterre et au Pays de Galles, l'objectif du travail de traduction a été de déterminer, dans la mesure du possible, quel concept de droit français correspond le mieux à un concept de droit anglais. En mettant en parallèle les deux systèmes juridiques, le lecteur, familier du système de droit dit civil qu'est le droit français, comprendra le fonctionnement du système de *common law* (droit coutumier) applicable en Angleterre et au Pays de Galles.

Ainsi, le lecteur ne sera pas surpris que le *Crown Prosecution Service*, dépendant de la Reine, se voit traduire par le très républicain Ministère public, ni que la plus haute juridiction, la *Supreme Court*, se voit dédoublée en Cour de cassation et Conseil d'État. Si les fonctions d'un *solicitor* peuvent être les mêmes qu'un avocat ou un notaire français, selon le domaine du droit dans lequel il exerce, un *barrister* est simplement un avocat; il n'a pas seulement pour rôle de plaider mais a aussi une fonction non négligeable de conseil. Quant au titre de *Queen's Counsel*, donné par la Reine aux *barristers* les plus méritants, si sa traduction par Conseiller de la Reine est littérale, elle n'est ni explicite ni exacte au vu de la réalité de leurs fonctions. Le statut de *Queen's*

Counsel correspond davantage à celui d'avocat aux Conseils, profession très réglementée en France dont les membres sont nommés par le garde des Sceaux. Certes, les fonctions respectives des deux professions présentent des divergences, mais cela découle de la différence même entre les systèmes de droit applicables respectivement Outre-Manche et en France.

La section *useful expressions* donne au lecteur les moyens de mettre lui-même en contexte, dans les deux langues, certains termes ou expressions relatifs à un point de droit. La section *further information* n'a d'autre objectif que d'attirer l'attention sur l'existence de faux-amis, d'homophones ou de points importants – tels que des écueils de langue – qui ne rentrent dans aucune autre section.

Enfin, l'originalité de l'ouvrage réside dans l'approche comparative des systèmes de droit anglais et français qui clôture chaque sujet. Cette approche de droit comparé ne prétend pas être une étude exhaustive, mais a pour but de mettre en exergue des points communs ou divergences qui pourront éclairer le lecteur sur les choix de traduction qui sont parfois faits et éventuellement, de lui donner des pistes pour poursuivre ses recherches dans un domaine précis.

L'ouvrage est divisé en trois parties. La première partie, composée de diverses fiches, présente la spécificité du système juridique de l'Angleterre et du Pays de Galles – par rapport aux systèmes des autres pays de l'Europe – ainsi qu'une présentation des juridictions et des professions du droit dans ces deux pays. Les deuxième et troisième parties sont relatives aux droits non contentieux et contentieux de l'Angleterre et du Pays de Galles. Chaque domaine juridique y est étudié, dans ses aspects non contentieux et contentieux. Ces parties sont divisées en chapitres (correspondant à un domaine du droit), eux-mêmes subdivisés en plusieurs fiches, chacune étant relative à un point de droit.

Quelques précisions complémentaires s'imposent.

Par application des dispositions de la section 6 de l'*Interpretation Act* de 1978, les mots de genre masculin incluent ici le féminin, ceux au pluriel incluent le singulier et inversement, sauf s'il est stipulé autrement. En revanche, et puisque le champ d'application de la loi de 1978 ne permet pas d'opérer une confusion entre les personnes physiques (*he* ou *she*) et les personnes morales (*it*), les auteurs ont choisi, lorsqu'un point de droit est susceptible de concerner les deux types de personnes juridiques (tel que le fait de passer un contrat), de prendre pour exemple l'individu masculin (*he*), sauf quand il doit en être autrement. Dans ce dernier cas, une indication spécifique sera donnée en tête de fiche, précisant qu'elle concerne une personne morale à l'exclusion d'une personne physique.

Quand il s'est agi de décrire, non pas des noms (n.), verbes (v.), adjectifs (adj.) ou adverbes (adv.), mais des noms composés ou des expressions, tels que *compos mentis*, *Individual Insolvency Register*, *proof of debt*, etc., les auteurs ont choisi de ne rien préciser. Les définitions figurant au glossaire permettront au lecteur de déduire du contexte l'usage qu'il peut faire des expressions ou groupes nominaux concernés.

Enfin, si cet ouvrage s'inscrit dans le cadre d'une étude de l'anglais juridique au travers du système applicable en Angleterre et au Pays de Galles, référence sera faite, de façon occasionnelle et appropriée, à la Grande-Bretagne et même, au Royaume-Uni. En revanche, l'expression Outre-Manche sera entendue comme faisant référence exclusive à l'Angleterre et au Pays de Galles.

Biographies

Géraldine Gadbin-George a dirigé la rédaction de cet ouvrage. Elle est Maître de conférences à l'Université Panthéon-Assas (Paris 2) et a exercé pendant plusieurs années les fonctions d'avocat et *solicitor*, tant en France qu'en Angleterre, ainsi que celle de magistrat administratif. Elle est titulaire d'un Doctorat en civilisation britannique, obtenu dans le cadre d'une convention de co-tutelle entre les Universités de Sussex (Grande-Bretagne) et Grenoble. Sa thèse a porté sur l'accès à la justice en Angleterre et au Pays de Galles au travers du rôle joué par les *Citizens Advice Bureaux*. Elle est membre de la *Solicitor Judges division* de la *Law Society* et inscrite au *Roll of solicitors*. Elle est l'auteur des fiches 2, 4, 5, 6, 25, 26, 40, 41, 42, 43, 44, 45, 46, 47, 48, 69, 70, 71, 72, 73, 74, 75, 76, 94, 95, 96, 97, 98, 99, 101, 115 et 136.

Anne Brunon-Ernst est ancienne élève de l'ENS Cachan, agrégée d'anglais et Docteur en civilisation britannique. Elle est Maître de conférences-HDR à l'Université Panthéon-Assas, où elle enseigne l'anglais juridique. Spécialiste de Jeremy Bentham, elle s'intéresse à l'héritage de Bentham dans la formation du concept de panoptisme et de biopolitique chez Foucault; parallèlement, elle travaille sur les questions proprement juridiques de la théorie benthamienne (droit civil, normativité juridique, législation indirecte). Elle a soutenu son habilitation à diriger des recherches à l'Université Sorbonne Nouvelle (Paris 3) en 2012. Elle est l'auteur des fiches 1, 13, 14, 15, 16, 17, 18, 19, 20, 21, 22, 23, 24, 85, 86, 87, 88, 89, 90, 91, 92, 93 et 100.

Armelle Sabatier est agrégée d'anglais et Docteur en littérature britannique. Elle est spécialiste du théâtre élisabéthain et jacobéen. Elle enseigne l'anglais juridique à l'Université Panthéon-Assas, où elle est Maître de conférences. Ses travaux de recherche sont en partie orientés vers les liens que le droit entretient depuis toujours avec la littérature. Elle est l'auteur des fiches 3, 27, 28, 29, 30, 31, 32, 33, 34, 53, 54, 55, 56, 62, 63, 64, 65, 102, 103, 104, 105, 106, 107, 108, 109, 119, 120, 121, 127, 128, 129, 130, 131 et 132.

Suhasini Vincent est titulaire d'un Doctorat en études anglophones de l'Université Sorbonne Nouvelle (Paris 3) et d'un Doctorat (*Ph. D*) de l'Université de Madras (Inde). Sa thèse, soutenue dans le cadre d'une co-tutelle entre les deux Universités, a porté sur l'Écriture métafictionnelle et littératures postcoloniales de la fiction indo-anglaise. En 2009, elle s'est vue décerner le deuxième prix « Jacqueline Bardolph » de la meilleure thèse soutenue sur des sujets concernant les pays du Commonwealth, organisé sous l'égide de la Société d'études des Pays du Commonwealth (SEPC). Elle est Maître de conférences à l'Université Panthéon-Assas, où elle enseigne l'anglais juridique et elle intervient en droit de la propriété intellectuelle à NEOMA Business

School (Reims). Elle est l'auteur des fiches 35, 36, 37, 38, 39, 49, 50, 51, 52, 57, 58, 59, 60, 61, 110, 111, 112, 113, 114, 116, 117, 118, 122, 123, 124, 125 et 126.

Justin Beplate a obtenu une double licence en droit et anglais à l'Université de Queensland (Australie), puis un doctorat en littérature à l'Université de Sydney (Australie) avant de devenir éditeur juridique, puis Maître de conférences à l'Université Panthéon-Assas, où il enseigne l'anglais juridique. Il est l'auteur des fiches 7, 8, 9, 10, 11, 12, 66, 67, 68, 77, 78, 79, 80, 81, 82, 83, 84, 133, 134 et 135.

PART 1

Presentation of the legal system of England and Wales

□ 1 EUROPEAN UNION LAW IN ENGLAND AND WALES

The purpose of this book is to focus on the law of England and Wales. However, as the United Kingdom joined the European Union (EU) in 1973, it must comply with EU law. The EU is governed by member States' representatives (elected or appointed) and EU civil servants in seven institutions, located in Brussels, Strasbourg, Luxembourg and Frankfurt. It has its own legal instruments (Treaties, Regulations, Directives, Decisions, Recommendations and Opinions) which have varying degrees of legal force.

The United Kingdom has seceded part of its sovereignty to the Union. The principle of supremacy of EU law flows from the Court of Justice of the European Union (CJEU)'s interpretation of Treaty provisions in *Costa v. Enel* (1964). The Union is regulated by Treaties, which govern the executive, legislative and judicial powers in the EU. The latest Treaty regulating the Union is the Treaty of Lisbon which establishes the Union in two treaties : the Treaty on the Functioning of the European Union (TFEU) and the Treaty on the European Union (TEU) (Article 1 TEU). The Lisbon Treaty now incorporates the Charter of Fundamental Rights of the European Union (CFREU) and the European Convention on Human Rights (ECHR) (Article 6 TEU).

The European Union, or Community as it was then called, was established by the Treaty of Rome (EC) in 1958, which gave a wider political basis to the European Coal and Steel Community (ECSC) post-war experiment. Since then, the political organisation of the Union has been amended many times, to meet the challenges of successive enlargements (from France, Belgium, Germany, Italy, Luxembourg and the Netherlands to 28 members to date). The latest change to the organisation of the Union was implemented by the Lisbon Treaty (2009), which was further amended by the European Stability Mechanism in 2013 to tackle the economic crisis.

The Union is now made up of seven institutions (Article 13 TEU) : the European Council, the Council, the Commission, the European Parliament (EP), the Court of Justice of the European Union, the European Central Bank (ECB) and the Court of Auditors. The Union is a political entity, which is still being built, and thus EU institutions do not fit into any of the traditional categories of the principle of separation of powers. EU institutions should be read through the lens of the protection of competing interests : the European Council and the Council protect the interests of the States, the Commission that of the Union and the EP that of the people of the 28 member States.

Primary legislation is generally introduced by the Commission. The EP then passes the bill with the help of the Council. There are two legislative procedures. The ordinary procedure (Article 294 TFEU) allows the Commission to make a proposal to the EP and the Council. In the first reading, the EP either adopts the Commission proposal or states to the Council the reasons why it is unable to do so. The Council then has three months to propose an amended bill to the EP, which in turn has three months to accept, reject or amend the legislative proposal in a second reading. If the EP and the Council are unable to reach an agreement, a Conciliation committee is set up and has to reach an agreement within six weeks. This agreed upon version of the bill, has to be consequently approved by a majority vote in the EP in a third reading, and finally by a qualified majority vote in the Council before it can become a EU law. The special procedure (Article 289 (2) TFEU) is a procedure whereby the EP does not have the right to submit amendments, but which allows the Council to adopt an act only if the EP has consented.

Secondary legislation (Regulations, Directives, Decisions, Recommendations and Opinions) can be taken by any EU institution, if it has been delegated temporary or permanent power to do so. Each EU legal instrument does not have the same binding value. EU legal theory distinguishes between vertical direct effect and horizontal direct effect.

Regulation provisions are capable of vertical and horizontal direct effect. They do not need any implementing measure to be applicable in a national legal order and are thus immediately enforceable as law.

Directives are also capable of vertical direct effect (*Van Duyn v. UK* in 1974), if the Directive is sufficiently clear, precise and unconditional (*Van Gend en Loos v. Nederlandse Administratie der Belastingen* in 1963). However they cannot impose an obligation upon an individual (*Marshall v. Southampton and South West Hampshire AHA* in 1986). The absence of horizontal direct effect of directives has been criticised. However several mechanisms, developed by case law, help to overturn this lack of horizontal direct effect in certain circumstances, through the indirect effect of Directives (*Van Colson and*

Kamann v. Land Nordrhein-Westfalen in 1984) and State liability (*Francovich v. Italy* in 1990).

Decisions are generally addressed to an individual, group of individuals or entity. They are binding only on those to whom they are addressed. The Lisbon Treaty established another category of decisions, which is used by the Common Foreign and Security Policy (CFSP) and are not addressed to anybody in particular.

Recommendations do not have any binding effect but they have persuasive value. They are mainly used in competition law.

Opinions do not have any binding effect and have a less persuasive value than Recommendations. They are used by institutions other than the Council, the Commission and the EP; that is mainly by the ECB.

The Court of Justice of the European Union is made up of the Court of Justice (previously known as the European Court of Justice/ECJ), the General Court (previously known as First Instance Court) and Specialized Courts (Article 19 TEU). The Court of Justice hears appeals from the General Court and has jurisdiction to hear preliminary references, infringement proceedings, actions for annulment and actions for failure to act. The General Court hears actions at first instance and appeals from the Specialised Courts and it has jurisdiction to hear preliminary rulings although it has not done so in practice.

GLOSSARY

- action for annulment : action which may be brought before the Court of Justice whereby the claimant requires the annulment of an act adopted by Union body, institution, office or agency on the grounds that it is contrary to EU law; *fr. : recours en annulation*
- action for failure to act : action which may be brought before the Court of Justice for the inaction of a Union body, institution, office or agency when it is deemed to be in violation of EU law; *fr. : recours en carence*
- Commission (n.) : European institution, which ensures the application of the Treaties (Article 17 TEU) through the drafting of the budget, the proposal of legislative acts, the application of the Treaties (direct and indirect administration; implementing and delegated acts) and the starting of infringement procedures against a member State under Article 258 TFEU; with the European Council and the Council which is the executive branch of the Union; to date, there is one Commissioner per member State in the College of Commissioners which is assisted by a staff of more than 200,000 civil servants; *fr. : Commission*
- Council (n.)/Council of Ministers : European institution, which gathers the representatives of each member State at ministerial level (Article 16 TEU); it includes COREPER, which is a group of ambassadors preparing the work of ministerial councils, and the Foreign Affairs Council which is presided upon by the High Representative for the European Union; *fr. : Conseil*

- Court of Auditors : European institution, which carries out the auditing functions of the Union (Article 285 TFEU) ; it does not have any prosecuting powers ; *fr. : Cour des comptes européenne*
- Court of Justice of the European Union (CJEU) : European institution, which ensures the correct interpretation and application of the Treaties (Article 19 TEU) ; *fr. : Cour de justice de l'Union européenne (CJUE)*
- decision (n.) : EU legal instrument, which is binding and does not require any national implementing legislation ; it may have a general application or may apply to a specific addressee (member State individual or concern) ; *fr. : décision*
- directive (n.) : legal instrument, which is binding upon member States as to the objectives to be achieved, but leaves to each member State the choice of form and means used to implement these aims ; *fr. : directive*
- European (adj.) Community (n.) (EC) : name given by the Treaty of Rome to the existing European Union ; *fr. : Communauté européenne*
- European (adj.) Council (n.) : European institution, which gathers the heads of state or government of member States (Article 15 TEU) ; formerly informal, the meetings were given some form of recognition in the Single European Act (SEA), then some specific functions in the Maastricht Treaty before becoming an institution in the Lisbon Treaty ; *fr. : Conseil de l'Europe*
- European (adj.) Parliament (n.) : European institution, which exercises the legislative and budgetary functions of the Union, with the Council ; it is a unicameral assembly, elected by direct universal suffrage in a free and secret ballot ; it is said to be made of the representatives of the Union's citizens (Article 14 TEU) ; to date there are 766 MEPs ; it also has supervisory powers over the Commission ; *fr. : Parlement européen*
- European (adj.) Union (n.) (EU) : name given to the political organisation which gathers 28 countries on the European continent ; name given by the Maastricht Treaty (1991) ; *fr. : Union européenne*
- European Central Bank (ECB) : European institution, which acts as the bank for the EU's single currency, the euro (Article 282 TFEU) ; it is part of the European System of Central Bank (ESCB) which includes National Central Banks (NCB) ; *fr. : Banque centrale européenne (BCE)*
- European Coal and Steel Community (ECSC) : organisation, which was established by the Treaty of Paris in 1952 and which aimed to abolish tariffs on coal and steel between France, Belgium, Luxembourg, Italy and Germany in an attempt to preserve peace and promote prosperity after two World Wars ; *fr. : Communauté du Charbon et de l'Acier*
- horizontal direct effect : effect of a legal provision whereby an individual has a remedy in a national court in an action against the state or an emanation of the state and against another individual ; *fr. : effet direct horizontal*
- infringement proceeding : action which may be brought before the Court of Justice on the grounds that a member State has failed to fulfil its obligations under EU law ; *fr. : procédure d'infraction*

- opinion (n.) : legal instrument, which does not have any binding force and is of persuasive value only; *fr. : opinion*
- preliminary (adj.) reference (n.) : reference by a national court regarding a question of interpretation of EU law to the Court of Justice; *fr. : procédure préjudicielle/renvoi prejudiciel*
- primary (ad.) legislation (n.) : refers to the Treaties; *fr. : législation primaire*
- qualified majority voting (QMV) : voting system, which allocates a certain number of votes to member States; it is a weighed voting system; the majority is reached when a majority of States and representatives of a majority of population in the EU agree to a decision; *fr. : vote à majorité qualifiée*
- recommendation (n.) : legal instrument, which does not have any binding force and is of persuasive value only; it is used as an instrument of indirect action to pave the way for future legislation; *fr. : recommandation*
- regulation (n.) : legal instrument, which is legally binding and does not need any further implementing act in order to be enforceable in national law; *fr. : règlement*
- secondary (adj.) legislation (n.) : legislation made under the Treaties; *fr. : législation secondaire*
- vertical direct effect : effect of a legal provision whereby an individual has a remedy in a national court in an action against the State or an emanation of the State; *fr. : effet direct vertical*

USEFUL EXPRESSIONS

- a reference for a preliminary ruling; *fr. : demande de décision préjudicielle*
- preliminary ruling proceedings before the CJEU; *fr. : procédure préjudicielle devant la CJUE/renvoi préjudiciel devant la CJUE*
- to avoid claims of (in)direct discrimination under Article 39 TFEU; *fr. : pour éviter des plaintes pour discrimination (in)directe*
- to be directly effective; *fr. : être d'effet direct*
- to be liable for damages for state liability; *fr. : être redevable du paiement de dommages et intérêts au titre de la responsabilité de l'État*
- to enforce a Directive against a State; *fr. : faire appliquer une directive contre un État*
- to fail to implement a Directive; *fr. : ne pas avoir mis en œuvre les dispositions d'une directive*
- to fulfil the Van Gend criteria; *fr. : répondre aux critères établis dans la jurisprudence Van Gend*
- to get/to have/to seek a remedy under EU law; *fr. : exercer un recours en droit européen*
- to give a preliminary ruling on; *fr. : statuer à titre préjudiciel sur*
- to have a horizontal direct effect; *fr. : avoir un effet direct horizontal*

- to have a vertical direct effect; *fr. : avoir un effet direct vertical*
- to implement a Directive incorrectly; *fr. : l'application incorrecte des dispositions de la directive*
- to rely on the provision of a Directive; *fr. : invoquer les dispositions de la directive*
- to satisfy the conditions for direct effect; *fr. : satisfaire aux conditions de l'effet direct*
- to suffer damage as contemplated by Article 101 TEU; *fr. : subir un préjudice tel qu'envisagé à l'article 101 TUE*

FURTHER INFORMATION

- the concept of jurisprudence in European legal English is synonymous with case law; in the context of EU law, both terms are used interchangeably; however, in the context of English law, the word jurisprudence refers to the science of law (*doctrine*); in the latter case, it is not to be confused with the French *jurisprudence* which is translated by case law in English
- each new Treaty re-numbers articles; for example, Treaty provisions relating to competition law previously as Articles 81 and 82 TEU, are now Articles 101 and 102 TEU; tables of equivalences are provided in books on EU Legislation
- the judicial power of the Union is mostly vested in the Court of Justice of the European Union, but the Commission is also allowed some judicial power under Article 105 TEU, related to competition law for example

COMPARATIVE APPROACH

Le Royaume-Uni étant membre de l'Union européenne, il est soumis aux mêmes règles que tous les autres membres de l'Union dans les domaines où les traités ont donné à l'Union autorité pour légiférer (articles 5, 13[2] et 352 TUE). Cependant et contrairement à la France, il est à noter que le Royaume-Uni a choisi de ne pas entrer dans un certain nombre de mécanismes (*opt out*), dont ceux de la zone Schengen et de la zone euro.

□ 2 PRESENTATION OF THE COMMON LAW SYSTEM

England and Wales have a common law system as opposed to a civil law one. Common law is a system of law revolving around case law, as opposed to statutes voted by Parliament. Case law is the group of precedents made by the courts through their decisions. The concept of precedent, also called *stare decisis*, means to adhere to, and apply, the decision made in previously decided cases. Therefore, a precedent is considered as binding on the lower courts if the particular dispute these lower courts have to solve raises similar factual and mostly, legal issues to those raised in the higher court case, which led to the creation of a precedent. An existing precedent may only have a persuasive value (as opposed to having a binding effect) if some of the issues (mostly legal) raised in the litigation differ from those in the case which gave rise to the precedent.

Vertical *stare decisis* is the principle whereby a higher court's precedents are binding on a lower court. The appellate committee of the House of Lords, which was replaced by the Supreme Court in October 2009 when the Constitutional Reform Act 2005 came into force, used to be bound by its own precedents (horizontal *stare decisis*). However, and further to Practice Statement [1966] 3 All ER 77, the Law Lords agreed to depart from their own precedents when they could result in injustice or restrain the development of the law.

Only the *ratio decidendi* of a court decision can form a precedent, as opposed to the *obiter dicta* which only ever has a persuasive value. *Ratio decidendi* is the actual legal ruling in a court decision. *Obiter dicta* consists of the comments or the reasoning which lead to a ruling. Not all court decisions give rise to a precedent. Only those court decisions, preferrably from a higher court, which change the judiciary's view on a particular legal issue can give rise to precedents. Case law makes the law evolve smoothly, in response to a need in a particular legal field.

There are three main reasons for the evolution or creation of case law : existing precedents may no longer be relevant to a particular legal field, no precedent exists in that field, or a statute passed by Parliament is unclear and needs to be construed by the judiciary. This last reason is paramount nowadays. Common law – through case law – used to be the main source of law as opposed to statutory law. However and under the influence of European law (see 1), the British legislator has been forced to pass an increasing amount of legislation. Therefore, nowadays and although Britain remains a common law jurisdiction, the increasing part played by statutes brings it closer to civil law countries, where the law voted by Parliament is paramount.

A distinction is often made between common law and equity, thus giving rise to precedents at common law and in equity. This distinction was important in the past when different courts had juridiction to hear of common law cases and equity cases. The distinction remains today, albeit to a limited extent, since the common law courts and equity courts were merged pursuant to the Judicature Acts 1881. Common law was seen as the law made by judges (this meaning remains today) as opposed to equity which consisted of the fair decisions made originally by the Lord Chancellor (the King's right hand man) and then by the equity courts, when the common law precedents failed to provide an adequate remedy for litigants. Courts now have the power to award remedies at common law and/or in equity, thus ensuring that a fair access to justice is granted to everyone. However antiquated this distinction might seem nowadays, it does remain. For further information on remedies at common law and in equity, see 84 and 93.

GLOSSARY

- appellate committee of the House of Lords : name given to the part of the House of Lords (the upper legislative house in the United Kingdom) which used to fulfil exclusively a judicial role (as the highest court of the land) before the creation of the Supreme Court; *fr. : ≈ Cour de cassation (ordre judiciaire)/≈ Conseil d'État (ordre administratif)*
- bind (v.) : have a compulsory effect; apply in a compulsory way; *fr. : lier*
- case law : group of legal principles or rulings (precedents) set by higher court which become binding on the lower courts which have to solve a dispute raising similar factual and mostly legal issues to the cases which gave rise to precedents; *fr. : jurisprudence*
- civil (adj.) law (n.) : codified legal system; it has updated legal codes which take account of the statutory changes brought by Parliament; the judge's role is to apply the provisions of the relevant code to a case and if unclear, interpret them; *fr. : droit civil*
- common (adj.) law (n.) : uncodified legal system (i.e. for which statutes and legal rules are not compiled together); it relies on the concept of case law or precedents; the judge's role is to make the law; *fr. : ≈ droit coutumier/ ≈ common law*
- construe (v.)/construction (n.) : interpret; *fr. : interpréter (v.)/interprétation (n.)*
- court (n.) : forum or place where justice is administered, where opposing litigants explain to the judge the nature of their dispute; the judge then hands down a decision; in England and Wales, there is a three-tier court system with first instance courts, appellate courts and a Supreme Court; *fr. : tribunal* (if in first instance)/*juridiction* (in all cases)
- dispute (n. or v.) : argument; *fr. : litige (n.)/contester (v.)*
- equity (n.) : system of law created, originally by the Lord Chancellor and subsequently by specialised – followed by ordinary – courts to supplement the common law when it was deemed unsatisfactory or insufficient to render a fair decision; *fr. : équité*
- issue (n.) : point, question; *fr. : point/question*
- judiciary (n.) : system of courts which interpret, apply or create (through case law) legal rules; also called the judicial system; *fr. : autorité judiciaire*
- jurisdiction (n.) : power conferred on the courts to hear a case; *fr. : compétence d'attribution*
- Law Lords : name given to the twelve judges (from the House of Lords but who only fulfilled a judicial role) who composed the appellate committee of the House of Lords; they had the title of Lord; they were part of the highest

court and subsequently became the Justices of the Supreme Court; *fr. : ≈ magistrats de la Cour de cassation/du Conseil d'État*

- legal (adj.) field (n.) : area of law; *fr. : domaine juridique*
- legislator (n.) : entity – the Parliament – which enacts laws; *fr. : législateur*
- litigation (n.) : contentious law; *fr. : droit contentieux*
- Lord Chancellor : now known as the Secretary of State for Justice; he supervises all of the Ministry of Justice business and is responsible for improving the criminal justice and prison system; he used to be the King's right hand man, in charge of rendering decisions in equity; until the Constitutional Reform Act 2005, he combined executive, legislative and judicial functions; his former legislative and judicial positions have now been transferred respectively to the Lord Speaker and the Lord Chief Justice; *fr. : ≈ Ministre de la Justice*
- merge (v.)/merger (n.) : combine two entities or things; *fr. : fusionner (v.)/ fusion (n.)*
- *obiter dicta :* from the Latin "by the way"; comments made by the court, which are different from the *ratio decidendi,* but logically lead to a legal ruling being rendered; *obiter dicta* only has a persuasive effect; *fr. : ≈ exposé des motifs (d'une décision)*
- precedent (n.) : legal ruling made by a court in relation to a specific dispute which binds courts of lower level when they have to resolve a case which raises similar factual or legal issues; all precedents form case law; *fr. : arrêt de jurisprudence*
- pursuant to : according to, by virtue of; *fr. : par application de/en vertu de*
- *ratio decidendi :* from the Latin "meaning of decision"; legal ruling which is essential in a court decision; *fr. : dispositif (d'une décision de justice)*
- remedy (n.) : in a legal context, means used by a court, mostly when exercising its civil jurisdiction, to enforce a right, impose a penalty or make any other appropriate and fair decision; a distinction is usually made between remedies at common law (damages or financial compensation) and in equity (injunction or specific performance); *fr. : mode de réparation (d'un préjudice)*
- ruling (n.) : legal issue determined by a court decision; *fr. : décision de justice*
- smoothly (adj.) : without problems or hurdles; evenly; *fr. : sans heurt/sans à coup*
- *stare decisis :* from the Latin "let the decision stand"; courts' policy to comply with decisions made in earlier cases, so long as they raised similar issues of fact and mostly, law; *fr. : ≈ autorité de la jurisprudence*
- statute (n.)/statutory (adj.) : law or Act of Parliament; *fr. : loi*
- Supreme Court : highest court in the United Kingdom which replaces the appellate committee of the House of Lords; its members are called Justices and replaced the former Law Lords; *fr. : ≈ Cour de cassation (ordre judiciaire)/ ≈ Conseil d'État (ordre administratif)*

USEFUL EXPRESSIONS

- to have jurisdiction to hear a case; *fr. : avoir compétence d'attribution pour connaître d'un dossier*
- this is an appellate court; *fr. : c'est une juridiction d'appel*
- case law should not be confused with jurisprudence; *fr. : il ne faut pas confondre la jurisprudence et la doctrine*
- this legal ruling is binding on the lower courts; *fr. : cet arrêt de principe lie les juridictions inférieures*
- this precedent binds lower courts/this precedent is binding on lower courts; *fr. : cette règle de jurisprudence lie les juridictions inférieures*
- the lower courts are bound by a higher court's precedent; *fr. : les juridictions inférieures sont liées par la jurisprudence définie par une juridiction supérieure*
- the Parliament's duty is to enact statutes; *fr. : le rôle du Parlement est de voter des lois*
- the court awards damages at common law and an injunction in equity; *fr. : le tribunal accorde des dommages et intérêts au titre de la common law et ordonne une injonction au titre de l'équité*

FURTHER INFORMATION

- a "common law country" used to be translated by *un pays coutumier*; however, and probably due to the fact that this French translation conveys the message of an antiquated legal system as opposed to the modern approach now taken by common law countries to the making of law, most authors tend to retain the expression "common law" in French
- case law is translated by *jurisprudence* as opposed to jurisprudence which is translated by *doctrine*
- the noun jurisdiction should not be confused with the French noun *juridiction* which is a court of justice
- likewise, a court should be translated by *tribunal*; the word tribunal also exists in English but refers to specialised courts whose judges are usually non-legally trained judges
- the English noun precedent should not be confused with the French adjective *précédent* which means former in English
- the title "Law Lord" used to be given to the judges from the appellate committee of the House of Lords; the House of Lords normally fulfils a legislative role; however, twelve Lords (the "Law Lords") were given a judicial role which was strictly separate from the legislative role of the other Lords; however, in 2005, the Constitutional Reform Act was passed which set up a Supreme Court; eleven of the twelve former Law Lords moved to the Supreme Court when it started work in October 2009, and thus became Justices of the Supreme Court; the Supreme Court has twelve Justices in total

COMPARATIVE APPROACH

La doctrine (*jurisprudence*) s'interroge de nos jours sur l'étendue des divergences qui perdurent encore entre le système de *common law* qui est celui applicable en Angleterre et au Pays de Galles, et celui de tradition civiliste applicable en France. Il est vrai que sous l'influence de l'Europe qui conduit à une forme d'harmonisation, un nombre croissant de lois est passé Outre-Manche, mettant ainsi davantage l'accent sur la loi votée par le Parlement plutôt que sur le droit créé par les juges par le biais de la jurisprudence (*case law*). Cependant, les systèmes de droit civil présentent, pour la plupart, la particularité d'être codifiés, ce qui n'est pas le cas Outre-Manche.

□ 3 COURT SYSTEM

Her Majesty's Court Service and the former Tribunals Service were unified under Her Majesty's Courts and Tribunals Service (HMCTS) in 2011. This single agency of the Ministry of Justice deals with the administration of courts and tribunals.

As civil litigation and criminal litigation have different purposes (as set out in this book), the English courts are divided between civil and criminal courts. A distinction is also drawn between inferior courts (tribunals or county courts), dealing with less important cases and superior courts (High Court, Crown Court and the Court of Appeal) hearing complex cases and appeals. The Judicial Committee of the Privy Council hears appeals from certain countries which are members of the Commonwealth. Tribunals deal with specialised cases such as disputes between employer and employee or immigration issues.

Civil courts

Civil cases can start either in a county court or in the High Court of Justice. There is one High Court based in London with several branches throughout England and Wales and various county courts. Since the Civil Procedure Rules 1999 (also known as the Woolf reform), civil cases have been divided into three different categories depending on the value of the claim or the complexity of the legal issues raised by a dispute : small claims, fast-track cases and multi-track cases. Small claims are exclusively heard in the small claims court, within the county courts. The way claims are usually allocated to a particular track varies depending on the complexity of the legal issues raised and the actual amount of the claim. Amounts for allocation are reviewed from time to time by the legislator.

Theoretically both county courts and the High Court can hear fast-track and multi-track cases although most multi-track cases are usually heard in the High Court.

The High Court comprises three divisions : the Chancery Division, the Queen's Bench Division (QBD) and the Family Division.

The Chancery Division has jurisdiction over claims related to companies, disputed wills, trusts, insolvency, tax, revenues, property law, mortgages, partnerships and intellectual property. It also has a divisional court hearing appeals from county courts. The Queen's Bench Division hears complex contract and tort cases. Two other specialised courts belong to this division – the Commercial Court, dealing with banking and insurance matters, and the Admiralty Court dealing with shipping law. Its divisional court can hear appeals for civil claims lying from a county court as well as some appeals lying from a criminal court on a point of law. The Family Division has jurisdiction to hear first instance cases and appeals related to all matrimonial matters, minors, legitimacy, adoption, domestic violence or cases arising from human fertilisation. As a divisional court, two High Court judges examine appeals from decisions coming from the family proceedings court (which is part of the magistrates' court) and county court when it involves family matters.

If a claimant or a defendant wishes to appeal a High Court decision, he can lodge an appeal to the Civil Division of the Court of Appeal. Since the Access to Justice Act 1999, a universal appeals system has applied to both civil and criminal cases. Almost all appeals are now subject to obtaining leave to appeal from the lower court. Appeals usually relate to issues of law.

Criminal courts

All criminal cases start in a magistrates' court irrespective of the nature of the offence. There are various magistrates' courts throughout England and Wales. When the case is too serious or triable on indictment, the magistrates commit it to the Crown Court which hears it in first instance. There is only one single Crown Court which sits in around 90 locations in England and Wales. 90 % of criminal cases are tried in magistrates' courts (summary and either way offences). The Crown Court has appellate jurisdiction over cases first tried in a magistrates' court. A case judged in the Crown Court can be appealed to the Criminal Division of the Court of Appeal.

Supreme Court

The Supreme Court of the United Kingdom (UKSC) has been the court of last resort for civil and criminal cases since its opening in October 2009. The Justices hear appeals for civil cases judged in the United Kingdom and for criminal cases judged in England, Wales and Northern Ireland. Most appeals to the Supreme Court come from the Court of Appeal on a question of general public importance.

Exceptions to the rule

The division between criminal and civil jurisdiction is not always clear, as a magistrates' court can examine some cases related to family law and licensing. The divisional court of the Queen's Bench Division can determine certain points of law in relation to criminal matters (e.g., a writ of *habeas corpus*).

Appeals can sometimes be lodged directly to the UKSC, thus avoiding the Court of Appeal. This is called the leapfrog procedure.

GLOSSARY

- adoption (n.) : see 63
- case (n.) : action brought to the court either by a prosecutor (in criminal matters) or a claimant (in civil matters); *fr. : dossier/affaire*
- company (n.) : see 13
- contract (n.) : see 7
- county court (n.) : inferior court hearing less complex civil claims below a fixed value of claim; *fr. : ≈ Tribunal d'instance*
- Court of Appeal : court hearing appeals from the three divisions of the High Court, the county courts, the Employment Appeal Tribunal, the Lands Tribunal and the Transport Tribunal; it has a criminal and a civil division; *fr. : Cour d'appel*
- Crown Court : criminal court which has original jurisdiction for indictable offences and sometimes for either-way offences. It is also an appellate court hearing appeals from magistrates'courts; *fr. : ≈ Cour d'assises (en première instance) ou chambre correctionnelle de la Cour d'appel (en appel)*
- disputed (adj.) will (n.) : see 132
- division (n.) : part of a court which is specialised in a certain legal field; *fr. : chambre*
- domestic (adj.) violence (n.) : incidents between members of a family; *fr. : violence conjugale*; see 131
- High Court of Justice : superior court hearing civil claims above a certain value of damages and/or complex cases; *fr. : ≈ Tribunal de grande instance*
- insolvency (n.) : see 94
- intellectual (adj.) property (n.) : see 35
- issue (n.) (factual or legal) : point of fact or law which the courts are required to consider in order to resolve a dispute; *fr. : point/question (de fait, de droit)*
- Judicial Committee of the Privy Council : final court of appeal for more than 20 Commonwealth countries; its decisions are not binding, but are persuasive; *fr. : Cour de cassation et Conseil d'État des territoires du Commonwealth*
- jurisdiction (n.) : power given to a court to hear a case; *fr. : compétence d'attribution*
- leapfrog (n.) : here, appeal made against a first instance decision directly to the Supreme Court, thus avoiding litigation before the Court of Appeal; *fr. : ≈ pourvoi direct devant la haute juridiction* (literally *saute-mouton*)
- leave (n.) : here, authorisation required from a lower court to appeal to a higher court; *fr. : autorisation*

- licensing (n.) : legal field which involves requiring an authorisation before opening a bar, public house or restaurant selling customers alcoholic drinks; *fr. : ≈ procédure d'autorisation d'ouverture de débit de boissons alcoolisées*
- lodge (v.) (an appeal) : apply to a higher court to reconsider a decision handed down by a lower court and which is disputed; *fr. : interjeter appel/ relever appel*
- magistrates' court : court which mostly has first instance criminal jurisdiction; it is a mandatory stage in any criminal matter, irrespective of the seriousness of the offence; it is also a trial court for summary offences and either-way offences if the defendant so chooses; it also has limited civil jurisdiction for some family matters and licensing applications; *fr. : ≈ Tribunal de police et/ou Tribunal correctionnel*
- mortgage (n.) : see 67
- offence (n.) : criminal action against a person or property; *fr. : infraction*
- partnership (n.) : see 13
- property law (n.) : see 66
- revenue (n.) : see 25
- Supreme Court of the United Kingdom (UKSC) : court of last resort for civil and criminal trials (except for Scotland) in the whole of the United Kingdom; *fr. : ≈ Cour de cassation (ordre judiciaire)/Conseil d'État (ordre administratif)*
- tax (n.) : see 25
- tort (n.) : see 85
- track (n.) : here, way by which cases are allocated to a particular procedural system within a court, depending on the amount of the claim and its complexity; there are three tracks : small claims, fast-track and multi-track; *fr. : voie (pour procédure accélérée, etc.)*

USEFUL EXPRESSIONS

- to appear in court; *fr. : comparaître devant une juridiction*
- to have jurisdiction over a case; *fr. : avoir compétence d'attribution pour connaître d'un dossier*
- to hear a case; *fr. : connaître d'une affaire*
- to try a case; *fr. : entendre un dossier dans le cadre d'un procès/juger une affaire*
- to appeal a decision/to lodge an appeal against a decision; *fr. : relever/interjeter appel d'un jugement*

FURTHER INFORMATION

- the English tribunal cannot be translated by the French *tribunal* which is a court; the jurisdiction of an English tribunal is not general but specialised and unlike a court, the judges of a tribunal may not have legal training

- likewise the French *cour* is reserved for courts having an appellate jurisdiction, save for the *cour d'assises* which has original jurisdiction to deal with serious crimes
- the French *juridiction* (court) does not correspond at all to the English jurisdiction (*compétence d'attribution*)
- in court decisions, the court where the case was heard is indicated under its abbreviated form; for example, a case heard in the Queen's Bench Division of the High Court of England and Wales will appear as EWHC (QBD)

COMPARATIVE APPROACH

Outre-Manche, il n'y a qu'un seul ordre de juridiction à l'inverse de la France qui en possède deux (ordres administratif et judiciaire). Au Royaume-Uni, la Cour Suprême dispose de 12 *Justices* (nom donné aux plus hauts magistrats) alors que la Cour de cassation seule (à l'exception du Conseil d'État) compte environ 130 juges. Cela explique sans doute, en partie, pourquoi le *Access to Justice Act* de 1999 a tenté de restreindre le nombre d'appels entendus par la *Court of Appeal* (et par voie de conséquence, les pourvois devant la *Supreme Court*) en instituant l'obligation d'obtenir une autorisation préalable (*prior leave*) de la juridiction de première instance (*first instance court*) ayant rendu la décision contestée.

En France, le principe du double degré de juridiction permet de contester, devant une juridiction supérieure, le bien fondé d'une décision rendue par une juridiction inférieure. En Angleterre et au Pays de Galles, le même principe trouve application mais est dénommé *three-tier system* ou système à trois étages (juridiction de première instance ou *first instance court*, Cour d'appel ou *Court of Appeal* et juge suprême ou *Supreme Court*). Des deux côtés de la Manche, le principe de *res judicata* (ou principe de l'autorité de la chose jugée) interdit à un tribunal de réexaminer une affaire qu'il a déjà jugée.

S'agissant des juridictions de première instance de l'ordre judiciaire, il y a une similitude évidente entre les *county courts*/Tribunaux d'instance et la *High Court*/Tribunal de Grande Instance, même si leurs compétences *ratione materie* respectives divergent du fait des pouvoirs différents que le législateur leur a confiés. En revanche, en l'absence d'un ordre administratif Outre-Manche, il n'existe pas de juridiction qui remplisse un rôle similaire aux Tribunaux administratifs en France; à cet égard, l'*Administrative Court* – juridiction spécialisée dépendant de la *Queen's Bench Division* de la *High Court* – a une compétence bien plus restreinte que celle du juge administratif français, même si l'*Administrative Court* a notamment le pouvoir de *judicial review* sur les décisions des autorités publiques (voir 76).

S'agissant des juridictions très spécifiques que sont les *tribunals*, qui sont spécialisés dans un domaine précis et dont les magistrats n'ont souvent pas de formation juridique approfondie, la France dispose d'un système assez similaire avec, par exemple, les tribunaux de commerce, les tribunaux des affaires de sécurité sociale (TASS) ou les conseils de prud'hommes.

□ 4 LEGAL PROFESSIONS

England and Wales have their own legal system. Legal professions include the solicitor and barrister professions and judges who may be professional or non-professional judges. Professional judges will be discussed below. Non-professional judges are for example those who work for the employment tribunals or the magistrates' courts.

Other professionals closely involved with the law are paralegals, licensed conveyancers, court clerks, court ushers, bailiffs and sheriffs. Paralegals assist solicitors and barristers in their daily tasks. Court clerks and ushers help with the administrative side of the courts. Bailiffs and sheriffs are mostly in charge of the service of legal documents, enforcement of court decisions, debt recovery or seeking payment of rent arrears, amongst other things.

For a long time solicitors were described as mere legal advisers as opposed to barristers who were seen as having mostly a role of representation in court. It was also believed that solicitors were generalists as opposed to barristers. Since the Courts and Legal Services Act 1990 and the Legal Services Act 2007, this description has no longer been appropriate as will be seen below.

In October 2013 there were 130,000 solicitors holding practising certificates. This is more than three times the number of solicitors who practised 30 years ago. In 2010 there were 15,500 self-employed practising barristers and about 1,400 Queen's Counsels (QC).

GLOSSARY

- arrears (n.) : sum of money owed which should have been paid earlier; *fr. : arriérés*
- bailiff (n.) : employee of Her Majesty's Courts & Tribunals Service attached to the county court; he is responsible for serving court documents and enforcing court orders (by recovering money owed or seizing and selling the goods of a debtor); *fr. : ≈ huissier*
- barrister (n.) : member of a legal profession whose professional body is the Bar; *fr. : ≈ avocat*
- court clerk : officer of the court who maintains the court records, administers oaths and generally deals with the daily administrative work of a court; *fr. : greffier*

- debt recovery : steps taken to obtain payment of outstanding monies; *fr. : recouvrement de créances*
- employment tribunal : see 120
- enforcement (n.)/enforce (v.) : all steps leading to the execution of a court decision; *fr. : exécution (d'une décision de justice)*
- judge (n.) : public officer who decides cases in a law court; *fr. : magistrat/juge*
- licensed (adj.) conveyancer (n.) : non-solicitor specialist working on behalf of clients buying or selling property; he has a licence i.e. is authorised to deal with all the usual stages of conveyancing; the Administration of Justice Act 1985 allowed the members of the profession to do conveyancing work and thus, compete with solicitors; *fr. : ≈ praticien de l'immobilier*
- magistrates' court : see 103
- paralegal (n.) : person who is not a qualified solicitor or barrister but who is educated and trained to perform legal tasks; *fr. : juriste/≈ clerc (d'avocat/de notaire)*
- practising (adj.) certificate (n.); document required each year from a solicitor before he may practise; the certificate can be obtained from the Solicitors' Regulation Authority, a branch of the Law Society which is the solicitors' professional body; a yearly fee is payable; *fr. : ≈ certificat annuel d'inscription à l'Ordre des avocats*
- service (n.) : in a legal context, delivery of a legal document to an entity; notification; *fr. : notification/signification*
- sheriff (n.) : High Court bailiff; he is paid by way of a percentage of the money collected or the realisation of assets he seizes; *fr. : ≈ huissier*
- solicitor (n.) : member of a legal profession whose professional body is the Law Society; *fr. : avocat/notaire* (depending on the context)
- court usher : person working for a court who decides the order of cases, ensures that the court files are secure, allows access to the courtroom and generally assists with the smooth running of a trial; *fr. : ≈ huissier-audiencier*

FURTHER INFORMATION

- a judge should be translated by *magistrat* or *juge*; a French *magistrat* should not be confused with a magistrate who is a non-professional judge working for the magistrates' courts
- before the creation of the Supreme Court as the highest judicial court, each solicitor used to be a "solicitor of the Supreme Court of England and Wales", formerly known as the Supeme Court of Judicature; the Supreme Court then consisted of the High Court, the Crown Court and the Court of Appeal; since the Supreme Court (highest judicial court) was created in 2005, solicitors have become known as "solicitors of the Senior Courts of England and Wales"

USEFUL EXPRESSIONS

- to fulfil a legal role; *fr. : remplir un rôle en matière juridique*
- to practise as a solicitor; *fr. : exercer comme avocat/notaire*
- to apply for a practising certificate; *fr. : requérir son inscription annuelle au tableau de l'Ordre des avocats*
- to seek payment of oustanding monies; *fr. : demander le paiement d'une créance*
- to serve a document on someone; *fr. : notifier/signifier un document à quelqu'un*

COMPARATIVE APPROACH

Il est difficile de comparer les professions juridiques qui existent en Angleterre et au Pays de Galles avec les professions françaises. Le *solicitor*, selon le domaine dans lequel il exerce, pourra être assimilé à un avocat ou à un notaire. Ainsi, s'il exerce dans les domaines du *conveyancing* (transactions immobilières) ou *probate* (droit des successions), il sera considéré comme un notaire. En revanche, s'il est spécialisé en matière contentieuse ou, s'agissant du droit non-contentieux, s'il donne par exemple des conseils aux entreprises, il est avocat.

Au contraire de la France qui est constituée de multiples barreaux, il n'y a qu'un seul barreau en Angleterre et au Pays de Galles. Le principe de la postulation n'y existe donc pas.

Le rôle de l'huissier de justice en France se rapproche davantage de celui de *sheriff* que de *bailiff*. En effet, bien qu'étant officier ministériel, il ne travaille pas directement dans le cadre d'un tribunal, même s'il ne peut exercer que dans le même ressort géographique que ce même tribunal.

S'agissant des *Queen's Counsels*, il n'existe pas vraiment d'équivalent à ce statut privilégié dont bénéficient certains *barristers*. En France, le statut d'avocat au Conseil d'État et à la Cour de cassation, nommé par le garde des Sceaux, est ce qui s'en rapproche le plus.

□ 5 ACADEMIC BACKGROUND OF THE LEGAL PROFESSIONS AND ORGANISATION

A prerequisite to becoming a solicitor, a barrister and subsquently a judge, is to have an undergraduate law degree (LLB) or equivalent (a degree in another subject followed by a one year conversion course called Common Professional Examination/Graduate Diploma in Law [CPE/GDL]).

Solicitors

After his degree, the prospective solicitor follows a one year full time (or two year part time) Legal Practice Course (LPC) at one of the Colleges of Law. Before commencing the LPC he must apply for student membership of the Solicitors Regulation Authority. Once he has taken and passed his LPC, he is admitted to the Roll of solicitors. He can start his two year training period with a firm of solicitors as a trainee solicitor. During the training phase, the trainee solicitor must pass the Professional Skills Course (PSC). The PSC consists of 12 days full time courses building on the vocational training provided in the Legal Practice Course.

At the end of his training period, he becomes a qualified solicitor. With a practising certificate, he can work in-house for a company or more generally, for a firm. Whilst doing his training, he will have acquired general experience in the litigation or non-litigation fields but is then likely to specialise in a particular legal field. The young solicitor will work as an assistant under the supervision of a partner. As an assistant solicitor he receives a salary. At some stage during his career he can hope to become a salaried partner and eventually, an equity partner in a firm. Trainee solicitors may only fulfil some of the duties of an experienced solicitor. For instance, trainee solicitors cannot be heard, i.e. appear, before certain courts. A solicitor who has been qualified for more than three years can set up his own firm and work as a sole practitioner.

Barristers

After his law degree the prospective barrister undertakes a one year full time (or two year part time) Bar Professional Training Course (BPTC) which is the vocational stage. It is given by a Law School or a College of Law. Once the prospective barrister has taken and passed his BPTC, he is eligible to be called to the Bar. This is a ceremony held at one of the Inns of Court. To qualify for Call the prospective barrister must have completed the vocational stage as well as 12 qualifying sessions which are educational sessions organised during a dinner party at the relevant Inn. The person called to the Bar has the title of barrister but can only practise once he has completed a one year pupillage training period in a set of barristers' chambers. Barristers are usually referred to as Counsel.

Pupillage is divided into two equal parts, a non-practising part (which is a period of observation) and a practising part. The pupil is shadowed by a barrister who acts as supervisor. By the end of their pupillage, prospective barristers are required to satisfactorily complete an Advocacy Training Course and a Practice Management course at their Inn.

After completing his training, the young barrister may obtain tenancy in a set of barristers' chambers as a self-employed barrister or work in-house as an employed barrister. Each set of chambers is headed by one (and sometimes two) Queen's Counsel(s) who is/are highly specialised barristers. They are said to take silk because of the silk lapels on their gown which makes it easier for judges to recognise them from a distance.

Other information

Members of the barrister profession may now apply for a transfer to become solicitors and likewise the other way round. This involves an examination to check that the applicant is able to convert to the other profession's duties. The respective professional bodies of solicitors and barristers are the Law Society and the Bar Council. However the Legal Services Act 2007 has brought the two professions closer by setting up the Legal Services Board, the independent body responsible for overseeing the regulation of lawyers in England and Wales. The 2007 Act also set up the Solicitors Regulation Authority (SRA), the independent regulatory body of the Law Society of England and Wales. The main mission of the SRA is to regulate the professional conduct of solicitors.

Judges

Solicitors and barristers who have practised for at least 5 or 7 years (depending on the nature of the judicial post they seek to hold) may apply to the Judicial Appointments Commission (JAC). The JAC is an independent commission that recommends candidates for judicial office. In fact most judges have usually practised in a firm of solicitors or a set of chambers for much longer than the 5 or 7 years required. Unlike France there is no specific school training judges straight after university. Since the implementation of the Tribunals, Courts and Enforcement Act of 2007 some (limited) judicial positions have become open to professions other than solicitors or barristers, such as legal executives, members of the Institute of Trade Mark Attorneys or Chartered Institute of Patent Attorneys.

Until recently only barristers could apply for a judicial appointment. Solicitors can now also apply. However research and statistics show that despite the fairly recent opening of the profession to solicitors, most aspiring judges are still barristers. The reason seems to be the work conditions of both professions : a set of chambers will always support a barrister who aspires to become a judge (it will improve its image) unlike a firm of solicitors which will see it as the possible loss of a fee earner.

Recent changes

The Legal Services Act 2007 enabled the creation of Alternative Business Structures (ABS). An ABS makes it possible for non-lawyers to invest in and own legal businesses. The creation of ABS will have an impact on the legal professions and on the way law firms are managed. It has been said that ABS would leave the door open for ethical problems such as conflicts of interest. It is too early to draw any definite conclusions but the legal professions will have to adapt themselves.

GLOSSARY

- admission to the Roll : having one name's down on a list of people duly authorised to practise as a solicitor; the admission gives rise to a ceremony organised by the Law Society where the new solicitor takes oath; *fr. : ≈ admission au barreau*

- assistant (adj.) solicitor (n.) : solicitor who works as an employee in a firm and who is (not yet) a partner; *fr. : ≈ avocat collaborateur/≈ clerc de notaire*
- Bar Council : professional body of barristers; *fr. : ≈ Ordre des avocats*
- call to the Bar : having one name's down on a list of people duly authorised to practise as a barrister; being called to the Bar gives rise to a ceremony organised by the Bar Council where the new barrister takes oath; *fr. : ≈ admission au barreau*
- Chambers (set of) (n.) : professional environment in which barristers generally work; they are tenants and rent an office and services from a Head of Chambers who is always a Queen's Counsel; *fr. : cabinet (de barristers)*
- College of Law/Law School : post-university professional school where aspiring solicitors and barristers are taught professional skills; *fr. : ≈ école des barreaux*
- Counsel (n.) : title usually given to barristers; *fr. : ≈ Maître*
- fee earner : name given to those (solicitors, legal executives, etc.) who charge clients fees for the work done on their behalf; *fr. : ≈ qui facture des honoraires*
- firm (n.) : here, group of solicitors, organised for example (but not exclusively) as a Limited Liability Partnership (LLP) who practise law; *fr. : ≈ cabinet d'avocat/≈ étude de notaires*
- hear (v.)/hearing (n.) : in a legal context, court appointment which follows an application to the judge; *fr. : entendre (dans le cadre d'une audience) (v.)/ audience (n.)*
- Inns of court : Gray's Inn, Lincoln's Inn, Middle Temple and Inner Temple; they used to be boarding schools for aspiring barristers; nowadays they are professional associations for barristers; it is mandatory for a barrister to belong to one of them; the twelve compulsory and very formal; dinners which are part of a barrister's training still take; place at the Inns; *fr. : ≈ Ordre local des avocats*
- Law Society : professional body of solicitors; *fr. : ≈ Ordre des avocats/≈ chambre des notaires*
- pass (v.) : when applied to an exam, means to succeed, to obtain the relevant diploma or qualification; *fr. : réussir (un examen)*
- practising (adj.) certificate (n.) : this is not a diploma but a document which is delivered on a yearly basis by the Law Society/Solicitors Regulatory Authority to a solicitor, at the latter's request, in order to practise law; *fr. : ≈ attestation d'exercice (d'une profession)*
- Queen's Counsel (QC) : specialised barrister with considerable expertise in a particular legal field; when becoming a QC, the barrister takes silk; *fr. : ≈ avocat au Conseil d'État et à la Cour de cassation*
- partner (n.) : as in a company, solicitor who runs a firm of solicitors; *fr. : avocat/ notaire associé*
- pupil (n.) : aspiring barrister doing his training; *fr. : élève avocat*

- qualified (adj.) : when applied to a solicitor, refers to someone who has finished his training and is able to start practising without being supervised by another (more experienced) colleague; *fr. : inscrit au grand tableau (de l'Ordre)*
- sole (adj.) practitioner (n.) : solicitor who set up his own firm, where he works by himself; *fr. : ≈ avocat à son compte*
- take (v.) : when applied to an exam, means going through the various exercises given at an exam; *fr. : passer (un examen)*
- trainee (n. or adj.) : someone who gains professional experience with a firm or company under the supervision of a more experienced colleague; *fr. : stagiaire*
- tenancy (n.)/tenant (n.) : because barristers are usually self-employed but work within a set of chambers, they pay rent to the head of chambers who is a Queen's Counsel; *fr. : ≈ locataire*
- in-house (adj.) : here, applies to solicitors or barristers who work exclusively for the legal department of a company to defend its sole interests (whether it is litigation or not); *fr. : juriste d'entreprise*

USEFUL EXPRESSIONS

- to apply for silk; *fr. : postuler pour devenir Queen's Counsel*
- to be called to the Bar; *fr. : être admis au barreau en tant que barrister*
- to work as an in-house solicitor; *fr. : travailler comme juriste d'entreprise*
- to take and fail an exam; *fr. : passer et échouer à un examen*

FURTHER INFORMATION

- do not confuse Counsel which is the title given to a barrister and the Bar Council which is the barristers' professional body
- the Inns of Courts derive their name from the fact that they used to be actual inns (*auberges*) where aspiring barristers were trained, fed and lived

COMPARATIVE APPROACH

La dualité des professions *solicitor/barrister* étant différente de celles d'avocat et notaire, il est difficile de comparer ces professions. Même si le système français autorise désormais les avocats collaborateurs à exercer en tant que salarié d'un cabinet, sous la direction d'associés, la majorité des avocats collaborateurs continue d'exercer à titre libéral, ce qui signifie qu'ils supportent l'ensemble des cotisations sociales qui reposeraient à défaut sur leur employeur s'ils étaient salariés. En revanche, en Angleterre et au Pays de Galles, être salarié est la règle pour les *solicitors* travaillant dans une *firm* jusqu'à ce qu'ils deviennent associés. En ce qui concerne les *barristers* travaillant en *chambers*, ils exercent tous à titre libéral.

S'agissant des magistrats (*judges*), la différence essentielle est qu'en Angleterre et au Pays de Galles, tous les magistrats professionnels ont précédemment exercé pendant plusieurs années le métier de *solicitor* ou *barrister*. En revanche, en France, les magistrats (de l'ordre judiciaire) suivent une formation à l'École Nationale de la Magistrature (ENM) à la sortie de l'université. Ceux de l'ordre administratif passent un concours (École Nationale d'Administration [ENA] ou assimilé).

☐ 6 SOLICITORS' AND BARRISTERS' DUTIES

Solicitors

A solicitor is usually the first contact of a client who requires legal advice (on a litigation or non-litigation matter), assistance or representation in court (for litigation matters). Unless he is a sole practitioner who is required to have a good knowledge of law in general, a solicitor is specialised in a particular legal field. Most solicitors work for firms composed of specialised departments. It is therefore erroneous to believe that solicitors are generalists.

Since the Courts and Legal Services Act 1990, solicitors doing litigation work have gained rights of audience before the higher courts (High Court, Crown Court, Court of Appeal and Supreme Court) and can become solicitor-advocates if they follow the appropriate training. Even before that reform, solicitors could plead a case before the lower courts including the magistrates' courts and the county courts and appear before certain higher courts for the hearing of specific applications.

For non-contentious legal matters, a solicitor will usually be the only professional instructed unless there is a very technical point on which the specialist advice of a barrister is sought. Likewise, regarding litigation matters, a solicitor will usually be able to deal with a case from its outset until its outcome. Counsel will mostly be instructed if specialist advice is required concerning the drafting of pleadings or a technical point of law, certain specialised pleadings must be drafted, or the client needs to be represented in a higher court and the solicitor has no rights of audience before them.

Barristers

Barristers' sets of chambers are all specialised in a particular legal field. A barrister gives specialist advice on a technical point of law. He organises "conferences with counsel" at his chambers, drafts specialised pleadings and attends court to represent a litigant, especially – but not only – before the higher courts. Barristers are normally bound by the Cab rank rule which means that a barrister who receives instructions is not supposed to turn them down even if the work does not correspond to what he usually does. However there are ways around it (such as lack of time to deal with the instructions, etc.). A 2013 Legal Services Board report considered the Cab rank rule as not being justified nowadays.

Barristers are usually instructed by solicitors. However other professionals such as chartered accountants or banks may wish to instruct them directly. Since the Public Access Rules 2004 members of the public have been able to instruct a barrister directly subject to certain conditions being fulfilled. But generally most still receive their briefs from solicitors who do the preparation work.

Barristers used to be immune from negligence actions, that is to say they could not be held professionally liable. The liability used to be transferred to the instructing solicitor. This changed with Arthur Hall v. Simons [2000] 3 AER 673, a landmark case heard by the Law Lords. Now a barrister can be held personally negligent.

GLOSSARY

- brief (n.) : here, set of instructions which a solicitor sends the barrister, asking him to give advice, draft pleadings or attend court; *fr. : ≈ instructions*
- chartered (adj.) accountant (n.) : professional designation given to accountants (specialists of finance and business) who belong to a professional body called an institute; members have to comply with ethical rules; *fr. : expert comptable*
- instructions (n.) : see brief; *fr. : ≈ instructions*
- Law Lords : see 2
- litigant (n.) : legal entity who resorts to contentious law to resolve a dispute; *fr. : justiciable*
- litigation (n.) : contentious law, involving a dispute between two or more parties; *fr. : droit contentieux*
- negligent (adj.)/negligence (n.) : see 86
- plead (v.) : verbally express one's legal arguments to a court; *fr. : plaider*
- pleadings (n.) : court documents exchanged by the claimant and the defendant (in a civil case) in the context of a court case; *fr. : actes de plaidoirie/ conclusions (droit civil)/mémoires (droit public)*
- rights of audience : right to do advocacy or plead a case in court; *fr. : droit de plaider*
- solicitor-advocate : title given to a solicitor who has obtained rights of audience before the higher courts after successfully going through specific training; *fr. : ≈ avocat pouvant plaider devant les juridictions supérieures*

USEFUL EXPRESSIONS

- to instruct counsel/to brief counsel; *fr. : saisir un barrister*

- to have rights of audience before the higher courts; *fr. : avoir le droit de plaider devant les juridictions supérieures*

FURTHER INFORMATION

- a litigant (*justiciable*) is different from a litigator who is a solicitor or barrister specialised in litigation
- after lenghty negotiations, solicitor-advocates were allowed to wear a wig in court in circumstances in which barristers would also wear one; initially barristers were reluctant to share this privilege which makes them easily recognisable in court

COMPARATIVE APPROACH

La réforme des *solicitor-advocates* a eu à ce jour un succès très mitigé. D'une part, les professions de *solicitor* et de *barrister* sont plus complémentaires que concurrentes. D'autre part, 95 % des dossiers contentieux donnent désormais lieu à des transactions bien avant l'audience de jugement (*trial*), réduisant de ce fait le besoin de plaider.

Depuis la réforme, un *solicitor-advocate* est encore plus similaire à un avocat qu'un simple *solicitor* (qui travaille au contentieux) puisqu'il peut plaider devant les juridictions dites supérieures, telles que la Cour d'appel (*Court of Appeal*).

La nature de la profession de *solicitor* fait qu'il est possible de trouver, au sein d'un même cabinet (*firm*) des avocats et des notaires, ce qui n'est à ce jour pas possible dans une structure française. Incidemment, on rappellera qu'en France, une loi n° 90-1259 du 31 décembre 1990 a fusionné l'ancienne profession de conseil juridique avec celle d'avocat. Quant à l'ancienne profession d'avoué près la Cour d'appel, qui a été fusionnée avec celle d'avocat par la loi n° 2011-94 du 25 janvier 2011, leur rôle a toujours été assuré, en Angleterre et au Pays de Galles, par les *solicitors* et *barristers*, comme pour les juridictions de première instance.

PART 2

Non-contentious law

1

Contract law

□ 7 INTRODUCTION

Contract law is the body of law governing the creation and enforcement of binding agreements entered into by contracting parties. Modern contract law has been shaped by 19th century economic theory and the doctrine of *laissez-faire*. Thus, courts have placed considerable importance on the concept of freedom of contract, taking the view that the contracting parties should be free to strike their own bargains with as little regulatory interference as possible.

The common law recognises certain types of promises as enforceable, while others will not be enforced by the courts. Enforceable promises are based on the notion of a bargain, in which there is an exchange of some kind. Promises which are gratuitous – i.e. for which nothing has been offered in exchange – are not binding (the exception to this is a special document called a deed, see the section on Consideration and Promissory Estoppel). Parties are free to make their own bargains, provided they are not illegal or otherwise contrary to public policy; however, these bargains will not be enforced unless the parties intended to be bound and something of legal value, known as consideration, was given in exchange for the original offer.

A contract may be bilateral or unilateral. Bilateral contracts are the most common type of agreement, created through the exchange of promises by contracting parties. The contractual obligations arise at the moment the promises are exchanged. In the case of unilateral contracts, one party promises to do something in the event that a certain act or service is performed, but there is no corresponding obligation on the promisee to undertake performance. Examples of unilateral agreements include a promise by a vendor to pay a real estate agent if he succeeds in selling his house, or a promise to pay a reward in exchange for information.

The elements of contract are traditionally presented as : an intention to create legal relations, an agreement, consisting of an offer and acceptance, and consideration. There are no formal requirements for most types of contract, though certain agreements (e.g. for the sale of land or the transfer of shares) must be drafted and executed in compliance with legislative requirements. The courts will not attempt to "second guess" the intentions of the parties; the terms of an agreement must be sufficiently certain before they will be enforced by the law. Vagueness about the price of goods, for example, or the duration of services to be provided will often render the agreement unenforceable. The parties may specify a particular mechanism by which such details are to be fixed (e.g. through independent arbitration), in which case the court may well regard the arrangement as binding. An agreement in which all parties have completed their obligations is known as an executed contract, whereas agreements yet to be performed are called executory contracts.

While the common law remains the foundation of contract law, these principles are being continuously modified or displaced by legislation, particularly in areas such as consumer rights, the sale of goods, and employment law. The effect of European law and human rights legislation is another area of constant development in relation to contract law.

GLOSSARY

- acceptance (n.) : see 8
- bargain (n. or v.) : the action of negotiating the terms of an agreement; the resulting agreement or compact; the notion of bargaining based on freely exchanged promises is central to common law principles of contract; *fr. : marchandage/négocier*
- bilateral (adj.) contract (n.) : an agreement based on mutual obligations; bilateral contracts are created upon the exchange of promises and bind both parties to their promises; *fr. : contrat synallagmatique*
- binding (adj.) : obligatory; involving a promise or agreement that cannot be broken; *fr. : qui lie*
- binding (adj.) agreement (n.) : enforceable agreement or contract; *fr. : convention obligatoire/accord juridiquement contraignant*
- consideration (n.) : see 9
- contracting (adj.) party (n.) : legal entity (individual, company, partnership, etc.) who enters into a contract; *fr. : contractant*
- deed (n.) : see 9
- draft (n. or v.) : preliminary or rough version of a document, plan, agreement, etc.; to draw up or prepare such a document; *fr. : projet (de contrat/ rédiger)*
- enforceable (adj.) : capable of being enforced (at law); *fr. : exécutoire*
- execute (v.) : put into effect or carry out; to execute a legal instrument (such as a contract or a deed) means to make it valid by signing it and observing any other formal requirements; *fr. : valider/signer*
- executed (adj.) contract (n.) : contract in which the parties have performed their respective obligations; *fr. : contrat exécuté*
- executory (adj.) contract (n.) : contract which has not yet been carried out, which remains to be performed; *fr. : contrat à exécuter*
- freedom of contract (n.) : ability of parties freely to enter into agreements without interference from the state; *fr. : liberté contractuelle*

- gratuitous (adj) : free; offered or provided without payment or charge; *fr. : gratuit*
- *laissez-faire* (doctrine of) (n.) : doctrinal belief that individuals should be free to conduct their commerce and other transactions with minimal interference from the government; non-interventionism; *fr. : laisser-faire*
- offer (n. or v.) : see 8
- promise (n. or v.) : undertaking to do or refrain from doing something, which may be the subject of a legally binding agreement; *fr. : promesse/ promettre*
- promisee (n.) : person to whom a promise is made; *fr. : bénéficiaire de la promesse*
- promisor (n.) : person who makes a promise; *fr. : promettant*
- public (adj.) policy (n.) : see 81
- unilateral (adj.) contract (n.) : agreement whereby the promisor undertakes to do something if a certain act is performed; in such a case, performance of the act constitutes acceptance of the offer, but there is no obligation to undertake performance (e.g. an offer to pay a reward in exchange for information); *fr. : contrat unilatéral*

USEFUL EXPRESSIONS

- to enter into a contract with someone; *fr. : contracter avec quelqu'un*
- parties to a contract; *fr. : les cocontractants*
- pursuant to the provisions/terms of the contract; *fr. : en vertu des clauses du contrat*
- this agreement is binding on the contracting parties; *fr. : cet accord lie les parties contractantes*
- to draft a contract; *fr. : rédiger un contrat*
- to enter into a contract with someone; *fr. : conclure un contrat/contracter avec quelqu'un*
- to be contrary to public policy; *fr. : être contraire à l'ordre public*
- to strike a deal/bargain with; *fr. : conclure un marché avec*

FURTHER INFORMATION

- the concept of bargain in contract law refers to the element of negotiation and exchange in binding agreements; the word bargain is often used in general English to refer to goods which are good value or surprisingly cheap (e.g. it was a real bargain; *fr. : c'était une véritable occasion*)
- the English word counterpart refers to either a copy of a legal document or a person who performs a function corresponding to another person in a different place; although it may be translated by the French noun *contrepartie* in some cases, it is never used to talk about compensation or indemnities

COMPARATIVE APPROACH

En France le droit des contrats fait partie du droit des obligations, un domaine qui est régi par le Code civil. En revanche, Outre-Manche, les principes régissant les contrats ont été développés par la jurisprudence anglaise (*case law*). Si le Parlement britannique intervient de plus en plus fréquemment dans la réglementation des contrats (contrats de travail et ce qui a trait à la protection du consommateur), il n'y a eu aucun projet de codification.

Les éléments constitutifs des contrats se ressemblent : en Angleterre et au Pays de Galles, les conditions d'intention (*intention*), l'accord entre les parties (*agreement*) et une contrepartie (*consideration*). En France, les éléments constitutifs du contrat sont le consentement, la capacité, l'objet et la cause.

La doctrine de l'autonomie de la volonté est centrale en droit français. C'est la volonté des parties contractuelles qui donne à une convention sa force obligatoire. En revanche, Outre-Manche, on met l'accent sur la notion de *bargain*, à savoir la négociation et l'échange d'intérêts entre les cocontractants.

Il existe une classification des contrats dans le Code civil qui ne trouve pas d'équivalent direct en droit commun. Bien que certaines classifications aient des équivalents (contrat synallagmatique/unilatéral, par exemple, correspond à *bilateral/unilateral contract* en anglais), d'autres distinctions, comme contrat à titre onéreux/contrat à titre gratuit, n'existent pas en tant que tels Outre-Manche.

□ 8 AGREEMENTS

Contractual obligations arise from a binding agreement between the parties. An agreement consists of an offer by one party (known as the offeror) and a corresponding acceptance by the other party (the offeree). Any legal entity can be a party to a contract : an individual, a partnership, a company, etc.

Offer

An offer exists where the offeror indicates his willingness to do something (or refrain from doing something) without further negotiation. An offer must be distinguished from an invitation to treat, where one party invites the other party to make an offer or enter into negotiations. An example of this would be an auction, where the seller invites bidders to make an offer to purchase the goods being auctioned (either with a reserve price or with no reserve). Displays in shop windows and advertisements are usually classified as invitations to treat, as are invitations by companies to submit a tender for goods or services.

An offeror can revoke his offer anytime before acceptance. An offer may also be terminated by rejection, by lapse of time, by failure to satisfy a condition precedent, or by the making of a counter-offer.

Acceptance

Agreement is formed when an offer is accepted by the offeree. The acceptance must be unqualified : that is, the offeree cannot impose any conditions or qualifications on the acceptance (i.e. the acceptance must mirror the offer made). A qualified acceptance is treated as a counter-offer, which the other party is then free to accept or reject. The acceptance may be explicit, or it may be inferred from the offeree's conduct. In the case of a unilateral offer (i.e. a promise made in the context of a unilateral contract), performance of the required act or service will constitute acceptance and entitle the promisee to enforce the original promise.

An agreement is not formed unless acceptance is communicated to the offeror. Silence will not amount to acceptance, unless there is no doubt that by remaining silent the offeree intended acceptance. In any event, an offeror can never stipulate that silence on the part of the offeree will be taken as acceptance. Communication can take any form, unless the offeror prescribes a particular method of acceptance. Often the communication will be instantaneous (e.g. by telephone or in person). However, in cases where there is a delay between sending and receiving the communication, the "postal acceptance rule" states that the agreement is formed at the moment the communication is sent. This means an agreement will exist even if the offeror never actually receives an acceptance sent by post. The application of the postal rule to modern forms of communication such as fax, e-mail, or text messaging remains uncertain. Although such messages are delivered instantaneously, they may not be read instantly if the office is closed or the receiving party is away from the receiving device. In practice, the decision of the courts will probably depend on the particular circumstances of the case, and whether or not the person accepting the offer was in a position to know that the communication had been ineffective.

The courts apply an objective test when determining whether or not an agreement exists, rather than inquiring into what the parties may have thought or intended. In other words, the question is whether or not a reasonable observer of the parties' words and actions would have concluded that there had been a meeting of the minds and that the parties were in agreement.

In the case of a unilateral contract the requirement of acceptance is waived. The offeree is under no obligation to perform the required act, but if he does undertake performance, the offer cannot be revoked and will become binding on completion of the act.

GLOSSARY

- acceptance (n.) : definite and unqualified assent to the terms of an offer which, provided the other elements of contract are satisfied, creates a legally binding agreement; for an acceptance to be valid it must be communicated to the offeror in the case of a bilateral contract; *fr. : acceptation*

- acceptance by conduct : implicit acceptance inferred from the actions or behaviour of the offeree; *fr. : ≈ acceptation implicite*
- agreement (n.) : consensus or accord reached between two or more legal persons; an agreement creates legally binding obligations where the other elements of contract are present; *fr. : accord*
- auction (n. or v.) : public sale whereby goods are sold by an auctioneer to the highest bidder (the party who offers the most money); the auctioneer's request for bids is treated as an invitation to treat; bidders are then free to make an offer, acceptance of which occurs when the auctioneer's hammer falls; *fr. : vente aux enchères*
- auction without reserve : auction where no minimum price is set and the owner undertakes not to bid in an attempt to raise the price of the goods; *fr. : vente aux enchères sans prix de réserve*
- bid (n. or v.) : price offered by a bidder in an auction or action of making a bid; *fr. : enchère/faire une enchère*
- binding (adj.) agreement (n.) : see 7
- communication (n.) : conveying or transmission of information; an offeree must communicate acceptance of the offer before an agreement will be formed (but see postal rule); *fr. : communication*
- condition precedent : term that suspends the validity of an agreement until a specified event has happened (e.g. an offer of employment which is subject to the provision of satisfactory references); failure to satisfy a condition precedent may have the effect of terminating an offer; *fr. : ≈ condition suspensive/condition préalable*
- counter-offer (n. or v.) : offer, often purporting to be an acceptance, which adds a qualification or changes the terms of the original offer, thus destroying it; it operates as a new offer which can be accepted or rejected; *fr. : contre-proposition*
- invitation to tender : procedure inviting vendors or contractors to submit competitive bids for the supply of goods or services; *fr. : appel d'offres*
- invitation to treat : situation in which one party invites another to make an offer; the display of goods in a shop window is an invitation to potential customers to make an offer for the goods, which can then be accepted or rejected by the vendor; *fr. : invitation à entrer en pourparlers*
- lapse of offer : period of time in which an offer remains open; if no time is specified by the offeror, the offer will lapse after a reasonable period of time has passed; *fr. : caducité de l'offre*
- legal (adj.) entity (n.) entity considered to have a legal personality conferring the ability to exercise rights and assume legal obligations; sometimes divided

into natural persons (human beings) and juristic persons (corporations and other legal entities); *fr. : personnalité juridique*

- meeting of the minds : concordance of intention between the parties to an agreement; *fr. : accord des volontés*
- mirror-image rule : principle that acceptance must correspond precisely with the terms of the offer; any variation or qualification will be treated as a counter-offer; *fr. : ≈ règle de l'équivalence des termes de l'offre et de l'acceptation*
- objective (adj.) test (n.) : test applied by the courts to determine whether an offer has been accepted; the question is whether a "reasonable man", examining the words and actions of the parties, would conclude that an agreement had been reached; *fr. : critère objectif*
- offer (n. or v.) : indication by one party (the offeror) to another (the offeree) that he is willing to do something or refrain from doing something; *fr. : offre*
- offeree (n.) : legal person to whom an offer is made; *fr. : destinataire de l'offre*
- offeror (n.) : legal person who makes an offer; *fr. : offrant(e)*
- postal acceptance rule : principle that acceptance of an offer by post is effective at the moment the letter is sent, and not when it is received; *fr. : ≈ théorie de l'émission*
- prescribed method of acceptance : procedure stipulated by an offeror for acceptance of his offer; where the procedure is mandatory (and subject to being reasonable), acceptance by any other means will not be valid; *fr. : méthode prescrite (pour l'acceptation)*
- revocation of offer : withdrawal or annulling of an offer before it has been accepted, effective from the moment the offeree becomes aware of the revocation; *fr. : révocation de l'offre*
- tender (n. or v.) : offer by one party to supply goods or carry out work for another party at a set price or rate; usually made in response to a general invitation by the second party calling on interested parties to submit a tender; tenders are treated as offers, acceptance of which will result in a binding contract; *fr. : soumission (à un appel d'offres)/faire une soumission*
- unilateral (adj.) contract (n.) : see 7
- unilateral (adj.) offer (n.) : promise to pay an amount of money or do something if the other party (the promisee) performs a certain action; the other party is under no obligation to perform the act, but if he does so he will be entitled to enforce the promise (e.g. an offer of reward in exchange for information); this type of offer gives rise to a unilateral contract, as opposed to a bilateral contract; *fr. : offre unilatérale*
- waive (v.)/waiver (n.) : action of relinquishing a right; refraining from insisting on a right or claim; *fr. : renoncer à/renonciation*
- withdraw (v.)/withdrawal (n.) : revoke or take back; an offer can be withdrawn any time before acceptance, although a unilateral offer cannot be withdrawn once the promisee has started performance of the required act; *fr. : retirer/retrait*

USEFUL EXPRESSIONS

- to enter into a binding agreement; *fr. : conclure une convention obligatoire*
- the offeree shall have 30 days to accept the offer, after which time the offer will lapse; *fr. : le destinataire de l'offre dispose d'un délai de 30 jours pour accepter l'offre, délai au terme duquel l'offre devient caduque*
- to be mere "puff" in an advertisement; *fr. : être une simple exagération dans une publicité*
- the offer is subject to the following conditions; *fr. : l'offre est soumise aux conditions suivantes*

FURTHER INFORMATION

- the word communication has a more restricted meaning in English than in its French counterpart; it is neither used to refer to public relations or publicity campaigns, nor to a paper delivered at a conference
- the French verb *traiter* cannot always be translated by to treat; e.g. *traiter avec quelqu'un* means to deal with/negotiate with someone; *traiter un dossier* means to deal with a file
- the word agreement has a wider meaning than the word contract; the latter refers to legally binding agreements only; the word accord would generally not be used in English to refer to an agreement between individuals, though it is often employed when referring to an agreement between employers and trade unions, or to official treaties (e.g. the Helsinki Accords of 1975)

COMPARATIVE APPROACH

Si le droit anglais a adopté une approche objective pour déterminer l'existence d'un accord menant à un contrat, le droit français est plus ouvert à une approche subjective. Le Code civil exige qu'on recherche quelle a été la commune intention des parties contractantes, alors que le droit anglais met davantage l'accent sur les circonstances extérieures telles que le comportement des parties, la nature de leurs échanges, etc.

La théorie de l'émission (*postal acceptance rule*) est toujours de jurisprudence constante Outre-Manche. En revanche, en France, la Cour de cassation semble pencher pour cette même théorie mais n'a pas encore réglé la question par un arrêt de principe.

□ 9 CONSIDERATION AND PROMISSORY ESTOPPEL

With the exception of deeds, a contract will not be enforceable unless something of value is given in exchange for the promise made by the offeree. This act or promise, which is effectively the price paid for the promise of the other party, is known as consideration. It often takes the form of money or goods with monetary value, but it can also be a promise to perform some act or not to do something (i.e. a forbearance).

It is often said that consideration need not be adequate but it must be sufficient, meaning there is no requirement that the consideration be of equal monetary value to the original promise, but rather that it has some value recognised at law. Love and affection, for example, are not sufficient to constitute valid consideration.

Consideration is often thought of as the price paid in exchange for the promise. Although it may be executed or executory, it cannot be past. Past consideration (an act done before any promise is made) cannot operate as valid consideration because it was not given in the context of an exchange (e.g. if X performed a service for Y, and Y subsequently promised to give X a bicycle by way of thanks, Y's promise would not be enforceable). Similarly, consideration for a promise cannot be given by a third party; it must always move from the promisee. If X offers to give something to Y in exchange for a promise by Z, Y cannot enforce X's offer as the "consideration" moved from Z.

If one party to a contract indicates to the other that he will not seek to enforce certain rights under the agreement, and the other party acts in reliance on this, the law takes the view that it would be unfair to allow the first party to go back on his promise even though it was unsupported by any consideration on the part of the other party. In such situations, the equitable doctrine of promissory estoppel will operate in order to estop (or prevent) the first party from retracting his promise not to enforce certain rights.

GLOSSARY

- consideration (n.) : in a contract, an act or promise by one party given in exchange for the other party's promise; must have some value recognised by law in order to be valid, though it need not have any relation of monetary equivalence; *fr. : ≈ contrepartie*
- deed (n.) : formal, written document signed in the presence of a witness; in contract law, promises contained in a deed do not require consideration to be enforceable; *fr. : acte notarié/acte authentique*
- enforceable (adj.) : capable of being enforced or compelled; promises made in a contract are enforceable at law; *fr. : exécutoire*
- estop (v.) : prevent or preclude; in certain cases, a party to a contract may be estopped from doing something because it would be inequitable; *fr. : ≈ empêcher*
- executed (adj.) consideration (n.) : act or forbearance performed in response to a promise; typical of unilateral agreements (e.g. giving information in response to an offer of a reward); *fr. : contrepartie parfaite*

- executory (adj.) consideration (n.) : promise given in exchange for a promise; this type of consideration is typical of a bilateral agreement (e.g. one party's promise to pay £100 in return for the other party's promise to sell his bicycle); *fr. : contrepartie promissoire*
- forbearance (n.) : action of abstaining or refraining from something; a promise to forbear from doing something may constitute good consideration for another party's promise; *fr. : abstention*
- go back on (v.) : change one's mind or renegue on a promise or commitment; *fr. : revenir sur/renier*
- good (adj.) consideration (n.) : consideration which the law recognises as having sufficient value to create a legally binding agreement; *fr. : contrepartie valable*
- past (adj.) consideration (n.) : act or promise; *fr. : contrepartie antérieure*
- promissory estoppel (n.) : equitable doctrine that operates where one party to a contract has represented, by words or conduct, that he will not insist on certain rights under the contract; if the other party acts in reliance on this representation, then the first party will be estopped (prevented) from going back on his representation; *fr. : ≈ principe d'interdiction de se contredire au détriment d'autrui/(non concedit venire contra factum proprium)*
- undertake (v.) : commit (oneself) to a course of action; *fr. : s'engager à*

USEFUL EXPRESSIONS

- consideration must move from the promisee; *fr. : la contrepartie doit émaner du bénéficiaire de la promesse*
- in consideration for the sum of; *fr. : moyennant la somme de*
- to be supported by good consideration; *fr. : être étayé par une contrepartie valable*
- to go back on a promise; *fr. : manquer à/revenir sur sa promesse*

FURTHER INFORMATION

- the word consideration is an uncountable noun, which means it cannot be used with the indefinite article "a"
- the verb to estop is a technical legal term, which would never be used in general English as a substitute for to stop or to prevent; in legal English it is often used in the passive form (e.g. to be estopped from doing something)

COMPARATIVE APPROACH

Le concept juridique de *consideration* est une particularité de la *common law* qui n'a pas d'équivalent dans les systèmes de droit civil comme celui de la France. Certains ont évoqué la similitude entre la notion de *conside-*

ration et celle de cause en droit français. Toutefois, la notion de *consideration* est de portée plus étroite que celle de la cause.

Le droit des contrats en France repose sur l'idée que les obligations naissent de la volonté des cocontractants, d'où le besoin d'une équivalence entre la valeur des promesses échangées. Cette idée est absente du droit anglais, où les tribunaux estiment que l'une des parties aurait pu faire une mauvaise affaire et que la valeur de la contrepartie n'a strictement aucun rapport avec la valeur de la promesse correspondante.

Le principe anglo-saxon *d'estoppel* a d'abord été reconnu par le droit arbitral où il a été consacré comme principe général du droit du commerce international avant d'être timidement évoqué par les juridictions françaises et notamment, la juridiction suprême (Civ. 1re, 3 février 2010, *Merial c/Klocke Verspackung*, pourvoi n° 08-21.288) mais le droit français demeure encore très attaché au principe d'autonomie de la volonté et à l'esprit de l'article 1134 du Code civil.

□ 10 INTENTION AND FORMALITIES OF CONTRACT

Intention

An agreement will not create an enforceable contract unless it can be proved that the parties intended to be bound by it. In a commercial or business context, there is a strong presumption that the parties intend to be bound by their respective promises. In a domestic situation, the presumption is reversed. For example, the court will assume that a promise made by a husband to his wife is not intended to give rise to legal relations. This presumption is rebuttable (as opposed to an irrebuttable presumption), which means that those interested can provide evidence that they intended their agreement to be binding. Conversely, there are circumstances where it can be shown that no intention to be bound exists, whether because of the actions of the parties or the existence of an honour clause relating to the agreement.

Formalities

There are very few formal requirements at common law for making an agreement legally enforceable. A contract can be either oral, written or a combination of the two. The terms of the agreement may be express or implied from conduct or from legislation. Certain agreements, such as a contract for the sale of land or the transfer of shares, are required by law to be in writing.

An agreement will not be binding unless the parties have the capacity to contract. The law regards certain classes of individuals – e.g. minors, the drunk and those who are not *compos mentis* – as having an impaired capacity to contract. Any contract entered into would be voidable or even potentially null and void.

Specific case of deeds

A deed is a special type of written document signed in the presence of a witness or, in the case of a company, affixed with a seal. Formal agreements or covenants are often made under seal and referred to as specialty agreements. Deeds become operative on delivery to the other party, though it is possible to deliver a deed that is specified to take effect at a future date or on fulfillment of a specified condition. This type of deed is known as a deed delivered by escrow. Agreements that are executed by way of a deed do not require any supporting consideration, and the parties' intention to be bound will be clear and not subject to rebuttal in the case of domestic agreements. Contracts which are not under seal (i.e. not deeds) are referred to as simple contracts (also known as parol contracts).

GLOSSARY

- bind (v.) : impose an obligation; oblige someone to undertake some action or other commitment; *fr. : obliger*
- capacity to contract : ability for a legal entity to enter into a legally binding agreement; *fr. : capacité à contracter*
- *compos mentis* (adj.) : of sound mind; in control of one's mind; *fr. : être sain d'esprit*
- covenant (n. or v.) : formal promise or agreement; used to refer to promises contained in a deed; the action of making a formal promise or agreement; *fr. : ≈ convention* or *engagement (n.)/s'engager or convenir (v.)*
- deed : see 9
- domestic (adj.) agreement (n.) : agreement between family members; there is a legal presumption that, in the absence of evidence to the contrary, domestic agreements are not intended to create legal relations; *fr. : accord familial*
- escrow agreement (n.) : when applied to a deed, it means that the deed is handed over by A to a third party who will hold on to it and pass it on to B when a specified condition (mentioned in the deed) has been met; *fr. : ≈ contrat de tierce détention*
- formal (adj.) agreement (n.) : agreement reached by observing certain formalities; *fr. : convention solennelle*
- honour clause (n.) : express statement that the parties intend an agreement to be binding in honour only, rather than in law; such agreements are not enforceable; *fr. : ≈ engagement sur l'honneur*
- intention (n.) : purpose or objective; in contract, an intention to create legal relations is required before the court will enforce the parties' promises; *fr. : intention*
- irrebuttable (adj.) presumption (n.) : presumption incapable of being rebutted or refuted; *fr. : présomption irréfragable*

- legal (adj.) relations (n.) : relationship between two or more parties in which legally binding, mutual obligations exist; *fr. : relations juridiques/lien de droit*
- null and void : devoid of force or legal validity; *fr. : nul et non avenu*
- parol contract : any binding agreement other than a deed; *fr. : convention verbale*
- presumption (n.) : inference or assumption in the absence of evidence to the contrary; in contract law, there is a presumption that agreements between family members are not intended to be binding, whereas commercial agreements are; *fr. : présomption*
- rebut (v.) : refute or disprove a statement, presumption, argument, etc.; *fr. : réfuter*
- rebuttable (adj.) presumption (n.) : presumption capable of being rebutted or refuted; *fr. : présomption simple*
- specialty agreement : contractual document in the form of a deed; *fr. : convention formelle*
- seal (n. or v.) : formal mark or adhesive device attached to a document to indicate authenticity or authority (traditionally in the form of impressed wax); the action of affixing a seal; *fr. : sceau (n.)/sceller (v.)*
- share (n.) : see 16
- simple (adj.) contract (n.) : agreement which is not under seal (i.e. not executed as a deed); *fr. : contrat sous seing privé*
- voidable (adj.) : see 77
- witness (n. or v.) : in contract law, a person who is present at the signing of a contract or other document and confirms this by countersigning it; the action of countersigning a document to confirm one's presence when it was signed by the principal signatories; a deed must be witnessed in order to be valid; *fr. : témoin (n.)/certifier (v.) (l'authenticité de)*

USEFUL EXPRESSIONS

- to affix one's seal to; *fr. : apposer son sceau sur*
- to execute a contract; *fr. : signer un contrat*
- intention to be bound by; *fr. : intention d'être lié par*
- to argue that a contract is null and void and dispute that it is merely voidable; *fr. : alléguer de ce qu'un contrat est nul et non avenu et contester qu'il n'est qu'annulable*
- to witness someone's signature; *fr. : certifier la signature de quelqu'un*

FURTHER INFORMATION

- to bind is an irregular verb (bound/bound) complex to use; to bind someone/ to be binding on someone means *lier quelqu'un*; to be bound by something means *être lié par quelque chose*

- the word deed refers to a formally executed contract but in general English, it is also used to refer to an action, particularly when referring to noble or heroic actions (e.g. he was rewarded for his brave deed); deed is not used as a verb in British English, although it is sometimes used in American English to mean the action of conveying or transferring something by deed
- outside the context of contract law, the word escrow also refers to a sum of money held in trust or as a security; an escrow account corresponds to *un compte sous séquestre*

Comparative approach

Les systèmes juridiques français et anglais requièrent qu'il y ait une intention juridique de contracter de la part des parties contractantes. C'est la raison pour laquelle on retrouve, dans les deux systèmes, la condition de la capacité juridique (*capacity to contract*) des cocontractants.

La loi française met l'accent sur le concept de bonne foi qui n'est pas aussi présent en droit anglais. Pour seul exemple et en matière de contrat de vente, on citera le principe de *caveat emptor* (c'est à l'acheteur d'être vigilant) applicable Outre-Manche. Ce principe n'est pas reconnu en temps que tel en France où, en cas de disproportion grave entre les prestations fournies respectivement par le vendeur et l'acheteur dans le domaine immobilier, l'acheteur est protégé par une éventuelle action en rescision pour lésion. Cependant, dans les deux systèmes, le droit européen est intervenu, notamment en droit de la consommation, pour accorder une plus grande protection aux acheteurs/consommateurs.

En France comme Outre-Manche, aucun document écrit n'est en général requis pour qu'un contrat soit exécutoire. Il existe cependant des exceptions : par exemple, une donation, hypothèque conventionnelle ou subrogation conventionnelle en France et un *written statement of employment particulars* en droit du travail Outre-Manche, qui est une sorte de contrat de travail résumé.

□ 11 PRIVITY OF CONTRACT, ASSIGNMENT AND AGENCY

Privity of contract

At common law, only the parties to a contract can sue to enforce rights under this contract. Under the doctrine of privity, third parties cannot seek to enforce any advantages that a contract may confer on them. They cannot be bound by the terms of a contract to which they are not a party. The doctrine of privity is a consequence of the requirement that parties must provide consideration before an agreement is binding.

Legislation now allows a third party to enforce any contractual term that confers a benefit on him, unless it is clear that this was not the contracting parties' intention.

Agency

There are other cases where agreements are affected by third parties' rights. An agent may enter into a contract on behalf of his principal. The agent acts as an intermediary rather than as a party, and the resulting agreement will be binding upon, and enforceable by, the principal. An agent may act by express authority, implied authority or apparent authority. There is apparent authority when the principal's past behaviour gives good reason to believe that a person has authority to act on his behalf. A contract entered into by an agent without authority is not binding on the principal unless he elects to ratify it.

Assignment

It is possible to assign (i.e. to transfer) contractual rights, subject to certain restrictions. For example, company X (the assignor) might decide to sell to company Y (the assignee) its right to recover certain debts owed by Z. Company Y is then entitled to enforce its contractual right to recover the debts from Z. The right to assign is usually governed by a specific assignment clause in the contract. However certain rights cannot be assigned such as the rights to the performance of personal services under an employment contract.

There are other limits to the assignment procedure. It is not possible to assign obligations under a contract unless the party entitled to the benefit of these obligations gives his assent. In the example above, Z could not assign the debt to another party without first obtaining X's consent. The relations between the original parties and a third party may be defined by substitution of an entirely new contract. This is known as novation, and should not be confused with assignment. For example, if X owes Y £500, and Y owes Z £500, all three parties may decide to extinguish the existing debts and replace them with a new agreement that X is to pay Z £500.

Collateral contract

This is another way to overcome the restrictions of the privity rule. This arises where an agreement between two parties is accompanied by a contract relating to the same subject matter between one of the contracting parties and a third party. The collateral contract functions as a kind of subsidiary agreement which induces a party to enter into the main contract. If X assures Y that certain goods are of good quality, and based on that assurance Y agrees to buy the goods from Z, under common law principles Y could not sue Z if the goods turn out to be poor quality (Z made no promise to this effect) and the doctrine of privity means that Y could not sue X (who is not a party to the contract). However, the court may find that a collateral contract existed between X and Y, whereby X made a promise as to quality in consideration of Y's promise to enter a contract with Z.

GLOSSARY

- absolute (adj.) assignment (n.) : unconditional transfer to the assignee of the assignor's entire interest (in property or under a contract); *fr. : cession absolue*
- agent (n.) : person who acts on behalf of another person (the principal); an agent is authorised to enter into contracts with a third party on behalf of the principal; *fr. : agent/préposé*
- apparent (adj.) authority (n.) : where a principal's behaviour has given a third party reason to believe that he had authorised another person to act as his agent, the principal will be bound by any subsequent agreement entered into on the basis of apparent authority; *fr. : autorité apparente*
- assign (v.)/assignment (n.) : transfer legal rights or obligations to another party or the transfer of this right; *fr. : céder (v.)/cession (n.)*
- assignee (n.) : one who receives an assignment; *fr. : cessionnaire*
- assignor (n.) : one who assigns a right; *fr. : cédant(e)*
- collateral (adj.) contract (n.) : subsidiary agreement which induces a party to enter into another, related agreement; sometimes used by courts to overcome the privity rule and enforce promises made by a third party; *fr. : convention annexe*
- express (adj.) authority (n.) : clear and explicit authority given to an agent to act on behalf of the principal; *fr. : autorisation expresse*
- implied (adj.) authority (n.) : authority which is implicit or suggested; an agent is authorised to enter into those contracts which are, by implication, required to carry out the principal's instructions; *fr. : pouvoir implicite*
- induce (v.) : fact of persuading a legal entity to do or refrain from doing something; *fr. : inciter*
- novation (n.) : act of substituting a new contract for an existing one, often involving the insertion of a new party; *fr. : contrat novatoire/novation*
- principal (n.) : party for whom an agent acts; *fr. : commettant*
- privity (n.) (doctrine of) : common law principle (now modified by legislation) by which only the actual parties to the contract can sue or be sued under the terms of the agreement; *fr. : doctrine de l'effet relatif des contrats*
- third party (n.) : in the context of contract law, legal entity other than those primarily concerned by an agreement; *fr. : tiers*

USEFUL EXPRESSIONS

- to be responsible to someone for something; *fr. : devoir répondre de quelque chose envers quelqu'un/être responsable de quelque chose à l'égard de quelqu'un*
- to act on behalf of someone; *fr. : agir pour le compte de quelqu'un*
- to assign a right to somebody; *fr. : faire cession d'un droit à quelqu'un*
- to confer a benefit on; *fr. : conférer un avantage à*
- to obtain the consent of; *fr. : obtenir l'aval de*

FURTHER INFORMATION

- do not confuse the English words principal (*commettant*) and principle (*principe*)
- the noun benefit refers to an advantage of some kind; it is never used to refer to the profits (*bénéfice*) made by commercial entities
- the French verb *assigner* means to issue a claim against someone (in court)

COMPARATIVE APPROACH

L'équivalent français de la doctrine de *privity of contract* (effet relatif des contrats) est prévu à l'article 1165 du Code civil qui stipule que les conventions n'ont d'effet qu'entre les parties contractantes. Une exception à cette règle est la stipulation pour autrui (*conferring a benefit on a third party*), qui permet à des tiers de faire respecter les promesses de contrats qui leur accordent un avantage.

□ 12 EXPRESS AND IMPLIED TERMS

The contents of an agreement, describing the rights and obligations of the parties, are contained in the terms of the contract. Terms explicitly agreed upon by the parties, whether written or otherwise, are known as express terms. However, it is common for contracts to contain implied terms as well : terms that give effect to the presumed intentions of the parties (terms implied in fact) or that are implied into the contract by local custom, usage, or legislation (e.g. the term implied into all contracts for the sale of goods that the goods be of satisfactory quality).

The parties generally make a number of representations in the course of negotiations, some of which are designed to induce the other party to enter into the contract. These representations will not necessarily form part of the contract, unless the parties make it clear that they are intended to be terms of any resulting agreement. A distinction is often made between terms and representations : the former are binding, and may give rise to an action for breach of contract; the latter are not contractual obligations, though false or misleading representations may affect the enforceability of any resulting agreement. If a statement is important in convincing the other party to enter into the contract, or is repeatedly made in a clear and emphatic manner, it is more likely that it will be treated as a term of the contract. Similarly, a statement is more likely to be incorporated as a term if it is made by a person with expert knowledge or skill than if it is made by an amateur with no special expertise in the subject matter of the contract.

Although oral statements may be incorporated as implied terms in certain circumstances, they cannot be presented as extrinsic evidence to contradict or change express terms in a written contract. This principle is known as the parol evidence rule.

The provisions of a written contract are set out in clauses. If the parties wish to exclude any terms not included in the document (other than terms implied by law), they may include an entire agreement clause to make this clear. Often clauses are included to cover specific eventualities such as an act of God or *force majeure*, or a variation of the agreement.

GLOSSARY

- act of God : event provoked by overwhelming natural forces (e.g. earthquake, flood, hurricane, etc.); many contracts include provisions dealing with acts of God; *fr. : fait de Dieu*
- clause (n.) : (numbered) subdivision of a contract stipulating a term or provision; *fr. : clause*
- entire agreement clause : clause stating that all the terms of the parties' agreement are contained in the contractual document; *fr. : ≈ clause d'intégralité (du contrat)*
- express (adj.) term (n.) : term of a contract explicitly agreed to by the parties, whether in writing or orally; *fr. : clause/disposition expresse*
- extrinsic (adj.) evidence (n.) : evidence concerning a subject in a document which is not found in the document itself; in contract, it is generally not capable of being used to contradict any express terms of the document; *fr. : preuve extrinsèque*
- *force majeure* clause : clause that deals with the contractual consequences of events outside the contracting parties' control, such as an earthquake, a hurricane, a strike, civil war, etc.; such a clause would often allow for delay, or even a total failure to perform the agreement, in the case of such an event; *fr. : clause de force majeure*
- implied (adj.) term (n.) : term that is not expressly provided for in the contract, but which is required in order to give effect to the parties' presumed intentions; some terms may be implied in law; *fr. : clause implicite*
- local (adj.) custom (n.) : common or habitual practice of a localised community; it may be the basis for implying a term into a contract (provided such a term does not contradict the express terms of the agreement); *fr. : coutume locale*
- parol evidence rule : common law principle that, subject to a number of defined exceptions, evidence extrinsic to a contractual document cannot be used to contradict or change the written terms of that document; *fr. : ≈ règle d'exclusion de la preuve extrinsèque/≈ règle de la preuve testimoniale*
- provision (n) : contractual term or statutory term; *fr. : disposition*
- representation (n.) : in contract law, it is a statement which, when made in the course of negotiations, does not, of itself, form part of a contract; *fr. : ≈ représentation/déclaration*

- term (n.) : promise or undertaking that forms part of a contract; provision; *fr. : clause*
- term implied in fact : provision implied to give effect to the subjective intentions of the parties; *fr. : clause implicite en fait*
- term implied in law : provision implied into certain types of contract by force of statute; *fr. : clause implicite en droit*
- term implied by usage : provision which a court implies into certain commercial contracts because they routinely form part of the standard terms used in agreements involving that particular trade or business; *fr. : clause implicite fondée sur l'usage*
- variation clause : clause that stipulates the manner in which a contract may be varied, usually by requiring changes to be in writing and signed by both parties; such a clause can, for example, be found in employment contracts; *fr. : ≈ clause évolutive/clause de variation*

USEFUL EXPRESSIONS

- to form part of the contract; *fr. : faire partie du contrat*
- the contract must be construed as meaning that; *fr. : le contrat doit être interprété comme signifiant que*
- to give effect to the intentions of the parties; *fr. : donner effet à l'intention des parties*
- to set out the terms of the agreement; *fr. : indiquer les termes de l'accord*
- pursuant to the terms of this contract; *fr. : en vertu des clauses de ce contrat*

FURTHER INFORMATION

- the words term and provision are often used synonymously when talking about contracts; however, the word provision has a wider meaning outside the context of contract law : we refer to the provisions of a statute (in the sense of the French *dispositions*), not the terms of a statute
- care should be taken not to confuse the word parol (as in parol contract e.g.) and parole, which in English means the conditional release of a prisoner (*liberté conditionnelle*); as for the French word *parole*, it refers to the fact of expressing oneself verbally

Comparative approach

Contrairement à la *common law*, le droit français insiste sur la notion de bonne foi et le Code civil stipule qu'on doit rechercher quelle a été la commune intention des parties contractantes, plutôt que de s'arrêter au sens littéral des termes. Le droit anglais accorde une importance considérable à l'idée de certitude dans le contrat, dans le but de promouvoir la stabilité et la sécurité des transactions. Cependant, Outre-Manche, l'apparition de la notion équitable *d'unconscionable behaviour* (comportement inadmissible) ainsi que certaines évolutions législatives récentes, notamment au niveau européen, conduisent à une plus grande similitude entre les droits des contrats français et anglais.

2

Company law

☐ 13 BUSINESS STRUCTURES

There are various types of business structures : sole proprietorships, partnerships, limited liability partnerships and companies. The creation of each business structure entails different formalities and liabilities.

Sole proprietorships are not incorporated. Although the sole proprietor or sole trader needs to register himself with HM Revenue and Customs, he does not need to file accounts. The liability of the sole proprietor is personal and unlimited.

In an ordinary partnership, two or more people (such as accountants or solicitors) organised as a firm agree to carry on business together with a view to making a profit. Each partner is considered as an agent of the firm and is thus jointly liable for the debts and obligations entered into by the partnership while he is a partner. Liability is personal and unlimited. Partners can also be jointly and severally liable.

Limited liability partnerships (LLP) are a special type of partnerships. They have a lot in common with companies (incorporation, corporate personality, limited liability, regulation by company law). This type of structure is used mostly by international professional firms. Members of the LLP are not liable for the debts and liabilities of the LLP. The LLP itself is liable unless there is evidence of fraudulent or wrongful trading.

There are various types of companies : private limited companies, with or without share capital, where the liability of members is limited, private unlimited companies with or without share capital, where owners are personally liable for the torts and breaches committed by themselves or the company's agents in the course of business on the whole value of their personal and business assets, and public limited companies which can sell shares to the public at large and which have limited liability for shareholders.

Generally an individual is personally liable for the whole value of his personal and business assets for the torts and breaches committed by himself and/or the company agents in the course of business. However there are differences based on whether the individual is a member or a shareholder. As the liability of members is limited by guarantee, members are thus liable up to the amount stated in the statement of guarantee. If their assets are insufficient to cover the liabilities, they will be declared bankrupt. The liability of shareholders is said to be limited by shares so they are liable up to the unpaid amount of their shares; if their shares are fully paid, they are not liable to contribute anymore. The company needs to register in order to become a legal entity, thus be incorporated. In some cases there is a requirement of a minimum capital.

GLOSSARY

- agent (n.) : when applied to a partnership, person authorised to act on behalf of a principal; *fr. : commandité*
- company (n.) : refers to various types of business structures, which provide limited liability for its members; it can be limited or unlimited; *fr. : société de capitaux*
- firm (n.) : business unit; *fr. : cabinet*
- HM Revenue and Customs : the United Kingdom's tax authority in charge of collecting taxes and preventing tax evasion; *fr. : Trésor public/fisc*
- incorporated business structure/body corporate/registered (adj.) company (n.) : business structure known as LLP or company which is created *via* the process of incorporation, that is through the formal registering of documents with the Registrar of Companies; *fr. : société immatriculée au Registre du Commerce et des Sociétés*
- joint (adj.) liability (n.) : type of liability whereby partners are liable together and as a whole for the torts and breaches committed by themselves or the company's agents in the course of business; *fr. : responsabilité conjointe*
- joint and several liability : type of liability whereby partners are liable in turn or as a whole until the wronged individual has recovered his losses fully; *fr. : responsabilité conjointe et solidaire*
- legal (adj.) entity (n.) : fact for a company to be considered as a person in its own right, as any other legal person; *fr. : personnalité juridique*
- limited (adj.) (ltd) : term which indicates the type of liability attached to the business structure : either limited or unlimited; when the liability is said to be limited (company and LLP), members are not liable, as a corporate person, whereas the business is; *fr. : limitée aux apports*
- limited (adj.) company (n.) : business structure where the liability of the owners for the torts and breaches committed by themselves or the company's agents in the course of business is limited by the value of their investment in the business; there are two types of limitations : by shares and by guarantee; *fr. : société à responsabilité limitée aux apports* (depending on the context, it could be a *société à responsabilité limitée [SARL], société anonyme [SA]* or a *société par actions simplifiée [SAS]*)
- limited (adj.) partnership (n.) : business structures regulated either under the Limited Partnership Act 1907 or the Limited Liability Partnership Act

2000 and creating a specialised form of partnership in which the liability of the partners is limited; *fr. : ≈ partenariat*

- listed (adj.) company (n.) : company which lists its shares on the stock market and must therefore comply with a certain number of statutory provisions; *fr. : société côtée en bourse*
- minimum capital requirement : minimum statutory amount of capital that a public company must have to be created; *fr. : capital minimum*
- partner (n.) : person who owns a business with other partners; *fr. : associé*
- partnership (n.) : business structure which is operated by two or more partners; the liability of partners is personal and unlimited except for limited or limited liability partnerships; *fr. : société de personnes*
- private (adj.) company (n.); business structure which is less stringently regulated than public companies as it is allowed neither to offer shares to the public at large, nor to list shares on the stock exchange; on creation, it only needs a nominal amount to comply with statutory requirements; *fr. : ≈ entreprise privée/société privée*
- public limited company (Plc) : business structure for which the shares can be sold to the general public; it has a substantial minimum capital; *fr. : ≈ société par actions*
- registration (n.) : process by which a company is registered; this involves registering certain documents with the Registrar of Companies; *fr. : immatriculation*
- share (n.) : see 14
- sole (adj.) practitioner (n.) : professional who owns all the assets of the business (like a solicitor who owns and runs his own firm); *fr. : personne exerçant en profession libérale/≈ EURL*
- sole (adj.) proprietor (n.)/sole (adj.) trader (n.) : person who owns all the assets of one of the most widespread forms of business structures; he is personally liable on the whole value of his personal and business assets; *fr. : entrepreneur d'une entreprise individuelle/≈ auto-entrepreneur*
- unlimited (adj.) company (n.) : business structure where owners are personally liable for the torts and breaches committed by themselves or the company's agents in the course of business on the whole value of their personal and business assets; *fr. : société à responsabilité indéfinie et solidaire/≈ société en nom collectif (SNC)* (depending on the context)
- unlimited (adj.) : the term indicates the type of liability attached to the business structure : either limited or unlimited; *fr. : indéfinie*
- wrongful (adj.) trading (n.) : see 100

USEFUL EXPRESSIONS

- limited by guarantee; *fr. : société à parts sociales limitée aux apports*
- limited by shares; *fr. : société par actions limitée aux apports*

- to register a company with the Registrar of Companies; *fr. : immatriculer une société au Registre du Commerce et des Sociétés*
- to set up a company; *fr. : monter une société*

FURTHER INFORMATION

- in the field of business structures, the main legal provisions to date are to be found in the Companies Act 2006 which superseded the Companies Act 1985
- public companies should not be confused with the French concept of *service public*

> COMPARATIVE APPROACH
>
> En Grande-Bretagne, la distinction majeure dans le droit des sociétés s'effectue par rapport à la nature des droits sociaux : existence de parts sociales (*private company*) ou à actions (*public company*). Cependant, en France, la distinction se fait par rapport à l'objet de la société ainsi constituée : civile ou commerciale, bien que cette distinction s'atténue progressivement.

□ 14 CAPITAL

Share capital and debt capital are the types of capital a company can raise.

Share capital

Shares have a nominal value and cannot be allotted below this value or at a discount, for fear that the sale will be declared void. However, the market value of a share can be above its nominal value, in this case the sale yields a premium. There is no authorised share capital as companies are no longer limited by the number of shares they can issue. Shares can be bought from the company or from a shareholder. Existing shareholders have a right of pre-emption. Some shares are not paid fully upon allotment, but are paid by instalments, thus creating a paid-up share capital. Not all shares confer the same rights, as there are several classes of shares (ordinary or preference shares). Variation of class rights will need to comply with additional formalities.

Capital maintenance regime guarantees that a company will only distribute capital in an authorised manner. A company may need to restructure its capital. To do so, a public company needs to adopt a special resolution and to be granted a court order affirming the reduction in the value of shares. A private company only needs to pass a special resolution backed by a statement of solvency. Redeemable shares and new statutory provisions allow greater flexibility to the general common law rule that companies are not allowed to buy their own capital. Private companies can now provide financial assistance by buying each other's shares.

Dividends can only be distributed out of profits available for the purpose i.e. accumulated/realised profits, less accumulated/realised losses. If dividends do not comply with the rule, the distribution will be unlawful.

Debt capital

A company can have debts, through loans, overdraft, mortgages and debenture stocks. These debts are acknowledged through secured or unsecured debentures. Secured creditors will be paid before unsecured creditors on the assets of the company. All debts need to be listed in a register of charges (for limited companies) or need to be registered with the Registrar of Companies within a certain period.

When the lender does not take possession of the property, then the loan is called a charge. Charges are fixed or floating. Fixed charges allow the mortgagor to claim the charged property in case of default. Floating charges allow the mortgagee more flexibility as the assets used as a security can be used and be re-applied to other securities of the same class. With both charges, first mortgagors take precedence over later ones for repossession in case of liquidation. A floating charge can become fixed in case of the occurrence of certain events (liquidation, etc.) thus causing crystallisation.

GLOSSARY

- accumulated (adj.) losses (n.) : refers to the past years' losses; *fr. : pertes cumulées*
- allot (v.) : when a person acquires members' rights through purchase; *fr. : attribuer (des droits)*
- capital maintenance : regime by which a company's capital is maintained at a certain level to protect creditors by preventing the capital from being returned to members; *fr. : ≈ réserves constituées*
- charge (n.) : security over the assets of a borrower/debtor which does not involve a transfer of ownership; *fr. : sûreté*
- crystallisation (n.) : process by which a floating charge becomes fixed; *fr. : cristallisation*
- debenture : document which acknowledges the debt a company owes towards an individual or an institution; *fr. : reconnaissance de dette*
- debenture stock : stock issued by a company which does not entitle the holder to be considered as a member, thus he is not entitled to dividends; however he will receive an interest on his loan to the company; *fr. : ≈ obligations/valeur mobilière donnant droit à l'attribution de titres de créances*
- debt capital/loan capital : capital a company can raise by borrowing from individuals or institutions; *fr. : capitaux d'emprunt*

- dividend (n.) : share of a company's profit distributed to shareholders; *fr. : dividende*
- financial (adj.) assistance (n.) : form of financial help (such as security, indemnity, gift, guarantee or loan) which substantially reduces the assets of the company helping another company in financial difficulties; *fr. : ≈ avancement de fonds, accord de prêts ou de sûretés en vue de l'achat d'actions par un tiers* (this is forbiddden under French law)
- fixed (adj.) charge (n.) : loan secured on a specific asset such as buildings; *fr. : sûreté réelle*
- floating (adj.) charge (n.) : loan secured on a class of changing asset such as raw materials; *fr. : sûreté « flottante »/droit de gage général*
- issue (n. or v.) : when a company creates shares; *fr. : émission (n.)/émettre (v.)*
- mortgagee (n.) : party to a mortgage who/which makes the loan; *fr. : créancier hypothécaire*
- mortgagor (n.) : party to a mortgage who/which benefits from the loan; *fr. : débiteur hypothécaire*
- overdraft (n.) : loan arrangement granted by a bank which allows withdrawal over the amount of money available in the account; *fr. : découvert*
- paid-up share capital : capital paid on allotment of shares; the amount to be paid by instalments is the called-up share capital, and the outstanding balance between the issued capital and the called-up share capital is the uncalled share capital; *fr. : capital social versé*
- pre-emption right : right given by the type of share; *fr. : droit de préemption*
- preference shares : shares which will confer to their owners more benefits than to holders of ordinary shares, such as preferential dividends or priority access to assets in case of liquidation; *fr. : actions privilégiées*
- realised (adj.) profits (n.) : actual as opposed to estimated profits; *fr. : profits réalisés*
- redeemable (adj.) shares (n.) : shares issued by a company to raise capital by allowing temporary membership to a shareholder; the shares will then be bought back by the issuing company at a fixed date; *fr. : ≈ actions rachetables*
- register of charges : register which records all the charges of an incorporated company; *fr. : ≈ registre des sûretés*
- secured (adj.) debenture (n.) : debt agreement which allows the lender some form of claim on the assets of the company in case of liquidation; *fr. : ≈ créance garantie*
- share (n.) : part of the company's share capital; *fr. : action*
- share capital : capital a company can raise through the selling of shares, also known as equity capital; *fr. : capital par actions*
- thing in action : intangible piece of property, formerly known as *chose* in action; *fr. : propriété immatérielle/propriété intangible*

- unsecured (adj.) debenture (n.) : debt agreement which does not provide the lender with some form of claim on the company's assets in case of liquidation; *fr. : créance non garantie*
- void (v.) : act of declaring an act not valid; *fr. : nul/non avenu*
- yield (n.) : amount of cash return for the possession of a share; *fr. : rendement/taux de rentabilité*

USEFUL EXPRESSIONS

- to dissipate assets; *fr. : dissiper des actifs*
- to incur debts; *fr. : s'endetter*
- to raise capital; *fr. : réunir des capitaux*

FURTHER INFORMATION

- a firm (in the sense of professional partnership) must not be confused with the French word *firme* which is a fairly colloquial name given to a big company

> COMPARATIVE APPROACH
>
> Outre-Manche, le droit des sociétés est influencé par le droit anglo-américain. Le cas de la création des actions privilégiées pour se calquer sur les *preference shares* (GB) et *preferred shares* (US) est significatif à cet égard.

□ 15 PRE-INCORPORATION AND INCORPORATION

The rules regulating a company during its formation are different from those which apply once the company is incorporated.

Corporate promoters are the people involved in the formation of a company. They have a fiduciary duty towards the unformed company and can be held personally liable for acts performed as the company's agent. Corporate promoters are necessary as a company cannot enter into any contract before incorporation for lack of contractual capacity. Once the company has been incorporated, pre-incorporation contacts will not apply unless they are subject to novation. Promoters will only be released from their liability under pre-incorporation contracts if there is an express or implied contractual term to that effect.

A company is usually incorporated by way of registration or more rarely, an Act of Parliament (as in the case of the company organising the 2012

London Olympic Games) or a Royal Charter (as in the case of the BBC). Registration involves filing various documents with the Registrar of Companies such as an application for registration setting out details of the company (structure chosen, name and address of the directors/officers, address of the head office, capital of the company and object of the company), together with the memorandum and articles of association and a statement of compliance. Upon payment of a registration fee, a certificate of registration is issued.

Once a company has been incorporated, it acquires a corporate personality. Depending on the type of business structure chosen, the company becomes liable both from a civil and criminal point of view (such as in case of white-collar crime like corporate manslaughter). If a company was only set up to save its members from being held liable, the court can decide to lift or pierce the corporate veil.

After incorporation, any third party (like, but not only, a potential creditor) may apply to Companies House for a company search which provides information such as the company's structure, its head office and the company's most recent accounts. A small fee is payable.

GLOSSARY

- accounts (n.) : records of all the financial transactions of a company; *fr. : comptabilité*
- application for registration : here, document provided by the promoter when registering his company; *fr. : demande d'enregistrement*
- articles of association : constitutional document which sets out the rules regulating the company's internal affairs; *fr. : statuts*
- Companies House : executive agency which incorporates and dissolves limited companies, stores statutory information and makes it available to the public; *fr. : ≈ administration du Registre du Commerce et des Sociétés*
- company search : detailed information about a company or a LLP; *fr. : extrait K-bis*
- contractual (adj.) capacity (n.) : power of a legal entity to enter into agreements; *fr. : capacité à contracter*
- corporate (adj.) manslaughter (n.) : liability of a company in case of accidental death caused by its activities; a successful prosecution could lead to the liquidation of the company; *fr. : ≈ homicide involontaire des personnes morales*
- corporate (adj.) personality (n.) : legal status given to a company once incorporated; it becomes a legal entity/legal person; *fr. : personnalité morale*
- corporate promoter : is defined in Whaley Bridge Calico Printing Co v Green (1880) as "a term not of law, but of business, usefully summing up in a single word a number of business operations familiar to the commercial world by which a company is generally brought into existence"; *fr. : ≈ promoteur d'entreprise*

- fiduciary (adj.) duty (n.) : legal duty to act exclusively in another legal person's interests; it usually includes both a duty of loyalty and a duty of care; *fr. : obligation fiduciaire*
- head office : official address of a legal entity; also known as registered office; *fr. : siège social*
- lift/pierce the corporate veil : fact for the courts to set aside the corporate personality of a company to impose liability on its members when the company was set up for fraudulent purposes, as a sham entity or to evade liability; *fr. : ≈ lever le voile de la personnalité morale/lever le voile corporatif*
- memorandum of association : document which provides basic information about a company at the time of its incorporation; before the Companies Act 2006, it was the most important constitutional document, now it is the articles of association; *fr. : acte constitutif*
- novation (n.) : here, process by which a contract is substituted by another; *fr. : novation*
- registered (adj.) company (n.) : company, which was incorporated by registration as opposed to unregistered company incorporated by an Act of Parliament or by a Royal Charter; *fr. : société immatriculée au Registre du Commerce et des Sociétés*
- registration (n.) : process by which a company becomes incorporated; *fr. : immatriculation au Registre du Commerce et des Sociétés*
- statement of compliance : document provided by the promoter when registering his company and stating that he has complied with the statutory requirements regarding the registration; *fr. : ≈ état de conformité*
- white-collar crime : non-violent crime committed within corporations for financial motives (e.g. fraud schemes); also known as corporate crime; *fr. : infraction en col blanc*

USEFUL EXPRESSIONS

- to be liable to someone for something; *fr. : être responsable de quelque chose à l'égard de quelqu'un*
- to do a company search; *fr. : demander un extrait K-bis*
- to draft the articles of association of a company; *fr. : rédiger les statuts d'une société*
- to file the company's accounts; *fr. : déposer les comptes de la société*
- to set up a company; *fr. : monter une société*

FURTHER INFORMATION

- in France and England and Wales, the word society refers to a community of people with shared customs, living together in an area; in French the word *société* is also the name for a company

COMPARATIVE APPROACH

Le domaine du droit des sociétés est de plus en plus régulé par les directives européennes. En ce qui concerne la formation et l'immatriculation d'une société, les exigences sont semblables en France et Outre-Manche. Outre-Manche, le *Registrar of Companies* est le directeur général du Registre du commerce et des sociétés et ce, au niveau national. Il a un statut différent des greffiers de commerce en France, qui sont des officiers publics et ministériels remplissant une mission pour le compte de l'État au niveau des juridictions concernées.

□ 16 DIRECTORS, SHAREHOLDERS AND MEMBERS

The constitution of a company is a contract between the company and its members and amongst the members themselves. There are powers beyond which a company is not allowed to act (*ultra vires*) and directors can be in breach of their contractual duties if they do. When an objects clause has been set at the time of constitution of the company, the latter can only enter into contracts related to its stated objects.

Articles and/or memorandum of association can be altered, but subject to statutory and common law limitations. More particularly, a constitution can only be altered if it is in the *bona fide* interest of the company. However it cannot force a member to buy more shares than he wishes to. Not all article provisions can be altered as some can now be entrenched, thus requiring unanimity for alteration.

Directors

Rights and duties of company directors are to be found in the Company Act 2006. *De jure*, *de facto* and shadow directors are subject to statutory provisions. Once the company has been incorporated, directors are appointed according to its articles, otherwise they are elected by members by passing an ordinary resolution. The power of the company originates from the decision taken by board meetings when there is a *quorum*.

A director has a number of duties. He must act within the company's powers, exercise reasonable skill, care and diligence on its behalf to promote the company and avoid conflicts of interests. He must be fully independent and not accept benefits from third parties. Any breach of these duties may result in disqualification and/or a civil or criminal court action (where an objective or subjective test will be applied, depending on the duty breached).

The approval of shareholders is required if the director wishes a longer service contract than that provided by articles of association, if the company loans money to directors, if payments are made for loss of office, if substantial property transactions are entered into by the board, if the director wishes relief from liability, etc.

There are several ways in which the office of a director may be terminated : occurrence of a specified event provided for in the articles, resignation, removal, disqualification and retirement.

Shareholders

Shareholders can exercise their power in a company by voting resolutions in meetings for public companies. Additionally members of private companies can exercise power through written resolution procedures. There are two types of meetings that members are allowed to attend : general meetings (which includes the Annual General Meeting or AGM) and class meetings, where only a certain class of members can attend. A resolution will only be valid if the notice is given and a *quorum* of members is present (members can appoint a proxy). There are several types of resolution : ordinary resolution and special resolution.

Members

There is a slight distinction to be made between members and shareholders. Members are company owners whose names have been entered on the register of members. This includes shareholders and people who have subscribed to the articles of association. On the other hand, shareholders will be considered as members only when their names have been entered on the register of members. For companies without equity capital, there will be no shareholders but only members.

GLOSSARY

- board of directors : name given to the directors of a company collectively; *fr. : conseil d'administration*
- *bona fide* (adj.) : in good faith; *fr. : bona fide/de bonne foi*
- director (n.) : term not defined in statutory provisions; however it includes both persons who have the title of director and persons who occupy the position of director, whatever name they are given; *fr. : directeur*
- disqualification (n.) : termination of a director's position which arises when the company becomes insolvent or, for example, when the director commits an indictable offence; *fr. : disqualification*
- membership right : right listed in the company's constitution and which includes the right to participate in general meetings, the way to count votes, the sale of shares, the allocation of dividends; *fr. : droit des membres (droit de vote, etc.)*
- objects clause : clause within the constitution which states the scope of the objects of the company; formerly compulsory, if they wish, companies can now have unrestricted objects and have unrestricted capacity to contract,

thus limiting *ultra vires* acts to persons outside the company; *fr. : clause définissant l'objet de la société*

- office (of a director) (n.) : position which has an existence independent from the director and is filled consequently by successive directors; *fr. : poste (de directeur)*
- ordinary (adj.) resolution (n.) : resolution which requires at least half the votes to pass; *fr. : résolution ordinaire*
- proxy (n.) : person appointed by another member to participate in a general meeting or document by which that power is given; *fr. : mandat/procuration* or *mandataire/titulaire d'une procuration*
- *quorum* (n.) : minimum number of people present to a meeting to ensure that the decisions taken at the meeting are valid; *fr. : quorum*
- removal (n.) : termination of a director's position by an ordinary resolution at a meeting; this does not deprive the director from his compensation package, which is referred to as a golden parachute, if the compensation seems excessive or unfair in the circumstances; *fr. : destitution*
- resignation (n.) : termination of a director's contract which arises when he decides to voluntarily relinquish his office; *fr. : démission*
- resolution (n.) : vote of members or directors in members' meeting or board meetings; *fr. : résolution*
- retirement (n.) : termination of a director's office which arises when he reaches the official retirement age or when articles provide for retirement in rotation; *fr. : départ à la retraite*
- shadow (adj.) director (n.) : person who neither has the title of director nor acts as a director but a person in accordance to which directors are accustomed to act; *fr. : administrateur de fait*
- shareholder (n.) : person who owns shares in a company; if the company does not have shares, it will have members; *fr. : actionnaire*
- special (adj.) resolution (n.) : resolution which requires at least 3/4 of the votes to pass; *fr. : résolution spéciale*
- *ultra vires* (adj.) : Latin phrase meaning beyond the scope of its powers; *fr. : ultra vires*
- *de jure* director : person who has been legally appointed the director of a company, according to the articles of association; *fr. : directeur de droit*
- *de facto* director : person who is not a *de jure* director, but who performs the acts and duties of a *de jure* director; *fr. : directeur de fait*

USEFUL EXPRESSIONS

- power is vested in someone; *fr. : le pouvoir incombe à quelqu'un*
- to act in good faith; *fr. : agir de bonne foi*
- to pass a resolution; *fr. : adopter une résolution*

- to summon up/to convene an AGM; *fr. : convoquer une assemblée générale des membres*
- misuse of company assets; *fr. : abus de biens sociaux*

FURTHER INFORMATION

- officers (in the sense of persons carrying out rights and obligations under an office) must not be confused with the French word *officier* which is the name given to somebody holding an official position on behalf of the government (*officier de l'état civil*) or a member of the armed forces (*officier*)

COMPARATIVE APPROACH

Un véritable droit pénal des sociétés s'est développé en France face à l'insuffisance du Code pénal à traiter les abus. Dorénavant, l'infraction la plus communément poursuivie est l'abus de biens sociaux, c'est-à-dire l'infraction consistant à faire un usage des biens de l'entreprise contraire aux intérêts de celle-ci. Si le droit anglais n'a pas de concept d'abus de biens sociaux, le type d'infraction comprise sous ce concept se retrouve dans les paragraphes 171 à 177 du *Companies Act* 2006 qui codifient les devoirs des directeurs, en se rapportant d'une manière ou d'une autre à l'intérêt de l'entreprise.

3

Commercial law

□ 17 INTRODUCTION

As any other type of contract, commercial contracts abide by the rules of contract law. Thus, a valid commercial contract needs an agreement (offer, acceptance and communication), the intention to create legal relations and consideration. Terms of commercial contracts are classified as express and implied (common law and statutory implied terms). If they are not statutory terms, they need to be incorporated to have legal effect. The classification of the term determines the seriousness of the breach (warranty, condition, terms, etc.).

Indeed, in case of breach, the aggrieved party has a certain number of remedies available to him (damages, liquidated or not, specific performance, execution order, etc.). Parties to the commercial contract can be discharged of their obligations under the contract when the contract has been fully performed, when there was a defect in formation (mistake, misrepresentation, duress, undue influence, etc.), or when an act makes the fulfilment of the obligations under the contract impossible (breach, rescission, frustration, etc.).

On account of involving two businesses, commercial contracts have specificities, which a purchase between an average consumer and a retailer does not contain. Moreover sales involving cross-border parties or shipments can create several types of contracts within one single transaction, depending on the type of security each party wishes to have : a contract between the buyer and the seller for the sale of goods, a contract between the agents and their principals (where the transaction was carried out through an agency agreement), a contract between the seller and the carrier for the shipment of the goods, an insurance contract for the insurance of goods against risks at different stages of the transfer of goods (storage, shipment, etc.), a contract between the buyer and his bank (where there is documentary credit), a contract between the issuing bank and the correspondent bank, a contract between the issuing bank and the seller, etc.

As a consequence, the following sections will develop points that are more specific to contracts of the commercial nature : specificities of commercial contracts, agency, non-consumer sale and supply of goods and services, international sales, payment mechanisms and commercial credit and security. The purpose here is to focus on commercial law as applicable to businesses. Therefore and even though a non-commercial person may take out a mortgage or act as a security for a financial transaction, reference will be made below to "it" rather than "he".

GLOSSARY

- acceptance (n.) : see 8
- agent (n.) : see 11
- average (adj.) consumer (n.) : term defined by EU law and which refers to a hypothetical consumer, whose acts or omissions are used as a standard against which the acts or omissions of businesses are assessed; *fr. : consommateur moyen*
- breach (n.) : see 77
- carrier (n.) : here, business or other legal entity which transports people or property; *fr. : transporteur*
- common law implied term : term of a contract which under the common law rules, forms part of an agreement although it is not expressly stated in the contract itself; *fr. : clause implicite/tacite au titre de la common law*
- communication (n.) : see 8
- condition (n.) : contractual term which must be satisfied for the other party to the contract to be duty bound to fulfil his own obligations under the contract; *fr. : condition*
- consideration (n.) : see 9
- correspondent (adj.) bank (n.) : financial institution which provides services on behalf of another one; *fr. : correspondant bancaire*
- damages (n.) : see 73
- discharge (n.) : see 77
- documentary (adj.) credit (n.) : conditional guarantee of payment whereby a bank will only pay a transporter (for example) after the goods are delivered and subject to being provided with a number of required documents; *fr. : crédit documentaire/lettre de crédit*
- duress (n.) : see 80
- enforcement order : see 4
- express (adj.) term (n.) : provisions in a contract which are expressed, that is which are expressly written down in the contract; *fr. : clause expresse/condition expresse*
- frustration (n.) : see 82
- intention (n.) : see 10
- issuing (adj.) bank (n.) : here, bank which opens a letter of credit or documentary credit; *fr. : banque émettrice*
- liquidated (adj.) damages (n.) : see 84

- misrepresentation (n.) : see different types of misrepresentation in 84
- mistake (n.) : see different types of misrepresentation in 78
- offer (n.) : see 8
- rescission (n.) : see 84
- remedies (n.) : see 2
- representation (n.) : see 79
- specific (adj.) performance (n.) : see 84
- statutory implied term : term of a contract which is implied by a specific statute and thus forms part of an agreement although it is not expressly stated in the contract itself; *fr. : ≈ clause implicite/tacite reconnue par la loi*
- term (n.) : see 12
- undue (adj.) influence (n.) : see 80
- warranty (n.) : legally binding promise or assurance that a factual statement is true; *fr. : garantie*

USEFUL EXPRESSIONS

- to rescind a contract/rescission of a contract; *fr. : résoudre un contrat/ordonner la résolution d'un contrat*

FURTHER INFORMATION

A chapter on commercial law cannot set aside the special quality of international trade :

- globalisation of trade means that an increasing number of British commercial transactions are made between either foreign partners or involve shipment from or to a foreign country
- moreover most of the concerns of international commerce overlap with British-based trade when it comes to the choice of the most appropriate financial instruments, commercial security, etc.
- English law and its courts can also be chosen by parties to a commercial contract (with or without any link to the UK) to govern an agreement and a venue, if a dispute is not settled out-of-court or by an arbitration tribunal and thus the case comes to litigation

COMPARATIVE APPROACH

L'Union européenne cherche depuis plusieurs années à harmoniser le droit commercial, afin de faciliter l'harmonisation des droits des pays membres et faciliter la libre circulation des personnes, biens et capitaux. À l'heure où le présent ouvrage était sous presse, le plus gros chantier en cours concernait un droit européen des contrats.

□ 18 COMMERCIAL CONTRACTS

The role of a commercial lawyer is to ensure the business efficacy of agreements entered into by his clients. Initial negotiation will begin with letters of intent, which do not aim to be binding and usually state so. A lock-out agreement can be entered into during the fixed period of negotiations. A battle of forms will ensue if each business has its standard terms of business.

The formal drafting of commercial contracts will minimise legal uncertainty by limiting the scope of legal default rules. Indeed, in case of ambiguity, the *contra proferem* rule applies. A commercial contract will include provisions relating to minimum terms as well as the obligations of the parties, to remedies in case of non-performance (self-help remedies, arbitration clauses, provisions for the payment of deposits, etc.), to choice of law and forum, in case of conflict, etc. It might also include *force majeure* and hardship clauses to deal with unanticipated events. Deposits and prepayments might be expected in some transactions to guarantee performance. Interest will be due on outstanding sums.

Unreasonable terms cannot be included in contracts, as clauses excluding or limiting liability in all circumstances. Statutes have set up a certain number of agencies to ensure compliance with legal provisions protecting consumers against aggressive practices and preventing anti-competitive commercial practices (the Office of Fair Trading, headed by the Director General, the Unfair Contract Terms Unit, etc.).

As for contracts, the rule of privity of contract applies, including statutory exceptions. However the issue of agency is of greater importance as business transactions are often carried out by agents (see 19).

GLOSSARY

- aggressive (adj.) practices (n.) : practices which cause the average consumer to decide upon a course of action he would not have taken otherwise; *fr. : pratiques aggressives*
- agreement to agree : pre-contractual agreement taken by the parties, which states that they agree to negotiate together in good faith; the agreement is usually not enforceable in court; *fr. : contrat subordonné à un accord/entente de principe/accord à fin de convention*
- battle of forms : process by which the negotiation of a commercial contract starts with an exchange of the standard terms of each business involved in order to establish which terms will apply in the contractual agreement under negotiation; it is not to be confused with conflict of laws; *fr. : conflit de conditions contractuelles*
- *contra proferem* rule : rule of interpretation which states that if a clause or term is ambiguous, amongst the range of possible interpretations, the courts will choose preferably the one which goes against the interest of the party

who/which drafted the clause/term rather than the one which goes against the party who/which agreed to the clause/term; *fr. : règle contra proferem*

- core (adj.) provisions (n.)/minimum (adj.) terms (n.) : provisions which are considered essential, although not fatal if omitted, to constitute a valid contract, such as price and date of performance; *fr. : dispositions essentielles*
- course of dealing : pattern of previous conduct between parties to an agreement; *fr. : conduite habituelle des affaires*
- deposit (n.) : amount of money paid by A to B before the full performance of B's obligations to A, to guarantee B will be paid; *fr. : acompte*
- director general of fair trading (DGFT) : head of the office of fair trading; *fr. : directeur de l'Autorité de la concurrence*
- exclusion (adj.) clauses (n.) : clauses excluding liability from contract; they are strictly regulated by the law; *fr. : clause d'exclusion*
- force majeure clause : clause included into contracts to determine the consequences on their obligations of events outside the control of the parties; *fr. : clause de force majeure*
- hardship clause : clause included into contracts to determine the consequences of a change in circumstances that would make the performance of obligations more difficult or onerous for the parties; *fr. : clause de sauvegarde*
- interpretation (n.) : refers to the rules to interpret commercial contracts; *fr. : interprétation*
- legal default rule : rule that is applied where a contract does not expressly mention the outcome in case of breach, frustration, performance and meaning of terms at common law; *fr. : règle par défaut*
- letter of intent : letter used when parties are negotiating a contract; it does not intend to be binding upon the parties; *fr. : lettre d'intention*
- liability (n.) : state of being legally responsible for something; *fr. : responsabilité*
- lock-out agreement : pre-contractual agreement taken by the parties, whereby A agrees to negotiate with nobody else but B for a fixed period of time; the agreement is usually enforceable in court; *fr. : accord de lock-out/≈ pré-accord temporaire d'exclusivité*
- novation (n.) : see 11
- office of fair trading (OFT) : independent professional organisation which enforces consumer protection and competition law; its powers are conferred by a wide range of Statutes amongst which the Consumer Protection from Unfair Trading Practices Regulations 2009 (UTPR); *fr. : commission de la concurrence* (formerly *Conseil de la concurrence*)
- outstanding (adj.) : here, sum due; *fr. : (somme) due*
- performance (n.) : in the context of commercial contracts, performance implies carrying out one's obligations under the contract; *fr. : réalisation/exécution*

- prepayment (n.) : payment made in advance to guarantee the other party that he/it will be paid for the performance of his/its obligations under the contract; *fr. : préfinancement*
- privity of contract : see 11
- reasonableness (n.) : in relation to exclusion clauses, reasonableness assesses whether, with the knowledge the parties had when they entered into the contract, the clause was reasonable to be included into the contract; *fr. : caractère raisonnable*
- self-help (n.) : methods of obtaining redress without resorting to litigation, for example withholding performance, set-off, deposits, interest, etc.; *fr. : ≈ auto-assistance*
- set-off (n. or v.) : principle governed by the rules of insolvency, which states that if party has a claim for payment against another, the latter can set-off the former's claim against any claim he has, as long as they are claims for liquidated amounts; *fr. : compensation (n.)/compenser (v.)*
- standard terms of business : terms of a contract which is standard to a business or an industry; *fr. : clauses commerciales standardisées*
- unfair standard term : term in a contract which is considered as unfair to one of the parties; the non exhaustive list of unfair provisions may be be found in Statutes; *fr. : clause abusive standardisée*
- Unfair Contract Terms Unit : unit within the Office of Fair Trading which was set up to enter into informal negotiations with business B further to business A's complaint, to persuade B to remove the unfair terms; if the negotiations are fruitless, the Unit may seek an injunction in court to ensure the non-application of the unfair terms by B; *fr. : unité chargée de la lutte contre les clauses commerciales abusives*

USEFUL EXPRESSIONS

- to invalidate a contract on grounds of undue influence; *fr. : invalider un contrat pour cause de dol*
- to vary a contract; *fr. : modifier un contrat*
- to set off A' debt against B's; *fr. : compenser la dette de A avec celle de B*
- to avoid a contract for mistake; *fr. : frapper un contrat de nullité/annuler un contrat pour cause d'erreur*
- interest accrues on the outstanding sums; *fr. : les intérêts courent sur les sommes restant dues*
- to settle a dispute amicably with a company; *fr. : résoudre de façon amiable un litige avec une société*

FURTHER INFORMATION

- the concept of rescission in English law (from the verb rescind) is much wider than the French concept of *rescision pour lésion*. Pursuant to the provisions of article 1674 of the French civil code, *rescision pour lésion* makes it possible for the purchaser of immovables (such as land) to seek the rescission of the sale if the sale price exceeded the actual value of the land by more than seven-twelfths

- the English rescission (n.) or rescind (v.) correspond to the French *résolution* (n.) or *résoudre* (v.) which means undoing the contract as if it had never existed; it must not be confused with the termination of a contract (from a moment in time and for the future) which corresponds to the French *résiliation*
- as for contract law, the provisions of the Contracts (Rights of Third Parties) Act 1999 still apply

COMPARATIVE APPROACH

Les règles relatives à l'exclusion de clauses abusives (*unfair terms*) dans les contrats ont été harmonisées dans l'Union européenne grâce à un certain nombre de directives, parmi lesquelles la Directive 2005/29/EEC. L'interdiction des clauses abusives s'applique donc de façon similaire en France et au Royaume-Uni.

□ 19 AGENCY

Agency is the process by which an agent acts on behalf of a principal, who is the beneficiary of the acts of the agent. There can be different sorts of agents : broker, commercial agent, commission agent, *del credere* agent, general agent, special agent, self-employed agent, etc.

The relationship between the agent and the principal is a fiduciary one akin to trust. Under the doctrine of privity of contract, modified by the Contracts (Rights of Third Parties) Act, the principal has rights and obligations arising under the contract entered into by his agent in his name. The rights and obligations of the agent to the third party will depend on whether the agency is disclosed or undisclosed and on the type of authority binding the principal to the agent (actual, apparent, usual, by ratification, by necessity, etc.).

The agent has duties towards his principal : he must fulfil his agency agreement with skill and care, obey the principal's instructions, perform his agreement personally; he should also avoid conflicts of interest, should not make a secret profit and should account for his actions. The agent has a right to be indemnified for his work and to a remedy. If most agreements can be terminated when obligations on both sides are fulfilled or by an act of one of the parties, some agreements are irrevocable and some can only revoked by the operation of the law.

Even in the absence of an express agency agreement, directors, officers, partners, employees and professionals can be considered in law as agents of their company, firm, etc. There are also alternatives to agencies, such as distributorship agreement (selective, sole, exclusive, etc.), franchising and subsidiary.

GLOSSARY

- actual (adj.) authority (n.) : authority which actually results from a prior agreement between the principal and the agent; *fr. : pouvoir effectif*
- agency agreement : contract which sets out the conditions under which the agency will be carried out by the principal and the agent; *fr. : contrat d'agence*
- agent (n.) : person who acts on behalf of a principal; *fr. : mandataire*
- apparent (adj.) authority (n.) : when the principal makes a representation to the third party (in most cases, the buyer) that the agent has authority and the third party relies on this representation; the principal cannot subsequently deny the agent's authority : he can be estopped from doing so; *fr. : pouvoir apparent*
- authority by necessity : when a person has authority to secure the interests of another party, which would be in immediate jeopardy if the former failed to act; *fr. : ≈ pouvoir par nécessité*
- authority by ratification : when the principal retrospectively approves of his agent entering into an agreement without his prior consent; *fr. : pouvoir de ratification*
- beneficiary (n.) : party who derives a benefit from an arrangement; *fr. : bénéficiaire*
- broker (n.) : agent who does not have the possession of the goods he is dealing with on behalf of his principal; *fr. : courtier*
- commercial (adj.) agent (n.) : agent who is entrusted with the sale of goods on behalf of a principal; he has the possession of the goods he is dealing with; *fr. : agent commercial/agent de commerce*
- commission agent : agent who is empowered to buy and sell property on behalf of the principal, but who is not privy to the sale contract; *fr. : commissionnaire*
- confirming house : legal entity like a business set in an exporting country which acts as an agent (negotiating and guaranteeing the transaction) on behalf of the principal who wishes to import into the country; *fr. : société de confirmation*
- *del credere* agent : agent who guarantees his principal the third party will pay, in exchange for a commission; *fr. : agent ducroire*
- director (n.) : see 16
- disclosed (adj.) agency (n.) : when the third party (usually the buyer) is aware that the seller is an agent, i.e. he is acting on behalf of a principal; *fr. : mandat explicite*

- distributorship agreement : agreement to buy goods in one country to sell them in the country of the distributor, who is an independent contractor; *fr. : contrat de distribution*
- employee (n.) : see 53
- exclusive (adj.) distributorship (n.) : distributorship agreement which allows one single distributor to sell some or all of the suppliers' products in an area; the supplier will refrain from granting another distributorship agreement to another distributor for the area, and from competing with the distributor; *fr. : contrat de distribution exclusif*
- fiduciary (adj.) : related to a trust relationship; *fr. : fiduciaire*
- general (adj.) agent (n.) : as opposed to the special agent, agent who acts on behalf of his principal for a series of transactions; *fr. : agent général*
- officer (n.) : see 16
- partner (n.) : see 13
- principal (n.) : party for whom an agent acts; *fr. : mandant*
- privity of contract : see 11
- professional (n.) : person engaged in a profession; *fr. : professions libérales*
- selective (adj.) distributorship (n.) : distributorship agreement which relies on a network of distributors who/which are asked to comply with minimum requirements but who/which do not have any exclusive rights; *fr. : contrat de distribution sélective*
- self-employed (adj.) agent (n.) : agent who acts as an independent worker; *fr. : mandataire indépendant/à son compte*
- sole (adj.) distributorship (n.) : distributorship agreement which allows one single distributor to sell some or all of the suppliers' products in an area; the supplier will refrain from granting another distributorship agreement to another distributor for the area, however the supplier can compete with the distributor; *fr. : contrat de distribution unique*
- special (adj.) agent (n.) : agent who acts on behalf of his principal for one transaction only; *fr. : agent pour une transaction unique*
- third (adj.) party (n.) : legal entity other than the parties involved in the main transaction who are here the principal and the agent; *fr. : tiers*
- trust (n.) : fiduciary relationship whereby B keeps A's property for the benefit of C; *fr. : trust*
- undisclosed (adj.) agency (n.) : when the third party (usually the buyer) is unaware that the seller is an agent, i.e. he is acting on behalf of a principal; *fr. : ≈ représentation non-divulguée*
- usual (adj.) authority (n.) : when the third party has implied the agent had the authority that any agent generally has in that particular position, even if the said agent was expressly denied part of that authority by the principal; *fr. : pouvoir habituel*

USEFUL EXPRESSIONS

- buyer; *fr. : acheteur*
- distributor; *fr. : distributeur*
- retailer; *fr. : détaillant*
- seller; *fr. : vendeur*
- supplier; *fr. : fournisseur*
- to vary a contract in an informal agreement; *fr. : modifier le contrat initial par un accord informel*

FURTHER INFORMATION

- distributorship needs to comply with the requirements of European Union competition law; any distributorship agreement must not hamper the free circulation of goods, services and capital within the Union and should conform to the terms of block exemptions
- a concern is the name given to a legal entity like a business or any commercial or industrial enterprise; a going concern is a business which has sufficient assets to continue trading

> COMPARATIVE APPROACH
>
> En droit français, le mandat peut se faire à titre gratuit, alors que le mandat en droit anglais ne peut être valable sans aucune forme de compensation pour le travail effectué par la mandataire dans le cadre de sa mission, et ce en vertu de la spécificité du droit des contrats de la *common law*.

□ 20 SALE AND SUPPLY OF GOODS AND SERVICES

The law makes a distinction between the sale of goods and the supply of services. Additionally the present section will only focus on non-consumer transactions. Indeed the rules pertaining to consumer transactions do not fall within the scope of commercial law since they offer a higher standard of protection to consumers. As any other type of contract, commercial contracts abide by the statutory provisions in the field. There are statutory implied terms that can be excluded only if the exclusion complies with the law relating to unfair contract terms.

Sale of goods

A sale of goods needs to be distinguished from other transactions, such as gift, bailment, barter, hire and hire purchase. Contracts relating to the sale of goods can involve different types of goods : existing goods and future goods; goods defined, goods unascertained and goods unascertained from a designated bulk source (e.g. : 5 tons of corn in a shipment bound from Athens).

Statutory provisions describe the duties of the parties to a sale of goods contract. The seller's duty is to deliver the goods. The buyer's duty it to pay for them and not to reject them, unless the other party has failed to perform his contractual obligation (under certain circumstances : breach of condition, wrong quantity, late delivery, non-delivery, defective delivery, etc.).

Amongst the statutory implied contractual conditions are the requirements that the goods be of a satisfactory quality and reasonably fit for the buyer's purpose. Commercial contracts will assess the quality in the light of its merchantability. Goods are said to have perished if they are considered as unmerchantable.

The owner (as opposed to the person in possession) of the property at the time of the damage bears costs (principle also known as *res perit domino*). Who owns the goods is therefore of importance to assess who will bear the risks. The general rule is that the seller retains title to the goods till they are paid for by the buyer.

Another rule, known as *nemo dat quod not habet*, states that if a seller purports to transfer a title to goods which he does not own, the buyer will not have any ownership right either. However, wishing to protect *bona fide* buyers, the law has developed statutory exceptions to the *nemo dat* rule (e.g. : estoppel in case of agency).

In case of breach of contract, the remedies available to the parties range from damages to orders that the parties perform their obligations under the contract and termination of the contract. The sellers have remedies available in the case of non-payment (suing for the price, right of lien, stoppage in transit, resale, reservation of title).

Supply of services

Amongst the statutory implied contractual conditions are the requirements that the supplier performs the service with reasonable skill and care. If the buyer wants to ensure that the supplier be obliged to achieve any given result, he should have a term expressly incorporated into the contract to that effect. Contrary to the sale of goods, it is customary for a contract for supply of services to include provisions for deposits and/or part-payments.

GLOSSARY

- bailment (n.) : transaction whereby the bailor transfers possession of the goods to the bailee to hold before transferring the possession back to the bailor in due course (e.g. : storage agreements); *fr. : dépôt/gage*
- barter (n.) : transaction whereby goods are transferred in exchange for goods and services instead of money; *fr. : troc/échange*

- *bona fide* : good faith; *fr. : bonne foi*
- breach (n.) : violation of a statute, an obligation or a rule; *fr. : violation*
- bulk (adj.) : mass of goods of the same kind which is contained in the same space and can be interchanged; *fr. : en vrac*
- delivery (n.) : transfer of the possession of goods voluntarily from the buyer to the seller; *fr. : livraison*
- deposit (n.) : see 18
- estoppel (n.) : legal principle which estops or forbids someone from relying on his previous behaviour, action or lack of action, to allege or deny a fact; estoppel purports to ensure that nobody will be wronged by the inconsistency or someone else's action or words; *fr. : ≈ interdiction de se prévaloir de sa propre défaillance*
- existing (adj.) goods (n.) : goods that are owned and possessed by the seller; *fr. : biens existants*
- future (adj.) goods (n.) : goods that are neither owned nor possessed by the seller but which are subject of a contract of a present sale; *fr. : biens futurs*
- gift (n.) : transaction whereby the ownership of the good is voluntarily transferred; *fr. : don/cadeau*
- goods (n.) defined (adj.)/specific (adj.) goods (n.)/ascertained (adj.) goods (n.) : goods which are specifically identified and agreed upon when the contract is entered into by the parties; *fr. : biens spécifiques*
- goods (n.) unascertained (adj.) : goods which are specifically not identified and agreed upon when the contract is entered into by the parties; *fr. : biens génériques*
- hire (n.) : transaction whereby the possession of the goods (and not the ownership) is transferred from the owner to the hirer for a payment (usually by instalments); *fr. : location*
- hire purchase : transaction whereby the possession of the goods is transferred from the owner to the hirer for a payment (usually by instalments) and the hirer is granted the opportunity to buy the goods at the end of the hire-purchase agreement, usually for a nominal price; *fr. : location-bail*
- merchantability (n.) : test used by the courts to determine whether the goods are merchantable (i.e. acceptable by a reasonable buyer without a price-reduction especially and additionally as long as the goods can be used for any purpose sold for); *fr. : qualité marchande*
- part (adj.) payment (n.) : sum of money paid, which is less than the amount due; it can be an instalment or payment paid on account; partial payment; *fr. : paiement partiel*
- property (n.)/ownership (n.)/title (n.) : general and absolute interest in goods, as opposed to special and limited interest; *fr. : propriété/titre*
- reject (v.) : fact of refusing to accept the goods under the contract; *fr. : rejeter*

- reservation of title clause : clause included into commercial contracts to ensure additional security to the seller by allowing him to retain title to the goods till they be paid for; *fr. : clause de réserve de propriété*
- right of lien : before the goods were transferred from the seller to the buyer, right to retain the possession of the goods (as opposed to the ownership) as security for payment of the price; *fr. : droit de gage/droit de rétention*

USEFUL EXPRESSIONS

- to fix a time for performance; *fr. : fixer une date pour l'exécution du contrat*
- to exercise a lien over goods; *fr. : exercer un droit de gage sur les biens/ marchandises*

FURTHER INFORMATION

- the current relevant statutory provisions in the field are the Sale of Goods Act 1979 (SoGA 1979) and the Supply of Goods and Services Act 1982 (SGSA 1982)
- additionally, the practitioner needs to be aware of provisions related to manufacturer's liability and to unfair terms in domestic contracts (Consumer Protection Act 1987, Unfair Contract Terms Act-UCTA1977, etc.) and EU legislation

COMPARATIVE APPROACH

Le domaine de la protection du consommateur est dominé par le droit européen. Les dispositions législatives contenues dans SoGA 1979 et SGSA 1982 qui ont trait aux transactions entre entreprises et particuliers sont harmonisées par des directives européennes. La protection du consommateur sera donc semblable en France et au Royaume-Uni.

□ 21 INTERNATIONAL SHIPPING AGREEMENTS

As the UK is an island, shipping agreements, be they national or international, have always been relevant to the practice of commercial transactions. International sales differ from standard sales as they involve transnational transactions, generally with issues specific to transnational carriage (conflict of law, sea transit, insurance, import/export licences, customs clearance, credit terms and fluctuations in currency).

A shipping transaction is evidenced by a contract of carriage, which is concluded between the shipper and the carrier. It will involve a certain number of transport documents (bill of lading (BOL), sea waybill, delivery order, mate's receipt, etc.). The type of bills (bearer bills, straight bills, order bills, etc.) determines how the contractual rights and liabilities are to be transferred to the new holders of documents.

The most common international sales contracts are f.o.b. and c.i.f. contracts. F.o.b. contracts guarantee the buyer that the goods will be delivered at a specific place without costs. There are different types of f.o.b. contracts (classic f.o.b. contracts, f.o.b. contracts with additional duties, modern f.o.b. contracts). The choice of contract determines the duties of the parties : the party who has to insure the goods and whether he has to do so, when the property passes (on shipment or on payment) and when the risk passes to someone else (usually on loading). Failure to nominate a ship can lead to the termination of the contract.

C.i.f. contracts guarantee that the seller will be responsible for the goods (supply, shipment and insurance) till they reach their final destination and the buyer pays for the goods upon tender of the shipping documents, and not on delivery. Under c.i.f. contracts, the seller has a duty to ship the goods, appropriate the goods for contract (send a notice of appropriation, if needed) and tender the shipping documents (BOL, insurance policy and invoice). The buyer may reject the goods on grounds that the BOL is inaccurate (bill not clean, received for shipment bill instead of shipped bill, consigned bill, etc.), that the insurance is ineffective (insurance certificate instead of insurance policy, failure to cover usual risks), or that the invoice does not identify the goods. A wronged buyer is often better off rejecting the documents (and thus the goods) than suing for damages. However, if the documents conform to the contract, the buyer must accept the goods even if they are damaged, unless otherwise provided. He will have a separate right to sue for the damage. If the buyer accepts documents, which do not correspond to the contract requirement, or if he resells the deals with them before they reach the shipping destination, he waives his right to reject them.

GLOSSARY

- appropriation (n.) : in the context of a commercial contract, for unascertained goods or unascertained goods from a designated bulk source, the fact that the goods are nominated; if the appropriation is unconditional, then property may pass from the seller to the buyer; *fr. : affectation de la marchandise au contrat*
- bearer bill (of lading) : transport document which allows delivery of the goods to the bearer of the bill exclusively; *fr. : connaissement au porteur*
- bill of lading (BOL or B/L) : transport document which evidences the contract, acts as a receipt for the goods and is a document of title, therefore it allows

transfer by endorsement or delivery without endorsement of the shipped goods; *fr. : connaissement/Bill of Lading*

- c.i.f. contract, "cost, insurance and freight" : contract of sale whereby the seller has to provide the goods, ship and insure them; *fr. : Coût, Assurance, Frêt (port d'embarquement convenu)*
- carrier (n.) : party who transports the goods; *fr. : transporteur*
- classic f.o.b. contract : contract of carriage between the seller and the carrier, for the account of the buyer, whereby the seller places the goods on board the ship he has nominated; the seller then gives the BOL to the buyer in exchange for the purchase price; *fr. : contrat f.o.b. classique*
- clean (adj.) : when relating to a BOL, the goods are not damaged or incomplete; the opposite of clean bill would be foul bill; *fr. : net*
- delivery order : transport document which is provided in relation to a contract for the carriage by sea of goods and which is an undertaking by the carrier to deliver the goods to the person identified in the order; *fr. : bon de livraison*
- f.o.b. contract with additional duties : contract of carriage between the seller and the carrier, for the account of the buyer, whereby the seller places the goods on board the ship; contrary to a classic f.o.b. contract, the buyer will have nominated the ship and/or arranged insurance; *fr. : contrat f.o.b. avec obligations supplémentaires*
- f.o.b. contract, "free on board" : contract which arranges that the goods will be delivered to an agreed upon location, free of charge, that is from the buyer's perspective; *fr. : contrat f.o.b./Franco Bord (port d'embarquement convenu)/chargé à bord*
- goods : tangible and moveable commodities; *fr. : marchandises*
- holder (of the BOL) (n.) : party with possession of the BOL as a result of an indorsement or party with possession of the bill as the result of any transaction; the lawful holder is understood to be the holder in good faith; *fr. : porteur/détenteur*
- insurance certificate : certificate issued as evidence of an insurance policy; it is not the insurance policy *per se* and has limited legal value; *fr. : certificat d'assurance*
- international (adj.) sale (n.) : sale whereby the place of business of at least one of the parties to the contract is not in the UK; an international sale generally involves moving goods from one country to another, but not necessarily so; *fr. : vente à l'international*
- invoice (n.) : document identifying the goods mentioned in the commercial contract; *fr. : récépissé/reçu/facture*
- mate's receipt : transport document which is a temporary receipt for goods on board a ship; the receipt will then be exchanged for a BOL; *fr. : reçu de bord*
- modern f.o.b. contract : contract of carriage between the buyer and the carrier, whereby the seller places the goods on board the ship, for the account of

the buyer; the BOL is given to the buyer directly; modern f.o.b. contracts are widely used; *fr. : contrat moderne f.o.b.*

- notice of appropriation : document evidencing the unconditional appropriation of goods and the passing of property; also known as notice of consignement; *fr. : document attestant de l'affectation de la marchandise au contrat*
- order bill (of lading) : transport document which allows delivery of the goods to the named party or order; order bills are widely used as they are transferable; *fr. : connaissement à ordre*
- received for shipment bill (of lading) : BOL which certifies the reception of the goods for shipment, as opposed to the placement of the goods on board the ship; *fr. : connaissement pour embarquement*
- sea waybill : transport document which is a receipt for goods (containing or evidencing a contract) and identifies the person to which the goods have to be delivered; *fr. : letters de transport maritime/sea waybill*
- shipped/shipped on board (BOL) : BOL which certifies the placement of the goods on board the ship; *fr. : connaissament embarqué*
- shipper (n.) : party who ships the goods; *fr. : expéditeur*
- straight (consigned) bills (of lading) : transport document which allows delivery of the goods to a named consignee exclusively; straight bills are used when the shipper has no intention of selling goods at sea; *fr. : connaissement nominatif/connaissement consigné*

USEFUL EXPRESSIONS

- a bill certifies the quantity and condition of goods; *fr. : le connaissement fait foi de la quantité et de l'état apparent des marchandises*
- consignee; *fr. : consignataire*
- delivery of the goods to the bearer of the bill; *fr. : livraison des marchandises au porteur du connaissement*
- document of title; *fr. : titre de propriété*
- endorsement; *fr. : endossement*
- foul bill; *fr. : connaissement avec réserves*
- INCOTERMS; *fr. : C.I.V./conditions internationales de vente*
- receipt for the goods; *fr. : reçu/récépissé pour les marchandises*
- the documents conform to the contract; *fr. : les documents sont conformes au contrat*
- the goods pass the ship's rail; *fr. : la marchandise passe le bastingage du navire*
- the property passes; *fr. : transfert de la propriété (des marchandises)*
- to evidence; *fr. : être la preuve de l'existence de/faire foi de*
- transferable; *fr. : négociable*

- transport document; *fr. : document de transport*
- to be on board a ship; *fr. : être à bord d'un navire*

FURTHER INFORMATION

- in English, the word "mate" can mean different things, depending on the context; in general English, a mate is a colloquial term to refer to a friend; however if the term is used by the seafaring community, it refers to an officer on board a ship, who works under the direct orders the captain of the ship
- in French, the word *connaissement* is reserved for maritime transport, whereas in American English, the term can cover all forms of transportation (sea, air and land)
- the French word *fret* refers both to the English word cargo and freight or transport, depending on the circumstances
- the law of international sales is often – but not always – English law; in this case, SoGA 1979 will apply but generally not UCTA 1977 (see 20); the High Court in London will then be the usual venue to hear the case unless the parties opt for arbitration (International Chamber of Commerce (ICC) or for maritime disputes, Chambre Arbitrale Maritime de Paris (CAMP) both being based in Paris)
- additionally, international sales will comply with international law and use standard forms of contracts (see GAFTA 100) or include standard terms (see the International Chamber of Commerce terms : INCOTERMS)
- in the Royal Navy, ships names of ships are prefixed by the abbreviation HMS (Her Majesty's Ship); this is not the case for the merchant navy

COMPARATIVE APPROACH

La notion de « passer la bastingage du navire » (*the goods pass the ship's rail*), qui était commune au droit français et anglais, a été supprimée, car elle ne correspondait plus à la réalité des navires containers. Il convient aussi de noter que les contrats f.o.b. américains sont différents de ceux utilisés en Angleterre et au Pays de Galles.

□ 22 BILL OF EXCHANGE

In any sale, whether domestic or international, sellers as well as buyers need to protect themselves against default payment or failure to deliver the goods. They do so by a number of payment mechanisms, known as bills of exchange, cheques, promissory notes, documentary credit, performance bonds, etc. The present section looks into bills of exchange and the following ones into other financial instruments.

The most common negotiable instrument is the bill of exchange. It is a contractual agreement between a drawer and a drawee to pay a third party. It needs to be supported by consideration. Each person who signs the bill becomes party to the bill (acceptor, accommodation parties, drawer, endorser, transferor, etc.). Additionally, there are two types of bills : inland bills and foreign bills.

The bill of exchange is defined in BoEA 1882, s.3(1) as an unconditional order addressed by the drawer to the drawee to pay money to a payee. To be valid, a bill of exchange needs to be made in writing and signed by the drawee. As the bill is transferable, the money will be paid by the drawer to the bearer, to the person named in the bill or to the order of that named person. The transfer of a bill will depend on the type of bill, and is usually effective through delivery and (general or special) endorsement. Bills are payable either on demand (a.k.a. "at sight" or "on presentation") or at a future time which is fixed or determinable. A holder can complete an incomplete bill by inserting the date, for example.

Except in cases of forged bills, which can only be enforced against the forger, holders are entitled to enforce a bill of exchange. There are a certain number of defences against the liability of a bill : the drawee's capacity to enter into a contractual relationship, the drawee's authority (as attested by his signature) to draw a bill, the delivery of the bill, etc.

At maturity, the bill needs to be honoured. A bill will be enforced by presentation and payment at the proper time and place, failure to do so can result in parties being released from liability. However, if the drawee fails to accept or to pay the bill, it is said to be dishonoured. The holder needs to notify the previous parties of the dishonoured bill, within a reasonable time. The holder can then start legal proceedings against the drawee or enforce the bill against another party liable on the bill.

GLOSSARY

- acceptor (n.) : party who/which accepts the bill; generally the acceptor is the drawee; *fr. : débiteur*
- accommodation party : party who/which lends his name to the bill to increase its marketable value; *fr. : avaliseur/donneur d'aval*
- bill of exchange : order by which the drawer orders the drawee (or payor, usually a bank) to pay a third party, known as the payee or the bearer, a sum of money; *fr. : lettre de change*
- drawee (n.) : person or institution (usually a bank) who/which is ordered by a bill of exchange to pay money to the payee; *fr. : tiré*
- drawer (n.) : person or institution who/which writes an order to another person or institution (usually a bank) for the payment of money owed to a third party, known as payee; *fr. : tireur*

- financial (adj.) instrument (n.) : document which evidences some contractual relationship and grants a right; as a payment mechanism, it serves as evidence of a right to enforce a debt; *fr. : effets de commerce*
- forger (n.)/forgery (n.)/forge (v.) : person who counterfeits a legal document; document which is counterfeited; or fact of counterfeiting; *fr. : faussaire (n.)/falsification (n.)/falsifier (v.)*
- general (adj.) endorsement (n.) : endorsement of a bill by the signature of the payee; *fr. : endossement général/approbation globale/fait d'entériner de manière générale*
- holder (n.) : person or institution who/which has the possession of a bill of exchange; *fr. : porteur*
- endorser (n.) : party who endorses the bill; *fr. : endosseur*
- inland bill of exchange : bill drawn and payable in the same country; *fr. : ≈ lettre de change à effet national*
- negotiable (adj.) : legally transferrable right; the opposite is non-negotiable; e.g. : bills of exchange; *fr. : négociable*
- payee (n.) : person or institution to whom/to which money is actually paid by the drawer under a bill of exchange issued by a drawer; *fr. : bénéficiaire/payé*
- special (adj.) endorsement (n.) : endorsement of a bill by the signature of the payee and the mention of the person or institution to which the bill is transferred; *fr. : endossement nominatif*
- transferable (adj.) : negotiable (see BoEA 1882); *fr. : transférable*
- transferor (n.) : party who/which transfers the bill; *fr. : cédant*

USEFUL EXPRESSIONS

- liability of the parties to the bill of exchange; *fr. : garantie solidaire des signataires de la lettre de change*
- order to pay at a fixed future time; *fr. : ordre de payer à échéance fixée*

FURTHER INFORMATION

- to date, the relevant legal provisions in the field of payment mechanism in international sales are to be found in the Bills of Exchange Act (BoEA) 1882

COMPARATIVE APPROACH

Les instruments de crédit propres au commerce international sont uniformisés et donc, ne présentent pas de différences notables entre le droit français et le droit anglais. En France, le fond et la forme de la lettre de change sont régis par le Code de commerce et en Grande-Bretagne par les *Bills of Exchange Act (BoEA) 1882*. En droit français, la mention « lettre de change » doit apparaître sur le document, sous peine de le disqualifier (sans pour autant rendre l'engagement contractuel nul entre les parties), alors que la mention n'est pas requise en droit anglais.

□ 23 OTHER FINANCIAL INSTRUMENTS

There are other financial instruments to secure a manufacturer from a buyer's default. Some of those instruments are used both in national trade and in international trade.

Cheque

A cheque is a form of bill of exchange, where the drawee is the bank. To be valid, a cheque must fulfil the requirements of a valid bill of exchange. However there are differences between cheques and bills of exchange : acceptance of the drawee is not needed, payment is on demand, a cheque may be crossed, there is no need for a notice of dishonour, and cheques need not be presented in due time. The assumption is that the bank has a mandate to act on the customer's instructions, unless the mandate is countermanded before payment.

Promissory notes

The law in force is similar to that covering bills of exchange. Promissory notes are promises made by the maker to another party, unconditionally promising to pay a certain sum at a certain date. The maker then becomes liable. To be enforceable, the promissory note needs to be delivered.

Documentary credit

It is an undertaking whereby a bank agrees to guarantee that the seller will be paid for the delivery of goods. Conversely, through this mechanism, the buyer also gets a guarantee that he will get the goods in exchange for the monies paid. This is done through a documentary bill. It is a bill of exchange presented for payment to the buyer, with the bill of lading and other shipping documents. Additionally the bank agrees to pay the seller if certain conditions are fulfilled. These agreements often need two banks to be operative, as the seller is notified by the correspondent's bank (located in his own country) that the buyer's credit in the issuing bank (located where the transaction takes place) is open, thus allowing him to ship the goods. The bank will honour payment if the conditions of credit are fulfilled by the seller, thus the customer needs to give specific instructions as to the documents to be presented for fulfilment of the seller's contractual obligations.

Performance bonds

They are mainly used to guarantee the buyer that the goods will be shipped. Failure on the part of the account party to ship the goods will result in payment by the account party to the buyer/beneficiary of sums agreed in the performance bond.

GLOSSARY

- account party : in a performance bond, party liable to pay the bank for all sums paid for on its behalf a.k.a. buyer; *fr. : donneur d'ordre*
- beneficiary (n.) : in a performance bond, party for whom/for which the bond is arranged and who/which will receive agreed upon sums if the account party fails to ship the goods; *fr. : bénéficiaire*
- cheque (n.) : bill of exchange drawn on a bank and payable on demand; *fr. : chèque*
- countermand (v.) : revoke or annul; *fr. : annuler*
- crossed cheque : traditionally, refers to two vertical lines printed on a cheque and containing the words A/C Payee; it restricted the right to cashing the cheque to the person named only and thus cannot be transferred; *fr. : chèque barré*
- delivery (n.) : here, transfer of possession; *fr. : livraison*
- documentary (adj.) credit (n.) : bill of exchange which is presented for payment to the buyer with the bill of lading and other shipping documents; *fr. : crédit documentaire/« crédoc »*
- drawee (n.) : see 22
- drawer (n.) : see 22
- enforceable (adj) : that which can be made or forced to be obeyed; *fr. : opposable/exécutoire*
- maker (n.) : here, party who makes a promissory note; *fr. : émetteur*
- mandate (n.) : proxy; *fr. : mandat*
- performance bond : security issued by a bank to guarantee fulfilment of certain contractual obligations; *fr. : garantie de bonne exécution/garantie de bonne fin*
- promissory (adj.) note (n.) : instrument by which one party promises another to pay a certain sum of money at a certain date; *fr. : billet à ordre*
- undertaking (n.) : here the term means a promise offered as a security for the performance of a particular act; the term can be found in civil law, where the promises made by parties to a contract, when considered independently, are called separately an undertaking; *fr. : engagement*

USEFUL EXPRESSIONS

- correspondent bank; *fr. : banque notificatrice*
- issuing bank; *fr. : banque émettrice*
- to stop a cheque; *fr. : faire opposition à un chèque*

FURTHER INFORMATION

- the English term “undertaking” takes on a variety of meanings; in the context of commercial law, it can be found in three cases : as a synonym of company or concern (*enterprise*); as a synonym of agreement (*engagement*); as a synonym of financial security (*effet de commerce*)
- note also that the “undertaker” is the name given in English to the man who prepares dead bodies and arranges funerals
- the International Chamber of Commerce (ICC) regulates the use of credits with the Uniform Customs and Practice relating to Documentary Credit. It is an arbitration court which helps resolve disputes out-of-court
- cheques are common means of payment for individuals, whereas other financial instruments detailed in the last two sections are reserved for businesses

COMPARATIVE APPROACH

Le crédit documentaire est soumis aux règlements des Règles et Usance Uniformes de la Chambre de Commerce Internationale basée à Paris. Les règles s’appliquant en droit français et en droit anglais sont dont uniformisées.

□ 24 COMMERCIAL CREDIT AND SECURITY

In any sale, sellers and buyers seek to insure themselves against default payment or failure to deliver the goods. They do so through specific financial instruments (see 22 and 23), but also through provision of credit and security.

Credit

There are different types of credit : loans (e.g. loan credit) and deferment payment obligations (e.g. sales credit). In the former case, the debtor gets money from the creditor and, in the latter case, the debtor postpones payment to the creditor, while enjoying the benefit of the goods or the service. Credit arrangements can be fixed-term or revolving.

Security

It can be real or personal. Real security can be consensual or non-consensual, possessory or non-possessory. There are different types of securities : pledge, lien, mortgage, equitable charges.

A pledge is created by any informal agreement, but in practice a letter of pledge is used in the banking system. Pledges need not be registered. A pledge gives power to the pledgee to sell the pledgor’s goods if he/it defaults. Pledgor’s goods in the possession of the pledgee can be subpledged, under condition. The limits of the use of pledges are that a pledge is not applicable to intangible goods. Pledges are usually terminated when the pledgor's debt is plaid to the pledgee.

Liens are rights of retention of property till the underlying debt is paid. There are two types of liens : general and special. The common law recognises that certain trades have a lien over their customer's property (ship's master, repairers, etc.). Liens might be created by contract or by statute. The lienee does not have the right to resell the goods at common law but he/it can do so as bailee under contractual and statutory provisions.

Mortgages provide that the mortgagor retains possession of the mortgaged property during the mortgage and has a right of redemption when the secured sums are paid. Any type of property can be mortgaged as long as the mortgage agreement is in writing for real property. The mortgagee can enforce his/its mortgage by foreclosure, seizure, implied right of sale and application to court for an order of sale.

Personal security differs from real security in that the former does not rely on the primary loan agreement to operate. Indeed personal security creates another secondary agreement independent from the principal contract. There are two types of personal securities : guarantees and indemnities. In the case of indemnity, the surety will guarantee that it/he will pay the manufacturer whether the buyer defaults or not. The surety then turns to the buyer for payment of the sums incurred on his/its behalf.

In the case of guarantees, the surety will pay the manufacturer/seller if the buyer defaults. As both contracts are related, if the principal contract is unenforceable, then the secondary contract will be too. As both the security agreement and the debt agreement are independent, the guarantor will remain liable even if the principal contract becomes unenforceable. The guarantor will be discharged from his/its liability if the debt is paid, if the debtor is discharged or by the operations of the law. Guarantees can be one-off or continuing, demand or conditional. They need to be evidenced by a written document signed by the guarantor. The guarantee can then be enforced as a contract. The rules of contract then apply to revocability and validity of the agreement. Guarantee terminates when the secured debts have been repaid in full. The guarantor is usually liable not only for the debts of the debtor, but he must also ensure the debtor's performance. In turn the guarantor can be indemnified by the debtor against all liabilities incurred and the guarantor can pursue any claim against the debtor (right of subrogation). Other types of personal security are letters of credit, performance guarantees and letters of comfort.

Courts can requalify a credit agreement into a security arrangement, if they consider that there was a disguised security arrangement instead of a genuine sale.

GLOSSARY

- bailee (n.) : person who holds goods without transfer of ownership; *fr. : dépositaire*

- conditional (adj.) guarantee (n.) : guarantee whereby the guarantor must pay the guarantee's debt only if specified circumstances come to pass; *fr. : garantie conditionnelle*
- consensual real security : security which is created by an agreement amongst the parties; *fr. : sûreté réelle immobilière conventionnelle*
- credit (n.) : provision allowing to postpone payment; *fr. : crédit*
- demand guarantee : guarantee whereby the guarantor must pay the guarantee's debt on first demand; *fr. : garantie sur demande*
- equitable (adj.) charge (n.) : here, interest in unregistered land imposing an obligation on the landowner in favour of another person; charges entered in the land charges register will be binding on future purchasers of the land; *fr. : charge*
- fixed-term credit : provision allowing to postpone payment at a fixed date; *fr. : ligne de crédit limitée dans le temps*
- foreclosure (n.) : process by which the mortgaged property is being repossessed by the mortgagee on grounds that the mortgagor is not fulfilling his obligations under the contract (i.e. : paying back his mortgage); *fr. : droit de saisie/exécution forcée*
- general (adj.) lien (n.) : form of security whereby the lienee retains any property belonging to the lienor, till his debts be paid off; *fr. : droit de gage général*
- guarantee (n.) : personal security given by a surety that he will pay a debt, if the debtor defaults; *fr. : cautionnement*
- indemnity (n.) : personal security which involves a third party guaranteeing he will pay the debtor's debts to the creditor, even if the debtor does not default; *fr. : garantie autonome*
- intangible (adj.) goods (n.) : goods which are incapable of being touched, incorporeal goods; in the present context, goods or services which increase the usefulness or utility of something (i.e. the ability to respond to a need), either directly or indirectly; *fr. : biens intangibles/biens immatériels*
- letter of comfort : letter addressed to the creditor-to-be reassuring him as to the creditworthiness of the debtor-to-be; it does not give rise to any contractual obligations; *fr. : ≈ lettre d'intention*
- letter of pledge : agreement used in the banking system, whereby the pledgor agrees to enter into a pledge agreement with the pledgee; a letter of pledge is entered into by the pledgor and the pledgee and sets out the rights and duties of the parties in respect to the pledged assets; *fr. : acte de nantissement*
- letter of credit : written instrument issued by a bank requiring someone (who may, or may not be specifically named) to advance money to the person named in the letter or the holder of the letter (if not named); *fr. : lettre de crédit*
- lien (n.) : possessory real security, whereby the lienee keeps the possession of the lienor's goods or documents until the latter pays the lienee for the work done on the said goods and documents; *fr. : gage*

- loan (n.) : money lent to the debtor on condition that the former will be paid back (with interest) by the creditor at a later date; *fr. : prêt*
- loan credit : money paid by the creditor to the debtor on condition that the former will be paid back (with interest) by the latter at a later date; for example, auto loan, student loan, equity loan, personal loan, etc.; *fr. : crédit/prêt*
- mortgage (n.) : non-possessory real security, whereby the mortgagor retains the ownership of an asset and agrees to transfer it to the mortgagee when he will have paid back his debt; *fr. : hypothèque*
- non-consensual real security : security which is created by the operation of the law; *fr. : ≈ sécurité immobilière non-consensuelle/judiciaire*
- non-possessory real security : security whereby the creditor's security interest is not based on his having possession of the goods; *fr. : sûreté réelle sans dépossession*
- one-off guarantee (n.) : guarantee which secures a single obligation; *fr. : garantie unique*
- order of sale : court order allowing the mortgagee to sell the mortgagor's property on account of his having defaulted; *fr. : ordre de saisie*
- performance guarantees : performance bonds : see 23
- personal (adj.) security (n.) : security which involves a third party guaranteeing he will pay the debtor's debts to the creditor, if certain circumstances come to pass; *fr. : sûreté personnelle*
- pledge (n.) : possessory real security, whereby the pledgee keeps the possession of the goods till payment by the pledgor; *fr. : ≈ nantissement*
- possessory real security : security whereby the creditor's security interest is based on his having possession of the goods; *fr. : sûreté réelle avec dépossession*
- real (adj.) security (n.) : security which grants property rights over the debtor's assets; e.g. factory plant, home, or cargo; *fr. : sûreté réelle*
- revolving (adj.) credit (n.) : provision allowing the credit line to remain open once the initial credit has been paid off; *fr. : crédit renouvelable/crédit revolving*
- right of subrogation : right to substitute one person for another in a credit claim; *fr. : droit de subrogation*
- sales credit : provision allowing the buyer to postpone his obligations under a contract of supply (e.g. sale price) to a later date; *fr. : vente à crédit*
- secured (adj.) : that which ensures the payment of a debt; *fr. : assorti d'une sûreté*
- seizure (n.) : process by which the mortgaged movable piece of property is being repossessed on grounds that the mortgagor is not fulfilling his obligations under the contract; seizure applies more particularly to bills of sale; *fr. : saisie*
- special (n.) lien (n.) : form of security whereby the lienee retains the property that relates to the lienor's debts, till they are discharged; *fr. : ≈ gage*
- surety (n.) : party who/which acts as a guarantee for a creditor; *fr. : cautionnement*

USEFUL EXPRESSIONS

- trade; *fr. : métier/commerce*
- there are special agencies to help individuals choose a trade; *fr. : il existe des bureaux d'information pour aider les gens à choisir un métier*
- contrary to lawyers, shopkeepers work in trade; *fr. : contrairement aux avocats, les marchands travaillent dans le commerce*
- payment default; *fr. : défaut de paiement*

FURTHER INFORMATION

- to date, the relevant legal provisions in the field of credit arrangements are the Consumer Credit Acts 1974 and 2006
- letters of comfort do not create any legal obligations between the parties

COMPARATIVE APPROACH

Depuis la réforme du 23 mars 2006, le droit français prévoit quatre types de sûretés réelles (nantissment, gage, hypothèque et antichrèse), qui se fondent sur la nature des biens (mobiliers ou immobiliers) et le type de sûreté (avec ou sans dépossession). Le droit anglais ne fait pas une telle distinction entre les biens mobiliers ou immobiliers et ne prévoit que trois formes de sûretés réelles (*mortgage, lien, pledge*). Le droit français ignore la distinction entre *pledge* et *lien.*

4

Tax law

□ 25 INDIVIDUALS AND EMPLOYEES

Tax is payable either to the central or local government. The person who pays tax is a taxpayer. Her Majesty's Revenue and Customs (HMRC) collects the central government's tax. The personal tax year runs from 6th April to 5th April in the subsequent year. Statutes provide for the rate of income tax and threshold of allowances.

Income tax is payable on taxable income such as earnings from employment or self-employment, state, company and personal pensions income, interest on most savings, dividends (income from shares), rental income and income derived from a trust. National insurance contributions (NIC) are payable when the earnings exceed a certain threshold. Payments stop when the employees/self-employed people reach state pension age. Voluntary NIC can be made by those who live abroad or are neither working nor claiming state benefits. A National Insurance number is allocated to everyone and must be disclosed when required to HMRC, an employer, the Department for Work and Pensions (including the Jobcentre) and the local council (for housing benefit claims).

The specificity of the system is that income tax and NIC owed by employees are collected by HMRC from the employers through the Pay As You Earn (PAYE) system.

Non-taxable income includes certain benefits, income from tax exempt accounts, working tax credit (WTC) and premium bond wins. Each United Kingdom resident for tax purposes gets a personal allowance which is an amount of taxable income which everyone can earn or receive each year tax-free. Tax credits can be granted which are non-taxable payments from the government. Working tax credit is given to those working on a low income. Child tax credit and/or child benefit is paid to those who look after a child, even not their own, so long as they pay towards his upkeep. Payment of the benefit will either stop when the child reaches 16 or a maximum of 20. However doing an advanced course at higher education level such as a university degree does not count.

Other tax allowances or reliefs include the married couple's allowance, tax-deductible expenses for employees or directors of a company (such as the cost of professional fees or subscriptions, business expenses, the cost of professional tools or specialist clothing). Conversely there is no tax allowance or relief applicable to company benefits paid to employees (such as company cars, medical insurance, accomodation or loans at a low interest rate). For those, the normal tax rate is payable.

Council tax is a local tax payable per dwelling or residential property. It replaces the former unpopular poll tax or community charge which was payable by each adult in a household. Council tax helps fund the services run by the local authorities. Other taxes applicable to individuals include Value Added Tax (VAT) which is discussed under the corporate or self-employed section.

GLOSSARY

- allowance (n.) : when applied to tax, annual exempt or tax-free amount to which someone may be entitled; *fr. : abattement fiscal*
- child benefit : benefit granted to one person only in a household if he is responsible for a child under 16 (or 20 maximum if the child follows approved education or training); *fr. : allocations familiales*
- child tax credit : tax credit which does not affect child benefit and which can be granted to someone in a household who is responsible for a child under 16 (or 20 if he is in approved education or training); *fr. : part fiscale de l'enfant*
- council tax : tax levied on households by local authorities to help fund the services provided by them; it is based on the number of people living in a property and its estimated value; it was introduced by the Local Government Finance Act 1992 and replaced the former community charge aka poll tax which was introduced by Margaret Thatcher; *fr. : taxe d'habitation*
- discount (n.) : reduction in the amount payable; *fr. : rabais/réduction*
- dwelling (n.) : place of residence like a flat or a house; *fr. : logement*
- earnings (n.) : money (like wages or profit) earned for work done or services rendered; *fr. : revenus*
- exemption (n.) : when applied to tax, activities which are not subject to tax requirements; *fr. : exemption d'impôts*
- financial (adj.) year (n.) : dates covered by a company's annual report and accounts submitted to the Companies Registry; it usually corresponds to the corporation tax accounting period; *fr. : année fiscale*
- HM Revenue & Customs (HMRC) : United Kingdom's tax authority often nicknamed "taxman"; *fr. : service des impôts/fisc*
- housing benefit : central government's help granted to low income people to help them pay their rent to the exclusion of hot water, heating or food; *fr. : aide personnalisée au logement (APL)*

- income tax : tax payable by employees, self-employed people (and even non-working people who have an income from a pension or savings) on some forms of income; *fr. : impôt sur le revenu*
- married couple's allowance : tax allowance granted to people who are married or in a civil partnership and live together, if one of them was born before April 1935; for marriages or civil partnerships contracted after 2005, the allowance is calculated on the basis of the highest earner's income; *fr. : parts fiscales des époux*
- National Insurance contributions (NIC) : contributions made by employees or self-employed people of 16 or over who earn more than a prescribed amount; such contributions build up someone's entitlement to certain state benefits, including the state pension, jobseeker's allowance, maternity allowance and bereavement benefits; *fr. : charges sociales*
- Pay As You Earn (PAYE) : see 26
- personal tax year : period of time for which someone is assessed for tax; *fr. : année fiscale (applicable aux personnes physiques)*
- poll tax : see council tax; *fr. : taxe d'habitation*
- relief (n.) : when applied to tax, amount deducted from the taxable profit; *fr. : dégrèvement fiscal*
- state pension : amount of money (usually paid on a monthly basis) which can be claimed from the state by someone after he retires; its amount depends on the duration of the National Insurance contributions made by the pensioner throughout his working life; there are various ways to complement the State pension; *fr. : retraite de base*
- tax credit : amount of money that a taxpayer can deduct from the amount of tax due to HMRC; *fr. : crédit d'impôt*
- taxman (n.) : nickname often given to the employees of central or local government tax authorities; *fr. : fisc*
- taxpayer (n.) : legal entity who owes tax; *fr. : contribuable*
- threshold (n.) : point which must be exceeded to be considered for benefits or tax credits; *fr. : seuil*

USEFUL EXPRESSIONS

- to levy/raise tax; *fr. : lever les impôts*
- to seek advice from the taxman; *fr. : demander l'avis du fisc*
- to apply for a tax exemption; *fr. : faire une demande d'exemption d'impôts*

FURTHER INFORMATION

- the phrase "death and taxes", which are both certain events in someone's life, are attributed to early 18th century English writer Daniel Defoe, author of *Robinson Crusoe*

- the community tax or "poll tax" (or tax on "each head") was criticised as it was a tax per adult resident living in a household; it was considered as unfair and replaced by the council tax

> COMPARATIVE APPROACH
>
> Au contraire du droit français qui requiert des contribuables (*taxpayers*) salariés qu'ils remplissent chaque année une déclaration d'impôts (*tax return form*), ce n'est pas le cas au Royaume-Uni où le principe du paiement de l'impôt à la source (*Pay As You Earn PAYE*) trouve application. S'agissant des crédits d'impôt (*tax credit*) ou dégrèvements fiscaux (*tax relief*), il est difficile de faire une comparaison entre les deux systèmes en raison de l'évolution permanente de la législation dans ces domaines.

□ 26 COMPANIES, PARTNERSHIPS OR SELF-EMPLOYED PEOPLE

Like individuals and employees, the taxation of companies is payable to HMRC or the local government. The financial year used for corporation tax purposes usually runs from 1st April to 31st March. Self-employed people run their own business and must comply with the rules applicable to employers and businesses. They must complete each year a self-assessment tax return form. This is used to calculate the tax and NIC payable. A penalty is payable for failure to comply with the relevant deadline. Businesses and corporations must settle different taxes. Pay As You Earn (PAYE) is the system used by HMRC to collect income tax and national insurance contributions (NIC) from employees and directors of limited companies. Both are deducted every month from the employees' earnings.

Value Added Tax (VAT)

This tax is charged to the end customer by VAT-registered businesses on most goods and services. The money is collected by the company or business on behalf of HMRC. Different rates of VAT apply. As opposed to the standard rate, the reduced rate applies to domestic fuel and power or the installation of energy-saving materials. Zero-rated items are children's clothes, public transport, food (save for that served in restaurants) and newspapers or books. Insurance premiums, events funded by charities or education expenses can be exempt from VAT, subject to some conditions being met.

Corporation tax

It is payable on the taxable profits of limited companies and other unincorporated bodies such as associations, clubs or charities. Taxable profits include trading profits, investment profits (except dividends) and capital gains. There are two rates of corporation tax (full and small-profits rate). Corporations must complete a self-assessment form for corporation tax which is filed with HMRC.

Stamp tax

There are four types of stamp tax. The annual tax on enveloped dwellings (ATED) is payable on high value residential property owned by companies. Stamp duty land tax (SDLT) is payable on the purchase of lease of land or property and sometimes on transfers of ownership of land or property. Stamp duty reserve tax is owed on shares and securities bought by a company through the stock market. Stamp duty used to be payable on property transactions before December 2003 and when acquiring shares using a stock transfer form.

Fuel duty

It is payable to HMRC by businesses which produce, import, warehouse, sell or deal in motor and heating fuels. Rates vary depending on the type of fuel. A relief may be granted to businesses who use certain oils or fuels for specific purposes or export them to foreign countries.

Business rates

They are a yearly tax payable to the local council to help pay for local services when a company, partnership or any form of business uses a building or part of a building for non-domestic purposes, including commercial purposes such as factories, warehouses, offices, pubs or shops. Reliefs are available in some geographical areas which are either granted automatically or on the business' application to the local council. Exemptions may also apply. The buildings used for disabled people's welfare or training, fish farms, buildings and land, places of public religious worship are exempted.

Capital allowances

They are a form of tax relief which can be claimed for what a business spends on certain assets that are owned and used in the business, subject to some conditions being met. Examples are capital allowances on plant and machinery, those relating to the renovation of buildings, research and development allowances, gifts to charity of staff help, trading stock or company equipment.

GLOSSARY

- annual tax on enveloped dwellings (ATED) : annual tax set up in April 2013 payable by companies which own high value residential property; previously called annual residential property tax; *fr. : ≈ taxe d'habitation & cotisation foncière des entreprises (CFE)*
- business rates : local taxes charged on most non-domestic (including commercial) properties to help pay towards local services; *fr. : impôts fonciers dûs par les entreprises*
- capital gain : profit resulting from the sale of real property, stock or a capital asset; *fr. : plus-value*

- corporation tax : tax payable to HMRC by limited companies and organisations such as associations, charities, clubs, cooperatives and other unincorporated bodies on their taxable profits; normally payable in four instalments; *fr. : impôt sur les sociétés*
- fuel duty : tax duty payable to HMRC if someone produces, imports, sells or deals in motor and heating fuels; *fr. : taxe générale sur les activités polluantes (TGAP)*
- Pay As You Earn (PAYE) : system by which an employer deducts income tax and NIC from the employee's gross pay before paying the employee's monthly salary; *fr. : imposition par une retenue à la source*
- self-assessment (n.) : term used to refer to the fact for a company, partnership or self-employed person to work out it/himself the amount of tax payable for an accounting period; once the self-assessment is done, the figures obtained must appear in the annual tax return; *fr. : auto-évaluation*
- stamp duty land tax (SDLT) : tax payable when the amount paid for property or land which is purchased or transferred is above a certain threshold; the transactions must be notified to HMRC on a stamp duty land tax return form even if no tax is due; *fr. : ≈ droits d'enregistrement et de timbres relatifs aux transactions immobilières*
- stamp duty reserve tax (SDRT) : tax payable on paperless transactions when buying shares; *fr. : ≈ impôt applicable aux transactions portant sur des actions cotées*
- tax return form : form completed annually by self-employed people, partnerships and companies and filed with HM Revenue & Customs declaring liability for taxation; *fr. : déclaration d'impôts*
- threshold (n.) : when applied to tax, amount above which tax is payable; *fr. : seuil*
- Value Added Tax (VAT) : indirect tax on the final customer which increases the actual price of goods or services; *fr. : taxe sur la valeur ajoutée*
- working tax credit : tax credit based on the hours worked and paid for; the system applies to employees or self-employed people; *fr. : crédit d'impôt pour travailleurs à bas revenus*

USEFUL EXPRESSIONS

- to be liable for tax; *fr. : être redevable d'un impôt*
- to owe VAT on goods and services; *fr. : être redevable de la TVA sur les biens et services*

FURTHER INFORMATION

- in 2013, current British Prime Minister David Cameron has made it his priority to fight against "phantom companies" (*sociétés fantômes*) which are only set up for the purposes of enabling tax evasion

COMPARATIVE APPROACH

En 2013, le taux de l'impôt sur les sociétés en Grande-Bretagne était de 23 % pour 2013, un taux réduit de 20 % s'appliquant aux petites et moyennes entreprises. En France, il était de 33 % (pour un chiffre d'affaires hors taxe supérieur à 7 630 000 euros), un taux réduit de 15 % s'appliquant à la fraction du bénéfice en dessous de 38 120 euros. En outre, en France, les sociétés acquittent une contribution sociale sur l'impôt sur les sociétés variant de 3,3 % à 5 % selon le montant du chiffre d'affaires.

S'agissant du taux normal de TVA, il est depuis janvier 2014 passé en France de 19,6 % à 20 %, et est donc aligné sur le taux applicable en Angleterre et au Pays de Galles.

5

Criminal law

☐ 27 INTRODUCTION

While civil litigation is primarily concerned with disputes opposing a claimant to a defendant, criminal law aims at punishing any conduct that the State regards as a potential or real threat to public order. The sentence passed by a court of law is perceived as a retribution for the committed offence, and can be regarded as deterrence. Other sentences can be given to rehabilitate the offender. The State mainly comprises the police which carry out investigations to collect evidence against a suspect and the Crown Prosecution Service (CPS) which may decide to prosecute the alleged offender. If prosecuted, the alleged offender will become the defendant.

A criminal offence requires two elements : *actus reus* and *mens rea*. The former is described as the guilty act as opposed to the latter which is the guilty mind. Criminal offences are ruled by common law, statute law or can be regulatory. There are three categories of offences. The least serious offences are summary or non-indictable offences. The most serious offences are indictable offences. The category in the middle consists of either-way offences. A distinction is sometimes drawn between offences against the person, property or the state. Military law sets out additional criminal offences that can be committed only by members of the British Armed Forces.

While *acteus reus* can be easily proved in most cases, an offender's state of mind is often complex to assess. His intention can either be direct or oblique, although in strict liability cases, criminal intention is not required. A criminal might have had the malice to commit a crime or could have conspired to act in a wrongful way or incited someone to do so (inchoate offences). Alternatively, an individual can unintentionally kill someone by omission or recklessness. An offender can be helped by accomplices.

Some offences against the person constitute both a criminal offence and a civil tort. They can result in criminal and/or civil liability, respectively before the criminal and civil courts.

GLOSSARY

- accomplice (n.) : individual helping the main offender to commit or cover up an offence; *fr. : complice*
- *actus reus* (n.) : Latin expression which defines the guilty act; it is the physical element of a crime which can consist of an act or an omission; *fr. : élément matériel de l'infraction*
- alleged (adj.) : supposed to have occurred or existed; *fr. : présumé*
- conspiracy (n.) : when several individuals agree to commit a crime; *fr. : complicité*
- criminal (adj.) offence (n.) : wrongful act violating a law; *fr. : infraction pénale*
- Crown Prosecution Service (CPS) : state legal institution in charge of prosecuting defendants on behalf of the Crown; *fr. : ≈ Ministère public/services du Procureur*
- defendant (n.) : here, legal entity who defends criminal proceedings; *fr. : prévenu/accusé*
- deterrence (n.) : here, the sentence imposed on an offender is seen as an example to stop other people from committing the same offence; *fr. : dissuasion*
- inchoate (adj.) offence (n.) : although the criminal act has not been committed, situation when a person attempts, incites or conspires to commit a crime; *fr. : ≈ infraction non accomplie/non consommée*
- incite (v.) : encourage someone to commit an offence; *fr. : inciter*
- indictable (adj.) offence (n.) : most serious offence, such as rape or murder, that is always heard in the Crown Court; *fr. : crime*
- intention (n.) : in a criminal context, the will to commit an offence; *fr. : intention criminelle*
- malice (n.)/maliciousness (n.) : deliberate and vicious desire to harm someone else; *fr. : malveillance*
- *mens rea* (n.) : Latin expression which defines the guilty mind; the criminal intent behind an offence; *fr. : élément moral de l'infraction*
- military (adj.) law (n.) : see 31
- oblique (adj.) intention (n.) : the offender does not want to cause the criminal act, but foresees the potential consequences of his action; *fr. : dol indirect*
- offence against the person : criminal action violating the physical integrity of an individual; *fr. : infraction contre la personne*
- offence against property : criminal act against a legal entity's property or goods; *fr. : infraction contre les biens*
- offences against the state : wrongful act against a government such as treason, terrorism or tax evasion; *fr. : crimes et délits contre la nation, l'État et la paix publique*
- offender (n.) : person who commits an offence; *fr. : délinquant/auteur d'une infraction*

- offence triable either-way : intermediary category of offences which can either be tried as a summary offence before the magistrates' courts (without a jury) or as an indictable offence before the Crown Court (with a jury if a non-guilty plea is filed) ; *fr. : ≈ délit*
- omission (n.) : here, failure to act which results in harm being sustained; *fr. : infraction d'omission*
- public (adj.) order (n.) : here, the well being, peace and safety of society; *fr. : ordre public*
- recklessness (n.) : unjustified risky act; *fr. : imprudence*
- rehabilitation (n.) : here, the sentence is given to reform the offender; *fr. : réhabilitation*
- retribution (n.) : here, the sentence aims at punishing the offender for the offence he has committed; *fr. : punition/châtiment*
- sentence (n.) : punishment inflicted for a criminal offence; *fr. : peine*
- strict (adj.) liability (n.) : term used in cases when the defendant's *mens rea* is not necessary to define his criminal act; *fr. : ≈ responsabilité sans faute pénale*
- summary (adj.) offence (n.)/non-indictable (adj.) offence (n.) : least serious offence which is always tried in the magistrates' courts; *fr. : ≈ contravention*

USEFUL EXPRESSIONS

- to break the law; *fr. : enfreindre la loi*
- to commit an offence; *fr. : commettre une infraction*
- to confess to committing an offence; *fr. : confesser la commission d'une infraction*

FURTHER INFORMATION

- criminal can be used both as a noun or an adjective
- the noun crime can be translated in French by *criminalité* or by *crime* which is the most serious type of offence
- penal is hardly ever used in England and Wales where the word criminal is preferred (as in criminal law)
- the word malice (which should be translated by *malveillance*) should not be confused with the French word *malice* (which means naughty or cheeky)
- the United Kingdom has long relinquished the distinction between felonies (the most serious offence) and misdemeanours (the less serious offence) which still applies in the United States; this old classification was ended by the Criminal Law Act 1967
- note the different spellings of offen*c*e in British English and American English (offen*s*e)
- the noun police is either singular or plural which means that you can either say "the police is" or "the police are"; however the "police force" is singular

Comparative approach

En droit pénal français, l'infraction pénale est déterminée par trois éléments (légal, matériel et moral) alors qu'en droit anglais, ce sont le *mens rea* et l'*actus reus* qui constituent l'infraction. Les infractions en France sont répertoriées par le Code pénal. Outre-Manche, les textes de loi votés par le Parlement (*statute law*) établissent la plupart des infractions pénales, mais certaines infractions sont définies par la *common law* et les règlements (*delegated legislation*).

Même si la classification des infractions pénales est ternaire dans les deux pays (contravention/délit/crime en France et *non-indictable offence* ou *summary offence/offence triable either-way/indictable offence* Outre-Manche), les catégories ne se correspondent pas toujours. Parfois, un délit peut correspondre à une *either-way offence* ou *summary offence.* L'infraction non accomplie (*inchoate offence*) n'a pas vraiment d'équivalent en droit pénal français.

Outre-Manche, il n'existe pas, comme en France, de possibilité de constitution de partie civile devant le juge pénal. En d'autres termes, la victime d'un délit civil qui est aussi une infraction pénale ne peut réclamer au juge pénal l'indemnisation de son préjudice. Elle devra en demander réparation au juge civil, dans le cadre d'une action séparée. Cependant et dans le cadre de la détermination de la peine à infliger, le juge pénal anglais peut parfois assortir la peine d'une ordonnance obligeant le condamné à indemniser les victimes. Cette ordonnance s'appelle un *compensartion order* et, contrairement aux dommages et intérêts traditionnellement accordées dans le cadre d'une action civile, tient compte des ressources (*financial means*) du prévenu/accusé.

Comme l'action pénale et l'action civile sont séparées Outre-Manche, l'adage français selon lequel « le pénal tient le civil en l'état » n'y a jamais reçu application. En France, cet adage a perdu de sa vigueur et, depuis l'entrée en vigueur du nouvel article 4 du Code de procédure pénale modifié par une loi du 5 mars 2007, ne s'applique désormais plus qu'à l'action en réparation de l'infraction.

□ 28 OFFENCES AGAINST THE PERSON

Offences against the person encompass any offence involving physical injury which can be fatal or not. They always imply one or several individuals, a perpetrator and a victim. They can start with threats, such as an assault or harassment, be followed by physical or sexual violence (battery, grievous bodily harm, kidnapping, sexual assault, or rape) and may end with the death of the victim (homicide, infanticide).

Fatal offences vary greatly according to the perpetrator's intention and the circumstances. When the intention is direct, the defendant will be charged with murder, attempted murder or assassination in the case of a politician's death, while death caused unintentionally is classified under the general term manslaughter. The law draws a distinction between negligence (involuntary manslaughter, gross negligence manslaughter, corporate manslaughter) and the intention to hurt but not kill the victim (voluntary manslaughter). Deaths occurring within suicide pacts are considered as manslaughter and not murder.

GLOSSARY

- assault (n.) : violent threat of bodily harm (as opposed to the actual infliction of violence) whilst showing someone's ability to cause that physical harm; it is both a criminal offence and a civil wrong; *fr. : ≈ agression* (essentially verbal)
- assassination (n.) : murder of an important person for political reasons; *fr. : ≈ assassinat à caractère politique*
- attempted (adj.) murder (n.) : when an individual intends to kill someone but is unsuccessful; *fr. : tentative de meurtre*
- battery (n.) : unlike assault, unlawful physical violence actually inflicted on someone (e.g. when stealing a handbag); *fr. : agression physique*
- corporate manslaughter : homicide committed by a company's representative responsible for the employees' health and safety; *fr. : ≈ homicide involontaire causé par une personne morale*
- grievous bodily harm (GBH) : serious injury inflicted on someone's body, including the nervous system and the brain; *fr. : coups et blessures volontaires*
- gross negligence manslaughter : criminal offence classified as involuntary manslaughter; the defendant is usually in breach of the duty of care he owed to the deceased (e.g. a doctor with his patient); *fr. : ≈ homicide involontaire par imprudence*
- harassment (n.) : causing someone distress by alarming or threatening the person; *fr. : harcèlement*
- homicide (n.) : general term to define any unlawful killings; *fr. : homicide*
- infanticide (n.) : when the mother and/or the father intentionally kill(s) their child(ren); *fr. : infanticide*
- injury (n.) : harm inflicted on a person; *fr. : blessure*
- involuntary (adj.) manslaughter (n.) : in criminal law, the situation when the defendant kills someone else by negligence or by acting recklessly; *fr. : homicide involontaire par négligence*
- kidnapping (n.) : when someone abducts another person; *fr. : enlèvement*
- manslaughter (n.) : when the defendant kills a person without the intention to do so; there are different types of manslaughter (gross negligence man-

slaughter, voluntary/involuntary manslaughter, etc.); *fr. : homicide involontaire*

- murder (n. or v.) : when the defendant kills a person intentionally; *fr. : meurtre (n.)/commettre (v.) un meurtre*
- rape (n. or v.) : intentional penetration of another individual's vagina, anus or mouth without consent; *fr. : viol (n.)/violer (v.)*
- sexual (adj.) assault (n.) : when an individual sexually touches another individual without his consent; *fr. : attouchements sexuels*
- suicide pact : agreement between consenting adults to die together; *fr. : pacte de suicide*
- voluntary (adj.) manslaughter (n.) : offence which is not considered as murder since there was no malice aforethought, but the intention to hurt is present; *fr. : homicide volontaire*

USEFUL EXPRESSIONS

- to cause someone GBH; *fr. : infliger/porter des coups et blessures à quelqu'un*
- to be guilty of murder; *fr. : être coupable de meurtre*

FURTHER INFORMATION

- corporate manslaughter is a form of corporate crime

COMPARATIVE APPROACH

Même si le droit anglais considère l'homicide involontaire comme une seule et même infraction, il est habituel d'introduire une distinction subtile entre *voluntary* et *involuntary manslaughter* qui permet aux juges d'apprécier plus finement les degrés d'intention dans un acte involontaire. *Voluntary manslaughter* est utilisé dans les cas où l'élément moral (ou *mens rea*) est présent mais amoindri par des circonstances atténuantes telles que la provocation, la jalousie ou dans le cadre de pacte de suicide (*suicide pact*). *Involuntary manslaughter* est plutôt invoqué dans les cas d'accidents de la route entraînant la mort.

Le délit de défaut d'assistance ou non-assistance, qui existe en droit français, n'existe pas en droit anglais sauf si une personne ne respecte pas son devoir de diligence (*duty of care*) envers la victime, comme, par exemple, dans certaines affaires de responsabilité médicale ou en cas de décès causé par une installation électrique défectueuse. Cela correspond à la notion de *gross negligence manslaughter* (homicide involontaire par imprudence) et ce sont les juges qui apprécient, au cas par cas, la définition et la portée de la notion de *duty of care* (obligation de faire attention à son prochain).

☐ 29 OFFENCES AGAINST PROPERTY

Criminal law punishes any wrongful or dishonest conduct towards property, whether it belongs to individuals, parternships, or companies. Damaging public property through littering or vandalism, is also a property offence. The destruction of property by arsonists is regarded as a serious offence which is triable on indictment.

Theft, which is triable either-way, generally refers to the illegal appropriation of someone's goods. Thieves can steal a few items in a shop (shoplifting), make off without payment, break into houses (burglary) or use guns and violence in a bank robbery for example. Handling stolen goods is also classified as a criminal offence. Criminals can illegally acquire money by threatening individuals through blackmail or extortion. Deception is another way of stealing money, though without any violence (money-laundering, embezzlement, forgery and counterfeit). If industrial espionage has existed for a long time, the development of new technologies has given way to new forms of crime such as hacking.

GLOSSARY

- arson (n.) : intentional act of setting fire to a public or private property; the person starting that fire is called an arsonist; *fr. : incendie criminel/acte de pyromanie*
- blackmail (n.) : threats against an individual in exchange for money or favours; *fr. : chantage*
- break into (v.) : illegally enter a property; *fr. : entrer par effraction*
- burglary (n.) : illegally entering a private property, for instance by breaking a door or a window, in order to steal money or goods; *fr. : cambriolage*
- counterfeiting (n.) : illegal copying of bank notes or any other valuable goods in order to deceive potential buyers; *fr. : contrefaçon*
- embezzlement (n.) : illegal appropriation of an individual's money and/or property through legal means; this offence can be committed by a trustee, a banker or an agent; *fr. : détournement*
- extortion (n.) : illegal appropriation of money by threatening someone; *fr. : extorsion*
- forgery (n.) : illegal creation or alteration of an official document in order to deceive authorities or individuals; *fr. : faux*
- hacking (n.) : illegal access to an individual's or a company's computing system; *fr. : piratage informatique*
- handling (v.) (stolen goods) : illegal possession of goods; *fr. : recel de biens*
- industrial (adj.) espionage (n.) : when a worker illegally collects secret information held by his company to transfer it to a rival company; *fr. : espionage industriel*

- littering (n.) : discarding used objects in a public place; *fr. : ≈ abandon de déchets*
- money laundering : illegal act consisting in transforming money acquired fraudulently into money gained honestly; *fr. : blanchiment d'argent*
- robbery (n.) : theft committed with violence and threats; for example in a bank; *fr. : vol aggravé*
- shoplifting (n.) : illegally taking an item from a shop; *fr. : vol à l'étalage*
- theft (n.) : general term to define the illegal appropriation of an individual's goods or property; *fr. : vol*
- thief (n.) (pl. thieves) : person who commits a theft; *fr. : voleur*
- vandalism (n.) : deliberate destruction or damage to public or private property; *fr. : vandalisme*

USEFUL EXPRESSIONS

- armed robbery; *fr. : vol à main armée*
- to hack into a company's computer system; *fr. : pirater le système informatique d'une société*
- to rob a bank; *fr. : braquer une banque*

FURTHER INFORMATION

- the French verb *voler* can be translated by two verbs in English, "to rob" and "to steal", which are used in different situations – while a thief steals a watch from an old lady, a pickpocket robs tourists

COMPARATIVE APPROACH

Il n'existe pas de différence notoire entre le droit français et le droit anglais en matière d'infraction contre les biens, si ce n'est éventuellement la qualification de l'infraction elle-même.

□ 30 CORPORATE CRIME

Corporate crime, also known as white-collar crime, comprises all the criminal offences committed by a corporation (business entity having a separate legal personality from the individuals running it) or by people acting on behalf of a corporation or other business entity. For example, a company is considered as a legal entity liable for its actions and whose wrongful acts can lead to criminal prosecutions. Legislation also provides for secondary liabilities offences to punish any senior officer who may have helped his company to commit a criminal offence.

Types of criminal offences

In the past, corporations could only be prosecuted in strict liability cases in which the duty of the corporation/company was at stake. When it came to cases of fraud or manslaughter, *mens rea* could hardly be proven. However, recent legislation has created new categories of criminal offences to fight against corporate crime. The Corporate Manslaughter and Corporate Homicide Act 2007 provides for the category of corporate manslaughter, a criminal offence punishing serious breach of a duty of care. The United Kingdom Bribery Act 2010 was also passed to fight against corporate corruption and bribery nationwide and overseas. Under this act, senior officers can be prosecuted for "failure to prevent bribery".

The Serious Fraud Office (SFO)

The role of the SFO is of paramount importance to punish fraudsters. This independent government department supervised by the Attorney General, investigates on serious fraud, bribery and corruption and if they have collected enough evidence, prosecutes the companies and the officers suspected of having committed corporate offences. Corporate fraud can encompass illegal activities such as asset stripping, fraudulent trading or false information. Corruption and bribery include different fraudulent actions such as illegal gratuity, extortion, corporate espionage or kickback.

If the corporation/company is convicted by a court of law, it can be sentenced to pay fines or to imprisonment.

GLOSSARY

- asset stripping : sale of the assets of an acquired company to raise money to pay the liabilities incurred during the purchase of that company; *fr. : démembrement d'actifs*
- bribery (n.) : here, giving or accepting money to influence a decision, the signing of a contract; *fr. : corruption*
- corporate crime : criminal offence committed by a corporation (i.e. a business entity having a separate legal personality from the people running it) or by individuals acting on behalf of a corporation or other business entity; *fr. : criminalité des entreprises*
- corporate espionage : act of stealing secret information from a company to sell it to another company; *fr. : espionage industriel*
- corporate manslaughter (n.) : see 28
- corruption (n.) : wrongful act committed by people who have leading positions within a business, such as a company director; *fr. : corruption*
- extortion (n.) : illegal use of one's position to obtain an advantage; *fr. : extorsion*

- fraud (n.) : dishonest and misleading action of a fraudster in order to make a profit; *fr. : fraude*
- fraudster (n.) : individual committing a fraud; *fr. : fraudeur*
- fraudulent (adj.) trading (n.) : when a company intends to defraud the other companies or partners it works with; *fr. : ≈ pratiques commerciales frauduleuses*
- illegal (adj.) gratuity (n.) : giving or accepting money to thank or be thanked for influencing a transaction; *fr. : gratification illégale*
- kickback (n.) : when a contract is about to be signed, an individual can demand a portion of the contract to secure the signing; *fr. : ≈ ristourne*

USEFUL EXPRESSIONS

- to defraud someone; *fr. : frauder au détriment de quelqu'un*
- something is done fraudulently; *fr. : quelque chose est frauduleux*

FURTHER INFORMATION

- the expression "white-collar crime" was invented in the United States in 1939 to refer to the various frauds committed by corporate or government officials

COMPARATIVE APPROACH

La lutte contre la criminalité en col blanc a pris depuis quelques années une dimension plus grande avec la création du Bureau Européen Anti-Fraude (*European Anti-Fraud Office*) ou (OLAF) dont le rôle est de protéger les intérêts financiers au sein de l'Union européenne, notamment en luttant contre la fraude et la corruption. En 2009, OLAF a lancé l'opération Diabolo II, une opération douanière internationale ayant pour objectif de combattre, par le biais de saisies, la contrefaçon de produits de luxe et de cigarettes.

□ 31 MILITARY CRIMINAL LAW

The British military, whose official title is Her Majesty's Armed Forces, is divided into three different branches – the Royal Air Force, the British Army and the Naval Service which encompasses the Royal Navy and the Royal Marines. The British monarch is at the head of the British Armed Forces since she is their commander-in-chief.

Although members of the Armed forces and civilians working for the Army (for example, civil servants, employees working on a military ship) are all subject to civil criminal law, they are likely to commit offences related to their positions. Accordingly, Service law sets out additional criminal offences that can be committed only by a service person, that is to say a member of the regular forces. Civilians working for the army have to comply with service discipline.

Service offences cover a wide range of situations where a serviceman (or even a civilian working for the Armed Forces) can break military law. Tensions between members of the army can lead to improper behaviour towards a superior or a subordinate which is regarded as misconduct or ill-treatment of subordinates. Mutiny, which implies a denial of authority, can jeopardise important operations. The misbehaviour of members of the Army while in operation can be harshly punished by law, especially in cases of looting, misconduct of operations or desertion. The criminal offence of assisting the enemy verges on high treason.

GLOSSARY

- assisting an enemy : offence consisting in providing the enemy with information and/or supplies or protecting an enemy; *fr. : ≈ trahison*
- British (adj.) Army (n.) : main branch of the British Armed Forces divided into a Regular and a Territorial Army; *fr. : ≈ Armée de terre*
- desertion (n.) : when a service person intentionally avoids service or flees any operation; *fr. : désertion*
- Her Majesty's Armed Forces (or British Armed Forces) : military institution; *fr. : forces armées*
- looting (n.) : stealing property or goods from people killed or captured during an operation led by the Armed Forces; *fr. : pillage*
- misconduct (n.) : threats or violent conduct directed at another officer; *fr. : insubordination*
- misconduct of operations : offence consisting in failing to carry out orders or carrying them out in an unprofessional or unethical way; *fr. : ≈ faute professionnelle dans le cadre d'une mission*
- mutiny (n.) : when a service person challenges authority or disobeys any order from a superior officer; *fr. : ≈ mouvement insurrectionnel*
- Naval (adj.) Service (n.) : branch of the Armed Forces at sea, including the Royal Navy, the Royal Marines and the Royal Fleet Auxiliary manned by civilian personnel in charge of the supply of ships; *fr. : ≈ Marine nationale*
- obstructing operations : offence consisting in delaying or preventing, whether intentionally or not, any operation led by the Armed Forces; *fr. : ≈ fait d'entraver les opérations*
- Royal (adj.) Air Force (n.) : branch of the Armed Forces operating with aircrafts; *fr ≈ Armée de l'air*

- Royal (adj.) Marines (n.) : branch of the Naval Service specialising in combat under extreme conditions; *fr. : ≈ force d'action navale*
- Royal (adj.) Navy (n.) : oldest branch of the British Armed Forces; naval force structured around ships and aircraft; *fr. : ≈ Marine nationale*
- service discipline : category of service law including offences such as ill-treatment of subordinates or failure to attend service which can be committed by a serviceman and a civilian working for the army; *fr. : ≈ discipline militaire*
- service offence : non-civilian criminal offence committed by a service person; *fr. : ≈ infraction d'ordre militaire*
- service (adj.) person (n.)/serviceman (n.) : member of the army and reservist; *fr. : ≈ militaire*
- treason (n.) : act of betraying one's country; *fr. : trahison*

USEFUL EXPRESSIONS

- to join the army; *fr. : s'engager dans l'armée*

FURTHER INFORMATION

- in the Royal Navy, when talking about crafts or vessels, a ship is anything above water as opposed to a boat which is below water (e.g. a submarine)
- in Britain, the name of all ships starts with HMS i.e. Her Majesty's Ship
- the English word services would be translated in French by *armées*
- the French equivalent of the Territorial Army is the *Armée de réserve*

> **COMPARATIVE APPROACH**
>
> Au Royaume Uni, le monarque remplit la fonction officielle du chef des armées (*commander-in-chief*) et tous les militaires font allégeance à la Reine. En revanche, le premier ministre britannique (*Prime minister*) et le ministre de la défense (*Secretary for Defence*) détiennent le pouvoir exécutif sur l'armée. À l'inverse, en France, c'est le Président de la République, élu au suffrage universel, qui est le chef des armées et qui décide des interventions militaires.

□ 32 THE ENGLISH POLICE

Police officers are civilians who, after completing the Initial Police Learning and Development Program over two years, are recruited in the police force. They are assisted in their operations by members of the public such as Police Community Support Officers (PCSO) who go through a one-year training program. Special constables work on a voluntary and part-time basis, and can be recruited by entrance and health tests.

The police forces are divided in two categories : the territorial police forces are responsible for the majority of policing in different police areas; the special police forces are national specialised forces such as the British Transport Police, the Ministry of Defence Police and the Civil Nuclear Constabulary. The London territorial police forces are represented by the Metropolitan Police and the City of London Police.

Serious offences are usually investigated by the Criminal Investigation Department (CID), a branch present in each territorial police forces. Detective chief inspectors and chief superintendents are in charge of these complex criminal cases. The Special Branch is also part of the territorial police forces and is in charge of counter-terrorism and national security issues. This branch works in cooperation with the secret services such as MI5 and MI6.

Various agencies such as the new National Crime Agency or the Serious Fraud Office which are not part of the police force, operate nationwide, fighting against high-profile crimes. The Crime and Disorder Committee has also been set up to scrutinise the actions of all the police forces.

Even though territorial police forces depend on local areas, the ranks of police officers, generally known as constables, are the same in England and Wales, with a few variations for the London police forces. The hierarchy of constables from bottom to top is as follows : police constable, sergeant, inspector, chief inspector, superintendent, chief superintendent, assistant chief constable, deputy chief constable and chief constable, the latter being at the head of a territorial police force.

GLOSSARY

- assistant chief constable/deputy chief constable : member of the police force who is below the deputy chief constable and assists the chief constable; *fr. : ≈ commissaire de police adjoint*
- British Transport Police : national police force in charge of policing the rail network in Great Britain; *fr. : police des transports britanniques*
- chief constable : head of the local police force; *fr. : ≈ commissaire divisionnaire de police*
- chief inspector : police officer senior to the inspector who can command small units; *fr. : ≈ lieutenant de police*
- chief superintendent : police officer senior to a superintendent; *fr. : ≈ commandant de police*
- City of London Police : territorial police force responsible for the City of London; *fr. : police de Londres*
- Civil Nuclear Constabulary : national police force responsible for any non military nuclear installation and material; *fr. : police responsable de la sécurité civile nucléaire*

- Crime and Disorder Committee (CDC) : local authority committee whose role is to review any police action related to crime and disorder; *fr. : ≈ police des polices*
- Criminal Investigation Department (CID) : branch of territorial police forces responsible for serious offences; *fr. : ≈ police judiciaire*
- detective chief inspector : senior officer working for the Criminal Investigation Department and supervising major investigations; he is below the detective chief superintendent; *fr. : ≈ officier de la police judiciaire*
- detective chief superintendent : commander of the Criminal Investigation department; *fr. : ≈ directeur de la police judiciaire*
- inspector (n.) : police officer senior to a sergeant; *fr. : ≈ brigadier chef de police*
- Metropolitan Police Service : territorial police force in charge of law enforcement in Greater London; *fr. : police du grand Londres*
- MI5 (Military Intelligence section 5) : branch of the British Secret Intelligence Service in charge of protecting the country from any threat within its borders; *fr. : ≈ Direction centrale du renseignement intérieur (DCRI)*
- MI6 (Military Intelligence section 6) : branch of the British Secret Intelligence Service responsible for protecting the country from any outside threats; *fr. : ≈ Direction générale de la sécurité extérieure (DGSE)*
- Ministry of Defense Police (MDP) : special police force in charge of the personnel, property of the Ministry of Defence and of any other defence interests; *fr. : ≈ police protégeant le ministère de la défense*
- National Crime Agency : governmental body in charge of any high level crime such as organised crime; *fr. : ≈ Office central de lutte contre le crime organisé*
- Police Community Support Officer (PCSO) : civilian supporting police operations; *fr. : ≈ police de proximité*
- police constable : lowest rank in the territorial police force; *fr. : ≈ gardien de la paix*
- police officer : general term applying to any member of the police forces; *fr. : ≈ agent de police*
- sergeant (n.) : police officer senior to a police constable; *fr. : ≈ brigadier de police*
- Serious Fraud Office (SFO) : legal body dealing with frauds worth over £5 million; *fr. : Direction générale de la répression des fraudes*
- Special branch : branch of all territorial police forces in charge of national security; *fr. : ≈ DCRI*
- special (adj.) constable (n.) : part-time police force volunteer who has full police powers and wears uniforms when on duty; *fr. : ≈ police de proximité*
- superintendent (n.) : police officer assisting the chief superintendent; *fr. : ≈ capitaine de police*

USEFUL EXPRESSIONS

- to join the police force; *fr. : entrer dans la police*
- traffic warden (n.); *fr. : agent de circulation*

FURTHER INFORMATION

- the Metropolitan Service is usually known and referred to in the press as "the Met"
- Scotland Yard refers to the headquarters of the Metropolitan Service
- "Bobby" is the informal and friendly term used to refer to police officers

COMPARATIVE APPROACH

Alors que la France possède une police civile (police nationale) et une police militaire (gendarmerie nationale), la police anglaise est seulement constituée d'agents civils (*civilians*).

Outre-Manche, il n'existe pas, à proprement parler, de police nationale, mais des polices locales dont la juridiction est circonscrite à une « région » en particulier (*police area*). Il existe des agences policières sur le plan national, spécialisées dans un domaine particulier comme les transports (*British Transport Police*). Les forces de police française s'appuient localement sur les polices municipales, mais les deux systèmes ne sont pas comparables.

□ 33 POLICE POWERS

When a police officer witnesses criminal activity (by catching someone red-handed) or has reasonable grounds to suspect that a crime has been committed or is about to be committed, he has the right to arrest the suspect without a warrant if he finds enough evidence to take him to the police station. These powers are usually known as stop and search. The police can ask a magistrate to issue a warrant such as an arrest warrant or a warrant to search a particular place. In certain circumstances set out in section 24A of the Police and Criminal Evidence Act 1984 (PACE), ordinary (non-police) people can arrest someone without a warrant.

After being brought to the police station by the arrestor, the arrestee is held in custody for at least 24 hours. This is a period of detention without charge. A custody officer searches the detainee even without his consent and informs him of his rights. Intimate searches are always carried out by an officer of the same sex. Police interviews are tape-recorded and the suspect has a right to legal advice. If he cannot afford a lawyer, a duty solicitor is made available to assist him.

If no evidence is found against the suspect, he will be released without charge. If the police gather evidence against the arrestee, they can decide to issue a caution, a reprimand or a warning to avoid any prosecution. The police can charge the suspect with minor offences. For other offences, the Crown Prosecution Service (CPS) is responsible for charging the suspect. A magistrate in a magistrates' court then decides to release the suspect on bail providing he turns up at trial (a sum of money is paid into court as a security) or keep him in detention until he is brought to trial. A detention warrant is subsequently delivered. For serious offences such as murder, the bail may be granted only by a judge of the Crown Court.

GLOSSARY

- arrest (n. or v.) : depriving a suspect of his freedom by taking him to the police station; *fr. : arrestation (n.)/arrêter (v.)*
- arrestee (n.) : person who is under arrest; *fr. : personne arrêtée*
- arrestor (n.) : police officer arresting the suspect; *fr. : officier chargé de l'arrestation*
- arrest warrant : court decision handed down by a magistrate (from the magistrates' court) authorising a suspect's arrest; *fr. : mandat d'arrêt*
- bail (n.) : legal system allowing a defendant to retain his freedom pending the outcome of his trial at court; usually a sum of money, called security, is paid into court and will be refunded provided the defendant attends his trial; *fr. : caution*
- bail sheet : legal document stating that the defendant is free until his trial provided he appears in court when required; *fr. : formulaire de caution*
- conditional (adj.) caution (n.) : pursuant to sections 22-27 of the Criminal Justice Act 2003, formal warning given to a suspect or a person who confessed to committing an offence; it is not a conviction, but it will appear on the person's criminal record; *fr. : ≈ avertissement assorti de conditions*
- charge (n. or v.) : formal accusation against someone alleging that there are grounds to believe that he committed an offence; *fr. : inculpation (n.)/ mettre (v.) en examen*
- consent (n.) : here, agreement given by someone who accepts to being searched (or his place being searched) for possible criminal evidence by a police officer; *fr. : consentement*
- custody (n.) : legal detention of a suspect in a police station cell for a limited period of time whilst an alleged offence (which may have been committed by the person in custody or witnesses by him) is being checked or investigated by the police; *fr. : garde à vue/détention provisoire*
- custody officer : police officer responsible for searching detainees in the police station; *fr. : ≈ officier de police chargé de la garde à vue*
- detainee (n.) : here, suspect kept in a police station; *fr. : détenu*
- detention without charge : statutory period of time during which a suspect can be kept in custody without being charged; *fr. : détention sans mise en examen*

- detention warrant : court decision handed down by a magistrate (from the magistrates' court) authorising someone's detention for a fixed period of time; *fr. : mandat de dépôt*
- duty solicitor : lawyer advising suspects in custody or interviewed by the police; solicitors may volunteer to be on duty or a rota system is organised by some local Law societies; *fr. : avocat commis d'office*
- intimate (adj.) search (n.) : search which includes looking for any object that the suspect might have concealed and which might be related to the commission of an offence; *fr. : fouille corporelle*
- police interview : any formal exchange between a suspect and police officers; *fr. : interrogatoire*
- police station (n.) : local headquarters of the police; *fr. : commissariat de police*
- release (v. or n.) without charge : to allow a suspect to walk out freely when no evidence is found to charge him with; *fr. : remettre (v.)/remise (n.) en liberté sans poursuite*
- red-handed (adj.) : fact of being caught in the process of committing an offence; *fr. : en flagrant délit*
- reprimand (n.) : severe rebuking of a person by a police officer made orally; *fr. : avertissement*
- search (n. ou v.) : general term referring to attempts at finding evidence either on the detainee when in custody or at his home with a search warrant; *fr. : fouille (n.)/perquisitionner (v.)*
- search warrant : legal document issued by a magistrate or a judge describing the place(s) to be searched and the item(s) to be seized; *fr. : ≈ mandat de perquisition*
- security (n.) : when bail is granted, money paid into a court's special account in order to ensure that the defendant attends court for his trial; *fr. : consignation/montant consigné*
- seizure (n.) : formal and authorised actions led by police officers to seize or get hold of any items that could be used as evidence; *fr. : saisie*
- stop and search : phrase to define the power of the police to search a person or a vehicle and to detain him provided that the constable has reasonable grounds for suspecting any criminal activity; *fr. : ≈ interpellation à fin de fouille*
- suspect (n and v.) : term defining a person whom the police have reasonable grounds to believe is related to the commission of an offence; *fr. : soupcon (n.)/ soupçonner (v.)*
- warning (n.) : reprimand given by the police to minors aged under 17; *fr. : avertissement*
- warrant (n.) : written information on oath presented to a magistrate, stating that the police suspect someone of having committed an offence; *fr. : mandat*

USEFUL EXPRESSIONS

- to be accused of; *fr. : être accusé de*
- to be under arrest; *fr. : être en état d'arrestation*
- to charge someone with an offence; *fr. : mettre quelqu'un en examen/inculper quelqu'un de la commission d'une infraction*
- to grant bail; *fr. : accorder la liberté sous caution*
- to have reasonable grounds to believe that someone committed an offence; *fr. : avoir de bonnes raisons au fond de croire que quelqu'un a commis une infraction*
- to hold someone in custody; *fr. : maintenir quelqu'un en garde à vue*
- to pay money into court by way of security; *fr. : consigner une somme d'argent dans un compte au tribunal à titre de garantie*
- to release someone on bail; *fr. : libérer quelqu'un sous caution*
- to withhold bail; *fr. : refuser la libération sous caution*
- to catch someone red-handed; *fr. : prendre quelqu'un la main dans le sac*

FURTHER INFORMATION

- the word custody has a double meaning in English, which refers both to *garde à vue* et *détention provisoire*; in the past, custody was used in divorce cases to refer to the French *garde des enfants*; this has been replaced by access

Comparative approach

Les forces de police ont des pouvoirs plus étendus Outre-Manche qu'en France. Elles bénéficient d'un pouvoir discrétionnaire en matière de poursuites judiciaires. Aucun organe ne contrôle leurs décisions de poursuivre ou non un suspect. Une fois que la police décide qu'une personne doit être mise en examen, elle transmet le dossier au ministère public (*Crown Prosecution Service*). Toutefois, la suprématie de la police a été amoindrie par l'article 28 (*section 28*) du *Criminal Justice Act* de 2003 qui a transféré une partie de ses compétences en matière d'inculpation au ministère public anglais (*Crown Prosecution Servive*). Le juge anglais intervient aussi pour délivrer des mandats d'arrêts et de perquisition ainsi que pour les décisions concernant les cautions (*bail*) ou la détention provisoire (*custody*).

Le système de mise en liberté sous caution (*release on bail*) est également typique des pays de *common law*, même si la France possède divers systèmes de libération restrictive des suspects, comme le placement sous contrôle judiciaire.

☐ 34 INVESTIGATING

In the course of a criminal investigation, the police forces try to collect as much compelling evidence as possible before potentially charging the suspect with the offence(s). In addition to *prima facie* evidence, the suspect may decide to confess to the cime. If no confession is made, police officers check the alibi given by the suspects, find any circumstantial or corroborating evidence, take the depositions of possible witnesses who are prepared to testify in court, and scrutinise any forensic evidence such as fingerprints or any DNA samples taken during custody. For homicides, a forensic pathologist carries out the autopsy of the corpse under the authority of the coroner in the presence of police officers. Hearsay evidence can sometimes be admissible under strict conditions. The police usually gather inculpatory evidence, but also take into account any exculpatory evidence in their decision whether or not to charge the suspect. When the police charge the suspect, the evidence is transferred to the Crown Prosecution Service which will decide to prosecute or not depending on the reliability of evidence.

GLOSSARY

- admissibility (n.) : here, type of evidence on which the parties may rely at trial; *fr. : recevabilité (de la preuve)*
- alibi (n.) : evidence showing that a suspected person cannot have committed a particular offence e.g. he was busy elsewhere; *fr. : alibi*
- circumstantial (adj.) evidence (n.) : indirect evidence inferred from a series of facts; *fr. : preuve circonstantielle*
- compelling (adj.) evidence (n.) : evidence which is considered as reliable and probative; *fr. : éléments probants*
- confess (v.) : admit being liable for an offence; *fr. : avouer/confesser*
- corroborating (adj.) evidence (n.) : additional evidence supporting the main evidence in criminal proceedings; *fr. : élément de preuve qui corrobore*
- coroner (n.) : an individual – who can be either a qualified lawyer or a medical doctor with some legal qualification – investigating on unnatural and violent deaths; *fr. : coroner*
- DNA sample : fragment of a mouth swab or of hair enabling to collect a suspect's DNA; *fr. : prélèvement ADN*
- deposition (n.) : written statement of a witness's testimony; *fr. : déposition*
- evidence (n.) : fact(s) showing that a suspect has committed or not an offence; *fr. : preuves*
- exculpatory (adj.) evidence (n.) : elements showing the suspect's innocence; *fr. : élément de preuve à décharge*
- fingerprint (n.) : impression of the hand and/or of a finger; *fr. : empreintes digitales*

- forensic (adj.) pathologist (n.) : medical doctor trained in the specialty of forensic pathology, that is to say the study of causes of death; *fr. : médecin légiste*
- give (v.) evidence/testify (v.) : when someone relates what he witnessed or knows in a police station or a court of law; *fr. : témoigner*
- hearsay (n.) : statement made (e.g. in court) by someone who is not a direct witness but heard of something through an actual witness; *fr. : ouï-dire*
- inculpatory (adj.) evidence (n.) : evidence showing the guilt of the suspect; *fr. : élement de preuve à charge*
- *prima facie* evidence : information which establishes a presumption that someone committed an offence; *fr. : commencement de preuve*
- reliability (n.) of evidence : evidence that cannot be denied; *fr. : ≈ fiabilité de la preuve*
- witness (n. or v.) : here, person who can give (direct first-hand) information related to a criminal offence; *fr. : témoin (n.)/témoigner (v.)*

USEFUL EXPRESSIONS

- to confess to committing an offence; *fr. : avouer avoir commis une infraction*
- to carry out an investigation; *fr. : mener une enquête*
- to fabricate/falsify evidence; *fr. : fabriquer des preuves*
- to investigate; *fr. : enquêter*
- to collect evidence; *fr. : rassembler des preuves*
- to take fingerprints; *fr. : relever des empreintes*

FURTHER INFORMATION

- the word evidence is always uncountable in English and can never be plural; in French it is translated into *les preuves* and *une preuve* is a piece of evidence; evidence is also a false friend and does not equate the French *évidence* which means an obvious fact

COMPARATIVE APPROACH

La différence majeure entre les enquêtes françaises et anglaises repose sur le rôle fondamental du juge d'instruction français qui n'existe pas Outre-Manche. En France, l'enquête de police est dirigée par le juge d'instruction qui instruit à charge ou à décharge. En Angleterre et au Pays de Galles, c'est la police qui mène l'enquête et transmet les preuves à charge au ministère public anglais (*CPS*). Le *CPS* décide s'il y a lieu de poursuivre le suspect.

6

Intellectual property law

☐ 35 INTRODUCTION

Intellectual property refers to creations of the human mind. It relates to information or knowledge, which can be consolidated in tangible objects at the same time in limitless number of copies at different locations in any part of the world. The property is not contained in those copies, but is present in the information or knowledge reproduced in the copies.

The general area of law that regulates the creation, use and exploitation of mental or creative labour is intellectual property law. It deals with the protection of intellectual creations, such as inventions, designs, brands, books, music, etc. It protects the interests of creators by giving them ownership rights over their creations. It protects rights relating to literary, artistic and scientific works, inventions in all fields of human endeavour, scientific discoveries and industrial designs. It ensures property protection over intangible things such as ideas, inventions and information. The four main types of intellectual property are copyright, designs, patents and trademarks.

Intellectual property is usually divided into two branches, namely industrial property and copyright. Industrial property protects inventions and takes a range of forms. These include patents to protect inventions, and industrial designs, which are aesthetic creations determining the appearance of industrial products. It also covers trademarks, service marks, layout designs, commercial names and designations, as well as geographical indications, and protection against unfair competition. Copyright protection regulates the creation and use that is made of a range of cultural goods.

The majority of developments regarding intellectual property law in England and Wales have had their origin in the European Community and, since the Maastricht treaty came into force in 1993, the European Union. The Intellectual Property Office (IPO) is the official government body responsible for granting Intellectual Property Rights.

GLOSSARY

- brand (n.) : trade name, symbol, sign or slogan that is used to identify and distinguish a product, service or business by evoking positive images or emotions in consumers, and may be protected through trademark; *fr. : ≈ signe désignant le produit*
- commercial (adj.) name (n.) : name used to identify a commercial product or service; *fr. : dénomination commerciale*
- competition (n.) : rivalry between two or more businesses; *fr. : concurrence*
- copyright (n.) : form of legal protection provided to the authors of original literary, dramatic, musical or artistic works that gives its creator, if the rights are sold, the sole right to reproduce, perform or display the protected work and is represented by the symbol ©; *fr. : droit d'auteur*
- design (n.) : appearance of the whole or part of a product resulting from its distinctive features like lines, contours, colours, shape, texture or materials; *fr. : dessin*
- designation (n.) : act of designating like giving a name or identifying a mark; *fr. : désignation*
- geographical (adj.) indication (n.) : place names used to identify products that come from these places and bear specific characteristics; *fr. : appellation géographique*
- grant (v.) : accord a right or a privilege; *fr. : conférer*
- human (adj.) endeavour (n.) : effort or attempt made by a human being to achieve something; *fr. : ≈ activité humaine*
- industrial (adj.) design (n.) : aesthetic or ornamental aspect of a two- or three-dimensional article with design features related to an industrial process; *fr. : dessin ou modèle industriel*
- industrial (adj.) property (n.) : category of intellectual property that includes patent, inventions, trademarks, industrial designs and geographic indications of source; *fr. : propriété industrielle*
- intellectual (adj.) property (n.) : generic term used to describe products of the intellect and includes copyright, designs, patents and trademarks; *fr. : propriété intellectuelle*
- invention (n.) : discovery or creation of a new manufactured product or a new composition or a new process or a new use for an existing material or any improvements made to any of these; *fr. : invention*
- item (n.) : single article or unit in a list or a collection; *fr. : article*
- knowledge (n.) : state of knowing specific information about something; *fr. : connaissance*
- labour (n.) : work or effort; *fr. : travail*
- layout (n.) : overall design of a page including elements such as page, type size, typeface, arrangement of titles, sub-titles and page numbers; *fr. : conception*
- ownership (n.) : legal right of possession; *fr. : propriété*

- patent (n.) : exclusive legal right enjoyed by an inventor or company to manufacture, sell and use his or its invention for a certain number of years thanks to the permission granted by a government; *fr. : brevet d'invention*
- regulate (v.) : control or direct according to a law or principle; *fr. : réglementer*
- service marks : distinctive signs which enable the identification of certain products or services as those produced by a particular person or enterprise, thus enabling the consumer to distinguish them from similar goods or services of others in the market; *fr. : marques de service*
- tangible (adj.) : capable of being touched or felt; *fr. : tangible*
- trademarks (n.) : registered brand or trade name comprising a combination of phrases, designs, symbols or words that enable a distinction of the goods of one party from the other competitors in the market; *fr. : marque (au sens juridique du terme)*

USEFUL EXPRESSIONS

- to incorporate a copyright symbol in protected works; *fr. : intégrer un symbole du droit d'auteur dans l'œuvre protégée*
- to protect copyright; *fr. : protéger les droits d'auteur*
- to be under the protection of copyright laws; *fr. : être protégé par la législation sur les droits d'auteur*

FURTHER INFORMATION

- the word brand (*signe désignant un produit*) in France is the term generally used by marketers who do not distinguish the difference between registered trademarks at the INPI (*signes protégés*) and unregistered trademarks (*signes non protégés*)
- the French word *signe* may denote a company name (*dénomination sociale*), trade name (*enseigne*) or a product name (*nom du produit*); a closely linked word is trademark (*marque*) which in the French context refers to trademarks and service marks (*marque de fabrique, de commerce ou de service*)
- in France, *marque* refers to a registered trademark (*marque enregistrée*) at the INPI; if the company name or trade name or product (*signes*) are not registered at the INPI, they will not fall under the category of a trademark (*marque*) in France
- the word development (*développement*) refers to significant changes in law in this context and must not be translated by the French word *exploitation* that refers to the act or the state of being developed
- the word labour (*travail*) must not be confused with the French word *labour* which is a farming word referring to plowing and tilling

COMPARATIVE APPROACH

En Grande Bretagne on n'utilise pas l'expression droits d'auteurs ou *author's rights* mais le mot *copyright*. Le terme *copyright* qui émane de la *common law* exprime la volonté de protéger les créateurs d'une œuvre des copieurs qui pourraient exercer une concurrence déloyale auprès d'eux. En revanche, le législateur français veille à la protection des droits d'auteurs pour que le créateur ou l'auteur d'une œuvre protégée puisse jouir, outre des prérogatives morales qui lui sont reconnues, d'un monopole de longue durée, attribué sans formalités, cessible à titre onéreux et dont la violation peut être sanctionnée pénalement.

□ 36 COPYRIGHT

Copyright refers to the area of intellectual property law that regulates the creation and use that is made of cultural property. In England and Wales, the Copyright, Designs and Patent Act 1988 (CDPA) details eight categories of works protected by a copyright law : literary, dramatic, musical and artistic works, films, sound recording, broadcasts and published editions. To be protected by copyright, the work must satisfy four requirements : it must be recorded in a material form, be original, sufficiently connected to the UK to qualify for protection under UK law and not be excluded from protection on public policy grounds.

As copyright is a property right, it is necessary to distinguish between two general categories of subject matter, namely authorial works and entrepreneurial works. This enables a distinction between the authors of the original creation who possess authorship rights, and the works created by entrepreneurs who possess neighbouring rights, related rights or *droits voisins*. Primary rights are conferred on the owner of the copyright, like the reproduction, distribution, rental or lending right, the public performance, communication, adaptation and authorisation right.

In addition to the economic rights that are granted to the first owner of copyright, the CDPA 1988 also confers moral rights like integrity right, the right to object to false attribution and the attribution or paternity right. The duration of literary, dramatic, musical and artistic works covers the life span of the author plus 70 years and is subject to the following exceptions : computer-generated works, Crown copyright, parliamentary copyright, artistic works used in designs, works of unknown authorship and unpublished works not in the public domain. The publication right is granted to any person who, after the expiry of copyright protection, publishes for the first time a previously unpublished literary, dramatic, musical, or artistic work or film.

GLOSSARY

- adaptation right : right to do any of the restricted acts in relation to an adaptation like reproduction in any material form, translation, issue of copies to the public, performance, dramatisation or broadcasts; *fr. : droit d'adaptation*
- artistic (adj.). work (n.) : work that is considered as artistic, falling under one of three categories irrespective of artistic quality – a graphic work (including painting, drawing, diagram, map, chart or plan, engraving, etching, lithograph, woodcut, or similar work), a photograph (excluding a film), a sculpture, or a collage; a work of architecture, being a building or fixed structure or a model; or a work of artistic craftsman; *fr. : œuvre artistique/production artistique*
- attribution (n.) : state of being named as the rightful author of a work; *fr. : attribution*
- author (n.) : creator of the original work of expression and the owner of the copyright; *fr. : auteur/créateur*
- authorial (adj.) : relating to or produced by an author; *fr. : relatif à un auteur*
- authorisation right : right owned by the copyright owner to authorise others to perform certain restricted activities; *fr. : droit d'autorisation*
- authorship right : right owned by the author or owner of the copyright enabling him to claim authorship of his work, and to object to activities that modify or distort his original work, as doing so would be prejudicial to his honour or reputation; *fr. : droit d'auteur*
- broadcasts (n.) : electronic transmission of visual means of communication in the form of images, sounds or other information to members of the public; *fr. : diffusion/émission/transmission*
- communication right : right owned by a copyright owner to communicate a work to the public as in the case of literary, dramatic, musical and artistic works, sound recordings, films, and broadcasts; *fr. : droit de communication*
- computer-generated work : work created by a computer program or software; *fr. : œuvre générée par ordinateur*
- copyright protection : protection provided by copyright law to authors of original works of intellectual creation; *fr. : protection des droits d'auteurs*
- Crown copyright : copyright that covers material created by civil servants, ministers, government departments and agencies or servants of the Crown that lasts for 125 years from the year in which the work was made; *f: droit d'auteur de la Couronne*
- distribution right : right to issue copies of the work to the public, and to distribute copies that were previously not available for circulation; *fr. : droit de distribution*
- dramatic (adj.) work (n.) : work that includes the scenario or script for films, plays and choreographic works; *fr. : œuvre dramatique*
- economic (adj.) right (n.) : right that enables the author of a work to derive financial reward from the ownership of the copyright; *fr. : droit économique*

- entrepreneur (n.) : person who has neighbouring rights to recreate and develop an existing work by using his technical, innovative and organisational skill; *fr. : ≈ entrepreneur*
- false (adj.) attribution (n.) : state of being named wrongly as the author of a work which one did not create; *fr. : fausse attribution*
- integrity right : right possessed by the copyright owner to object to derogatory treatment of a work or any part of it; *fr. : droit à l'intégrité*
- literary (adj.) work (n.) : any work other than a musical or dramatic work, which is written, spoken or sung (including a computer program, a database, etc.); *fr. : œuvre littéraire*
- material (adj.) form (n.) : storage or fixation of literary, dramatic and musical works in a visible form; *fr. : forme matérielle ou support matériel*
- lending (adj.) right (n.) : right to make a copy of the work available for use, on terms that it will be returned, through an establishment which is accessible to the public; *fr. : droit de prêt*
- moral (adj.) rights (n.) : rights that safeguard an author's non-pecuniary or non-economic interests and protect his works against uses which are prejudicial to an author's moral interests; *fr. : droit moral*
- musical (adj.) work (n.) : work consisting of music exclusive of any words or action that is intended to be sung, spoken or performed with the music; *fr. : œuvre musicale*
- neighbouring (adj.) right (n.) : derivative right that enables the user who is not the author of the work to develop or use existing authorial works to create a derivative work; *fr. : droit voisin*
- original (adj.) creation (n.) : work that is considered innovative and creative when the author has exercised the requisite intellectual qualities, labour, skill or effort, in producing the novel intellectual creation; *fr. : création originale*
- parliamentary (adj.) copyright (n.) : copyright that covers information and works made by or under the direction or control of the House of Commons or the House of Lords; *fr. : droit d'auteur du Parlement*
- paternity right : right that ensures that authors and directors are named and recognition is attributed to them; *fr. : droit de paternité*
- primary (adj.) rights (n.) : rights that the law confers on the copyright owner that set out the scope of copyright to determine the types of activity which, unless done with the copyright owner's consent, amount to an infringement of the owner's copyright; *fr. : ≈ droits essentiels*
- property rights : right that is capable of being owned and sold and is capable of being licensed; *fr. : droits de propriété*
- public (adj.) domain (n.) : status of a creative work whose copyright or patent has reached its expiry date or has never received copyright protection; *fr. : domaine public*
- public (adj.) policy (n.) : system of laws and regulatory measures promulgated by a government entity; *fr. : politique gouvernementale*

- public performance right : right that protects owners of copyright in dramatic works by ensuring that the playing or showing of the work in public is an act protected by the copyright in a sound recording, film or broadcast; *fr. : droit de représentation publique*
- publication right : right that is granted without formality to any person who, after the expiry of copyright protection, publishes for the first time a previously unpublished literary, dramatic, musical, or artistic work or film; *fr. : droit de publication*
- published (adj.) edition (n.) : published version of the whole or any part of one or more literary, dramatic or musical works; *fr. : édition publiée*
- rental (adj.) right (n.) : right to rent the work and make it available for direct or indirect economic or commercial advantage; *fr. : droit de location*
- reproduction right : right to copy the work that is granted to owners of copyright; *fr. : droits de reproduction*
- requirement (n.) : condition required by law; *fr. : exigence juridique*
- sound recording : recording of sound and reproduction of the entire or partial production on a medium that can be used by the public; *fr. : enregistrement sonore*
- span (n.) : period of time; *fr. : durée*
- unpublished (adj.) : not available in print for distribution and sale; *fr. : non publiée*

USEFUL EXPRESSIONS

- to object to false attribution of paternity; *fr. : s'opposer à la fausse attribution de la paternité*
- an object that is excluded from copyright protection; *fr. : un objet qui est exclu de la protection du droit d'auteur*
- to confer rights of ownership to someone; *fr. : conférer des droits de propriété à quelqu'un*
- to grant the right to use a picture; *fr. : conférer ou accorder le droit d'utilisation d'une image*
- to receive a government grant; *fr. : recevoir une subvention du gouvernement*

FURTHER INFORMATION

- the word copy (*exemplaire*) must not be confused with the French word *copie* which refers to a duplicate or a replica or a reproduction

Comparative approach

La principale différence entre le *copyright* anglo-saxon et le système français des droits d'auteur est l'importance accordée aux droits moraux.

Outre-Manche, les droits patrimoniaux ont une plus grande incidence que les droits moraux. En revanche, en France, le législateur vise à garantir non seulement les intérêts économiques, mais aussi la notion de droit moral en conférant à l'auteur, indépendamment de ses droits patrimoniaux, le droit de revendiquer la paternité de son œuvre et d'empêcher toute modification susceptible de porter préjudice à son honneur ou à sa réputation.

□ 37 DESIGNS

Designs in intellectual property encompass industrial, graphic, urban planning, fashion, stage, costume, product and packaging design. As the art of designing is concerned with the nature and appearance of objects, it may be easily copied and thus deserves protection.

In England and Wales, there are currently five different ways in which a design may be protected : UK registered design, registered community design right, unregistered community design right, copyright protection of design drawings for artistic works, two-dimensional designs and surface decoration and UK unregistered design right.

In order to be registered as a national or community design or to receive protection as an unregistered community design, six criteria have to be considered : protectable design, novelty, "individual character", visibility, entitlement, and not conflict with earlier relevant rights.

After identification of the design, it is necessary to ascertain its state of the art, its interest to the informed user, and the protection that can be afforded to the design. Copyright can provide two forms of protection : direct protection by protecting the form and decoration of articles as artistic works, or indirect protection by protecting the author of a preliminary document on which a design is based.

As with copyright, unregistered design right is granted automatically on creation of a design. In order to establish the existence of an unregistered design right, it is necessary to show that there is a "design" which falls outside the exclusions from design right, that is original enough to be considered for design protection. Additionally, in order for a design to be protected by unregistered design right it is necessary to ensure that it does not fall within the list of "excluded" features contained in section 213 of the Copyright, Designs and Patents Act 1988.

The unregistered design right lasts for 15 years from its creation and date when it was first recorded into an article; or for 10 years from the date in which the articles made to the design were made available for sale or hire; whichever is earlier.

GLOSSARY

- entitlement (n.) : right granted by law or contract permitting the right holder to be eligible or entitled to a protected design; *fr. : droit inhérent*
- community design : industrial design right that applies in the EU and has both registered and unregistered forms; *fr. : dessin ou modèle communautaire*
- costume design : fabrication of stage clothes or apparel, or outfits for the overall appearance of a character of a performer; *fr. : conception de costumes*
- criteria (n.) : standard rule, application or test by which a decision can be made; *fr. : critères*
- design right : specific legal protection available to unregistered designs in the UK; *fr. : droit relatif à un dessin*
- direct protection : copyright protection that is offered directly to artistic and creative works; *fr. : protection directe*
- fashion design : application of art, aesthetics and design concepts to clothing and accessories; *fr. : création de mode*
- graphic (adj.) design (n.) : creative process that uses images and typography, thus combining art and technology to communicate ideas; *fr. : conception graphique*
- indirect (adj.) protection (n.) : copyright protection that is offered indirectly to design drawings through the copyright in the documents which were used during the process of devising the finished design; *fr. : protection indirecte*
- individual (adj.) character (n.) : trait that shows how the overall impression of the design is different from the appearance of other already known designs; *fr. : caractère individuel*
- industrial (adj.) design (n.) : see 35
- informed (adj.) user (n.) : person who is familiar with the kind of product in question and is aware of the amount of design freedom he can avail; *fr. : utilisateur averti*
- novelty (n.) : characteristic that distinguishes a product from an existing product and the state of the art, thus enabling a classification as new; *fr. : nouveauté*
- packaging (adj.) design (n.) : conceiving the best packaging system for a product by considering the size, shape, colour, closure, appearance, protection and labelling aspects that would suit the product; *fr. : conception d'emballage*
- product design : process of creating a new product which involves creating its style, deciding on its mechanical architecture, selecting materials and processes and engineering the various components necessary to make the final product; *fr. : conception du produit*
- registered community design : monopoly right that grants the design owner the exclusive right to make, use, sell, import and export any product embodying the registered design; *fr. : dessin ou modèle communautaire enregistré*

- registered (adj.) design (n.) : legal provision which protects the overall visual appearance of a product or a part of a product; *fr. : dessin déposé*
- stage design : also known as scenic or production design, it refers to the art of creating an aesthetic space for performance with the right scenery, lighting, sound and costumes; *fr. : scénographie de théâtre*
- unregistered community design : design right that provides protection against the copying of the design for a restricted period of 3 years from first disclosure and serves to protect transitory designs which are market tested before application is made for a registered design; *fr. : dessin ou modèle communautaire non enregistré*
- unregistered (adj.) design (n.) : design right that can be exercised without a formal registration process and is automatically acquired by a designer upon creation of an original design; *fr. : dessin ou modèle non enregistré*
- urban (adj.) planning (n.) : branch of architecture that deals with the design and organisation of community space, urban space and activities; *fr. : planification et amènagement urbain*
- visibility (n.) : part that is noticeable in use as its parts are considered as novel and possessing individual characteristics that are protectable; *fr. : visibilité*

USEFUL EXPRESSIONS

- to ascertain how to protect information; *fr. : déterminer comment protéger les informations*
- to conflict with the interests of the design holder; *fr. : être en conflit avec les interêts du titulaire du dessin*
- in the event of a conflict between the parties; *fr. : en cas de conflit entre les parties*
- to register a design; *fr. : faire enregistrer un dessin*
- to make an application for registration; *fr. : faire une demande d'enregistrement*

FURTHER INFORMATION

- the French adverb *actuellement* is translated in English by the adverb currently
- the English verb design is translated by *concevoir* in French

Comparative approach

À côté des dessins et modèles déposés, la législation britannique connaît un régime de dessins et modèles non déposés (*unregistered design right*) selon lequel la protection normalement conférée au créateur est en outre subordonnée à deux conditions de fond, distinctes de la nouveauté et du caractère individuel des dessins et modèles déposés, à savoir l'originalité et le rattachement suffisant avec le Royaume-Uni ou l'Union européenne. Au lieu de suivre le modèle adopté par les autres pays de la communauté européenne qui instituent une même condition de caractère individuel, le Code français de la propriété intellectuelle présente la particularité d'y substituer une exigence de caractère propre.

□ 38 PATENTS

A patent is a legal document that confers a 20-year monopoly on the patentee. The applicant for a patent is required to disclose its invention so that it can be used by a person skilled in the art. In return, the state follows the guidelines set by the Patent Office and issues the applicant with a patent that gives him the exclusive right to control the way that its patented invention is exploited.

The patent system in England and Wales operates on the first to file system, whereby the first person to file an acceptable application for an invention should be granted a patent over the invention. Patents are known either as British patents or European patents and are granted by two authorities : the UK Intellectual Property Office (IPO) and the European Patent Office (EPO).

Unlike copyright, which arises automatically on creation of the work, patents are only granted after the applicant satisfies the following requirements of registration : patentable subject matter, novelty, inventive step and ownership. Patents in Britain and the EU are made up of four key parts : an abstract, a description of the invention, one or more claims and any drawings referred to in the description or claims. Claims vary from case to case and may be classified as product claims, process claims, product-by process claims, representative claims and functional claims.

Patents may be classified under one of the following schemes that respect the norms set by the World Intellectual Property Organisation (WIPO) : International Patent Classification (IPC), the Cooperative Patent Classification (CPC) and the United Kingdom classification (UKC).

Patent agents assist applicants to choose either to make a "full application" or opt for an "early filing". After publication of the patent application, if third parties do not oppose the grant of a patent, the application moves to the stage of substantive examination to ascertain whether the application complies with the requirements of the Patents Act 1977, or in the case of the EPO, the European Patent Convention 2000.

GLOSSARY

- abstract (n.) : brief summary of the technical features of an invention, containing the title of the invention, a concise summary of the matter contained in the specification and an indication of the technical field to which the invention belongs; *fr. : synthèse*

- applicant (n.) : person who applies for a patent; *fr. : déposant*
- ascertain (v.) : to make certain; *fr. : vérifier/déterminer*
- British (adj.) patent (n.) : patent issued by the IPO that is subject to British law; *fr. : brevet britannique*
- confer (v.) : grant; *fr. : conférer*
- cooperative patent classification : patent classification that contains 250,000 groups and a hierarchical structure based upon the IPC, which replaced the former European Classification System (ECLA) on 1st January 2013; *fr. : ≈ classification coopérative des brevets*
- description (n.) : account of the background of the invention, summarising the prior art, referring to the existing art, outlining the technical problem that the invention attempts to solve and the solutions that it offers; *fr. : description*
- disclose (v.) : make information known to the public; *fr. : divulguer/révéler*
- drawing (n.) : graphic representation of an invention or idea; *fr. : dessin*
- early (adj.) filing (n.) : provision permitting an applicant to give an indication that a patent is sought, as well as offering him a twelve-month breathing-space in which he can decide whether he wishes to pursue a patent or not. *fr. : dépôt de demande de brevet anticipé*
- European (adj.) patent (n.) : patent issued by the EPO in Munich which applies to all contracting states in the EU; *fr. : brevet européen*
- exclusive (adj.) right (n.) : right that can be exercised only by the owner of the copyright; *fr. : droit exclusif*
- first to file : legal concept that establishes that the right to a grant of a patent for an invention lies with the first applicant who files for protection of his invention and applies regardless of the date of the actual invention; *fr. : système du premier déposant*
- full (adj.) application (n.) : patent application that contains a request for grant of a patent, a description of the invention, one or more claims, any drawings referred to in the description or the claims and an abstract. *fr. : dossier complet*
- functional (adj.) claim (n.) : claim that defines the invention by referring to the function that the invention performs, its performance or its purpose, rather than the structure or elements of the invention; *fr. : ≈ demande relative à la fonction de l'invention*
- guideline (n.) : principle that sets standards or determines the course of action; *fr. : directive/instruction*
- international patent classification : classification of 70,000 subdivisions or groups of different types of technical information maintained by the WIPO; *fr. : classification internationale des brevets*
- invention (n.) : see 35

- inventive (adj.) step (n.) : feature of an invention that contains technical advance when compared to the existing know-how, and can be identified by a person skilled in that area of technology; *fr. : activité inventive*
- monopoly (n.) : exclusive control and right to use an invention; *fr. : monopole*
- norm (n.) : rule or standard; *fr. : norme*
- novelty (n.) : see 37
- ownership (n.) : see 35
- patent agent : person who assists in the drafting and processing of patents, offers advice on the exploitation of patents, and acts as a go-between uniting the technical-scientific domains with the legal and commercial process; *fr. : agent de brevet*
- patentable subject matter : art, process, machine, manufacture or composition of matter are subject matter protected by the Patent Act and does not take into account the quality of the subject; *fr. : objet brevetable*
- patentee (n.) : person to whom a patent has been granted officially and whose patent is classified in a patent classification; *fr. : breveté*
- patented (adj.) invention (n.) : invention that has qualified for the grant of a patent; *fr. : invention brevetée*
- product-by process claim : if a product already exists but a new process is devised for producing that product, this hybrid claim covers both the process and the product produced by the process; *fr. : ≈ demande de type produit-par-procédé*
- process claim : claim that protects activities or actions such as methods, processes or uses; *fr. : ≈ demande relative au process*
- product claim : claim for a product *per se* that confers protection over all uses of that product, no matter how the product was derived; *fr. : ≈ demande touchant au produit*
- publication (n.) : stage in the patent application process when the application is published and made available for public inspection, thus informing third parties that the application has been made; *fr. : publication*
- registration (n.) : act of recording the patent registration in a register, thus giving the registrant priority against anyone who has an earlier unregistered right, subject to the proviso that the registrant had no notice of the earlier right; *fr. : enregistrement/dépôt*
- substantive (adj.) examination (n.) : detailed examination of a patent application by a patent examiner to determine whether a patent should be granted or not; *fr. : examen de fond*
- third (adj.) party (n.) : legal term for any individual who does not have a direct link with a legal transaction but who might be affected by it; *fr. : tiers*
- United Kingdom classification : classification of patent application in the UK prior to 1st July 2007; *fr. : classification des brevets au Royaume-Uni*

USEFUL EXPRESSIONS

- to comply with patent requirements; *fr. : se conformer aux critères de brevetabilité*
- in compliance with the Patent Act; *fr. : en conformité avec la loi sur les brevets*
- to file a dossier; *fr. : déposer un dossier*
- to opt for a European patent; *fr. : opter pour un brevet européen*
- to opt out of the international patent system; *fr. : sortir du système international des brevets*
- to satisfy the inventive step requirement; *fr. : remplir le critère d'activité inventive*

FURTHER INFORMATION

- the word office (*bureau*) must not be confused with the French word *office* which has other meanings of religious service, pantry or official designation
- to operate (*fonctionner*) must not be confused with the French word *opérer*

COMPARATIVE APPROACH

La Grande Bretagne et la France ont opté pour le système du premier déposant ou *first to file system* selon lequel le droit au titre de propriété industrielle appartient à la personne qui justifie de la date de dépôt de brevet la plus ancienne. Ce système du premier déposant s'oppose au système du *first to invent* ou du premier inventeur suivi par le régime américain où le droit au titre de brevet appartient à l'inventeur qui réussit à prouver qu'il a été le premier à réaliser l'invention.

□ 39 TRADEMARKS

In England and Wales, the Trade Marks Act (TMA) 1994 establishes two legal regimes, which transform signs into forms of intellectual property. They are the common law of passing off and the statutory regime which regulate certain signs or symbols, usually words or pictures. They are used in trade in connection with particular goods or services. This legal protection enables the proprietors of trademarks to prevent other traders from using the signs on the same or similar goods or services.

The Law of Passing Off

Under the law of passing off, the sign must have been used in trade so as to have acquired a reputation. This legal provision allows trader A to prevent a competitor B from passing their goods off as it they were A's. In order to succeed in an action for passing off, a claimant must establish that the claimant has goodwill that the defendant made a misrepresentation that is likely to deceive the public and the misrepresentation damages the goodwill of the claimant.

The Statutory Regime

In contrast with the law of passing off, in the statutory regime, the sign must have been registered, either at the UK Trade Mark Registry or at the Community Trade Mark Office (OHIM). A trademark may be registered as an ordinary trademark, a certification trademark or a collective trademark.

A mark may be revoked on the following grounds : of non-use in five years following the date of completion of the registration, suspension for an uninterrupted period of five years, generic use in trade or deceptive for misleading the public.

Section 46/Article 50 provides that a mark may be revoked on the grounds of non-use in five years following the date of completion of the registration; suspension for an uninterrupted period of five years; generic use in trade; or deceptive for misleading the public.

To regulate geographical indications or designations for regional and traditional food names within Europe, Article 22 of the agreement relating to Trade Related Aspects of Intellectual Property Rights (TRIPS) stipulates the need to specify the indication of origin by distinguishing between appellations of origin and geographical indications. In keeping with EU regulations, new laws in England and Wales have included protected designation of origin (PDO), protected geographical indication (PGI), and traditional speciality guaranteed (TSG).

GLOSSARY

- appellations (of origin) : kind of geographical indication in product naming to indicate that the product possesses specific qualities that are essentially due to the geographical environment in which it was produced; *fr. : appellation d'origine*
- certification trademark : mark indicating that the goods and services in connection with which it is used are certified by the proprietor of the mark in respect of origin, material, mode of manufacture, quality or other characteristics; *fr. : marque de certification*
- collective (adj.) trademark (n.) : mark distinguishing the goods or services of members of the association which is the proprietor of the mark from those of other undertakings, thus serving as a sign of membership; *fr. : marque collective*
- deceive (v.) : give a false impression; *fr. : tromper*
- deceptive (adj.) : likely to deceive or mislead; *fr. : frauduleux*
- distinguish (v.) : identify differences; *fr. : distinguer*
- goodwill (n.) : favourable reputation and regular patronage that is enjoyed by an established and well-run business; *fr. : fonds de commerce/clientèle*

- generic (adj.) use (n.) : words that are used to designate the accepted and recognized description of a class of goods or services as in the case of computer software or facial tissue; *fr. : usage générique*
- geographical (adj.) indication (n.) : see 35
- legal (adj.) regime (n.) : general framework of legal rules and principles that govern a country; *fr. : régime juridique*
- mislead (v.) : lead in the wrong direction; *fr. : tromper*
- misrepresentation (n.) : false material assertion of facts inducing a party to enter into a contract; *fr. : erreur (vice du consentement)*
- ordinary (adj.) trademark (n.) : mark that distinguishes the goods and services of one particular trader from those of other traders; *fr. : marque ordinaire*
- passing off : common law provision which can be used to enforce unregistered trademark rights, and prevent the infringer from misrepresenting his goods and services as being the goods and services of the claimant as in the case of the use of slogans and visual images that have become part of the goodwill or reputation of the product; *fr. : loi sur la concurrence déloyale/passing off*
- protected (adj.) designation (n.) (of origin) : term used to describe foodstuffs that are produced, processed and prepared traditionally and entirely in a given geographic area, and are thus entitled to bear the name of the place of origin; *fr. : appellation d'origine protégée*
- protected geographical indication : term used to describe foodstuffs that are at least partially manufactured within the specific region and indicate the geographic link with the area due to the traditional method of preparation in at least one of the stages of production, processing or preparation; *fr. : indication de provenance*
- sign (n.) : word, logo, name, symbol or a combination thereof, used by a producer or a vendor to distinguish a particular product or service; *fr. : signe*
- trade symbols : symbol ™ is used to inform potential infringers that a slogan, logo or other indicator is being claimed as a trademark; *fr. : symbole de marque*
- trader (n.) : person who is engaged in trade or business; *fr. : commerçant/négociant*
- traditional speciality guaranteed : term used to protect traditional food products of specific character whose raw materials, production methods and processing are of a traditional nature, thus granting the producer an exclusive right over the registered product name; *fr. : spécialité traditionnelle garantie*

USEFUL EXPRESSIONS

- to pass off a mark; *fr. : faire une tentative de substitution de marque*
- an act of passing off; *fr. : une action en concurrence déloyale*
- to revoke on the grounds of; *fr. : révoquer pour des motifs de*

- the revocation of a trademark; *fr. : la révocation d'une marque*
- to trade goods and services; *fr. : échanger des biens et des services*
- to take part in trade fairs; *fr. : participer à des foires commerciales*

FURTHER INFORMATION

- the word agreement (*accord/contract*) must not be confused with the French word *agrément* which has other meanings of ornamental or pleasure
- the verb to prevent (*empêcher*) must not be confused with the French verb *prévenir* which means to warn

COMPARATIVE APPROACH

La marque de certification en Grande Bretagne indique que les produits sur lesquels elle est utilisée ont été obtenus selon certaines normes qui ont été définies et contrôlées par le propriétaire de la marque. C'est une forme voisine de la marque collective française. En France, la marque collective de certification est déposée pour des produits qui se caractérisent par des traits précis quant à leur nature, leurs propriétés ou leurs qualités. Pour bénéficier d'une marque collective déposée, quatre critères doivent être satisfaits : être originaire de la région et être un produit authentique, artisanal et naturel.

7

Insurance law

□ 40 INTRODUCTION

Insurance is a contractual system in which a legal entity, the policyholder – who may be the insured or not – pays an insurer a premium in exchange for the insurer's promise that he will provide the insured with a service if a particular risk guaranteed becomes a reality. Insurance is a financial protection against a risk, but it cannot make the risk disappear. The policyholder will usually be the insured but this is not always the case, as for life insurance or companies' group insurance policies.

Within his company, the insurer sets up a community of risks by bringing together the largest number of similar risks. The premium rate takes into account factors such as the previous occurrence of similar risks and the likelihood of any further future occurrence. Whilst calculating the premium, the insurer tries to limit the risk of his financial exposure if the risk becomes real and exceeds its expected scope. When the risk to insure is great, it may be spread between various insurers through coinsurance. A lead insurer will deal with the file on behalf of his colleagues. To cover the risk to which they are themselves exposed, insurance companies may also resort to reinsurance. Within the insurance business, various categories of people play a paramount role : brokers, agents, underwriters and actuaries.

Unlike most insurers who are companies, Lloyd's of London which has a predominant place in the insurance/reinsurance business is a corporate body. The Lloyd's Names scandal arose in the late 1980s and early 1990s. A United States court then awarded plaintiffs substantial punitive damages in an asbestosis and pollution litigation. The defendants were insured/reinsured by Lloyd's. The specificity of Lloyd's was to be organised in syndicates whose members were called Names. Membership of a syndicate was different from owning shares in a company. Its duration was limited but the financial exposure extended as far as the Names' own assets. The substantial order for damages rendered by the United States court resulted in many Names being made personally bankrupt.

In most cases, an insurer will be an insurance company represented by an individual. For the sake of ease, the insurer and the insured will be referred to as a "he", who may also be an individual or a company, partnership, etc.

GLOSSARY

- actuary (n.) : insurance specialist who assesses the likelihood of a risk occurring, tries to reduce this occurrence and the impact of the risk if it ever occurs; *fr. : actuaire*
- agent (n.) : here, person who works for a specific insurance company and is in charge of a particular geographical area; he only sells that particular insurer's policies to the end customer (the policyholder or insured); *fr. : agent d'assurance*
- broker (n.) : insurance professional who offers advice and searches the market to buy the most appropriate policy from an underwriter for the end customer (the policyholder or insured) whom he represents; *fr. : courtier d'assurance*
- coassurance (n.)/coassure (v.) : practice in which an important risk to be insured is distributed between various insurers with whom the policyholder signs a contract for a percentage of the cover; one of the insurers (the lead insurer) will be in charge of the file, on his own behalf and that of the coinsured insurers; *fr. : coassurance*
- community of risks : groups of risks set up by an insurer to ensure a similar protection to all of them; *fr. : mutualisation des risques*
- in-house (adj.) : here, refers to the actuaries, solicitors or other professionals who are employed by the company/firm and work exclusively for it; *fr. : en interne*
- insured (n. or adj.) : person or entity who has the benefit of an insurance policy when the risk covered occurs; the insured is not necessarily the same person as the policyholder who contracts with the insurer; *fr. : assuré/bénéficiaire de la police*
- insurer (n.) : legal entity (usually a company) which grants an insurance cover (usually a financial cover) for a possible risk in exchange of a premium; *fr. : assureur*
- Lloyd's Name : name given to the members of the syndicates who belong to Lloyd's of London; *fr. : Names de Lloyds*
- plaintiff (n.) : legal entity who sues a defendant before the United States courts; this was also the name given to those suing defendants in Britain until the Civil Procedure Rules 1999 (it was then replaced by the word claimant); *fr. : demandeur*
- policy (n.) : insurance contract which the policyholder/insured and the insurer enter into to provide cover to an insured, should a specific event occur; *fr. : police (d'assurances)*
- premium (n.) : amount paid by the policyholder/insured (usually a yearly sum) to an insurer in exchange for cover; *fr. : prime (d'assurance)*
- reinsurance (n.)/reinsure (v.) : practice where the insurer transfers part of the risk insured to another insurer (the reinsurer) with whom the policyholder has no direct contact; *fr. : réassurance*
- risk (n.) : likelihood that an event will occur against which the policyholder/insured seeks cover from the insurer; *fr. : aléa*

- underwriter (n.)/underwrite (v.) : insurance specialist accountable to an insurance company who runs a portfolio of risks and decides if and how an insured's risk should be covered and for what premium; *fr. : souscripteur d'assurance*

USEFUL EXPRESSIONS

- to take out/subscribe an insurance policy; *fr. : souscrire une police d'assurance*
- the likelihood of the risk occurrence in a year is; *fr. : la probabilité de la survenance du risque est*
- to work out the premium rate; *fr. : calculer le taux de prime*
- in return for insurance cover; *fr. : en contrepartie de la couverture d'assurance*
- insurance protects against a risk; *fr. : l'assurance est une garantie contre un aléa*

FURTHER INFORMATION

- do not confuse "to insure" which relates to the insurance business and "to ensure" which means "to ascertain" or "to make sure"
- likewise "to assure" something means to say something with near certainty or assurance
- an insurance "policy" (*police*) should not be confused with the "police" force

COMPARATIVE APPROACH

Le marché de l'assurance est un marché international et il est courant que les assureurs britanniques et français travaillent ensemble, par le biais de la coassurance ou réassurance, ou au contraire, aient des intérêts opposés dans le cadre de contentieux (*litigation*). Comme Outre-Manche, l'assurance française repose sur la notion d'aléa (*risk*) et les dispositions des polices (*provisions of insurance policies*) se ressemblent, les assureurs français n'hésitant pas à rédiger leurs contrats en anglais, ce qui facilite l'établissement de contrats de coassurance ou réassurance. Contrairement à l'Angleterre et au Pays de Galles où le droit n'est pas codifié, le droit des assurances français est régi par le Code des assurances.

□ 41 INSURANCE POLICIES IN GENERAL

Unlike commercial contracts which revolve around the principle of *caveat emptor*, insurance contracts are based on the *ubberimae fidei* principle. Prior to entering into the contract, the proposed policyholder/insured must complete a proposal form at the insurer's request. The information given enables the insurer to determine the insured's needs in relation to a particular risk, if previous insurance claims were made as well as the likelihood of a risk occurrence in the future. A temporary cover note is usually issued by the insurer pending the preparation of the contract. The policy sets out the terms of the contract which the insurer and the insured enter into. Reference is expressly made in the policy to the insurer's general and special conditions (or schedule) which are part of the contract. The schedule contains the conditions which are specific to a particular insured.

The information which appears in the contract includes details of the policyholder, the insured (who is not necessarily the same legal entity as the policyholder) and the insurer, the amount of the premium, the nature of the risk covered, the extent of the cover, possible exclusions, exemptions or excess to be borne by the insured and the inception date. Damage caused by civil war is usually excluded from cover. Conversely *force majeure* events may be insured. Excess is a sum of money which the insurer requires the policyholder/insured to meet as the first part of any claim. The balance of the claim is then paid by the insurer within the policy limits. Excess can be compulsory, voluntary, per claim or annual aggregate. The inception date is that on which insurance cover becomes effective. Unless otherwise stated, an insurance policy is usually taken out for a year. It is renewed unless either party gives advanced notice of its termination before the anniversary date. The notice period is set by statute. A renewal notice is sent out to the policyholder/insured a few weeks before the termination date.

GLOSSARY

- annual aggregate excess : amount by which the annual applicable coverage limit is reduced in order to determine the amount of the insured's recovery; this amount is irrespective of the number of claims made to the insurer per policy; *fr. : franchise annuelle*
- *caveat emptor :* Latin expression meaning "let the buyer beware"; the buyer should take the necessary precautions before purchasing goods or services; *fr. : ≈ que l'acheteur prenne ses précautions*
- cover (n. or v.)/coverage (n.) : protection granted by the insurance company to the insured in the event of the occurrence of the risks insured; *fr. : garantie*
- cover note : temporary document issued by the insurer pending finalisation of the actual policy; *fr. : note de couverture*
- deductible/excess (n.) : sum of money set out in the policy which is borne by the insured before he is entitled to payment by the insurer; *fr. : franchise*
- endorsement (n.)/endorse (v.) : document annexed to the insurance policy setting out specific points; it is an integral part of the insurance contract; *fr. : avenant*
- *force majeure* insurance : concept inspired from French law which insures events beyond the control of parties to a contract such as, but not exclusively, flood, earthquake, fire or epidemics; *fr. : force majeure*

- general (adj.) conditions (n.) : terms of an insurance contract which apply to all those who subscribe a policy with a specific insurer; *fr. : conditions générales*
- inception date : date stated in the policy on which the insurance cover comes into force; *fr. : date d'entrée en vigueur*
- notice period : here, amount of time which an insurer must give the policyholder (or which the policyholder must give the insurer) to notify him of a particular event (for example, making a claim or terminating the contract); *fr. : délai de préavis*
- occurrence (n.) : event by which, or moment the risk becomes real and may give rise to an insurance claim; *fr. : survenance d'un sinistre*
- policyholder (n.) : person (other than the insurer) who is a party to an insurance contract and is entitled to enforce the insurer's obligations to provide benefits to the insured; the policyholder is the legal owner of the policy who may be different from the insured who receives payment or benefits; *fr. : souscripteur*
- proposal form : questionnaire which the proposed policyholder/insured must complete at the insurer's request to enable the latter to determine the nature of the risk to cover and the likelihood of its occurrence; *fr. : questionnaire (d'assurance)*
- renewal notice : document sent by the insurer to the policyholder some time before the anniversary date of the policy, reminding him of the renewal and the need to settle the premium; *fr. : notice de renouvellement*
- schedule (n.) : as opposed to the general conditions, specific terms of an insurance contract which apply to a particular policyholder; *fr. : conditions particulières*
- *uberrimae fidei* : duty of utmost good faith required when entering into a contract; *fr. : obligation d'extrême bonne foi*

USEFUL EXPRESSIONS

- to complete a form/to fill in a form; *fr. : remplir un formulaire*
- to construe an insurance policy; *fr. : interpréter une police d'assurance*
- to give someone notice of; *fr. : informer quelqu'un de*
- to seek renewal of; *fr. : solliciter le renouvellement de*
- to assess the risk; *fr. : évaluer le risque*
- provisions of an insurance contract; *fr. : dispositions d'une police d'assurance*

FURTHER INFORMATION

- the courts of England and Wales have given a slightly different interpretation from the French ones to the concept of *force majeure*; the need to consider case law should therefore be borne in mind when coming across that legal term

COMPARATIVE APPROACH

Comme en Angleterre et au Pays de Galles, le droit français des assurances fait une distinction entre les notions de souscripteur (*policyholder*) et d'assuré (*insured*). S'agissant du concept de franchise (*excess*), le droit français distingue entre la franchise relative ou simple et la franchise absolue. La première permet à l'assuré d'être intégralement indemnisé dès que le montant de la franchise est dépassé. Dans le second cas, l'indemnisation n'aura lieu que si le montant du sinistre est supérieur à la franchise, auquel cas l'assuré recevra la différence entre le montant du sinistre et celui de la franchise. Il n'y a pas de véritable équivalent de ces concepts en droit anglais et donc, aucune traduction littérale n'est possible.

□ 42 DIFFERENT TYPES OF INSURANCE

Various classifications are possible. A distinction is often made between life-related (or long-term) insurance and non-life (or general) insurance, the latter being split between property insurance and liability insurance. A life insurance policy is taken out by an individual or a corporation/company : in the latter case, this is a group insurance which provides cover to a specific community. Banks often take out group insurance to protect themselves against the risk of death of people to whom loans are granted. Health insurance is also a life-related insurance and is taken out by people who want to see their health expenses and treatment covered by the insurance company in case of illness, sick leave or disability following an accident. Another distinction can be made by taking into account the natural elements responsible or that cause the risk. This usually refers to the transport industry and includes aviation insurance, marine and non-marine insurance. The last distinction takes into account the risk borne by the insured : commercial or industrial risk, personal risk or agricultural risk insurance. On top of that, there are contingency risk or special risk insurance policies (such as credit insurance, legal expenses insurance) which cover the risks not otherwise included in a specific category.

GLOSSARY

- agricultural risk insurance : insurance which provides cover against the risks usually related to the profession; it includes crop insurance which protects field owners against the destruction of crops by hail, storms, etc.; *fr. : assurance des risques agricoles*
- aviation insurance : insurance which covers the liability incurred by aircraft manufacturers as well as the risks related to aircrafts and satellites; *fr. : assurance aérienne*

- commercial and industrial risk insurance : insurance geared towards the occurrence of damage during the exercise of a commercial or industrial activity; *fr. : assurance des risques industriels et commerciaux*
- contigency risk/special risk insurance : insurance covering a risk which does not fall within the scope of a general insurance; *fr. : assurance risques spéciaux*
- credit insurance : insurance which covers someone against the insolvency risk or a legal entity; *fr. : assurance crédit*
- group insurance : policy usually taken out by a corporation to give insurance coverage to a group of people (e.g. employees); *fr. : assurance groupe*
- health insurance : insurance covering medical treatment and costs in case of illness, sick leave or disability following an accident; *fr. : assurance maladie/ mutuelle*
- legal expenses insurance (LEI) : insurance which provides coverage against the potential costs of legal action against the insured; *fr. : assurance protection juridique*
- liability insurance : together with property insurance, one of the two types of non-life or general insurance; it provides cover against damage resulting from a legal entity's liability; *fr. : assurance de responsabilité*
- life-related (adj.) insurance/long-term (adj.) care insurance (n.) : insurance which includes life, life related or health insurance; grants coverage for damage sustained by people as opposed to property; *fr. : assurance de personnes*
- marine insurance : insurance coverage which applies to damage sustained by boats, ships, cargo, terminals and any maritime transport by which property is conveyed; *fr. : assurance maritime*
- non-life insurance/general insurance : insurance (such as car insurance) which provides cover for any type of damage which is non-life related; *fr. : assurance dommages*
- non-marine insurance : insurance geared towards anything non-marine such as personal accident, property, liability, business interruption or machinery breakdown insurance; *fr. : assurance terrestre*
- personal (lines) risk insurance : insurance coverage given to someone who sustains personal injury or death; *fr. : assurance de particuliers*
- property insurance : together with liability insurance, one of the two types of non-life or general insurance; *fr. : assurance de choses*

USEFUL EXPRESSIONS

- to insure someone against a risk; *fr. : assurer quelqu'un contre un risque*
- to be insured against a risk; *fr. : être assuré contre un risque*

FURTHER INFORMATION

- like the French concept of *assurance groupe*, that of group insurance is misleading as it implies that a policy is taken out by a group of people as policyholders; this is not the case; in fact, it is taken out by a legal entity (as policyholder), such as an employer, on the lives of a group of people (e.g. employees) who will be the insureds

COMPARATIVE APPROACH

Les principales catégories d'assurance qui existent en France sont similaires à celles qu'on trouve en Angleterre et au Pays de Galles. Ainsi, on retrouve notamment les assurances de personnes (*life related insurance*) et celles de dommages (*non-life insurance*). Parmi les assurances de personnes, l'assurance maladie ou complémentaire santé (communément appelée mutuelle) présente une originalité puisque contrairement au système anglais de la *National Health Service* (NHS) qui couvre l'intégralité des frais médicaux dispensés par les établissements et docteurs affiliés dans le pays, la sécurité sociale française ne rembourse qu'une partie des frais engagés.

Outre-Manche, une *mutual insurance company* est une société spécialisée dans l'activité d'assurance, dont le capital appartient intégralement aux souscripteurs (*policyholders*) de polices.

□ 43 SPECIFIC CASE : LIFE AND LIFE-RELATED INSURANCE

They depend on the duration of someone's life. Examples include convertible insurance, unit-linked insurance, term insurance, with or without profit insurance, universal life insurance or level premium insurance. A life-related insurance policy can be a joint one.

The main two categories are term insurance and whole-of-life policies.

With term insurance, the policyholder chooses the period of time for which he wants cover and the amount to be covered. The policy pays out to the designated beneficiaries if the policyholder dies within the term. If not, the policy does not pay out but the premiums paid are not returned. Two sorts of term insurance exist i.e. level-term and decreasing-term insurance.

If the policyholder dies within the specified term, the level-term insurance policy pays out a lump sum. The monthly or annual premiums paid, stay level as will the amount covered for throughout the term. It is a good way of protecting a family after death or to cover an interest-only mortgage which is not covered by an endowment policy. The amount covered for under a decreasing-term life insurance policy decreases over the term of the policy. It can be used for a debt that reduces as time goes on. Family income benefit life insurance is a type of decreasing term policy for which, in case of death, a regular income or annuity (as opposed to a lump sum) is paid out to beneficiaries until a previously agreed upon expiry date.

A whole-of-life insurance policy is an ongoing policy which pays out upon the policyholder's death.

GLOSSARY

- annuity (n.) : series of payments periodically received over a specified period of time; *fr. : rente*
- convertible (adj.) insurance (n.) : insurance terms which can be changed throughout the policy's life; *fr. : assurance convertible*
- decreasing-term life insurance policy : life policy providing a death benefit which decreases at a pre-set rate over the life of the policy; *fr. : assurance-vie décroissante*
- endowment policy : insurance policy by which a sum of money is either paid to the insured at maturity if he is still alive or to a designated person if the policyholder dies before a specific date; *fr. : assurance mixte*
- joint life insurance : insurance taken out on behalf of two people; it will be paid out on a first death or second death basis as stated in the policy; *fr. : assurance-vie sur deux têtes*
- level premium insurance : insurance for which the premium paid remains the same throughout the duration of the policy; *fr. : assurance-vie à prime nivelée*
- level-term insurance : insurance for which the premium paid by the policyholder only remains even for a set period of time but may change/increase after the expiry of that set period; *fr. : assurance-vie temporaire*
- lump (adj.) sum (n.) : as opposed to a payment by instalments or annuities, single amount of money paid out; *fr. : capital*
- term insurance : insurance which provides coverage at a fixed rate of payments for a limited term or period of time; *fr. : assurance temporaire*
- unit-linked (adj.) insurance (n.) : insurance which includes a death benefit and is directly linked to some investments made by the insurance company; *fr. : assurance à capital variable*
- universal life insurance : insurance in which the premium can be altered as the policyholder's circumstances change; *fr. : assurance-vie à garantie variable*
- with/without profit insurance policy : policy for which the policyholder either shares (with profit) or does not share (without profit) the benefits made by the insurance company when it invests the policyholder's insurance premiums; *fr. : police avec/sans participation aux bénéfices*
- whole-of-life insurance/whole life insurance : life insurance policy which remains in force during the period of the insured's whole life; *fr. : assurance vie entière*

USEFUL EXPRESSIONS

- to purchase a life insurance policy; *fr. : acheter une police d'assurance-vie*
- to take out a joint insurance policy with one's spouse; *fr. : souscrire une assurance-vie conjointement avec son époux*
- the surrender value of a life insurance policy; *fr. : la valeur de rachat d'une police d'assurance-vie*

FURTHER INFORMATION

- life insurance is often confused with life assurance; however, life assurance is often construed as being a more hybrid mixture of investment and insurance than life insurance

COMPARATIVE APPROACH

Plus que le régime des assurances-vie lui-même, il est intéressant de se pencher sur les divergences entre les régimes d'imposition appliquées aux assurances-vie en France et Outre-Manche. En Angleterre et au Pays de Galles, les intérêts annuels versés par des banques ou organismes assimilés sont soumis à un prélèvement à la source (*pay as you earn – PAYE*) au taux réduit (*reduced rate*). Cela concerne notamment les intérêts versés par les compagnies d'assurance au titre de contrats d'assurance-vie. Si le contribuable n'est pas assujetti à l'impôt sur le revenu, il peut demander le versement des intérêts bruts (*gross interest*). En France, l'assurance-vie est encore considérée, en 2013, comme faisant partie du patrimoine. De ce fait, le contrat entre dans l'assiette de calcul de l'Impôt de Solidarité sur la Fortune. Les intérêts sont soumis au paiement de prélèvements sociaux (*social contributions*) et s'agissant de l'imposition, les contribuables peuvent choisir le prélèvement forfaitaire libératoire prélevé directement par l'assureur au moment des retraits, ou d'intégrer leurs gains à leur impôt sur le revenu.

□ 44 SPECIFIC CASE : HOME INSURANCE

Home insurance, which is a form of personal lines insurance, may include buildings, contents or possession and home emergency insurance.

Buildings insurance

Home owners who have a mortgage are usually required to take out buildings insurance by the bank which gives them a loan. In other cases, buildings insurance is not compulsory. For those who own a flat in a block, buildings insurance is usually taken out by the freeholder, sometimes through a management company, but will be paid by the flat owner through the service charges.

Buildings insurance usually covers damage caused by fire, earthquakes, theft or attempted theft, floods, storms, subsidence, vandalism or falling trees. Insurance cover should include the cost of rebuilding the home if it is damaged, including any possible demolition costs as well as architects' and builders' fees. People who live in high risk flooding zones should ascertain that floods are covered by their policy. Likewise, those who made a claim for subsidence (as opposed to settlement) in the previous year may find it difficult to get insurance cover from a different insurer if they decide to switch companies.

With a sum-insured policy, the insurance premium will depend on the likely rebuilding cost of the home. With a bedroom-rated policy, the premium is calculated on the basis of the number of bedrooms in the house and the rebuilding costs are irrelevant.

Accidental damage cover is usually included in buildings insurance. It provides cover for damage accidentally caused to the building or fixtures and fittings (such as broken glass or damaged baths or sinks). Buildings insurance usually covers the property owner's legal liability for damage caused to someone else's property (including underground cables or pipes).

Home contents insurance

It usually covers damage to one's possessions due to fire, earthquakes, theft or attempted theft, vandalism, subsidence, flood, falling trees and similar natural calamities. Contents insurance also covers the cost of accommodation and storage if the occupier cannot live in his house because of damage like fire, contents of outbuildings, the cost of replacement keys and locks if they are lost, theft of cash from the house and the house occupier's legal liability if a visitor is injured in the house, as well as limited accidental damage cover (e.g. glass in furniture). The insured will either get new-for-old or an indemnity cover. New-for-old applies when the insurer pays the full cost of repairing the damaged items or the sum necessary to replace them with an equivalent item. For indemnity policies, a deduction for wear, tear and depreciation is made before payment to the insured is effected.

An extended cover can be granted in exchange of payment of an extra premium. All risks cover or personal possessions cover can be added to the contents policy to cover damage of possessions away from home, like a mobile phone or credit cards.

Legal expenses cover may be included in house contents insurance in exchange for an additional premium. It covers the cost of litigation either as a claimant or defendant as well as any award of the opponent's legal costs.

For all home contents insurance exclusions or an excess may apply.

Home emergency insurance

It normally covers events such as the urgent need to repair a burst pipe, boiler, electricity problem or blocked drains. Some insurers may include it in the home insurance cover or as an extended service for an additional premium.

GLOSSARY

- bedroom-rated home insurance : the insurance and the relevant premium are based on the number of bedrooms in a house regardless of their size; *fr. : ≈ assurance habitation en fonction du nombre de chambres*
- buildings insurance : insurance providing coverage for damage to the structure of a building or house; *fr. : assurance du bâtiment*
- contents insurance : insurance covering loss or damage to a person's personal possessions which are in his house; *fr. : assurance du contenu*
- excess (n.) : see 41
- fixtures and fittings : generally, a fixture is construed as meaning house items attached to the floor or walls (radiators, built-in cupboards, plugs, wallpaper, etc.) and a fitting refers to house items which are free standing or hung to the wall by a nail (carpets, curtains, lampshades, etc.); *fr. : installations et aménagements intérieurs*
- freehold (n.) : see 67
- home insurance : insurance which protects a house in case of theft, natural disaster or vandalism; *fr. : assurance habitation*
- new-for-old replacement value/replacement-as-new value : indemnity is paid to the insured which corresponds to the replacement value of items or property damaged or lost without any deduction for wear and tear; *fr. : valeur à neuf*
- personal lines insurance : insurance sold to individuals (rather than groups, companies or businesses which take out commercial lines insurance) which includes specialist insurances like car or home insurance; *fr. : assurance des particuliers*
- settlement (n.)/settle (v.) : disruption or distortion of a building through for example, the adjustement of a new building to the ground; *fr. : tassement*
- subsidence (n.)/subside (v.) : damage affecting the solidity or stability of a building or its services; this may occur when the ground is unable to support the weight of the building; *fr. : affaissement*
- sum-insured buildings insurance : insurance which provides cover for the cost of rebuilding a house irrespective of the extent of the damage sustained; therefore the sum insured may be above or below the current market value of the property; *fr. : ≈ assurance calculée sur la valeur de reconstruction*
- wear and tear : depreciation or damage which occurs through regular use or ageing; *fr. : vétusté*

USEFUL EXPRESSIONS

- the due date of annual premiums; *fr. : l'échéance de prime annuelle*
- an index-linked insurance policy; *fr. : une police d'assurance indexée*
- in the event of a claim; *fr. : en cas de sinistre*

- the cost of replacement-as-new less wear and tear; *fr. : le prix du neuf moins la vétusté*

FURTHER INFORMATION

- the settlement of a building (*tassement*) is different from the settlement of a sum of money (*règlement/paiement*) or the settlement of a litigation case (*règlement amiable d'un contentieux*)

COMPARATIVE APPROACH

En France, la notion de *bedroom-rated home insurance* n'existe pas. L'assurance habitation tient compte du nombre total de pièces habitables et pas seulement de chambres. Les propriétaires qui font construire ou font effectuer certains travaux de rénovation doivent souscrire une assurance dommage-ouvrage qui les garantit contre les dommages de nature décennale qui peuvent affecter la solidité de l'ouvrage ou le rendent impropre à sa destination. Cette police correspond à la *building defects insurance*, qui garantit les désordres affectant la structure (*structural damage*) de l'ouvrage.

□ 45 SPECIFIC CASE : CAR INSURANCE

Three types of cover are available. Third party car insurance covers against damage which the driver/policyholder and/or his passengers cause to another person or his property during the accident. Damage to the policyholder or his car is not covered. Third party, fire and theft car insurance goes further than ordinary third party cover. Should the car be damaged or destroyed by fire or stolen, the cost of repair or replacement of the vehicle is covered. Comprehensive car insurance goes further than third party, fire and theft by covering damage to the policyholder's car in case of accident. In emergency cases, the policyholder can drive cars other than his own with third-party cover. Named drivers (or additional drivers) can be added on to somebody else's policy and drive that person's car without taking out a separate insurance policy of their own.

Medical expenses are sometimes included in car insurance policies. Motor legal protection is also included in most policies and covers the cost of legal action resulting from a car insurance claim. A courtesy car will usually be made available by the insurer whilst the car is repaired by an approved repairer after sustaining an accident. Whilst calculating the premium, the insurer will take into account the no-claims bonus (NCB) of the proposed policyholder/insured. Any claim made to an insurer will invalidate the NCB built up unless special NCB protection was taken out. Most policies include an excess the extent of which is set out in the insurance contract. If a car is stolen or written off following an accident, the insured will usually be awarded the market value of the car by the insurer.

GLOSSARY

- approved (adj.) repairer (n.) : repair service or mechanic who is accredited by an insurance company; getting the repair work done by a non-approved person will normally result in the insurer's refusal to provide cover; *fr. : réparateur agréé*
- comprehensive car insurance : extension of third party, fire and theft car insurance which also covers the damage caused to the policyholder's car; *fr. : assurance tous risques*
- courtesy car : replacement car made available by an insurer to an insured (subject to the terms of the policy) whilst e.g. a car is being repaired after an accident; *fr. : voiture de courtoisie*
- market value : amount for which something can be sold at a particular time on a specific market; *fr. : valeur vénale*
- named (adj.) driver (n.) : person whose name is expressly mentioned in the schedule of a car insurance policy as being allowed to drive a particular car; *fr. : conducteur nommément désigné*
- no-claims bonus (NCB) : reduction on a car insurance premium if no claim is made within a specified period; *fr. : bonus-malus*
- third party car insurance : insurance providing cover against damage which the driver/policyholder and/or his passengers cause to another person or his property during the accident; *fr. : assurance au tiers*
- third party, fire and theft car insurance : insurance which covers damage to the policyholder's car in case of fire, theft or attempted fire and theft; it is thus an extension of third party car insurance; *fr. : assurance au tiers, vol et incendie*
- write (v.) off : here, fact for an insurance company to state that a car is no longer roadworthy after an accident and/or that the cost of repair would exceed its market value; *fr. : mettre en épave*

USEFUL EXPRESSIONS

- to fulfil an obligation to insure; *fr. : satisfaire à l'obligation d'assurance*
- to be disqualified from driving; *fr. : se voir retirer son permis de conduire*
- to insure a company car; *fr. : assurer une voiture de fonction*

FURTHER INFORMATION

- when a car is written off, it usually has to be scrapped i.e. sent to the scrapyard (*envoyée à la casse*)

COMPARATIVE APPROACH

L'assurance voiture est obligatoire en France et Outre-Manche. En France, on peut déterminer deux grands types d'assurance : d'une part, la police de base est l'assurance au tiers (*third party car insurance*) ou assurance responsabilité civile (*civil liability*), obligatoire depuis 1958. Elle couvre les dommages matériels et/ou corporels qu'un conducteur cause à un tiers, qu'il s'agisse de quelqu'un dans un autre véhicule, d'un piéton, cycliste ou même de l'un de ses passagers. Cependant, le conducteur n'est pas indemnisé du préjudice qu'il se cause à lui-même. D'autre part, l'autre grande catégorie d'assurance française est l'assurance tous risques (*fully comprehensive car insurance*). Outre les garanties dues aux tiers, elle couvre le préjudice subi (*damage sustained*) par le conducteur et son véhicule, lorsqu'il en est responsable ou lorsque le responsable n'est pas déterminé ou ne peut être identifié.

La France et le Royaume-Uni n'ont pas la même façon de calculer le bonus-malus. En France, pour atteindre le taux de bonus maximal (*maximum no-claims bonus rate*) qui est de 50 %, il faut treize ans sans avoir causé d'accident. Et en cas d'accident responsable, le conducteur ne perd pas totalement son bonus mais seulement un pourcentage de celui-ci. Outre-Manche, il faut conduire quatre ans sans être responsable d'un accident pour obtenir un taux de bonus entre 60 et 65 %. Ce taux n'augmente pas, même si l'attitude du conducteur est exemplaire pendant de nombreuses années supplémentaires. Mais la survenance d'un seul accident responsable suffit à anéantir le bonus. Il faudra alors être de nouveau assuré pendant quatre ans sans causer d'accident pour revenir au taux de bonus maximal.

□ 46 SPECIFIC CASE : HEALTH OR PRIVATE MEDICAL INSURANCE (PMI)

The National Health Service (NHS) was set up in 1948 following the publication of the Social Insurance and Allied Services report (or Beveridge report) in 1942 which provided that the population should be protected from the "cradle to the grave". The NHS is a universal free health service but people may take out PMI for example, to avoid long NHS waiting lists when they have to see a specialist or undergo surgery. Many employers provide health insurance to their employees but PMI may be taken out individually. PMI covers consultations, nursing and hospital care and surgery but not accidents or emergency treatments. Depending on the extent of the cover, the policyholder may be treated in an NHS or private hospital. Should a specialist's fees (which are usually higher than a general practitioner's or an ordinary physician's) exceed the agreed figure set out in the policy, the policyholder will pay for the shortfall. Like car insurance policies, most health insurance policies include a no-claims bonus if no claim is made for a certain time. The amount of the premiums increases over time as the risk of illness increases with age.

GLOSSARY

- consultation (n.) : here, meeting between an individual and a physician who advises him on his medical condition and if need be, on the medical treatment recommended; it may also be the review by a specialised physician or advice previously given by a general practitioner; *fr. : consultation (médicale)*
- emergency treatment : provision of healthcare services by a physician which requires acting urgently in view of the patient's condition; *fr. : traitement (médical) d'urgence*
- general (adj.) practitioner (n.) (GP) : physician providing medical care in relation to a large variety of medical problems; *fr. : médecin généraliste*
- health (n.) : state of not being ill or injured; *fr. : santé*
- no-claims bonus : see 45
- nursing (n.) : using one's clinical judgement to provide people with care when they have health problems; *fr. : ≈ soins infirmiers*
- physician (n.) : medical doctor who practises general medicine (general practitioner or GP) as opposed to being specialised in a particular field; *fr. : médecin généraliste*
- private medical insurance (PMI) : privately paid substitute for the National Health Service; PMI provides advantages to the subscriber (doctors, dentists or surgeons from the private sector, quicker access to surgeries) in exchange for payment of a premium; *fr. : assurance mutuelle de santé*
- shortfall (n.) : deficit, shortage of something; *fr. : manque/insuffisance*
- surgery (n.) : branch of medicine requiring an incision of the body to treat an illness or cure a medical condition; *fr. : chirurgie*
- waiting (adj.) list (n.) : number of people queuing or waiting for something; *fr. : liste d'attente*

USEFUL EXPRESSIONS

- the carrier of a disease; *fr. : le porteur d'une maladie*
- a deferred/waiting period can apply to health insurance; *fr. : un délai de carence peut s'appliquer à l'assurance maladie*
- to join the queue in the NHS; *fr. : faire la queue à la NHS*
- to undergo surgery; *fr. : subir une opération*

FURTHER INFORMATION

- the noun physician (*médecin généraliste*) should not be confused with physicist (*physicien*)
- in 1983, "dread disease" or critical illness insurance was created; people can take out insurance against the risk of contracting cancer for instance
- Bupa is a British healthcare organisation which provides private health insurance (and related); Bupa runs private hospitals, has accredited doctors and provides nursing and residential care for elderly people

COMPARATIVE APPROACH

En France, la Couverture Maladie Universelle (CMU) permet à tous d'accéder aux services de la sécurité sociale et de voir couvrir ou rembourser un pourcentage de ses dépenses de santé (*medical expenses*) (consultations médicales, médicaments, opérations...). Si la sécurité sociale s'apparente plus ou moins à la *National Health Service*, le système français s'en distingue en ce qu'il assure une couverture moindre. En effet, l'État français, financé par les contributions faites par les travailleurs et les employeurs, ne prend en charge qu'une partie des frais médicaux, par le biais de la Caisse Primaire d'Assurance Maladie (CPAM). Le solde est en partie financé par la mutuelle qu'une très grande majorité de français souscrit auprès de sociétés privées, en échange d'un tarif. Les mutuelles sont une spécificité du système français.

□ 47 SPECIFIC CASE : INDUSTRIAL RISKS INSURANCE

Any commercial or industrial operation (including manufacturing, heavy industrial, utilities or services) must be covered by Industrial Risks Insurance. It covers physical injury and damage to all real and personal properties. More specifically, business interruption insurance covers the loss of profit due to damage to the property insured, employers and public/products liability, burglary, glass breakage, loss of money and accidental damage. It reflects the exposure faced by the industrial or commercial business. It defines the maximum indemnity period insured (starting when the damage occurred and ending when the business results are no longer affected by the damage), the turnover, the gross profit and the ratio turnover/gross profit.

GLOSSARY

- burglary (n.) : see 29
- business interruption insurance : insurance which covers a business loss of profit when an industrial risk occurs; *fr. : assurance perte d'exploitation*

- employers' liability : liability incurred by employers for damages caused to employees in the course of employment; *fr. : responsabilité des employeurs*
- gross (adj.) profit (n.) : here, insured part of the turnover after deducting the charges which vary depending on that turnover; *fr. : bénéfice brut*
- indemnity period : period of time covered by the insurance policy; *fr. : période d'indemnisation*
- industrial (adj.) risks (n.) : risks or dangers potentially faced by any commercial or industrial venture; *fr. : risques industriels*
- public (adj.) liability (n.) : responsibility of a commercial or industrial business which arises from the physical and/or property damage sustained by a third-party such as a subcontractor, a visitor, a member of the public or even a trespasser; *fr. : ≈ responsabilité civile*
- products liability : responsibility of people like manufacturers, suppliers, distributors or retailers which results from claims arising out of the use, handling or consumption of a product; *fr. : responsabilité des produits*
- ratio (n.) : relative proportion of two things; *fr. : rapport*
- real (adj.) property (n.) : real estate or immovables which include land and buildings; *fr. : immobilier*
- turnover (n.) : gross income of the business; *fr. : chiffre d'affaires*
- utilities (n.) : gas, water, electricity, telephone or sewage as well as other services of public interest; *fr. : services d'intérêt général*

USEFUL EXPRESSIONS

- insurance indemnity period; *fr. : période d'indemnisation de l'assurance*
- ratio of gross profit to turnover; *fr. : rapport bénéfice brut/chiffre d'affaires*
- business interruption insurance covers some standing charges; *fr. : l'assurance perte d'exploitation garantit certains frais généraux permanents*

FURTHER INFORMATION

- the opposite of gross profit (*bénéfice brut*) is nett profit (*bénéfice net*)
- turnover (*chiffres d'affaires*) must not be confused with turnout (*participation*), to a vote for example

COMPARATIVE APPROACH

En France, la responsabilité des employeurs (*employers' liability*) pour les dommages subis par leurs employés dans le cadre de leur travail n'est pas un risque assurable en tant que tel. En effet, l'indemnisation des salariés est assurée par le biais de la sécurité sociale financée par les contributions mensuelles. Cependant, dans certains cas, les salariés concernés peuvent, si nécessaire, engager un recours contre leur employeur pour obtenir réparation du préjudice subi (*compensation for the damage sustained*) pour faute inexcusable (*inexcusable breach of duty*).

□ 48 SPECIFIC CASE : CONTRACTORS' ALL RISKS INSURANCE AND MACHINERY BREAKDOWN INSURANCE

Building works take time. The building contractor or principal usually takes out a contractors' all risks policy to cover damage to the works whilst they are done. On-site equipment and stock may also be covered for an additional premium. This policy covers the liability of all those involved on-site which usually includes the principal, architect, contractors and sub-contractors. Coverage applies until the works are completed and accepted. The contractors may then wish to take out a cover extension for the maintenance period. Machinery breakdown insurance purports to indemnify the insured for damage sustained by machinery described in the insurance policy. For instance, the damage may occur through the defect affecting the machinery or the user's negligence.

GLOSSARY

- acceptance of (construction) works : formal procedure by which the owner of the property or his agent accept the works as completed; *fr. : réception des travaux*
- contractors' all risks insurance : insurance which covers accidental damage or damage caused during the building works to machinery (and potentially on-site stock and equipment) by fire or other perils; the works covered are those carried out by any of the parties involved on-site i.e. architects, contractors or sub-contractors; *fr. : assurance tous risques chantiers*
- machinery breakdown insurance : insurance which covers damage caused to machinery or equipment described in the relevant policy; *fr. : assurance bris de machine*
- maintenance period : period following completion of a building project during which the contractor remains liable for maintenance issues; *fr. : période d'entretien*
- negligence (n.) : see 86
- principal (n.) : person who supervises all those (architects, contractors or sub-contractors) involved in building works or person who orders the works; *fr. : maître d'œuvre* (if supervisor of the works)/*maître d'ouvrage* (if person who ordered the works)

- sub-contractor (n.) : person with whom a contractor enters into an agreement with a view to carrying out specified works on behalf of a principal; *fr. : sous-contractant*

FURTHER INFORMATION

- principal (*maître d'œuvre/d'ouvrage* depending on the context) should not be confused with principle (*principe*)

COMPARATIVE APPROACH

En France, l'assurance tous risques chantiers (*contractors' all risks insurance*) est souvent souscrite par le maître d'ouvrage ou le maître d'œuvre pour ce qui des dommages en cours de chantier. S'agissant des dommages de nature décennale survenus après réception des travaux, il est conseillé au propriétaire de souscrire une assurance dommage-ouvrage. Ce type de police permet au propriétaire de se voir rapidement indemnisé de tout dommage affectant la solidité de l'ouvrage ou le rendant impropre à sa destination (C. civ., art. 1792), sans préjudice de la recherche des responsabilités parmi les intervenants aux travaux. En Angleterre et au Pays de Galles, elle correspond à la *building defects insurance*. Elle est en général souscrite pour dix ans.

8

Environmental law

□ 49 INTRODUCTION

Definition and scope

Environmental law can be defined as the legal standards set by governments to preserve environmental quality and natural resources. It covers a wide range of environmental issues like atmospheric pollution, habitat protection, hazardous waste management, land management, marine pollution controls, noise control, water regulation, wildlife conservation and planning for sustainable development.

As a member of the Organisation for Economic Co-operation and Development (OECD), the UK follows the OECD's green growth strategy to encourage sustainable economic development. Promoted by the Sustainable Development Commission (SDC) in 2010, the commission aims at reconciling the increasing demands of economic and social development to protect scarce environmental resources, by finding ways and means of meeting the needs of the present generation without depleting the earth's finite natural resources needed for the use of future generations. The UK has also charted a course of action to encourage green growth and a green economy.

International and national environmental law

International environmental law includes agreements amongst different nations such as treaties (thus falling within the scope of public international law) or between citizens or corporations of different nations (in which case this is a matter of private international law).

National environmental law refers to "soft law" adopted in England and Wales which is not binding in itself as well as "hard law" or international principles which are binding on the area concerned and may also govern the area's relations with other regions of the UK or the EU or other continents.

As the standards set forth in these laws aim at protecting the environment, environmental law inevitably involves regulating or interfering with the rights of ordinary citizens so that society as a whole may benefit from its protection. UK legislation must of course abide by the Community environmental legislation adopted by the EU.

GLOSSARY

- agreement (n.) : here, act of creating a pact between two parties or countries; *fr. : accord*
- atmospheric (adj.) pollution (n.) : pollution of the air caused by a release of gases, chemicals and particles that can cause harm to humans, animals and vegetation; *fr. : pollution atmosphérique*
- Community environmental legislation : environmental measures taken by the European Commission aimed at improving the quality of life and the environment for the European community at large (legislation includes the enactment of directives and regulations to ensure the enforcement action); *fr. : droit communautaire de l'environnement*
- binding (adj.) : legally enforceable by law; *fr. : juridiquement contraignant/qui lie*
- environmental (adj.) issues (n.) : aspects of human activity that may adversely affect biodiversity, ozone depletion, climate change, global warming and the management of resources; *fr. : questions environnementales*
- environmental (adj.) quality (n.) : standard set to ensure the protection of natural resources to enable human beings to enjoy a good quality of life; *fr. : qualité environnementale*
- green (adj.) growth (n.) : strategy elaborated by the OECD to encourage governmental policies that protect ecosystems, and foster economic and social development, while ensuring at the same time that the natural resources are consumed sensibly without being depleted completely; *fr. : croissance verte*
- habitat protection : act of safeguarding the natural environment of wildlife species as it is critical for their survival; *fr. : protection de l'habitat*
- hard (adj.) law (n.) : domestic statutes or international treaties that are legally binding; *fr. : normes juridiques contraignantes*
- hazardous waste management : process of monitoring the disposal of dangerous waste materials and offering recycling solutions that can create renewable sources of energy; *fr. : gestion des déchets dangereux*
- international environmental law : legally binding environmental treaties signed between different nations to tackle a wide range of environmental issues; *fr. : droit international de l'environnement*
- international (adj.) principle (n.) : guideline contained in an international document like the Universal Declaration of Human Rights or the 1992 Rio Declaration on Environment or Development which serves as a standard for protecting a cause; *fr. : principe international*
- land management : process of regulating the use of land and its resources in rural and urban areas and ensuring that steps are taken to prevent degradation and harm to the environment; *fr. : gestion de l'espace*
- legality (n.) : state of conforming to legal principles; *fr. : légalité/caractère légal*

- marine pollution control : measure taken to prevent pollution to the oceans and protect marine life from litter, illegal dumping, oil spills and sewage; *fr. : contrôle de la pollution marine*
- natural (adj.) resource (n.) : substance or material that is found in a natural form like sunlight, air, water or land; *fr. : ressource naturelle*
- noise control : strategy to reduce the impact of domestic, industrial, indoor or outdoor noise; *fr. : lutte contre le bruit*
- private international law : law governing agreements, rules and regulations made between private citizens or parties of different countries; *fr. : droit international privé*
- public international law : law governing legal relations between states and nations resulting in the signing of national treaties and agreements; *fr. : droit international public*
- soft (adj.) law (n.) : newly established rules and laws that are flexible, easy to change and are not binding at both domestic and international levels; *fr. : normes juridiques non-contraignantes*
- sustainable (adj.) development (n.) : economic progress achieved through the proper use of natural resources without compromising the capacity of future generations to fulfil their needs; *fr. : développement durable*
- treaty (n.) : agreements between nations or with international organisations that are binding on the signatories; *fr. : traité*
- water regulation : method of controlling the consumption of water, finding and applying ways of recycling this scarce commodity; *fr. : réglementation des eaux*
- wildlife conservation : strategy adopted to protect endangered wildlife species and their habitat by making individuals and corporations aware of the need to conserve ecosystems; *fr. : conservation de la faune*

USEFUL EXPRESSIONS

- to abide by the terms of an agreement; *fr. : se conformer aux termes d'un accord*
- to conserve resources; *fr. : conserver les ressources*
- the conservation of nature; *fr. : la conservation de la nature*
- to enter into an international agreement; *fr. : signer une convention internationale*
- to interfere with someone's rights; *fr. : porter atteinte aux droits de quelqu'un*
- an interference with the exploitation of natural resources; *fr. : une entrave à l'exploitation des ressources naturelles*
- to preserve the quality of life; *fr. : préserver la qualité de vie*
- the preservation of endangered species; *fr. : la protection des races menacées*
- to regulate European energy policy; *fr. : réglementer la politique énergétique européenne*

- the regulation of environmental pollution; *fr. : réglementation de la pollution environnementale*
- a regulating authority; *fr. : une autorité compétente*

FURTHER INFORMATION

- the word issue (*problème/question*) refers to a topic of discussion or matter of interest; it must not be translated by the French adjective *issu* which is the fact of stemming from or descending from, nor should it be confused with the French noun *issue* which is an exit or the outcome of something
- the word standard (*norme*) refers to a requirement or level required and must not be translated by the French word *standard* that may also refer to a switchboard
- the adjective sustainable (*durable*) refers to the idea of being sustained, and must not be translated by the French word *soutenable* which is the act of defending one's opinions or ideas

COMPARATIVE APPROACH

Le concept de développement durable (*sustainable development*) a été mentionné pour la première fois dans le rapport Bruntland de 1987 publié par la Commission mondiale sur l'environnement et le développement de l'Organisation des Nations unies (*United Nations World Commission on Environment and Development* [WCED]). Au niveau international, la France et le Royaume-Uni, qui sont membres du G8, se sont engagés à suivre une politique de transparence en mettant en exergue l'importance de la croissance verte (*green growth*) et du développement durable de la planète dans le cadre de la croissance économique.

L'Agence européenne pour l'environnement (*European Environment Agency* [EEA]) est une agence de l'Union européenne créée en 1993, regroupant 32 pays membres (dont la France et le Royaume-Uni) dont le rôle est de fournir aux peuples et à leurs gouvernements des informations indépendantes sur l'environnement et de veiller à la mise en œuvre d'une politique environnementale commune (*common environmental policy*).

□ 50 ENVIRONMENTAL LAW SOURCES

Environmental governance is influenced by the interaction between the sources of environmental law : hard and soft environmental law. As opposed to soft law, hard law has a binding effect.

Hard environmental law

Hard Law in environmental governance refers to international agreements, principles and rules that are binding on states in their relations with other states. In England and Wales, hard law environmental treaties conform to international legal rules laid out by the United Nations Environment Programme (UNEP). Hard environmental law consists of instruments such as international treaties, protocols or agreements agreed upon amongst nations. Judicial decisions of international significance enumerated under Article 38 (1) of the 1946 Statute of the International Court of Justice (ICJ) also have a binding effect. The ICJ Statute describes the law to be applied by the ICJ when deciding cases within its jurisdiction and is the most authoritative enumeration of the sources of international environmental law.

Hard environmental law involves three characteristics : high degree of legal obligation, precise wording and delegation of interpretation or enforcement to an international court or tribunal. It binds England and Wales to international agreements and commitments. The country is required to create enforcement mechanisms like committees and dispute-settlement bodies to legally enact the commitments made in environmental treaties.

Soft environmental law

Soft environmental law includes the principles set by the governments of England and Wales to respect certain norms and incorporate them into national environmental policy. This body of law is not enforceable in itself (it has no binding effect) but its rules offer a flexible set of guidelines that help in the shaping of environmental policy.

Soft environmental law contains three legal dimensions : no legal obligation, abstract wording and it leaves room for political manoeuvring by providing greater flexibility for decision-making. It is a useful tool for non-state actors like state administrative agencies, non-governmental organisations (NGOs) or international environmental organisations.

GLOSSARY

- abstract (adj.) wording (n.) : statement made in a general context without any concrete references to laws or regulations; *fr. : formulation abstraite*
- accords (n.) : agreement or consent made by two parties or countries regarding an issue of important mutual concern; *fr. : accords*
- agreement (n.) : see 49
- binding (adj.) : see 49
- commitment (n.) : act of making a promise or a pledge to do something; *fr. : engagement*
- conform (v. or adj.) : here, adhering to generally accepted norms of behaviour; *fr. : se conformer à/être conforme à*
- decision-making : act of deciding on the right course of action; *fr. : prise de décisions*
- delegation of interpretation : process of empowering an authority to interpret and implement legislation; *fr. : ≈ délégation du pouvoir d'interprétation*

- dispute-settlement : process of solving a dispute by some form of Alternative Dispute Resolution (ADR); *fr. : règlement des différends*
- enforceable (adj.) : relating to the capacity of being obeyed, enforced or observed; *fr. : exécutoire*
- enforcement mechanism : here, measure taken to protect the environment by setting up legal instruments and agreements between countries or regions; *fr. : mécanisme d'exécution/coercitif/de mise en œuvre*
- environmental (adj.) governance (n.) : process of making environmental decisions that involve the government, citizens, businesses and non-government organisations; *fr. : gouvernance environnementale*
- guideline (n.) : principle used to set a standard for a course of action; *fr. : ligne directrice*
- international (adj.) court (n.) : court like e.g. the International Court of Justice (ICJ) in the Hague, formed by nations through treaties or agreements that comes under the authority of an international organisation like the United Nations; *fr. : Tribunal international/Cour internationale*
- legal (adj.) obligation (n.) : duty or responsibility to carry out the terms of a rule, regulation or contract; *fr. : obligation légale*
- legal (adj.) sanction (n.) : legally approved penalty to enforce law and punish an offender; *fr. : ≈ sanction (administrative ou judiciaire)*
- non-binding (adj.) : not comprising the power to obligate or bind a person to an agreement or treaty; *fr. : juridiquement non-contraignant/n'ayant pas un effet liant*
- non-governmental (adj.) organisation (n.) : non-profit group at local, national or international level, composed of individuals who strive towards a common goal of protecting the interests of a particular group, cause or society like developing projects to protect the global environment, protecting flora and fauna, preserving national parks, conserving water resources, etc.; *fr. : organisation non-gouvernementale*
- pact (n.) : agreement or treaty signed between nations for purposes of mutual benefit; *fr. : pacte*
- policy (n.) : plan of action conceived by a government, a party or an organisation to execute a programme, procedure or protocol aimed at achieving an intended result; *fr. : politique (gouvernementale ou d'une organisation, etc.)*
- precise (adj.) wording (n.) : use of specific or precise terms to draft a document, statute or regulation; *fr. : précision du langage*
- protocol (n.) : sub-agreement of a treaty that gives legal force to matters agreed upon between nations; *fr. : protocole*
- treaty (n.) : see 49

USEFUL EXPRESSIONS

- to grant rights and protections; *fr. : accorder des droits et assurer des protections*

- in accordance with the law; *fr. : conformément à la loi*
- to act accordingly; *fr. : agir en conséquence*
- to conform to international norms; *fr. : être conforme aux normes internationales*
- an agreement under negotiation; *fr. : un accord en cours de négociation*
- to have green fingers; *fr. : avoir la main verte*
- to renege on a committment; *fr. : revenir sur un engagement*

IMPORTANT INFORMATION

- the word legal instrument (*outil juridique*) refers to a formal legal document, and must not be translated by the French word *instrument* which refers specifically to musical, measurement instruments or tools
- the word policy (*politique*) must not be confused with the French word *police* referring to the law enforcement police force
- the word statute (*loi*) must not be confused with the French word *statut* that refers to a person's position or standing in society

COMPARATIVE APPROACH

En France, le droit de l'environnement est une matière jeune puisque le Code de l'environnement a été publié pour la première fois en 2000. Sa partie législative regroupe en grande partie des lois précédemment dispersées. En 2005, une Charte de l'environnement a été intégrée dans le bloc de constitutionnalité, consacrant ainsi la valeur juridique supérieure de ce domaine du droit.

Outre-Manche, l'absence de codification rend l'identification des textes, et l'appréciation de leur valeur juridique, plus complexe. Un texte important est le *Environmental Protection Act*, une loi promulguée en 1990 et qui définit l'environnement comme étant tout ce qui touche à l'air, l'eau ou la terre.

☐ 51 ENVIRONMENTAL FRAMEWORK, STANDARDS AND PRINCIPLES

National framework

The UK Environmental Observation Framework (UKEOF) launched in 2008, is a partnership of public sector organisations that work in collaboration with government devolved administrations, environment observation agencies and voluntary groups. The aim of the UKEOF is to make the best use of the country's environmental observations and data at both national and international levels.

At the national level, observations are made by the member organisations of the UKEOF at environmental domain-based workshops. These observations are drafted in a statement of need. A statement of need contains a report of the statutory and organisational requirements needed to tackle the challenges related to the changing natural environment. England and Wales have a decision support framework that prioritises areas for environmental observations based on sound evidence of a need to protect the environment. Discussion-governance forums enable the organisation to decide on the right implementation methods.

In England and Wales, the Environment Protection Act (EPA) of 1990 and the amended EPA of 1995 provide the fundamental structure to protect natural resources and regulate pollution control. The HRA of 1998 which incorporated the ECHR into UK law offers further statutory protection of public rights and judicial review provides further protection by making it possible to question the legality of public environmental decision-making.

International framework

The UK participates in the global endeavour to ensure that environmental information is successfully exchanged in three stages.

The first step requires an "information exchange obligation" as specified in Principle 9 of the Rio Declaration of 1992 regarding scientific cooperation and policy coordination. The document signed at the United Nations Conference on Environment and Development at Rio de Janeiro (3-14 June 1992) detailed the 27 principles that nations must follow to protect global environment and developmental systems.

The second phase necessitates "reporting and providing information" of trans-boundary harm as mentioned in the Kyoto Protocol of 1997. The final stage is set for "eco-auditing and environmental auditing" to enable the UK to gauge its environmental footprint and establish the environmental cost. While the Kyoto protocol was valid only until 2012, the Doha Amendment to the Kyoto Protocol (2012) includes new commitments and extends the commitment period of the protocol to December 2020.

Environmental norms

Environmental standards in England and Wales fall under the following categories : emission standards in air water and soil, quality standards concerning noise levels for aeroplanes, air quality standards for sulphur dioxide levels and water quality standards, process standards for regulating hazardous activity and preventing accidents, product standards in relation to pharmaceuticals, food packaging and labelling, and environmental management standards like the ISO 9000 and the ISO 14021 for providing certification.

Proactive environmental principles

Proactive environmental law in the UK necessitates the application of the principles of the "polluter pays" principle, the public participation principle and the precautionary principle to mitigate harm and protect scarce resources.

The principle of "polluter pays" or Extended Producer Responsibility (EPR) defined by the OECD stresses the fact that the polluter should pay for any costs that arise from harm caused to the environment, or damage to individuals caused by pollution as in the case of landfill taxes (2012) where polluters have to pay for the costs of waste disposal.

The public participation principle introduced by the United Nations Conference on Environment and Development in 1992 at the Rio conference is a concept that encourages democratic participation of the public in governmental decision making. The UK follows this principle of encouraging citizens to engage in environmental policy making. Thus it opens access to environmental information for all.

The precautionary principle developed by the Commission of the European Communities asserts that failure to take preventative action cannot be justified by the absence of scientific proof regarding a risk of environmental harm. This is the case of genetically modified organisms (GMOs) where the UK adopts a precautionary approach to genetically modified (GM) crops in the light of the lack of scientific evidence and uncertainty of the effects.

GLOSSARY

- air quality standard : requirement regarding the concentration of pollutants in the atmosphere based on an evaluation of the effects of each pollutant on human health, flora and fauna; *fr. : norme de qualité de l'air*
- devolved (adj.) administration (n.) : transfer of administrative powers to assemblies and governments of the regions of Northern Ireland, Scotland and Wales; *fr. : ≈ autorité déconcentrée*
- discussion-governance forum : public meeting place for open discussions on environmental issues and the framing of rules and regulations for implementing decisions; *fr. : forum de débats consacrés à la gouvernance*
- eco-auditing : tool for evaluating environmental performance with the goal of safeguarding the environment by assessing environmental practices and by considering how environmental regulatory requirements are met; *fr. : système d'audit environnemental*
- emission standard : requirement that sets the limits for the levels of discharges of organic and inorganic matter into air, water and soil with the intention of protecting the environment; *fr. : normes d'émission*
- environmental (adj.) auditing (n.) : financial tool used by business organisations to assess the environmental impact of their operations, thus enabling them to decrease waste, recycle and predict the impact of a project on the environment; *fr. : audit environnemental*

- environmental domain-based workshop : gathering of experts from environmental organisations in the UK to address the challenges of protecting the changing natural environment; *fr. : atelier environnemental*
- environmental (adj.) footprint (n.) : tool for measuring human dependence on the ecosystem by calculating human demand on scarce depleting resources; *fr. : empreinte environnementale*
- environmental (adj.) management standard (n.) : requirement for companies to obtain an accreditation or certification like an ISO certification to ensure that they comply with certain standards regarding environmental issues; *fr. : norme de gestion de l'environnement*
- environmental (adj.) standard (n.) : norm established by the European Environmental Agency regarding emission controls and imposing regulatory measures like quality, process and product standards; *fr. : normes environnementales*
- food packaging : industry involved in packing and preserving food according to the required climatic conditions and requirements in the food distribution chain; *fr. : emballage alimentaire*
- global (adj.) endeavour (n.) : international effort to accomplish a common purpose; *fr. : effort mondial*
- hazardous (adj.) : dangerous, risky or perilous; *fr. : dangereux*
- implementation method : manner of executing a policy or plan of action; *fr. : méthode de mise en œuvre*
- international (adj.) framework (n.) : global approach that favours a joint-effort of cooperation between nations to solve problems or implement international agreements; *fr. : cadre international*
- ISO : environmental management standard developed by the International Standard Organisation which serves as a tool to guarantee the quality of products or services; *fr. : norme ISO*
- judicial (adj.) review (n.) : see 76
- Kyoto Protocol : international treaty that commits its signing nations to reduce emission levels that was adopted in Kyoto on 11th December 1997; *fr. : protocole de Kyoto*
- labelling (n.) : act of identifying or designating a product or a service; *fr. : étiquetage*
- launch (v. or n.) : begin (a project); *fr. : lancer/lancement (projet)*
- noise level : measurement of sound as units or decibels; *fr. : niveau sonore*
- partnership (n.) : here, arrangement or contract between two or more persons, organisations or nations with the intention of sharing responsibility and achieving a common goal; *fr. : partenariat*
- policy coordination : strategic measure taken by an authority to execute the terms of a treaty or implement a project; *fr. : coordination des politiques*
- "polluter pays" principle : concept according to which the polluter is liable to pay for any cost incurred for rectifying damage caused to the environment; *fr. : principe du pollueur-payeur*

- precautionary (adj.) measure (n.) : steps taken in advance to avert possible danger or harm; *fr. : mesure préventive*
- public participation principle : principle that recognises the right of the public to engage in the decision making process and is considered as a vital part of democratic governance; *fr. : principe de la participation du public*
- proactive (adj.) regulation (n.) : precautions taken by an authority like foreseeing the occurrence of harm and taking measures to avert the problem; *fr. : réglementation proactive*
- prioritise (v.)/priority (n.) : fact of ranking or rating an area or domain as a top priority; *fr. : accorder la priorité/priorité*
- process standard : requirement regarding manufacturing, installations or process-related activity to regulate the right means of production and prevent accidents; *fr. : normalisation des processus*
- product standard : requirement regarding scientific or product-related information of chemicals on food packaging and labelling to ensure safe usage and to warn users of its likely hazards and drawbacks; *fr. : norme applicable aux produits*
- public (adj.) funding (n.) : expenditure for public projects that is financed at the expense of the taxpayer; *fr. : financement public*
- quality (adj.) standard (n.) : here, requirement that sets the permissible level of pollution with reference to noise controls, levels of sulphur dioxide in air, and water quality; *fr. : norme de qualité*
- Rio Declaration : document signed at the United Nations Conference on Environment and Development at Rio de Janeiro in 1992; *fr. : déclaration de Rio*
- sound (adj.) : when applied to evidence, convincing proof or indication; *fr. : (preuve) solide*
- sustainable (adj.) development (n.) : see 49
- statement of need : document containing the observations made by experts in domain-based workshops regarding environmental issues that affect the UK; *fr. : énoncé des besoins*
- tackle (v.) : face or confront; *fr. : affronter/faire face à*
- trans-boundary harm : damage that can span, traverse and affect countries connected by rivers or by other natural borderlines; *fr. : dommages transfrontaliers*
- voluntary (adj.) group (n.) : association that works to support a cause; *fr. : groupe bénévole*

USEFUL EXPRESSIONS

- to gauge the extent of the problem; *fr. : mesurer l'étendue du problème*
- to standardise the legal framework; *fr. : harmoniser le cadre juridique*
- to meet environmental standards; *fr. : respecter les normes environnementales*
- to necessitate a careful study; *fr. : exiger une étude approfondie*

- to partner in research projects; *fr. : s'associer aux projets de recherches*
- to prioritise environmental protection; *fr. : accorder la priorité à la protection de l'environnement*
- to tackle environmental challenges; *fr. : relever des défis environnementaux*

FURTHER INFORMATION

- the word emission (*émission*) refers to the emitting of smoke or gas
- the verb gauge (*évaluer*) refers to the act of determining, estimating or measuring, and must not be confused with the French word *gage* which has the meanings of forfeiting something

COMPARATIVE APPROACH

En 2010, la Commission européenne a choisi d'utiliser le concept de l'empreinte écologique comme un des indicateurs du développement durable. Suite à cette décision, Outre-Manche, le *Department for Environment, Food and Rural Affairs* (DEFRA) (ministère de l'environnement) a entrepris d'évaluer son empreinte. L'Angleterre, le Pays de Galles, l'Écosse et l'Irlande du Nord ont désormais pour objectif la création d'une « *one planet economy* » afin de stabiliser l'empreinte écologique. Quant à la France, c'est le Service de l'observation et des statistiques (SOeS) au sein du ministère de l'écologie et du développement durable et de l'énergie qui a pour mission de recueillir les statistiques en matière d'énergie, d'environnement et de développement durable. Il diffuse ensuite les données relatives à l'empreinte carbone de la France et définit aussi les indicateurs du développement durable permettant d'élaborer une stratégie à long terme.

□ 52 SUSTAINABLE DEVELOPMENT AND GREEN GROWTH

UK's Sustainable Development policy is based on the Brundtland Commission Report of 1987. Named after Norway's former Prime Minister Gro Harlem Brundtland, the commission's report (1983-87) entitled "Our Common Future" identified the environmental, economic and social aspects that affect sustainability on the planet.

The Environmental Agency (EA), a non-departmental public body, established by the 1995 Environment Act is the environmental protection regulator in England and Wales responsible for protecting the environment through the integrated management of air, land and water. It has specific responsibilities in the domains of conservation, fisheries, flood defence, pollution prevention and control, recreation and navigation, and water resources.

In 2000, the Sustainable Development Commission (SDC) was set up in the UK to help decision makers and advisors adopt sustainable development as the operating system of choice in the four governments of the UK. The SDC encourages action at grassroots and individual level and welcomes their advice and recommendations to achieve sustainable development.

At the Big Sustainability Summit of 2011, plans were unveiled to create a new, citizen-led network and establish a world-class sustainability knowledge hub amongst leading universities. In this conference held on 1st March 2011, representatives from environmental groups and organisations in the UK met to plan sustainable development, provide advice, create lobbies, and scrutinise government initiative in this area.

Sustainable Development promotes the idea that social, environmental and economic development are all achievable and attainable within the limits of our earth's natural resources, but at the same time it highlights the importance of protecting the natural resource base and the environment. Simultaneously, through the adoption of the concept of green growth, the UK aims at managing natural resources and assets wisely, so that development today does not compromise economic growth in the future.

Sustainable Development strategies include the definition of environmental objectives and targets, the publication of a set of indicators in areas such as air quality, water quality, land, wildlife and habitats to ensure their protection in spite of social and economic change, environmental education, the creation of schemes to improve relationships between industry and government, the need for environmental regulation and the use of fiscal instruments including taxation of pollution, the agenda and priorities for sustainable development, and the need to respect environmental rights. Sustainable development funding in the country is derived from three main sources : charging schemes, flood defence levies and government grants.

GLOSSARY

- achievable (adj.) : relating to the possibility of obtaining or making something happen; *fr. : réalisable*
- attainable (adj.) : relating to something that can be accomplished; *fr. : accessible*
- charging (adj.) scheme (n.) : system of charging users for environmental licences in order to recover implementation costs; *fr. : système de tarification*
- citizen-led network : interconnected group with a common purpose that is organised and led by citizens; *fr. : réseau organisé par les citoyens*
- conservation (n.) : act of protecting the environment or natural resources from degradation; *fr. : conservation*
- economic (adj.) development (n.) : progress obtained in the standard of living due to planned and sustained actions of policy and decision makers in government; *fr. : développement économique*

- environmental (adj.) development (n.) : action taken to protect natural resources and improve the quality of life through sustained efforts to protect the environment; *fr. : dévelopment environnemental*
- environmental (adj.) education (n.) : study of the relationship between natural and human systems that enables a deeper understanding of environmental issues and considers ways and means of solving problems; *fr. : éducation en matière d'environnement*
- environmental (adj.) regulation (n.) : laws pertaining to the regulation of air, water, land and other environmental matters; *fr. : réglementation en matière environnementale*
- fisheries (n.) : industry that is involved in the catching, processing and selling of fish and other aquatic species; *fr. : pêche*
- flood defence : structure like an artificial channel, dam or reservoir built to deal with a rise in water level caused by heavy rainfall and flooding of water; *fr. : protection contre les inondations*
- flood defence levy : charging scheme under the Community Infrastructure Levy Regulations of 2010 by which local authorities can raise funds from developers undertaking new building projects; the money is used to develop flood defences; *fr. : système de tarification pour la protection contre les inondations*
- government grant : financial assistance awarded by the government to a legal entity for business, charity, education or research purposes; *fr. : subvention du gouvernment*
- grassroots (n.) : here, ordinary citizens who do not belong to the class of political leaders or elite; *fr. : ≈ représentation communautaire*
- fiscal (adj.) instrument (n.) : tool in the fiscal system like taxes or subsidies that can help raise funds for public spending; *fr. : ≈ instrument fiscal*
- integrated (adj.) management (n.) : system that combines various processes to work as a unified whole with common objectives; *fr. : système de gestion intégrée*
- knowledge hub (n.) : forum providing resources, news and information; *fr. : pôle du savoir*
- natural (adj.) resource base (n.) : reserve of natural resources like land, water and forests that are needed for human and animal survival and existence; *fr. : base de ressources naturelles*
- non-departmental (adj.) public body (n.) : department or body that plays a role in the work of national government, but is not connected with a government department or ministerial authority; *fr. : organisme public non-ministériel*
- water resources : sources of water that can be potentially used for industrial, domestic, agricultural and recreational purposes; *fr. : ressources en eau*
- taxation of pollution : fiscal tool of levying taxes on hazardous wastes and pollution as a way of punishing offenders responsible for environmental pollution; *fr. : taxation de la pollution*

USEFUL EXPRESSIONS

- to reduce CO_2 emissions; *fr. : réduire les émissions de* CO_2
- an achievable environmental goal; *fr. : un objectif réalisable dans le domaine de l'environnement*
- to adopt a grassroots approach; *fr. : adopter une stratégie d'approche populaire*
- to be granted ISO certification; *fr. : se voir accorder la certification ISO*
- to levy a landfilling tax; *fr. : imposer une taxe sur la mise en décharge des déchets*
- with regard to sustainable development; *fr. : en matière de développement durable*

FURTHER INFORMATION

- the verb achieve (*atteindre*) must not be confused with the French verb *achever* meaning to kill or complete something
- the noun agenda (*programme*) refers to the order of events in a meeting or a list of things to be done; the French noun *agenda* refers to a diary or a notebook organiser
- the noun scheme (*dispositif, système*) refers to a systematic plan of action and must not be translated by the French noun *schéma* that refers to a diagram or outline

COMPARATIVE APPROACH

Dans le cadre de la politique de développement durable, le Royaume-Uni et la France ont pris des initiatives pour élaborer des pactes écologiques en prenant des mesures pour adapter leurs budgets nationaux en tenant compte des priorités environnementales.

La France a organisé une série de rencontres politiques afin de fixer des objectifs à long terme. Les projets intitulés Grenelle 1 (2009) et Grenelle 2 (2010) ont été présentés devant une commission mixte paritaire composée de sénateurs et députés avant d'être adoptés par le Parlement. Six chantiers majeurs ont été lancés à savoir habitat et urbanisme, transport, énergie, biodiversité et agriculture, santé et environnement, et gouvernance et information.

Au Royaume-Uni, le Parlement a aussi adopté une initiative phare en 2011, intitulée le *Green Deal* pour mettre en place des mesures d'efficacité énergétique. Par un système innovant de financement de travaux de rénovation énergétique, ce projet aide les particuliers à emprunter des fonds et à limiter les coûts initiaux.

9

Employment law

□ 53 DIFFERENT TYPES OF STATUS IN THE LABOUR MARKET

Despite its image of a flexible employment system, England and Wales have gradually integrated European labour legislation, thus providing people in the workplace with a minimum of statutory protection. We will focus here on the private sector to the exclusion of the public sector which employs civil servants. In the private sector, various positions can be held – worker, employee, self-employed and contractor, director and office holder. These statuses determine different rights, duties and statutory protections.

Employees

They are the most protected individuals in the workplace insofar as they are entitled to all the statutory employment rights (see 56). Any breach of these rights gives rise to actions in court for unfair or wrongful dismissal (see 119). They usually have signed a contract of employment, accepting that their work is controlled by the employer in exchange for a salary. Their relation with their employer is based on a mutuality of obligations. They can work full time or part time. Being present in the workplace is not compulsory as employees can be homeworkers thanks to telecommuting.

Workers

Workers are an intermediary category between employee and self-employed. They have signed a contract of employment and their contractual relation with the employer who is not a customer relies on a mutuality of obligations. They can sometimes be allowed to employ sub-contractors. They benefit from most of the statutory protections, except for unfair dismissal claims and statutory redundancy pay.

Flexible statuses for workers have recently been created to meet with the fluctuations or unexpected demands of businesses. Employers can contract out with temporary work agencies which provide agency workers for a day or a week. After 12 weeks of work, these workers are entitled to some statutory employment rights such as the national minimum wage. Casual workers (such as seasonal workers but not exclusively) are not part of the permanent staff, but carry out work when the employer needs them. They are protected against discrimination, are entitled to be paid at the national minimum wage rate and their working hours have to comply with the statutory regulations. However, they cannot benefit from other statutory rights such as sick pay or maternity/ paternity leave.

Self-employed and contractor

Self-employed individuals or independent contractors can hire sub-contractors to carry out the work they have contracted for with their employer. The latter does not have to pay for statutory sick pay or paid holiday or maternity leave. Self-employed workers have to register with Her Majesty's Revenue and Customs (HMRC).

Director and office holder

Company directors are usually at the head of limited companies. They are considered as office holders. This status includes people who have not signed a contract and have been appointed to different positions in a company or an organisation.

Other statuses

Beginners in a job can be either apprentices who are taught the skills of the job by their employer or a trainee who usually follows and observes an employee at work for a short period of time.

GLOSSARY

- agency worker : individual working temporarily for an employer who hired him via a temporary work agency; *fr. : intérimaire*
- apprentice (n.) : individual learning a trade or a specialty by working for an employer who teaches him the skills; *fr. : apprenti*
- casual (adj.) worker (n.) : person who is employed on an "as and when required" basis; he must be treated as an employee whilst the contract is applicable; the business which resorts to casual workers must make clear that the contract is casual or else, it could be construed as an ordinary contract of employment; *fr. : travailleur intérimaire*
- civil (adj.) servant (n.) : individual working in the public sector; *fr. : fonctionnaire*
- contractor (n.) : independent/self-employed worker who provides services for a business under a contract for services; he is not an employee; *fr. : travailleur indépendant/≈ membre d'une profession libérale/≈ auto-entrepreneur*
- director : see 16
- employee (n.) : individual who has signed a contract of employment with his employer; in exchange for a salary, the employee's work is controlled by the employer who is under the statutory obligation to provide work for him; the

employee benefits from all the statutory employment rights; *fr. : employé/ salarié*

- employer (n.) : individual at the head of a business or a company, who is independent; *fr. : employeur*
- full (adj.) time (n.) : hours of work in the statutory limit of 48 hours a week; it is calculated on the basis of an average over 17 weeks; employees may choose to opt out of this system; self-employed people are not subject to a statutory working limit; *fr. : temps plein*
- Her Majesty's Revenue and Customs (HMRC) : see 25
- homeworker (n.) : individual, whether an employee or self-employed, whose workplace is at home and not on the premises of their office or factory; *fr. : travailleur à domicile*
- independent (adj.) contractor (n.) : self-employed individual working for an employer for a fixed period of time and for a precise type of work; *fr. : travailleur indépendant*
- labour market : situation in terms of employment; *fr. : marché du travail*
- limited (adj.) company (n.) : see 13
- national minimum wage : lowest wage (determined by statute) which an employer may lawfully pay his employees; *fr. : ≈ salaire minimum interprofessionnel de croissance (SMIC)*
- office holder : person who occupies a post which was existing before he took it and will still exist when he leaves it; the person can be appointed to that post; *fr. : ≈ titulaire d'un métier à responsabilité/≈ d'une charge*
- part (adj.) time (n.) : applies to any type of working pattern which represents fewer hours than a full-time employment; *fr. : temps partiel*
- seasonal (adj.) worker (n.) : special type of worker mostly working in tourism or to respond to an occasional demand in shops (like the run up to Christmas); usually they are considered as employees for the period for which they are engaged and enjoy the same statutory rights; *fr. : travailleur saisonnier*
- self-employed (adj.) worker (n.) : individual offering their services and skills to employers for a limited period of time and for a certain type of activity; they pay their own taxes, cannot claim sick pay, maternity/paternity leave; *fr. : travailleur indépendant/≈ membre d'une profession libérale/≈ auto-entrepreneur*
- staff (n.) : group of employees working for the same employer; *fr. : personnel*
- statutory sick pay : see 56
- sub-contractor (n.) : worker hired by an independent contractor to perform work they have not contracted for directly with the main employer; *fr. : sous-traitant*
- telecommuting (n.)/teleworking (n.) : work carried out at home, made possible by new technologies such as internet, teletex or satellites; *fr. : télétravail*

- temporary work agency : individual or company providing companies or businesses with temporary workers; *fr. : agence intérimaire*
- trainee (n.) : individual learning a job by observing an employee at work for a short period of time; *fr. : stagiaire*
- worker (n.) : intermediary category between employee and self-employed; *fr. : ≈ travailleur*

USEFUL EXPRESSIONS

- apprenticeship; *fr. : apprentissage*
- to work as a freelance worker; *fr. : travailler en indépendant*
- shop-floor workers; *fr. : les ouvriers*
- telecommuting/teleworking; *fr. : télétravail*

FURTHER INFORMATION

- commercial agents are considered as self-employed; they usually negotiate on behalf of another person
- the term civil servant refers to the fact that those working for the Crown fulfil a service for society as a whole; French *fonctionnaires* fulfil a *service public* and are also available to help the people as a whole

Comparative approach

Si les catégories de travailleurs sont assez similaires en France et Outre-Manche (sous l'influence, en partie, de la législation européenne), la catégorie intermédiaire de *worker* ne connaît pas vraiment d'équivalent en droit français. De même, le statut français d'auto-entrepreneur qui bénéficie de certaines déductions fiscales par rapport aux artisans ou aux autres professions indépendantes, n'existe pas en Angleterre et au Pays de Galles.

□ 54 CONTRACT OF EMPLOYMENT

Pursuant to the Employment Act 2002, a contract of employment is understood as a "contract of service". It can be express or implied and made orally or in writing. As the statutory definition is rather vague, judges rely on caselaw which has devised a number of tests to determine if the parties are actually bound by a contract of employment. They usually combine the "integration" test to examine if the employee is part of the employer's company, with the "economic reality", the "mutuality of obligations" and the control tests. Many cases in court revolve around the problematic definition of the status of the people in the workplace since employees, workers or sub-contractors do not benefit from the same statutory protection (as will be seen below).

A contract of employment may grant more rights than legislation. In any case, it cannot be more restrictive which means than the statutory rights of employees cannot be reduced by a contract of employment.

Statement of particulars

If the employer is not under a statutory duty to give his employee a written contract of employment, he must give him a written statement of particulars within two months of hiring him. This document sets out the employee's/worker's main rights and duties : names of the parties to the contract, date of implementation, remuneration or salary, working hours, details of paid holidays, bank holidays, statutory sick pay and pension scheme. The employer must also specify the length of the notice period in case of termination of contract, the type of contract and add any existing collective agreement. The employer is under the obligation to give his employee a monthly pay slip setting out the gross wage, the various deductions including PAYE (pay as you earn) and the net wage that is to be paid each month. The statement of particulars should give information about the possible disciplinary procedure and give the employee the name of a person to contact in case of grievances. Should disputes or conflicts arise with his employer, the employee can attend a disciplinary hearing with a colleague or a trade union representative. The employee is entitled to be informed of the reasons for his dismissal.

Flexible contracts

Contracts of employment can vary greatly and some of them are highly flexible. Types of contracts include fixed-term and long-term contracts which usually include probationary/trial periods in their provisions, key and zero-hour contracts which are beneficial to some professions such as shop-workers, offer no regular working hours and give way to job insecurity.

GLOSSARY

- bank holiday : public holiday when workers get time off or are paid extra if they work; *fr. : ≈ jour férié*
- collective (adj.) agreement (n.) : document signed by employers and trade union representatives in a particular field, stating the rights and duties of employees at work; a collective agreement may offer more protection and/or more rights than legislation; in any case, it cannot be more restrictive than legislation; *fr. : convention collective*
- contract of employment : agreement by which an employer hires an employee or a worker for a certain type of work in exchange of a remuneration; *fr. : contrat de travail*
- contract of service : agreement struck between an employer and an employee in which the former gives a remuneration for the services carried out by the

latter; it is to be distinguished from the phrase "contract for services" (*contrat de service*) which is used for self-employed workers; *fr. : ≈ contrat de travail*

- control test : test devised by common law to determine the nature of the relationship between an employer and an employee; if the work is controlled by the employer, then the person doing the work is regarded as an employee; otherwise, he is considered as self-employed; *fr. : ≈ lien de subordination hiérarchique*
- deduction (n.) : amount of money that is withdrawn on the employee's pay slip, such as taxes (e.g. PAYE) or National Insurance contributions; *fr. : déductions salariales*
- economic (adj.) reality (n.) : test devised by common law to determine whether the worker is working for his own account (self-employed) or is dependent on his employer (employee); *fr. : réalité économique*
- fixed-term contract : contract of employment signed for a limited period of time; *fr. : ≈ contrat à durée déterminée (CDD)*
- grievance (n.) : complaint made by an employee who argues he has been wronged; *fr. : réclamation*
- gross (adj.) wage (n.) : monthly sum of money paid to the employee before any deduction; *fr. : salaire brut*
- job insecurity : situation in which the worker's or employees's future is uncertain; *fr. : précarité*
- integration test : test devised by common law to determine whether the employee or the worker is an integral part of the employer's business and benefits from the usual statutory protections; if not, it means he is self-employed; *fr. : ≈ test de l'intégration*
- key-contract (n.) : contract of employment guaranteeing work but not on a regular basis; *fr. : ≈ contrat de travail forfaitaire clé en mains*
- long-term contract : contract of employment signed on a long-term basis, indicating no expiry date; *fr. : contrat à durée indéterminée (CDI)*
- net (adj.) wage (n.) : sum of money paid to the employee after all the deductions through the PAYE system; *fr. : salaire net*
- notice period : period of time between the notification of the dismissal and the end of the contract when the employee must work in cases of termination of contract, such as dismissal, expiry or redundancy; *fr. : délai de préavis*
- paid (adj.) holiday (n.) : statutory time off when the employee is paid; *fr. : congés payés*
- PAYE (pay as you earn) : tax system by which tax is automatically deducted from the employee's monthly wage; *fr. : système de prélèvement des impôts à la source*
- pay slip : monthly document enumerating the gross wage, all the deductions, and indicating the net wage; *fr. : fiche de paie*
- pension scheme : system enabling working individuals to save money for their retirement through occupational, personal or stakeholder pensions; *fr. : régime de retraite*

- probationary (adj.) period (n.)/trial period : period of work when the worker starts his job and is observed by the employer before possibly signing a long-term contract if the observation process is deemed satisfactory in terms of work quality; *fr. : période d'essai*
- provision (n.) : here, term of a contract of employment; *fr. : disposition*
- remuneration (n.) : amount of money given for the work done; wage and salary are two different aspects of remuneration; *fr. : rémunération*
- salary (n.) : amount of money received by a working individual on a yearly basis; *fr. : salaire annuel*
- statutory (adj.) protection (n.) : protection given by statute law, i.e., law voted in Parliament; *fr. : protection légale*
- statutory sick pay (SSP) : weekly sum of money fixed by the legislator and which is paid by the employer to an employee for a period of up to 28 weeks if the employee qualifies for it; paid time off when an employee is sick; *fr. : congé maladie*
- trade union (n.) : see 121
- trial period : please see probationary period above
- wage (n.) : amount of money received by a working individual each month; *fr. : salaire mensuel*
- working (adj.) hours (n.) : number of hours an employee works on a weekly basis; *fr. : heures de travail*
- written statement of particulars : written extract from the contract of employment, stating the main terms and conditions of employment; this document is compulsory; *fr. : ≈ conditions particulières du contrat*
- zero-hour contract : contract of employment stating that the worker is required to work only when his employer needs him; his working hours are flexible and subject to fluctuations; the remuneration is calculated according to the number of worked hours; *fr. : contrat « zéro heure »*

USEFUL EXPRESSIONS

- to apply for a job; *fr. : poser sa candidature à/postuler pour un emploi*
- to appoint someone to a position; *fr. : nommer quelqu'un à un poste*
- to be a job seeker; *fr. : être demandeur d'emploi*
- to enrol someone into a private pension scheme; *fr. : inscrire quelqu'un à un régime de retraite privé*
- to earn a living/money; *fr. : gagner sa vie/de l'argent*
- to follow a training scheme; *fr. : suivre un programme de formation*
- to hire someone; *fr. : embaucher quelqu'un*
- the labour market; *fr. : le marché du travail*
- to offload labour; *fr. : débaucher*
- to rely on skilled labour force/workforce; *fr. : s'appuyer sur la main d'œuvre qualifiée*

- to serve a notice period; *fr. : effectuer sa période de préavis*
- under-employment; *fr. : le travail précaire*

FURTHER INFORMATION

- the verb "to bind" is an irregular verb and can used in different ways; while a contract is said to be *binding* on the parties, the parties *are bound* by a contract
- wage and salary cover different aspects of remuneration; while wage refers to the remuneration given every month, salary is used when giving the amount earned in a year

COMPARATIVE APPROACH

Même si la législation européenne impose un contrat écrit pour toute embauche, la France, l'Angleterre et le Pays de Galles ne se conforment pas à cette réglementation de la même façon. Outre-Manche, un *written statement of particulars* résume, par écrit, les points essentiels en cas de contrat verbal. En France, en cas de non-remise d'un contrat écrit à l'employé par l'employeur, l'employé est considéré comme étant embauché à titre indéterminé et à temps complet, le premier bulletin de salaire se substituant au contrat écrit. Un contrat de travail écrit est toutefois obligatoire pour les CDD et les temps partiels. Les contrats de travail restent plus flexibles Outre-Manche, en particulier les contrats dits zéro-heure (*zero-hour contract*) où l'employé ne travaille pas régulièrement et perçoit une rémunération uniquement pour les heures effectuées. Ce genre de contrat n'existe pas en France.

□ 55 EMPLOYER'S RIGHTS AND DUTIES

The relationship between an employer and an employee relies on a mutuality of obligations. These obligations may derive from the terms of a contract of employment and the collective agreement applicable in a particular professional field. A contract of employment (like a collective agreement) may grant more rights than statute to employees but cannot be more restrictive. The employer's and employee's obligations can also derive from implied terms in fact and in law. Implied terms in fact derive from the specific needs of some professions. Implied terms in law are based on common law and statutory law.

Financial issues

The employer must pay a wage to an employee even if he has no work to give him. He can give performance and/or discretionary bonuses to his employee. He has the duty to indemnify him from any expenses incurred by the job.

Although an employee has the right to ask for some time off for training, the employer is under no obligation to accept, and if he does he does not have to pay him. An employer has the right to refuse to allow flexible working to an employee unless the latter wants to take care of his child(ren) or a dependent adult.

Any employer has the right to spend money to control his employees' means of communication in the workplace, such as their use of internet access or phone calls and can also use CCTV cameras provided their employees are informed of such monitoring.

Health and safety

The employer owes a reasonable duty of care to his employees and workers in relation to any potential negligence that could occur in the workplace. The employer must provide the people who work for him with a safe and secure environment. An employer with five employees or more must issue a written health and safety policy, describing exactly the procedure applicable – who is supposed to do what, how (calling emergency services or a representative in the company), and when they should react. If there are fewer than five employees, there is no such statutory obligation. However, the employer is advised to assess potential hazards, keep a record of them and anticipate any risks his employees might be exposed to. After identifying them, the employer must take measures to control them.

The employer must prevent any industrial accidents or prescribed diseases, such as exposure to dangerous substances (exposure to asbestos used to be a major problem in the workplace but is now strictly regulated). It is compulsory to comply with fire regulations, which implies providing escape routes and giving access to fire extinguishers. Equipment and machinery may harm people in the workplace and have to be checked and tested on a regular basis. Communication with the employees or workers on any hazards they might have noticed at work is also part of the employer's duties. Regular training of employees and workers on health and safety issues can reduce injuries at work.

Controlling health and safety risks in the workplace is of paramount importance for an employer. Employees injured at work may claim an Industrial Injuries Disablement Benefit. An employer can be held liable (either directly or vicariously) for any accident and be ordered to pay damages to his employees or any third party who may have sustained a loss through an employee's negligence (e.g. when using machinery at work). In extreme circumstances, the employer's attitude may amount to a criminal offence and he could be prosecuted.

GLOSSARY

- asbestos (n.) : building material that was formerly used for insulation and which presents a health hazard for humans or animals when asbestos dust is inhaled; *fr. : amiante*

- bonus (n.) : extra sum of money given to the employee by the employer, which is usually performance related; *fr. : prime*
- duty of care : see 86
- escape route : track usually marked by a colour, that is to be followed to get out of the premises in case of fire; *fr. : sortie de secours*
- expense (n.) : here, sum of money spent by the employee whilst performing his work duties, such as paying for a train ticket to go to a work meeting, etc.; *fr. : ≈ dépense liée au travail/frais de travail*
- fire extinguisher : device used to put out a fire or delay it; *fr. : extincteur*
- fire regulation : rule related to the measures that should be taken in case of fire; for example, following the evacuation plan, closing all the doors; *fr. : règlementation en cas d'incendie*
- harm (n. and v.) : hurt or injure someone; *fr. : blessure (n.)/blesser (v.)*
- hazard (n. and v.) : synomym for danger; *fr. : danger (n.)/mettre en danger (v.)*
- health and safety policy : written statement describing the actions and the measures to prevent any accident at work and protect the employees' health; *fr. : mesures de sécurité*
- indemnify (v.) : cover costs incurred in the performance of a job; *fr. : indemniser*
- industrial (adj.) accident (n.) : incident taking place at work and causing personal injury; the employee can be partly or completely disabled as a result of the accident; *fr. : accident du travail*
- Industrial Injuries Disablement Benefit : sum of money paid weekly by the state when an employee has become disabled after an accident in his workplace or has developed a prescribed disease; *fr. : ≈ indemnisation des accidents du travail*
- injury (n.) : harm sustained by someone; *fr. : blessure*
- issue (n.) : particular question or point; *fr. : question/sujet/point*
- negligence (n.) : see 86
- prescribed (adj.) disease (n.) (PDs) : disease or injury which results from a risk arising from a person's work; governmental regulations give an official list of PDs; *fr. : maladie professionnelle*
- prosecute (v.) : see 102
- risk (n.) : here, possibility of causing or being inflicted with harm or injury; *fr. : risque*
- training (n.) : here, programme designed to teach employees about certain aspects of their work or on health and safety regulations; *fr. : formation*
- vicariously (adv.) liable (adj.) : responsible for someone else's negligence; *fr. : responsible du fait d'autrui*
- workplace (n.) : place where employees work; it can be a factory, a shop or an office, etc.; *fr. : lieu de travail*

USEFUL EXPRESSIONS

- this machine is a fire hazard; *fr. : cette machine présente un risque d'incendie*
- hazardous products; *fr. : produits dangereux*
- to be liable for someone's injuries; *fr. : être responsable des blessures de quelqu'un*
- to follow a training programme; *fr. : suivre un stage de formation*
- to incur expenses; *fr. : engendrer des frais*
- to owe a duty to someone/to owe someone a duty; *fr. : avoir un devoir envers quelqu'un*

FURTHER INFORMATION

- the noun hazard is a false friend and cannot be translated by the French *hasard* (chance or coincidence in English)

COMPARATIVE APPROACH

Les réglementations en matière de sécurité au travail sont similaires en France et Outre-Manche.

□ 56 EMPLOYEES' RIGHTS AND DUTIES

As is the case for employers, the rights and obligations of employees may derive from the terms of a contract of employment or may be implied in law or in fact. If a collective agreement is applicable to the employee's professional field, it can only grant the employee more rights than statute.

Rights

Employees and workers have been entitled to the national minimum wage since 1998. Employees have 28 days of paid annual leave and can take maternity or paternity leave, depending on their status. However, the working hours limit is still the highest in Europe, the maximum being currently 48 hours a week even though a worker, and sometimes an employee, may opt out of this scheme in order to work more. Whatever their status, members of the workforce are protected from all sorts of discrimination, whether it be related to age, gender, disability or religion (see 58). Employees have a statutory right to equal pay. Any breach of anti-discrimination law (whether direct or indirect) or equal pay rights can give rise to claims in court.

Employees are entitled to be absent from work when they are sick. In this case, they receive occupational sick pay. They are also entitled to take time off when they are pregnant or want to raise their child(ren). Ordinary maternity leave enables a pregnant woman to take twenty six weeks off. In terms of Statutory Maternity Pay, a woman is paid 90 % of her salary for the first six weeks, and then her remuneration is calculated according to the statutory rate which is updated every year. A woman can take additional maternity leave to take care of her new-born child for another twenty six weeks. After a whole year away, the employee has the right to return to her job, and if this is not possible, her employer must offer her an alternative position.

A woman can also apply for parental leave to have more time to raise her child. Fathers also have the right to claim for paternity leave and are allowed to take two weeks off within the first two months of the child's birth. They receive the Statutory Paternity Pay. Adopting parents have the right to take an adoption leave and benefit from the same statutory rights as a pregnant woman. An employee can also ask for flexible working to take care of a child or a dependent adult.

Duties

The employee must perform his work with normal care and skill, and follow the instructions given by his employers unless they are likely to put other colleagues' health or security in jeopardy. On top of adapting to the changes in the workplace and cooperating in a team, employees must try to preserve trust and confidence with their employer. The employee must be loyal to his employer. This duty implies that the employee should report any wrongdoing and/or misconduct of a colleague. Keeping information or trade secrets confidential is also incumbent on the employee. An employer has the right to add any restrictive provisions to the contract of employment to prevent the employee from disclosing any or some information related to his work.

GLOSSARY

- adoption leave : in case of an adoption, a woman or one of the civil partners is entitled to take time off to care for the adopted child; *fr. : congé pour adoption*
- confidence (n.) : here, synonym for trust; *fr. : confiance*
- confidentiality (n.) : respect of secrecy; *fr. : confidentialité*
- direct (adj.)/indirect (adj.) discrimination (n.) : see 59
- disclose (v.) : here, reveal secret information; *fr. : révéler*
- equal (adj.) pay (n.) principle : anti-discrimination rule stating that salary should be calculated according to the individual's skills and performance and not on differences in gender, religion, ethnic origin or disability; *fr. : principe de l'égalité des rémunérations*
- flexible (adj.) working (n.) : any change to some of the terms and conditions of employment (mostly relating to the time or number of working hours) so that the employee can take care of his child or of a dependent adult; *fr. : travail flexible*
- loyalty (n.) : quality of being faithful; *fr. : loyauté*

- maternity leave (AML) : statutory period of 26 weeks of absence from work which a woman can take before and after giving birth to look after herself and her new born child; *fr. : congé de maternité*
- misconduct (n.) : dishonest or unreasonable behaviour; *fr. : faute*
- negligence (n.) : see 86
- occupational (adj.) sick pay (n.) : amount of money given to a sick employee and paid by the employer; *fr. : indemnité de congé maladie*
- parental (adj.) leave (n.) : time of absence from work which can be taken by the mother or the father to raise a child; no remuneration is received during that time, subject to the terms of the collective agreement; *fr. : congé parental*
- paternity leave : the father or one of the civil partners who has not claimed for an adoption leave is entitled to two weeks off to support the mother or the other civil partner within the first 56 days of the new-born child(ren); *fr. : congé de paternité*
- provision (n.) : see 12
- skill (n.) : ability in a certain field which has been developed by training and/or experience; *fr. : compétence*
- Statutory Maternity Pay (SMP) : legal rate to be paid by the employer to a woman on maternity leave; *fr. : ≈ indemnité journalière de congé maternité*
- Statutory Paternity Pay (SPP) : legal rate to be paid by the employer to a father who is on paternity leave; *fr. : ≈ indemnité journalière de congé de paternité*
- wrongdoing (n.) : wrong, dishonest or illegal act committed by an employee at work; *fr. : acte répréhensible*

USEFUL EXPRESSIONS

- to be liable to an employer for something; *fr. : être responsable de quelque chose à l'égard d'un employeur*
- to be on sick/maternity leave; *fr. : être en congé maladie ou de maternité*
- to comply with/abide by the terms of a contract; *fr. : se conformer aux dispositions d'un contrat*
- expected week of childbirth; *fr. : date prévue de l'accouchement*
- to get pregnant; *fr. : tomber enceinte*
- to have a holiday entitlement; *fr. : avoir un droit aux congés*

FURTHER INFORMATION

- same-sex couples are entitled to adoption and paternity leave the same way as heterosexual couples are; one of the parents takes an adoption leave or a maternity leave and the other parent has the right to take the statutory two weeks off

- a “garden leave” clause (*clause de dispense d’exécution du préavis*) is an express contractual provision dispensing the employee from carrying out his work duties, usually during some or all of a notice period; this is construed as a way to protect confidential information at work
- whistleblowing (*dénonciation*) is the fact for someone who witnesses or suspects wrongdoing in his workplace such as a breach to environmental law, or a criminal offence, to report it either to his employer or to prescribed organisations; a whitsleblower cannot be dismissed for reporting wrongdoing

Comparative approach

Même si le droit du travail anglais s’est, depuis quelques années, mis en conformité avec le droit européen, en instaurant, par exemple, un salaire minimum, les salariés y sont toujours moins bien protégés que leurs homologues européens. La durée moyenne du temps de travail (48 heures hebdomadaires) est supérieure à celle pratiquée dans le reste de l’Europe et notamment en France (35 heures par semaine).

En France, la durée du congé de maternité (*maternity leave*) est plus courte qu’en Angleterre et au Pays de Galles puisqu’elle est de l’ordre de 16 semaines contre 26 semaines. Les indemnités journalières en cas de congé maternité ou de paternité sont plus avantageuses en France. Les congés parentaux et les congés pour adoption existent dans les deux pays. Les employées sont protégées de la même façon lors de la reprise du travail.

Les devoirs du salarié envers l’employeur sont similaires en Angleterre et au Pays de Galles et en France. Le non-respect de ces devoirs peut entraîner un licenciement dans les deux pays.

10

Human rights and immigration law

□ 57 HUMAN RIGHTS – GENERAL INFORMATION

Human rights are universal freedoms and entitlements that each person possesses. The word "human" underlines the basic equality of all people and the fact that all "human beings" are equally worthy of basic respect. A human right is a pre-existing claim of a human being to obligate the state to legally do or refrain from doing something to an individual.

The Human Rights Act (HRA) 1998 guarantees substantive rights and procedural rights to UK citizens and requires public authorities to act in accordance with the European Convention on Human Rights (ECHR). Those rights in the HRA that set forth the individual and collective rights are known as substantive rights. They ensure the normal legal order of society. The procedural rights in the HRA provide the implementation mechanisms to remedy violations and ensure compliance.

The HRA sets out clearly those non-derogable (or absolute) rights, derogable rights and qualified rights which must be respected by the UK Parliament. It applies to existing law and law to be enacted in the future which must comply with its provisions.

Because it incorporated the ECHR into British law, the underlying idea of the HRA was to make access to justice for human rights violations quicker for people residing in the UK. Before it came into force, individuals who felt that their rights had been violated had to take their case to the European Court of Human Rights in Strasbourg (ECtHR), which was a lengthy and expensive process. It is now possible to seek from the UK national courts the enforcement of rights guaranteed to them. However, if dissatisfied with a UK court decision, an individual may still bring a claim before the ECtHR but this can only be done after all domestic remedies are exhausted.

GLOSSARY

- absolute (adj.) right (n.) : right that is so fundamental that it must never be limited or restricted in any way as in the case of the right to a fair trial; *fr. : droit absolu*
- collective (adj.) right (n.) : right that is held by each individual member in society, but collectively for the benefit of the whole collective group in society; *fr. : droit collectif*
- compliance (n.) (with) : act of conforming to something; *fr. : respect (de)*
- derogable (adj.) right (n.) : human right that can be suspended by a state during a time of public emergency without the fear of violating human rights norms; *fr. : droit susceptible de dérogation/droit non-absolu*
- entitlement (n.) : claim upon a state enabling an individual to assert, exercise and protect a right; *fr. : droit*
- freedom (n.) : right to act according to one's will in the absence of any law limiting such an act; *fr. : liberté*
- fundamental (adj.) freedom (n.) : right that is fundamental to the protection of human dignity as it is universal; it refers to the fact that all human beings are born with the right to enjoy it; *fr. : droit fundamental*
- human (adj.) rights (n.) : legally enforceable claim or entitlement held by an individual vis-à-vis government authority, for the protection of the inherent human dignity of a human being; *fr. : droits de l'Homme*
- individual (adj.) right (n.) : right that is held by each individual in society, regardless of his belonging to a group; *fr. : droit individuel*
- limited (adj.) right (n.) : right that limits an individual's right to liberty (e.g. if someone is legally detained in a removal centre for immigration purposes); *fr. : droit limité*
- non-derogable (adj.) right (n.) : human right that cannot be suspended by a state as the state is bound to guarantee such a right at all times, including a time of public emergency; *fr. : droit non-susceptible de dérogation/droit intangible*
- obligate (v.) : bind or compel someone or an authority to act in a particular way due to legal ties and obligations; *fr. : obliger*
- qualified (adj.) right (n.) : right that may be restricted, either partly or completely, in order to protect the rights of all individuals in society, as in the case of imposed limitations to an individual's right to the freedom of expression, if such an act may provoke racial hatred; *fr. : droit non absolu/droit assorti de conditions*
- procedural (adj.) right (n.) : right that permits the state to take procedural action, remedy human rights violations and determine the manner of implementing substantive human rights; *fr. : droit procédural*
- public (adj.) authority (n.) : person or authority whose functions are of a public nature like central and local government agencies, courts, tribunals, removal centres and prisons; *fr. : autorité publique*
- refrain (v.) from : prevent from doing something; *fr. : s'abstenir de*

- substantive (adj.) rights (n.) : individual rights and freedoms that an individual possesses in society, like the right to expression, association, movement and religious freedom; *fr. : droits substantiels*
- universal (adj.) freedom (n.) : liberty which that applies to all persons at all times; *fr. : liberté universelle*
- underline (v.) : emphasise the importance of something; *fr. : souligner*

USEFUL EXPRESSIONS

- to act in accordance with human rights norms; *fr. : agir conformément aux normes en matière de droits de l'Homme*
- to have the right to the freedom of expression; *fr. : avoir le droit à la liberté d'expression*
- to comply with/to abide by the provisions of the ECHR; *fr. : se conformer aux dispositions de la CEDH*
- to grant the right to human dignity; *fr. : accorder le droit à la dignité humaine*
- to require compliance with the ECHR; *fr. : exiger de satisfaire les dispositions de la CEDH*

FURTHER INFORMATION

- the word compliance (*respect*) refers to the act of conforming to the law and must not be translated by the French word *complaisance* which refers to kindness or indulgence
- the word process (*processus*) refers to a series of steps or actions to be accomplished in order to achieve a result and must not be translated by the French word *procès* that refers to a court trial

COMPARATIVE APPROACH

En France, l'article 1 de la Déclaration universelle des droits de l'Homme et du citoyen adopté le 26 août 1789 par l'Assemblée nationale, qui a valeur constitutionnelle, dispose que les hommes naissent et demeurent libres et égaux en droits. En plus de ce texte fondateur, dès 1947, l'État français a créé une commission nationale consultative des droits de l'Homme (CNCDH) qui a un rôle de conseil et est garant des droits fondamentaux accordés aux citoyens pour l'exercice des libertés publiques.

En revanche, au Royaume-Uni où l'ordre juridique britannique est caractérisé par l'absence *prima facie* de Constitution écrite, il n'y avait aucun texte énumérant les droits fondamentaux des citoyens jusqu'à l'adoption du *Human Rights Act* de 1998. Donc, avant 1998, les citoyens avaient la liberté de faire tout ce qui n'était pas spécifiquement interdit par la *common law*.

☐ 58 BASIC SUBSTANTIVE RIGHTS

Freedom of thought, conscience and religion, of expression, of assembly and association, right to privacy and protection of property are the basic substantive rights protected by the HRA.

The freedom of speech and expression (Article 9) of the HRA offers protection against indoctrination by the State and protects forms of expression in written or spoken words, action and any expressive medium. Members of Parliament also enjoy parliamentary privilege and legal immunity which protects them from defamation actions of libel and slander.

Religious freedom in the UK has to be exercised with due regard to other rights like the right to respect for private and family life (Article 8), freedom of expression (Article 10) and freedom of assembly (Article 11). As the right protected by Article 9 is broadly defined as an all-encompassing right, atheism, scepticism, and agnosticism are given the same protection under the ECHR Convention as established religious faiths.

The right to privacy (Article 8) protects four distinct interests : the right to private life, family life, home and correspondence. The respect for one's private life includes respect for individual sexuality, respect of private and confidential information, personal data protection, right not to be subject to unlawful state surveillance, right to control the dissemination of information about one's private life and right to information. The state is thus obliged to take positive measures to forbid extreme breaches of these rights by private individuals including tort actions like defamation, trespass, nuisance and breaches in the protection of confidential information.

Article 11 of the HRA imposes two types of obligations on the state. There is a negative obligation of not restricting peaceful assembly. There is also a positive obligation of guaranteeing reasonable and appropriate measures to protect individuals who want to exercise their right to peaceful assembly. However the right to strike is not considered as a constitutional right.

The basic list of substantive rights drawn up in the original European Convention in 1950 has since been supplemented by a number of protocols that set out additional rights like the right of peaceful enjoyment of personal possessions (1st protocol) and the right to education (2nd protocol).

GLOSSARY

- agnosticism (n.) : doctrine that is based on the tenet that there exists no proof of the existence or non-existence of God; *fr. : agnosticisme*
- all-encompassing (adj.) right (n.) : right that is broad in scope offering blanket sanctions against human rights violations; *fr. : droit universel*
- assembly (n.) : act of people gathering together; *fr. : réunion*
- association (n.) : act of forming groups, organising and getting together with the aim of addressing certain common issues of concern to society at large; *fr. : association*

- atheism (n.) : philosophy that rejects belief in God; *fr. : athéisme*
- confidential (adj.) information (n.) : data, correspondence, material and documents which contain information that is privileged and protected on the grounds of confidentiality; *fr. : informations confidentielles*
- conscience (n.) : internal dictates of the human mind permitting an individual to make decisions on how he sees the world and rightly act in a given situation; *fr. : conscience*
- correspondence (n.) : written or digital communication like letters, e-mails and notes which may be exchanged between two or more parties; *fr. : correspondance*
- personal data protection : data or information which is related to an identifiable individual; *fr. : protection des données à caractère personnel*
- defamation (n.) : act of making derogatory statements about an individual in order to lower a person in the regard of other members of society, as in actions of libel and slander; *fr. : diffamation*
- dissemination (n.) : act of transmitting, circulating and broadcasting information to a wide public; *fr. : diffusion*
- expression (n.) : act of externalising beliefs, ideas, information and opinions through writing, speech, art or symbols; *fr. : expression*
- expressive (adj.) medium (n.) : means of conveying ideas by means of mass communication; *fr. : moyen d'expression*
- indoctrination (n.) : process of teaching or inculcating a doctrine or ideology; *fr. : endoctrinement*
- legal (adj.) immunity (n.) : protection from tort actions like defamation, offered to members of Parliament for statements made during proceedings in Parliament; *fr. : immunité judiciaire*
- libel (n.) : defamation in a permanent form that is printed, published and communicated to a third party in the form of writing, print, broadcast or electronic communication; *fr. : diffamation écrite*
- negative (adj.) obligation (n.) : duty of the state to refrain from forcing an individual to do something he is not obliged to do; *fr. : obligation négative*
- nuisance (n.) : area of tort law that takes legal action to redress harm done to one's property and may be classified as private nuisance or public nuisance; *fr. : délit civil de nuisance*
- parliamentary (adj.) privilege (n.) : legal immunity granted to members of parliament protecting freedom of speech in debate or during proceedings in Parliament; *fr. : privilège parlementaire*
- positive (adj.) obligation (n.) : duty of the state to establish an appropriate legislative system or framework to ensure the protection of human rights; *fr. : obligation positive*
- privacy (n.) : state of enjoying freedom to live one's private life with minimum interference from others, in particular from public authorities and the state; *fr. : vie privée*

- property (n.) : possession of tangible possessions like land and goods, and of intangible assets like copyrights and patents; *fr. : propriété*
- protocol (n.) : international legal instrument which is created to amend an existing treaty; *fr. : protocole*
- thought (n.) : faculty of mental thinking; *fr. : pensée*
- scepticism (n.) : doctrine based on the principle of disbelief that propagates the ideas that knowledge is uncertain and all knowledge is unattainable; *fr. : scepticisme*
- slander (n.) : defamatory statement made orally or verbally in a temporary form; *fr. : diffamation orale/calomnie*
- speech (n.) : faculty of expressing thought and ideas through articulated speech; *fr. : parole*
- state surveillance : monitoring of activities or conversations by government authorities over persons or groups considered as potentially dangerous to public safety; *fr. : surveillance de l'État*
- strike (v. or n.) : stopping work as a protest against dissatisfactory working conditions; *fr. : grève*
- trespass (n.) : tort action which invades the protected interests of another person as in assault, battery and damage to property, land or goods; *fr. : délit civil d'intrusion*

USEFUL EXPRESSIONS

- a breach of human rights/to breach human rights standards; *fr. : une violation des droits de l'Homme/violer les droits de l'Homme*
- to exercise one's right to free expression; *fr. : exercer son droit à s'exprimer librement*
- to enjoy the right to the freedom of expression; *fr. : jouir du droit de la liberté d'expression*
- with due regard to human rights norms; *fr. : en tenant dûment compte des normes relatives aux droits de l'Homme*

FURTHER INFORMATION

- the word breach (*violation*) meaning infringement, must not be confused with the French word *brèche* that refers to a fracture or a rupture
- the word libel (*diffamation écrite*) refers to a tort action of damaging a person's reputation and must not be translated by the French word *libellé* that refers to the manner in which a text is drafted
- the word tort (*responsabilité délictuelle*) must not be confused with the French word *tort* as used in *avoir tort* which means to be wrong

COMPARATIVE APPROACH

Au Royaume-Uni l'immunité parlementaire (*parliamentary privilege*) garantie par l'Article 9 de la *Bill of Rights* 1689 vise à protéger le libre débat parlementaire et à préserver la séparation des pouvoirs législatif et judiciaire (*legislative power and judiciary*). La portée du privilège de liberté d'expression du parlementaire a souvent été remise en question par les juges Outre-Manche.

En France, l'Article 26 de la Constitution du 4 octobre 1958 établit qu'aucun membre du Parlement ne peut être poursuivi devant un tribunal du fait des opinions exprimées ou votes émis par lui au Parlement, consacrant ainsi le principe de l'immunité parlementaire. Cette immunité est limitée aux seules questions liées aux actes directement rattachables à leurs fonctions parlementaires, tels que les propos tenus durant les discussions au sein des groupes ou dans le cadre des missions ou rédaction de rapports.

□ 59 FORMAL PROCEDURAL RIGHTS

Procedural guarantees of the HRA ensure the right to a fair trial (Article 6) in both criminal and civil cases and prohibit discrimination (Article 14).

The right to a fair trial includes the right to due process rights, minimum rights to a fair procedure and is based on the fundamental adversarial principle or *audi alteram partem* (as opposed to the inquisitorial principle). The UK is required under Article 3 of the ECHR to ensure that no individual shall be subject to torture or to inhumane or degrading punishment and it imposes three obligations on the state : negative obligation, positive obligation and procedural obligation.

Absence of retrospective law (or *ex post facto* law) is thanks to Article 7 of the HRA that provides effective safeguards against such law to prevent arbitrary prosecution, conviction and punishment or sentence. It stipulates that no one shall be held guilty of any criminal offence on account of any act or omission which did not constitute a criminal offence under national or international law at the time when it was committed; nor shall a heavier penalty be imposed than the one that was applicable at the time the criminal offence was committed.

In the UK, the death penalty was abolished in all circumstances including high treason by the Crime and Disorder Act 1998. It was replaced with a maximum sentence of life imprisonment. When the 13th protocol to the ECHR became mandatory and binding on the UK, death penalty in exceptional circumstances was also forbidden for crimes under military law or in wartime.

Article 14 of the HRA requires that all the rights and freedoms contained in the HRA must be protected and applied without discrimination. In the UK until 2010, six strands of protection against discrimination existed to ban inequality : race, gender, disability, faith, sexuality and age. Since the passing of the Equality Act in 2010, three more characteristics have been included to the list of protected characteristics, namely gender reassignment, marriage and civil partnerships, pregnancy and maternity. The Act includes a new public sector equality duty that obliges public bodies to ensure the elimination of direct and indirect discrimination.

GLOSSARY

- arbitrary (adj.) : based on individual discretion and not grounded by law or statute; *fr. : arbitraire*
- adversarial (adj.) principle (n.)/*audi alteram partem* (Latin) : legal maxim that insists on hearing all the parties or all sides of an argument in order to grant the right to a fair trial; its opposite is the inquisitorial principe; *fr. : principe du contradictoire applicable (ici, applicable dans un système accusatoire)*
- binding (adj.) : legally enforceable by law; *fr. : juridiquement contraignant/ayant un effet liant*
- conviction (n.) : process of finding a person guilty of a criminal act in a court of law; *fr. : condamnation/reconnaissance de responsabilité pénale*
- degrading (adj.) : debasing or humiliating; *fr. : dégradant*
- direct (adj.) discrimination (n.) : less favourable, differential treatment to one group than another on the grounds of sex or race or another protected characteristic; *fr. : discrimination directe*
- disability (n.) : state of being physically or mentally handicapped; *fr. : handicap*
- discrimination (n.) : unequal treatment of people and making a distinction in favour of or against a group of people; *fr. : discrimination*
- due process right : right that ensures that formal legal proceedings are carried out in fairness as in the case of a right to a lawyer, the right to examine witnesses, or the right to be heard by an impartial court; *fr. : droit à une procédure régulière*
- fair (adj.) procedure (n.) : obligation of the state to ensure that a civil or criminal trial complies with substantive and procedural human rights as in the case of the right for an accused to be promptly informed of the accusation against him in a language that he understands; *fr. : procédure équitable*
- fair (adj.) trial (n.) : requirement that judicial issues be resolved through legal proceedings which are fair to all parties as in the case of access to a neutral and fair court or the right to be presumed innocent until proven guilty; *fr. : procès équitable*
- faith (n.) : belief in God or in other religious doctrines; *fr. : foi*

- gender reassignment : surgical procedures that physically change a person's gender from male to female or from female to male; *fr. : réaffectation sexuelle/ changement de sexe*
- high (adj.) treason (n.) : act of criminal disloyalty against one's country; *fr. : haute trahison*
- impose (v.) (on) : enforce or establish (as law); *fr. : imposer (à)*
- indirect (adj.) discrimination (n.) : discriminatory treatment which is neutral on its surface, but which has disparate and unequal impact on different groups of people as in the case of discrimination on the grounds of disability, age or harassment; *fr. : discrimination indirecte*
- inequality (n.) : condition of being unequal or suffering from disparity; *fr. : inégalité*
- inhumane (adj.) : cruel and lacking in compassion; *fr. : inhumain*
- mandatory (adj.) : compulsory or obligatory in nature; *fr. : obligatoire*
- minimum (adj.) right (n.) : basic rights that ensure an individual lives with human dignity; *fr. : droit minimum*
- negative (adj.) obligation (n.) : see 58
- omission (n.) : act of leaving out, omitting or neglecting to do something; *fr. : omission*
- positive (adj.) obligation (n.) : see 58
- protected (adj.) characteristic (n.) : equality trait that protects groups from discrimination by specifying nine strands on the grounds upon which discrimination is unlawful; *fr. : caractéristique protégée*
- procedural (adj.) guarantee (n.) : legal measure that ensures the proper administration of justice and contains procedures that respect substantive and procedural norms; *fr. : garantie procédurale*
- prosecution (n.) : act of prosecuting and conducting legal proceedings against a person; *fr. : poursuite pénale*
- requirement (n.) : condition required by law; *fr. : exigence juridique*
- retrospective (adj.) law (n.) : *ex post facto* or after-the-fact law that punishes an act as a criminal offence, even though it was not a crime under the law at the time when it was committed; *fr. : loi rétroactive*
- safeguard (n.) : measure to protect the rights of a citizen; *fr. : mesure de protection/sauvegarde*
- sentence (n. or v.) : criminal punishment imposed on someone who was found guilty of the commission of an offence; sentence occurs after conviction; *fr. : peine*
- strand (n.) : element or trait that composes a part of a larger group of elements; *fr. : volet de protection*
- torture (n.) : act of inflicting physical pain or subjecting a person to cruel or unusual punishment; *fr. : torture*

USEFUL EXPRESSIONS

- to be binding on a state; *fr. : s'appliquer à un État/lier un État*
- mandatory procedural guarantee; *fr. : garantie procédurale obligatoire*
- to prohibit discrimination; *fr. : interdire la discrimination*
- to be subject to torture; *fr. : être soumis à la torture*

FURTHER INFORMATION

- the word mandatory (*obligatoire*) refers to the nature of an act being compulsory and must not be confused with the French word *mandat* which means a term of office or a postal money order

Comparative approach

En France, même si le principe fondamental de l'égalité de droit devant la loi est garanti par les articles 1 et 6 de la Déclaration du 26 août 1789 et l'article 1 de la Constitution du 4 octobre 1958, elle accuse un retard face au Royaume-Uni qui s'est doté d'une instance spécialisée dans la poursuite des comportements discriminatoires dès 1919.

En France tous les citoyens peuvent saisir directement le Défenseur des droits qui est une autorité constitutionnelle indépendante chargée de veiller à la protection des droits et des libertés des individus. Inscrite dans la Constitution depuis le 23 juillet 2008 et instituée par la loi organique et la loi ordinaire du 29 mars 2011, elle regroupe diverses missions.

En ce qui concerne le champ d'application des comportements prohibés, la France reconnaît trois formes de discrimination : directe si l'inégalité se fonde sur un critère prohibé, indirecte lorsqu'une règle, une pratique ou un critère apparemment neutre a un effet défavorable sur un groupe visé par un critère de discrimination, ou sous la forme d'un harcèlement.

□ 60 HUMAN RIGHTS ISSUES AND DEBATES

Right to life

In the UK, the right to life is a basic civil and political right protected by Article 2 of the HRA. Though this right is guaranteed by law, it has often been subject to debate regarding its scope particularly at the beginning and the end of life. Even though the UK permits the termination of pregnancy with the Abortion Act 1967, pro-life advocates continue to demand an answer to the question of whether the unborn child falls under the category of "everyone" in the right to life. Euthanasia is also a subject of on-going discussion in the UK between the proponents and opponents of euthanasia debating on whether the act of deliberately ending a person's life to relieve suffering by active or passive euthanasia or assisted suicide is considered as illegal.

In *R (Debbie Purdy) v. Director of Public Prosecutions* [2009] UKHL 44, its last landmark decision before it became the Supreme Court in October 2009, the appellate committee of the House of Lords invited the Director of Public Prosecutions to prepare a policy document setting out the elements which would be taken into account when deciding whether someone should be prosecuted for assisted suicide. This document has not yet been released.

Right to strike

If the right to strike is embedded in the right to association provided for in Article 11 of the ECHR, UK law only recognises the existence of "trade disputes", thus limiting the grounds for action by excluding agency workers and outsourced employees. In the 1970s, the Conservative government under Margaret Thatcher crushed the power of the trade unions by outlawing mass picketing, enforcing a system of pre-strike ballots and requiring union leaders to be regularly re-elected to keep their posts. Thus, the right to strike does not exist and is a debatable issue, as the UK violates International Labor Organisation (ILO) standards by restricting strikes and other related activities like picketing, go-slows and work-to-rule.

Prisoners' right to vote

Since the 1870 Forfeiture Act, convicted prisoners in the UK have been banned from voting. Voting rights for prisoners has been a subject of debate in recent years as UK human rights law is not in line with the ECHR, which grants all individuals of voting age the right to vote regardless of their criminal status. The Representation of the People Act 1983 prohibits convicted prisoners from voting in parliamentary and local government elections. However, under the provisions of the Representation of the People Act 2000, an individual in jail on remand may still be entitled to vote.

In Hirst v UK 2005, the ECtHR held that the UK failed to comply with Article 3 of Protocol 1 of the ECHR. Pressure was put on the UK to fall in line with the rest of Europe on prisoners' voting rights. Since David Cameron's election in 2010 as head of the conservative-liberal coalition government, Britain has refused to grant convicted prisoners the right to vote.

The UK's restriction on prisoners only applies to those who are convicted and that once a convicted criminal is released from prison, he may resume voting. But the right to vote is also denied to those convicted of illegal election practices and to patients detained in psychiatric institutions due to the nature of the crimes committed.

GLOSSARY

- active (adj.) euthanasia (n.) : deliberate medical treatment to ensure the death of an individual suffering from a terminal illness; *fr. : euthanasie active*

- agency worker : individual employed by an employment agency, who possesses a contract of employment permitting him to be assigned to work for a person other than the employment agency; *fr. : travailleur intérimaire*
- assisted (adj.) suicide (n.) : termination of life with the help of a person who assists in giving effect to the suicide; *fr. : suicide assisté*
- civil (adj.) right (n.) : right that ensures the respect of a person in a civil society as in the case of the right to equality; *fr. : droit civil*
- ban (v. or n.) : forbid or prohibit by law; *fr. : interdire*
- crime-specific policy : procedure relating to a particular crime; *fr. : politique spécifique de criminalité*
- convicted (adj.) prisoner (n.) : person found guilty of a crime who is placed in lawful detention; *fr. : prisonnier condamné*
- debatable (adj.) issue (n.) : argument or discussion that is open to dispute and is questionable; *fr. : point discutable/point qui fait l'objet d'un débat*
- debate (v. or n.) : engage in a formal discussion or argument about opposing views; *fr. : débattre/débat*
- detain (v.) : keep an individual under custody or temporary confinement; *fr. : détenir*
- euthanasia (n.) : act of terminating the life of a person suffering from terminal illness through the administration of lethal injections or suspending medical treatment; *fr. : euthanasie*
- go-slow (n.) : protest that is shown through a deliberate reduction in the rate of production; *fr. : travail au ralenti*
- ground (n.) : condition that provides the basis or foundation for an argument; *fr. : motif*
- on-going (adj.) : currently taking place or underway; *fr. : en cours*
- outsourced (adj.) employee (n.) : workforce which is recruited from outside a company and which is contracted to a third party for work purposes and for a set period of time; *fr. : employé délégué/employé mis à disposition*
- passive (adj.) euthanasia (n.) : death of an individual suffering from terminal medical illness that is caused by medical professionals' decisions to stop life-supporting machines or discontinue life-extending drugs; *fr. : euthanasie passive*
- picketing (n.) : protest organised outside the workplace to try to persuade workers not to perform their tasks; *fr. : piquetage/piquet de grève*
- pregnancy (n.) : state of being pregnant that covers the period from conception to birth; *fr. : grossesse*
- pre-strike (adj.) ballot (n.) : vote for industrial action that takes place before a union takes action; *fr. : referendum avant grève*
- pro-life (adj.) advocate (n.) : person who believes in the right to life and opposes acts of euthanasia, abortion or assisted suicide; *fr. : personne qui soutient le droit la vie*
- procure (v.) : do an act in order to obtain something; *fr. : se procurer*

- political (adj.) right (n.) : right that assures everyone the opportunity to take part in the making of governmental public policy by giving him the right to participate; *fr. : droit politique*
- proponent (n.) : person in favour of something (as opposed to an opponent); *fr. : partisan*
- remand (v. or n.) : in a criminal context, to send the accused person back to custody; *fr. : placer en détention*
- strike (v.) : see 58
- trade dispute (n.) : disagreement between workers and employees pertaining to termination of services, unfair dismissals, dissatisfactory work conditions; *fr. : différend commercial*
- unborn (adj.) : not yet delivered from the mother's womb; *fr. : non-né/à naître*
- work-to-rule (n.) : act of doing the strictest minimum at work by following work regulations strictly (e.g. in the context of industrial action), thus severely disrupting normal operations; *fr. : grève du zèle*

USEFUL EXPRESSIONS

- a ban on euthanasia; *fr. : une interdiction de l'euthanasie*
- to ban the right to strike; *fr. : interdire le droit de grève*
- to guarantee the right to human dignity; *fr. : garantir le droit fundamental à la dignité humaine*

FURTHER INFORMATION

- the word ban (*interdire* or *interdiction*) must not be confused with the French word *ban* meaning a proclamation or wedding bans (before a wedding)
- the word pregnancy (*grossesse*) refers to the condition of being pregnant with a baby and must not be translated by the French word *prégnance* that refers to the significance of the state of mind or vitality

COMPARATIVE APPROACH

Outre-Manche, le droit ne reconnaît pas le droit de grève (*right to strike*) de manière explicite. Le salarié (*employee*) gréviste doit donc éventuellement faire face à toutes les sanctions de droit commun en raison de l'inexécution de son contrat de travail. Des immunités sont prévues par la loi mais uniquement si le mouvement répond à un certain nombre de critères.

En France, le droit de grève est un droit constitutionnel reconnu dans le préambule de la Constitution du 27 octobre 1946. Cependant, il ne fait pas l'objet d'une définition formelle. En conséquence, il n'existe aucune réglementation législative concernant l'étendue du droit de grève et les conditions régissant son exercice. L'article L. 521-1 du Code du travail protège le salarié gréviste de toute pénalité possible, sauf en cas de délit grave (*serious offence*). Le licenciement d'un employé en raison de sa participation en grève est nul et non avenu car il est considéré comme une simple suspension dans le contrat de travail.

À l'exception du Royaume-Uni, presque tous les pays d'Europe ont instauré un service minimum en cas de grève dans les services essentiels. En France, le service minimum s'applique depuis 2008 dans les transports en commun et les écoles. Un préavis de grève est donné dans un délai prévu par la loi pour permettre aux autorités d'organiser le service minimum.

S'agissant du droit de vote (*right to vote*), contrairement à son homologue britannique qui a toujours refusé de se plier aux exigences européennes, en France, le simple fait d'être détenu ne prive pas du droit de vote. Seuls ceux auxquels les tribunaux ont interdit le droit de vote et d'élection sont privés de leur capacité électorale pendant le délai fixé par le jugement (*court order*). En plus, l'incapacité électorale ne prend effet que lorsque la condamnation est définitive (*final conviction*), c'est-à-dire quand les voies de recours (appel et recours en cassation) sont épuisées ou quand les délais de recours sont expirés.

□ 61 IMMIGRATION RIGHTS

Right of abode

In the UK, the state has the power to decide who are its nationals, and uses its immigration law to prevent the entry and residence of non-nationals. The Immigration Control Act 1971 gave the right of abode in the UK to those it defined as "patrials", i.e. British citizens, British overseas citizens, British overseas territory citizens, British subjects, British nationals residing overseas and British protected persons. British nationality may be obtained by registration or naturalisation or by making an asylum claim.

Registration

Registration is an entitlement and those who are entitled to register are children of British citizens by descent, if either the child and both parents have lived in the country for three years prior to the date of the application or if the application is made for registration within twelve months of the child's birth, and providing at least one of the parents was a citizen otherwise than by descent. This provision limits the transmission of citizenship by descent to one generation by birth and a second generation by registration. The entitlement to registration carries a requirement of good character except in the case of children under ten.

Naturalisation

There is no entitlement to naturalisation. The Secretary of State (also known as the Home Secretary) exercises his discretionary power to decide who should be naturalised. Applicants must satisfy the following criteria : be of "full age and capacity", have completed the qualifying three-year period of residence, be of "good character", make a pledge of loyalty to the UK, and take the oath of allegiance to uphold the democratic values and fulfil the duties of a citizen. To obtain citizenship, the applicant has to show intention of making his future home in the UK.

Right to asylum

The right to asylum is possible only for asylum seekers residing in the UK. Three kinds of claims can be made to the UK Border Agency to support the right to asylum : "*sur place*" claim relating to the 1951 Geneva Convention, human rights claim as laid down in the ECHR, and asylum qualification claim as in the EU Qualification Directive. Once a claim is made, asylum seekers are protected from removal during the waiting period.

GLOSSARY

- abode (n.) : place of residence, home or dwelling place; *fr. : résidence/domicile*
- asylum (n.) : refuge offered to a person who has been extradited or deported by a foreign country; *fr. : asile*
- asylum qualification : common criteria that identify the characteristics for international protection of refugees; *fr. : ≈ qualification pour l'asile*
- British (adj.) citizen (n.) : individual born in the UK who has acquired British citizenship by birth on British soil; *fr. : citoyen britannique*
- British national residing overseas : individual who is entitled to nationality by connection with Hong Kong before it was passed back to China; *fr. : ressortissant britannique résidant à l'étranger*
- British (adj.) nationality (n.) : citizenship acquired by one of the six forms of nationality : British citizenship, British overseas citizenship, British overseas territory citizenship, British national overseas, British protected person and British subject; *fr. : nationalité britannique*
- British overseas citizen : individual who under the British Nationality Act 1983 qualifies for this citizenship if he did not automatically become a British citizen or a British overseas territories citizen before 1st January 1983; *fr. : citoyen britannique d'outre-mer*
- British overseas territory citizen : individual who was a UK and Colonies citizen before 1st January 1983 and who automatically became a British citizen due to his connection with a British overseas territory or through an ancestor; *fr. : citoyen d'un territoire britannique d'outre mer*

- British protected person : individual who is a former national of countries which did not form part of the British Empire, but which were under the protection of Britain; *fr. : citoyen d'un protectorat britannique*
- British (adj.) subject (n.) : individual who was a British subject and a citizen of Ireland prior to 1949 and who did not acquire another form of citizenship or who applied to remain as a British subject; *fr. : sujet britannique*
- citizenship (n.) : state of possessing rights, duties and privileges of a citizen; *fr. : citoyenneté*
- descent (n.) : state of originating from an ancestor that offers an individual the opportunity to claim lineage; *fr. : souche/origine*
- full (adj.) age (n.) : age of 18 when an individual can assume the rights and responsibilities of adults in society; *fr. : âge de la majorité*
- full (adj.) capacity (n.) : state of being *compos mentis*, of sound mind; *fr. : capacité*
- good (adj.) character (n.) : requirement for British nationality, whereby the applicant must show respect for the rights and freedoms of the UK, observe UK laws, and fulfil his duties and obligations as a resident; *fr. : intégrité/comportement du « bon père de famille »*
- human rights claim : claim made on the basis of the protected rights of the ECHR whereby it is possible for an asylum seeker to apply to remain in the UK if removing him constitutes a breach of his rights; *fr. : ≈ revendication pour faire valoir ses droits de l'homme*
- immigration law : branch of law that specifies the procedural requirements and regulations regarding entry of foreigners into the country; *fr. : loi sur l'immigration*
- national (n.) : individual belonging to a nation; *fr. : ressortissant*
- naturalisation (n.) : process whereby a foreign-born person is granted citizenship; *fr. : naturalisation*
- oath (of allegiance) (n.) : promise made by a citizen to stand loyal to a country; *fr. : serment (d'allégeance)*
- pledge (n.) : solemn, binding promise of loyalty; *fr. : vœu/engagement*
- registration (n.) : method of acquiring citizenship by filling in an application form if an individual satisfies all the requirements; *fr. : enregistrement*
- removal (n.) : process of deporting an asylum seeker; *fr. : mesure d'éloignement*
- residence (n.) : dwelling place or place of abode; *fr. : résidence*
- "*sur place*" claim : claim made by asylum seekers on the grounds of persecution or well-founded grounds of such persecution and the impossibility of finding asylum in another country as stipulated in the Geneva Convention relating to status of refugees (1951); *fr. : ≈ d'asile introduite « sur place »*
- transmission (n.) : act of passing on the right of citizenship to the next generation; *fr. : transmission*

- waiting (adj.) period (n.) : time span between the application and the decision granting asylum or not; *fr. : ≈ temps d'attente/délai de carence*

USEFUL EXPRESSIONS

- to seek asylum in the UK; *fr. : requérir le droit d'asile au Royaume-Uni*
- to grant/to refuse naturalisation; *fr. : accorder/refuser la naturalisation*
- to obtain British citizenship; *fr. : obtenir la citoyenneté britannique*
- to qualify for asylum; *fr. : remplir les conditions nécessaires pour obtenir l'asile*

FURTHER INFORMATION

- the word discretion (*discrétion*) refers to the power to decide and act and must not be confused with the quality of being discrete or the French word *discrétion* that refers to tact
- the word prior (*précédent*) meaning formerly must not be confused with the Latin words of *a priori* used frequently in French and which refer to deductive reasoning made earlier

COMPARATIVE APPROACH

À l'heure actuelle, le Royaume-Uni privilégie le droit du sol (*jus soli*), tandis que la France suit une politique de la nationalité basée sur une combinaison du droit du sang et de droit du sol (*jus sanguinis*).

Au Royaume-Uni, depuis le *British Nationality Act* 1981, le droit du sol est appliqué d'une façon conditionnelle. Il ne suffit pas d'être né sur le sol britannique pour acquérir la nationalité britannique. Pour un enfant né de parents étrangers, l'obtention de la nationalité britannique est soumise à la condition que les parents soient en possession d'un titre de séjour permanent.

En France, une loi du 26 juin 1889 réitère le principe du droit du sol apparu pendant l'Ancien Régime. Il permet l'intégration progressive des étrangers par la naturalisation. La loi du 19 octobre 1945 modifiée en 1973 autorise la transmission de la nationalité française par filiation ou par la naissance sur le sol français. La loi du 16 mars 1998 ajoute une condition nécessaire, celle de la « manifestation de volonté » : un enfant ayant obtenu la nationalité française ne devient citoyen français qu'à partir de 18 ans, âge d'acquisition du droit de vote, quand il exprime sa volonté d'acquérir la nationalité. Ce critère a été supprimé par la loi du 26 novembre 2003 qui a mis l'accent sur le besoin d'intégration des immigrés, en exigeant de leur part une connaissance suffisante de l'histoire et de la culture de la France, la signature d'une charte des droits et devoirs et le respect des principes de la République française.

11

Family law

□ 62 MARRIAGE AND COHABITATION

Heterosexual and same-sex couples can choose either to make their relationship official through marriage or simply to cohabit. The rights and duties of married and unmarried couples vary greatly. Civil partnerships still exist.

Marriage

Pursuant to the Marriage (Same-Sex Couples) Act 2013, the relationship of heterosexual or same-sex couples can be formalised through marriage. Marriage can be conducted either by a Superintendent Registrar for a civil ceremony in a register office, or a Church of England clergyman or any other religious representative. While the new legislation makes civil ceremonies lawful for same-sex couples, it creates no statutory obligation upon religious authorities which are free to conduct a religious ceremony for same-sex couples or not.

To be valid, the couple must give advanced notice of their marriage and their union must be recorded in the marriage register. A marriage certificate is issued after the celebration of the ceremony, hence providing evidence of the new marital status. When married, women can take their husband's name, create a double-barrelled surname or keep their maiden name. When getting married, spouses acquire rights but also have duties.

The husband has automatic parental responsibility towards any child(ren) born within wedlock. However, the Marriage Act (Same-Sex Couples) 2013 did not extend this presumption to lesbian couples. Married couples must share household expenses or provide for household allowance. They share everything, whether it be their inherited and matrimonial property or their assets (whether acquired prior to or during marriage) and liabilities (debts incurred prior to or during marriage). Before getting married, couples can enter into pre-nuptial contracts or sign post-nuptial contracts after marriage in order to protect a part of their property and assets in case of a marriage breakdown. Should a spouse die during marriage, the surviving spouse is entitled to a part or the whole of the deceased's estate.

Civil partnerships which were implemented in December 2005 (Civil Partnership Act 2004) allow exclusively same-sex couples to register a civil partnership and thereby acquire virtually the same rights and responsibilities as married couples. The new legislation on same-sex marriage enables the conversion of existing civil partnerships into marriage.

Cohabitation

Cohabitation is the alternative to marriage for those who do not wish to tie the knot. Cohabiting couples have fewer rights and almost no obligations towards their cohabitee. Financial support is not compulsory. If one cohabitant dies intestate, the other has no right to claim any inheritance. However, a cohabiting couple can sign a cohabitation contract to decide how their property should be distributed in the event of separation. In cases of domestic violence, cohabitants can apply for non-molestation orders and be protected the same way as married couples.

GLOSSARY

- assets (n.) : anything tangible or intangible (like real estate, cash, jewellery, shares, etc.) which can be controlled or owned and has or is likely to produce positive economic value; *fr. : actif*
- civil (adj.) partnership (n.) : before the Marriage (Same-Sex Couples) Act 2013, an alternative to marriage exclusively for same-sex couples which virtually grants them the same rights and duties as married couples; *fr. : ≈ pacte civil de solidarité/Pacs*
- civil (adj.) ceremony (n.) : non-religious marriage usually conducted by a Registrar; *fr. : mariage civil*
- cohabitation contract : legal document signed by cohabitants to provide for the redistribution of their property in case of separation; *fr. : convention signée entre concubins*
- cohabiting (adj.) couple (n.) (or cohabitees/cohabitants) (n.) : non-married couple living under the same roof who have fewer rights and duties than married couples or civil partners; *fr. : concubins*
- double-barrelled (adj.) surname (n.) : hyphenated last name when a wife joins her husband's surname and her maiden name; *fr. : nom composé*
- duty of household expenses : each spouse has a duty to support the other financially; *fr. : obligation de contribution aux charges du mariage*
- estate (n.) : here, all the deceased's assets and liabilities; the assets include property, possessions (shares, insurance policies, etc.) and money the deceased owned at the time of his death, and some gifts made up to seven years before he died; the liabilities include the deceased's debts; *fr. : patrimoine successoral*
- household (n.) : group of people living in the same accommodation; *fr. : foyer*
- household allowance : minimum financial support to run the matrimonial home, including food; *fr. : devoir de secours*

- inherited (adj.) property (n.) : here, property acquired by inheritance during the marriage; *fr. : ≈ biens de famille*
- intestate (adj.) : person who dies without drawing up a will; *fr. : ab intestat*
- liabilities (n.) : as opposed to assets what a legal entity owes, such as debts; *fr. : passif*
- marital (adj.) property (n.) : property acquired by the joint efforts of the parties during marriage; *fr. : biens communs du couple*
- marriage breakdown : see 127
- marriage certificate : legal document signed on the day of the ceremony, proving the marital status of the couple; *fr. : certificat de mariage*
- marriage register : official record of the ceremonies conducted by a Registrar; *fr. : ≈ registre de l'État civil (faisant état des mariages)*
- matrimonial (adj.) home (n.) : home occupied by spouses; *fr. : domicile conjugal*
- non-molestation order : in cases of domestic violence (harrasment or threat), judicial decision ordering the abuser not to molest the victim who is also the applicant; *fr. : ordonnance de protection*
- notice of marriage : form signed by both parties that has to be submitted to the Registrar eight weeks before marriage; *fr. : publication des bans*
- parental (adj.) responsibility (n.) : legal authority over a child; *fr. : autorité parentale*
- pre-nuptial (adj.) contract (n.)/pre-nups : private agreement entered into before marriage by two parties who wish to provide for the division of their assets in case of divorce; *fr. : ≈ contrat de mariage (antérieur)*
- post-nuptial (adj.) contract (n.) : private agreement entered into after marriage has taken place provided the two parties are still living together; *fr. : ≈ contrat de mariage (postérieur)*
- register office : local building approved by government where civil ceremonies are conducted; *fr. : service/bureau de l'état civil*
- Registrar of Marriages/Superintendent registrar : official representative working in the register office who can conduct civil marriage; *fr. : ≈ officier de l'état civil*
- religious (adj.) ceremony (n.) : religious marriage conducted by any representative of a religion; *fr. : mariage religieux*
- spouse (n.) : one of the parties in a marriage; *fr. : conjoint*
- wedlock (n.) : synonym for marriage; *fr. : mariage/liens du mariage*

USEFUL EXPRESSIONS

- to enter into a pre-nuptial/post-nuptial agreement; *fr. : signer un contrat de mariage*
- to give the bride away; *fr. : conduire la mariée à l'autel*

- to keep one's maiden name; *fr. : garder son nom de jeune fille*
- to list assets; *fr. : faire la liste des biens*
- to register a civil partnership; *fr. : ≈ signer un Pacs/se pacser*

FURTHER INFORMATION

- there is a difference between the meaning of marriage and wedding : marriage defines the legal relationship unlike wedding which refers to the ceremony
- "to get married" and "to marry" are not used the same way – while you can get married in church, you marry someone for life

COMPARATIVE APPROACH

En Angleterre et au Pays de Galles, le mariage civil n'est pas nécessairement obligatoire. Le mariage religieux anglican, juif et chez les Quakers est reconnu. Pour les autres groupes religieux, le mariage civil est obligatoire même si un mariage religieux est célébré. La polygamie reste interdite.

Contrairement à la France, le mariage Outre-Manche n'est pas soumis au système du régime matrimonial. La séparation de biens, la communauté réduite aux acquêts n'existent pas dans le droit de la famille anglais. Lorsqu'un couple se marie, tous les biens sont susceptibles d'être partagés par un juge en cas de divorce, autant ceux acquis avant et pendant le mariage, que ceux dont l'un des conjoints a personnellement hérité ou peut hériter à l'avenir. L'absence d'une codification du mariage encourage certains couples à signer un contrat prénuptial qui prévoit le partage des biens en cas de séparation. Ce type de contrat n'est pas à proprement parler l'équivalent du contrat de mariage français dans la mesure où le contrat pré-nuptial peut être rédigé comme n'importe quel contrat. Toutefois, la garde des enfants ne rentre pas en ligne de compte, et demeure le domaine réservé du juge si les parents ne parviennent pas à trouver un accord.

Le mariage homosexuel est maintenant reconnu dans les deux pays.

□ 63 CHILDREN AND PARENTS

Family law has recently had to cope with a wide range of new situations, including the development of assisted reproductive techniques and the recognition of same-sex couples' rights to adopt. Family can be defined in many ways depending on the situation. From the nuclear family to kinship, and stepfamilies, this term refers to a wide range of relationships – including the in-laws – that evolve throughout a person's lifetime.

Parental responsibility

Genetic parenthood does not automatically imply parental responsibility in law as parents raising a child do not always share his DNA. Although the common law defines legal parenthood by genetic parentage, the Human Fertilisation and Embryology Act 2008 prescribes that the person who gives birth to the child is the child's legal mother. Ever since then, a distinction has been drawn between genetic and gestational motherhood. This distinction can give rise to legal issues in surrogacy cases as the surrogate mother who has no genetic link to the child, is considered as the legal mother of the child since she carries it and gives birth to it. A child can also be brought up by adoptive parents or a guardian.

Surrogacy

Surrogacy is legal in England and Wales. Usually, a commissioning couple strikes a surrogacy arrangement with a surrogate mother who agrees to carry their genetic child and give birth to it. The couple does not have the right to pay the surrogate mother, but has to meet the expenses incurred by the pregnancy. On the day of birth, the surrogate mother gives up the child for adoption so that the genetic mother's name can be added to the birth certificate next to the father's. Since the arrangement is not binding on the parties, the surrogate mother has the right to refuse to give up the child for adoption and keep him. The commissioning couple has then to make a claim in court, applying for a parental order and as well as a residence order.

Adoption

Adoption is open to anyone over 21, whether they be a single person, a couple, or two people of different or the same sex. Still, pursuant to international conventions, the consent of the biological parents is always required for the adoptive parents – the adopters – to become the legal parents of the adopted child – the adoptee. Before the adoption order is issued by a judge, the child can stay with foster parents.

GLOSSARY

- adopt (v.) : transfer the legal rights of biological parents in respect of their biological child(ren) to another person/couple; *fr. : adopter*
- adoptee (n.) : adopted child; *fr. enfant adopté*
- adopter (n.) : person adopting the child; *fr. adoptant*
- adoption (n.) : when a person acquires the legal rights of biological parents; *fr. : adoption (simple* or *plénière)*
- assisted (adj.) reproduction (n.) : medical technique enabling parents with low fertility to conceive a child; *fr. : procréation médicalement assistée (PMA)*

- binding (adj.) : here, agreement creating obligations on the parties; *fr. : à caractère obligatoire/qui lie*
- birth certificate : official document stating the name, date and place of birth of the child as well as his parents' details; *fr. : certificat de naissance*
- foster parents : parents who do not have parental responsibility and are only able to provide day-to-day care to the child before his/her adoption; *fr. : famille d'accueil*
- genetic (adj.) mother (n.) : mother who has genetic link with the child through her fertilised egg; *fr. : mère génitrice*
- genetic (adj.) parentage (n.) : link which is genetically determined between the parents and the child; *fr. : filiation par procréation charnelle*
- gestational (adj.) mother (n.) : person who gives birth to the child; *fr. : mère gestatrice*
- guardian (n.) : person who is given legal responsibility for a child by a judge when the child's parents are both deceased or when the legal responsibility of the parent(s) has been suspended; *fr. : tuteur*
- in-laws (n.) : family of the other party to a marriage or a civil partnership; *fr. : belle famille*
- kinship (n.) : larger family group where members are related by blood or marriage; *fr. : liens de parenté*
- nuclear (adj.) family (n.) : family unit composed of parents and their dependent children; *fr. : noyau familial*
- parentage (n.) : lineage, origin of a child; *fr. : filiation*
- parental (adj.) responsibility (n.) : legal authority over a child, including rights and duties, and powers; *fr. : autorité parentale*
- parental (adj.) order (n.) : in surrogacy cases, court decision extinguishing the surrogate mother's parental rights to transfer parental responsibility to the commissioning couple; *fr. : ordonnance de transfert de l'autorité parentale*
- parenthood (n.) : state of being a parent; *fr. : parentalité*
- residence order : order which defines who will be the primary carer of the child and where he will live; *fr. : ordonnance désignant la résidence habituelle de l'enfant*
- stepfamily (n.) : family where the child lives with one of his genetic parents and his new wife or husband (stepmother or stepfather), and the step-parent's child(ren) who become(s) his/her stepbrother(s) or stepsister(s); *fr. : ≈ famille recomposée*
- surrogacy (n.) : situation in which a woman carries a baby for a low-fertlity couple; *fr. : gestation pour autrui (GPA)*
- surrogacy arrangement : agreement struck between the surrogate mother and the genetic couple; *fr. : ≈ accord pour une GPA*
- surrogate (adj.) mother (n.) : woman who carries a child for another couple and who has no genetic link with the child; *fr. : mère porteuse*

USEFUL EXPRESSIONS

- genetic engineering; *fr. : manipulation génétique*
- to give parental responsibility; *fr. : accorder l'autorité parentale*
- to issue an adoption order; *fr. : délivrer une ordonnance d'adoption*
- next of kin; *fr. : famille*
- to have siblings; *fr. : avoir des frères et sœurs*
- sperm donor; *fr. : donneur de sperme*

FURTHER INFORMATION

- stepfamily/in-laws : unlike French, which uses the same generic term (*belle famille*), English draws a distinction between the family of one's spouse (the in-laws), and the family of a new wife or husband who has married one of the child's parents (the stepfamily); the legal consequences are different since a stepmother may be given parental responsibility over the child while a mother-in law can have some contact rights over a child born within her son/daughter's marriage
- mother/father-in-law : the mother and the father of the other party within a marriage or a civil partnership; *fr. belle-mère/beau-père*
- stepbrother/stepsister (n.) : the child(ren) of the step-parent; *fr. : demi-frère/ demi-sœur*
- stepmother/stepfather (or step-parent) : person who marries the mother or the father of a child; *fr. belle-mère/beau-père*

COMPARATIVE APPROACH

Contrairement à la France, la gestation pour autrui (GPA) (*surrogacy*) est autorisée en Angleterre et au Pays de Galles. Les mères porteuses (*surrogate mothers*) n'ont pas le droit de percevoir d'indemnisation financière, mais le couple doit suppléer aux dépenses occasionnées lors de la grossesse dans une limite raisonnable. Au regard de la loi, seule la mère gestatrice, c'est-à-dire celle qui porte et donne naissance à l'enfant, est la mère de l'enfant. Si le père géniteur est lui aussi reconnu comme le père de l'enfant, la mère porteuse doit renoncer à ses droits le jour de la naissance afin que la mère génétique ait la possibilité d'adopter l'enfant. Ce genre de procédure peut parfois créer des situations conflictuelles si la mère porteuse refuse de donner l'enfant qu'elle a porté, mais qui ne partage pas nécessairement son patrimoine génétique. Etant donné que la loi ne reconnaît pas l'accord passé entre une mère porteuse et les futurs parents, il ne peut être pris en compte par une juridiction et un juge aux affaires familiales tranchera un éventuel litige en tenant compte de l'intérêt supérieur de l'enfant.

Outre-Manche, les couples homosexuels ont également le droit d'avoir recours à la GPA et d'adopter des enfants. En France, la GPA est interdite, mais les couples homosexuels ont le droit d'adopter des enfants depuis la loi sur le mariage pour tous de 2013.

12

Probate/inheritance law

□ 64 WHAT IS INHERITANCE LAW ?

Upon someone's death, his estate will be dealt with by a personal representative (PR) who will be either an executor (if a will was drawn up) or an administrator (if no will was made). It is not compulsory to make a will. A person who does not have a will dies intestate. The PR's duty is to determine the contents of the estate, identify the assets and liabilities, find out who the heirs and beneficiaries are, settle the deceased's debts and distribute the residue of the estate between the heirs and other beneficiaries.

Intestacy

If no will was ever made, the estate is distributed to the "next of kin" according to certain statutory rules. If the deceased had a surviving spouse but no children, parents, siblings and their children, the spouse inherits everything. If there are children, the spouse gets the personal chattels, £250 000 and a life interest in half the remainder. The children get the other half immediately, but wait until the death of the other parent to get the other half.

If there is no surviving spouse but the deceased left children, they share the estate equally. If there is no surviving spouse or children, the estate is distributed amongst the relatives. The priority order is as follows : parents, siblings or their children, grandparents, uncles/aunts or their children and the Crown.

Drawing up a will

A will is a way for someone to anticipate and organise how his estate will be distributed upon his demise. A will is drawn up by a person over eighteen who is *compos mentis*. It is possible to draw up one's own will or to have it drawn up by a solicitor. A handwritten will is called a holographic will. All wills should be signed in the presence of two witnesses. For evidential reasons, a will should be dated. Although a will can be kept at home, a copy is usually filed with the principal registry of the family division of the High Court, a district registry or probate sub-registry as evidence of its existence and date. Should the testator decide to amend his will, he must first revoke the first will through a codicil.

In his will, the testator must appoint an executor who will administer his will after his death. He has a lot of leeway and can give anyone (surviving spouse, children, other family member or even a third party such as a charity) a life interest in a property, the bare ownership of a property or the property itself, in whole or part. He can also make a pecuniary legacy. Sometimes, a gift with reservation of benefit is made in the deceased's lifetime.

English law makes it possible to disinherit one's children but this is not possible as against the surviving spouse. Unreasonable clauses or those contrary to public order or good morals are forbidden in wills. Likewise, if the testator indicates clearly who inherits his personal effects such as jewellery, they cannot be used by the estate to pay off debts or inheritance tax.

GLOSSARY

- assets (n.) : valuable property that a legal entity owns, uses or benefits from; *fr. : actif*
- bare (adj.) ownership (n.) : owning a property without having the right to use it, the right vesting with someone who has a beneficial or life interest in the property; *fr. : nue-propriété*
- beneficiary (n.) : here, individual receiving money and/or possessions from the deceased; *fr. : bénéficiaire*
- chattels (n.) : personal belongings or objects of the deceased; *fr. : biens meubles* (as opposed to *immeubles* or immovables)
- codicil (n.) : alterations to the provisions of a will, usually made by a solicitor; *fr. : codicille*
- *compos mentis* : of sound mind; *fr. : sain d'esprit*
- deceased (n. or adj.) : dead person; *fr. : défunt*
- demise (n.) : death, fact of disappearing; *fr. : mort/disparition*
- disinherit (v.) : act of not bequeathing property or money to a potential heir, of depriving him of the deceased's estate; *fr. : déshériter*
- estate (n.) : here, all the deceased's assets and liabilities; the assets include property, possessions (shares, insurance policies, etc.) and money the deceased owned at the time of his death, and some gifts made up to seven years before he died; the liabilities include the deceased's debts; *fr. : patrimoine successoral*
- executor (n.)/executrix (n.) : person chosen in the will to manage the estate and take care of the person's wishes after his death; he may be a solicitor, a friend, a relative, a bank or the Public Trustee in England and Wales; *fr. : exécuteur/exécutrice testamentaire*
- gift (n.) with reservation of benefit (n.) : property you give to someone in your lifetime; the person is no longer the owner, but has the right to live in it until he dies; *fr. : ≈ donation de son vivant avec réserve du bénéfice*
- heir (n.) : individual who is entitled to inherit from a deceased person; he can be the surviving spouse, children, brothers and sisters, uncles and aunts, friends or even third parties (e.g. a charitable organisation); *fr. : héritier*

- holographic (adj.) will (n.) : handwritten document in which the testator expresses his last wishes as to how his estate should be disposed of after his death; *fr. : testament olographe*
- inherit (v.) : receive a part or the whole of a deceased's assets; *fr. : hériter*
- inheritance law : laws regulating the distribution of the deceased's assets; *fr. : droit des successions*
- intestate (adj.) : person who dies without drawing up a will; *fr. : ab intestat*
- liabilities (n.) : unlike assests, the money that one individual owes, such as debts; *fr. : passif*
- life interest (in a property) : here, fact of occupying a property until one's death without even having the bare ownership of it; *fr. : droit d'usufruit*
- next of kin : person or persons most closely related by blood to another person; *fr. : membres de la famille proche*
- pecuniary (adj.) legacy (n.) : monetary gift made in a will; *fr. : ≈ don d'argent par voie testamentaire*
- personal (adj.) representative (n.) (PR) : individual acting on behalf of the deceased to administer his will; he pays off the debts from the deceased's estate and distributes the residue to the beneficiaries according to the deceased's wishes; *fr. : ≈ exécuteur testamentaire/liquidateur de la succession*
- Principal Registry of the Family Division of the High Court : official place where wills can be filed for keeping and evidence purposes; *fr. : ≈ Fichier central des dispositions de dernières volontés (FCDDV)*
- residue (n.) : what is left once the debts and inheritance taxes have been paid off and the assets are distributed according to the deceased's will; *fr. : ≈ quotité disponible*
- revoke (v.) : here, fact of cancelling the effects of a will; *fr. : révoquer (un testament)*
- settle (v.) : here, effect payment; *fr. : s'acquitter de/payer*
- siblings (n.) : people having one or both parents in common; *fr. : frères et sœurs* (including *demi-frères et demi-sœurs*)
- surviving (adj.) spouse (n.) : husband or wife who becomes a widower or widow on his/her spouse's death; *fr. : conjoint survivant*
- testator (n.) : individual drawing up a will; *fr. : testateur*

USEFUL EXPRESSIONS

- bequest (n. or v.); *fr. : legs*
- to draw up a will; *fr. : rédiger un testament*
- to die intestate; *fr. : mourir ab intestat*
- to receive a bequest; *fr. : recevoir une part d'héritage/un legs*
- to give one's surviving spouse a life interest in a property; *fr. : donner à son conjoint survivant un droit d'usufruit sur une propriété*

FURTHER INFORMATION

- in English, testament has a broader meaning than the term will; in the context of probate, will refers to the legal document drawn up by an individual; testament can have a figurative meaning in a historical commentary for instance; it also refers to the divisions of the Bible where capitalised
- the "h" in the word heir is not pronounced (it is mute) to avoid any confusion with the term hair (*cheveux*); the article "an" is also used before heir

COMPARATIVE APPROACH

Si les règles régissant la rédaction d'un testament sont similaires en France et Outre-Manche, les règles de transmission sont différentes. Outre-Manche, il est possible de déshériter ses enfants au profit d'un tiers, tel qu'un organisme caritatif (*charity*). Le concept d'héritier réservataire (≈ *heir with automatic claim on part of the deceased's estate*) n'existe donc pas en droit anglais. Par voie de conséquence, la notion de pacte successoral (≈ *agreement as to succession*) *stricto sensu* non plus. En France, les héritiers réservataires ont automatiquement droit à la quotité disponible (≈ *disposable part of the estate*), sauf en cas d'ingratitude (consacrée par l'article 955 du Code civil) ou autre cause d'indignité successorale.

Si les successions *ab intestat* (*intestacy*) existent des deux côtés de la Manche, les règles de transmission divergent également même si en France, une loi n° 2001-1135 du 3 décembre 2001 a nettement amélioré la situation du conjoint survivant (*surviving spouse*) en France.

□ 65 ADMINISTERING AN ESTATE

When an individual dies, his estate must be administered or in other words, wound up. His debts must be settled and his assets distributed amongst the beneficiaries. This process is called probate. If the deceased died intestate, the process is undertaken by an administrator who is usually a close relative of the deceased (the order of priority to act as administrator is as follows : surviving spouse or civil partner, the children, parents, siblings, grandparents and uncles/aunts). If the deceased made a will, an executor, appointed in the will, is in charge.

In order to deal with the estate, the administrator or executor respectively need to make an application to the probate registry for the grant of letters of administration or grant of probate. The administrator/executor can then identify all the liabilities and assets. Liabilities (inheritance tax, probate fees and other debts) must be paid first. Whatever remains is used to distribute the residue to the beneficiaries under the will or according to the law in case of intestacy.

A beneficiary (whether the deceased died intestate or not) can disclaim inheritance. Alternatively he can apply for a deed of variation if he does not want to receive all the property or money that was left to him.

When the liabilities have been paid and the assets distributed, the administrator/executor must prepare the estate accounts which he signs with the beneficiaries. The probate process is then over.

GLOSSARY

- administrator (n.) : individual, usually the next of kin, who is in charge of administering the estate of the deceased when the latter left no will or when his will is not valid; *fr. : ≈ administrateur/liquidateur de la succession*
- deed of variation : alteration to the will made by the beneficiary who does not wish to receive part of the assets the deceased left him; *fr. : ≈ renonciation partielle à une succession*
- disclaim (v.) : when applied to inheritance, fact of refusing the provisions of a will; *fr. : renoncer (à la succession)*
- disposal of assets : distribution of the deceased's estate; *fr. : partage des biens de la succession*
- estate (n.) : here, the deceased's property, goods, and money after deducting liabilities; *fr. : ≈ patrimoine de la succession*
- estate accounts : legal document indicating that the assets have been duly distributed and the liabilities have been paid; *fr. : ≈ comptes de succession*
- grant (n.) : here, document issued by the probate registry of the High Court which names the deceased's personal representative and gives him power to deal with the deceased's estate; there are two types of grant : grant of letters of administration when the deceased died intestate (appointing an administrator) and grant of probate when a will was drawn up (confirming the appointment of an executor); *fr. : ≈ acte d'homologation/acte de notoriété*
- inherit (v.) : receive property and/or goods after an individual's death; *fr. : hériter*
- inheritance (n.) : property, money or goods received by an individual after someone's death; *fr. : héritage*
- inheritance tax : money that has to be paid to Her Majesty's Revenue and Customs (HMRC) before the distribution of the deceased's estate; *fr. : droits de succession*
- intestate (adv.) : someone who has left no will or whose will is not valid; *fr. : ab intestat*
- probate (n.) : legal document allowing the executor to distribute the estate of the deceased according to his wishes; *fr. : ≈ action successorale*
- wind up (v.) : here, administer someone's estate by paying the deceased's liabilities and distributing any remaining assets; *fr. : liquider (la succession)*

USEFUL EXPRESSIONS

- legacy; *fr. : héritage*
- to levy a tax; *fr. : prélever un impôt*
- to outlive someone; *fr. : survivre à quelqu'un*
- to receive a bequest; *fr. : recevoir un héritage*
- to approve the estate accounts; *fr. : approuver les comptes de succession*

FURTHER INFORMATION

- in England, the phrase "law of succession" is seldom used to refer to the French *droit des successions*, but is often used for the Royal family

COMPARATIVE APPROACH

Outre-Manche, le patrimoine successoral du défunt (*deceased's estate*) sert en priorité à payer les droits de succession (*inheritance tax*), les frais y afférant et les dettes du défunt. Le passif non apuré (pour le cas où l'actif serait insuffisant) meurt avec le défunt et n'est donc pas transmis aux héritiers.

En revanche, en France, nombreux sont ceux qui, ayant accepté une succession purement et simplement, se retrouvent contraints d'acquitter les dettes du défunt sur leur patrimoine personnel et donc, au-delà de ce qu'ils ont pu recevoir au titre de la succession. Cela explique pourquoi le droit français a mis en place la procédure d'acceptation d'une succession à concurrence de l'actif net.

13

Property law

☐ 66 INTRODUCTION

Real property includes land and the physical things either attached to it (buildings, etc.) or found beneath its surface (minerals, etc.). These are known as corporeal hereditaments, because they are tangible things and can be passed on to one's heirs. However, real property also encompasses intangible things, or incorporeal hereditaments, such as a right of way over neighbouring land (easement) or the right to exploit the resources of another's land in a certain way (*profits à prendre*).

Legal and equitable interests

Proprietary interests can exist both at law and in equity. A right of way over land may, for example, exist as a legal easement; but where the legal formalities for creating such a legal interest have not been followed, it may still be recognised as an equitable easement giving rise to certain rights and obligations. This classification of interests as legal or equitable will affect the remedies available to redress any infringement of a party's rights.

Registration

Modern land law has, through the progressive implementation of the Land Registration Acts (1925 and 2002), increasingly moved towards a system of entering title to land in a centralised register called the land register. The aim is to simplify conveyancing and make the process of establishing title to land more transparent. The improvement brought by the Land Registration Act 2002 is to leave the door open to the electronic signing of all property transfers in the near future.

GLOSSARY

- conveyancing (n.) : transfer of legal title of property from one legal entity to another; *fr. : transfert de propriété*
- corporeal (adj.) hereditament (n.) : permanent object (like coal) which is tangible and confined to the land; *fr. : patrimoine foncier corporel/immeuble par nature*

- easement (n.) : see 67
- heir (n.) : person entitled to inherit the property of a deceased person; *fr. : héritier*
- hereditament (n.) : proprietary interests, whether in corporeal or incorporeal form, capable of being inherited; *fr. : patrimoine foncier/bien immobilier (susceptible de transfert dans le cadre d'une succession)*
- incorporeal (adj.) hereditament (n.) : intangible proprietary interests, such as a right of way or other easement; *fr. : patrimoine foncier incorporel/immeubles par l'objet auquel ils s'appliquent*
- land (n.) : those parts of the earth's surface, including the airspace above and subsoil below, that are subject to legal ownership; *fr. : terre*
- land register : here, the central register used to record title to land in England and Wales; information such as property ownership, property boundaries and registration of property (which may change in case of transfer, death or divorce) appears in the register; *fr. : registre du cadastre*
- own (v.)/ownership (n.) : possess something as proprietor or owner; the state of having a legal right of possession; *fr. : ≈ posséder (v.)/droit de propriété (n.)*
- *profits à prendre* : see 67
- property (n.) : anything capable of being owned; may be classified as either real property (land and other hereditaments) or personal property (all other types of property); *fr. : biens/propriété*
- proprietary (adj.) rights (n.) : here, rights concerning the use, occupation or ownership of land; *fr. : droits de propriété*
- real (adj.) property (n.) : land and incorporeal hereditaments; *fr. : biens immobiliers/immeubles*
- registered (adj.) owner (n.) : when applied to land, legal entity registered as having the freehold title to land; *fr. : propriétaire inscrit au cadastre*
- title to land : legal entity's right of ownership of land; *fr. : titre de propriété*

USEFUL EXPRESSIONS

- to dispose of real property; *fr. : aliéner des biens immobiliers*
- to establish one's title; *fr. : faire la preuve de son droit*
- to establish ownership of a property; *fr. : faire établir un droit de propriété*

FURTHER INFORMATION

- the verb "to own" has a wider meaning in English than mere possession (one may possess something without necessarily owning it)
- conversely, the English noun "proprietor" is more restricted in scope than the French *propriétaire*; it would not normally be used to refer to the owner of things such as cars or animals

COMPARATIVE APPROACH

Le droit français fait une distinction entre les meubles (*movables*) et les immeubles (*immovables*). En vertu de l'article 517 du Code civil, les biens sont immeubles par leur nature, leur destination ou l'objet auquel ils s'appliquent. Les « immeubles par nature » correspondent aux *corporeal hereditaments*. Les « immeubles par l'objet auquel ils s'appliquent » et plus particulièrement les droits réels immobiliers s'apparentent aux *incorporeal hereditaments*. En revanche, il n'est pas aisé de trouver un point de comparaison aux « immeubles par destination ».

En ce qui concerne le droit en Angleterre et au Pays de Galles, la distinction en *common law* entre un intérêt *legal* et un intérêt *equitable* ajoute considérablement à la complexité du droit foncier et ne trouve pas d'équivalent en droit français.

□ 67 LEGAL INTERESTS IN LAND

The Crown is the ultimate owner of all land in England and Wales. This means that when someone buys land (or real property), he acquires an estate in the land rather than absolute ownership. There are two principal types of legal estate in land : freehold and leasehold.

Estates in land

Freehold estate is the expression commonly used to refer to an estate in fee simple absolute in possession. When we say that someone "owns" land, we are really saying that he has an estate in fee simple. The term fee simple means the land can be inherited by anyone, and such estates normally last for an unlimited period of time. A leasehold estate is sometimes referred to as a term of years absolute, referring to the fact that the estate lasts for a limited period of time. The term of the lease can be for as long as the owner agrees to, though 99-year leases are commonly used as a matter of historical convention. It is rare to find long-term leases exceeding 999 years, though in theory there is nothing to prevent this. If the owner of a property (the landlord) leases it to a tenant, the tenant will enjoy certain legal rights to possession and use of the land as a result of the leasehold estate.

It should be noted that a third type of legal estate in land, known as commonhold, has been introduced by recent legislation. In a block of flats, for example, certain areas such as lifts or stairwells may be owned and managed by an association, whose legal right to control those areas arises from its commonhold estate. This form of estate is, however, of relatively limited significance in practice.

Legal interests in land

As well as estates in land, English law recognises legal interests in land. In modern property law, these legal interests are confined to mortgages and easements. Any other interest in land will exist in equity rather than at law. A mortgage is created as a form of security for a loan. The lender, or mortgagee, acquires a proprietary interest in land purchased by the mortgagor with the loan monies. This proprietary interest terminates once the loan is repaid. The most common example is the case of a home buyer who takes out a mortgage with his bank.

An easement refers to a right enjoyed by a land owner to benefit in some way from a neighbour's land. The most common example is where a landowner has a right of way through an adjoining property. The categories of easements are not closed, however, and may include a wide variety of beneficial interests. The dominant tenement is the land which benefits from the easement, while the other property is referred to as the servient tenement. Closely related to the concept of easements is *profits à prendre*. This interest, which may exist both in law and equity, consists in the right to take resources or produce from another's land, or to use it for grazing animals.

GLOSSARY

- commonhold estate : way of owning land, introduced by the Commonhold and Leasehold Reform Act 2002, allowing the common areas of certain developments (e.g., an apartment block) to be owned by a commonhold association; *fr. : ≈ parties communes* (as opposed to *parties privatives)*
- dominant (adj.) tenement (n.) : land which has the benefit of an easement over adjoining property (the servient tenement); *fr. : fonds dominant*
- easement (n.) : right enjoyed by a landowner to benefit from neighbouring land; *fr. : servitude*
- estate (n.) : here, period of time for which a person's tenure in land lasts; indefinite tenure is called an estate in fee simple (or freehold), whereas tenure for a limited duration is a term of years absolute (or leasehold); *fr. : ≈ droit réel foncier*
- fee simple absolute in possession : legal estate conferring indefinite tenure in land; more commonly known as the freehold estate, it is the most complete form of ownership possible; *fr. : ≈ bien immobilier tenu en propriété perpétuelle*
- freehold (adj.) estate (n.) : common name for estate of fee simple absolute in possession; *fr. : ≈ bien immobilier tenu en propriété perpétuelle*
- lease (n.) : contract granting one person (the tenant or lessee) exclusive possession of property owned by another (the landlord) for an agreed period; *fr. : bail*
- leasehold estate : common name for term of years absolute; *fr. : ≈ tenure à bail*
- lessee (n.) : person to whom a lease is granted; also known as a tenant; *fr. : locataire*
- lessor (n.) : person who grants a lease; also known as a landlord; *fr. : bailleur*

- mortgage (n. and v.) : type of interest in property conveyed to a lender (the mortgagee) as security for a loan by the owner (the mortgagor); the mortgagee's proprietary interest terminates once the loan is repaid; *fr. : hypothèque/hypothéquer*
- mortgagee (n.) : lender of money under a mortgage; *fr. : créancier hypothécaire*
- mortgagor (n.) : borrower who offers land as security for a loan; *fr. : débiteur hypothécaire*
- *profits à prendre* : right to take resources or produce from another's land, or use it to graze livestock; *fr. : profits à prendre*
- right of way : right to pass through another's land, whether by way of a public right, an easement or a licence; *fr. : servitude de passage*
- servient (adj.) tenement (n.) : land that is subject to an easement or some other encumbrance that benefits other land; *fr. : fonds servant*
- title to land : see 66
- tenancy (n.) : landholder's interest; more commonly used in restricted sense as a synonym for leasehold; *fr. : location*
- tenant (n.) : lessee; *fr. : locataire*
- tenement (n.) : piece of land owned by a legal entity; *fr. : ≈ parcelle/≈ fonds*
- term of years absolute : legal estate conferring tenure in land for a limited period by way of a lease; more commonly known as a leasehold estate; *fr. : ≈ tenure à bail*

USEFUL EXPRESSIONS

- the acquisition of freehold title; *fr. : acquisition de titres de pleine propriété*
- to take out a mortgage; *fr. : souscrire une hypothèque*
- to pay off a mortgage; *fr. : purger une hypothèque*

FURTHER INFORMATION

- the word estate is commonly used to refer to a large house in the country surrounded by an extensive landholding, of the kind owned by aristocratic families; a housing estate, on the other hand, refers to an area of subsidised housing or collection of council flats

COMPARATIVE APPROACH

Contrairement à l'idée du *Crown estate* de la *common law*, le droit de la propriété en France est, au moins en principe, un droit absolu (*absolute right*), même s'il peut être restreint en cas d'expropriation pour cause d'utilité publique. En pratique, en Angleterre et au Pays de Galles, il est difficile de distinguer la notion de *freehold estate* de celle de propriété absolue.

La notion de *leasehold estate* Outre-Manche crée un droit de propriété alors qu'en droit français, les baux relèvent du domaine du contrat.

□ 68 EQUITABLE INTERESTS IN LAND

Any proprietary right that is neither an estate nor a legal interest (i.e. a legal easement or mortgage) will exist as an equitable interest in land. It is possible, for example, to have an equitable mortgage or an equitable easement. Often these equitable interests will arise where certain formalities in the creation of proprietary rights have not been followed, but the courts will recognise the right in order to prevent unfairness or injustice. It should be noted that the range of equitable interests in land is large and various, and it is beyond the scope of this work to attempt an exhaustive overview of the subject.

Trusts of land

A trust is an arrangement whereby a person settles property to one or more trustees, who hold the property for the benefit of another person (the beneficiary). Historically, strict settlements were used to create a series of beneficial interests in favour of a succession of persons, often for the purpose of keeping the property interests of wealthy or aristocratic families intact. While strict settlements still continue in force, settlements of land today will always take effect as trusts of land. This means the legal estate will be vested in the trustees of land, who have broad powers to deal with the land in a manner consistent with the interests of the beneficiaries.

Licences

A licence is a permission to enter upon or to use land for an agreed purpose. Although a licence affects rights in the use of land, strictly speaking it is a personal arrangement between a licensor and a licensee rather than a proprietary interest. At its most simple, a bare licence is an express or implied permission to enter someone's property (i.e. it protects the licensee from claims in trespass). Where the grant of a licence is given for consideration a contractual licence will arise. Although licences will generally not bind third parties, there are some circumstances where equity will intervene to protect the interests of a licensee.

GLOSSARY

- bare (adj.) licence (n.) : permission, freely given, to enter or use land for a specific purpose; *fr. : ≈ autorisation inconditionnelle*
- beneficiary (n.) : legal entity who benefits from something; *fr. : bénéficiaire*

- contractual (adj.) licence (n.) : authorisation granted in exchange for something of value; such a licence cannot be freely revoked during the period agreed upon by the parties; *fr. : autorisation contractuelle*
- co-ownership (n.) : see 135
- equitable interest in land : beneficial interest in property existing in equity rather than at law; the beneficiaries of a trust in land have an equitable interest in the land which can be enforced against other parties, including the legal owner of such land (the trustee); *fr. : ≈ intérêt en équité dans la propriété*
- legal (adj.) estate (n.) : right of ownership at common law; *fr. : ≈ propriété*
- legal (adj.) title (n.) : legal right to ownership of property; *fr. : titre*
- licence (n.) : personal arrangement whereby a landowner (licensor) grants another person permission to enter the land, or to use it for an agreed purpose; *fr. : autorisation*
- strict (adj.) settlement (n.) : trust conferring successive beneficial interests in land; historically used to keep land within a settlor's family, such settlements now exist as trusts of land; *fr. : ≈ arrangements patrimoniaux*
- trustee (n.) : entity with nominal title to property held in trust for the benefit of another (the beneficiary); *fr. : ≈ fidéicommissaire/≈ administrateur d'un trust*
- trust of land : arrangement imposed by statute whereby land owned by more than one person, or by a number of persons in succession, is held under a trust; a trust of land would be imposed, for example, on property owned jointly by a husband and wife (who would often be both trustees and beneficiaries of the trust of land); *fr. : trust foncier/≈ propriété détenue en fiducie*

USEFUL EXPRESSIONS

- to hold property in trust for one's children; *fr. : tenir des biens par fidéicommis à l'intention de ses enfants*
- to grant a licence to enter land; *fr. : accorder une permission de passer par un terrain*

FURTHER INFORMATION

- care should be taken not to confuse the concept of a settlement in land law with the idea of a settlement in litigation (whereby parties agree to settle a matter outside of court)

COMPARATIVE APPROACH

Le développement considérable des principes d'*equity* en Angleterre et au Pays de Galles ne connaît pas d'équivalent en France, où les juges donnent priorité à l'application des codes en vigueur par rapport à la jurisprudence (*case law*). Même si, Outre-Manche, la distinction entre les intérêts en droit et en équité est devenue académique, maintenant que les juridictions ont une compétence commune dans les deux domaines, la classification d'un intérêt foncier comme *legal* ou *equitable* aura des répercussions sur la nature des remèdes qui seront éventuellement accordés à une partie lésée.

☐ 69 SPECIFIC CASE OF HOUSE CONVEYANCING

Buying or selling a home involves three main stages. In this chapter, we will assume that the vendor and purchaser are individuals and have instructed a solicitor as opposed to a licensed conveyancer. An essential principle of conveyancing is *caveat emptor* or "let the buyer beware". The burden is on the purchaser to ensure that the property complies with his expectations.

Prior to exchanging contracts

After visiting a property, a prospective purchaser expresses his interest in buying it to the vendor. He makes a financial offer to the vendor which may be lower than the actual sale price. An agreement is hopefully reached over the sale price. If the solicitors operate under the Law Society's TransAction Protocol, the vendor's solicitor will send the purchaser's solicitor a package which includes the draft sale contract, a copy of previous title deeds, a property information form (which dispenses the solicitor from conducting some of the preliminary enquiries which must otherwise be carried out) and a fixtures, fittings and contents form (indicating which ones are included in the purchase and which others will be removed).

The purchaser's solicitor checks the title to property to ensure, amongst other things, that the vendor is the registered owner. He makes local authority searches with the aid of the local council. He also makes preliminary enquiries through the vendor's solicitor. These include whether there are any disputes relating to the property (such as, but not exclusively, neighbouring disputes), planning permissions or constraints (e.g. if the property or part of it is listed), where the exact boundaries of the property are and who is liable for the maintenance of hedges, if there are rights of way, restrictive covenants (e.g. it may be forbidden to have pets in a flat), what insurance policies were taken out by the vendor and covering which risks, whether the property's utilities (gas, water and electricity) are the property's own, go *via* a neighbour's property or are shared with him. Other searches may include coal mining searches for example. If the property is leasehold, the purchaser's solicitor will find out who the managing agent and the freehold owner are, and if the vendor is up to date with payment of the services charges.

Once an agreement has been reached by both solicitors over the draft contract, a completion date is fixed. Completion is different from the exchange of agreements which may be signed before an estate agent. Exchange and completion constitute two different stages of the conveyancing process. Solicitors usually allow at least two weeks between exchange of agreements and completion, in case one of the parties (purchaser or vendor) is involved in a chain of sales. Before exchanging, the purchaser should ensure that he will have sufficient funds to purchase the property, which usually involves taking out a mortgage. Before giving his formal consent at the exchange stage, he should also make sure he agrees with the results of the various searches carried out. Any problem or query should be addressed before the exchange of agreements.

A usual fear of the purchaser at this stage is gazumping which may occur, if the vendor, after giving his verbal agreement to a prospective purchaser's price offer, decides to accept a higher offer from a different prospective buyer. Although legal in practice, gazumping is considered as an unfair practice. It is still very much in use and regularly disrupts conveyancing chains.

Exchange of contracts

Upon exchanging contracts, the purchaser hands over a non-refundable deposit which is usually 10 % of the purchase price but may be negotiated. Should the purchaser be in the process of selling his existing property, he might take out a bridging loan to pay the deposit on the new property. The deposit is not recoverable once paid, e.g. the purchaser pulls out of the sale. Both parties exchange contracts by signing them. Both parties are then bound by the agreement. Should the purchaser pull out, he will lose the deposit and might be sued for breach of contract. Gazumping is no longer possible at this stage.

Once contracts have been exchanged, the purchaser's solicitor prepares the draft transfer document which transfers the title of the property from the vendor to the buyer. This transfer document is signed by both parties. If the purchaser took out a mortgage, the mortgage documents can now be finalised to ensure that the purchase monies are available on the completion date. Final searches and enquiries are carried out, such as a land registry search, to make sure that there are no registrations against the vendor (such as undisclosed mortgages). In the run-up to completion, other steps must be taken such as paying land registry fees and stamp duty. The purchaser should also take out an insurance policy on his new property.

Completion

On the day of completion, a formal deed is signed through the purchaser's and vendor's solicitors. The balance of the purchase price is paid. The transfer documents, the title deeds and the keys to the property are handed over to the purchaser. Some more steps must be taken by the purchaser, directly or through his solicitor, such as registering the transfer of ownership with the land registry and informing the freehold owner of the transfer (if the purchaser bought a leasehold property). A copy of the deeds will be sent to the mortage lender who will keep them until the property is sold or the mortage is paid off.

Once the stamp duty is paid, the purchaser's solicitor sends him a statement of completion setting out the main steps of the financial transactions.

GLOSSARY

- bridging loan : short-term loan to cover an interval between two property transactions (purchase of a new property before the existing one is sold); *fr. : crédit-relais*
- *caveat emptor :* legal principle whereby the buyer cannot recover damages from the vendor for defects on the property that render it unfit for ordinary purposes; however this principle will not apply if the vendor made a misrepresentation of an aspect of the property which amounts to fraud or otherwise concealed a latent defect; *fr. : ≈ que l'acheteur soit vigilant*
- chain (n.) : situation which occurs when a purchaser of property relies on completion of the sale of his existing property in order to finalise the purchase of the new property; *fr. : ≈ chaîne (de ventes immobilières)*
- completion (n.) : stage of the conveyancing process when legal title to property is passed from the vendor to the purchaser; the buyer takes possession of the property; completion is the second stage of the procedure after the exchange of contracts; *fr. : ≈ acte authentique de vente (immobilière)*
- comply (v.) (with) : meet with one's expectations; *fr. : se conformer (à)*
- conveyancing (n.) : transfer of legal title of property from one legal entity to another; *fr. : transfert de propriété*
- deposit (n. or v.) : payment of a contractual percentage of the purchase price pending completion; this amount is forfeited if the purchaser pulls out; *fr. : acompte*
- exchange (n. or v.) : here, formal commitment from the purchaser to buy, and from the vendor to sell, a property; the subsequent stage of the conveyancing procedure is completion; *fr. : compromis de vente (immobilière)*
- fixtures and fittings : a fixture is considered as any item bolted to the floor or walls, and a fitting as any item that is free standing or hung by a nail; *fr. : ≈ agencements et équipements*
- freehold (n.) : property which is fully owned; a freeholder has full responsibility for the maintenance and repairs of the property; *fr. : ≈ pleine propriété*
- gazumping (n.) : when the vendor of a property accepts a verbal offer from a potential purchaser (thus reaching a binding verbal agreement), but then accepts a higher offer from a rival buyer, therefore being in breach of the initial agreement; *fr. : ≈ acceptation après accord d'une offre plus élevée*
- land registry search : consultation of the land register (in exchange of a fee) which gives the purchaser relevant information about the property he intends to buy such as a title register, title plan or flood risk indicator; *fr. : ≈ recherche cadastrale*
- leasehold (n.) : the property is owned for the duration specified in the lease; the freehold owner grants the leasehold owner the right to live on the

property; at the end of the lease the property comes back to the possession of the freehold owner; during the leasehold period, the lease indicates who bears the cost of maintainance and repair; *fr. : ≈ bail à long terme*

- licensed (adj.) conveyancer (n.) : see 4
- listed (adj.) : when applied to a building, placed on the Statutory List of Buildings of Special Architectural or Historic Interest and thus, subject to restrictions relating to any amendment which might affect the property's architectural interest; there are various grades of listed buildings; *fr. : classé*
- local authority search : enquiry sent by the purchaser's solicitor to the local authority, as part of the conveyancing procedure, to find out whether e.g. the local authority plans to build a road near the property or if the owner of neighbouring property has applied for planning permission to develop his land; *fr. : ≈ recherche cadastrale et d'urbanisme de la commune*
- managing (adj.) agent (n.) : someone who works for a property management company which manages, controls and deals with the general supervision of a property (usually a block of flats); *fr. : syndic*
- mortgage (n.) : loan granted by a bank or building society on the security of a property and which is repayable over a set number of years; *fr. : hypothèque*
- mortgagee (n.) : bank or building society which lends money in exchange of a security over a property; *fr. : créancier hypothécaire*
- mortgagor (n.) : borrower in a mortgage (usually a prospective homeowner); *fr. : débiteur hypothécaire*
- preliminary (adj.) enquiries (n.) : initial enquiries about a property made by the prospective buyer to the vendor, which the vendor must answer before the exchange of contracts; *fr. : ≈ demande de renseignements/≈ enquête préliminaire*
- pull out (v.) : when applied to the sale of property, fact for the purchaser (usually) to come back on his promise to buy the property; if the deposit has been paid to the vendor, it will be forfeited and the vendor may also sue the prospective purchaser for damages; *fr. : se retirer/se désister*
- purchaser (n.) : legal entity who buys a property; *fr. : acheteur*
- restrictive (adj.) covenant (n.) : restriction on the use of property; should someone violate a covenant, any person who is benefited by the covenants (usually a neighbour) may sue to enforce the restrictions; *fr. : clause restrictive*
- right of way : easement; privilege to pass over the land of someone else; the holder of the right of way can only have a reasonable enjoyment of the land, whereas the landowner retains the privileges of ownership; *fr. : servitude de passage*
- service charges : expenses usually payable by a tenant to a landlord; should the tenant ask for details of the service charge payable and should the landlord refuse, the landlord can be prosecuted; *fr. : charges locatives*
- stamp duty : tax (Stamp Duty Land Tax [SDLT]) payable on the transfer of property; in November 2013, it represented between 1 % and 7 % of the

whole purchase price so long as the latter was above £125,000; no stamp duty is payable below this sum; *fr. : droit de timbre*
- title to property : all the rights in a property in which a party has a legal or equitable interest; *fr. : titre de propriété*
- transfer document : document which transfers the title to property from the vendor to the buyer; *fr. : acte de transfert (de propriété)*
- utilities (n.) : here, water, gas, electricity and litter collection; *fr. : ≈ services publics*
- vendor (n.) : legal entity who sells a property; *fr. : vendeur*

USEFUL EXPRESSIONS

- to be part of a chain; *fr. : faire partie d'une chaîne de transactions immobilières*
- exchange takes place before completion; *fr. : le compromis de vente a lieu avant l'acte authentique*
- title to property is passed on to the new owner; *fr. : le titre de propriété est transféré au nouveau propriétaire*
- the deposit is paid upon exchange taking place; *fr. : l'acompte est acquitté au moment de l'établissement du compromis de vente*
- the purchaser needs to take out a bridging loan; *fr. : l'acquéreur doit souscrire un crédit-relais*
- the property is listed; *fr. : la propriété est classée*

FURTHER INFORMATION

- chains are frequent in England and Wales and therefore, bridging loans are also common as the purchaser of a place may have to wait a few weeks or months before selling his existing property
- the word gazump started being used in the 1920s when gangsters started conning a person by artificially bidding the price up
- gazumping is an illegal but frequent practice; it is difficult to prove as it usually occurs after a verbal acceptance by the vendor of a first purchaser's offer but before written contracts are exchanged

COMPARATIVE APPROACH

Une divergence importante concernant les transactions immobilières en France et en Angleterre et au Pays de Galles est que la règle *caveat emptor* ne trouve pas application en droit français où l'acheteur peut engager une action à l'encontre du vendeur sur le fondement des vices cachés. Cette action (sur le fondement de l'article 1641 du Code civil) est ouverte dans un délai de 2 ans à compter de la vente dès lors que le défaut, qui existait au moment de l'acquisition, rend le produit impropre à l'usage auquel on le destine. Cependant, il convient de préciser qu'en Angleterre et au Pays de Galles, la règle de *caveat emptor* ne s'applique pas en cas de fraude ou quand le vendeur a délibérément voulu tromper l'acquéreur.

Le principe du *gazumping*, toléré en Angleterre et au Pays de Galles, est interdit en Écosse et en France.

Sous ces réserves, la procédure de *conveyancing* est très similaire à la procédure applicable en France, elle aussi constituée de deux étapes. La première prévoit la signature d'un compromis/acte synallagmatique de vente (*exchange*), assorti ou non de conditions suspensives (*conditions precedent to* ou *"subject to" conditions*), et le paiement d'un dépôt de garantie (*deposit*). L'acte peut être sous seing privé ou notarié. La seconde étape est la signature de l'acte de vente lui-même (*completion*), qui ne surviend qu'en cas de non-réalisation des conditions suspensives. L'acte doit être notarié (*deed*). Le solde du prix (*remainder of the purchase price*) est acquitté ce jour là.

□ 70 SPECIFIC CASE : TENANCY AGREEMENTS

A tenancy agreement is a contract between one landlord and one tenant (at least). The landlord can be an individual or a company or a partnership. For this chapter, we will assume that the landlord is an individual. The tenancy agreement sets out the terms and conditions of the tenancy. It can be verbal or in writing and, in both cases, the landlord and tenant will have rights and duties. The tenancy relates to someone's accomodation as opposed to commercial premises (which give rise to a special lease). There are essentially two types of tenancy which have given rise to specific statutory protection : the tenancy is fixed-term if it runs for a period of time; it is periodic if it runs on a weekly or monthly basis.

However it is always possible for the landlord and the tenant to negotiate other contractual terms, so long as the tenant is granted at least the minimum protection granted by the law and the terms and conditions of the tenancy agreement are fair. A tenancy can be in connection with furnished or unfurnished accomodation.

Assured shorthold tenancy (AST)

This is the most common form of tenancy agreement. The landlord must be a private legal entity as opposed to a local council or housing association, he must not live in the property, the agreement must have started after 15th January 1989 and the property must be the tenant's main accommodation (as opposed to a holiday home). The rent must be between £250 a year (or £1,000 in London) and £100,000 a year. This type of tenancy is called "assured shorthold" : the tenant has security of tenure in the premises for at least 6 months during which he is protected from an early termination.

Other types of tenancy

They are less common than ASTs. A "regulated tenancy" is one which started before 15th January 1989. The tenant can apply for a "fair rent". An "assured tenancy" can only apply to a tenancy which started between 15th January 1989 and 27th February 1997. Both the regulated tenancy and the assured tenancy give the tenant substantial protection from eviction.

The landlord may give someone a licence. The boundary between a licence and some forms of tenancy is not always clear. A licence is usually construed as giving less protection to someone who merely has the landlord's permission to live in a property but does not have a legal right as such to live there.

A tenancy can also be a "non regulated" one. In this case, the landlord is a resident landlord, which means that he and the tenant have lived in the same property since the start of the letting. For example, a furnished room let out by a resident landlord to a lodger is either a form of tenancy which is "not regulated" or a licence.

Minimum terms and conditions

The tenancy agreement should include the respective names of the landlord and tenant, the property address and a description of it, the start and end date of the agreement, the rental price (including how and when it is paid or reviewed), the amount of the deposit (and if it can be withheld, and to what extent, should the tenant cause damage), which bills should be paid by the landlord or the tenant and the landlord's and tenant's respective duties. The tenancy agreement may also specify who is responsible for minor repairs (substantial repairs being done by the landlord), when and how the agreement can be terminated, if this can be done at a date earlier than the contractual term and how and whether the property can be sublet. It is frequent for pets not to be allowed in rented accommodation.

GLOSSARY

- assured shorthold tenancy (AST) : form of residential tenancy which is standard if the tenant moved in after 28th February 1997, granted for an initial minimum of 6 months during which the tenant has security of tenure, for which rent is paid to a non-resident landlord; *fr. : ≈ contrat de location/bail d'une durée minimale avec garanties*
- assured (adj.) tenancy (n.) : form of residential tenancy which was standard for tenants who moved in between 15th January 1989 and 28th February 1997, granted for a minimum guaranteed period of time during which the tenant has security of tenure, for which rent is paid to a non-resident landlord; *fr. : ≈ contrat de location/bail d'une durée minimale avec garanties*
- deposit (n.) : sum payable as a pledge for a contract; *fr. : dépôt de garantie*
- eviction (n.) : action of throwing out, expelling someone from a property; *fr. : expulsion*

- furnished (adj.) : equipped with furniture; *fr. : meublé*
- housing (adj.) association (n.) : organisation, usually a non-profit organisation, which lets out property to low income people; *fr. : ≈ association d'aide au logement*
- landlord (n.) : legal entity who rents out a property which he owns; *fr. : propriétaire-bailleur*
- licence (n.) : here, written or verbal authorisation given by a landlord to someone, allowing him to live in a property with the landlord in exchange for payment of a sum of money; *fr. : ≈ contrat de location/bail informel*
- lodger (n.) : when applied to a licence or a tenancy which is "not regulated", someone who usually rents a furnished room in a property with a resident landlord; *fr. : ≈ pensionnaire*
- non-regulated (adj.) tenancy (n.) : tenancy which is not regulated (see below); *fr. : ≈ bail non soumis à réglementation*
- pet (n.) : domestic or tamed animal; *fr. : animal domestique*
- premises (n.) : property, house, flat or building; *fr. : locaux/lieux*
- regulated (adj.) tenancy (n.) : letting of premises after the 15th January 1989 by a non-resident private landlord who rents out the place for a fair rent; this does not apply if the tenant receives board or other services such as cooking or cleaning; *fr. : ≈ bail soumis à réglementation*
- security of tenure : guarantees from which a tenant can benefit for the duration of his tenancy agreement; *fr. : garantie de maintien dans les lieux*
- tenancy (n.) : occupation or possession of a property as a tenant; *fr. : location*
- tenant (n.) : person who occupies property rented out by a landlord; *fr. : locataire-preneur*

USEFUL EXPRESSIONS

- to rent out a property; *fr. : louer un bien immobilier*
- it is let out on a short/long term basis; *fr. : c'est loué à court/long terme*
- to be bound by the terms of the tenancy agreement; *fr. : être lié par les termes d'un contrat de bail*

FURTHER INFORMATION

- the plural word "premises" must not be confused with its singular form "premise" which is a former statement on which an argument is based (for example : it is based on the premise that; *fr. : c'est basé sur l'hypothèse que*)
- council houses correspond to the French *habitations à loyer modéré* (HLM) and, as in France, they are subject to a specific legal regime
- the person who runs a public house (commonly known as pub) is called a pub landlord or publican

COMPARATIVE APPROACH

En Angleterre et au Pays de Galles, la législation relative aux baux d'habitation a beaucoup évolué depuis trente ans et selon les dates d'entrée dans les lieux, des locataires voisins peuvent dès lors être assujettis à des régimes très différents. En France, le droit commun du bail est régi par les articles 1708 à 1710 et 1713 à 1751 du Code civil et par la loi n° 89-462 du 6 juillet 1989 tendant à améliorer les rapports locatifs. En France, le propriétaire et le locataire doivent impérativement être liés par un contrat écrit, qu'il soit sous seing privé ou en la forme authentique. La durée du bail, pour un logement vide, est de 3 ans si le propriétaire est une personne physique ou 6 ans s'il est une personne morale.

En France, la location de logements meublés est assujettie à des règles différentes. Ainsi, la durée minimale du bail n'est que d'un an tacitement reconductible. Cette formule connaît depuis 2010 un succès croissant puisqu'elle présente notamment des avantages fiscaux pour les propriétaires.

En juin 2013, le gouvernement a déposé à l'Assemblée Nationale le projet de loi Alur (accès au logement et urbanisme rénové) qui, s'il est adopté, devrait entraîner de nombreuses modifications concernant le logement et la copropriété en général.

□ 71 LANDLORD'S AND TENANT'S RESPONSIBILITIES

Landlord's responsibilities

Regarding the tenant's welfare and for the duration of the tenancy agreement, the landlord must ensure that the property is safe and free from health hazards, that the fire safety regulations are complied with, and that all electricity and gas equipment is maintained on a regular basis. The landlord is responsible for important repairs such as those affecting the property structure, plumbing installations including (but not only) heating and hot water systems. Of course the landlord should bear the cost of those works. Should works be necessary, the landlord must give his tenant at least 24 hours' notice that he wishes to enter the premises. No such notice is necessary in case of emergency. If the landlord fails to do the works promptly, the tenant can have them done and then seek reimbursement of the costs incurred from the landlord. The landlord should protect the tenant's deposit by paying it into a government-approved scheme.

Should an inspection be carried out by the Housing Health and Safety Rating System (HHSRS) and reveal some non-compliance with the law, an enforcement notice must be served on the landlord who must take action promptly.

Tenant's responsibilities

The tenant should comply with all his obligations, which may derive from a written or verbal tenancy agreement so long as they are reasonable and in compliance with the law. He should keep up to date with the rent as and when required. Rent is usually payable in advance, on a weekly or monthly basis. Bills relating to electricity, telephone or gas are generally payable by the tenant as well as council tax and a TV licence. If the landlord is responsible for the maintenance of the exterior and structure of the property, the plumbing, central heating, electricity wiring as well as the extensive repairs and maintenance of the exterior and the structure of the property, the tenant must look after and maintain internal decorations, equipment and furniture (if the property is let out furnished), deal with minor maintenance, comply with specific restrictive covenants (like a prohibition to have pets or to smoke).

The tenant should also give access to his landlord as and when reasonably required (for instance, to carry out works). He should not cause nuisance to anyone and, in particular, his neighbours. He should not abandon the property without duly informing his landlord and settling any outstanding monies.

GLOSSARY

- council tax : see 25
- enforcement notice : notification to carry out a breach; *fr. : injonction (d'exécuter)*
- housing benefit : means tested governmental financial help which is intended to enable poorer people to meet their housing costs for rented accommodation; *fr. : ≈ aide au logement*
- income tax : see 25
- maintenance (n.) : steps taken to preserve the state of property; *fr. : entretien*
- mortgage (n.) : see 67
- notice period : here, period of time which one party must allow before taking a particular step; *fr. : délai de préavis*
- nuisance (n.) : see 90
- restrictive (adj.) covenant (n.) : contractual provision which limits the use (or prohibits certain uses) of a property; *fr. : clause restrictive*
- TV licence : form of tax payable by those who own a television; *fr. : redevance télévision*

USEFUL EXPRESSIONS

- to give someone a month's notice to do something; *fr. : donner à quelqu'un un mois de préavis pour faire quelque chose*

- to comply with restrictive covenants; *fr. : se conformer à des clauses restrictives*
- to let out a house; *fr. : donner à bail une maison*
- restrictive covenants are attached to the lease; *fr. : le contrat de bail est assorti de clauses restrictives*

FURTHER INFORMATION

- council tax is the successor of the much criticised community charge (aka poll tax)

COMPARATIVE APPROACH

Il n'y a pas de divergence majeure entre les droits et devoirs des propriétaires-bailleurs (*landlords*) et locataires-preneurs (*tenants*) en France et en Angleterre et au Pays de Galles.

□ 72 TERMINATION OF A TENANCY AGREEMENT

By the landlord

In England and Wales, the law allegedly tends to protect the weaker party i.e. the tenant. If the tenancy agreement contains a break clause, this will be applied like any contractual provision. However the landlord's right to possession cannot be exercised during the first 6 months of the tenancy. In the absence of a break clause, it is possible for a landlord, in some circumstances, to bring the tenancy agreement to an end before the contractually set date.

The landlord can terminate an "assured shorthold tenancy" if the following conditions are fulfilled : the tenant must be given at least 2 months' notice to quit, the date he must leave is at least 6 months after the initial agreement began (this initial agreement may have since then been renewed). Last but not least, the rule is that the landlord cannot ask the tenant to leave before the end of the period (for a periodic tenancy) or the fixed-term (for a fixed-term tenancy). However, during the fixed-term, the landlord may ask his tenant to leave if he wants possession under the Housing Act 1988. This may be because the tenant owes arrears of rent, the landlord wants to move back into the property or the landlord is aware (and can prove) that the tenant has used the property for illegal purposes (as a brothel or to sell drugs). In those cases, the notice period (for giving the tenant his notice to quit) may be reduced from 2 months minimum down to 2 weeks in some (rare) cases.

To terminate an "assured tenancy" the landlord must prove that he needs possession under the Housing Act 1988.

For other types of tenancy (if, for example, the landlord has a lodger) the landlord should give his tenant reasonable notice to quit. Usually this corresponds to the rental payment period which means that if the tenant pays on a monthly basis, the landlord must give him a month's notice.

By the tenant

A written tenancy agreement should indicate the notice period which a tenant must comply with to bring the contract to an end. For a fixed-term tenancy, the notice period cannot be less than 2 months before the normal end date of the fixed-term. For a periodic tenancy the tenant gives notice at the end of a rent period. The rent period corresponds to a rent term. If rent is paid on a monthly basis, the tenant must give a month's notice. Should the tenant insist on leaving the premises before the end of the notice period, the landlord may insist that rent be paid until the end of the tenancy, unless a contractual break clause specifies otherwise.

Consequences

If a property was let out on an assured shorthold tenancy which started after 6th April 2007, the landlord will have had a statutory obligation to pay the tenant's deposit in a tenancy deposit protection (TDP) scheme which is a government-backed scheme. The deposit must be paid into a TDP scheme within 30 days of entry. When the tenancy agreement comes to an end, the tenant is entitled to his deposit back within 10 days of the tenancy ending.

The landlord cannot withhold part of the deposit because of general wear and tear to the condition of the property (for example, worn out carpets). Conversely if the tenant left hook holes in the wall or stained the carpet, the landlord is entitled to deduct the cost of repair or the cost which must be incurred to change the carpet for example.

GLOSSARY

- arrears (n.) : sums which are still due; *fr. : arriérés*
- break clause : contractual clause which allows a party to terminate a contract early; *fr. : clause de résiliation*
- lodger (n.) : person who usually rents a furnished room in someone else's house; *fr. : ≈ locataire d'une chambre meublée*
- tenancy deposit protection (TDP) : government-backed scheme by which the tenant's deposit must be paid into a specially protected account; it is a guarantee provided to the tenant that the landlord will not use the deposit for his own use; *fr. : ≈ protection pour le dépôt de garantie des locataires-preneurs*
- wear and tear : decrease in value of an asset which may be damaged by the passage of time; *fr. : usure normale*

USEFUL EXPRESSIONS

- to repossess a house; *fr. : reprendre possession de sa maison*
- the rent fell due last week; *fr. : le loyer était dû la semaine dernière*
- to give a month's notice to quit; *fr. : donner un mois de préavis avant de quitter les lieux*
- to forfeit a deposit; *fr. : perdre son dépôt de garantie*
- the landlord must allow normal wear and tear; *fr. : le propriétaire-bailleur doit accepter l'usure normale*
- the monies outstanding correspond to rent arrears; *fr. : les sommes dues correspondent à des arriérés de loyers*

FURTHER INFORMATION

- government-backed schemes like the tenancy deposit protection (TDP) were introduced to protect the tenant against the possible dilapidation of his deposit by the landlord

COMPARATIVE APPROACH

En France, le propriétaire-bailleur peut mettre un terme au contrat de location à l'échéance du bail (en donnant un préavis de 6 mois), en appliquant une clause de résiliation (*break clause*) ou en saisissant le juge en cas de non-paiement de loyers. Quant au locataire-preneur, il peut donner congé à tout moment dès lors qu'il respecte un délai de préavis de 3 mois. Cependant, ce délai peut être réduit à 1 mois en cas de mutation.

En France, l'article L. 613-3 du Code de la construction et de l'habitation prévoit une trêve hivernale de plusieurs mois pendant lesquels un locataire ne peut être expulsé pour non-paiement de loyers. Il n'existe pas de protection similaire en Angleterre et au Pays de Galles.

PART 3

Litigation

1

Presentation of litigation

□ 73 CIVIL LITIGATION AND SCOPE

Litigation consists of the various steps involved in the court resolution of a dispute. When applied to civil law, it opposes two different litigants or more who are involved in a civil dispute (for example, revolving around negligence, breach of contract, etc.). Civil law is often opposed to criminal law. The purpose of civil law is to grant the aggrieved party a remedy at common law (damages or financial compensation) or in equity (injunction or specific performance). Conversely, criminal law aims at punishing someone for an offence he committed. Just like criminal law, civil law is divided into substantive law and procedural law.

The Civil Procedure Rules (CPR) – also known as the Woolf reform – were introduced in 1998 to govern the procedure that is followed within the civil court system. The "overriding objective" of the CPR, as expressed by Lord Woolf, is to enable the courts to deal with cases justly and at proportionate cost. In other words, access to justice should be made easier for litigants by simplifying the former procedural rules, getting rid of legalese and making it cheaper to go to court, for example, by making it possible to dispense with the services of a litigator in a range of cases (e.g. small claims).

Litigators tend to use the Green Book (or Civil Court practice book) and the White Book published on a yearly basis. The former examines procedure in the civil courts and contains the updated CPR as well as the Supreme Court Rules and Practice Directions. The latter provides guidance on civil procedure and an update on the latest reforms.

GLOSSARY

- aggrieved (adj.) party (n.) : party who sustained a loss or damage, or various heads of damage; *fr. : partie lésée/partie qui a subi un préjudice*
- common law : legal system on which the law of England and Wales is based and which mostly consists of case law (court precedents) rather than statutes; *fr. : common law/droit coutumier*

- conversely (adv.) : saying the reverse or opposite of something else; *fr. : inversement*
- court (n.) : judge or body of people presided over by a judge who must render a decision in view of the evidence adduced to them; *fr. : tribunal (première instance)/juridiction (tous niveaux)*
- damages (n.) : financial compensation which may be awarded by a court to compensate a loss sustained; damages are a common law remedy; *fr. : dommages et intérêts*
- dispense (v.) with : give up what is not necessary; *fr. : se dispenser de*
- dispute (n.) : in a legal context, argument between two or more parties; *fr. : litige*
- equity (n.) : justice applied as a complement to common law when the latter is inappropriate, insufficient or inexistent to render a fair decision; *fr. : équité*
- legalese (n.) : technical and specialised vocabulary of the legal profession and the judiciary; usually used in a derogatory context; *fr. : jargon juridique*
- litigant (n.) : legal entity who claims or defends court proceedings; *fr. : justiciable*
- litigator (n.) : lawyer (solicitor or barrister) specialised in litigation; *fr. : avocat spécialiste du contentieux*
- litigation (n.) : act of taking legal action, usually by issuing court proceedings with a view to resolving a dispute; *fr. : droit contentieux*
- offence (n.) : see 27
- overriding (adj.) objective (n.) : in the particular context of the CPR, aim of these rules which is to ensure that cases are dealt with fairly, expeditiously and proportionately, in view of the complexity, value and importance of the claim and the parties' respective financial means; *fr. : objectif primordial*
- practice direction : supplemental protocol to litigation rules; *fr. : ≈ circulaire d'application*
- procedural (adj.) law (n.) : way in which substantive rights can be enforced; *fr. : règles de procédure*
- small (adj.) claims (n.) : see 75
- specific (adj.) performance (n.) : equitable remedy granted by the court requiring someone to do something; *fr. : obligation de faire*
- substantive (adj.) law (n.) : written law (sometimes passed by way of statutes) that defines legal entities' rights and duties (such as civil rights and responsibilities); *fr. : règles de fond*
- Supreme Court : highest court in the United Kingdom set up by the Constitutional Reform Act 2005; not to be mistaken with a different concept which was used before 2005, when the "Supreme Court" (of Judicature) comprised the higher courts, i.e. the High Court, the Court of Appeal and the Crown Court; *fr. : ≈ Cour de cassation (ordre judiciaire)/≈ Conseil d'État (ordre administratif)*

- update (n. or v.) : act of making something more modern, bringing up to date; *fr. : mise à jour (n.)/mettre à jour (v.)*

USEFUL EXPRESSIONS

- to go to court; *fr. : aller au tribunal/saisir une juridiction*
- a litigant instructs a litigator; *fr. : un justiciable mandate un avocat spécialiste du contentieux*
- to abide by/to comply with the overriding objective of the CPR; *fr. : se conformer à l'objectif primordial du Code de procédure civile*

FURTHER INFORMATION

- the noun damages, in its plural form, should not be confused with its singular form damage (*préjudice*)
- the words litigant and litigator refer to two different categories of people who choose court dispute resolution
- in a legal context, the word argument can be used in two different contexts; it either refers to the dispute between two parties or more, alternatively, it can refer to the reasoning underpinning a decision

> COMPARATIVE APPROACH
>
> L'entrée en vigueur des CPR a marqué un tournant important en adoptant un système de codification assez similaire à celui du Code de procédure civile (CPC) français. Aujourd'hui et ainsi qu'il a été dit ci-dessus, le *Green Book* et le *White Book* ont une signification, et recouvrent une réalité, différentes d'avant 1998.

□ 74 ALTERNATIVES TO CIVIL LITIGATION

Since the implementation of the CPR, the parties to a dispute have been strongly encouraged to find alternative ways of settling that dispute, other than by going to court. Court litigation should be used as a last resort. Failure by a party to consider alternatives to litigation may result in being penalised when the time comes for the court to determine costs.

Pre-action protocols

The development of pre-action protocols was recommended by Lord Woolf in his final Access to Justice Report of 1996. Pre-action protocols for personal injury claims, the resolution of clinical disputes, disease and illness claims, professional negligence, judicial review, defamation, construction and engineering disputes, housing disrepair cases, possession claims based on rent arrears, possession claims based on mortgage or home purchase plan or arrears in respect of residential property, and low value personal injury claims in road traffic accidents, are now in force.

The purpose of pre-action protocols is to settle a dispute without the need for litigation or alternatively, narrow down the issues in dispute if the case goes to court. Pre-action should not be used by one party to secure an advantage over another. Pre-action requires the parties to exchange information and documentation before the issue of a court claim, to act in a reasonable and proportionate manner and if a court claim is made, to ensure the efficient management of the case by the court. The proposed claimant must send the proposed defendant a letter of claim, setting out the main issues in dispute. The letter of claim should be supported by key written evidence, if available. The defendant's written acknowledgment (i.e. his written reply to the claim letter), which may include a counterclaim, should be sent to the proposed claimant within 14 days of receipt of the original letter. If no amicable settlement is possible, the parties should try to reduce the scope of the disputed issues, thus dispensing the court from dealing with it.

In some rare cases, pre-action rules will not apply, for instance when they would expose one of the parties to his claim being time-barred, due to the expiry of the relevant limitation period.

Alternative Dispute Resolution (ADR)

There are various alternatives to the court resolution of a dispute. ADR may include resorting to an ombudsman, conciliation, an arbitrator or a mediator. An arbitrator's decision is the only one which is normally binding on the parties. Should one of the parties be dissatisfied with the award made by he arbitrator, no further action can be taken. The decisions made through other forms of ADR are not usually binding, unless the parties agree to give them a binding effect. This means that a subsequent court action is possible. Should the parties ignore ADR and then be required by the court to disclose evidence of their attempts to settle the case amicably, costs sanctions may be imposed on the party at fault.

GLOSSARY

- acknowledgment (n.) : formal response in reply to something done; *fr. : accusé de réception*
- alternative dispute resolution (ADR) : way of resolving a dispute outside a court; *fr. : ≈ autre moyen de régler un conflit*
- arbitration (n.) : form of ADR; the arbitrator's award, based on written evidence, is legally binding; this means that the claimant can take court action if the arbitrator's decision is deemed unsatisfactory; most arbitrators are part of the Chartered Institute of Arbitrators; many trade agreements contain an arbitration clause, making it compulsory for the parties to resort to arbitra-

tion in case of dispute; a fee is normally payable when instructing an arbitrator; the parties may opt for a non-binding arbitration; *fr. : arbitrage*

- case management : under the CPR, process by which a judge, who is in charge of a particular case, will manage the case on a regular basis to make sure that a number of steps are taken by the parties, thus ensuring progress; *fr. : procédure de mise en état*
- claimant (n.) : legal entity who starts a court action against a defendant, by issuing court proceedings; before the CPR came into force, he was called the plaintiff; *fr. : demandeur (ordre judiciaire)/requérant (ordre administratif)*
- claim (n.) : document issued by the claimant, and then served on the defendant, setting out the facts of a case and the legal grounds on which the claimant intends to rely; before the CPR, it was called a writ; *fr. : assignation (ordre judiciaire)/requête (n.) (ordre administatif)*
- claim letter/letter of claim : letter sent by the proposed claimant to the proposed defendant setting out the facts of a case and the legal grounds on which the claimant intends to rely; under the pre-CPR system, it was called a letter before action; *fr. : lettre de mise en demeure (avant assignation)*
- clinical (adj.) dispute (n.) : legal dispute involving the alleged liability of a medical practitioner (doctor, surgeon, consultant, nurse, etc.) which is either sought directly or indirectly (the claim being made, e.g., against the hospital employing him); *fr. : responsabilité médicale*
- conciliation (n.) : form of ADR; conciliation is normally non-binding unless specified otherwise; the conciliator does not seek evidence or call witnesses; no written decision is made; *fr. : procédure de conciliation*
- costs (n.) : court issue fees, expert's fees, solicitor's or barrister's fees as well as any disbursement relating to the litigation; *fr. : dépens*
- counterclaim (n. or v.) : document, similar to a claim, made by the defendant against the claimant after being served with the claimant's claim; the counterclaim should be part of the defendant's defence; this is called a defence and counterclaim; *fr. : demande reconventionnelle*
- defamation (n.) : see 89
- defendant (n.) : legal entity who defends a court claim; the defendant may make a counterclaim against the claimant when he files his defence with the court; *fr. : conclusions en défense (ordre judiciaire)/mémoire en défense (ordre administratif)*
- evidence (n. or v.) : body of facts in a case which support an assertion; *fr. : éléments de preuve*
- implement (v.)/implementation (n.) : put into effect; *fr. : exécuter (v.)/exécution (n.)*
- issue (n.) : point or question; *fr. : question/point*
- judicial (adj.) review (n.) : see 76
- limitation period : period of time within which a claim must be issued; failure to comply with that period will result in the claim being time-barred; *fr. : délai de prescription*

- mediation (n.) : form of ADR which is normally not binding; the mediator, whose decision is called a resolution, acts as go-between; the parties may opt for a binding mediation; a small claims mediation service deals with court claims under £10,000; *fr. : médiation*
- mortgage (n.) : see 69
- ombudsman (n.) : person instructed in the context of ADR whose ruling or recommendation is not binding, thus allowing a dissatisfied claimant to take subsequent court action; the ombudsman's services are free of charge; the services covered by most banks, building societies or insurance companies are usually covered by the Financial Ombudsman Services (FOS); *fr. : ombudsman*
- personal injury claim : claim made by someone who sustained personal injury (e.g. in an accident); *fr. : ≈ demande d'indemnisation pour préjudice corporel*
- pre-action protocol : protocol strongly encouraging the parties to a dispute to take a number of steps to try to settle their claim amicably i.e. without a court resolution; *fr. : ≈ protocole précédant une action en justice*
- possession claim : see 136
- professional (adj.) negligence (n.) : form of negligence (see 86) which applies to a professional who breaches the duty of care he owes someone; *fr. : responsabilité civile professionnelle*
- purpose (n.) : objective; *fr. : but*
- settle (v.)/settlement (n.) : determination of a legal dispute without the need to resort to a court action; *fr. : règlement amiable (d'un litige)*
- time-barred (adj.) : being unable to proceed with a legal claim, due to the expiry of the limitation period; *fr. : prescrit*

USEFUL EXPRESSIONS

- to raise a factual issue; *fr. : soulever une question de fait*
- to be time-barred; *fr. : être prescrit*
- the limitation period is 3 years from the time the cause of action accrues; *fr. : le délai de prescription est de 3 ans à compter de la survenance de la cause de l'action*
- to reach an amicable settlement/to settle a dispute amicably; *fr. : arriver à un accord amiable*
- unlike a mediator's decision, an arbitrator's is binding on the parties; *fr. : contrairement à la décision du médiateur, la sentence de l'arbitre lie les parties*

FURTHER INFORMATION

- the word claimant should not be translated by *plaignant* which gives it a criminal connotation (with the underlying idea of a *plainte*)
- the most commonly used forms of ADR are mediation and arbitration

Comparative approach

En France, une ordonnance n° 2011-1540 du 16 novembre 2011 a été prise par application de la loi du 17 mai 2011 de simplification et d'amélioration de la qualité du droit, portant transposition de la directive européenne n° 2008/52/CE du Parlement européen et du Conseil du 21 mai 2008, encourageant la médiation en matière civile et commerciale.

Bien avant ces dispositions et dans certains domaines, les justiciables étaient déjà contraints de tenter de résoudre leurs litiges à l'amiable. Ainsi, la procédure de conciliation est depuis longtemps obligatoire dans le cadre de tout litige pendant devant le conseil de prud'hommes. Une audience de conciliation est aussi obligatoire en matière de divorce devant le tribunal de grande instance, et il est courant que des accords de conciliation soient entérinés par les tribunaux de commerce.

Les raisons motivant le recours à l'arbitrage, la médiation ou la conciliation, sont les mêmes en France qu'en Angleterre et au Pays de Galles : limiter le coût engendré par les actions en justice ainsi que réduire l'encombrement des tribunaux.

□ 75 VARIOUS STAGES OF CIVIL LITIGATION

A party who is dissatisfied with the non-binding decision rendered by way of ADR may resort to the court resolution of the dispute. The system in force in England and Wales is an adversarial one : the parties' role is to adduce the evidence supporting the legal grounds on which they rely; the court's mission is to consider this evidence and, in view of it, take a decision.

Parties to the litigation

The claimant used to be called a plaintiff before the CPR came into force. The defendant may bring a third party action against another legal entity, the third party defendant. On appeal (both before the Court of Appeal or the Supreme Court) an appellant is opposed to a respondent. The appellant is the person who lodges an appeal against the decision rendered or handed down by a lower court. At any stage of the court proceedings (whether before the first instance, appellate or Supreme Court), any party may wish to make a specific application or lodge a petition. The party who makes an application is an applicant and the party who defends it is the respondent. Likewise, the party who lodges a petition is a petitioner and the party who defends it is a respondent. It is important to understand that the party who appeals or alternatively, makes an application or lodges a petition may be any of the parties to the litigation.

The CPR created Group Litigation Orders (GLO) which are reminiscent of United States class actions.

Various stages of the litigation

Before court proceedings are issued, the claimant should consider how to fund his case. He can enter into a conditional fee agreement (CFAs also called "no win no fee") with his solicitor and barrister (if the latter is instructed). CFAs are particularly used in personal injury cases. Alternatively the claimant may have previously taken out legal expense insurance (LEI) or may subsequently subscribe an after the event insurance (AEI). Otherwise the claimant may benefit from legal aid if he passes the merits and means test. The legal aid system was recently reformed by the Legal Aid, Sentencing and Punishment of Offenders Act 2012 (LASPO) which came into effect on 1st April 2013.

The claimant must have standing in order to bring a claim against a defendant. The claimant must send the defendant a claim letter, informing him of the issues in dispute and inviting him to settle the claim. The litigation starts when the claimant issues a claim out of court, with which particulars of claim must be enclosed. The particulars give details of the claim. The claim and particulars must be served on the defendant by a set date. Failure to serve the particulars of claim with the claim may prompt the defendant to apply to strike out the claim. An issue fee is payable when the claim is issued.

Upon being served with the court proceedings, the defendant must indicate to the claimant and to the court whether he intends to defend the court action. Failure to respond is likely to result in the claimant entering default judgment against the defendant. If he informs the claimant and the court of his intention to defend the claim, the defence – and any possible counterclaim – must be served on the claimant, and filed with the court, within 28 days of service of the claim. If the contents of the defence are weak, the claimant may obtain summary judgment against the defendant. A third party claim may be issued and served by the defendant against a third party. The defendant may seek legal aid to fund his case, may use his own funding or may have subscribed the appropriate legal expenses insurance policy.

Further pleadings may be exchanged between the parties, such as the claimant's reply to the defendant's defence. All court documents must be accompanied by a statement of truth verifying the truth of the information contained in those documents.

At any time until trial and, as part of a strategy, any party (usually the defendant to a claim) may make a Part 36 payment, i.e. a payment into court of the reasonable sum which he believes is due to the opposing party. Such payment is made for tactical reasons and may result in costs sanctions if the interested party fails to accept that sum as settlement, and this sum is later deemed reasonable by the court.

Case management

If the system is adversarial which means that the parties conduct the litigation, the CPR introduced a case management system – starting with ADR – to ensure that the parties comply with the CPR's overriding objective. A judge has the duty to manage each case to ensure that no unnecessary, costly or time consuming step is taken. The judge will also encourage the parties to settle the case amicably as and when appropriate. A timetable will be set to ensure that various steps are taken by the parties within a certain time frame and various case management conferences may be organised, throughout the litigation, to ensure that the parties comply with this timetable.

Another major step taken at the outset of the case management stage is the allocation of the case to the appropriate track. The CPR set up three different tracks to which each case might be allocated, depending on its nature, complexity and the amount of the claim. Although it is the judge in charge of case management who will take the relevant decision, the norm is that cases involving a claim below £50,000 will be heard in a county court, and those above this sum in the High Court. Small claims jurisdiction, which involves a simplified procedure (to enable people to appear as litigants in person without the need to instruct a solicitor), relates to claims up to £10,000. The fast-track applies to claims between £10,000 and £25,000. The norm is also that High Court cases are allocated to the multi-track system, with more complex procedural rules owing to the difficulty of the legal issues potentially raised in the case. Claims between £25,000 and £50,000 will either be fast-track or mutli-track, in the county courts or the High Court.

Since the Legal Aid, Sentencing and Punishment of Offenders Act 2012 (LAPSO, also called Jackson reform) which came into force in April 2013, the parties to the litigation have been required, in the most complex cases, to prepare a detailed costs budget setting out the anticipated costs of proceedings. Should any of the parties wish to depart from this forecast budget, the changes need to be approved by the court. Approval will not be given to a budget change unless the relevant party shows that he had a "good reason" to do so. Here again, the underlying message is to comply with the overriding objective of the CPR, by ensuring that the richer party will not prolong the litigation to the poorer party's detriment.

Disclosure

Under the pre-CPR system, disclosure was called discovery. The disclosure process makes it compulsory for each party to the litigation to disclose all the documents he intends to rely on, including the documents which adversely affect his own case or support another party's case. Documents covered by legal professional privilege are excluded.

Witness statements and expert evidence

Witness statements should be exchanged by the parties if they seek to rely on such evidence at trial. Each statement must be certified to be true by the witness. The court's permission is required if a party intends to rely on expert evidence at trial. Each party may instruct his own independent expert of all parties may apply to the court for a single joint expert (SJE). SJEs could not be instructed before the CPR came into force. An expert witness' duty is to the court, not to the party who instructs him.

Trial

Civil trial is determined by the judge alone without a jury except for some civil fraud or defamation cases. Before trial, counsel for each party drafts a skeleton argument, which is exchanged with the other parties' skeleton arguments and filed with the court. When trial starts, both parties' barristers set out their case. They call their witnesses and experts and the examination-in-chief, cross examination and re-examination process then take place. Both parties' counsel then sum up the evidence and make submissions on legal issues. The standard of proof in civil litigation is the balance of probabilities, contrary to criminal law where the defendant's guilt must be proven beyond reasonable doubt. The judge then takes his decision based on the evidence put before him.

Judgment is usually reserved until a later date. So far as costs are concerned, the LAPSO reform brought some major changes to the rules formerly applicable. Regarding orders for costs, if the parties were subject to the costs budgeting regime implemented by the Jackson reform (which is the case for most cases nowadays), the winning party will usually recover from the losing party whatever sum was agreed in the budget submitted to the judge at the case management conference. Otherwise and subject to the special provisions, which apply to small claims, the old rule whereby costs follow the event should apply i.e., the losing party should pay the winner's costs or a substantial part of them. Making an unmeritorious claim or failing to accept a Part 36 payment may result in costs sanctions.

Appeal

The usual rule is that the dissatisfied party must obtain leave from the court before lodging an appeal.

GLOSSARY

- adversarial (adj.) system (n.) : procedural system in which the parties have the conduct of the case; they exchange their arguments, documents, witness and expert reports; the judge is passive throughout the trial and at the end of it, merely draws conclusions on the grounds of the evidence adduced by the parties; *fr. : système accusatoire*
- after the event insurance (AEI) : form of legal expenses insurance (LEI) subscribed after the cause of action emerged to protect against the insurable event of losing a case based on that cause of action; *fr. : ≈ assurance protection juridique souscrite après survenance de l'événement déclenchant le litige*
- appellant (n.) : person who appeals against a decision; *fr. : appelant*
- applicant (n.) : person who makes an application to the court (e.g. for payment on account of damages); *fr. : demandeur*
- barrister (n.) : see 4
- case management : procedural stage introduced by the CPR whereby a judge in charge of a case imposes on the parties to take a number of steps such as

abiding by deadlines for the exchange of pleadings, of documents (including witness statements or expert reports) and attending at least one case management conference; *fr. : procédure de mise en état*

- conditional fee agreement (CFA) : agreement between a client and his solicitor and barrister (if instructed) by which the solicitor/barrister can charge a success fee on top of the normal fee if the case is successful; should the case be unsuccessful, the CFA usually provides that a reduced fee may be charged or alternatively, no fee at all; *fr. : ≈ convention d'honoraires conditionnelle*
- cross-examination (n.) : questioning of a hostile witness in court; *fr. : ≈ contre-interrogatoire (d'un témoin)*
- default judgment : judgment which the claimant can enter into if the defendant fails to defend his case; *fr. : jugement par défaut*
- disclosure (n.) : procedural stage requiring all the parties to disclose to each other all the information and documentation which relate to the case and are in their possession, even if it may adversely affect their individual interests; *fr. : procédure de communication de pièces*
- examination-in-chief (n.) : questioning of a witness by the party who called him to give evidence; *fr. : ≈ interrogatoire (d'un témoin)*
- fast-track claims : claims to which simplified procedural rules apply to speed up the judicial process; *fr. : ≈ demandes traitées par la voie rapide*
- Group Litigation Order (GLO) : court order which provides for the simultaneous case management of claims which raise common or related factual or legal issues; *fr. : ≈ action de groupe*
- leave (n.) : here, autorisation; *fr. : autorisation*
- legal (adj.) aid (n.) : loan of public money granted to a litigant who passes a means and merits test, to fund a court case; *fr. : aide juridictionnelle*
- legal expenses insurance (LEI) : type of insurance which covers a policyholder against the possible costs of a legal action which someone can bring against him; *fr. : assurance protection juridique*
- legal professional privilege : privilege or protection which attaches to a client (as opposed to his solicitor) in a client/solicitor relationship; it can only be waived by the client; *fr. : ≈ confidentialité des échanges professionnels entre client et avocat*
- litigant in person : person who goes to court (as claimant or defendant) without seeking a solicitor's assistance or representation; *fr. : justiciable comparaissant en personne*
- order for costs : judge's decision, at the end of the litigation, deciding which party will bear the financial costs of the litigation; the usual rule is that the losing party will pay for his own costs, plus a substantial part of the winner's costs; we say that "costs follow the event"; *fr. : condamnation aux dépens/ ≈ condamnation au titre de l'article 700 du Code de procédure civile (CPC) (ordre judiciaire)/≈ condamnation au titre de l'article L. 761-1 du Code de justice administrative (CJA) (ordre administratif)*

- payment into court (Part 36 payment) : sum of money which for tactical reasons, a party pays into a special court bank account as payment or part-payment of a claim made against him; costs sanctions may result from the other party's failure to accept the sum paid; *fr. : consignation (au greffe)*
- particulars of claim : document which the claimant must file with the court and serve on the defendant at the same time as the claim form; it sets out the details of the claim; *fr. : assignation (ordre judiciaire)/requête (ordre administratif)*
- petitioner (n.) : party who makes a specific application to the court (e.g. a divorce petition); *fr. : demandeur/requérant*
- pleadings (n.) : documents (claim and particulars of claim, defence, reply, etc.) which the parties to the litigation serve on each other and which set out the factual and legal issues on which they rely; *fr. : actes de procédure*
- re-examination (n.) : after the cross-examination stage, last chance given by a party to question the witness he called at trial; *fr. : ≈ nouvel interrogatoire (d'un témoin)*
- reserved (adj.) : when applied to a court decision, fact that the court's actual decision will be handed down a few days later; *fr. : mise en délibéré*
- respondent (n.) : person who defends an application, a petition or an appeal; *fr. : défendeur/intimé* (depending on the circumstances)
- serve (on) (v.) : bring to the attention of someone in an official way; *fr. : notifier/signifier*
- skeleton argument (n.) : list of the main legal points to which each party (or his solicitor/barrister) will refer when making submissions in court; *fr. : ≈ résumé des notes de plaidoirie*
- small (adj.) claims (n.) : claims involving a small sum (determined by statute) to which specific procedural rules apply; *fr. : ≈ petits litiges (relevant du juge de proximité)*
- solicitor (n.) : see 4
- statement of truth : statement made by all the parties to the litigation confirming the accuracy of the contents of their pleadings; *fr. : ≈ attestation de véracité*
- submissions (n.) : overview of the case expressed verbally by each party at trial; there are opening and closing submissions which are made respectively at the start and end of trial; *fr. : ≈ présentation du dossier/≈ plaidoirie*
- summary judgment : accelerated way of obtaining a judgment; *fr. : ≈ ordonnance de référé*
- trial (n.) : when a case is tried, judicial examination and determination of factual and legal issues arising from a dispute between two parties or more, which results in a judgment being handed down; *fr. : procès*
- witness statement : written summary of the evidence which a witness will give at trial; it is mandatory for the parties' respective witness statements be disclosed to each there well before trial; *fr. : déclaration de témoin*

USEFUL EXPRESSIONS

- "costs follow the event"; *fr. : les frais et dépens suivent le sort du principal*
- to find in favour of the claimant; *fr. : trancher en faveur du demandeur/ donner gain de cause au demandeur*
- to plead a case/to make oral submissions on a case; *fr. : plaider un dossier*
- to hand down/to render a decision; *fr. : rendre un jugement*
- to apply to the court for £500 on account of damages; *fr. : demander au tribunal £500 à titre de provision à valoir sur les dommages et intérêts*
- the court makes an order for costs in favour of the defendant; *fr. : le tribunal ordonne la condamnation du demandeur à payer les frais et dépens du défendeur*

FURTHER INFORMATION

- the Jackson reforms have been very unpopular with the legal professions, including some judges; even before the costs reform came into force, the Court of Appeal held in *Henry v. News Group Newspapers* [2013] EWCA Civ 19 that there was "good reason" for a claimant's original costs estimate to go over budget by more than £268,000
- a trial (where a case is tried or *procès*) is different from a hearing (*audience*) when a party's specific application or petition is heard
- the statement of truth is different from an oath; in a statement of truth, the relevant party to the litigation states : "I believe that the facts stated in this (named document) are true"

COMPARATIVE APPROACH

Depuis l'entrée en vigueur des CPR, les règles de procédure applicables en Angleterre et au Pays de Galles ne sont pas sans rappeler le système français : le juge de proximité près du tribunal d'instance qui a compétence pour connaître des petits litiges de la vie quotidienne, rappelle le juge qui traite des *small claims*. Pour le reste, la distinction entre le tribunal d'instance et tribunal de grande instance, et leurs règles respectives de compétence, rappelle la divergence entre les *fast-track* et *multi-track* désormais en vigueur devant les *county courts* et la *High court*. Le système de *case management* semble avoir été copié sur celui de la mise en état applicable en France.

Cependant, la ressemblance n'est que superficielle. En effet, à l'inverse du système accusatoire en vigueur Outre-Manche, le système procédural applicable en France, en matière civile, est inquisitoire. Le rôle moins important des parties dans la conduite du procès (et par voie de conséquence, le rôle plus déterminant du juge) a des répercussions sur le déroulement de la procédure et aussi sur son coût. En France, l'accent est mis sur les actes de procédure (*pleadings*) écrits, les témoins (*witnesses*) n'ayant pas l'opportunité de s'exprimer devant le tribunal. S'agissant des experts, la situation est similaire. En outre, l'étendue du devoir de communication de pièces (*disclosure*) est bien moindre en France qu'Outre-Manche. La procédure étant plus simple en France, l'audience des plaidoiries (*closing submissions*) est plus courte. Par voie de conséquence, le coût de traitement d'un dossier est bien moindre que celui qui serait engendré dans un dossier équivalent en Angleterre et au Pays de Galles.

Sur le point particulier de l'aide juridictionnelle (*legal aid*), si le bénéficiaire doit satisfaire à des conditions de ressources (*means test*) et relatives au bien fondé de la demande (*merits test*), une différence majeure existe entre les deux systèmes : en France, le bénéficiaire de l'aide est pris en charge, ce qui veut dire qu'il se voit donner, à titre définitif, de l'argent public pour financer son action en justice; en revanche, en Angleterre et au Pays de Galles, un système de récupération (*clawback*) existe qui permet au bureau d'aide juridictionnelle (*legal aid board*) et donc, aux contribuables, de se rembourser sur toutes sommes qui pourraient être allouées en justice au bénéficiaire de l'aide.

En ce qui concerne le concept de *Group Litigation*, qui rappelle, dans une certaine mesure, celui de class action aux États-Unis, la France tente de prendre modèle sur l'Angleterre et le Pays de Galles puisque le Sénat doit réexaminer en dernière lecture, courant 2014, un projet de loi sur la consommation autorisant les actions de groupe, qui permettraient aux consommateurs s'estimant lésés d'agir ensemble en justice.

On a ci-dessous traduit le concept de *summary judgment* par ≈ ordonnance de référé. Leur point commun est le fait que dans les deux cas, la décision de justice est rendue dans de brefs délais. Cependant, ils divergent dès lors que, contrairement à l'assignation en référé qui doit être accompagnée d'une action au fond (*application on the merits*), la demande de *summary judgment* se suffit à elle-même.

□ 76 OTHER FORM OF LITIGATION : JUDICIAL REVIEW

Scope of judicial review

Judicial review enables a judge to review a decision or action of a public body. It is a way for the claimant to challenge the procedure followed by a public body when reaching a decision, rather than the actual lawfulness of this decision. The court's powers are thus limited. The court cannot substitute what it thinks is the correct decision but will inform the public body of its error to prompt it to take a further lawful decision. For example, judicial review may be sought against a decision relating to prisoners' rights, a decision of an immigration authority or of a local authority when it exercises its power to provide welfare benefits or takes a decision under the Town and Country Planning Act 1990.

Judicial review can be used when all avenues of appeal have been exhausted. It is different from an appeal to a higher court which involves disputing the decision's legal grounds and merits. A claim for judicial review must be filed within 3 months after the grounds to make the claim first arose. The claimant will then be time-barred. A protocol exists which is a code of good practice setting out the steps which parties should follow before making a claim for judicial review. This protocol is not appropriate where the claimant has an urgent case, for example in case of failure of a local housing authority to arrange for the interim accomodation of a homeless claimant. It is not appropriate either where the defendant, i.e. the public body which took the disputed decision does not have the legal power to change the decision being challenged, for example in the immigration field.

Most judicial reviews are dealt with by the Administrative Court which is a specialised division of the Queen's Bench Division of the High Court (see 3). However, since 1st November 2013, immigration judicial reviews have been transferred to the Upper Tribunal Immigration and Asylum Chamber (see 122 to 126).

The government launched a public consultation which closed on 1st November 2013 inviting views on the possible reform of judicial review. Its purpose is to find ways to cut down on the increasing number of unmeritorious applications for judicial review which results in delaying tactics. The government is also considering an amendment of the rules relating to the requirement of standing.

Alternatives to judicial review

Discussion and negotiation are alternatives to litigation. Ombudsmen (like the Local Government Ombudsmen or the Parliamentary and Health Service Ombudsmen) can deal with complaints. However, this is only possible before a court action is commenced. Mediation, i.e. negotiation carried out by an independent neutral party, as well as other forms of alternative dispute resolution (ADR), are possible. However no party can be forced to resort to those alternatives.

GLOSSARY

- alternative dispute resolution (ADR) : see 74
- arise (v.) : take place, happen; *fr. : survenir*
- challenge (v. or n.) : here, disputing the validity of something; *fr. : contester (v.)/contestation (n.)*
- delay (v.) : postpone, adjourn to a later date; *fr. : retarder*

- judicial (adj.) review (n.) : court proceeding in which a judge reviews the lawfulness of a decision or action made by a public body; *fr. : ≈ voie de recours judiciaire à l'encontre d'une décision administrative*
- lawfulness (n.) : compliance with the law; *fr. : légalité*
- litigation (n.) : contentious law, usually requiring a court of justice to settle the dispute; *fr. : droit contentieux*
- mediation (n.) : see 74
- ombudsman (n.) : person, sometimes appointed by the central government or a local authority, who acts as mediator to try to resolve a dispute; *fr. : ombudsman*
- on the merits : here, a decision or court order based upon the facts presented in evidence and the law applied to that evidence; *fr. : bien fondé*
- planning (n.) : here, urbanism; *fr. : urbanisme*
- standing (n.) : interest which gives the legal capacity to issue legal proceedings against someone; *fr. : intérêt à agir*
- time-barred (adj.) : when the limitation period has expired; *fr. : prescrit*
- unmeritorious (adj.) : unworthy, without merit; *fr. : non-fondé*

USEFUL EXPRESSIONS

- to rely on legal grounds; *fr. : invoquer des moyens de droit*
- to consider the merits of a claim; *fr. : étudier le bien fondé d'une demande*
- an unmeritorious claim; *fr. : une demande non-fondée*
- the claimant must have standing; *fr. : le requérant doit avoir un intérêt à agir*

FURTHER INFORMATION

- judicial review in England and Wales should not be confused with judicial review in the United States which consists of the federal courts' power to review the constitutionality of the federal executive or legislative acts (*Marbury v. Madison* 1803) or that of the states' executive, legislative or judicial acts (*Fletcher v. Peck* 1810)

Comparative approach

Le concept de *judicial review* est difficilement comparable à une quelconque voie de recours en France, tant devant l'ordre judiciaire que l'ordre administratif. Ce n'est pas une voie d'appel, puisque le recours en *judicial review* n'est possible que lorsque les délais d'appel sont épuisés.

Ce n'est pas l'équivalent d'un recours gracieux à une personne publique, auteur de la décision contestée, puisque c'est un recours au tribunal. Ce n'est pas davantage un recours pour excès de pouvoir ou de plein contentieux, puisque le juge saisi du recours en *judicial review* n'a ni le pouvoir d'annuler la décision contestée, ni d'accorder une indemnisation, ni de substituer une autre décision à celle contestée, mais simplement d'inviter l'autorité publique à revoir sa décision.

Le recours à fins de *judicial review* ne peut davantage être comparé à l'opposition (il ne s'agit pas de contester un jugement par défaut), au contredit (il n'y a pas de problème de compétence d'un juge puisque la *judicial review* s'exerce à l'encontre d'une décision administrative et non juridictionnelle), à la tierce opposition (aucun tiers ne conteste une décision judiciaire) ou au recours en révision (il ne s'agit pas de modifier un jugement pour cause de fraude, etc.).

On peut simplement qualifier le concept de *judicial review* de voie de recours judiciaire à l'encontre d'une décision administrative. Si c'est en général l'*Administrative Court* (une juridiction spécialisée de la *Queen's Bench Division* de la *High Court*) qui connaît des *judicial reviews* (sous réserve, entre autres exemples, du contentieux de l'immigration), cette juridiction ne peut pas vraiment être comparée aux tribunaux administratifs français (voir 3).

2

Contract law and litigation

□ 77 DISCHARGE OF CONTRACT

Where all obligations under an agreement are performed by the contracting parties, the contract is said to be discharged (or at an end). Disputes may arise, however, as to what constitutes performance. Traditionally, the rules for performance were quite strict : even minor departures from requirements laid down by the contract allowed the other party to claim non-performance. This potential for hardship caused by such a rigorous approach has been mitigated in more recent years. If there has been substantial performance, with only relatively minor defects, the party performing the work will be entitled to claim payment for the goods or services provided, less any money required to fix the defects. Whether there has been substantial performance is an issue of fact in each case; however, it will not be applicable where the defect concerns breach of a condition. In some cases, one party may accept, of his own free choice, partial performance of the other's obligations; in such cases payment for the part-performance will be enforceable. Finally, a party may be prevented by the other party from performing its contractual obligations, in which case an action will be open for breach of contract.

The following chapters will look at the main ways in which a contract may be discharged, avoided or set aside by the courts, whether for breach of contract or because of some vitiating factor in the contract's formation (such as misrepresentation, undue influence or duress).

A basic distinction needs to be made at the start between contracts which are void and those which are voidable. A void contract is an agreement that never had any legal force in the first place (i.e. it was void *ab initio*), whether because it lacked an essential element such as capacity or consideration, or because it was illegal or otherwise contrary to public policy. Voidable contracts, on the other hand, are capable of being binding agreements. If a person is induced to enter into an agreement through misrepresentation, for example, he will have the choice either to affirm the resulting contract or to rescind it. If he opts for rescission, the contract will be set aside and the parties put back (as far as possible) in their pre-contractual positions.

Where parties fail to perform their contractual obligations they will be in breach of contract. The various remedies available for breach, including termination and damages, are discussed in the chapters that follow; however, it should be noted at this stage that concepts such as rescission and voidable contracts do not apply in such circumstances.

GLOSSARY

- affirm (v.) : see 83
- avoid (a contract) (v.) : cancel a contract which cannot be continued, thus putting an end to the parties' agreement; *fr. : résoudre/annuler/invalider (un contrat)*
- binding (adj.) : see 7
- breach (n. and v.) : failure to observe or perform (contractual) obligations; the action of committing such a breach; *fr. : rupture/violation (n.)/rompre (v.)*
- condition (n) : see 83
- consideration (n.) : see 9
- damages (n.) : see 73
- defective performance : performance of contractual obligations which is imperfect or faulty in some way; amongst other things, an action for damages can be brought in respect of any defects; *fr. : mauvaise exécution contractuelle*
- discharge (v. or n.) : here, bring to an end or release from contractual obligations; *fr. : éteindre (v.)/extinction (n.) (d'une obligation contractuelle)*
- duress (n.) : see 80
- illegal (adj.) : see 81
- induce (v.) : persuade or influence; *fr. : persuader*
- misrepresentation (n.) : see 79
- partial/part-performance : performance of contractual obligations which falls short of full performance; *fr. : exécution partielle*
- repudiation (n.) : see 83
- rescission (n.)/rescind (v.) : see 84
- set aside (a contract) (v.) : annul or cancel the effect of a contract found to be either void or voidable; *fr. : résoudre/invalider/annuler (un contrat)*
- termination (n.)/terminate (v.) : see 83
- undue (adj.) influence (n.) : see 80
- vitiating factor : element or circumstance that impairs the validity of a contract; any factor that renders, or has the potential to render, an agreement devoid of any legal force; *fr. : vice (affectant/susceptible d'affecter la validité d'un contrat)*
- void (adj.) : invalid; of no legal effect; *fr. : frappé de nullité (absolue)*

- voidable (adj) : capable of being set aside or rescinded by one of the contracting parties; *fr. : annulable/susceptible de nullité (relative)*

USEFUL EXPRESSIONS

- an action to set aside (a contract) for duress; *fr. : action en nullité pour violence*
- to seek from the court an order that the defendant pay the claimant damages for breach of contract; *fr. : présenter au tribunal une demande de condamnation du défendeur à payer au demandeur des dommages-intérêts pour rupture de contrat*
- to seek damages as compensation for the various heads of damage sustained; *fr. : demander des dommages et intérêts au titre des divers chefs de préjudice subis*

FURTHER INFORMATION

- in general English the word breach may have the sense of *rupture* (e.g. to breach the enemy's defences; a breach in the dam); in contract law, however, the two words are not interchangeable (it is not possible to "rupture" a contract)
- the noun damages, in the sense of financial compensation, is always plural; take care not to confuse this with the uncountable noun damage (*préjudice*)
- it is common to use the verb discharge in the passive form (e.g. the contract was discharged; they were discharged from their obligations)

COMPARATIVE APPROACH

Le droit français opère une distinction marquée entre les contrats civils et commerciaux, les litiges y afférant relevant de deux juridictions différentes. Outre-Manche, la distinction existe mais elle est moins prononcée (*cf.* les chapitres sur les *commercial contracts*).

En droit français où le principe « pas de nullité sans texte » trouve application, les textes – en l'espèce, les articles 1109 et suivants du Code civil – définissent précisément les causes de nullité absolue ou relative. Parmi ces dernières, on trouve les vices du consentement (erreur, dol et violence) qui présentent une similitude non négligeable avec les notions de *mistake*, *misrepresentation*, *duress* et *undue influence* étudiées ci-dessous.

On verra que contrairement à la France, ces divers concepts sont surtout issus de la *common law* (mais il y a quelques exceptions). Outre-Manche, les causes de nullité relative ou absolue peuvent être assimilées à ce qui rend un contrat respectivement *voidable* ou *void.*

□ 78 MISTAKE

In some cases, where one or more of the parties is mistaken about some aspect of the agreement the validity of the contract may be called into question. Mistake will never affect the validity of a contract unless it can be shown that it preceded the agreement and that it induced the mistaken party, or parties, to enter into the contract.

Mistake is divided into common mistake and cross-purposes mistake.

Common mistake

A common mistake occurs when both parties make the same mistake. For instance, John bought a work of art from Sarah which both parties believed was an original Rodin, but which turned out to be a fake. A common mistake will only render a contract void if it is fundamental – it robs the agreement of all substance, or makes its performance radically different from that envisaged by the parties. The courts regard mistakes about the existence of the subject matter as fundamental, so if the subject matter of the agreement has, unknown to both parties, ceased to exist, then the contract may be void.

Generally, a common mistake as to some quality of the goods or subject matter will not be operative – it will not affect the validity of the contract, even in situations where the attribute or quality is important. The law in this area is complex and not always entirely consistent. However, the guiding principle is that a common mistake as to quality (as opposed to existence) will only be operative where the lack of this quality renders the goods or subject matter "essentially different" from that which it was believed to be.

Cross-purposes mistake

Often the mistake is not a common one, and it turns out that the parties, labouring under different misunderstandings, are at cross purposes. Such mistakes will rarely make a contract void. Where only one of the parties has misunderstood some aspect of the agreement, this is referred to as a unilateral mistake. The contract will be valid unless the misunderstanding concerns the fundamental nature of the offer and the other party was aware of this mistake (or should have been aware of it). A mistake by one party as to the identity of the other will not be operative, unless it can be shown that the other's identity was of fundamental importance to the agreement.

Where the parties have each made different mistakes about the subject matter, the court will generally attempt to give effect to the intentions of the parties. However, if they are at such cross-purposes that it would be impossible for a reasonable observer to say what they had agreed to, then the contract may be declared void.

Mistake may also be operative in the case of a deed. If one of the parties was fundamentally mistaken as to the nature of the transaction embodied by a deed, such a mistake can be used as a defence to any proceedings brought by the other party in reliance on the deed.

GLOSSARY

- cross-purposes mistake : mistake deriving from one party's erroneous understanding about the other party's intention or purpose; *fr. : ≈ erreur menant à une absence de consensualisme/≈ erreur sur la nature du contrat*
- common (adj.) mistake (n.) : single mistake shared by both parties to a contract; *fr. : erreur commune « vice du consentement »*
- deed (n.) : see 9
- fundamental (adj.) mistake (n.) : mistake which is basic or essential; generally, only fundamental mistakes will be operative under common law; *fr. : ≈ erreur-obstacle*
- identical (adj.) mistake (n.) : (see "common mistake"); *fr. : erreur commune « vice du consentement »*
- misconception (n) : incorrect view or opinion; misunderstanding; *fr. : idée erronée/malentendu*
- mistake as to the identity (of the other party) : mistake relating to the identity of the person with whom a contract was entered into; *fr. : erreur sur la personne/erreur sur l'identité du cocontractant*
- mistake as to quality : mistake concerning the attributes or distinctive characteristics of something; in contract law such mistakes are rarely operative; *fr. : ≈ erreur sur la qualité/≈ erreur sur la substance*
- mistake as to the existence of the subject matter : mistaken belief by both parties that the subject matter of a contract exists, when in fact it does not (e.g., where goods have been destroyed without the parties' knowledge); *fr. : ≈ erreur sur l'existence de la chose objet du contrat*
- misunderstand (v.) : interpret the words or actions of another in the wrong way; miscomprehend; *fr. : mal comprendre*
- misunderstanding (n.) : failure to understand or interpret something; *fr. : méprise*
- mutual (adj.) mistake (n.) : (see "common mistake"); *fr. : erreur commune*
- operative (adj.) : having effect, functioning; *fr. : fonctionnel*
- precede (v.) : come before; a mistake must precede a contract to be operative; *fr. : précéder*
- rectification (n.) : equitable remedy allowing the correction of a contractual document which does not accurately express the intention of the parties; *fr. : rectification*
- render (v.) : make; *fr. : rendre*
- shared (adj.) mistake (n.) : (see "common mistake"); *fr. : erreur commune*
- unilateral (adj.) mistake (n.) : mistake by only one party to a contract; such mistakes are rarely operative in contract law; *fr. : erreur unilatérale*

USEFUL EXPRESSIONS

- to be at cross-purposes with someone; *fr. : comprendre quelqu'un de travers*
- to be labouring under a misunderstanding about something; *fr. : se tromper sur quelque chose*
- to call something into question; *fr. : mettre en cause/contester quelque chose*
- to draw a fine distinction between two concepts; *fr. : faire une distinction subtile entre deux concepts*
- to render the contract void; *fr. : entraîner l'annulation du contrat*

FURTHER INFORMATION

- the expression "common mistake" has a particular meaning in the context of contract law, and should not be confused with the general English sense of a mistake which occurs quite often (*erreur courante*); in other areas of law, the adjective "common" may be used to signify "of relatively minor importance"; e.g. a common assault in criminal law

COMPARATIVE APPROACH

Les principes du consensualisme et de l'autonomie de la volonté sont importants en droit des contrats des deux côtés de la Manche. Le domaine de l'erreur, vice du consentement en droit français, est plus large que la simple *mistake* et on pourrait dire qu'il inclut aussi la notion de *misrepresentation* (*cf.* ci-dessous). Si le concept de *mistake* est issu de la *common law*, celui d'erreur ressort de l'article 1110 du Code civil.

L'influence de la jurisprudence et de la *case law* montre des rapprochements intéressants entre les concepts de *mistake* et d'erreur. À titre d'exemple, la célèbre affaire du Poussin (Civ. 1re, n° 82-12237, 13 décembre 1983) portait sur l'erreur sur les qualités substantielles que le vendeur aurait commise en cédant à prix bas à un musée, un tableau qui s'est ultérieurement révélé de Nicolas Poussin (pour lequel un prix plus élevé aurait pu être négocié). Dans le dossier *Leaf v. International Galleries* [1950] 2 KB 86, l'*errans*, M. Leaf, a cru acheter à une galerie un tableau de John Constable qui s'est avéré n'être qu'une copie. Il a engagé une action en résolution à l'encontre du vendeur pour *mistake* et *innocent misrepresentation*. Dans les deux affaires, les deux juridictions ont constaté la faible durée du délai de prescription (*limitation period*) en la matière, l'action étant d'ailleurs prescrite dans l'affaire Leaf.

À titre de second exemple, si l'erreur sur la personne ou sur l'identité du cocontractant trouve en droit anglais un quasi-équivalent avec la notion de *mistake as to identity*, la jurisprudence en Angleterre et au Pays de Galles n'y inclut pas les erreurs relatives aux attributs ou au caractère de l'autre partie (telles que la respectabilité, la solvabilité, etc.)

□ 79 MISREPRESENTATION

A misrepresentation occurs when, in the course of negotiating a contract, one party (the representor) makes an untrue statement of fact to induce the other party (the representee) to enter into the contract. The misrepresentation may be written, oral, or even by conduct.

There are therefore three elements required for a statement to constitute an actionable misrepresentation : the statement must be false; it must be a statement of fact, as opposed to mere opinion or a statement of future intention; and it must have acted as an inducement to enter into the contract. A false statement of law is not a misrepresentation, nor is a statement of opinion (unless the representator had no reasonable grounds for holding that opinion) or intention. Mere "sales talk", which is typically used by a sales person to sell a product to a customer, will normally not count as statements of fact.

Although silence will generally not count as a misrepresentation, the law has recognised a duty to disclose information in a number of specific circumstances. Examples of this include contracts requiring utmost good faith (e.g. an insurance contract) or an agreement between parties in a fiduciary relationship (e.g. a trustee and a beneficiary). Remaining silent about a material fact in such circumstances may amount to a misrepresentation.

If the false statement of fact played no part in the representee's decision to enter into the contract then it cannot be relied on to set aside the agreement; a misrepresentation will be actionable only if it was an inducement for the representee to enter into the contract.

There are a number of different types of misrepresentation recognised by common law and statute. Fraudulent misrepresentation occurs where a party makes a false statement which they know (or believe) to be untrue. The courts have also recognised negligent misrepresentation under common law principles of tort law, imposing a duty on anyone professing expert knowledge or skill to use reasonable care to ensure the accuracy of any representations made to induce other parties to enter a contract. Under the provisions of current legislation like the Misrepresentation Act 1967, however, there is no requirement to prove negligence to claim damages for a misrepresentation. The representor will be liable unless he can show that it was an innocent misrepresentation – he believed the statement to be true at the time it was made, and there were reasonable grounds for that belief.

GLOSSARY

- actionable (adj) : subject to, or giving a sufficient basis for, an action at law; *fr. : passible d'une action en justice*
- contract of utmost good faith : type of contract in which the parties are required by law to disclose all material facts before entering into the contract; failure to do so renders the contract voidable (e.g. insurance contracts); *fr. : contrat basé sur la bonne foi*

- disclose (v.)/disclosure (n.) : act of making information known (often refers to information of a restricted or private nature); full disclosure of material facts is required in contracts of insurance and other contracts of utmost good faith; *fr. : communiquer (v.)/communication (n.) (d'informations ou de documents)*
- false (adj.) representation (n.) : statement which is untrue; *fr. : fausse assertion*
- fiduciary (adj.) relationship (n.) : relationship in which one party holding a special position of trust or confidence is required to act for the benefit of another (e.g. the relationship between a trustee and beneficiary); *fr. : relation fiduciaire/≈ rapport de confiance*
- fraudulent (adj.) misrepresentation (n.) : false statement which the maker knows, or believes, to be false; *fr. : assertion frauduleuse et inexacte*
- induce (v.) : persuade or influence; *fr. : persuader/influencer/convaincre*
- inducement (n.) : something which persuades or influences a person to do something; *fr. : motivation*
- innocent (adj.) misrepresentation (n.) : false representation which the representor believed, upon reasonable grounds, to be true at the time it was made; *fr. : assertion inexacte qui n'est pas faite exprès*
- material (adj.) fact (n.) : relevant or important fact; only misrepresentations about facts material to the subject matter of a contract are actionable; *fr. : fait pertinent*
- misrepresent (v.)/misrepresentation (n.) : giving a false or imperfect representation or account; false or misleading statement; *fr. : présenter (un fait) de manière inexacte (v.)/assertion inexacte (n.)*
- negligent (adj.) misrepresentation (n.) : false statement of fact made by a person without due care; *fr. : assertion inexacte engageant la responsabilité civile quasi-délictuelle*
- representation (n.) : portrayal or description, by words or by conduct, of the qualities or nature of something or someone; *fr. : assertion*
- representation by conduct : assertion implied from the conduct of a party; *fr. : assertion tacite*
- representation of fact : assertion about a fact; only assertions of fact can form the basis of actionable misrepresentation in contract law; *fr. : assertion de fait*
- representation of law : assertion concerning the law; such representations are generally not actionable as misrepresentations; *fr. : assertion de droit*
- representee (n.) : person or entity to whom a representation is made; *fr. : personne à l'encontre de qui l'assertion est faite*
- representor (n.) : person or entity who makes a representation; *fr. : auteur de l'assertion*
- sales talk : promotional speech or demonstration designed to persuade a potential customer to purchase something; generally not regarded by law as actionable misrepresentations; *fr. : boniment*

- statement (n.) : expression of something in speech or writing; enunciation; *fr. : déclaration*

USEFUL EXPRESSIONS

- to have reasonable grounds for believing; *fr. : avoir de bonnes raisons de croire*
- to count as; *fr. : compter comme*
- to play a part in something; *fr. : contribuer à quelque chose*
- to rely on a representation; *fr. : se fier à une assertion*

FURTHER INFORMATION

- negligent misrepresentation uses the tortious concept of negligence; negligence should not be translated by *négligence* but by *responsabilité civile quasi-délictuelle*
- it is generally preferrable to use the verb "enter into" rather than "enter" when talking about contracts or negotiations (e.g. the parties entered into the contract after lengthy discussions)
- the noun statement has different uses in legal English; in contract law, it generally refers to any enunciation made by a party in the course of negotiations; however, it may be used in other contexts to refer to a formal, written declaration or deposition

COMPARATIVE APPROACH

Les notions de *misrepresentation* et de *mistake* peuvent être comparées, conjointement, à celle de l'erreur en droit français (C. civ., art. 1110), même si la jurisprudence leur a souvent donné un champ d'application quelque peu différent. Contrairement à l'erreur du droit français qui doit toujours être prouvée par l'*errans*, l'intervention du législateur, Outre-Manche, avec la *Misrepresentation Act* 1967, a permis de renverser la charge de la preuve pour les seules *misrepresentations* rentrant dans le champ de la loi (le défendeur à l'action en *misrepresentation* étant présumé responsable, cette présomption étant simple [*rebuttable*] et non pas irréfragable [*irrebuttable*]).

□ 80 DURESS AND UNDUE INFLUENCE

Where a party to a contract obtains the consent of the other party through threats or undue influence, the contract will be voidable. There are two related concepts to deal with such cases : the common law doctrine of duress, and the equitable doctrine of undue influence.

Duress

The following elements must be present for a finding of duress : there was illegitimate pressure exerted by one of the contracting parties on the other; this pressure induced the claimant to enter into the contract; the claimant protested against this pressure either at the time or shortly after the contract was formed. Duress implies some measure of compulsion or coercion : the idea that the claimant was compelled to enter into the contract due to pressure, whether economic or otherwise, exerted by the other contracting party. Duress may take the form of threats to person, property, or financial well-being (economic duress). In all cases the courts will not find duress if the claimant is presented with some practical alternative, or if the pressure was "legitimate" (e.g. a threat to alter the terms of an existing contract). Further, in cases where illegitimate pressure was exerted but the victim did nothing to protest until long after the contract was formed, the courts will be unlikely to uphold a claim of duress.

Undue influence

Undue influence arises where one party uses his influence over another to prevent that person from exercising their independent judgment. A party that has been persuaded to enter into a contract through the exercise of undue influence can seek to have the contract set aside.

Undue influence may be actual or presumed. For actual undue influence the claimant must show that he entered into a contract as a direct result of that influence. If, however, there is a special relationship of trust between the parties, and one party enters into an agreement that is obviously disadvantageous to their own interests, the law will presume the existence of undue influence. The onus will then be on the other party to rebut, or disprove, this presumption (which is thus not irrebuttable). There are a number of examples where a relationship of trust is presumed to exist, including that of parent and child, doctor and patient, trustee and beneficiary, or religious adviser and disciple. However, current caselaw has found that no such special relationship exists between husband and wife. A relationship of trust may also arise from the circumstances of a particular case.

Undue influence and third parties

In some cases, a person may use his influence to persuade someone to enter into an agreement with another party. If, for example, a husband exerts undue influence on his wife to sign a contract with their bank providing security for a loan, the question is whether the contractual rights of the bank can be affected by the impropriety of a third party (i.e. the husband). The courts have held that such a contract could be avoided (in the sense of made void) by the wife if the bank had either actual or "constructive" (presumed) notice of the impropriety. To prevent having constructive notice imputed to them by law, the bank would have to show that it took reasonable steps to ascertain that the wife was aware of the implications of the proposed transaction before signing the contract.

GLOSSARY

- coerce (v.)/coercion (n.) : compel someone to do something by force or threats; the action of coercing someone; *fr. : contraindre (v.)/coercition (n.)*
- compel (v.)/compulsion (n.) : force or oblige; action of being forced or constrained to do something; *fr. : obliger (v.)/contrainte (n.)*
- constructive (adj.) notice (n.) : awareness or knowledge (about a fact or state of affairs) which the law presumes a legal entity to have; *fr. : ≈ connaissance présumée*
- duress (n.) : illegitimate constraint or pressure put on the free exercise of another's will or judgement; *fr. : violence*
- economic (adj.) duress (n.) : pressure or threats, often indirect, directed towards the financial well-being of a person or entity; *fr. : contrainte économique*
- exert (v.) : to exercise or bring to bear a force or quality; *fr. : exercer*
- illegitimate (adj) : not in accordance with legal rules or accepted standards; unauthorised; *fr. : illégitime*
- impropriety (n.) : failure to observe proper procedure or standard of behaviour; *fr. : incorrection*
- induce (v.) : see 77
- irrebuttable (adj.) : which cannot be rebutted or refuted; *fr. : irréfragable*
- onus (n.) : see 85
- presume (v.)/presumption (n.) : concept or idea that is taken to be true on the basis of probability; *fr. : présumer (v.)/présomption (n.)*
- relationship of trust : special relationship between contracting parties arising by virtue of the trust or confidence which one party places in the other (e.g. parent and child, solicitor and client, doctor and patient, etc.); *fr. : relation de confiance*
- threat (n.) : declaration of intention to inflict injury or other harm on someone; *fr. : menace*
- undue (adj.) influence (n.) : power which A has over B to influence B's behaviour and prevent B from exercising an independent judgment about A's own interests; equitable doctrine that allows agreements formed in such conditions to be set aside; *fr. : dol/manœuvres dolosives*

USEFUL EXPRESSIONS

- to put pressure on someone to do something; *fr. : faire pression sur quelqu'un pour qu'il fasse quelque chose*
- to threaten someone with something; *fr. : menacer quelqu'un de quelque chose*
- to reverse the burden of proof; *fr. : renverser la charge de la preuve*

- the defendant is presumed liable, but this presumption is rebuttable; *fr. : le défendeur est présumé responsable mais la présomption n'est pas irréfragable/la présomption est simple*

FURTHER INFORMATION

- the nouns threat and menace are not always interchangeable in English; while both terms are used to refer to something which poses a danger, a statement of intention to cause harm is a threat rather than a menace

COMPARATIVE APPROACH

Les concepts de *duress* et d'*undue influence* se recoupent dans une large mesure avec ceux de violence et de dol en droit français. Cependant, là encore, le dol et la violence ressortent des dispositions du Code civil (art. 1111 à 1116 inclus) alors que la *duress* et l'*undue influence* sont respectivement issus de la *common law* et de *l'equity*.

□ 81 ILLEGALITY AND UNFAIRNESS

Illegal contracts

A contract may be illegal at the time it was formed, due to some statutory or common law prohibition concerning the subject matter of the agreement. Examples of agreements which are illegal at common law include contracts to commit (or benefit from) a crime, contracts promoting public corruption, or contracts aimed at defrauding the tax office (HM Revenue & Customs). These agreements are considered contrary to public policy and therefore void. Other types of contract, such as those restricting competition in a commercial context, are illegal under specific statutes. In some cases a contract may be lawful at the time of formation, but is performed in an illegal way.

Consequences of illegality

An agreement which is illegal at the time of its formation will be treated as if it never existed as a binding contract; it will therefore be void *ab initio*. As a result, neither party can rely on the contract to sue the other to recover money or property already transferred. The court may make exceptions where one of the parties is less at fault than the other, in which case the victim may be able to recover property transferred to the "guilty" party. Where the contract was lawful at the time of formation but performed in an illegal way, the consequences will depend on the knowledge of the contracting parties. If both parties were aware of the illegal mode of performance, the contract will be void. If, on the other hand, one of the parties was unaware that the other party was carrying out the contract in an illegal way, then this "innocent" party may seek to enforce the agreement. In certain cases the court may be prepared to sever or strike out the illegal elements of a contract, provided they are a relatively unimportant part of the agreement and their removal would not destroy the nature of the contract. Some contracts include a severability clause to indicate the intentions of the parties in the event that the court finds parts of the agreement to be illegal or otherwise invalid.

Contracts in restraint of trade

Contracts which seek to limit a person's right to trade freely or use his or her skills for payment are an important aspect of commercial dealings. Such agreements are common, for example, when a vendor sells a business or where a skilled employee leaves a company, the aim being to prevent the vendor/employee from setting up a business in the same area and attracting clients away from their former business/employer. Whether or not such contracts are enforceable depends on a complex set of rules under both common law and statute. As a general principle, however, any agreement that seeks to place a restraint on trade will be void unless it can be shown to be reasonable and not contrary to public policy. While employers may legitimately seek to protect trade secrets or good will, restrictions designed merely to prevent competition will not be enforceable.

Exemption clauses

In some cases the terms of a contract, though not illegal, are considered to be so unfair to one of the parties that the law will intervene to prevent an injustice. The most significant instance of this concerns exemption clauses : contractual provisions which seek to exclude or limit the liability of one of the parties in the event of a breach of contract. Common law judges have, in more recent times, been wary of enforcing such clauses and developed stringent tests for their incorporation and interpretation. Any ambiguity in the clause will be interpreted in such a way as to restrict or nullify its operation. The more onerous the clause, the more difficult it will be to rely on it. Such clauses are now covered by statutory law under the Unfair Contract Terms Act 1977, which is particularly focused on regulating the use of exemption clauses in relation to agreements between a business and a consumer. The legislation makes it clear that certain types of liability cannot be excluded (e.g. liability for death or personal injury resulting from negligence). In other cases, such as indemnity clauses or exemption for non-performance, the party seeking to rely on the clause must satisfy the court that it is fair and reasonable.

GLOSSARY

- consumer (n.) : purchaser of goods and services for personal use; *fr. : consommateur/-trice*
- defraud (v.) : illegal action consisting in taking or keeping money, goods or property by cheating or deceiving someone; *fr. : frauder*

- exemption clause : contractual term that seeks to exclude or restrict one party's liability under the agreement in the event of a specified breach; *fr. : clause d'exonération*
- exclusion clause : term in a contract purporting to exclude one party's liability for specified breaches of contract; a type of exemption clause dealing with exclusions rather than limitations of liability; *fr. : clause d'exclusion*
- good will : see 39
- illegal (adj) contract (n.) : agreement prohibited either by statute or at common law on the basis of public policy; *fr. : contrat frappé d'illégalité*
- indemnity clause : contractual term providing that one party will compensate the other in the event of any loss arising from the contract; *fr. : ≈ clause pénale*
- onerous (adj) : burdensome; involving heavy or oppressive obligations; *fr. : pénible*
- public (adj.) policy (n.) : broadly shared interests of a community or society; contracts which attack or subvert these interests will be illegal at common law; *fr. : intérêt général/ordre public*
- reasonable (adj.) : fair or moderate; (of person) having fair and sensible judgement; *fr. : raisonnable/agissant en « bon père de famille »*
- restraint of trade clause : contractual term limiting a party's right to exercise his trade or carry on business within a particular area and/or time period; to be valid such clauses must not offend public policy and must be reasonable; *fr. : clause de non-concurrence*
- sever (v.)/severance (n.) : cutting off; to sever an illegal term is to excise it from the main body of the contract; *fr. : couper (v.)/retrait (n.)*
- severability clause : contractual term indicating the parties' express wish to sever certain parts of the contract in the event that a court finds them to be illegal or invalid; *fr. : ≈ clause salvatrice*
- strike out (v) : annul or render void; delete or cancel the effect of (a clause or provision); *fr. : annuler*
- subject matter : object of a contract; *fr. : objet (du contrat)*
- unfair (adj.) : not in accordance with rules or standards; unjust or inequitable; *fr. : injuste*
- void *ab initio :* void from the beginning; a contract which is void *ab initio* never came into existence in the first place; *fr. : nul ab initio*

USEFUL EXPRESSIONS

- to exclude the liability of a party in the event of; *fr. : exclure la responsabilité d'une partie en cas de*
- an agreement containing a restraint of trade clause; *fr. : une convention qui contient une clause de non-concurrence*

- to limit liability for breach of contract; *fr. : limiter la responsabilité en cas de rupture de contrat*

FURTHER INFORMATION

- the word interdiction is rarely used in English, apart from certain ecclesiastical, legal or military contexts; it should not be used as a general substitute for prohibition
- competition in a commercial context cannot be translated as *concurrence*; the meaning of concurrence in English is restricted to the sense of an accordance or a coincidence in time of events

COMPARATIVE APPROACH

Les tribunaux français, comme ceux de l'Angleterre et du Pays de Galles, frappent régulièrement de nullité les contrats qui sont illégaux ou contraires à l'ordre public. Faire une « mauvaise affaire » ne donne pas droit à la résolution d'un contrat, ni en France ni Outre-Manche. Cependant, la notion de caractère abusif a un rôle de plus en plus important dans les deux pays grâce à la législation, et surtout au droit européen. L'hostilité des tribunaux français envers des clauses d'exonération égale celle des tribunaux Outre-Manche. Ces clauses sont interprétées de façon restrictive. En revanche, le concept de clause pénale en droit français a un champ d'application un peu plus large que celui de *penalty clause* ou *indemnity clause*, car la clause pénale englobe toute clause qui vise à assurer l'exécution d'un contrat. La validité des clauses pénales en droit français est protégée par l'article 1152 du Code civil, même si les tribunaux sanctionneront les clauses imposant le paiement à titre de dommages et intérêts d'une somme manifestement excessive.

□ 82 FRUSTRATION

The doctrine of frustration operates where some event occurs which, through no fault of the parties, makes its performance impossible or illegal. The agreement is said to be frustrated and the contractual obligations of the parties come to an end.

One theory behind the doctrine is that it gives effect to the implied intentions of the parties at the time the contract was made. The parties are taken to have implicitly agreed that they would no longer be bound in the event of the frustrating event. However, the more generally preferred view today is that courts may intervene to impose a fair solution where the obligation under an agreement is, because of the change in circumstances, completely different to that envisaged by the parties when the contract was made. Rather than appeal to the presumed intentions of the parties, the courts seek to do justice in a situation which is not the fault of either party.

Frustration usually falls into one of three categories : impossibility (e.g. the subject matter of the contract is destroyed, or a person required to perform the contract is no longer available due to illness or some other reason) ; illegality (e.g. due to a change in the law) ; and changed circumstances, such that the central or commercial purpose of the agreement is completely destroyed and performance would be pointless.

Exceptions

The courts have recognised a number of circumstances where the doctrine of frustration will not apply, despite the occurrence of an intervening event making performance impossible. This will be the case, for example, where the parties had considered (or ought to have considered) the relevant event at the time the contract was formed, or where the contract expressly requires performance under any circumstances. Likewise, a contract will not be frustrated by an event due to the fault of one of the parties, or an event that makes performance more onerous or expensive, but not impossible.

Effect

At common law a contract will be discharged at the point in time at which the frustrating event occurs. This does not mean the contract is void *ab initio*; although the parties are released from their contractual obligations, they will still be bound by any obligations incurred before the contract was frustrated. If a party received advance payment under the contract but failed to perform the corresponding service, he would be obliged to repay the amount. Under common law principles, however, advance money would not be repayable where there had been part performance (however minimal). This situation is now governed by legislation which provides that money transferred prior to frustration of the contract is recoverable, though the amount will be reduced by any expenses incurred by the recipient in performance of the contract. The legislative framework further provides that any party receiving a benefit from part performance of a contract (prior to its frustration) may be required to pay a just sum in return for the benefit.

GLOSSARY

- discharge (n. or v.) : here, release from or termination of (contractual) obligation; *fr. : résiliation/décharge des obligations résultant d'un contrat (n.)* or *résilier/décharger des obligations d'un contrat (v.)*
- fair solution theory : theory behind doctrine of frustration which justifies court intervention where the original purpose and obligations of contracting parties are frustrated by a change in circumstances; this theory focuses on the need to impose a fair solution rather than the existence of some implied term giving effect to the presumed intentions of the parties; *fr. : ≈ théorie de la solution équitable*

- frustrating (adj.) event (n.) : intervening event, following the formation of a contract, which makes its performance impossible or illegal, or which otherwise prevents its main purpose from being achieved; *fr. : ≈ évènement rendant impossible l'exécution d'un contrat*
- frustration (n.)/frustrate (v.) : doctrine allowing for discharge of contractual obligations where an unforeseen event prevents the parties from achieving the main purpose of the agreement or renders its performance impossible or illegal; to thwart or defeat (the purpose or performance of a contract); *fr. : ≈ théorie de l'imprévision/≈ rendre un contrat impossible à exécuter*
- incur (v.) : become liable to or subject to something (usually through one's own actions); *fr. : encourir*
- onerous (adj.) : involving heavy or burdensome obligations; difficult or laborious; *fr. : pénible/lourd*
- part performance : carrying out of (contractual) obligations which falls short of complete performance; partial or incomplete performance; *fr. : exécution partielle*
- pointless (adj.) : having no sense or purpose; *fr. : inutile/dénué de sens*
- recipient (n.) : person who receives something; *fr. : récipiendaire*
- recoverable (adj.) : capable of being (legally) regained or retrieved; *fr. : recouvrable*
- void *ab initio* : see 81

USEFUL EXPRESSIONS

- to incur substantial losses; *fr. : subir des pertes importantes*
- to be discharged from one's responsibilities; *fr. : être libéré de ses obligations*
- the contract was frustrated by an intervening event; *fr. : l'exécution du contrat a été rendue impossible par la survenance d'un évènement*

FURTHER INFORMATION

- the verb frustrate has two senses in English : to prevent, or to cause annoyance
- the verb discharge is often used in the passive form (e.g. the contract was discharged); it is also used in a number of common collocations in other areas of the law (e.g. the prisoner/jury/accused was discharged)

COMPARATIVE APPROACH

La loi française n'a pas d'équivalent direct de la doctrine de *frustration*. Tant en France qu'en Angleterre et au Pays de Galles, l'exécution d'un contrat peut devenir impossible suite à l'intervention d'un événement imprévisible.

La notion de force majeure existe en France et aussi en Angleterre et au Pays de Galles où on se réfère d'ailleurs à la *force majeure*. Cependant, le concept de *frustration* a un domaine d'application beaucoup plus extensif.

□ 83 TERMINATION FOR BREACH

A contract is breached where one of the parties either fails to perform his obligations under the contract (actual breach) or indicates his intention not to do so (anticipatory breach). Although the innocent party will always be entitled to sue for damages, whether or not he can terminate the contract depends on the nature of the breach. The three types of breach that may give rise to termination are repudiation, breach of a condition, or serious breach of an innominate term. In each of these cases the wronged party has the choice either to terminate the contract or to affirm it.

Repudiation

Where one party gives clear indications that they no longer intend to perform their contractual obligations, the other party can treat this as a repudiation or anticipatory breach of the contract. Repudiation may be expressed in words or implied from conduct. The courts will not find repudiation, however, unless there has been conduct that is clearly inconsistent with continuation of the contract (e.g. where a person agrees to sell goods to someone, but before the agreed delivery date he sells those goods to another). Where repudiation of a contract occurs, the innocent party is entitled to treat the contract as discharged and to sue for damages for any loss incurred.

Actual breach : conditions, warranties and innominate terms

Where there is an actual breach of contract, the consequences will depend on the nature of the term breached. Contractual terms can be divided into three main categories : conditions, warranties, and innominate terms. A condition is an essential term of the contract. Breach of a condition is therefore treated as a fundamental breach of contract allowing the other party to terminate the agreement. Warranties are non-essential terms, breach of which does not entail serious consequences. A wronged party may sue for damages for breach of a warranty, but is not entitled to terminate the contract. Often parties will specify in a contract which terms are intended to be conditions or warranties; in other cases the importance of the term will be governed by traditional usage (e.g. time clauses in commercial agreements are often treated as conditions). Innominate (or intermediate) terms do not neatly fit into either of the above categories; their breach may, depending on the circumstances, result in either serious or trivial consequences. The injured party will only be entitled to terminate the contract if the breach is sufficiently serious; if it is not a fundamental breach the consequences will be the same as for a warranty.

Affirmation or termination

Contracts are not automatically discharged by breaches, no matter how serious. The wronged party can elect whether to terminate or affirm the contract (in either case, an action for damages for breach will also be open). A serious breach is treated as a repudiation, whether actual or anticipatory, of obligations under the contract, but the wronged party must "accept" that repudiation before the contract will be treated as discharged. Further, any decision to treat the contract as discharged must be made known to the other party. Usually this will be expressly communicated in clear language; however, the courts have found that silence may, in some circumstances, be sufficient to communicate acceptance of the repudiation.

GLOSSARY

- affirm (v.)/affirmation (n.) : decision by the innocent party, following a breach or other event giving rise to a right to end a contract, to treat the contract as continuing in force; *fr. : ≈ considérer un contrat comme exécutoire/ ≈ confirmation du caractère exécutoire d'un contrat*
- anticipatory (adj.) breach (n.) : indication, conveyed by words or conduct of a contracting party, of an intention to breach the contract in the future; *fr. : rupture anticipée*
- breach (n. and v.) : see 77
- condition (n.) : essential or important term of a contract, breach of which will entail a right to terminate the contract; *fr. : ≈ clause impérative*
- discharge (n. and v.) : see 77
- entail (v.) : necessitate or produce as a (logical) consequence; *fr. : entraîner*
- innominate (adj.) term (n.) : intermediate contractual term that is neither condition nor warranty; consequences for breaching such a term depend on whether or not it was a fundamental breach; *fr. : ≈ clause non-nominée*
- repudiation (n.) : indication by a contracting party that he no longer intends to be bound by the contract; *fr. : répudiation*
- repudiatory (adj.) breach (n.) : breach amounting to repudiation of a contract; *fr. : répudiation*
- terminate (v.)/termination (n.) : bring to an end (a contract); action of discharging a contract (for breach or other cause); *fr. : résilier (v.)/résiliation (n.)*
- time clause : provision in a contract specifying the time or period in which acts are to be performed; where time is of the essence, the clause will function as a condition; *fr. : ≈ clause stipulant un délai d'exécution*
- trivial (adj.) : of little importance; insignificant or minor; *fr. : insignifiant*
- warranty (n.) : contractual term, breach of which does not entitle the wronged party to terminate the contract; *fr. : ≈ clause non-impérative*
- wronged (adj.) party (n.) : party who is innocent of any breach or other wrongdoing; injured party; *fr. : partie lésée*

USEFUL EXPRESSIONS

- to fail to perform (one's) obligations under a contract; *fr. : manquer à son devoir d'exécution de ses obligations contractuelles*
- to treat the contract as discharged; *fr. : considérer le contrat comme résilié*
- the party elected to terminate the contract; *fr. : la partie a choisi de mettre fin à la convention*

FURTHER INFORMATION

- although the word warranty has the technical meaning described above in contract law, it is most commonly used to mean a written guarantee issued by a manufacturer to a purchaser ("under warranty" means *sous garantie*); the corresponding verb, "warrant", means to guarantee (e.g. to warrant the truth of something); used as a noun, however, "warrant" refers to an official document authorising an arrest or a search of premises (*mandat d'arrêt, mandat de perquisition, etc.*)
- the verb "resile" is sometimes used in English to talk about drawing back from or retracting a promise or statement (e.g. he resiled from his original commitment); however, in contract law the French verb *résilier* would normally be translated as "to terminate"

COMPARATIVE APPROACH

Le Code civil prévoit qu'une condition résolutoire est sous-entendue dans les contrats synallagmatiques où l'une des deux parties ne satisfait pas à son engagement. Une résolution partielle avec réduction du prix, par exemple, pourrait être accordée par un juge français mais ne serait pas ouverte en droit anglais. La notion de *termination* en droit anglais correspond à la résiliation du contrat en droit français. Quant au concept français de résolution (rétroactive) d'un contrat, il correspond davantage à la *rescission*, *discharge* ou *avoidance* d'un contrat Outre-Manche.

□ 84 REMEDIES

Remedies in contract law can be divided into common law remedies, which are available as a matter of right, and equitable remedies, which always remain at the discretion of the court. In addition, the contract itself may expressly provide for remedies agreed to by the parties as applicable in the event of breach.

Damages

The usual common law remedy for breach is damages : money awarded to the wronged party in order to compensate him for any losses suffered as a result of the breach. The aim of the courts in awarding damages is to put innocent parties in the position they would have been in if the contract had been performed (*restitutio in integrum*). Traditionally damages are aimed at compensating pecuniary losses only, although more recent cases have allowed recovery for mental distress or loss of amenity in certain cases.

Losses are calculated on the basis of either expectation or reliance. Where the parties expected a certain result from the contract, damages may seek to put injured parties in the position they would have been had the contract been performed. Compensation for loss of expectation (or loss of bargain) is the most common basis for calculating damages in practice. However, an alternative method is to put claimants in the position they were in before the contract; this approach compensates for wasted expenditure and other losses actually incurred in reliance on the broken agreement. Sometimes this will be the only basis available : for example, in situations where it would be difficult to do much more than speculate about the expectation losses. Injured parties cannot claim reliance damages, however, if it can be shown that they would have made a loss had the agreement been performed. Under the bad bargain rule, such parties will only receive nominal damages for the breach.

Restitution

Restitution is a common law remedy requiring the return of money or property to its rightful owner. If money is paid under a contract, and there is no adequate performance in return, the payer may seek repayment (or restitution) of the money. This remedy is available even where it turns out that no contract exists, whether because it was not properly formed in the first place, or because it is void for illegality, or for some other reason. Restitution is designed to prevent the unjust enrichment of another party. Similarly, where parties receive no money for work performed or goods supplied, and are not able to sue for the money under an existing contract, they may claim a reasonable price for their performance through an action known as a *quantum meruit.*

Action for an agreed sum

If a party performs his contractual obligations and is not paid the agreed price for performance, he can seek to enforce the other party's promise to pay. Such a proceeding, known as an action for an agreed sum, is a claim for a debt rather than a damages claim.

Specific performance

Unlike the remedies described above, which are all common law remedies available as of right once a breach is proved, specific performance is an equitable remedy awarded at the discretion of the court. Specific performance is a court order compelling a person to fulfill his contractual obligations. It will only be granted in cases where damages would be inadequate (e.g. if a seller refused to complete in a contract for the sale of a house, the court may order the seller to fulfill his contractual obligations). Specific performance will not be ordered to enforce an employment contract, nor will it be available where a contract has been obtained by unfair means or where it could cause great hardship to a party.

Rescission

Rescission is an equitable remedy that sets aside (or rescinds) a voidable contract and returns the parties to their pre-contract position. Misrepresentation, mistake, undue influence, duress or nondisclosure (e.g. in insurance contracts) may all, in certain circumstances, give rise to a voidable contract which can be rescinded by the wronged party. Rescission should not be confused with termination, which arises as a result of breach of contract, or frustration. A court will not order rescission where it is impossible to restore the parties to their pre-contractual position, or where third parties have acquired rights under the contract.

Rectification and *non est factum*

Two remedies apply specifically in the case of mistakes relating to written documents. Rectification is an equitable remedy which alters the "mistaken" terms of a document in order to reflect the true agreement of the parties. *Non est factum* ("this is not my deed") is a common law remedy that avoids a contract created when a person signs a document that they believe to be something completely different from what it actually is. This remedy will not be available unless the claimant can show he was fundamentally mistaken about the nature of the document that, through no carelessness on his own part, he was tricked into signing.

Liquidated damages

Liquidated damages refer to an amount agreed upon by the parties as being payable in damages in the event of breach. The courts will generally give effect to a liquidated damages clause, providing it represents a genuine attempt to estimate the losses arising from the relevant breach. If, on the other hand, the agreed sum amounts to a penalty for breaching the contract, rather than a genuine pre-estimate of compensation payable, then the clause will be invalid. The court will strike out penalty clauses and proceed to award damages on the usual common law principles.

GLOSSARY

- action for an agreed sum : common law claim for recovery of a debt owed under a contract; *fr. : action en recouvrement de créance*
- damages : see 73
- defective (adj.) performance (n.) : see 77
- expectation losses : loss of expected or anticipated benefits under a contract that is not performed; used to calculate compensation for a lost bargain; *fr. : ≈ perte d'un gain*
- expenditure (n.) : action of spending money; amount (of money) laid out or spent; *fr. : dépense(s)*

- liquidated (adj.) damages (n.) : amount of money agreed to in advance by contracting parties as the amount payable by way of damages in the event the contract is breached; *fr. : dommages-intérêts liquidés*
- loss (n.) : detriment or disadvantage resulting from being deprived of something or incurring expense (often due to another's wrongdoing); *fr. : perte*
- loss of amenity : loss of quality of life caused by an injury or damage; *fr. : préjudice d'agrément*
- nominal (adj.) damages (n.) : very small sum of money awarded as a symbol to someone by way of compensation for damage sustained; *fr. : dommages et intérêts d'un montant symbolique*
- *non est factum* : claim that an agreement or document was not the claimant's; sometimes relied upon where a person signs a document believing it to be something completely different from what it is; *fr. : défense de non est factum*
- pecuniary (adj.) loss (n.) : financial loss; traditionally, parties seeking compensation for a breach of contract could only claim damages for their pecuniary losses; however, non-pecuniary losses may now be recoverable in certain circumstances; *fr. : préjudice financier*
- penalty clause : contractual term, often purporting to be a liquidated damages clause, which fixes an excessive amount of money payable in the event of a breach and therefore operates to penalise the defaulting party; penalty clauses are not enforceable; *fr. : clause pénale*
- *quantum meruit* : legal principle entitling a person to recover a reasonable sum for the provision of goods or services; may apply where contract is silent about the amount due, or where there is no contract and the provider seeks restitution for goods or services which have benefitted the other party; *fr. : quantum meruit*
- rectification (n.) : see 78
- remedy (n.) : see 2
- rescission (n.)/rescind (v.) : equitable remedy allowing courts to set aside a voidable contract and return the parties to the position they were in before the contract was made; parties may rescind a contract in certain cases of misrepresentation, mistake, undue influence, duress or nondisclosure; *fr. : résolution (n.)/résoudre (v.)*
- restitution (n) : common law remedy requiring the return of money or property to its rightful owner, or payment of money to prevent the unjust enrichment of another party; *fr. : restitution*
- rightful (adj.) : having a lawful or legitimate right to (property or title); *fr. : légitime*
- specific (adj.) performance (n.) : equitable remedy compelling a person to perform his contractual obligations; *fr. : exécution forcée*
- unjust (adj.) enrichment (n.) principle by which noone should profit at someone else's expense without making restitution for the reasonable value of the benefits which were unfairly received; *fr. : enrichissement sans cause*

- unliquidated (adj.) damages (n.) : damages for an amount determined by the court (rather than by the parties : see liquidated damages); *fr. : dommages-intérêts non-liquidés*
- voidable (adj.) contract (n.) : see 77

USEFUL EXPRESSIONS

- the court has the power to award damages; *fr. : le tribunal a le pouvoir d'allouer des dommages-intérêts*
- the court exercises its discretionary power; *fr. : le tribunal exerce son pouvoir discrétionnaire*
- to suffer a loss; *fr. : subir un préjudice*
- the contract was set aside for undue influence; *fr. : le contrat a été invalidé pour dol*
- to take the necessary steps to enforce a contract; *fr. : prendre les dispositions nécessaires pour procéder à l'exécution d'un contrat*

FURTHER INFORMATION

- the English word prejudice is used to mean either a detriment or, more commonly, a preconceived idea; it is not used in the sense of a loss or injury
- where expenditure refers to money, the corresponding verb is usually to spend; the verb to expend is more commonly employed for non-pecuniary expenditures (e.g. to expend resources, energy, time, etc.)
- rescission (*résolution*) and termination (*résiliation*) are not interchangeable terms; rescission refers to the setting aside of voidable contracts (which are then treated as never having existed), whereas termination refers to the ending of contractual obligations because of a breach
- likewise, the English noun rescission should not be translated by *rescision pour lésion* which is dealt with in article 1674 of the *Code civil* and refers exclusively to sales of immovables

COMPARATIVE APPROACH

Tant en France qu'en Angleterre et au Pays de Galles, en cas d'inexécution d'une partie ou de la totalité des obligations découlant d'un contrat, la partie lésée aura tendance à demander la condamnation de son cocontractant à lui verser des dommages et intérêts et/ou, selon la nature du contrat, son exécution forcée. Cependant, le système de *common law* est beaucoup plus réceptif que le droit français au besoin pour le demandeur de minimiser son propre préjudice.

3

Tort litigation

□ 85 INTRODUCTION

Tort law is a branch of civil law and can be defined as the set of rules, which provides remedies for damage caused by the tortfeasor to the victim. Damage includes injury to the person (physical and moral), damage to physical property, damage to financial interests, injury to reputation, etc.

The aim of tort is to prevent or compensate harm and not punish the wrongdoer. Contrary to a criminal act (i.e. public wrong), a tort is a private wrong. The suit will be filed by the person wronged, since the wrongful act affects one person (or set of persons) only, and not society as a whole. Redress will then require the author of the loss to do or to refrain from doing something for the benefit of the one who suffered the loss. In a majority of cases coming before the courts, the claimant will either sue the defendant for financial compensation (i.e. damages) for the injury he has suffered or seek an injunction to prevent the harm from happening again In a claim under the law of tort, the onus is on the claimant to show that the defendant has breached his duty towards him.

Tort law creates universal legal obligations, i.e. the obligations do not arise from a contractual agreement, but are fixed by law. Moreover tort is not concerned with issues of who is morally culpable, but with liability between persons, be they natural or artificial. In some cases the same act can be sued both in a civil court for damages and in a criminal court for a guilty verdict.

The law of tort derives its legal principles both from case law (e.g. the seminal case *Donoghue v. Stevenson* [1932] UKHL 100 which establishes the neighbour principle) and from mandatory statutory provisions (such as the Consumer Protection Act 1987 for consumer liability).

There are four types of tort, which are developed in the following sections : negligence, nuisance, defamation and trespass. Separate sections will also deal with statutory torts and remedies in tort. Torts can be committed both by moral and by legal entities, that is by individuals, and by companies or partnerships (see 13). However, in the present chapter, for the sake of conciseness, claimants and defendants, victims and wrongdoers, etc., will be referred to as he/him/his, whatever the gender, number and legal status. Thus the third person masculine singular will not preclude a given statement to apply to women and commercial entities as well as to men.

GLOSSARY

- claimant (n.) : legal person who initiates civil legal proceedings against a defendant; was called plaintiff before the Civil Procedure Rules 1998; *fr. : demandeur*
- damage (n.) : injury, loss or harm caused to a legal entity, property or reputation; damage needs to be compensable otherwise the claimant does not have a legal remedy; the term damage is uncountable; *fr. : dommage/préjudice*
- damages (n.) : financial compensation awarded to the claimant by the courts in a civil case, and paid for by the defendant; *fr. : compensation financière/indemnisation/dommages et intérêts*
- injunction (n.) : here, court order which requires one party to the case to do or to refrain from doing something for the benefit of the other party; it is an equitable remedy; *fr. : injonction de faire/injonction de ne pas faire*
- liability (n.) : here, legal obligation or duty; a claim in tort arises out of the breach of one's duty to others; the court establishes the liability of a defendant, i.e. it finds the defendant liable/responsible for the wrong committed; *fr. : responsabilité*
- onus (n.)/burden of proof : obligation for one party to provide evidence in order to establish the facts; in a civil case, the burden lies with the claimant to adduce evidence to satisfy the standard of proof on a balance of probabilities; *fr. : charge de la preuve*
- remedy (n.) : form of redress denied or granted by the courts to a claimant; *fr. : réparation du dommage, du préjudice/remède*
- tortfeasor (n.) : legal entity who commits a tort; wrongdoer; *fr. : auteur du préjudice/du dommage*

USEFUL EXPRESSIONS

- alleged wrong; *fr. : fait dommageable*
- the burden of proof/onus is on the claimant to prove; *fr. : la charge de la preuve incombe au demandeur*
- to adduce evidence of something; *fr. : rapporter la preuve de quelque chose*
- to apply to the court for redress/to seek redress from the court/to apply to the court for a remedy; *fr. : solliciter un remède de la juridiction*
- to award/grant someone a remedy; *fr. : allouer/attribuer à quelqu'un réparation*
- to be entitled to a remedy; *fr. : avoir droit à réparation*

- to be awarded a remedy for the damage sustained; *fr. : se voir attribuer réparation du préjudice subi*
- to cause someone damage/a loss; *fr. : causer un dommage/préjudice à quelqu'un*
- to grant redress; *fr. : accorder réparation*
- to issue legal proceedings against/to sue someone; *fr. : engager une action à l'encontre de quelqu'un*
- to win a case against the defendant/to succeed against the defendant; *fr. : gagner une affaire contre le défendeur*

FURTHER INFORMATION

- the word claimant should not be translated by *plaignant* which in French can be associated with criminal proceedings
- neighbour principle : common law principle which lies at the foundation of the tort of negligence; the neighbour is not the person living next door to you, but refers to any person who can be closely and directly affected by the acts of the defendant; the principle implies that anyone should be in contemplation of the claimant when doing something
- there is no equivalent in England and Wales of the French *constitution de partie civile*; this is why in some cases the same act can give rise to a civil action (claim for damages) and a criminal one (for a guilty verdict)
- the English word prejudice means *préjugé* in French
- do not confuse the words damages (*dommages et intérêts*) and damage (*préjudice*)

COMPARATIVE APPROACH

Le concept anglais de *tort* correspond à la responsabilité délictuelle en droit français qui, avec le droit des contrats (*contract law*) forme le droit de la responsabilité civile. *Negligence*, qui est l'une des composantes de *tort law*, correspond au droit de la responsabilité quasi-délictuelle. La responsabilité délictuelle est fondée sur le concept de délit civil (*tort*) par opposition au délit pénal (*criminal offence*). Cependant certains *torts* présentent à la fois le caractère d'un délit civil et pénal.

☐ 86 NEGLIGENCE

Negligence is a civil tort only. It can be defined as the tort of causing foreseeable damage by unreasonable conduct, where there is a duty to take care. Typical cases of negligence include a car accident where someone sustains an injury or consumer disputes. Professional negligence is a growing area of negligence.

In order to establish negligence, the claimant must prove on a balance of probabilities that the defendant owed him a duty of care (the standard of care will be adapted to circumstances), that the duty was breached and that as a consequence of the breach, he sustained damage (this is the causal link). Two other requirements were subsequently added by caselaw : the damage must be foreseeable and not too remote. Additionally, it must be fair, just and reasonable to impose such a duty on the defendant. The objective test of the reasonable man applies.

When all these elements are satisfied by the claimant, there are a certain number of defences that a defendant can avail of in an action in tort. Some defences will prevent the claimant from recovering from the defendant's breach of duty and others will only adapt the quantum of damages to the level of involvement of each party. In all cases, if the claimant has delayed too much in bringing the claim, he may be barred from claiming (see 88).

The claimant comes to court to seek redress. The courts can offer several types of remedies : damages, injunction and restitution of property (see 93).

GLOSSARY

- breach (n.) : one of the elements of negligence at common law where it applies to the defendant's duty of care; *fr. : violation/manquement*
- causation (n.) : one of the elements of negligence at common law where the claimant must show that the damage flows from the breach; one test to establish causation (amongst other possible tests) is the "but for" test, which states that but for the act of the defendant, or if the defendant had not done an act, the claimant would not have suffered a loss; *fr. : lien de causalité*
- duty of care (to someone) : one of the elements of negligence at common law; it is the legal obligation for one party to avoid by his acts or omissions to cause harm to another party; there is neither a duty to the public at large nor a general duty to act; however if an individual member of the public decides to intervene, he has a duty not to make matters worse; when there is a recognised duty situation, there is no need to prove duty; *fr. : ≈ obligation d'attention/de prendre soin de son prochain*
- foreseeability (n.)/foreseeable (adj.) : test to determine whether damage to the claimant would have been in the contemplation of a reasonable man; the claimant must be a foreseeable victim without necessarily being identifiable by the defendant; *fr. : prévisibilité*
- reasonable (adj.) man (n.) : phrase which states the standard of care expected by a hypothetical individual who is considered as a reasonably careful member of the public; *fr. : bon père de famille*
- remote (adj.) damage (n.) : loss sustained by the claimant which is not a direct consequence of the defendant's breach of duty and thus, should not give rise to an award of damages from the court; in order to give rise to an award of damages, the damage sustained by the claimant must not be too remote from the defendant's breach of duty; *fr. : ≈ préjudice indirect*

USEFUL EXPRESSIONS

- breach of duty; *fr. : manquement à une obligation*
- the burden lies with the claimant to establish; *fr. : la charge de la preuve incombe au demandeur d'établir*
- the damage arises from the breach; *fr. : le préjudice découle du manquement*
- the damage must not be remote from the breach of duty; *fr. : le préjudice doit être une conséquence du fait dommageable/le lien de causalité doit être suffisant entre le fait dommageable et le préjudice*
- to be liable to someone for something; *fr. : être responsable de quelque chose à l'égard de quelqu'un*
- to be sued for negligence; *fr. : faire l'objet d'une action en responsabilité quasi-délictuelle*
- to breach one's duty/to be in breach of one's duty; *fr. : violer/manquer à son obligation*
- to cause foreseeable damage to someone; *fr. : causer un préjudice prévisible à quelqu'un*
- to claim under the law of tort; *fr. : présenter une demande au titre de la responsabilité délictuelle*
- to discharge a duty; *fr. : s'acquitter d'un(e) devoir/obligation*
- to establish the elements of negligence; *fr. : établir les éléments constitutifs de la responsabilité quasi-délictuelle*
- to fail to establish a legal requirement; *fr. : manquer à son obligation légale d'établir quelque chose*
- to have a claim in tort; *fr. : avoir un recours sur le fondement de la responsabilité délictuelle*
- to inflict damage on someone; *fr. : infliger un préjudice à quelqu'un*
- to owe someone something (like a duty of care); *fr. : être redevable de quelque chose envers quelqu'un (comme d'une obligation d'attention)*
- to recover damages from someone; *fr. : recouvrer des dommages et intérêts de quelqu'un*
- to succeed against someone in a negligence suit; *fr. : gagner à l'encontre de quelqu'un dans le cadre d'une action judiciaire en responsabilité quasi-délictuelle*

FURTHER INFORMATION

- *Donoghue v. Stevenson* (1932) is a seminal case in the tort of negligence; in its narrow rule (the *ratio decidendi*), the case establishes the liability of manufacturers to the ultimate consumer when there is no possibility of intermediate examination; in its broad rule, it states that individuals have a duty not to harm their neighbours, in a legal sense

- remoteness can be translated by the French *éloignement*; when applied to negligence, it refers to which part(s) of the claimant's loss or harm the defendant should be liable for; the issue of remoteness of the damage answers the question : in respect of what consequences of an established duty can the injured party recover ?
- the English word deed can be translated by *action* (the fact of doing something, a negligent deed e.g.) or *acte notarié* (document notarised by a solicitor, e.g. for conveyancing)

COMPARATIVE APPROACH

En droit français, la responsabilité quasi-délictuelle est régie par l'article 1382 du Code civil. Si les deux autres conditions (préjudice ou *damage* et lien de causalité ou *causal link*) sont semblables en droit français et en droit anglais, la différence essentielle entre les deux types de responsabilités repose sur la notion de faute, qui est absente du *tort* anglais. Pour engager la responsabilité quasi-délictuelle de quelqu'un, il faut donc démontrer sa faute en France et le manquement à une obligation de prendre soin de son prochain (*breach of duty of care*), en Angleterre et au Pays de Galles.

Le concept anglais du *reasonable man* (également connu sous le nom de *man on the Clapham omnibus*) correspond exactement au concept français de « bon père de famille ».

Contrairement au droit français, il n'y a pas d'obligation d'assistance à personne en danger en droit anglais. À noter donc les deux traductions suivantes :

– omission of a legal duty, *fr. : inexécution d'une obligation légale*;

– positive duty to act; *fr. : devoir d'assistance.*

□ 87 SPECIAL CASES OF NEGLIGENCE

Economic loss and psychiatric damage are two specific types of negligence.

Economic loss

When it comes to economic loss, the common law identifies two categories of damage : consequential economic damage and pure economic loss. Consequential economic damage is economic damage flowing from the physical damage to the claimant's property. It follows the principles in negligence actions (see 86).

Pure economic loss is the purely financial loss suffered which does not entail any physical damage. A typical case of pure economic loss would involve misleading financial advice for example, as in the seminal case *Hedley Byrne & Co Ltd v. Heller & Partners Ltd* [1964] AC 465. To establish a claim in pure economic loss the claimant needs to establish a proximate relationship by looking at whether the advice was required for a purpose, this purpose was made known and the advice was acted upon without further inquiry. The courts will consider that the advisor breached his duty if his actions fell below the standard of the reasonable expert. Causation is established thanks to the "but for" test. Moreover, the losses must not be too remote. In cases of pure economic loss, no damages can be granted unless the loss is due to a negligent statement and when the relationship between the parties meets the special relationship criteria.

Psychiatric damage

Psychiatric damage is the damage flowing from witnessing with unaided senses an accident in which a loved one is involved. Psychiatric damage is not to be confused with distress and mental anguish (see 93). A typical case of psychiatric damage would involve seeing a family member being hit by a car. In order to succeed in his claim, the claimant must establish that he was a foreseeable claimant on account of the love he had for the victim, that he was at the scene in the immediate aftermath of the accident and that he witnessed the scene with his own unaided senses.

Because the proximity criterion is essential in establishing psychiatric damage, the courts distinguish between primary and secondary victims. Courts will also look at whether an ordinary person of normal fortitude or ordinary phlegm would suffer if placed in similar circumstances. A claimant can only bring an action for psychiatric damage if he has a recognised medical condition.

GLOSSARY

- primary (adj.) victim (n.) : person involved in the accident or the rescue; *fr. : victime directe/immédiate*
- proximity (n.) : proximity of time and place; this means that the person wishing to claim under psychiatric damage must prove that he was at the scene at the time of the accident or in its immediate aftermath; *fr. : lien de proximité*
- secondary (adj.) victim (n.) : person who is not involved in the accident or the rescue, but who has a relation of proximity to the person injured; *fr. : victime par ricochet*
- special (adj.) relationship (n.) : additional criteria to establish negligence in cases of pure economic loss whereby the claimant and the defendant have a relationship of proximity which justifies imposing a duty on the defendant; *fr. : ≈ relation de proximité*

- unaided (adj.) senses (n.) : perception through the individual's own senses of vision, hearing, smell and/or touch; the term implies that the individual's perception should not be mediated through a verbal description of the facts or a running commentary on television, for example; *fr. : ≈ par ses propres sens*

USEFUL EXPRESSIONS

- pure economic loss; *fr. : préjudice exclusivement financier*
- consequential damage; *fr. : préjudice qui découle de l'acte dommageable*
- post-traumatic stress disorder (PTSD) is a recognised mental condition; *fr. : le trouble du stress post-traumatique est une pathologie pyschiatrique répertoriée*
- psychiatric damage; *fr. : préjudice psychologique*
- to bring an action based on the grounds of negligence; *fr. : engager une action sur le fondement de la responsabilité quasi-délictuelle*
- to witness a horrific incident; *fr. : être le témoin d'un horrible accident*

FURTHER INFORMATION

- primary and secondary victims (*victimes immédiates et par ricochet*) must not be confused with first and second victims (*première et deuxième victimes*)

COMPARATIVE APPROACH

Il n'y a jamais eu de définition harmonisée de *pure economic loss* en droit comparé. L'une des raisons est que la plupart des systèmes juridiques européens (mis à part les systèmes de *common law* et allemand) ne reconnaissent pas l'existence du concept de *pure economic loss* ou bien ne le considèrent pas comme un type de préjudice indépendant. Le concept juridique de *pure economic loss* se situe à la frontière du préjudice indemnisable et non-indemnisable.

Il convient de ne pas confondre *psychological damage* ni avec le préjudice moral ni avec le préjudice psychologique en droit français. Le préjudice moral regroupe l'ensemble des atteintes qui n'affectent pas directement un patrimoine. Il inclut donc aussi la souffrance lors de la perte d'un être cher, la peur et l'angoisse. Il s'apparente au type de préjudice nommé *injury to the person (physical and moral)* en droit anglais, mais pourrait aussi comprendre certaines situations couvertes par le terme *psychological damage*, lorsque les conditions de proximité sont réunies. En droit français, le préjudice psychologique est surtout utilisé en droit du travail. Il recouvre les souffrances psychiques endurées et ne requiert pas, pour son indemnisation, les mêmes conditions strictes que le concept de *psychological damage* en droit anglais.

88 DEFENCES

When the claimant has established in fact the existence of the negligent act, there are a certain number of general defences available to the defendant.

Causation

Causation is an essential element in establishing negligence. If the claimant is unable to establish a causal link between the defendant's negligent act and the injuries caused or the loss sustained, the claimant will not be able to recover for the damage caused by the negligent act. For example, the defendant will avoid liability if it can be shown that an intervening act breaks the chain of causation between the negligent act and the harm sustained (also known as *novus actus interveniens*).

In complex cases where the exact cause of the damage is not known, the claimant can recover thanks to a common law rule, which states that the claimant need neither establish duty nor prove breach, but only show causation, when the negligent act was sufficiently under the control of the defendant (also known as *res ipsa loquitur* or "the thing speaks for itself").

On the other hand, once causation is established, the defendant cannot avoid liability by claiming that he could not have foreseen the full extent of the claimant's injuries. Indeed the common law has a rule, which states that you take your claimants as you find them (also known as the "egg-shell skull" rule). However the courts will take into account the pre-existing medical condition before assessing the amount of damages to be granted.

Consent

Lack of consent can be another defence available. When it comes to the claimant's consent, there are two competing doctrines. The first one claims that the claimant agreed to be injured by the defendant. This defence is more particularly applicable in sports where the sportsmen are aware of the dangers of playing sports. However courts are wary of applying the defence in other contexts on account of a common law doctrine, which implies that knowledge of a danger does not amount to accepting the risks entailed in the venture (also known as *sciens is non volent*).

Necessity

Necessity is a defence, which can be used if the defendant proves that the harm inflicted to the claimant arose out of an intentional interference to people or property in order to prevent greater damage.

Apportionment of liability/shared liability

Liability can be apportioned or shared between the claimant and the defendant (as when the claimant contributed to the extent of his injuries by not wearing a helmet when riding his motorbike). This is known as contributory negligence and the onus is on the defendant to prove it. The claimant's damages will be proportionate to the court's assessment of his contribution to his own loss.

Liability can also be shared amongst several tortfeasors. Liability can be joint, several or joint and several. This will affect the way a claimant may seek to recover payment of the damages awarded to him. Joint, several and joint and several liability are forms of primary liability.

Vicarious liability makes the defendant liable for the torts committed by another individual, as in cases of employer-employee relationship. For the employer to be held vicariously liable, the worker must be an employee who has committed a tort in the course of his employment. This is a form of secondary liability.

Illegality

Illegality is a defence, which bars a claimant from establishing a claim that would help him profit from his illegal act. This is also known as *exturpi causa non oritur actio*.

GLOSSARY

- consent (n.) : defence which states that the claimant is barred from recovering on grounds that he consented to his injuries or loss; consent needs to be distinguished from legal consent, which prevents the tort from arising in the first place, for example a boxer who understands he will be punched in the game; *fr. : consentement*
- contributory (adj.) negligence (n.) : defence which alleges that the claimant contributed to his injuries; *fr. : contribution/participation (de la victime) à la réalisation de son propre dommage*
- egg-shell skull principle : legal principle which takes into account the victim's pre-existing medical condition; *fr. : affection médicale préexistante*
- joint and several liability : each party is independently liable for the full extent of the damage resulting from the negligent act; payment of the full damages ordered by the court can be sought by the claimant against any of the defendants held liable who can subsequently seek reimbursement from his co-defendants; *fr. : responsabilité conjointe et solidaire*
- joint (adj.) liability (n.) : when various legal persons are held liable together for the claimant's loss; no specific percentage of liability is determined by the court; *fr. : responsibilité conjointe*
- necessity (n.) : defence used if the defendant proves that the damage sustained by the claimant arose out of an intentional interference to people/property to prevent an even greater damage; *fr. : état de nécessité*
- secondary (adj.) liability (n.) : as opposed to primary liability, liability affecting the defendant for the tort(s) of another person; *fr. : ≈ responsabilité subsidiaire*

- several liability : each of the defendants is liable for his own type of liability; *fr. : responsabilité solidaire*
- vicarious (adj.) liability (n.) : secondary liability A may incur for damage caused to C by the tort of B; there must be a particular relationship between A and B and B's tort should be related to the relationship; *fr. : responsabilité pour autrui*

USEFUL EXPRESSIONS

- the court held that B and C should be held liable jointly and severally; *fr. : le tribunal a jugé que B et C devraient être tenus responsables conjointement et solidairement*
- to assess damages; *fr. : évaluer le montant des dommages et intérêts*
- to be held contributorily negligent; *fr. : voir sa responsabilité quasi-délictuelle retenue pour avoir contribué à la réalisation de son propre dommage*

FURTHER INFORMATION

- primary and secondary liability (*responsabilité primaire/subsidiaire* or *directe/indirecte*) must not be confused with primary and secondary victims (*victimes immédiates* and *par ricochet*)
- illegal (action against the law) must not be confused with unlawful (action in contravention of the rules in a specific context) or illicit (action which custom or society forbids or disapproves of)

COMPARATIVE APPROACH

Contrairement au droit français (C. civ., art. 1384 al. 4) où les parents sont tenus de supporter les conséquences des actes dommageables commis par leur enfant, le droit anglais ne retient la responsabilité des parents que s'ils ont manqué à leur obligation de se conformer à leur *duty of care* et donc, s'ils ont personnellement engagé leur responsabilité quasi-délictuelle (*negligence*). Il n'y a donc pas, à proprement parler, de responsabilité des parents du fait de la *negligence* de leurs enfants en Angleterre et au Pays de Galles.

Il existe une divergence majeure entre le système d'indemnisation des préjudices corporels en France et Outre-Manche. Outre-Manche, les juridictions appliquent un principe d'indemnisation globale du préjudice subi (*once and for all settlement*) alors qu'en France, les tribunaux n'hésitent pas, en cas d'aggravation du préjudice, à accorder à la victime des dommages et intérêts complémentaires.

□ 89 DEFAMATION

Defamation can be defined as the publication of a statement, which reflects on a person's reputation and tends to lower him in the estimation of right-thinking members of society generally or tends to make them shun or avoid him. To establish defamation, three elements must be proved : the statement made is defamatory, it refers to the claimant and it is communicated to at least one person other than the claimant.

Defamation takes the form of two separate torts : slander and libel. Slander occurs when the defamatory act is in temporary form and libel when it is in permanent form. As a consequence of this distinction, slander requires special damage being proved whereas libel is actionable *per se* and can be prosecuted as an offence. A defamation case is tried by a judge and a jury in the High Court. The jury will assess the quantum of damages, which can be nominal, aggravated or contemptuous.

There are four specialised defences : justification, fair comment, absolute or qualified privilege and offer of amends under statutory provisions. If the claimant manages to prove malice, the defendant's defence fails. In the 2010s, the tort of defamation has been more particularly relevant concerning the freedom of speech in relation to the press. There have been calls for a blanket protection for the press relative to political discussion and information. The courts try to strike a balance between the duty and interest of members of the public to know a fact and the defendant's right to privacy.

GLOSSARY

- actionable *per se* : sufficient, by itself, to justify legal action in court, without the need to adduce evidence of damage being sustained; *fr. : ≈ justifiant intrinsèquement le bien-fondé d'une action en justice*
- blanket protection : generic protection; *fr. : ≈ protection générale*
- comment (n.) : statement of opinion, as opposed to statement of fact; *fr. : commentaires/propos*
- duty-interest test : right to know test which establishes whether it is/was in the interest of the public to communicate or publish the defamatory statement; *fr. : ≈ test de l'intérêt général par rapport à l'intérêt privé*
- fair (adj.) comment (n.) : the fairness of the comment is judged by the objective standard of whether a fair-minded person could honestly express the opinion in question; *fr. : ≈ exception de commentaire juste*
- justification (n.) : test whether the opinion, however exaggerated, obstinate or prejudiced, was honestly held by the person expressing it; true test; *fr. : ≈ exception de vérité*
- libel (n.) : written or other permanent form of defamation; *fr. : ≈ diffamation écrite/permanente*

- malice (n.) : defence which aims to establish that the defendant did not honestly believe that what he said was true, that is, that he was either aware that it was not true or indifferent to its truth or falsity; *fr. : intention de nuire*
- qualified (adj.) : limited; *fr. : restreint*
- slander (n.) : verbal or non-permanent form of defamation; *fr. : diffamation verbale/non-permanente*

USEFUL EXPRESSIONS

- absolute or qualified privilege; *fr. : immunité absolue ou restreinte*
- false representation; *fr. : fausse déclaration*
- false statement; *fr. : fausse affirmation/allégation*
- freedom of speech; *fr. : liberté d'expression*
- good name; *fr. : réputation/renom*
- malicious falsehood; *fr. : calomnie dans l'intention de nuire*
- public figure; *fr. : personnalité/personne connue*
- publication; *fr. : diffusion/publication*
- the claimant's claim stands; *fr. : la demande en justice du demandeur est recevable*
- to be privileged; *fr. : jouir de l'immunité*
- to be sued for defamation; *fr. : être poursuivi en diffamation*
- to dismiss someone's claim; *fr. : débouter quelqu'un de sa demande*
- to make an offer of amends; *fr. : faire amende honorable*
- to tarnish/harm someone's reputation; *fr. : porter atteinte à la reputation de quelqu'un*

FURTHER INFORMATION

- the English word malice should not be confused with its French counterpart (*malice*) which means playful/naughty

Comparative approach

Jusqu'à très récemment, le droit anglais n'avait pas de principe juridique permettant la protection de la vie privée. Cette protection passait par des actions en diffamation. L'adoption du *Human Rights Act 1998* a permis de créer un droit à la vie privée autonome grâce à son article 8.

Si, Outre-Manche, une différence est faite entre diffamation permanente/écrite (*libel*) ou non-permanente/verbale (*slander*), le droit français distingue entre les diffamations publique ou non-publique. Tout comme en Angleterre et au Pays de Galles, la diffamation en France peut être poursuivie sur un plan civil ou pénal (article R. 621-1 du Code pénal).

En France, la liberté de la presse est toujours majoritairement régie par la loi du 29 juillet 1881. En Grande-Bretagne, le *Defamation Act 2013* apporte des modifications substantielles au droit jurisprudentiel (*Reynolds criteria*) et législatif (*Defamation Act 1952*) dans le domaine du délit de diffamation, et ce au-delà de la diffamation par voie de presse. Dans les deux pays, les critères objectifs pour établir un acte diffamatoire sont semblables, en l'espèce : (1) la publication (2) d'une allégation (3) concernant un fait précis (4) qui porte atteinte à l'honneur ou à la considération de l'individu concerné.

□ 90 NUISANCE

Nuisance is a tort, which aims to remedy interferences affecting an individual or a representative cross-section of a class of people who may be affected by it. There are two types of nuisance : private and public. Unlike private nuisance, public nuisance is a crime as well as a tort and can be prosecuted. Examples of public nuisance include obstructing a public highway but also holding a music festival without authorisation, blocking a right-of-way or even selling food which is unfit for human consumption. Most requirements to claim and remedies are similar in both torts.

To assess the reasonableness of the interference, courts will strike a balance between the occupier's right to use his land as he sees fit and the neighbour's right to the quiet enjoyment of his land. Factors such as the character of the neighbourhood, the abnormal sensitivity of the claimant, the duration of the nuisance (which must be continuous or recurrent), the public benefit derived from the act causing the nuisance, the maliciousness of the act, the existence of natural hasards affecting the use and enjoyment of land and negligence will be considered by the courts. In addition to reasonableness, foreseeability and remoteness of the harm needs to be considered when making a claim.

Only the owner or the occupier with a right of exclusive possession can sue the creator of the nuisance for the physical harm to land and/or the quiet enjoyment of land. The occupier will be liable if the act is under his control, if it is that of an independent contractor, if it is caused by an unlawful trespasser or by a predecessor in title (if the present occupier adopted or continued the nuisance). The landlord will be liable if he authorised the nuisance, if the nuisance existed at the time he starting letting his property, and if he failed to remedy to the cause of the nuisance.

There are a certain number of effective defences available to the defendant, amongst which prescription, statutory authority allowing the nuisance, contributory negligence, the claimant's consent and acts of God or nature. However stating that the claimant came to the nuisance is an ineffective defence.

To succeed in private nuisance, the claimant must have an interest in land whereas for public nuisance this is not necessary. Thus for public nuisance a non-occupier can seek payment of damages for injury to the person or to property. There are three forms of remedies : injunction (when money cannot compensate adequately), damages (for physical damage, personal discomfort and the recovery of reasonable remedial expenditure) and abatement. Criminal prosecution is possible for public nuisance only.

GLOSSARY

- abatement (n.) : here, suppression or termination of the nuisance; *fr. : suppression*
- act of God : unavoidable intervening event, such as a natural catastrophe, also known as act of nature; an individual cannot reasonably be asked to protect himself against the occurrence of such an event but can be insured against it; *fr. : fait de Dieu/≈ événement fortuit et imprévu*
- highway (n.) : British word (as opposed to US meaning of motorway) which refers to a road which can be accessed by the public; *fr. : voie publique*
- illegal (adj.) : act which is both unlawful and criminal; *fr. : illégal*
- landlord (n.) : rightful owner of property who lets it out to a tenant, who is a legal entity who occupies or possesses a property and pays rent for the right to do so; *fr. : propriétaire-bailleur*
- malice (n.) : intentional wrongdoing; *fr. : intention de nuire*
- natural (adj.) hasards (n.) : natural threat that has a negative effect on humans and nature; in a nuisance case, the claimant is asked to take reasonable steps to minimise a known risk; *fr. : catastrophes naturelle*
- occupier (n.) : person who is allowed by the owner to occupy the property; *fr. : occupant/preneur*
- predecessor in title : former owner of premises; *fr. : précédent propriétaire*
- prescription (n.)/limitation period : time limit during which a person is allowed to claim; the right to claim is subsequently extinguished; *fr. : délai de prescription*
- private (adj.) nuisance (n.) : unlawful interference with a person's use of land or some right over, or in connection with it; *fr. : troubles de voisinage*
- public (adj.) nuisance (n.) : tort which materially affects the reasonable comforts and convenience of life of a representative cross-section of a class of people; *fr. : troubles à l'ordre public*
- remedial (adj.) expenditure (n.) : cost of trying to remedy the nuisance; *fr. : coût de remise en état*
- right-of-way : right to go across someone's property; *fr. : servitude de passage légale* (as opposed to *conventionnelle)*
- trespasser (n.) : person who is not invited upon the property by the owner or the occupier; his presence on the land is unlawful and he can be sued in the tort of trespass; *fr. : intrus*

USEFUL EXPRESSIONS

- a legal person's right to the quiet enjoyment of his land; *fr. : droit d'une personne physique ou morale à la jouissance paisible de sa propriété*
- the limitation period has expired, the claimant is time barred; *fr. : le délai de prescription a expiré, le demandeur est prescrit*
- to lodge a claim for public nuisance against; *fr. : engager une action pour troubles à l'ordre public à l'encontre de*

FURTHER INFORMATION

- the English word hasard means danger and should therefore not be confused with the French word *hasard*, meaning luck or chance (*chance*)
- statutory nuisance is the statutory protection offered to people whose quiet enjoyment of their property is disturbed by a nuisance (smells, noise, etc.); light for example has been considered as a nuisance since the Clean Neighbourhood and Environment Act 2005; under the umbrella of statutory nuisance, an individual can seek the help from a local authority or can apply to a Magistrates' court; in both cases an abatement notice or an order should be served on the persons at the origin of the nuisance

COMPARATIVE APPROACH

Si, jusqu'à récemment, le concept de *common law* dénommé *nuisance* était surtout utilisé Outre-Manche pour arbitrer les troubles de voisinage et à l'ordre public, de nos jours, son application s'étend au droit de l'environnement.

Le régime statutaire de protection de l'environnement en France et en Grande-Bretagne (*statutory nuisance*), permettant de résoudre les litiges de pollution industrielle et agricole, est semblable. Cependant, le droit français exige des justiciables un intérêt à agir (*fact of having standing*) requis par l'article 31 du Code de procédure civile, qui est plus strict que le critère de *interest in land* exigé du justiciable britannique.

□ 91 TRESPASS

Trespass is the tort of interfering with another person's rights (to his own person, his land or his goods). It is actionable *per se* as damage is not a pre-requisite to a court action. The act needs to be intentional, if not the appropriate means of redress will be found in an action in negligence. In order to sue in trespass the claimant needs to establish a direct interference to his person, land or goods (chattels) and that this interference was voluntary. However the defendant can be an innocent trespasser. The courts can grant damages or an injunction.

Trespass is a civil tort. However in some rare instances, a trespasser can be prosecuted, as when a trespasser breaches poaching laws or enters public land (e.g. railways) or trespasses with the intent of residing (e.g. squatters).

Trespass to the person is defined as a direct interference to a person's body, liberty or rights. There are three main individual torts : battery, assault and false imprisonment. Trespass to land is the tort committed by the defendant when he enters upon land in possession of the claimant, remains on it, places or projects an object upon it. Any person in exclusive possession of the trespassed land can sue. This includes the landowner, the tenant and/or the owner-occupier. Trespass to goods is the tort committed by the defendant when he interferes with the goods of another person.

In the case of trespass to the person, the defendant can argue that the claimant gave his consent, that a lawful arrest took place (with a valid warrant), or that he acted in defence of a person, property or out of necessity (with a reasonable and proportionate use of force and without retaliation). In cases of trespasses to land and to goods, the defendant can raise the defences of the licensed or authorised user, the exercise of a right of distress, and mistake.

Despite the fact that trespasses to person and to land are actionable *per se*, a claim in trespass to goods needs to prove damage to the goods and that the claimant was in possession of the goods at the time of the alleged interference. The available remedies in cases of trespass are damages and/or orders for the return of the goods or the payment of their value.

GLOSSARY

- actionable *per se* : see 89
- assault (n.) : tort which consists in the claimant's reasonable apprehension of force inflicted on him by the defendant; intention is necessary which means that omission does not constitute assault; *fr. : menace/tentative d'agression*
- battery (n.) : tort which consists in applying force to another person; the claimant needs to establish a deliberate physical contact and an intentional act on the part of the defendant, but no intention to injure is required; *fr. : violence physique/voie de fait*
- distress (n.) : here, act of seizing the property of a tenant, debtor or wrongdoer to compensate for a claim against him; *fr. : ≈ saisie d'un bien*
- false (adj.) imprisonment (n.) : tort which consists in inflicting bodily restraint on the claimant, without the express or implied authorisation of the law; *fr. : détention illégale/séquestration arbitraire/emprisonnement injustifié*
- goods (n.)/chattels (n.) : movables; *fr. : biens meubles*
- intentional (adj.) tort (n.) : tort such as assault, battery, trespass to land and some cases of negligence, which requires evidence of the wrongdoer's intention to carry out the tortious act; *fr. : ≈ délit civil intentionnel*

- licence (n.) : form of consent/authorisation given by a licensor to a licencee; *fr. : autorisation*
- nominal (adj.) damages (n.) : symbolic sum awarded by the courts by way of compensation of a loss; *fr. : euro symbolique à titre d'indemnisation*
- occupier (n.) : person who has a sufficient degree of control over given premises; *fr. : occupant*
- premises (n.) : fixed or moveable construction like a house, pub, boat, car or plane; *fr. : lieux*
- trespass to goods : wrongful physical interference with goods which are in someone else's possession; *fr. : ≈ atteinte aux biens d'autrui*
- trespass to land : common law tort, actionable *per se*, which is committed when someone intentionally enters the land of someone else without a lawful excuse; *fr. : ≈ entrée sans autorisation sur la propriété d'autrui*
- trespass to the person : unlawful intrusion which interferes with someone's person (for example, battery); *fr. : ≈ voie de fait (au sens civil, et non administratif du terme)*
- visitor (n.) : person entering somebody else's property for the exercise of a right conferred by law; *fr. : visiteur*

USEFUL EXPRESSIONS

- a landowner; *fr. : un propriétaire d'un bien immobilier (terrain, maison, etc.)*
- the rightful owner; *fr. : le proprétaire légitime*
- title to land/goods; *fr. : titre de propriété (immobilière/mobilière)*
- to act in good faith; *fr. : agir de bonne foi*
- to be a prerequisite condition to something; *fr. : être une condition préalable à quelque chose*

FURTHER INFORMATION

- eviction from a property corresponds to *expulsion* and must not be confused with deportation which is the *expulsion* of unauthorised/illegal migrants
- trespass must not be confused with *trépas* which means death

COMPARATIVE APPROACH

Il n'y a pas vraiment d'équivalent à la notion de *trespass to property* en France. Bien entendu, le droit à la propriété privée est protégé et nul n'est censé s'introduire sans autorisation chez quelqu'un. Cependant, le propriétaire d'un terrain enclavé (fonds dominant) peut prétendre à une servitude de passage sur le terrain de son voisin (fonds servant). De la même façon et afin de promouvoir le droit d'accès à la nature, toute personne peut traverser à pied, voire installer un bivouac sur tout terrain non clos, sauf interdiction expresse contraire. Bien entendu, si ce terrain s'avère privé, le propriétaire peut demander à l'intrus de quitter son terrain.

En ce qui concerne la notion de *trespass to the person*, la voie de fait en droit civil français s'en rapproche le plus, même si, là encore, elle n'est pas clairement définie. Une voie de fait est constituée quand quelqu'un provoque quelqu'un d'autre et s'en prend physiquement à lui. Un tel comportement peut être pénalement répréhensible.

En ce qui concerne la notion de *trespass to goods*, l'article 322-1 du Code pénal punit d'une peine d'emprisonnement et/ou d'une amende « la destruction, la dégradation ou la détérioration d'un bien appartenant à autrui ».

☐ 92 STATUTORY TORTS

The rules of tort are normally judge-made. However Parliament has created some statutory torts which impose duties on individuals, companies and public bodies. Product liability, occupiers' liability and employers' liability protect tenants, employees, customers and consumers. Statutory provisions are incorporated into contracts expressly or impliedly. Exemption clauses are only lawful if they do not violate enactments and if they are not onerous.

In order to make a valid claim for breach of a statutory duty, some conditions must be fulfilled : the statute must allow a civil claim, the claimant must be owed a duty under the statute, the damage alleged by the claimant must be within the scope of the statute, the defendant must have breached a statutory duty and the defendant's breach must have caused the claimant's loss.

Some breaches in statutory duties will not allow the claimant to recover for consequential or economic damage, but only for death or physical injuries. A closer look at the statutory provisions regulating the field will provide all relevant information concerning the potential claimants and defendants, the type of breach covered (defect, etc.), the type of injury sustained, the relevant authority and the categories of damages that can be claimed as well as the defences allowed.

GLOSSARY

- breach of duty : fact of not complying with an obligation; *fr. : ≈ violation d'une obligation*
- consumer (n.) : according to statutory definition, a consumer is any person who wishes to be supplied with goods for his private use, with services or facilities for a purpose other than business, or with accommodation for a purpose other than business; *fr. : consommateur*

- customer (n.) : party to a standard form contract who deals on the basis of written standard terms of business of the other party to the contract who/which him/itself runs a business; *fr. : client*
- defect (n.)/defective (adj.) : when a product is not of marketable quality and/or its safety is below the standards usually expected; *fr. : désordre/affecté d'un désordre*
- enactment (n.) : any piece of legislation (including delegated legislation) which has legal effect; *fr. : loi/texte ayant force de loi*
- exemption clause : clause in a contract excluding/restricting any liability, by making it subject to restrictive or onerous conditions; or excluding/restricting any right or remedy in respect of liability, subjecting a person to any prejudice in consequence of the pursuance of any such right or remedy; or excluding/restricting rules of evidence or procedure; *fr. : clause d'exemption/clause dérogatoire/clause d'exception*
- incorporate (v.)/incorporation (n.) : include/inclusion; *fr. : incorporer/incorporation*
- liability (n.) : in the context of statutory liability, liability arising in the course of any business or from the occupation of any premises used for the occupier's business purposes; *fr. : responsabilité*
- onerous (adj.) clause (n.) : unusual clause; *fr. : clause onéreuse*
- personal (adj.) injury (n.) : injury which includes any disease or impairment of physical or mental condition; *fr. : préjudice corporel*
- producer (n.) : person who manufactured the goods or in the case of a non-manufactured substance, person who won or abstracted it; *fr. : producteur*
- product (n.) : here, any goods or electricity or product which is comprised in another product (like a component part or raw material); *fr. : produit*
- statutory (adj.) : granted or defined by the law voted by Parliament; *fr. : législatif*

USEFUL EXPRESSIONS

- defective goods; *fr. : produits défectueux*
- in the course of/outside the course of their employment; *fr. : dans le cadre/en dehors du cadre de leur travail*
- pursuant to/according to a law; *fr. : en vertu d'une loi*
- statutory provisions; *fr. : dispositions législatives*

FURTHER INFORMATION

- industrial does not mean *industriel* but *relatif au travail*
- statutory torts do not only refer to the torts as covered in legislation voted by Parliament but also texts like regulations (*règlements*)

COMPARATIVE APPROACH

Le droit européen joue un rôle de plus en plus important dans les domaines de la protection des consommateurs et des travailleurs. Les débats récurrents concernant le temps de travail occultent l'harmonisation croissante des conditions de travail en Europe; pour preuve, la quantité de directives dans le domaine. Cependant, comme la régulation dans ce domaine se fait au moyen de directives, elle laisse aux États membres un peu de latitude pour mettre en œuvre les objectifs à atteindre (voir 1).

□ 93 REMEDIES

Damages

There are two main categories of damages i.e. liquidated or unliquidated damages (or damages "at large"). Another distinction is often made between general and special damages. The purpose of most (but not all) damages is to put the victim of the tort back in the situation in which he was in before the tort was committed. This is called *restitutio in integrum.* Payment of damages can be made as a lump sum or by instalments. A payment on account of damages can also be made pending the final decision of the court. For personal injury cases a periodical payment order (PPO) or structured settlement can also be made.

Should the claimant sustain damage to his property, the award of damages will either correspond to the reduction in the property value at the time and place of destruction, or to the replacement value (based on market prices) if the property was destroyed.

For personal injury, the damages awarded should cover all the claimant's losses, be they past, present or future (compensation for the various heads of damage sustained, reimbursement of expenses, accrued interest if relevant and legal costs). For physical damage, loss is divided into non-pecuniary loss (pain and suffering, mental anguish, loss of amenities, loss of earning capacity, "lost years" but also cosmetic damage) and pecuniary loss. The court can also award aggravated and/or contemptuous damages, aesthetic damages, nominal damages or statutory damages, but no exemplary damages.

Injunction

Contrary to damages, which are a common law remedy, an injunction is an equitable (thus discretionary) remedy. Both remedies (damages and/or injunction) can be awarded simultaneously or in lieu of each other. Several types of injunction are available (mandatory, prohibitory, interlocutory/provisional, final/perpetual, etc.).

GLOSSARY

- aesthetic (adj.) damages (n.) : damages granted to a party when the breach has caused serious and permanent disfiguration; *fr. : indemnisation du préjudice esthétique*
- aggravated (adj.) damages (n.) : damages which compensate the claimant for mental distress when the injury was caused or its extent increased by the manner in which the defendant committed the wrong or his subsequent behaviour; *fr. : ≈ dommages et intérêts à titre d'indemnisation d'un préjudice intangible*
- cosmetic (adj.) damage (n.) : damage to the appearance of a covered item which does not affect the use one can make of the item (e.g. damage to the body of a car); *fr. : ≈ préjudice affectant l'esthétique d'un bien*
- damages "at large" : the amount of damages is not yet determined/liquidated and will be assessed by the court; *fr. : ≈ dommages et intérêts non-liquidés*
- damages *in lieu :* financial compensation granted by the court as a substitute for something else (injunction, performance of a contract, etc.); *fr. : dommages et intérêts accordés à titre de substitut*
- discretionary (adj.) remedy (n.) : remedy which is awarded if a court decision grants it; *fr. : remède discrétionnaire*
- exemplary (adj.) damages (n.) : punitive damages granted by the United States courts but not in the United Kingdom; awarded to punish the defendant for his deliberate wrongdoing which disregarded the claimant's rights; also known as punitive damages; *fr. : dommages et intérêts punitifs*
- final (adj.) injunction (n.)/perpetual (adj.) injunction (n.) : injunction which is granted at the end of the litigation; *fr. : injonction permanente*
- general (adj.) damages (n.) : financial compensation awarded for the heads of damage usually sustained in similar circumstances; *fr. : ≈ dommages et intérêts généraux*
- heads of damage : types of loss sustained; *fr. : chefs de préjudice*
- instalments (n.) : differs from the payment of a lump sum of money in that payments are spread out in time (usually monthly instalments); *fr. : rente*
- interlocutory (adj.) injunction (n.)/interim (adj.) injunction (n.) : injunction issued temporarily, pending the outcome of the litigation; *fr. : ≈ injonction interlocutoire*
- legal (adj.) costs (n.) : amount of money granted by the court to the winning party in order to compensate for the reasonable costs incurred in the action; *fr. : dépens*
- liquidated (adj.) damages (n.) : the amount of compensation awarded to the claimant is set out specifically in the court judgment or agreed with the defendant by way of a settlement agreement; *fr. : dommages et intérêts liquidés*
- loss of amenity : head of loss which takes into account the fact that the claimant's injuries deprive him of some enjoyment, such as not being to able to practice a hobby; *fr. : préjudice d'agrément*

- loss of earning capacity : head of loss which aims to compensate the disadvantage the claimant will be subjected to on the labour market during his working life; *fr. : perte d'une chance (de revenus)*
- lump sum : once and for all settlement i.e. amount of money awarded in one go to the claimant; *fr. : capital*
- mandatory (adj.) injunction (n.) : court decision ordering a legal entity to stop a particular act or thing; *fr. : injonction de faire*
- mental (adj.) anguish (n.) : head of loss which takes into account the claimant's mental distress caused by the defendant's negligent act; *fr. : troubles de l'anxiété*
- nominal (adj.) damages (n.) : small sum given by way of compensation when the rights of the claimant have been infringed but there is no actual damage caused by the tortious act; *fr. : indemnisation de principe*
- pain and suffering : it includes suffering arising from the injury itself, the medical treatment and mental suffering caused by the awareness of the effects of the injuries on the patient; *fr. : prix de la douleur/premium doloris*
- payment on account/interim payment : payment of a sum of money pending the court's decision on the actual amount of damages to award; *fr. : paiement à titre de provision*
- periodical payment order (PPO) : court order by which the court sets up a structured settlement plan; a monthly sum is paid to the victim which can be linked to an earning index and can be varied by the courts to meet the victim's changing needs; *fr. : ≈ jugement ordonnant des paiements étalés dans le temps*
- prohibitory (adj.) injunction (n.) : court decision ordering a legal entity to stop a particular act or thing; *fr. : injonction de ne pas faire*
- *restitutio in integrum :* common law doctrine which states that the aim of damages in tort law is to put the claimant in the position he would have been in, had the tort not been committed; *fr. : restitutio in integrum/restitution intégrale*
- special (adj.) damages (n.)/consequential (adj.) damages (n.) : financial compensation awarded for the particular heads of damage sustained by the claimant in specific circumstances; *fr. : ≈ dommages et intérêts spéciaux*
- statutory (adj.) damages (n.) : damages which are set by the law as voted by Parliament rather than assessed according to the degree of damage sustained by the claimant; *fr. : dommages et intérêts statutaires*
- unliquidated (adj.) damages (n.) : as opposed to liquidated damages, only the right of the claimant to compensation is established, no fixed amount being determined for the damages; *fr. : dommages et intérêts non-liquidés/non-déterminés*
- upon the merits : defence which relies on the justice of the cause, not on its technicality; *fr. : sur le fond/au fond*

USEFUL EXPRESSIONS

- heads of damage; *fr. : chefs de préjudice*
- interest accrues on that sum at the rate of %; *fr. : les intérêts courent sur cette somme au taux de %*
- to apply for payment on account of damages; *fr. : requérir en justice le paiement d'une provision à valoir sur les dommages et intérêts*
- to assess damages; *fr. : évaluer les dommages-intérêts*
- to award/grant damages to the victim; *fr. : accorder des dommages-intérêts à la victime*
- to grant an injunction; *fr. : ordonner une injonction/enjoindre*
- to seek an injunction from the court that the defendant be ordered to do something; *fr. : présenter une demande d'injonction au tribunal tendant à ce qu'il ordonne au défendeur de faire quelque chose*

FURTHER INFORMATION

- one should never say : "the claimant sustained various damages" as damages refer to the financial compensation awarded to the victim of a tort; instead one should say : "the claimant sustained (or suffered) various heads of damage"
- English law does not enable the victim of a tort to go back to court to seek a further award of damages if the loss he sustained becomes worse over time; this means that the French concept of *aggravation* is not recognised in English law and should not be confused with the type of financial compensation called aggravated damages which can be granted in specific circumstances

Comparative approach

Le droit de la responsabilité délictuelle (*tort*) et quasi-délictuelle (*negligence*) français, comme en Angleterre et au Pays de Galles, vise à accorder à la victime la meilleure réparation possible en tenant compte des circonstances de l'espèce. Les juges ont identifié des chefs de préjudice (*heads of damage*) similaires. L'indemnisation peut se faire par le biais d'un capital (*lump sum*) ou d'une rente (*instalments*), une demande de provision à valoir sur les dommages et intérêts (*claim for payment on account of damages*) pouvant être formée par la victime en début de procédure (*litigation*).

Cependant, on peut identifier deux différences importantes entre ces systèmes juridiques.

Pour un même préjudice corporel (*personal injury*), par exemple, les juges français ont tendance à accorder une indemnisation plus faible en France qu'Outre-Manche. La raison est qu'en France, il est possible de retourner devant le juge pour solliciter des dommages et intérêts complémentaires si le préjudice s'aggrave. Cela est impossible Outre-Manche (où le règlement *once and for all* est en vigueur), ce qui explique pourquoi les juges ont tendance à être un peu plus généreux.

L'autre différence concerne le nombre de procédures d'injonction disponibles en France : injonction de payer, de faire et de ne pas faire. À noter toutefois que l'injonction de payer n'est pas applicable dans le cas de recouvrement de créances au titre des préjudices causés.

4

Insolvency procedures and company law remedies

□ 94 INTRODUCTION

An individual (but this is also true of a partnership or a company) is insolvent when he becomes unable to pay his debts when they fall due. In other words, the assets of the debtor are insufficient to meet his liabilities to creditors. Insolvency law is currently based on the Insolvency Act 1986. The purpose of insolvency law is to strike a balance between the need to avoid bankruptcy or liquidation if at all possible whilst protecting the creditors' interests. Various procedures are available by which the sums owed to creditors will be paid in full or in part. These insolvency procedures must not be confused with voluntary procedures which may be initiated by an individual or a company irrespective of their financial situation.

Official receivers (OR) and insolvency practitioners (IP) handle insolvency procedures. ORs are civil servants and court officers. They deal with the early stages of bankruptcy and compulsory liquidation by investigating the individual's, the partnership's or the company's affairs. IPs are in the private sector and are usually accountants or solicitors. They must be authorised to act as IP by a recognised professional body (RPB). Details of the relevant OR or IP can be found at the Individual Insolvency Register (for an individual or a partnership) or Companies House (for a company).

Creditors must make themselves known and file a claim with the OR or the IP. A report is later sent to them giving information on the debtor's assets and liabilities. Creditors will be notified in due course of any distribution of money (or not) before the case is closed.

GLOSSARY

- assets (n.) : any property of value owned by a legal entity (whether an individual, a partnership or a company); assets can be tangible (in a physical form like real estate or stock) or intangible; *fr. : actif*

- bankruptcy (n.) : insolvency procedure which applies to an individual including a sole practitioner or a member of a partnership, but not to a company; *fr. : faillite personnelle*
- case (n.) : here, legal matter; *fr. : dossier/affaire*
- civil (adj.) servant (n.) : in Britain, someone employed by the Crown or more generally, the government or a public authority; *fr. : fonctionnaire*
- company (n.) : see 13
- compulsory (adj.) liquidation (n.) : liquidation which follows a court order handed down further to an unpaid creditor's petition; an OR takes control of the company but an IP may be appointed if there are assets to pay his costs; *fr. : liquidation judiciaire*
- Companies House (n.) : see 15
- court officer : person who assists the effective operation of justice; *fr. : ≈ officier ministériel*
- creditor (n.) : person or legal entity who is owed money; *fr. : créancier*
- debt (n.) : monetary sum due to an individual or a corporate creditor, for goods supplied or services rendered; *fr. : dette*
- debtor (n.) : person or legal entity who owes money to someone else; *fr. : débiteur*
- due (adj.) : owed as a debt or payable; *fr. : dû*
- insolvency (n.)/insolvent (adj.) : fact for someone, a partnership or a company to be unable to pays one's debts; *fr. : insolvabilité/situation de cessation de paiements*
- insolvency law : law which relates to insolvency procedures; *fr. : droit des procédures collectives*
- insolvency practitioner (IP) : person authorised by the relevant professional body to deal with insolvency matters; he can act as trustee in bankruptcy, supervisor of a voluntary arrangement, administrator or liquidator of a company; *fr. : ≈ administrateur/liquidateur* (for companies)/≈ *syndic de faillite* (for individuals)/≈ *administrateur judiciaire*/≈ *mandataire judiciaire*
- insolvency procedures : legal steps which can be taken when an individual, a partnership or a company is not able to meet his/its debts to creditors; *fr. : procédures collectives*
- Individual Insolvency Register (IIR) : register which is regularly updated and contains information on bankruptcies, debt relief orders, individual and fast-track voluntary arrangements, bankruptcy restriction orders or undertakings; *fr. : ≈ registre des faillites personnelles*
- liabilities (n.) : as opposed to assets; *fr. : passif* (as opposed to *actif*)
- liability (n.) : legal obligation towards a person; *fr. : responsabilité*
- liquidation (n.) : winding up of a company's affairs, involving the sale of a company's assets, cessation or sale of its activities or operations, distribution of the proceeds of sale amongst creditors and distribution to the shareholders of any surplus; *fr. : liquidation*

- official (adj.) receiver (n.) (OR) : civil servant and court officer who first intervenes in any bankruptcy or compulsory liquidation; *fr. : ≈ juge-commissaire*
- partnership (n.) : see 13
- solvency (n.)/solvent (adj.) : degree to which the assets exceed the liabilities; *fr. : solvabilité*

USEFUL EXPRESSIONS

- assets are insufficient to meet liabilities; *fr. : l'actif est insuffisant pour désintéresser le passif*
- the amount due and owing; *fr. : le montant dû*
- to be indebted to someone/to owe someone money; *fr. : être endetté à l'égard de quelqu'un*
- to fall due/become due; *fr. : venir à échéance/devenir exigible*
- to file a claim with a court; *fr. : déposer une demande en justice*
- to go bust/to go belly up (colloquial)/to be wound up; *fr. : être liquidée (for a company)*
- payment of debts/liabilities; *fr. : apurement du passif*

FURTHER INFORMATION

- the noun company (*société*) should not be translated by *compagnie*
- because it is colloquial, the "winding up" of a company is used indifferently to refer to the dissolution and the liquidation of a company; however, these correspond to slightly different moments of the procedure; the dissolution occurs 3 months after the liquidation of a company
- the word debt is ambiguous as it is often used to describe both a *créance* or a *dette*
- an IP is usually a solicitor i.e. a legal professional; it is difficult to translate in French as depending on the solicitor's field of expertise, the solicitor can be a *notaire* (if he deals with conveyancing or probate) or, in most other cases, an *avocat*

COMPARATIVE APPROACH

Les grandes réformes du droit des procédures collectives et des faillites (*insolvency law*) ont été passées à une époque similaire en France et en Angleterre et au Pays de Galles (*Insolvency Act 1986* complétée par l'*Enterprise Act 2002* et loi du 25 janvier 1985 refondue en 2005). Si les procédures se ressemblent en ce qu'elles ont pour objectif de protéger les intérêts des créanciers, il reste des divergences fondamentales. Le concept anglais de *Official receiver* n'existe pas vraiment en France, même s'il se rapproche un peu de celui du juge-commissaire. De même, il n'existe pas davantage de période d'observation telle qu'on l'applique en France, même si le système *d'administration,* étudié ci-dessous, présente avec elle quelques ressemblances dès lors que le dirigeant est dessaisi de son entreprise dès le déclenchement de la procédure.

□ 95 BANKUPTCY AND COMPULSORY LIQUIDATION

Bankruptcy

It applies to individuals including members of a partnership or sole traders. A creditor, the supervisor of an individual voluntary arrangement (which is not complied with) or the individual debtor himself can file a bankruptcy petition with the court. This usually happens when a statutory demand remains unsatisfied i.e. when a debt has not been settled within 21 days of service. A bankruptcy order is made by the court. If no IP is appointed, an OR acts as receiver and trustee. He manages the bankrupt's estate and realises any available assets save for some personal items. The fees and costs of the proceedings are paid first. The creditors are then paid according to a statutory priority list. There are restrictions to the right to trade of an undischarged bankrupt. Leave from the court is required to run a company or be a company director. The undischarged bankrupt must inform those with whom he intends to do business of the name under which he used to trade. This is meant to ensure that they are aware of his previous financial difficulties and his present situation. Discharge from bankruptcy is automatic after 12 months running from the bankruptcy order. Alternatively a notice can be filed with the court by the OR seeking an earlier discharge. A bankruptcy restrictions order can be made against the bankrupt extending the bankruptcy restrictions up to 15 years.

Compulsory liquidation

This procedure applies to companies or partnerships. The creditors can lodge a petition with the court seeking a winding up order. This occurs when there are outstanding monies owed by the company/partnership to its creditors. After the winding up order, the OR acts as liquidator or trustee until an IP is usually appointed. The OR informs all known creditors of the situation. A creditors' meeting is summoned up after the creditors have returned a proof of debt form duly completed. The role of the liquidator is to pay all the fees and costs relating to the liquidation and realise the company's assets with a view to paying the creditors according to a priority list which is binding. The director of a liquidated company can become the director of another company save if he was judged bankrupt as a person or disqualified. He may be required by the court to contribute to the assets of the new company he joins and may not be allowed to use the name of the former company to which he belonged.

GLOSSARY

- assets (n.) : see 94
- bankruptcy (n.) : see 94
- binding (adj.) : here, which is compulsory/mandatory and must be complied with or applied; *fr. : qui lie/qui a force obligatoire*
- complete (v.) : to fill in (a form); *fr. : remplir (un formulaire)*
- compulsory (adj.) liquidation (n.) : see 94
- costs (n.) : here, disbursements; *fr. : débours* (or *dépens* if in a legal/judicial context; see 74)
- creditors' meeting (n.) : meeting usually summoned up to decide which IP to appoint in a bankruptcy or liquidation or to consider proposals in the case of administration or voluntary arrangement; *fr. : réunion des créanciers*
- director (n.) : see 16
- discharge (v.)/discharged (adj.) : when a bankrupt person is released from liability; this occurs usually within 12 months from the court's bankruptcy order; the bankrupt does not recover his former assets; *fr. : réhabiliter (v.)/ réhabilitation (n.)*
- disqualification (n.) : sanction ordered by a court forbidding someone from running a company; *fr. : interdiction de gérer*
- estate (n.) : here, bankrupt's legal and equitable interests in property; *fr. : patrimoine*
- fees (n.) : sum of money owed to a professional for advice or services rendered; *fr. : honoraires*
- leave (n.) : synonym for authorisation; *fr. : autorisation*
- liquidator (n.) : person appointed to administer the liquidation of a company; *fr. : liquidateur*
- outstanding (adj.) monies (n.) : sums due and owing; *fr. : sommes dues*
- priority list : statutory list determining the order in which creditors should be paid; *fr. : ordre de paiement (des créanciers)*
- proof of debt : form completed by each creditor at the liquidator's request, setting out details of his claim against the company, including its amount and how it arose; *fr. : déclaration de créance*
- realise (v.) : convert assets into cash by selling them; *fr. : vente*
- receiver (n.) : person usually appointed by the court to run a company or deal with a bankrupt's estate for a period of time; his task is to sell the debtor's assets to pay back creditors insofar as possible; *fr. : ≈ administrateur*
- service (n.)/serve (v.) : in a legal context, bringing some documents to the attention of someone in an official way; *fr. : notification*
- statutory (adj.) : deriving from a statute; *fr. : législatif*
- statutory (adj.) demand (n.) : formal notice served on a debtor requiring him to pay a debt within 21 days failure of which may result in bankruptcy

proceedings being issued; *fr. : ≈ mise en demeure avant assignation à fin de faillite*

- summon up (v.) : convene, call together (e.g. a meeting); *fr. : convoquer*
- trustee (n.) : in the context of insolvency law, title often given to an IP appointed in a bankruptcy; *fr. : ≈ mandataire*
- undischarged (adj.) : when applied to someone bankrupt, means that he has not been released from bankruptcy yet; *fr. : non réhabilité*
- winding up order : court order obtained further to the petition (usually from a creditor) which constitutes the first step towards a court liquidation; *fr. : jugement de mise en liquidation judiciaire*

USEFUL EXPRESSIONS

- to comply with/abide by; *fr. : se conformer à*
- to give leave to do; *fr. : donner l'autorisation de faire*
- to summon up/convene a meeting; *fr. : convoquer à une réunion*
- to effect service of a document on someone/to serve a document on someone; *fr. : notifier/signifier un document à quelqu'un*

FURTHER INFORMATION

- "to qualify for" means "to meet the requirements of"
- "winding up" someone, as opposed to a company, means to tease someone
- in a judicial context, the court usually makes an "order for costs" against the losing party to the litigation, ordering it to reimburse all the disbursements incurred (such as the issue fee for the claim or experts' fees, etc.); in France, the equivalent would be a *condamnation aux dépens* which (for civil, as opposed to public law cases) is made pursuant to article 700 of the *Code de procédure civile*

Comparative approach

En Angleterre et au Pays de Galles, le concept de *bankruptcy* (procédure applicable aux individus en état de cessation des paiments) concerne à la fois les personnes physiques dont les dépenses excèdent les revenus, et les anciens dirigeants de personnes morales dont la responsabilité personnelle est engagée. Outre-Manche, il n'existe pas, comme en France, une véritable procédure de surendettement. De même, la procédure de *statutory demand*, qui donne au débiteur une dernière chance avant d'enclencher la procédure de *bankruptcy*, ne trouve pas d'équivalent en droit français.

□ 96 PROCEDURE AND PAYMENT OF CREDITORS

Within 12 weeks of the court order (for bankruptcy or compulsory liquidation), the OR notifies all known creditors of this order. An IP can be appointed in lieu of the OR if there are substantial assets. After the court order, no legal actions can be brought by unsecured creditors against the individual/company without the court's approval. The OR/IP acts as trustee/liquidator. He sends all known creditors a report setting out the individual's or company's assets and liabilities as well as a proof of debt form to all known creditors if he intends to hold a creditors meeting. The form is completed and returned to him. This meeting is compulsory if required by 25 % of the creditors (in terms of value of money owed). A creditors' committee (for bankruptcy) or liquidation committee (for liquidations) can be appointed. These committees decide whether to engage into litigation (to recover outstanding monies) or continue with the bankrupt's or company's business. When the insolvency process is completed i.e. a list of remaining assets/liabilities has been drawn, the OR informs the creditors of his intention to apply to the Secretary of State for release. Conversely the IP holds a final creditors' meeting to be released from his duties. Both OR/IP give a list of receipts/payments.

Regarding distribution, fixed charge holders are not affected by the winding up of a company. They are the creditors who took out a security over one of the company's assets before it became insolvent. They can take the relevant assets, proportionately to their number, before they are sold by the trustee/liquidator. Whatever monies are left after the company's remaining assets have been realised will be shared amongst the creditors on a proportionate basis, by way of a dividend, depending on the category to which they belong. The Insolvency Act 1986 sets out a binding priority list of the different categories.

According to this priority list, the charge holders (secured creditors) are the first to get paid when the assets are sold. The IP has priority over his fees for work carried out in connection with the administration or winding up of the company. Then come preferential creditors such as employees in respect of their wages (limited to four months) and contributions to pension schemes. They are followed by creditors holding a floating charge over an asset (such as a debenture, unsecured creditors, those to whom interest is payable on debts followed by the shareholders). Any decision of the OR/IP to reject a creditor's claim may be disputed in court.

GLOSSARY

- administration (n.) : here, insolvency procedure (usually pronounced by a judge) which allows a company to carry on trading but stops any legal action against a company unless the administrator or a court allows it to proceed; *fr. : ≈ procédure de sauvegarde*

- charge (n. or v.) : security over the assets of a borrower/debtor which does not involve a transfer of ownership; *fr. : sûreté*
- committee (n.) (creditors' or liquidation) : group of creditors who work with the IP to supervise his task; the creditors' committee is discretionary; *fr. : ≈ syndicat des créanciers*
- debenture (n.) : document (which will usually contain a floating charge) by which a company acknowledges a debt and undertakes to pay back a sum of money which it received on loan from the holder of the document; *fr. : reconnaissance de dette*
- dividend (n.) : see 14
- fixed (adj.) charge (n.) : charge taken out by a lender over particular assets of a company (usually property although it could apply to shares or goodwill) which the company cannot dispose of without the lender's consent; *fr. : sûreté réelle* (if applicable to property)
- floating (adj.) charge (n.) : charge taken by a lender over the general assets of a company (such as stock); the company may use and dispose of these assets (like stock) without the secured creditor's consent; it can convert to a fixed charge over these assets in the occurrence of certain events listed in the charge document; *fr. : sûreté « flottante »/droit de gage général*
- pension scheme (n.) : see 54
- preferential (adj.) creditor (n.) : creditor who has a preferential debt (such as employees' claim for arrears of pay, some unpaid pension contributions but unlike Crown debts like PAYE or VAT) who is paid ahead of an ordinary creditor; *fr. : créancier privilégié*
- realise (v.) : sell; *fr. : vendre/céder*
- release (n. or v.) : here, discharge of one's obligations; *fr. : décharge (n.)/ décharger (v.)*
- secured (adj.) creditor (n.) : refers to a creditor who has a security like a charge or a mortgage over some or all of a company's property; *fr. : créancier privilégié*
- security (n.) : fixed or floating charge taken to secure the repayment of a debt; *fr. : sûreté*
- shareholder (n.) : see 16
- unsecured (adj.) creditor (n.) : creditor who does not hold any security over a company's property; last in the list of creditors, just before shareholders; *fr. : créancier chirographaire*
- wage (n.) : see 54

USEFUL EXPRESSIONS

- to go into administration; *fr. : faire l'objet d'une procédure de sauvegarde*
- to be secured by a fixed charge over assets; *fr. : être garanti par une sûreté réelle sur des actifs*
- to convene a creditors' committee; *fr. : convoquer un syndicat de créanciers*

FURTHER INFORMATION

- the adjective unsecured as in unsecured creditor (*créancier chirographaire*) must not be confused with an insecure person who lacks confidence (*personne peu sûre d'elle*)
- the noun security (*sûreté*) is different from the word safety (*sécurité*)
- there is a difference between the liquidation and the dissolution of a company; the former refers to the sale of all the company's assets and the latter to the actual closure of the company

COMPARATIVE APPROACH

En France, le « syndicat » des créanciers (*creditors' committee*) n'a pas vraiment de pouvoirs. En ce qui concerne le paiement des créanciers, il existe aussi un ordre de paiement des créanciers (*creditors' priority list*). On distingue les créanciers privilégiés (*preferential creditors*) tels que les salariés (*employees*), le fisc (*taxman*) et ceux bénéficiant d'une sûreté réelle (*fixed charge*) et les créanciers chirographaires (*unsecured creditors*) qui ne sont détenteurs que d'une créance simple.

□ 97 VOLUNTARY ARRANGEMENT

There are individual voluntary arrangements (IVA), fast-track voluntary arrangement (FTVA) or company voluntary arrangements (CVA). The first two are an alternative to an individual's bankruptcy, the latter to a company's liquidation. They only apply to non-priority debts.

IVA or CVA

An IVA or a CVA is a composition, i.e. a formal arrangement of an individual or a company with his/its creditors, whereby the whole debt or part of it in case of forfeiture will be paid back over a fixed period of time. A moratorium is drawn by an IP (as opposed to an OR) who will put forward a proposal to the creditors. The IP summons up a creditors' meeting where the proposal will be accepted or rejected. The agreement of a set percentage of the creditors (by debt value) on the IP's proposal is required to make the IVA or CVA binding on all the creditors, irrespective of whether they took part in the vote or not. The creditors' approval of the IVA or CVA must be endorsed by a court order. Default of a debtor under an IVA will usually result in a bankruptcy order. Likewise under a CVA, most CVA proposals provide for the supervisor to lodge a winding-up petition in case of default.

FTVA

An alternative to an IVA is the FTVA. It differs from it in that it is less formal and can only occur after the bankruptcy order has been made. The debtor himself drafts a proposal to put to his creditors and sends it to the OR (as opposed to an IP) who in turn may approve it and submit it to the creditors for their agreement. If approved by a majority (by debt value) of the creditors, the OR will act as supervisor and ensure that the agreement is implemented. The OR charges a fixed fee which means that the FTVA is cheaper than an IVA.

GLOSSARY

- company voluntary arrangement (CVA) : insolvency procedure which applies to companies and is an alternative to liquidation; it is a renegotiation of all the sums owed to all the creditors, and is only valid if/when approved by a creditors' meeting and vote; *fr. : moratoire amiable entre créanciers*
- default (n.) : failure to do something, such as comply with an obligation; *fr. : manquement*
- draft (v. or n.) : synonym for write; *fr. : rédiger*
- endorse (v.)/endorsement (n.) : to sign or ratify a document; *fr. : signer/ratifier*
- fast-track voluntary arrangement (FTVA) : less formal and faster alternative to IVA; *fr. : moratoire amiable entre créanciers*
- forfeiture (n.)/forfeit (v.) : here, fact for a creditor of giving up or surrendering part of the monies due to the debtor; *fr. : renoncement*
- implement (v.) : make something work or come into force; *fr. : mettre en œuvre*
- individual voluntary arrangement (IVA) : insolvency procedure which applies to individuals and is an alternative to bankruptcy; it is a renegotiation of all the sums owed to all the creditors, and is only valid if/when approved by a creditors' meeting and vote; *fr. : moratoire amiable entre créanciers*

USEFUL EXPRESSIONS

- to reach an agreement with; *fr. : arriver à un accord avec*
- to surrender/forfeit a sum of money; *fr. : renoncer à une somme d'argent*

FURTHER INFORMATION

- the noun forfeiture (*renoncement*) must not be confused with *forfaiture* which is an abuse of authority

COMPARATIVE APPROACH

En France, comme en Angleterre et au Pays de Galles, un moratoire amiable avec les créanciers (par opposition au moratoire judiciaire) est possible, tant dans le cadre des procédures collectives affectant les sociétés que des procédures de faillite. C'est un bon moyen pour l'individu ou la société concernée d'oxygéner sa trésorerie.

☐ 98 ADMINISTRATION AND ADMINISTRATIVE RECEIVERSHIP

Like the CVA, they are alternatives to a company's liquidation. They also enable the company to remain alive (i.e. not be dissolved) and to continue trading as a "going concern". Recent changes to both systems were brought by the Enterprise Act 2002.

Administration

When a company goes into administration, an administrator (who must be an IP) is appointed to manage the company's affairs. He acts as an officer of the court and aims at rescuing the company whenever possible. The company benefits from a protection (limited in time) from the legal actions of creditors who might want to try to recover their monies. Thus a creditor cannot petition for the winding up of a company whilst it is in administration. If the administrator is not successful in rescuing the company, he can move the company to a CVA or pronounce the dissolution of the company.

Administrative receivership

When a company goes into administrative receivership, an administrative receiver (who must be an IP) is appointed by a creditor to a company. It is a prerequisite that this creditor has a charge over the company's assets to secure its debt before an administrative receiver can be appointed. The creditor will often be a bank with whom the company took out a loan and who secured a mortgage over the assets of the company. The bank will have obtained a debenture from the company, which is a document giving the creditor a charge over the company's assets. The role of the receiver is to find the best way for the creditor to recover its outstanding monies. He may reach the view that the company should continue trading under his supervision, that it should be sold as a going concern, in whole or in part, or that is should cease trading and its assets sold one by one.

GLOSSARY

- administration (n.) : procedure by which an administrator is appointed by the court to try to rescue a company in financial difficulty; *fr. : ≈ administration judiciaire*
- administrator (n.) : IP appointed in an administration; *fr. : ≈ administrateur*
- administrative (adj.) receivership (n.) : non-court procedure by which an IP controls a company's assets under the terms of a security arrangement (e.g. charge) with a view to carrying on trading or selling part or all the assets to pay off preferential creditors; *fr. : ≈ redressement non-judiciaire/≈ administration confiée à un séquestre*
- composition (n.) : agreement between a debtor and his creditors by which the latter agree to receive a reduced amount in full and final settlement of their claim; *fr. : moratoire/concordat*

- debenture (n.) : see 14
- going concern : refers to a business or company which is or continues trading, for instance when it is sold; *fr. : poursuite d'activité*
- prerequisite (n.) : thing required as a prior condition to something else; *fr. : condition sine qua non*
- winding up petition : petition filed with the court, usually by a creditor, seeking an order that a company be put into compulsory liquidation; *fr. : demande d'ouverture d'une procédure de liquidation judiciaire*

USEFUL EXPRESSIONS

- to sign a composition agreement with creditors; *fr. : signer un concordat avec des créanciers*
- to petition for the winding up of a company; *fr. : demander l'ouverture d'une procédure de liquidation judiciaire à l'encontre d'une société*
- to sell a business as a going concern; *fr. : vendre une entreprise en activité*
- to go into liquidation; *fr. : faire l'objet d'une liquidation*

FURTHER INFORMATION

- the expression "as a going concern" should not be confused with the noun concern (*inquiétude*)

COMPARATIVE APPROACH

Le concept d'*administrative receivership* (redressement non-judiciaire) est une particularité du droit applicable en Angleterre et au Pays de Galles qui ne trouve pas vraiment d'équivalent en France. Elle suspend les fonctions du dirigeant de la société et peut de ce fait être comparée à l'ouverture d'une période d'observation, même si celle-ci n'a pas de véritable existence comme en France.

□ 99 VOLUNTARY PROCEDURES : SPECIFIC CASE OF VOLUNTARY BANKRUPTCY AND LIQUIDATION

Voluntary bankruptcy

An individual may elect to file for voluntary bankruptcy. This is usually done to have better control over one's affairs than when a creditor initiates the procedure.

Voluntary liquidation and alternative

There are two kinds of voluntary liquidation of a company. Shareholders can voluntarily wind up the company by voting and passing a special resolution to stop trading. This is called creditors' voluntary liquidation and it can occur when the company cannot pay its debts. Sometimes a company is solvent and can pay its debts but one of its members wants to close it down. This is members' voluntary liquidation.

An alternative to voluntary liquidation of a company is its "striking off" the Companies' Register. This can only apply to a limited company if the company is solvent, has settled all its debts, has not traded, sold off any stock or changed names in the last 3 months, is not threatened with liquidation and has no agreement with its creditors (such as a CVA). Once struck off, the company will no longer exist.

GLOSSARY

- Companies' Register : see 15 (Companies House)
- creditors' voluntary liquidation (CVL) : when a shareholders' resolution leads to the winding-up of an insolvent company; *fr. : liquidation volontaire à la demande des créanciers*
- elect (v.) : synonym for to choose; *fr. : choisir*
- file (v.) : synonym for to lodge; *fr. : déposer/enrôler*
- members' voluntary liquidation (MVL) : liquidation pronounced at a member's request; the company may still be solvent and in a position to pay its debts; it is usually a tax-efficient way for the company to distribute its remaining assets to the shareholders; the distribution to the shareholders is considered as capital receipts rather than income; *fr. : liquidation volontaire à la demande des membres (de la société)*
- resolution (n.) : corporate action which gives rise to a vote; it can be a members' resolution (ordinary or special) or a directors' resolution; an ordinary members' resolution (or of a class of members) is passed by a simple majority; a special members' resolution of the members (or of a class of members) is passed by a majority of not less than 75 %; a directors' resolution is passed by a simple majority; *fr. : résolution*
- shareholder (n.) : see 16
- solvent (adj.)/solvency (n.) : state of a legal entity who has enough assets to settle his liabilities; *fr. : solvable (adj.)/solvabilité (n.)*
- strike off (v.) : remove, cross off; *fr. : radier*
- trade (v. or n.) : activity of buying or selling goods or doing any form of commercial business; *fr. : ≈ commerce*
- voluntary (adj.) bankruptcy (n.) : as opposed to an involuntary bankruptcy filed with the bankruptcy court by a creditor, the debtor himself initiates the voluntary bankrutpcy when his assets are insufficient to meet his liabilities; *fr. : ≈ faillite personnelle volontaire*

- voluntary (adj.) liquidation (n.) : the winding up of a company occurs at the request of members of the company; *fr. : ≈ mise en liquidation volontaire*

USEFUL EXPRESSIONS

- to file for bankruptcy; *fr. : déposer une demande à fin de faillite personnelle*
- to apply to be struck off the Companies' Register; *fr. : demander la radiation au Registre du Commerce et des Sociétés*

FURTHER INFORMATION

- in France and pursuant to article L. 654-1 *et seq* of the *Code de commerce*, the *banqueroute* is a criminal offence punishable by a prison sentence and/or a fine; amongst many things, it may consist of fraudulently trying to postpone the liquidation of a company, distraining assets or mismanaging accounts
- as opposed to a compulsory liquidation which is the result of a court order, a voluntary liquidation results from a resolution of the company

COMPARATIVE APPROACH

Le concept anglais de *creditors' voluntary liquidation* n'existe pas en France. En revanche, il est courant de procéder à la dissolution anticipée d'une société et donc, volontaire (*members' voluntary liquidation*). Par exemple, s'agissant des sociétés à responsabilité limitée (SARL), les associés prennent la décision en assemblée générale extraordinaire en vue de la radiation (*striking off*) de la société du registre du commerce et des sociétés (RCS) (*register of Companies' House*).

En ce qui concerne la faillite personnelle (*bankruptcy*), il faut évoquer la procédure française de surendettement, prévue à l'article L. 330-1 du Code de la consommation. Ce régime applicable au débiteur, personne physique de bonne foi, qui ne peut face à ses dettes non professionnelles exigibles et à échoir, permet à la commission compétente d'ordonner un report ou rééchelonnement du paiement des dettes et même, si la situation du débiteur est irrémédiablement compromise, une procédure de rétablissement personnel qui consiste en une annulation de l'ensemble des dettes avec ou sans liquidation judiciaire. Cela correspond à une forme de faillite personnelle.

Dans un arrêt de 2010 (Civ. 2e, 21 janvier 2010, nº 08-19.984), la Cour de cassation a confirmé sa jurisprudence antérieure en jugeant que le dirigeant d'une SARL ne relevait pas de la loi sur les procédures collectives du seul fait de son statut de gérant. Dès lors, il peut bénéficier de la procédure de surendettement, mais uniquement pour ses dettes personnelles et non professionnelles.

□ 100 BUSINESS STRUCTURES & SHAREHOLDER'S REMEDIES

If the shareholder of a company seeks redress for a grievance, there are various remedies available to him. He can enforce the company's constitution, start a derivative claim or sue on grounds of unfair prejudice. Companies are legal entities and, pursuant to *Foss v Harbottle* (1843) 67 ER 189, do not allow rights to third parties. However there are now exceptions to this rule. These exceptions are covered by the derivative claim principle which was originally a common law principle before the statutory derivative claim was created by Sections 260-264 of the Company Act 2006.

A derivative claim allows a member or shareholder to sue a third party (often an insider) on behalf of the company, in cases where the company itself is unlikely to seek redress against the third party. A minority shareholder, a member or a person to whom shares have been transferred by the operation of the law can bring a derivative claim against a director or any other person who might have caused harm to the company's interests (officers, employees, etc.) irrespective of whether a director has derived a benefit from an actual or proposed act or omission which causes negligence, default or breach of trust.

To pursue a claim, the member/shareholder must first obtain the court's authorisation. Amongst other tests, the claimant must satisfy the court that he has a *prima facie* case. In order to avoid double recovery, through both derivative and personal claims, the ability of members to recover is limited by the no-reflective loss principle. Members can also petition the court on grounds that the company has carried out business in a way that was unfair and prejudicial to the interests of a section of members. An instance of unfair prejudicial conduct is when a the company's sole director has paid himself an excessive salary. The court can grant several remedies, amongst which orders restricting the ability of the company to do an act, to conduct its internal affairs, to change its constitution or to purchase the claimant's shares.

GLOSSARY

- breach of trust : negligent or fraudulent violation by a trustee, or someone else in a fiduciary relationship, of the terms of a trust; *fr. : ≈ abus de confiance*
- common law derivative claim : prior to the introduction of statutory derivative claims by the Companies Act 2006, the common law derivative claim was allowed when the grievance was an illegal or *ultra vires* act, when it breached members' rights, when it was not passed by a special resolution or when it related to some fraud committed against the minority of members; *fr. : ≈ action ut singuli découlant de la common law*
- default (n.) : failure to perform an act that was prescribed by the law; *fr. : défaillance/manquement*

- fraudulent (adj.) trading (n.) : under the statutory definition in the Insolvency Act, in the course of winding up a company, when the business of the company has been carried out with the purpose of defrauding creditors; it is a criminal offence; *fr. : pratique commerciale frauduleuse*
- no-reflective loss principle : principle whereby members are not allowed to recover the loss that corresponds to the actual loss of the company; *fr. : ≈ principe contre la double indemnisation*
- *prima facie* (adj.) test (n.) : here, test establishing whether a member's claim has any obvious merits; *fr. : ≈ à première vue*
- statutory derivative claim : introduced by the Companies Act 2006, claim allowing shareholders or members to take action on behalf of the company against a third party (usually an insider : director, officer or employee) which has acted against the interests of the company; *fr. : ≈ action ut singuli découlant de la loi*
- unfair prejudicial conduct : when the affairs of a company have been carried out in a manner that is prejudicial to the interests of all or part of members; *fr. : ≈ comportement injuste dont il résulte des conséquences dommageables*
- wrongful (adj.) trading (n.) : under the statutory definition in the Insolvency Act, when directors continue trading when they knew or ought to have known that the company would go into liquidation; it is a civil offence and a lesser offence than fraudulent trading; *fr. : ≈ négligence sanctionnable*

FURTHER INFORMATION

- in the field of shareholders' remedies, the main legal provisions to date are to be found in the Insolvency Act 1986 and the Companies Act 2006

USEFUL EXPRESSIONS

- expenses incurred in the litigation; *fr. : dépenses occasionnées par la procédure*
- to restore the company to the position it was in before it went into liquidation; *fr. : remettre la société dans la position dans laquelle elle était avant d'entrer en liquidation*

COMPARATIVE APPROACH

Il n'y a pas de procédure de *derivative claim* en droit français. Les actionnaires minoritaires sont protégés par d'éventuelles actions en responsabilité : actions individuelles (lorsque le préjudice a été commis par un administrateur), les actions *ut universi* (exercées par les représentants légaux de la société) et actions *ut singuli* (exercées par les actionnaires eux-mêmes).

5
Tax litigation

□ 101 GENERAL RULES

There are two types of litigation which relate to tax disputes i.e. civil and criminal litigation.

Criminal litigation

The central government (represented by HMRC) or local taxman may prosecute any taxpayer (individual or corporate) for tax evasion (also called tax fraud). Fraud must not be confused with tax avoidance or tax planning which are not criminal offences. Tax evasion consists of hiding one's income and wealth to avoid paying tax. It also consists of claiming tax relief to which someone is not entitled. In April 2010 the Crown Prosecution Service and the Revenue and Customs Prosecutions Office merged to join forces against tax evasion. This service is now called the CPS Central Fraud Group. In January 2013 the Director of Public Prosecutions announced his intention to split co-defendants in multi-party prosecutions into separate trials. Reasons for doing so may include the better chance for the prosecutor and the judge to obtain confessions from the defendant and/or evidence relating to a co-defendant.

Tax fraud and evasion are criminal offences which may lead to the fraudster's imprisonment and/or payment of a fine as well as any tax arrears. The court which has jurisdiction to try tax matters may be the magistrates' court (for example, for non-payment of council tax) or the Crown Court, depending on the seriousness of the offence.

Civil litigation

A legal entity may dispute the amount of tax or duty he has to pay or the penalty imposed on him. The first instance jurisdiction to deal with tax disputes lies with the First-tier Tribunal (tax chamber) which was set up on 1st April 2009. It replaces the four former separate tax tribunals which were the General Commissioners, the Special Commissioners, VAT & Duties and section 706 Tribunals. The First-tier Tribunals can hear all appeals (specific name given to the claim lodged against a tax decision) relating to all types of tax, whether direct or indirect such as income tax, corporation tax, capital gains tax, inheritance tax, stamp duty land tax, PAYE coding notices, national insurance contributions, VAT and duties such as custom duties, excise duties or landfill tax.

The jurisdiction of the tax tribunal is UK-wide and thus, extends beyond the borders of England and Wales. The First-tier Tribunal (tax chamber) is independent from HM Revenue & Customs (HMRC).

The onward appeal from a First-tier Tribunal (tax chamber) decision lies with the Upper Tribunal (Tax and Chancery chamber). This appeal is not heard as of right : prior leave must be obtained from the First-tier Tribunal. Appeals are heard by panels which may consist of legally qualified judges, non-legally qualified expert members or a mixture of the two.

GLOSSARY

- arrears (n.) : sums still due and owing; *fr. : arriérés*
- capital gains tax : tax on the profit or the gain made when selling or otherwise disposing of assets (such as property or shares); a tax-free allowance is available; *fr. : impôt sur les revenus du capital*
- corporation tax : tax on the taxable profits of limited companies, unincorporated bodies, associations and other clubs or societies; *fr. : impôt sur les sociétés*
- direct (adj.) tax (n.) : tax levied directly on an individual or organisation, such as income tax or corporation tax; *fr. : impôt direct*
- income tax : tax on some income such as earnings from employment or self-employment, pensions, savings, rental income, income paid on a trust, dividends (on shares) etc.; *fr. : impôt sur le revenu*
- indirect (adj.) tax (n.) : tax usually levied on goods or services such as VAT; *fr. : impôt indirect*
- inheritance tax : tax paid on an estate on someone's death; it can also be payable on gifts or trusts made during someone's lifetime; it is only payable when the value of the deceased's estate exceeds a certain threshold; *fr. : impôt sur les successions*
- landfill tax : tax on the disposal of waste; *fr. : taxe de mise en décharge*
- national insurance contributions : see 25
- offence (n.) : see 27
- stamp duty land tax : tax payable on the transfer of property; *fr. : droit de timbre*
- tax avoidance : fact of taking advantage, by means that are within the law, of loopholes or lack of clarity in the law to reduce a tax bill; avoidance is not in itself a criminal offence; *fr. : évitement fiscale*
- tax evasion : form of illegal tax non-compliance by which a taxpayer tries to evade taxes; tax evasion is a criminal offence; *fr. : évasion fiscale*
- tax planning : form of tax avoidance, in which the taxpayer organises his affairs to gain tax advantages or to avoid a double taxation; planning is not in itself a criminal offence; *fr. : planification fiscale*
- tax relief : reduction in the amount of tax payable; *fr. : allègement/dégrèvement fiscal*

USEFUL EXPRESSIONS

- to be prosecuted for tax fraud; *fr. : être mis en examen pour fraude fiscale*
- prior leave must be obtained before lodging an appeal against a first instance decision; *fr. : une autorisation préalable doit être obtenue avant de relever appel d'une décision de première instance*
- to be convicted of tax evasion; *fr. : être condamné pour évasion fiscale*
- it is granted as of right; *fr. : c'est accordé de plein droit*

FURTHER INFORMATION

- in Attorney General's References n°s 86 and 87 of 1999 [2001] 1 Cr App R (S) 141, the Attorney General identified the aggravating features of tax and excise evasion for sentencing purposes; these features include the sophisticated nature of the fraud, the use of a specific scheme, a breach of trust, the fraudulent obtaining of money pursuant to the scheme coupled with the suppression of profits, the amount of loss to the taxman, the personal benefit to the defendant, and the concealment of the fraudulent nature of the claims at audit

COMPARATIVE APPROACH

Les règles contentieuses en Angleterre et au Pays de Galles sont faciles à appréhender puisqu'il n'y existe qu'un seul ordre de juridiction. En revanche, en France, les deux ordres de juridiction (ordre administratif et ordre judiciaire) peuvent avoir compétence, selon la nature du contentieux. Ainsi, s'agissant de l'établissement de l'impôt, le juge administratif est compétent en matière d'impôt sur le revenu, impôt sur les sociétés, taxe d'habitation et taxe foncière, taxe professionnelle et TVA. En revanche, le juge judiciaire est compétent s'agissant des contributions indirectes, impôt de solidarité sur la fortune (ISF), droit de timbre et droits d'enregistrement (sur les ventes immobilières, successions ou donations). En ce qui concerne le recouvrement de l'imposition, le juge judiciaire est compétent lorsque le contentieux vise l'opposition aux poursuites. En revanche, le juge compétent est le même que pour l'établissement de l'impôt si le contentieux est relatif à l'obligation de payer.

6

Criminal litigation

□ 102 INTRODUCTION

Criminal procedure rules are determined by common law and statute law in compliance with the European Convention on Human Rights that was integrated into British law with the Human Rights Act (HRA) 1998. Any UK citizen is entitled to a have a fair trial pursuant to Article 6 of the HRA whether it be for civil or criminal litigation. Regarding criminal cases, Article 6 specifies basic procedural rights. The defendant should be notified of the charge(s) against him within a reasonable period of time. He is to be considered as "innocent until proven guilty", under the presumption of innocence principle. He should be given enough time to prepare his defence. He has the right to defend himself, or if he chooses a lawyer, the state has to help him face legal costs through legal aid. He is entitled to call witnesses for his defence and to cross-examine the prosecution witnesses.

Unlike the inquisitorial system that is dominant in civil law countries, criminal litigation in common law countries relies on the adversarial system opposing two parties to the trial, the prosecution and the defendant. In the course of the trial, the defendant's guilt has to be proved beyond reasonable doubt. While on one hand, the burden of proof is on the prosecution who has to convince the judge and sometimes the jury of the defendant's guilt, on the other hand the defence has to challenge the evidence presented by the prosecution and show the defendant's innocence. The judge does not take part in the questioning of the parties' witnesses even though he can intervene to remind the prosecution, the defence lawyer or some witnesses of the courtroom procedure. The judge is expected to play the role of a fair and independent arbiter in the course of the trial.

Once the prosecution has decided to prosecute the defendant, a written charge and a requisition are issued describing the charges brought against the defendant and ordering him to appear in a magistrates' court to answer the charges. A summons is drawn by a magistrate and sent to the defendant to inform him of the charges pending against him and indicating the date he must appear in court.

GLOSSARY

- adversarial (adj.) system (n.) : legal system that prevails in common law countries; it implies that the criminal trial opposes two parties while the judge, who is responsible for the courtroom procedure, remains neutral so as to reach the fairest decision; the adversarial system is opposed to the inquisitorial system; *fr. : système accusatoire*
- beyond reasonable doubt : criminal standard of proof required when deciding a defendant's guilt; the jury or judge should only ever convict someone if all their doubts were cleared after hearing all the evidence; *fr. : ≈ intime conviction*
- burden of proof : onus to prove someone's (civil) liability or (criminal) guilt; *fr. : charge de la preuve*
- cross-examine (v.) : questioning of a witness by the opposite party to the trial; *fr. : faire subir un contre-interrogatoire*
- defendant (n.) : in a criminal case, party who is charged with an offence and is brought to trial by the prosecution; *fr. : ≈ prévenu/accusé*
- guilt (n.) : in criminal law, state of having committed an offence that is punished by law; *fr. : culpabilité*
- innocent until proven guilty : before and during the trial, the defendant must be considered and treated as innocent so that he can benefit from a fair trial; *fr. : ≈ présomption d'innocence*
- inquisitorial (adj.) system (n.) : legal system prevailing in civil law countries like France; the judge plays an active role by leading the trial; *fr. : système inquisitoire*
- legal (adj.) aid (n.) : financial help provided by the state to ensure that a defendant can benefit from a lawyer to advise, assist or represent him before the courts; *fr. : aide juridictionnelle*
- prosecution (n.) : party to the trial in charge of proving the defendant's guilt; *fr. : ≈ Ministère public*
- requisition (n) : legal document drawn by the prosecution requiring the defendant to appear before a magistrates' court to hear and answer the charges; *fr. : ≈ accusation formelle/réquisition*
- summons (n.) : here, legal document issued by a magistrate describing the accusation as well as the time and place the defendant must appear in court; *fr. : ≈ citation à comparaître*

USEFUL EXPRESSIONS

- to be found guilty; *fr. : être déclaré coupable*
- to prosecute someone; *fr. : poursuivre quelqu'un devant les juridictions pénales*
- to seek someone's conviction; *fr. : rechercher la condamnation de quelqu'un*

FURTHER INFORMATION

- the verb to prosecute can be used only for criminal proceedings; the French *poursuivre* in civil cases can be translated by to sue or to bring an action against someone and also applies to a criminal prosecution
- in law reports, a criminal case is presented as follows : R v. X, that should be read as Regina against X; Regina is the Latin term referring to the Queen (Rex is used when the monarch is a king) who is constitutionally the Head of State; this also the reason why the prosecution who works on behalf of the State is named Crown Prosecution Service and is usually referred to under its abbreviated form of the Crown (or of course CPS)

COMPARATIVE APPROACH

Si la procédure pénale Outre-Manche est accusatoire, elle présente un caractère plus inquisitoire en France où le président de la juridiction conduit et dirige les débats. Dans le cadre de la procédure accusatoire, la justice nait naturellement des échanges contradictoires des parties. En revanche, un système inquisitoire requiert l'intervention, en l'espèce le juge, pour trancher un différend entre les parties.

Cependant, il ne faut pas exagérer l'importance des divergences entre les systèmes applicables des deux côtés de la Manche. La création du *Crown Prosecution Service* en 1986 a permis d'accroître le rôle des procureurs impliqués au stade de l'enquête. Quant à la France, l'audience de jugement est contradictoire, teintant donc fortement d'accusatoire le système normalement inquisitoire.

En Angleterre et au Pays de Galles, l'interrogation des témoins (notamment le contre-interrogatoire ou *cross-examination*) et les plaidoiries pénales sont plus « théâtrales » qu'en France, obéissant à un cérémonial très formel.

□ 103 CRIMINAL JURISDICTION AND PERSONNEL

First instance jurisdiction

Ordinary jurisdiction

The criminal first instance court system is structured around one set of inferior courts, the magistrates' courts, and a superior court, the Crown Court.

Save for cases for which there is a specialised jurisdiction (like the Youth court), all criminal cases start in a magistrates' court whether they relate to a summary, triable either-way or indictable offence.

Magistrates consider the nature of the offence (to see if the case may be tried by them or be committed to the Crown Court). They grant bails, hear the defendant's plea of guilty or not guilty during the arraignment, and judge 90 % of criminal cases. They are always assisted by a clerk who guides them when confronted with a legal difficulty. When magistrates reach the conclusion that they do not have the power to hear a particular offence (offence triable either way or indictable offence), they commit the case to the Crown Court during committal proceedings.

Summary offences, also called non-indictable offences (the least serious offences), are always tried in magistrates' courts, usually by a panel of two or three magistrates, or sometimes by a professional judge (such as a district judge) sitting alone. There is no jury trial in the magistrates' courts.

Most offences triable either way (the intermediate category of offences) will also be tried by the magistrates' courts. However, the defendant can choose to have his case heard by a jury in the Crown Court. This may be for tactical reasons (e.g. to have the benefit of a trial by jury which does not exist in the magistrates' courts or have the case heard by professional legally qualified judges). This choice is expressed at the hearing in the magistrates' court where the defendant will explain that he wishes his case to be heard by the Crown Court.

Like all other offences, indictable offences (also called offences triable on indictment) first come before the magistrates' courts before being committed to the Crown Court for trial.

Specialised criminal jurisdiction

Coroners' courts examine suspicious deaths in general. Juveniles are usually tried in youth courts. In the wake of notorious miscarriages of justice, a Criminal Cases Review Commission was set up to scrutinise potentially wrongful convictions.

Appellate jurisdiction

As well as being a first instance trial court for some either-way offences and all non-indictable offences, the Crown Court is also a court of appeal for cases first tried in the magistrates' court. Appeals from the Crown Court are then lodged with the criminal division of the Court of Appeals. Although primarily a civil court, the divisional court of the Queen's Bench Division of the High Court can hear some appeals from criminal courts on certain points of law. The Supreme Court of the United Kingdom remains the court of last resort but only examines points of law (as opposed to fact).

Personnel

Magistrates sitting in the magistrates' courts are lay people (i.e. non professional judges), also known as Justices of the Peace or JP. They usually have no real legal qualification but were selected because of their interest in justice and they subsequently get some limited legal training. The clerk who assists the magistrates is a legally qualified person who can be either a former solicitor or barrister. Occasionally a legally qualified judge (usually a district judge) will try a magistrates' court case.

The judges of the Crown Court, Court of Appeals and of course Supreme Court, are all legally qualified people. They are all former solicitors or more commonly, barristers, who applied to the judiciary after practising as solicitors/barristers for a number of years determined by statute.

Clerks also assist judges in the Crown Court and Court of Appeals where their role is also important : they ensure the smooth running of the day to day running of a case, liaising with solicitors/barristers and prisons when the defendant is jailed. They also play a part at trial where they call witnesses and generally assist the judges in so far as possible.

GLOSSARY

- appellate (adj.) jurisdiction (n.) : power and authority to examine an appeal; *fr. : compétence d'attribution en appel*
- arraignment (n.) : when the judge officially reads the charges pressed against the defendant during a pre-trial hearing; *fr. : ≈ audience de première comparution*
- clerk (n.) : person who assists the judges in a court; in the magistrates' court, the clerk is usually a former solicitor or barrister; *fr. : greffier*
- commit (v.) : here, the magistrates decide that an either-way or indictable offence should be heard in the Crown Court; *fr. : ≈ renvoyer une affaire (devant la cour d'assises)*
- committal (adj.) proceedings (n.) : preliminary hearing when magistrates decide if there is sufficient evidence for the case to be tried in the Crown court; *fr. : audience préliminaire*
- coroner : see 34
- Criminal Cases Review Commission : independent body responsible for investigating suspected miscarriages of justice; *fr. : commission de révision des condamnations pénales*
- Crown Court : criminal court which has original jurisdiction for indictable offences and sometimes for either-way offences; it is also an appellate court hearing appeals from the magistrates' courts; *fr. : ≈ Cour d'assises/tribunal correctionnel (*depending on the nature of the offence*)*
- district (adj.) judge (n.) : professional judge sitting in some courts; *fr. : juge/magistrat*
- first (adj.) instance (n.) : court before which a case is first heard before potentially being subject to an appeal to a higher court; *fr. : première instance*
- indict (v.) : in criminal law, formal procedure consisting in charging someone with one or several offences in order to bring the defendant to trial; *fr. : ≈ inculper/mettre en examen*
- indictable (adj.)offences (n.)/offences triable on indictment : see 27

- Justice of the Peace : magistrates from the magistrates' courts; *fr. : juge de paix*
- magistrate (n.) : non-professional judge sitting in the magistrates' court; *fr. : ≈ juge de proximité/juge du tribunal de police* (depending on the nature of the offence)
- magistrates' court : here, criminal court of first instance hearing summary offences and most of either-way offences; *fr. : ≈ juge de proximité/tribunal de police/tribunal correctionnel* (depending on the nature of the offence)
- miscarriage of justice : wrongful conviction; *fr. : erreur judiciaire*
- offences triable either way : see 27
- summary offences/non-indictable (adj.) offences (n.) : see 27
- Supreme Court of the United Kingdom (UKSC) : court of last resort for civil and criminal trials (except for Scotland) in the whole of the United Kingdom; *fr. : ≈ Cour de cassation*
- try (v.) : fact for a court to hear and determine a case at trial; *fr. : ≈ entendre dans le cadre d'un procès*
- youth court : court hearing cases other than homicide involving defendants who are under 18; *fr. : tribunal pour mineurs*

USEFUL EXPRESSIONS

- to appear/turn up in court; *fr. : se présenter devant un juge*
- to be committed to the Crown court for trial; *fr. : être renvoyé devant le Tribunal correctionnel/Cour d'assises pour son procès*
- to appear before the court; *fr. : comparaître devant la juridiction*
- to be tried for theft; *fr. : être jugé pour vol*

FURTHER INFORMATION

- as opposed to a French *magistrat*, an English magistrate is not a professional judge
- the legal meaning of the verb try (*juger quelqu'un dans le cadre d'un procès*) must not be confused with the ordinary meaning of that verb (*essayer*)

Comparative approach

Il y a deux différences essentielles entre les systèmes français et anglais de droit pénal, l'une concernant les juges et l'autre, le fonctionnement de la justice pénale lui-même.

En France, les magistrats judiciaires sont issus de l'École Nationale de la Magistrature (ENM). Outre-Manche, il n'y a pas d'équivalent de l'ENM et tous les juges (à l'exception des *magistrates*) sont d'anciens *solicitors* ou *barristers*.

Le système de la comparution obligatoire devant les *magistrates' courts*, quelle que soit la nature de l'infraction – précédant éventuellement un renvoi devant la *Crown court* – est spécifique au système applicable en Angleterre et au Pays de Galles. Les trois types d'infractions existant en France et Outre-Manche ne se correspondent pas nécessairement : certains délits français peuvent, Outre-Manche, être considérés comme des contraventions, ou au contraire des crimes. En France, les trois types d'infractions sont jugés par des juridictions distinctes en première instance : le juge de proximité pour les quatre premières catégories de contraventions, le Tribunal de police pour les contraventions de cinquième classe, le Tribunal correctionnel pour les délits et la Cour d'assises pour les crimes. Outre-Manche, il y a un recoupement entre les juridictions compétentes, s'agissant des *either-way offences*, infractions pour lesquelles l'accusé lui-même a le choix de la juridiction qui le jugera. Son choix est en général guidé par la volonté, ou non, d'avoir des juges professionnels et éventuellement, un jury devant la *Crown Court* (s'il plaide non coupable).

□ 104 PARTIES TO THE TRIAL

In the adversarial system, the trial opposes two parties : the prosecution, represented by the Crown Prosecution Service (CPS), and the defendant. Although private individuals can initiate prosecutions, this procedure is seldom chosen by the victims' families.

Prosecutor

The Crown Prosecution Service (CPS) was created by the Prosecution of Offences Act 1985. It is headed by the Director of Public Prosecutions (DPP). Although his actions are supervised by the Attorney General who represents the CPS in Parliament, he does not depend on the Secretary of State for Justice who has neither authority nor influence over his decisions. Below the DPP, the Chief Executive supervises cases and prosecutions on a daily basis. Chief Crown Prosecutors are senior lawyers in charge of prosecutions and acting as representatives of the CPS within the community. Prosecutors prepare cases and appear in court.

Upon receiving evidence collected by the police, the CPS does not automatically prosecute each case. It abides by the Code for Crown Prosecutions which sets out two main tests. The evidential test is the first stage when the CPS assesses the reliability and admissibility of evidence and decides if it can realistically win the case in court. The second point raised is the public interest : the underlying idea of a prosecution is that it may lead to someone being convicted and thus, help protect society from criminals. If the two tests are not conclusive, the CPS discontinues prosecution. Should the case pass these two tests, the CPS officially prosecutes the defendant(s) in order to seek a conviction.

Defendant

The defendant can be either an individual or a company in the case of corporate crime. In this chapter, the term defendant is understood as one individual. The defendant can appear in court with other co-defendants who are charged with the same or different offences. Sometimes, they have acted only as accomplices.

When the defendant appears in a magistrates' court for the arraignment to hear the charges pressed against him, he can plead guilty or not guilty to all or some of the charges. In the case of summary offences, if the defendant pleads guilty to committing an offence, the magistrates usually pass the sentence on him the same day. When it comes to a guilty plea for an either-way offence, the procedure is not always straightforward as the magistrates can only give a maximum of 12 months' imprisonment. The magistrates first hear the prosecution and then the defence lawyer (who always speaks last). The CPS is under no obligation to accept the plea. The prosecutor must make sure that the sentence that the court can potentially pass is proportionate to the seriousness of the offence, and take into consideration the victim's interests as well as the society's interests. The guilty plea procedure enables the defendant to avoid a trial, but not a mandatory sentence. If the sentence is to exceed one year imprisonment, the magistrates commit the case to the Crown Court that will then pass the appropriate sentence. Guilty pleas to indictable offences are automatically committed to the Crown Court.

Should the defendant choose to plead not guilty, a trial will be organised within a reasonable period of time. Pursuant to Article 6 of the ECHR, the defendant has the right to be assisted by counsel. In order to alleviate the seriousness of the charges, the defendant can opt for defences showing his diminished responsibility in case of insanity, automatism or mistake. Other defences can rely on extenuating circumstances such as self-defence, duress, necessity, and sometimes marital coercion.

GLOSSARY

- accomplice (n.) : individual helping a criminal to commit an offence; *fr. : complice*
- arraignement hearing : pre-trial hearing when the prosecution reads to the defendant the charges brought against him; the defendant has a chance to plead guilty or not guilty to those charges; *fr. : ≈ audience de première comparution*
- automatism (n.) : type of defence relying on the fact that the defendant does not control some parts of his body or some movements; *fr. : automatisme*
- co-accused/defendant (n.) : legal entity accused in the same case as the defendant, either as an accomplice or for the same offence; *fr. : co-accusé*

- convict (v. or n.) : find someone guilty as charged; *fr. : condamner/juger coupable*
- counsel (n.) : synonym for lawyer who advises, assists and represents clients in court; *fr. : avocat*
- Crown Prosecution Service (CPS) : state legal institution in charge of prosecuting defendants on behalf of the Crown; the CPS is a party to the criminal trial; *fr. : ≈ ministère public*
- defendant (n.) : see 102
- Director of Public Prosecutions (DPP) : head of the CPS; *fr. : ≈ Procureur général*
- discontinue (v.) : stop something; when applied to a prosecution, it means that the CPS decides not to institute proceedings; *fr. : classer sans suite*
- duress (n.) : defence purporting to show that the defendant was compelled to commit the offence he is charged with; *fr. : contrainte*
- insanity (n.) : defence purporting to show that the defendant was mentally disturbed or not fully aware of his actions when he committed the offence(s); *fr. : folie*
- intoxication (n.) : defence used when the defendant committed an offence after consuming drugs or alcohol with or without consent; *fr. : intoxication (volontaire ou involontaire)*
- marital (adj.) coercion (n.) : defence in which the defendant claims that to have been forced to commit the offence(s) by his spouse; *fr. : contrainte maritale*
- mistake (n.) : defence purporting to show that the defendant unintentionally committed the offence; *fr. : erreur de fait*
- necessity (n.) : defence purporting to show that extreme circumstances pushed the defendant to act in a certain way; e.g. trespassing on a property to save someone from drowning; *fr. : état de nécessité*
- plea (n.) : depending on whether it is a guilty or not guilty plea, defendant's decision to admit or deny that he committed the offence with which he is charged; *fr. : ≈ reconnaissance de culpabilité (*guilty plea*)/fait de plaider non-coupable (*not guilty plea*)*
- plead (v.) : here, act of admitting or denying the commission of an offence; *fr. : plaider (coupable ou non coupable)*
- prosecutor (n.) : former solicitor or barrister with several years' experience who prepares criminal cases and appears in court on behalf of the Crown; *fr. : ≈ procureur*
- Secretary of State for Justice : member of the Cabinet in charge of the Ministry of Justice; *fr. : ≈ garde des Sceaux*
- self-defence (n.) : defence purporting to show that the defendant's attempts to protect his life led to a wrongful action; *fr. : ≈ légitime défense*
- sentence (v. or n.) : see 27

USEFUL EXPRESSIONS

- to prosecute someone for theft; *fr. : poursuivre quelqu'un pénalement pour vol*
- to plead guilty to a criminal offence; *fr. : plaider coupable d'avoir commis une infraction pénale*
- to confess to committing an offence; *fr. : confesser avoir commis une infraction*

FURTHER INFORMATION

- the status of Attorney General exists both in the UK and the US, but does not cover the same political reality; while in the UK, he is an MP sitting in the House of Commons, the US Attorney General acts as the Secretary for Justice and is a member of the President's cabinet (≈ *garde des Sceaux*)
- as opposed to the US where plea bargaining is common, it is not well perceived in England and Wales where no bargaining is ever supposed to take place between the prosecutor and the defendant over the sentence itself; at most, plea bargaining is tolerated only to the extent that the prosecutor and the defendant can agree that the defendant pleads guilty to one offence and the prosecutor drops the remainder of the potential charges
- pursuant to the Constitutional Reform Act 2005, the office of Lord Chancellor was removed to improve the separation of the judiciary and the political sphere; the member of the Cabinet responsible for the Ministry of Justice is now known by the more neutral phrase Secretary of State for Justice; still, the word Lord Chancellor is still in use
- counsel (lawyer) should not be confused with council (local government)

COMPARATIVE APPROACH

Alors que le Parquet français dépend du pouvoir exécutif, plus particulièrement du garde des Sceaux qui est son chef hiérarchique, le *Crown Prosecution Service* dépend de *l'Attorney General* qui n'est pas membre du gouvernement à l'instar du *Secretary for Justice* (garde des Sceaux). Cette indépendance est relative dans la mesure où *l'Attorney General* a le pouvoir d'arrêter des poursuites.

Si, contrairement aux États-Unis, le Ministère public Outre-Manche est peu enclin au *plea bargaining* – qui consiste à plaider coupable de la commission d'une infraction en échange d'une moindre peine ou de l'abandon de certaines charges – le législateur français a introduit en 2004 la procédure de comparution sur reconnaissance préalable de culpabilité (CRPC) aussi connue sous l'appellation de « plaider-coupable ». Cela donne au ministère public une marge de manœuvre pour négocier (d'où le mot *bargaining*) avec le prévenu en lui proposant, directement et sans procès, une peine réduite s'il reconnaît les faits qui lui sont reprochés.

Un point commun entre les procédures pénales anglaise et française est celui de l'opportunité des poursuites, l'obligation de poursuivre ne s'imposant au Procureur ou au CPS que lorsque l'infraction ou les circonstances de sa commission ont un caractère tel que la poursuite est nécessaire dans l'intérêt public.

□ 105 JURY

Criminal courts in which a trial by jury is available

Trial by jury is only available in the Crown Court but not in the magistrates' courts. Jury trial may occur in two types of cases : for indictable offences where the defendant has pleaded not guilty, and for triable-either-way offences which end up being tried in the Crown Court. In the latter case, this may occur either when the magistrates commit a case to the Crown Court or when the defendant elects to be judged by a jury in the Crown Court.

The right to a jury trial in the Crown Court following a non-guilty plea is not absolute. Under Section 44 (4 & 5) of the Criminal Justice Act 2003 the Crown Court will not hold a jury trial when there is "evidence of a real and present danger" of jury tampering. If the trial has already started, the judge can decide to discharge the empanelled jury.

Because juries only deal with issues of fact as opposed to law, no jury trial is available in the Court of Appeals or in the Supreme Court.

Formation of a jury

A jury must be empanelled. Jury service is a civic duty for registered electors aged between 18 and 75. To be eligible, potential jurors must have a clear criminal record, be in fit mental condition and have resided in the UK for at least 5 years. Before the trial starts, a pool of twenty potential jurors is called by the judge who sends them a written summons. On the day of the jury selection, twelve names are called randomly from the venire and the chosen jurors sit in the jury box. Once the jury has been empanelled, each juror takes oath. The jurors are then informed that from then on (throughout trial and after trial) their freedom of speech is restrained : jurors do not have the right to discuss the case with anyone during and after trial and if they do so, they can be charged with contempt of court and be fined or imprisoned. Once the jury is sworn in, the trial can start.

Role of the jury

The jury is the judge of fact as opposed to the Crown Court judge who is the judge of law. This explains why there are no jury trials at the Court of Appeals or the Supreme Court as they essentially hear legal (as opposed to factual) issues. Jurors must be fair and unbiased. They hear the prosecutor's and the defendant's evidence. At the end of the trial, the judge gives some instructions (summing up) to the jurors before they retire to the jury room to deliberate.

A foreman is chosen by the jurors to represent them. He is in charge of leading the discussions and giving the verdict once a decision is made. The court usher usually stands outside the jury room during deliberations in order to ensure that the jurors are not in contact with any third party. The judge does not take part in the deliberations. During the deliberations, the jurors consider the evidence adduced and decide whether it is sufficient to find the defendant guilty "beyond reasonable doubt" of a particular offence. They reach a verdict of guilty or not guilty (either unanimoulsy or with an acceptable majority), based on the factual evidence heard and seen.

When the deliberations are over, the jury is called back into court. The jury foreman delivers the verdict. If this is a guilty verdict, the conviction is followed by the sentence which is determined by the judge only.

GLOSSARY

- adduce (v.) : here, fact for the CPS and the defendant to disclose the evidence on which they respectively rely to prove their case; *fr. : produire des éléments de preuve aux débats*
- contempt of court : act that challenges or denies the authority of a legal representative or that breaches procedural rules; *fr. : ≈ outrage à magistrat*
- conviction (n.) court decision reached by a jury or a judge whereby the defendant is found guilty of the offence with which he was charged; *fr. : condamnation*
- criminal (adj.) record (n.) : legal document stating former convictions; *fr. : casier judiciaire*
- deliberation (n.) : discussions and debates between jurors in order to reach a verdict; *fr. : délibérations*
- deliver (v.) : here, act of reading the verdict in open court, usually performed by the foreman of the jury; *fr. : lire le verdict*
- discharge (v.) : here, decision by the judge to dimiss the empanelled jury; *fr. : renvoyer un jury*
- elect (v.) : choose; *fr. : choisir*
- empanel (v.) (a jury) : select the jurors of a jury; *fr. : constituer un jury*
- foreman (n.)/foreperson (n.) : juror chosen by his fellow jurors to lead the debates and deliver the final verdict; *fr. : président du jury*
- issue (n.) : here, a point of fact (issue of fact) or law (issue of law); *fr. : question/point*
- juror (n.) : member of a jury; *fr. : juré*
- jury (n.) : in criminal cases, 12 lay people randomly selected to hear evidence at trial and reach a verdict; *fr. : jury*

- jury box : place in the courtroom where the jurors are seated; *fr. : banc des jurés*
- jury room/deliberation room : secret place where the jurors can freely debate; *fr. : salle des délibérations*
- jury tampering : unlawful attempt at influencing or manipulating a jury; *fr. : ≈ subornation des jurés*
- reach (v.) : when applied to a verdict, decision as to whether the defendant is guilty or not guilty; *fr. : parvenir (à un verdict)*
- sentence (n. or v.) : see 27
- summing up (n.) : here, instructions given by the judge to the jury; *fr. : instructions au jury*
- summons (n.) : here, official document issued by a judge whereby a potential juror is required to appear in court for jury selection; *fr. : convocation au tribunal*
- swear (v.) in (a jury) : here, select the jurors and arrange for them to take the oath; *fr. : assermenter un jury*
- take the oath/swear on oath : official and solemn act of swearing in court either to remain fair (for a juror) or to tell the truth (for a witness); *fr. : prêter serment*
- usher (n.) : here, member of the court staff, in charge of keeping order in the courtroom; *fr. : huissier-audiencier*
- venire (n.) : here, lists of potential jurors; *fr. : ≈ liste annuelle des jurés*

USEFUL EXPRESSIONS

- to take part in deliberations; *fr. : participer aux délibérations*
- to reach a guilty verdict despite a not-guilty plea; *fr. : rendre un verdict de culpabilité en dépit du fait d'avoir plaidé non-coupable*

FURTHER INFORMATION

- during the selection and oath process, the jurors either swear on a religious book (such as the Bible) or affirm when they object to a (religious) oath; in the latter case they read the following text : "I swear […] that I will faithfully try the defendant and give a true verdict according to the evidence"
- unlike the US where the system of peremptory challenges remains whilst selecting jurors, the Criminal Justice Act 1988 replaced them with the random selection of twelve jurors from a venire of twenty people

COMPARATIVE APPROACH

Alors que les jurés anglais siègent à la *Crown court* dans le cadre de procès relatifs à des crimes (≈ *indictable offences*), comme leurs homologues français qui siègent en Cour d'assises, ils peuvent aussi connaître de certains délits (≈ *either-way offences*) qui peuvent être jugés à la *Crown court.*

S'il y a Outre-Manche 12 jurés, il n'y en a que 6 en première instance en France et 9 en appel. Le système français, même si le principe du contradictoire y est applicable, présente un aspect plus inquisitorial (*inquisitorial*) que le système applicable en Angleterre et au Pays de Galles : à l'inverse du système anglais, l'accusé n'a pas le choix de plaider coupable ou non-coupable; c'est le juge (au Tribunal de police ou correctionnel) et le jury (à la Cour d'assises) qui ont pour mission d'étudier les éléments de preuve pour retenir, ou non, la culpabilité du prévenu/de l'accusé.

En France, le gouvernement a lancé en 2012, à titre d'expérimentation, un système de jurés populaires dans les Tribunaux correctionnels (citoyens-assesseurs) mais cette expérience a été abandonnée dès mars 2013.

□ 106 CRIMINAL TRIAL

Preliminary stages before the trial

Before the trial, the defendant is entitled to ask the judge to dismiss the offence he is charged with. The prosecution can issue a notice of opposition. The prosecution has a duty to disclose evidence to the opposing party – information and details of the prosecution case must be available for the defendant. The prosecution must write a formal indictment, indicating the counts and the charges pressed against the defendant. When complex cases are to be heard in the Crown Court, such as fraud cases, or when an application for a trial without jury has been sent to the court, the judges can order a preparatory hearing where the prosecution presents a case statement to which the defendant can object. Even though trials are usually held in public and are open to the press whose members sit on the press bench, the court can restrict reporting or access by the public, and can sometimes order a trial in private.

Summoning witnesses

Once the accused has entered a plea of not guilty, the trial can begin. Each party has the right to call witnesses testifying for them, or experts who are under the legal obligation to give objective opinions in court. Witnesses who have agreed to give evidence in court usually receive a witness summons indicating the time and place they are required to appear in court. Some individuals can be sometimes compelled to testify in court. The defendant usually stands in the dock.

Trial procedure

The criminal trial starts with the prosecution's opening speech summarising the case, and presenting the main inculpatory evidence. Then, the prosecutor calls his witnesses and/or experts. When testifying in person, a witness sits in the witness box and takes an oath or solemnly affirms that he will tell the truth. The prosecution asks questions to the witness (examination-in-chief) who is then cross-examined by the defence. The prosecution has the possibility to re-examine his witness. This order of questioning witnesses is the same for the defence. Evidence of a witness can be provided in writing – the statement is read and summarised in court. Hearsay evidence is admissible. The court usher is in charge of presenting exhibits to the judge and/or the jury. Court proceedings are recorded by a stenographer. At the end, each party delivers a closing speech, focussing on the main evidence and facts revealed at trial. If the defendant is found guilty, the defence counsel usually gives a plea in mitigation, asking the judge to be lenient when passing the sentence.

Suspending a trial

Under some circumstances such as suspicion of interfering with witnesses or obstruction to the course of justice, the judge can adjourn the trial. When the case is remanded, the defendant can be released on bail or kept in custody pending a new date for the trial to continue.

GLOSSARY

- adjourn (v.) : suspend the hearing of the case and postpone it to a later date; *fr. : ordonner un renvoi*
- affirm (v.) : solemnly promise to tell the truth at trial without taking the oath on a religious book; *fr. : prêter serment*
- closing (adj.) speech (n.) : formal speech delivered first by the prosecution, and then by the defence counsel at the end of the trial; each summarises the main facts and evidence presented at trial; *fr. : plaidoirie*
- compellable (adj.) witness (n.) : witness who can be forced to give evidence in court; *fr. : ≈ témoin cité à comparaître*
- count (n.) : charge brought against the defendant; *fr. : chef d'inculpation*
- cross-examination (n.) : questioning of a witness by the opposing party in the trial; *fr. : contre-interrogatoire de témoins de la partie adverse*
- disclose (v.) : when applied to evidence, obligation imposed on one party to show all his evidence to the other party to a trial; *fr. : communiquer (des pièces)*
- dock (n.) : area where the defendant sits during the trial; *fr. : box des accusés*
- examination-in-chief : stage in the trial when each party questions witnesses testifying in their favour; *fr. : ≈ interrogatoire de (ses propres) témoins*
- exhibit (n.) : document or object presented as evidence at trial; *fr. : pièce à conviction*
- give (v.) evidence/testify (v.) : to make a statement, usually based on personal knowledge, about facts related to the offence; *fr. : témoigner*
- indictment (n.) : legal document describing the charges brought against the defendant; *fr. : mise en examen*

- interfere (v.) with : here, manipulate or threaten witnesses; *fr. : suborner (un témoin)*
- notice (n.) of opposition (n.) : when the prosecution states that it is opposed to the defendant's dismissal of the offence he is charged with; *fr. : ≈ notification de rejet*
- obstruct (v.) : when applied to the course of justice, intentional action to delay or hinder the criminal procedure; *fr. : entraver le cours de la justice*
- opening (adj.) speech (n.) : speech delivered by both the prosecution and the defence counsel at the start of a trial; its purpose is to introduce their views on the case; *fr. : ≈ plaidoirie d'ouverture*
- plea in mitigation : in case of a guilty verdict, the defence lawyer tries to convince the juge to be lenient with his client; *fr. : plaidoirie à fin de reconnaissance de circonstances atténuantes*
- preparatory (adj.) hearing (n.) : preliminary hearing that can be ordered by a judge in the Crown Court; *fr. : audience préliminaire*
- press bench (n.) : area where members of the press are seated; *fr. : banc de la presse*
- re-examination (n.) : stage in the trial when each party has the right to ask questions to the witnesses testifying in their favour in order to rectify some facts or allegations further to cross-examination by the other party; *fr. : ≈ seconde audition des témoins*
- remand (v.) : here, adjourn a case until a later date; *fr. : renvoyer*
- stenographer (n.) : member of court staff in charge of recording proceedings as the witnesses and the different parties speak; a written transcript can be required subsequently by the parties; *fr. : sténographe judiciaire*
- take an oath : see 105
- trial in private/in chambers : trial from which the public and the press are excluded; *fr. : procès à huis clos*
- usher (n.) : member of court staff responsible for passing around papers, objects or any other piece of evidence in the course of the trial; *fr. : huissier*
- witness box : area where witnesses sit to give evidence in court; *fr. : barre des témoins*
- witness summons : legal document requiring a witness to attend court; *fr. : convocation des témoins*

USEFUL EXPRESSIONS

- to adduce evidence showing that; *fr. : verser des preuves montrant que*
- alleged (adj.); *fr. : présumé*
- to plead guilty (adj.); *fr. : plaider coupable*
- to rebut evidence (n.); *fr. : réfuter une preuve*

FURTHER INFORMATION

- the old French phrase *voir dire* is used in English and American law, but does not refer to the same process; whilst in English law, *voir dire* describes the moment in a trial when a judge can ask the jury to go out so as to decide a dispute between the prosecutor and the defence regarding the admissibility of some evidence, in the US, *voir dire* means the selection of potential jurors
- the oath taken by witnesses testifying in court reads as follows : "I swear by... (according to religious belief)/I do solemnly, sincerely and truly declare and affirm that the evidence I shall give shall be the truth the whole truth and nothing but the truth"

COMPARATIVE APPROACH

En France, les témoins ne jurent pas sur la Bible, alors qu'Outre-Manche, les témoins prêtent serment sur le livre sacré correspondant à leur confession religieuse. Cependant, pour les athées ou certains groupes religieux refusant de jurer sur la Bible (comme les *Quakers*), il existe une formule permettant de prêter serment sans livre sacré.

Le déroulement du procès en France, teinté d'inquisitoire, est différent de la procédure applicable Outre-Manche qui est vraiment accusatoire.

□ 107 MILITARY TRIAL

Military courts hear cases involving all members of the British Armed forces as well as civilians subject to service discipline. Most offences committed by a serviceman are brought before Commanding Officers (CO) during a summary hearing. The defendant is entitled to choose to be tried before the Court Martial which usually deals with the most serious service offences. If a CO finds the defendant guilty as charged, he can pass different sentences on the accused such as reduction in rank, or detention in a unit guardhouse. The defendant can appeal the decision in the Summary Appeal Court presided by a Judge Advocate who reconsiders the charge(s) and the punishment along with two other officers. A second appeal may be lodged to the High Court of Justice.

Civilians subject to service discipline can only be tried either in the Service Civilian Court (SCC) or the Court Martial for serious offences. In the SCC, a Judge Advocate sitting alone, hears offences that would be normally tried in a magistrates' court. Appeals lie in the Court Martial. Should the offence be triable on indictment, the case is committed to the Court Martial where a Judge Advocate along with a Board consisting of civilian members will hear the case. The Board only reaches a verdict on the defendant's guilt.

The Court Martial, which has original jurisdiction over serious offences, is presided over by a Judge Advocate and includes a Board, a jury composed of between three and seven officers. Unlike the Crown Court juries, the Board decides the guilt or innocence of the defendant and takes part in the deliberations over the sentence with the Judge Advocate. The accused can be sentenced to imprisonment, dismissal or fines. Appeals to the decision are made to the Court Martial Appeal Court, and a second appeal can be lodged to the UKSC.

GLOSSARY

- board (n.) : here, jury sitting in a Court Martial either composed of civilian members (for trials involving civilians subject to service discipline) or of officers (when the defendant is a serviceman); *fr. : ≈ jury militaire*
- Commanding (adj.) Officer (n.) (CO) : officer at the head of a unit's command who is also in charge of discipline; *fr. : ≈ commandant*
- Court Martial : military court which has original jurisdiction over serious service offences; it is also a court of appeal for case tried in a summary hearing; *fr. : cour martiale*
- Court Martial Appeal Court : appellate court in which Lords and Ladies Justices of Appeal sitting usually in the civilian Court of Appeal hear appeals from the Court Martial; *fr. : ≈ cour d'appel martiale*
- dismissal (n.) : here, termination of employment with the Armed forces as a way of punishing the defendant for committing an offence; *fr. : renvoi (pour déshonneur, etc.)*
- fine (n.) : sentence consisting in paying a certain amount of money to the State; *fr. : amende*
- Judge Advocate : senior judge sitting in the Service Civilian Court and the Court Martial; *fr. : ≈ Président du tribunal militaire*
- reduction in rank : demotion of the defendant to a lower rank of seniority; *fr. : rétrogradation*
- Service Civilian Court (SCC) : military court which has jurisdiction over discipline offences committed by civilians; *fr. : ≈ tribunal militaire pour les civils*
- summary (adj.) hearing (n.) : speedy trial of most service offences corresponding to the offences usually heard in a Magistrates'court; *fr. : audience sommaire*

USEFUL EXPRESSIONS

- to be court-martialed; *fr. : être traduit en cour martiale*
- to be demoted to a lower rank; *fr. : être rétrogadé vers un poste d'un niveau plus faible*

FURTHER INFORMATION

- the Military force has its own in-house lawyers (qualified solicitors or barristers who joined the Army, Navy, etc.)

> **COMPARATIVE APPROACH**
>
> En France, les tribunaux militaires ont été supprimés en 2011. Les militaires sont désormais jugés dans les même tribunaux que les civils. Le Royaume-Uni a conservé ses tribunaux militaires.

☐ 108 CONVICTING AND SENTENCING

Conviction

When a judge is not convinced by the evidence adduced by the prosecution (for non-indictable offences and either-way-offences dealt with in the magistrates courts) or when a jury delivers a non-guilty verdict (for indictable offences or either-way-offences committed to the Crown Court), the court acquits the defendant. With an acquittal, the accused is said to have been exonerated by the court. Conversely when a judge or a jury finds someone guilty of an offence beyond reasonable doubt, the defendant/accused is convicted.

Sentence

A jury (if present) never deals with the sentencing of an accused. This is a legal role fulfilled by the judge. If the defendant is present, the judge explains the nature of the sentence passed on him, the possible consequences of failing to comply with a court order and the defendant's right to appeal the decision within a limited period of time.

A conviction may lead to a variety of sentences. Therefore punishment depends on the nature of the offence and mitigating factors (aggravating or extenuating circumstances). A defendant can be given consecutive sentences. In the event of a suspended prison sentence, the court delivers a supervision order. The defendant can also be released on probation.

In the magistrates' courts, the magistrates can order an absolute or conditional discharge, which implies that the defendant is able to leave the court. Penalties can range from fines, curfew orders, community service orders to custodial sentences. A magistrate cannot sentence someone to more than six months in prison. In the Crown Court, the convict can be sentenced to life imprisonment. In the case of a murder conviction, he is given a mandatory life sentence, implying that he will be eligible for parole after a fixed period of time. The courts are also allowed to issue confiscation orders and even compensation orders.

Compensation order

Pursuant to the Powers of Criminal Courts (Sentencing) Act 2000 (PCC(S)A) the criminal judge may, and sometimes must, make a compensation order as an ancillary order to someone's sentencing. A compensation order cannot be interpreted as a way to reduce the sentence itself. It is a way for the convict to compensate, to some extent, the personal injury, distress, loss or damage he may have caused someone. Ancillary orders such as exclusion orders can also aim at preventing the offender from relapsing. As opposed to the Crown Court, the amount of compensation awarded by the magistrates' courts is limited by statute. Importantly, and contrary to the damages usually awarded by courts as compensation for a loss sustained, the criminal courts must take into account the convict's financial resources when making a compensation order.

GLOSSARY

- absolute (adj.) discharge (n.) : here, the convicted defendant can walk out of court freely without any conditions; *fr. : libération inconditionnelle*
- acquit (v.) : declare that the defendant is innocent of the offence with which he was charged; this may also imply that the evidence provided was insufficient to prove the defendant's guilt beyond reasonable doubt; *fr. : acquitter* (for indictable offences)*/relaxer* (for the other types of offences)
- aggravating (adj.) factor/circumstance (n.) : element of an offence increasing its seriousness; e.g. recidivism; *fr. : circonstances aggravantes*
- ancillary (adj.) order (n.) : court decision which is annexed to, or secondary to the main order by which a sentence is given to the defendant; it purports to compensate any loss or prevent the offender from relapsing; this type of order can include compensation order, anti-social behaviour order, deprivation or confiscation order; *fr. : ≈ ordonnance*
- community sentence : sentence given for minor offences such as assault; the convict will have to do unpaid work for the community, like cleaning pavements or removing graffiti; *fr. : travaux d'intérêt général*
- community service order : court decision issued by a magistrate whereby the convict is sentenced to work for the community for a fixed number of hours; *fr. : peine de travail d'intérêt général*
- compensation order : criminal court decision which is ancillary to the judge's decision to sentence someone, whereby the convict may be ordered to pay for any personal injury, distress, loss or damage he may have caused; this is not a way to negotiate the sentence; as opposed to ordinary damages which aim at compensating the actual loss sustained by someone, the criminal judge must take into account the convict's financial resources; *fr. : ≈ ordonnance d'indemnisation*
- conditional (adj.) discharge (n.) : court decision whereby the convict can walk out of court freely provided he undertakes to comply with some conditions; *fr. : libération conditionnelle*
- confiscation order : court decision whereby the convict's property is taken by the State; *fr. : confiscation*
- convict (v.) : find the defendant guilty of an offence; *fr. : condamner*
- conviction (n.) : see 105

- curfew order : court decision handed down by a magistrate whereby the convict is not allowed to leave his house at certain hours of the day, usually at night; *fr. : couvre-feu*
- custodial (adj.) sentence (n.) : court decision handed down by a magistrate or a judge whereby the convict is deprived of his freedom and placed in prison; *fr. : peine de prison/de détention/privative de liberté*
- exclusion order : criminal court decision ancillary to the main sentence which prohibits the defendant from visiting a particular place or area for a fixed period of time; *fr. : ≈ ordonnance faisant injonction de ne pas fréquenter un lieu*
- extenuating (adj.) circumstances (n.) : elements of a crime alleviating the seriousness of the offence; e. g insanity; *fr. : circonstances atténuantes*
- fine (n.) : court decision handed down in a magistrates' court sentencing the defendant to paying a certain amount of money to the State; *fr. : amende*
- life imprisonment : sentence passed by the Crown Court whereby the defendant is sentenced to spend his life (or at least a number of years determined by statute) in prison; *fr. : peine de prison à vie*
- mandatory (adj.) sentence (n.) : compulsory minimum period of time a convicted defendant must spend in prison before being considered for parole; *fr. : peine incompressible*
- mitigating (adj.) factor (n.) : element that can reduce the severity of the sentence passed for an offence; *fr. : circonstance atténuante*
- parole (n.) : release of a prisoner before the end of his prison sentence provided he can show good behaviour; *fr. : liberté conditionnelle*
- probation (n.) : period of time when a convicted person is released subject to good behaviour; the commission of another crime or failure to observe the conditions of his probation will result in a prison sentence; *fr. : liberté surveillée*
- relapse (n. or v.) : here, to commit a wrongful act again; *fr. : récidive*
- sentence (n. or v.) : see 27
- supervision order : court decision whereby a defendant who has been given a suspended sentence is placed under the supervision of a local (police or court) officer; *fr. : placement sous contrôle judiciaire*
- suspended prison sentence : prison sentence that the convict is not required to serve immediately; however, should the convicted defendant commit another offence within a certain time, the initial prison sentence might have to be served if ordered by the court along with any sentence passed for the second offence; *fr. : peine de prison avec sursis*

USEFUL EXPRESSIONS

- to serve a sentence; *fr. : effectuer une peine*
- to receive a prison sentence; *fr. : se voir infliger une peine d'emprisonnement*

- to pass a sentence of imprisonment on someone; *fr. : prononcer une peine de prison à l'encontre de quelqu'un*

FURTHER INFORMATION

- to convict and to sentence are not used the same way; the conviction is the recognition by the court of someone's guilt and the sentence is the punishment inflicted on someone
- conviction (*condamnation*) should not be confused with the French noun *conviction* which means belief
- if the noun acquittal is used in English law indistinctively for the three types of offences, the French *acquittement* only applies to crimes heard by the *cour d'assises* as opposed to the other two types of offences (*contraventions* and *délits*) which lead to a *relaxe* by the *juge de proximité*, the *Tribunal de police* and the *Tribunal correctionnel*
- in England and Wales, it is said that "the punishment must fit the crime"

> COMPARATIVE APPROACH
>
> En France, en cas de multiplicité d'infractions commises, il est possible de solliciter du tribunal la confusion des peines. Cela consiste, quand deux peines au moins sont en concours et donnent lieu à des poursuites pénales séparées, à faire absorber la plus faible par la plus forte. Ce cumul n'est pas automatique et doit faire l'objet d'une demande spécifique du prévenu. En Angleterre et au Pays de Galles, un système similaire existe connu sous l'appellation : *Offences to be Taken Into Consideration* (TICs). Là encore, une demande expresse doit être formée à l'effet d'obtenir du juge qu'il veuille bien fusionner les peines pour ne retenir que la plus importante. Le juge exerce son pouvoir discrétionnaire.

□ 109 APPEAL AND REVIEW

Appealing a decision from a magistrates' court

The defendant can lodge an appeal against his conviction and the sentence he was given. If he chose to plead guilty, he can only appeal against the sentence. The appeal against his conviction is based on points of fact or law. A new hearing usually takes place in the Crown Court before a judge and two or four magistrates. The defendant can also appeal "by way of case stated" to the Divisional Court of the Queen's Bench Division (one branch of the High Court of Justice) only on a point of law. In the event of an alleged wrongful deprivation of freedom, it is possible to apply for a writ of *Habeas Corpus* in this court. The prosecution may also lodge an appeal.

Appealing from the Crown Court

A defendant judged in a trial for indictment in the Crown Court can apply for leave to appeal against his conviction and the sentence. The appeal lies in the Court of Appeal, Criminal Division. The Court of Appeal allows an appeal on a point of law, on irregularities at trial or if the verdict of the jury (on factual issues) is unsatisfactory. The prosecution must also apply for leave to appeal. The appeal must be linked to the offences included in the indictment and lodged only if the decision terminates the trial, as in acquittals.

Effects of an appeal

After examining any new evidence (when relevant) or alleged breach of procedural rules, the judge can either allow the appeal, giving a right of appeal to the appellant, or dismiss it. During the appeal, the opposing party to the appellant becomes the respondent. Once the arguments brought up by each party have been heard and evidence has been scrutinised, the court can either uphold, reverse or vary a ruling or quash the criminal conviction. In the case of reversing or varying a ruling, the Court of Appeal can order a resumption of the Crown Court proceedings, a new trial or order the acquittal of the defendant. Both the prosecution and the defendant have a right to appeal the decision to the UK Supreme Court, subject to leave being granted. The Criminal Cases Review Commission is responsible for examining a suspected miscarriage of justice. The Divisional Court of the Queen's Bench Division can issue a mandatory order, imposing a re-trial.

Double jeopardy

Double jeopardy used to be a fundamental common law principle implying that an acquitted defendant could not be prosecuted a second time for the same offence. Nevertheless, section 75 of the Criminal Justice Act 2003 introduced an exception to this rule. In the case of a "qualifying sentence" carrying life imprisonment, a new trial can be allowed against an acquitted defendant. The "qualifying offence" encompasses murder, manslaughter, arson and rape. The prosecution can apply for an order to quash the acquittal (section 76) and ask for a retrial provided new and compelling evidence can be brought up in court (section 78). The decision to quash an acquittal must be made in the interests of justice (section 79).

GLOSSARY

- acquittal (n.) : see 108
- allow (v.) (an appeal) : decision handed down by an appellate court authorising the appellant to appeal against a lower court's decision; *fr. : autoriser (un appel)/faire droit (à une requête en appel)*
- appeal (n. and v.) : legal procedure whereby one of the parties to the trial can challenge a lower court decision before a higher court; *fr. : interjeter/relever appel*

- appellant (n.) : person appealing against a court decision; *fr. : appelant*
- compelling (adj.) evidence (n.) : here, substantial and reliable evidence; *fr. : ≈ preuve irréfutable*
- culprit (n.) : guilty person; *fr. : coupable*
- dismiss (v.) : here, decision handed down by an appellate court rejecting the appellant's appeal; *fr. : rejeter (un appel)*
- leave (n.) : here, permission, authorisation granted by a judge to appeal a decision; *fr. : autorisation (de relever appel)*
- miscarriage of justice : conviction of someone for an offence he has not committed; alternatively, fact of not convicting someone who was guilty of an offence; *fr. : erreur judiciaire*
- quash (v.) : here, decision handed by an appellate court holding that the conviction made by the first-instance court is null and void; *fr. : annuler (une condamnation pénale)*
- respondent (n.) : opposing party to the appellant in an appeal; *fr. : intimé*
- reverse/overrule/overturn (v.) : decision handed down by a court of appeal reaching an opposite decision to the first-instance court's; *fr. : infirmer*
- uphold/affirm/confirm (v.) : decision handed down by a court of appeal reaching the same decision as the first-instance court's; *fr. : confirmer*

USEFUL EXPRESSIONS

- to apply for leave to appeal; *fr. : solliciter l'autorisation de relever appel*
- to grant leave to appeal; *fr. : accorder l'autorisation de relever appel*
- to lodge an appeal against a first instance decision/an appellate decision; *fr. : interjeter appel d'une décision de première instance/se pourvoir en cassation à l'encontre d'une décision d'appel*

FURTHER INFORMATION

- in law reports, an appeal is presented as follows : In Re v. X
- while the common law principle of double jeopardy does not apply in cases of serious crimes in the United Kingdom, the United States has never changed this principle enshrined in the Fifth Amendment of the US Bill of Rights and incorporated at the state level

Comparative approach

Comme en droit français, la peine ordonnée en Angleterre et au Pays de Galles est susceptible de se trouver aggravée en cas d'appel interjeté par le prévenu/accusé. En revanche, une divergence importante entre les deux droits réside dans le fait que l'appel, de même que le pourvoi (*appeal to the Supreme Court*) est beaucoup plus restreint Outre-Manche qu'en France, en raison de la procédure complexe que constitue la demande d'autorisation (*application for leave to appeal*) en vigueur dans de nombreux cas.

7

Intellectual property litigation

□ 110 INTRODUCTION

An infringement of intellectual property right occurs when a person who is not the owner of the intellectual property exercises exclusive rights without the permission of the owner. To establish infringement of intellectual property, it is necessary to prove that the infringer has copied the whole or a substantial part of the owner's product or material. When he takes legal action against an infringer, the owner of the intellectual property right must prove that the precise property in respect of those rights exists, that the infringer's product is a copy (in whole or part) of one of his products, and that the infringer made his product without his licence or authority.

The owner of intellectual property can take the following actions against the infringer : send a letter before action, propose negotiations to hopefully reach an out-of-court settlement, request HM Revenue and Customs to seize infringing imported goods for a 10-day period while seeking a court order (if relevant) or initiate legal proceedings in court.

In copyright infringement proceedings, the material, product or service covered by the particular intellectual property right must be precisely identified. Likewise in the case of patent infringement, the exact scope of the invention, patent specification and protection characteristics must be clearly stated. If a court decides that an intellectual property right has been infringed, it can award any of the following remedies : injunction, damages, account of profits and destruction of infringing material.

Trademark infringement and design infringement may be criminal offences (and thus give rise to a prosecution) as well as be actionable in civil law. In England and Wales criminal provisions are set out in the Copyright, Designs and Patent Act 1988 and the Fraudulent Act 2006 for intellectual property crimes like counterfeiting and piracy.

GLOSSARY

- account (of profits) : method of compensation whereby the copyright owner can sue the infringer for the amount profited from the breach of the copyright; *fr. : restitution des bénéfices*
- counterfeiting (n.) : process of fraudulently altering and distributing a product that is of lesser value than the original product; *fr. : contrefaçon*
- design infringement : unauthorised manufacture or importation for sale or the unauthorised sale or hire of articles incorporating or embodying the registered design; *fr. : contrefaçon des dessins ou modèles*
- exclusive (adj.) right (n.) : see 38
- infringe (v.) : violate or break the terms of a contract; *fr. : empiéter/enfreindre*
- infringer (n.) : person who violates the rights of an individual or an organisation by distributing material protected by copyright without authorisation; *fr. : contrefacteur/contrevenant*
- infringement (n.) : breach of copyright when either the whole or a substantial part of the author's restricted rights are used by another person; *fr. : violation/infraction*
- infringing (adj.) material (n.) : infrastructure that enables free distribution, transmission and downloading of music, films, television programs and books; *fr. : copies illicites*
- injunction (n.) : order issued by a court to a party to do something or refrain from doing a particular act; *fr. : injonction*
- letter before action : formal notice demanding the infringer to perform a legal obligation and respect the specific terms of copyright; *fr. : lettre de mise en demeure*
- licence (n.) : formal permission or authorisation from a government authority; *fr. : licence*
- patent infringement : unauthorised manufacture, use or sale of a patented invention which the patent owner has not authorised; *fr. : contrefaçon de brevet/violation de brevet*
- patent specification : disclosure or written description of an invention that is drafted to specify the written requirements for patentability; *fr. : description du brevet*
- piracy (n.) : unauthorised use of patented, copyrighted material and ideas; *fr. : exploitation illicite*
- trademark infringement : unauthorised use of a trademark or service mark on competing or related goods and services; *fr. : contrefaçon de la marque*

USEFUL EXPRESSIONS

- to infringe copyright protection/an infringement of copyright; *fr. : enfreindre le droit d'auteur/violation du droit d'auteur*

- to settle a claim/to make an out of court settlement; *fr. : régler un litige en dehors du cadre judiciaire*
- to seek a court order; *fr. : requérir une décision de justice*

FURTHER INFORMATION

- the word account (*compte*) must not be confused with the French word *acompte* which means a deposit/down payment
- the word actually (*réellement*) must not be confused with the French word *actuellement* which means currently/at present
- the word demand (*revendication*) must not be confused with the French word *demande* which means demand/application

COMPARATIVE APPROACH

Outre-Manche, la juridiction qui tranche les litiges de propriété intellectuelle est la *Chancery Division* instituée au sein de la *High Court*. En France, les actions civiles et les demandes relatives à la propriété littéraire et artistique, y compris lorsqu'elles portent également sur une question connexe de concurrence déloyale, sont exclusivement portées devant les tribunaux de grande instance (TGI).

□ 111 COPYRIGHT INFRINGEMENT AND DEFENCES

Copyright law draws a distinction between primary and secondary infringement.

Primary infringement

It concerns individuals who are directly involved in the reproduction, performance and adaptation of the copyright work. The claimant must prove on a balance of probabilities (which is the usual standard of proof applicable in civil cases) that the defendant carried out an activity which falls within the copyright owner's control, a causal link to show that the defendant's work was derived from the copyright work and that the act was carried out in relation to the work or a substantial part of it. The claimant may use direct evidence or resort to an inference of derivation to prove the infringement. A substantiality question may be considered to find out if the restricted act has been carried out in relation to the work or a substantial part of it. In order to divide a work into copyright protected and unprotected parts, three principles are applied : the relevancy norm, the originality criterion and the principle of non-protection of ideas.

Secondary infringement

This form of accessorial infringement refers to infringers in a commercial context who deal with infringing copies and facilitate such copying or public performances. Copyright law recognises the need to provide owners with protection against those who abet the primary infringer. The defendant can only be found liable if the claimant shows that the defendant knew or had reason to know that the activities in question were wrongful.

Defences available

The defendant may rely on fair dealing defence, defence of incidental use, library use defence, defence for library copying and lending, defences that relate to copying carried out for pedagogical purposes and cultural preservation, artistic works defence and defences for computer programs that permit making back-up copies.

GLOSSARY

- abet (v.) : help or assist; *fr. : assister/encourager*
- accessorial (adj.) infringement (n.) : act of secondary infringement whereby the infringer provides assistance to the primary infringer to copy, distribute and communicate the material to the public; *fr. : contrefaçon accessoire*
- back-up copy : data which is copied and stored for use in case the original data gets corrupted or damaged; *fr. : copie de sécurité*
- causal (adj.) link (n.) : in order to prove infringement, the copyright owner has to show the similarity between the works, that the defendant had access and an opportunity to copy the work and establish a direct connection between the two; *fr. : lien de causalité*
- copying (n.) : make a reproduction or copy of an original work; *fr. : reproduction/copie*
- derivation (n.) : process of finding similarities between works, coupled with evidence that the defendant had access to and a chance to copy the copyright work; *fr. : dérivation*
- direct (adj.) evidence (n.) : evidence that directly suggests the guilt of an infringer as in the case of a witness seeing the act of copying a work; *fr. : preuves directes*
- fair dealing defence : defence for copyright infringement concerning uses of content (*e.g.* research, review and reporting current events); *fr. : défense de l'utilisation équitable*
- incidental (adj.) use (n.) : as a defence, the defendant demonstrates that copyright is not infringed by the incidental or accidental inclusion of a work in an artistic work (*e.g.* a film); *fr. : utilisation accessoire*
- inference (n.) : process of arriving at logical conclusions from premises known or assumed to be true; *fr. : conclusion*

- lending (n.) : grant the use of a work temporarily on condition that it will be returned; *fr. : prêt*
- library use defence : special defence which allows librarians to copy articles or the whole or part of a work for research; this includes lending copyright works to the public; *fr. : défense tirée de l'utilisation par une bibliothèque*
- originality (adj.) criterion (n.) : factor by which a person will only infringe a copyright work which reflects an author's original work; *fr. : critère d'originalité*
- pedagogical (adj.) purposes (n.) : material used for educational use; *fr. : à des fins pédagogiques*
- primary (adj.) infringement (n.) : offence for which there is no requirement to prove knowledge or intention of infringement on the infringer's part; *fr. : contrefaçon directe*
- primary (adj.) infringer (n.) : person who is liable for the primary infringement of a copyright work; *fr. : contrefacteur/contrevenant direct*
- protected (adj.) parts (n.) : elements of a work which are original and thus merit copyright protection; *fr. : données protégées*
- relevancy (adj.) norm (n.) : only elements of the work that are relevant to the type of work in question can receive copyright protection; *fr. : notion de pertinence*
- reproduction (n.) : act of copying an original work; *fr. : reproduction*
- restricted (adj.) act (n.) : activity that falls within the copyright owner's rights; it constitutes a copyright infringement; *fr. : acte réservé à l'autorisation du titulaire de droit*
- secondary (adj.) infringement (n.) : act of infringement carried out by secondary infringers who assist the primary infringer; knowledge or intention on the ingringer's part is required; *fr. : contrefaçon secondaire*
- substantiality (adj.) question (n.) : question that arises in an infringement action as to whether the restricted act has been carried out in relation to the work or a substantial part of it; *fr. : condition de substantialité*
- unprotected (adj.) parts (n.) : elements of the work that are not protected by copyright (e.g. the underlying idea behind a work); *fr. : données non protégées*
- wrongful (adj.) : unjust, unlawful or illegal; *fr. : illicite*

USEFUL EXPRESSIONS

- derivative work; *fr. : œuvre dérivée*
- to be liable for a breach of copyright; *fr. : être responsable d'une violation de copyright*
- to be liable to someone; *fr. : être responsible envers quelqu'un*
- to rely upon a valid defence; *fr. : invoquer une défense légitime*

FURTHER INFORMATION

- the word evidence (*preuve*) must not be confused with the French word *evidence* which has the meaning of the facts of the obvious fact
- the word dealing (*utilisation*) in this context means that the defendant has made use of the work and it does not imply that a transaction has taken place between the parties

> COMPARATIVE APPROACH
>
> Tandis qu'en Grande Bretagne, le concept de *fair dealing* favorise le droit des utilisateurs en reconnaissant la validité de clauses générales susceptibles de s'appliquer à de nombreuses situations, en France, la loi relative aux droits d'auteurs et aux droits voisins dans la société de l'information (DADVSI) protège les intérêts légitimes de l'auteur en énumérant les exceptions qui peuvent porter atteinte à l'exploitation normale de l'œuvre.

□ 112 DESIGN INFRINGEMENT AND DEFENCES

The owner of an Unregistered Design Right has the exclusive right to reproduce the design for commercial purposes. It decides whether to allow someone else to reproduce his designs. He can oppose any unauthorised act of primary or secondary infringement. Infringement of design rights includes commercial dealings with infringing articles, being in possession of them for commercial purposes or importing the merchandise into the country.

If proceedings are issued in court, the unregistered design owner must be able to identify with precision each and every design the defendant relies upon and prove that the defendant's activities fall within the scope of the protected rights. The claimant must show that there has been substantive infringement, whereby there exists a causal link between the two designs and the existence of a substantial similarity between his own work and the one which the defendant reproduced in whole or a substantial part of it.

In a situation where copyright and unregistered design rights both exist, section 51 of the CDPA 1988 provides the following defence : making an article to the design does not infringe copyright, but might nevertheless still infringe unregistered design right.

GLOSSARY

- causal (adj.) link (n.) : see 111
- commercial (adj.) dealing (n.) : method or manner of conduct while doing business; *fr. : opération commerciale*

- design right : see 37
- exclusive (adj.) right : see 38
- infringement (n.) : see 110
- merchandise (n.) : goods and commodities that are bought and sold in business; *fr. : marchandise*
- substantive (adj.) infringement (n.) : if the defendant's product contains the essential elements of one of the design claims, the product may substantially infringe the design right; *fr. : violation des formes substantielles*

USEFUL EXPRESSIONS

- to authorise the use of a design; *fr. : autoriser l'utilisation d'un dessin*
- the legal authorisation to represent an applicant; *fr. : l'autorisation légale de représenter le déposant*
- persons authorised to sign; *fr. : personnes habilitées à signer*
- within the scope of design protection; *fr. : dans le champ de la protection du dessin*

FURTHER INFORMATION

- the word profit (*bénéfice*) must not be confused with the French word *profiter* which means to take advantage of

COMPARATIVE APPROACH

Outre-Manche, la *Chancery Division* de la *High Court* a une compétence concurrente à celle des *county courts* en matière de dessins ou modèles non déposés. Il existe aussi une chambre spécialisée appelée la *Patents county court* qui arbitre des litiges en matière de dessin ou modèle enregistré qui posent, à titre accessoire, une question de droit d'auteur. En France, les TGI ont compétence pour se prononcer sur ce type de litige.

□ 113 PATENT INFRINGEMENT AND DEFENCES

A distinction must be made between direct and indirect patent infringement.

Direct patent infringement

Direct infringement involves some immediate engagement with the patented product or process. Direct infringement takes place irrespective of the knowledge of the defendant, except in a situation where an infringer uses a process or "offers a process for use" under section 60(1) (b) of the Patents Act 1977.

In the course of litigation, the patentee (who is the claimant) must prove that the defendant performed without the patentee's consent one of the activities that fall within the patent owner's control. As liability is absolute in relation to a patent for a product or where a product has been obtained directly from a patented process, there is no need for a patentee to prove that the defendant knew that he was infringing. Thus, an act which is an independent, accidental or unintentional creation of the same invention will constitute patent infringement.

Indirect patent infringement

Indirect infringement applies where a person facilitates the act of infringement. A patent is infringed when a person contributes to, but does not participate directly in the infringement. The patentee must establish that the means supplied by the defendant relate to an essential element of the invention. The supplier must have the knowledge requirement that the means are both "suitable" for and are "intended" to be used in putting the invention into effect. The supplier must also know that the commercial product exemption does not apply in the circumstances.

Defence

The defendant in a patent suit may rely on the following defences : private commercial use, experimental purpose, prior use, biotechnological invention and farmer's privilege.

GLOSSARY

- biotechnological (adj.) invention (n.) : inventions applied in the fields of agriculture, agroindustry and industry that use living organisms to make, improve or modify products; *fr. : invention biotechnologique*
- consent (n.) : agreement or permission regarding a course of action; *fr. : accord/consentement*
- exemption (n.) : the state of being exempt; *fr. : exemption*
- experimental (adj.) purpose (n.) : if the purpose of the activity is to discover something unknown or to test a hypothesis, immunity will be considered for this act that is regarded as an experiment; *fr. : fins expérimentales*
- farmer's privilege : defence where a farmer uses the product of his harvest for propagation on his farm, after there has been some form of commercialisation of plant-propagation material to the farmer by the patent owner for agricultural purposes; *fr. : privilège de l'agriculteur*
- invention (n.) : see 35
- means (n.) : method, instrument or medium used to obtain a result; *fr. : moyens*

- patentee (n.) : see 38
- patented (adj.) : protected by patent; *fr. : breveté*

USEFUL EXPRESSIONS

- to exempt someone from any form of liability; *fr. : exempter quelqu'un de toute forme de responsabilité*
- to request exemption from something; *fr. : faire une demande d'exemption de quelque chose*
- to be exempted from payment; *fr. : être dispensé du paiement*
- to find a suitable solution; *fr. : trouver une solution appropriée*

IMPORTANT INFORMATION

- the word engagement (*engagement*) meaning a commitment can also refer to a meeting or a *rendez-vous*

COMPARATIVE APPROACH

En Angleterre, une chambre spécialisée au sein du *Chancery Division* de la *High Court* appelée la *Patents Court* est autorisée à juger des contestations portant sur les brevets déposés. En France, les TGI peuvent se prononcer sur la validité des brevets européens.

□ 114 TRADEMARK INFRINGEMENT DEFENCES

Sections 10(1)-(3) the CPDA 1988 provides that in order to prove trademark infringement, the owner of the trademark has to show that the defendant used the trademark or brand "in the course of trade".

Trademark infringement occurs in the following situations : when the marks and goods or services are identical, when there is a likelihood of confusion or association with the registered mark due to its similarity, when the defendant uses the existing reputation of the owner's mark to take unfair advantage of it to promote his own trademark or when the defendant's mark is detrimental to the distinctive character, or reputation of the registered trademark.

As in the case of patents and registered designs, liability for trademark infringement is strict. To infringe a trademark, there is no requirement for knowledge, intention or derivation on the part of the defendant. However the trademark owner must show that the mark was "used in the course of trade" to establish infringement. In contrast with passing-off, damage does not have to be established by the trademark owner. There is not even a requirement that the mark has been used for the trademark owner to succeed in his legal action.

The infringer of a trademark may use one of the following defences : use of a registered trademark, use of name or address, descriptive use, use to indicate the intended purpose of a product or service, comparative advertising or local uses.

GLOSSARY

- brand (n.) : see 35
- comparative (adj.) advertising (n.) : strategy that uses a direct comparison between specific competing products to demonstrate that one product is better than another one and thus entice consumers to purchase the obviously superior product; *fr. : publicité comparative*
- course (of trade) : general transactions that take place customarily in the management of trade or business; *fr. : cours d'opérations commerciales*
- derivation (n.) : see 111
- detrimental (adj.) : causing harm, damage or injury; *fr. : préjudiciable*
- distinctive (adj.) : characteristic or typical; *fr. : spécifique*
- intended (adj.) purpose (n.) : something that is meant to be used for a specific or planned event or use; *fr. : usage prévu*
- knowledge (n.) : see 35
- likelihood (n.) : probability or chance of something happening; *fr. : probabilité*
- registered (adj.) trademark (n.) : trademark registered with the IPO that bears the symbol ®, and gives the trademark owner the exclusive right to use the mark for the goods or services that it covers in the UK; *fr. : marque déposée*
- registered (adj.) design (n.) : see 37
- reputation (n.) : state of holding a person or thing in high esteem or regard; *fr. : réputation*
- requirement (n.) : see 36

USEFUL EXPRESSIONS

- to demonstrate the relevance of an argument; *fr. : démontrer la pertinence d'un argument*
- demonstration of compliance; *fr. : preuve de la conformité*
- in contrast with EU law; *fr. : à l'opposé de la politique de l'Union européenne*

IMPORTANT INFORMATION

- the word damage (*préjudice*) must not be confused with the French word *dommage* which has other meanings of pity and shame

COMPARATIVE APPROACH

En Angleterre, la *Chancery Division* instituée au sein de la *High Court* a une compétence exclusive en matière de marques et tromperies commerciales en première instance. En France, les demandes de saisie-contrefaçon et autres mesures conservatoires, sont à soumettre aux commissaires de police, juges d'instance ou présidents du TGI.

8

Insurance litigation

☐ 115 GENERAL RULES

There can be three types of disputes in insurance law.

Firstly, a dispute can arise between an insurer and the policyholder/insured. The insurer may deny coverage, the insurer or the insured may have withheld relevant information when the policy was entered into or the insurer and insured disagree over the construction of a clause. In some cases, a formal complaint can be made with the Financial Ombudsman who will investigate the matter to try to solve it. If he does not succeed and in all other cases, it is always possible to resort to Alternative Dispute Resolution (ADR) or court litigation.

Secondly an insurer may have indemnified his insured before some liability issues with a third party are resolved. The insurer is then subrogated in his insured's rights. The insurer can then attempt ADR to resolve the dispute with the third party and if unsuccesful, begin court litigation. An example would be a car accident in which an insured cyclist is indemnified by his own insurer. The insurer will then have to resolve the liability issues with the car driver and/or his own insurer.

Thirdly disputes may arise between insurers in connection with a coassurance or reinsurance legal issue.

Since 1st April 2013 the small claims court jurisdictional limit has been increased to £10,000. If the claim is above that amount, the county courts or High Court will have jurisdiction.

GLOSSARY

- alternative dispute resolution (ADR) : see 74
- construction (n.) : here, interpretation; *fr. : interprétation*
- jurisdiction (n.) : court's power to deal with a case and hand down the relevant decision; *fr. : compétence d'attribution*
- Ombudsman (n.) : person who provides independent advice to try to settle a dispute; *fr. : médiateur/protecteur du citoyen/Défenseur des droits*

- small claims procedure : see 75
- subrogation (n.) : substitution of one person (here, the insurer) to another (here, the insured) with reference to a lawful claim as against a third party, when the insurer has already indemnified the insured; the insurer is then entitled to exercise the rights of his insured as against the third party; *fr. : subrogation*

USEFUL EXPRESSIONS

- to be subrogated in someone's rights; *fr. : être subrogé dans les droits de/venir aux droits de*
- this policy can be construed as meaning; *fr. : cette police peut être interprétée comme signifiant*
- claims departments of an insurance company; *fr. : service sinistres d'une compagnie d'assurances*
- to deny coverage; *fr. : refuser la couverture*
- to construe a clause; *fr. : interpréter une clause*
- to deny cover; *fr. : dénier/refuser la garantie*
- to resort to litigation; *fr. : avoir recours au contentieux*

FURTHER INFORMATION

- insurers often opt for ADR to avoid litigation with each other which can be very costly

Comparative approach

Comme Outre-Manche, il est possible en France de recourir à la médiation (*mediation*), à l'arbitrage (*arbitration*) ou à une action contentieuse (*litigation*) en cas de désaccord entre assureur et assuré sur le bien fondé de la garantie. De même, il est courant qu'un assureur indemnise son assuré, se retrouvant ainsi subrogé dans ses droits et de ce fait, habilité à exercer à sa place toute action en responsabilité à l'encontre d'un tiers.

9

Environmental litigation

□ 116 INTRODUCTION

Environment law seeks to punish harm caused to the environment by human activity and works within a national and international, legal and ethical framework. It involves protecting the environment by limiting or preventing human activity that may cause damage.

To combat environmental crime committed by the corporate world, the Environment Protection Act (EPA) of 1990 (and its later versions) mandates certain pollution-reducing technology to limit the levels of pollution for power plants and factories. It makes provisions for the improved control of pollution arising from certain industrial processes, thus re-enacting the provisions of the Control of Pollution Act of 1974 relating to waste on land. The EPA also established a system of sanctions if environmental crime is committed.

The Department for Environment, Food and Rural Affairs (DEFRA) is the ministerial department that works directly in England to improve the environment. DEFRA negotiates with the devolved administrations in Wales, Scotland and Northern Ireland, and coordinates environmental regulations whilst keeping in mind European and international obligations.

Environmental law is influenced by theoretical analysis and the work of economists and political scientists, resulting in the adoption of specific principles that help regulate and influence its scope. The principles that govern environmental policy and regulatory standards today in the UK are sustainable development, the precautionary principle, the "polluter pays" principle and the public participation principle. These principles endeavour to reconcile the conflicting demands of economic and social development against resource management and protection through sustainable development.

GLOSSARY

- commit (v.) : perform a criminal act; *fr. : commettre (une infraction)*
- conflicting (adj.) : relating to contradictory or incompatible actions; *fr. : contradictoire/conflictuel*

- corporate (adj.) world (n.) : business environment in large companies where there is an obligation to respect laws and ethics while doing trade and commerce; *fr. : monde de l'entreprise*
- devolved (adj.) administration (n.) : see 51
- endeavour (v.) : make a purposeful effort to attain or obtain something; *fr. : s'efforcer de*
- environmental (adj.) crime (n.) : criminal damage caused to the environment; *fr. : infraction contre l'environnement*
- environmental (adj.) policy (n.) : mechanism laid in place by a government or a business in order to comply with the environmental law of the country; *fr. : politique environnementale/politique en matière d'environnement*
- environmental (adj.) regulation (n.) : at a national level, law enacted by Parliament or text adopted by a government to protect the environment and regulate environmental policy; *fr. : réglementation environnementale*
- harm (n.) : damage or injury inflicted on a person or thing; *fr. : dommage/ préjudice*
- mandate (v.) : authorise or make obligatory or mandatory; *fr. : imposer*
- political (adj.) scientist (n.) : expert of political science who studies the science and theory of government; *fr. : politologue*
- "polluter pays" principle (n.) : see 51
- pollution-reducing (adj.) technology (n.) : use of tools and equipment that have been conceived with the intent of decreasing pollution to the environment; *fr. : technologies de reduction de la pollution*
- precautionary (adj.) principle (n.) : idea of foreseeing possible catastrophes and taking preventive action as a means of protecting the environment; *fr. : principe de précaution*
- provisions (n.) : clause or legal instrument providing for the application of law; *fr. : dispositions*
- public participation principle : see 51
- reconcile (v.) : bring together or compose by integrating together; *fr. : concilier*
- regulatory (adj.) standards (n.) : norms followed throughout the UK to ensure that environmental policy is applied in synergy and functions harmoniously; *fr. : normes réglementaires*
- resource management : process of using available natural resources wisely so that they are not completely depleted, but are allocated also for use by future generations; *fr. : gestion des ressources*
- scope (n.) : complete range or extent of activity; *fr. : portée/champ d'application*

USEFUL EXPRESSIONS

- to endeavour to protect the environment; *fr. : s'efforcer de protéger l'environnement*

- to mandate use of green technology; *fr. : rendre obligatoire l'usage des technologies vertes*
- a mandatory requirement; *fr. : une exigence à caractère obligatoire*

FURTHER INFORMATION

- the verb coordinate (*coordonner*) referring to the act of working together, must not be confused with the French noun *coordonnées* which refers to personal details such as an address or a phone number

COMPARATIVE APPROACH

En Angleterre, le *Department for Environment, Food and Rural Affairs* (DEFRA) est l'exécutif chargé de protéger l'environnement. L'*Environmental Agency* (agence nationale de l'environnement), le *Health and Safety Executive* (exécutif chargé de la santé et de la sécurité), le *Crown Prosecution Service* (service du procureur), *HM Customs and Excise* (le service des douanes) et le *Pesticide Safety Directorate* (la direction britannique pour la sécurité des pesticides) mettent leurs moyens en commun pour protéger l'environnement, atteindre les objectifs fixés en haut-lieu et sanctionner les auteurs d'infractions au droit de l'environnement.

En France, le ministère de l'Écologie, du développement durable et de l'énergie est assisté, au niveau régional, de la Direction régionale de l'environnement, de l'aménagement et du logement (DREAL) (sous l'autorité du Préfet de région) et au niveau départemental, des Directions départementales des territoires (DDT) et Directions départementales des territoires et de la mer (DDTM) (sous l'autorité du Préfet), pour mettre en œuvre les politiques publiques relatives à la promotion du développent durable.

□ 117 REGULATORY STRATEGIES AND JURISDICTION

Environmental regulation in England and Wales is based on two elements : the reactive regulation of providing remedies for pollution and the proactive regulation of foreseeing and applying precautionary measures to change behaviours and make citizens aware of the risks of environmental damage. An example of the former is the willingness to limit the use of genetically modified crops and genetically modified organisms. An example of the latter is the new "green deal" policy implemented by the government and the landfill tax raised on waste disposal. The reactive regulatory strategies aim at establishing liability for polluting the environment and considering the provision of remedies.

Three different courts have first-instance jurisdiction to hear environmental cases. The First-Tier (Environment) Tribunal – which was set up in 2010 pursuant to the Tribunals, Courts and Enforcement Act 2007 – has jurisdiction, amongst other things, to hear appeals against the imposition of civil sanctions issued by the Environment Agency. It also checks compliance with the Convention on Access to Information, Public Participation in Decision-making and Access to Justice in Environmental matters of 25 June 1998 (Aarhus convention).

Under Section 82 of the 1990 EPA, the magistrates' courts have criminal jurisdiction to deal with some environmental offences. The county courts have civil jurisdiction to grant damages for loss or nuisance caused by non-eco-friendly acts and/or to issue an injunction to stop these acts causing damage to the environment.

As for appeals and depending on the decision appealed against, they are made either to the High Court, a Magistrates' court or the General Regulatory Chamber (Environment).

GLOSSARY

- civil (adj.) sanction (n.) : as opposed to a criminal sanction, penalty awarded for violating the law like a fine or community service; *fr. : sanction civile*
- environment (adj.) tribunal (n.) : tribunal that has original jurisdiction to deal with various contentious environmental issues; *fr. : ≈ juridiction ayant compétence pour connaître des questions d'environnement*
- first-tier (adj.) : when applied to a court, refers to the fact that it first hears of any dispute; first-tier court decisions may then be appealed against; *fr. : de première instance*
- genetically modified organisms : organisms like plants, animals, fish, insects, bacteria and yeast that have been altered through the use of genetic engineering techniques to permit gene transfer; *fr. : organismes génétiquement modifiés*
- genetically modified crops : plants whose DNA have been altered or transferred by means of genetic engineering techniques; *fr. : cultures génétiquement modifiées*
- green (adj.) deal (n.) : government policy of granting loans to house owners to install energy saving green technology that will enable them to reduce their energy bills in the long run; *fr. : nouveau contrat vert*
- injunction (n.) : court order requiring one of the parties to the litigation to perform a particular act or restrain from indulging in a particular act; *fr. : injonction*
- jurisdiction (n.) : power given to a court or tribunal to interpret and apply law; *fr. : compétence d'attribution*
- landfill tax : amount of money levied by the government from entities which fill up land that is used for the disposal of waste, that permits the government to generate funds for environmental protection; *fr. : taxe de mise en décharge*

- waste (adj.) disposal (n.) : manner of getting rid of waste by collecting, monitoring, and selectively recycling waste materials; *fr. : élimination des déchets*

USEFUL EXPRESSIONS

- to assess environmental impact; *fr. : évaluer l'impact sur l'environnement*
- an assessing body; *fr. : un organisme d'évaluation*
- to mitigate risks or harm; *fr. : atténuer les risques ou le préjudice*
- risk mitigation; *fr. : limitation des risques*
- to take precautions to avoid damage to the environment; *fr. : prendre des précautions pour éviter de causer un dommage à l'environnement*

IMPORTANT INFORMATION

- the word tier (*niveau*) referring to the level of jurisdiction, must not be confused with the French word *tiers* referring to a third of a quantity or a third party

COMPARATIVE APPROACH

Outre-Manche et comme dans la majorité des juridictions, les magistrats du *First-Tier (Environment) Tribunal* sont d'anciens avocats qui peuvent justifier de plusieurs années d'expérience (le chiffre étant déterminé par la loi), notamment en droit de l'environnement.

En France, une majorité de questions de nature environnementale est traitée, en première instance, par les tribunaux administratifs, constitués de magistrats recrutés par le biais de l'École Nationale d'Administration (ENA) ou sur concours spécifique. Comme Outre-Manche, le juge administratif français dispose d'un pouvoir d'injonction et d'astreinte mais en dépit de cela, il n'a pas de vrai moyen de faire procéder à l'exécution de ses décisions.

À l'instar de son voisin, la France applique les grands principes environnementaux tels que le principe pollueur-payeur, le principe de prévention, le principe de précaution et le principe de participation. Avec la loi Barnier de 1995, ces quatre principes sont devenus des principes généraux du droit de l'environnement français.

□ 118 SANCTIONS AND ENFORCEMENT

In England and Wales, the Environment Protection Act (EPA) was passed in 1990. It implemented a system of fixed penalty notices to punish environmental offenders. The Regulatory Enforcement and Sanctions Act of 2008 favours a sanctions-based approach to environmental regulation in cases of corporate liability and individual negligence.

Companies involved in environmental offences frequently cast blame on third parties or categorise harm as an unavoidable accident caused by employees. So the legislator passed tort laws establishing that liability could ensue vicariously, thus making companies liable for acts or omissions of their employees during their work schedules.

In cases of individual negligence, offenders are strictly liable for their acts, be it a criminal offence or an act of civil tort or negligence. Strictly liable offences include littering, fly posting, graffiti, abandoned vehicles and waste disposal. Fixed penalty notices are issued for offences for which appropriate and sufficient evidence exist. Depending on the nature of the criminal offence, trial will take place before the magistrates' courts or the Crown Court.

Educational programmes or environmental campaigns are other tools for dealing with environmental crime and anti-social behaviour.

GLOSSARY

- abandoned (adj.) vehicle (n.) : cars, vans, automobiles that have been left unattended by owners who wish to get rid of them; *fr. : véhicule abandonné*
- anti-social (adj.) behaviour (n.) : hostile or disruptive manner of conducting oneself as opposed to established norms of society; *fr. : comportement anti-social*
- corporate (adj.) liability (n.) : legal responsibility of a corporation for criminal acts or omissions that can harm others in society; *fr. : responsabilité des personnes morales*
- criminal (adj.) damage (n.) : offence of injury caused to property by negligence or wilful destruction that is actionable by law; *fr. : ≈ préjudice engendré par une infraction pénale*
- educational (adj.) programme (n.) : here, course or part of the curriculum aimed at informing and educating youth about the need to preserve the environment for future generations; *fr. : programme éducatif*
- ensue (v.) : be the consequence or the result of; *fr. : découler*
- environmental (adj.) campaign (n.) : movement organised to make citizens aware of the need to protect the environment; *fr. : campagne en faveur de l'environnement*
- environmental (adj.) offender (n.) : legal entity which violates environmental regulations and causes harm to the environment; *fr. : ≈ personne (physique ou morale) qui commet une infraction en matière environnementale/ délinquant écologique*
- environmental (adj.) regulation (n.) : see 52
- fixed penalty notice : issuance of a warning to offenders involved in anti-social behaviour or environmental crime by enforcing a pre-determined fine; *fr. : ≈ notification d'une amende fixe*

- fly posting : illegal act of placing advertising leaflets or flyers in public areas; *fr. : affichage sauvage*
- graffiti (n.) : offence of causing damage to public property by scribbling, drawing or inscribing messages on walls; *fr. : graffiti*
- littering (n.) : act of carelessly discarding waste in public spaces; *fr. : ≈ dépôt d'ordures*
- negligence (n.) : see 85
- sanctions-based (adj.) approach (n.) : method of regulating the protection of the environment by awarding penalties or sanctions to offenders; *fr. : approche fondée sur les sanctions*
- third party : individual not directly involved in the affair or offence; *fr. : tiers*
- tort : see 85
- vicarious (adj.) liability (n.) : indirect responsibility for an act committed by an employee; *fr. : responsabilité du fait d'autrui*
- waste (adj.) disposal (n.) : see 117

USEFUL EXPRESSIONS

- to campaign for the protection of environment; *fr. : faire campagne pour la protection de l'environnement*
- an awareness campaign; *fr. : une campagne de sensibilisation*
- to raise environmental issues; *fr. : soulever des questions environnementales*

FURTHER INFORMATION

- the adjective vicarious refers to the act of accepting indirect responsibility for an act committed by others (*responsabilité pour autrui*)

COMPARATIVE APPROACH

Au Royaume-Uni, le *Crown Prosecution Service* (CPS) (ministère public) est chargé des poursuites à l'encontre de ceux qui commettent des infractions au droit de l'environnement. Les juridictions compétentes en la matière sont les *magistrates' courts* ou la *Crown Court.*

En France, la délinquance écologique est susceptible de faire l'objet de poursuites devant les juridictions répressives telles que le Tribunal correctionnel. Mais de telles poursuites pénales peuvent être évitées en cas de transaction dite pénale, rendue possible par l'ordonnance n° 2012-34 du 11 janvier 2012 portant simplification, réforme et harmonisation des dispositions de police administrative et de police judiciaire du Code de l'environnement.

Le nouvel article L. 173-12-1 du Code de l'environnement permet à l'autorité administrative, tant que l'action publique n'a pas été mise en œuvre, de tenter de transiger avec les auteurs de contraventions et délits environnementaux. L'idée de ces transactions pénales est de combler les carences d'un droit pénal de l'environnement existant, mais parfois peu efficace.

10

Employment litigation

□ 119 TERMINATION OF EMPLOYMENT

There are four ways in which a contract of employment can come to an end: the expiry of the fixed-term for fixed-term contracts; for a long-term contract, the employee can resign, he can be dismissed or made redundant.

Resignation

If an employee or a worker wishes to leave his job, the most effective way is to send the employer a written resignation letter and respect the notice period stated in the contract of employment. If there is no notice period, two weeks' notice is the usual notice given.

Redundancy

When faced with economic difficulties, an employer may decide to reduce his workforce when some members no longer appear necessary. The selection of the employee(s) to be made redundant must be based on fair criteria and the employer has to comply with any applicable anti-discrimination laws to avoid a claim for unfair dismissal. The employer can offer voluntary redundancy. Before laying off an employee, the employer has the duty to inform him, offer any alternative employment within the company, or find some retraining programmes. A notice period before the end of employment is compulsory. The employee has the right to have a consultation with his employer. In case of collective redundancies (20 or more people), the consultation is held between the employer and a representative of the employees. An employee who has worked for more than two years is entitled to a redundancy package and can claim unemployment benefit from the state. An employee who is on a short-term or temporary lay-off can also claim statutory redundancy pay if he does not work for a month. Some company directors are entitled to golden parachutes included in their contract. The grounds for redundancy can give rise to a court action for unfair redundancy dismissal.

Dismissal

An employee can be subject to a summary dismissal or an ordinary dismissal. In both cases, the employer can propose a compromise agreement to his employee. While receiving some benefits such as severance payment, the employee signs a legal document stating that he will not bring any claim against his employer in the future. Summary dismissal may occur when the employee's behaviour can be considered as gross misconduct, such as being violent toward colleagues. In this case the dismissal is immediate and there is no need for the employer to respect the notice period.

For an ordinary dismissal, the employer must comply with strict rules which derive from statute and may have been complemented by collective agreements (which tend to give more protection to the employees). Non-compliance may result in a subsequent action for unfair dismissal. After carefully investigating any suspicion of misconduct or poor performance at work by hearing witnesses or collecting information, the employer sends a written notification to the employee inviting him to attend a disciplinary hearing, and setting out the allegation made against the employee and the main evidence gathered against him. The employee can attend the disciplinary hearing with someone else (usually a trade union representative or another colleague). After the hearing, the employer must inform his employee of his decision. Should this be a dismissal decision, the employee has the right to appeal the decision reached at the disciplinary hearing.

The employee has the right to ask for a written statement from his employer if he has been employed for a year. The statement must be sent within 14 days. The employer must comply with the notice period specified in the contract or the statutory notice period which is usually calculated according to the number of months or years the employee has worked for the employer. An employee who has been dismissed cannot claim any benefit. However any jobseeker is entitled to a Job Seeker Allowance (JSA) while looking for work.

GLOSSARY

- compromise agreement : agreement reached by the employer and the employee setting out the conditions in which the contract of employment is terminated; this legal document usually includes financial terms and a binding promise from the employee not to sue his former employer for unfair dismissal; *fr. : ≈ rupture conventionnelle de contrat*
- consultation (n.) : mandatory meeting which must take place between an employee and his employer when the latter wishes to make the employee redundant; the reasons for redundancy must be explained and the employer must inform the employee of any alternatives; in case of collective redundancies (20 employees or more), a representative for the employees will meet with the employer; *fr. : entretien préalable au licenciement pour motif économique*
- disciplinary (adj.) hearing (n.) : meeting when the employer informs the employee that his performance at work is below what is expected or that he

has behaved in a unreasonable way; this may lead to a dismissal; *fr. : entretien préalable au licenciement pour motif personnel*
- dismissal (n.) : termination of the contract of employment because of the employee's poor performance or reluctance to adapt; *fr. : licenciement pour motif personnel*
- fixed-term contract : contract of employment signed for a limited period of time; *fr. : ≈ contrat à durée déterminée (CDD)*
- golden (adj.) parachute (n.) : very substantial severance payment made to the former executive of a company, usually when he is made redundant; *fr. : parachute doré*
- gross (adj.) misconduct (n.) : here, employee's behaviour at work which is deemed totally unreasonable by an employer, like fraud or theft; *fr. : faute grave/inexcusable*
- Job Seeker Allowance (JSA) : weekly benefit paid to individuals looking for a job; *fr. : allocation chômage*
- lay (v.) off : terminate a contract of employment by dismissing someone; *fr. : renvoyer (quelqu'un)*
- misconduct (n.) : here, employee's behaviour deemed inappropriate by an employer, usually during working hours; *fr. : comportement fautif*
- poor (adj.) performance (n.) : level of work below the average or what is normally expected from someone at work; *fr. : insuffisance professionnelle*
- redundancy (n.) : termination of employment for economic reasons; *fr. : licenciement pour motif économique*
- redundancy package : this package includes the various payments to which an employee made redundant is entitled, such as redundancy payment, unpaid salary, compensation, holiday pay; *fr. : indemnités de licenciement*
- resign (v.)/resignation (n.) : when the employee decides to terminate his contract; *fr. : démissioner*
- retraining (adj.) programme (n.) : courses to teach new skills to employees so that they can get another job more quickly; *fr. : ≈ programme de conversion*
- severance payment : monetary compensation given upon termination of contract; *fr. : indemnité de départ*
- summary (adj.) dismissal (n.) : laying-off of an employee according to an accelerated procedure, for example when the employee was caught stealing; *fr. : ≈ licenciement sans préavis*
- unemployment benefit : sum of money given by the State to help unemployed people while they look for a new job; *fr. : indemnité de chômage*
- unfair (adj.) dismissal (n.) : unreasonable breach by the employer of statutory employment rights; *fr. : licenciement sans cause réelle et sérieuse*
- voluntary (adj.) redundancy (n.) : when an employer has lawful reasons to make a certain number of his employees redundant, he can ask for volunteers usually, but not always, amongst those who are near retirement age; whenever the employer's offer for voluntary redundancy is accepted by an employee, compensation must be given to the employee; *fr. : départ volontaire*

- warning (n.) : here, letter from the employer informing the employee that evidence of poor performance or misconduct at work has been gathered, that he is invited to attend a disciplinary hearing on a particular date (accompanied by a colleague or a trade union representative) and that he could be dismissed if this behaviour is recurrent; *fr. : avertissement*

USEFUL EXPRESSIONS

- to register with the Jobcentre; *fr. : s'inscrire à Pôle Emploi*
- to be fired/sacked; *fr. : être licencié pour motif personnel*
- to hire someone; *fr. : embaucher quelqu'un*
- to be on the dole (colloquial); *fr. : être au chômage*
- to lay someone off; *fr. : licencier quelqu'un*
- to make someone redundant; *fr. : licencier quelqu'un pour motif économique*
- to hand in one's resignation letter; *fr. : remettre sa lettre de démission*
- to be entitled to welfare benefit (n.)/entitlement (n.); *fr. : prestations sociales*

FURTHER INFORMATION

- the original meaning of redundancy is the state of no longer being needed or useful; applied to the labour market, it means that an employer can no longer make use of someone's skills, because he does not have any work left for him to do

COMPARATIVE APPROACH

Les procédures de licenciement françaises et anglaises sont assez comparables ainsi que les motifs de licenciement. Le droit du travail français fixe, cependant, des délais réglementaires entre l'entretien et la notification qui n'existent pas vraiment en droit anglais. Les travailleurs anglais ont également droit aux allocations chômage dont le montant est toutefois nettement inférieur à celui alloué aux chômeurs français qui sont mieux protégés.

□ 120 DISPUTES

Mediation and arbitration

Conflicts in the workplace should always be dealt with in the early stages to avoid any claims in court. Should any grievance be raised at work, between members of the workforce, or between an employer and an employee, a formal meeting between the parties is usually organised to determine the causes of the conflict and examine the possible solutions.

Mediation is a good alternative to court litigation to try to solve a dispute. An impartial mediator is responsible for hearing parties and trying to restore the working relations between individuals. No binding decisions are made. The Advisory, Conciliation and Arbitration Service (ACAS) can help, advise and provide mediators. Collective mediations between trade unions and employers can also be supervised by independent arbitrators. Arbitration is an alternative option to avoid court proceedings provided the parties agree to it and comply with the arbitrator's decision. Unlike mediation, the decisions of an arbitrator are binding.

Court dispute resolution

Should the dispute not be settled amicably or through mediation/arbitration and depending on its nature, a claim may be brought either in civil courts, such as the county courts or the High Court, or in specialised tribunals (Employment Tribunal (ET) and the Employment Appeal Tribunal (EAT) for appeals on a point of law). Awards of damages by the ET are capped. Before the claim is heard by a tribunal, conciliation before an ACAS representative is proposed to the parties as a way to try to solve the dispute without holding a trial. One qualified lawyer and two lay people, representing respectively employers' organisations and trade unions, usually sit in the ET. Judges of the High Court, experienced in employment law, sit in the EAT to hear appeals lying from the ET on points of law.

Most claims are for wrongful or unfair dismissal. In a claim for wrongful dismissal, the employee argues that the employer is in repudiatory breach of contract. This may arise when the employee was dismissed without notice or less notice than that defined by statute. For employees hired on a fixed-term contract, a breach of contract can occur if the employer dismisses them before the contractual expiry date. Claims can be brought both before civil courts and tribunals. The remedies usually awarded are compensation calculated on the contractual benefits the employee was normally entitled to.

Unfair dismissal claims can be brought only before an ET and within three months of the dismissal. Some dismissals are automatically held to be unfair if the employee shows that he/she was laid off because he was member of a trade union, or she was pregnant. Three remedies are then possible – reinstatement, re-engagement or compensation. Constructive dismissal is part of unfair dismissal and is related to the employer's conduct. If the latter shows that he no longer wishes to work with his employee or if he acts in a way that amounts to a repudiatory breach of contract, then the employee can terminate the contract and seek compensation.

GLOSSARY

- arbitration (n.) : part of Alternative Dispute Resolution (ADR); an independent arbitrator examines the evidence and any documents before reaching his decision which is binding; *fr. : arbitrage*
- cap (v. or n.) : limit; *fr. : limite*

- conciliation (n.) : here, formal meeting between the parties which can be held by an ACAS representative as a way to try to resolve an employment dispute amicably and thus, avoid a court/tribunal action; *fr. : conciliation*
- constructive (adj.) dismissal (n.) : when an employer acts as if he wanted to end an employee's contract, but does not do it, the employee is entitled to consider that he is dismissed and is allowed to claim compensation; *fr. : licenciement déguisé*
- Employment Tribunal (ET) : inferior court specialised in employment law where a lawyer and two elected representatives of employers and employees examine claims for unfair and wrongful dismissals; the damages this court can award are limited; *fr. : ≈ conseil des prud'hommes*
- Employment Appeal Tribunal (EAT) : inferior court hearing appeals from ET on points of law; *fr. : ≈ chambre sociale de la cour d'appel*
- grievance (n.) : complaint made by an employee who argues he has been wronged; *fr. : réclamation*
- mediation (n.) : part of Alternative Dispute Resolution (ADR); a mediator examines the evidence and any documents before reaching his decision; contrary to arbitration, his decision is not binding; *fr. : médiation*
- re-engagement (n.) : court decision handed down by a tribunal or a court in the case of unfair dismissal; the employer is obliged to hire the dismissed employee again but gives him a different position; *fr. : ≈ ré-embauche*
- reinstatement (n.) : court decision handed down by a court or a tribunal reversing the effect of an unfair dismissal so that the dismissed employee gets his job back; *fr. : réintégration*
- unfair (adj.) dismissal (n.) : see 119
- wrongful (adj.) dismissal (n.) : breach by the employer of contractual terms; *fr. : licenciement abusif*

USEFUL EXPRESSIONS

- to reach an agreement; *fr. : trouver un accord*
- to resort to mediation; *fr. : avoir recours à la médiation*
- to be bound by an arbitrator's ruling; *fr. : être lié par la décision d'un arbitre*
- to sue someone for unfair dismissal; *fr. : engager une action à l'encontre de quelqu'un pour licenciement sans cause réelle et sérieuse*

FURTHER INFORMATION

- the noun tribunal cannot automatically be translated by the French *tribunal* as the jurisdictional scope of the English tribunal is much narrower than its French counterpart

COMPARATIVE APPROACH

Contrairement à l'*Employment Tribunal* où siège un juge, le conseil des prud'hommes en France n'est pas composé de juristes, mais seulement de conseillers représentant les salariés et les employeurs. Si la procédure de conciliation est simplement recommandée par ACAS, elle est obligatoire en France dans le cadre de toute action devant le conseil de prud'hommes.

□ 121 TRADE UNION

Most English and Welsh trade unions are part of the Trade Union Congress (TUC), the main national trade union. Although membership has steadily decreased over the past decades, trade unions remain the most structured force to defend workers' rights and negotiate collective agreements with employers. This type of organisation must first be registered in the list of trade unions. A certification officer examines the application and checks that the organisation complies with the main legal criteria of a trade union, such as independence. A listing is then issued, giving the organisation statutory recognition.

One of the main activities of a trade union is collective bargaining with the employers so as to sign a collective agreement. Trade union representatives can also advise employees on their rights and accompany them to grievance or disciplinary hearings. In the event of a collective grievance, the trade unions first try to negotiate with the employers. Should conciliation attempts fail, they may decide to start industrial action. Workers can go on strike, or initiate work-to-rule or begin go-slow actions. Trade unions can also demonstrate against decisions taken by the government or measures voted by the Parliament.

Current legislation has vastly reduced the power of trade unions by making most industrial actions unlawful. If they benefit from some immunities, trade unions can be sued for liability in tort.

GLOSSARY

- certification officer : civil servant in charge of registering workers' organisations and employers' associations on the list of trade unions; *fr. : ≈ autorité habilitée à délivrer une certification*
- collective (adj.) agreement (n.) : mutual decisions reached by trade unions and employers, usually to improve the employees' working conditions or rights in a particular professional field; *fr. : convention collective*
- collective (adj.) bargaining (n.) : process by which trade unions negotiate workers' collective rights with employers; *fr. : négociation syndicale*

- collective (adj.) grievance (n.) : complaint made by a group of employees; *fr. : revendication*
- demonstrate (v.) : act of walking down the streets with posters to complain about a particular situation; *fr. : manifester*
- disciplinary (adj.) hearing (n.) : see 119
- go-slow action : when the workforce slows down work so as to cause delays or even disruptions for their employer's business activities; *fr. : ≈ opération escargot/travail au ralenti*
- immunity (n.) : here, protection given by the law, preventing employers from suing trade union representatives in certain cases; *fr. : immunité*
- industrial (adj.) action (n.) : situation in which dissatisfied workers decide to stop work in order to make their grievances or claims heard; *fr. : grève*
- listing (n.) : here, official document containing the names of recognised trade union and employers' association; *fr. : registre des syndicats*
- membership (n.) : act of being affiliated to an organisation; *fr. : adhésion*
- strike (n.) : situation when workers temporarily or completely stop work; industrial action; *fr. : grève*
- tort (n.) : see 86
- trade union (n.) : legal organisation duly registered which defends workers' rights; *fr. : syndicat*
- work-to-rule : industrial action in which employees only do the minimum required by the rules of their contract; this usually causes slowdown; *fr. : grève du zèle*

USEFUL EXPRESSIONS

- to go on strike; *fr. : se mettre en grève*
- labour unrest; *fr. : agitation ouvrière*
- stoppage (n.); *fr. : débrayage*
- to be a unionised worker; *fr. : être un travailleur syndiqué*
- wage settlement; *fr. : accord salarial*

FURTHER INFORMATION

- employers also have their own associations defending their interests, such as the Confederation of British Industry or the Federation of Small Businesses

COMPARATIVE APPROACH

L'organisation syndicale est différente dans les deux pays. La création d'un syndicat est plus réglementée en Angleterre dans la mesure où un syndicat doit être enregistré sur le registre des syndicats (*listing*) après vérifications de certains critères. La marge de manœuvre des syndicats anglais a été sévèrement réduite sous Margaret Thatcher, portant un coup aux organisations syndicales. Même si les syndicats français jouissent de davantage de droits que leurs homologues anglais, le nombre d'adhésions est un des plus faibles en Europe.

11

Immigration litigation

□ 122 IMMIGRATION LAW AND RELATED HUMAN RIGHTS

Immigrants in the UK are entitled to protection of their civil and fundamental rights under the European Convention of Human Rights (ECHR). No public authority can infringe on an immigrant's basic rights while he awaits leave to enter into the country.

Legal provisions relating to immigration law in the UK are based on the Common European Asylum System (CEAS). The aim of this system, which was endorsed by the European Parliament in June 2013, is to provide asylum seekers with better access to the asylum procedure, protect their rights by ensuring fair and humane treatment, guarantee quicker and better asylum decisions and grant protection according to international norms to those suffering from the fear of persecution.

Pursuant to the Immigration Act 1971, the UK, the Channel Islands, the Isle of Man and the Republic of Ireland are referred to as the Common Travel Area. Entry to the area from outside is subject to strict control but once duly authorised in one of the relevant jurisdictions, any person is free of immigration control. However the UK has refused to sign the Schengen agreement and expressly opted out of the European Council Directive 2003/86/EC on family reunification. By refusing to accept any common visa rules with the EU, the UK has manifested its preference for an "island status" by adopting a policy of "managed migration".

The UK Border Agency, which controls immigration, has taken measures to prevent the asylum route from being abused by those who want to come to the UK for purely economic reasons, to encourage migrants to return home and to exercise strict control over applications for family reunion. To prevent illegal or unauthorised immigration and overstaying in the country, the Secretary of State of the Home Office (a.k.a the Home Secretary) has the power to detain or deport and enforce the departure of illegal or unauthorised migrants. He has the authority to issue a deprivation of nationality order if it is in the public interest to do so.

Immigration authorities control aliens after entry in the country, overseas and at the borders. There are Entry Clearance Officers for overseas decisions and Immigration Officers (IO) at border controls operated by the UK Border Agency. Unsuccessful immigration and asylum applicants have a right to appeal and have their cases heard at a two-tier tribunal, created under the Tribunals, Courts and Enforcement Act 2007. This Act came into force in February 2010 and a two-tier system replaced the former one-tier Asylum and Immigration Tribunal.

GLOSSARY

- abuse (v. or n.) : to misuse or use incorrectly; *fr. : abus*
- alien (n.) : foreign resident without the citizenship of the country; *fr. : étranger*
- appeal (v. or n.) : request to review an unsuccessful application for asylum; *fr. : relever appel (d'une décision)/appel*
- asylum seeker : person who seeks refugee status in a foreign country due to fear of persecution for reasons of religion, race, opinion or social group in his own country; *fr. : demandeur d'asile*
- border (n.) : frontier line that separates one country from another; *fr. : frontière*
- border control : law enforcement force of the immigration services that checks entry of aliens into the UK; *fr. : contrôle aux frontières*
- Common Travel Area : free travel zone where routine immigration checks are not carried out as a person who travels in this area possesses permission to enter this space composed of the UK, the Republic of Ireland, the Channel Islands and the Isle of Man; *fr. : zone commune de circulation/zone de déplacement sans frontière*
- deport (v.) : evict or transfer an alien from a country to his homeland or to another country willing to offer him asylum; *fr. : expulser*
- deprivation (n.) : when applied to nationality, refers to the act of denying or withdrawing the right to citizenship of a country; *fr. : déchéance (d'un droit)*
- detain (v.) : withhold or restrain a person from proceeding into a country; *fr. : détenir*
- enforce (v.) : impose a rule or a law; *fr. : faire respecter/exécuter*
- entry clearance officer : personnel of UK Border Agency who is entrusted with the duty of verifying travel documents and who may grant leave to enter into the UK; *fr. : ≈ officier chargé d'autoriser l'entrée dans le pays*
- Home Office : main government department responsible for securing the UK border and controlling immigration; *fr. : ministère de l'intérieur britannique*
- illegal (adj.) migrant (n.) : individual who enters fraudulently into the UK and enters its border without going through entry clearance procedures; *fr. : immigré clandestin*
- immigration (n.) : process of aliens entering into a country with the intention of obtaining leave to remain; *fr. : immigration*

- Immigration Officer : personnel of the UK Border Agency who examines travel documents to grant leave to enter into the UK; *fr. : ≈ agent d'immigration*
- island status : policy of the UK whereby it shows willingness to remain separate and function independently from the European continental mainland, thus remaining a "closed" island; *fr. : ≈ statut de nation insulaire*
- managed (adj.) migration (n.) : policy of the UK government to facilitate the migration of skilled workers and innovators whose skills could be beneficial to the country, thus permitting only certain categories of people to enter and stay; *fr. : émigration encadrée*
- overseas (n.) : countries abroad or situated across the seas; *fr. : étranger/ d'outre-mer*
- overstaying (n.) : act of extending one's stay (usually beyond the validity of a visa); *fr. : dépassement de la période de résidence autorisée*
- refugee (n.) : person seeking asylum in a foreign country due to political upheaval or persecution in his country of origin; *fr. : réfugié*
- Schengen zone agreement : zone permitting the free movement of people from the countries of the EU that have signed the agreement (agreement which the UK has not signed), thus enabling them to travel, live or work in the area covered by the treaty; *fr. : zone Schengen*
- unauthorised (adj.) migrant (n.) : irregular, clandestine, or undocumented with reference to migration; *fr. : migrant en situation irrégulière*

USEFUL EXPRESSIONS

- a skilled immigrant; *fr. : immigrant qualifié*
- to apply for asylum; *fr. : demander l'asile*
- to be vested with a power; *fr. : être investi d'un pouvoir*
- to emigrate to another country; *fr. : émigrer dans un autre pays*
- to migrate to another country; *fr. : migrer vers un autre pays*
- to repatriate illegal migrants to their country of origin; *fr. : rapatrier des migrants clandestins dans leur pays d'origine*
- to strip someone of his nationality; *fr. : déchoir quelqu'un de sa nationalité*
- to deport someone; *fr. : expulser quelqu'un*

FURTHER INFORMATION

- the word provision (*disposition*) refers to a stipulated condition in law and must not be confused with the act of providing or supplying goods or the French word *provision* that refers to funds, stock and supply
- the word mutual (*mutuel*) referring to a reciprocal relationship in English and French, must not be confused with the French noun *mutuelle* meaning private health insurance

Comparative approach

Si, contrairement à la France, le Royaume-Uni a refusé de signer l'accord de Schengen sur la libre circulation des personnes et de ratifier la directive européenne 2003/86/EC sur le droit au regroupement familial, les politiques de contrôle des migrations que leurs gouvernements respectifs appliquent sont assez similaires. D'ailleurs, lors d'un sommet franco-britannique qui s'est tenu le 6 juillet 2009, les représentants des gouvernements alors en place ont fait une déclaration commune sur l'immigration, réaffirmant solennellement leur engagement à lutter contre l'immigration clandestine.

□ 123 ASYLUM PROCESS AND APPEALS

In 2007, a new process of dealing with asylum claims called the New Asylum Model was set up in the UK. An asylum seeker is assigned a case owner before going through the following steps : screening interview, first reporting event and substantive interview. Alternatively he may be chosen for a fast track application process.

Refugee status is granted only if the asylum seeker can show that it is reasonably likely that his fear of being persecuted will materialise if he is forced to return to his country. Persecution could be for reasons of race, religion, nationality, membership of a particular social group or political opinion. A White list of safe countries of origin was drawn up which refers to the countries where there is no serious risk of persecution.

If an application for asylum is refused, the asylum seeker has the right to appeal to the First-Tier Tribunal (Asylum and Immigration Chamber). For onward appeals, they are made to the Upper Tribunal composed of specialist immigration judges. An appeal can be made on the grounds of racial discrimination, human rights violation or if the decision which is disputed does not comply with immigration legislation. This new two-tier system was set up by the Tribunals, Courts and Enforcement Act 2007.

After an unsuccessful application, the asylum seeker has to choose between the options of a voluntary return or an enforced removal. The Voluntary Assisted Return and Reintegration Programme (VARRP) is a scheme opened to asylum applicants whose application has been refused or who have been granted limited leave to remain. The VARRP offers a package help scheme to help rejected asylum seekers to set up a business, receive training or education to make a new beginning in the home country. The Assisted Voluntary Return of Irregular Migrants (AVRIM) is a programme for illegal immigrants not belonging to the EU, which makes travel arrangements and obtains travel documents for aliens. The Assisted Voluntary Return for Families and

Children (AVRFC) helps both asylum seekers and illegal or unauthorised migrants by offering help to families with at least one child under the age of 18, and for individuals under the age of 18.

GLOSSARY

- assign (v.) : delegate a task to someone; *fr. : confier à*
- assisted voluntary return : assistance offered to unsuccessful asylum applicants by the UK Border Agency to return to their country of origin and establish a new life; *fr. : aide au retour volontaire*
- asylum claim : application for protection by an asylum seeker made to the Secretary for State for the consideration of asylum or humanitarian protection; *fr. : demande d'asile*
- enforced (adj.) removal (n.) : act of forcefully evicting an unsuccessful asylum seeker from the UK by placing him in a detention centre and arranging for his removal; *fr. : éloignement forcé*
- fast track application : request for an asylum decision to be made within a week at one of the removal centres while the asylum seeker is held in detention; *fr. : ≈ procédure de demande accélérée*
- first reporting event : meeting organised to get the asylum applicant to meet the case owner who will deal with the case; *fr. : ≈ premier entretien*
- likelihood (n.) : possibility or probability of an occurrence; *fr. : probabilité*
- materialise (v.) : to become possible or real; *fr. : concrétiser*
- racial (adj.) discrimination (n.) : treating an individual abusively or differently on the grounds of race; *fr. : discrimination raciale*
- refugee status : protection granted to successful asylum seekers granting them authorisation to remain in the UK; *fr. : statut de réfugié*
- safe (adj.) country (n.) : country from which its inhabitants do not constantly flee for their lives and do not usually need protection under the Geneva Convention; *fr. : pays sûr*
- screening (adj.) interview (n.) : initial meeting with the asylum seeker in which the UK Border Agency runs checks to see if the applicant has made prior claims for asylum in the country, and attributes a reference number to the application; *fr. : ≈ entretien de filtrage*
- substantive (adj.) interview (n.) : asylum interview when the asylum applicant describes his case to the case owner and details the reasons for his fear of persecution in his home country; *fr. : ≈ entretien avec explication des motifs*
- White (adj.) list (n.) : list of countries considered as safe (as opposed to black liste) permitting UK Border agency to process applicants from such countries through the fast track system; *fr. : ≈ liste des pays sûrs*
- voluntary (adj.) return (n.) : option granted by the UK Border Agency to unsuccessful asylum seekers to return to their country of origin; *fr. : retour voluntaire*

USEFUL EXPRESSIONS

- to fill in/to complete an application; *fr. : remplir un formulaire de demande*
- to have a well-founded fear of being persecuted; *fr. : avoir une crainte fondée d'être persécuté*
- to make an asylum application; *fr. : introduire une demande d'asile*
- to meet someone by prior appointment; *fr. : rencontrer quelqu'un sur rendez-vous*

FURTHER INFORMATION

- the word application (*formulaire de demande*) meaning a document for making a request, must not be confused with the French word *application* referring to the action of implementing or enforcing a decision
- the word report (*faire un rapport*) refers to the action of informing someone of something at a specific meeting and must not be confused with the French word *report* that refers to the action of postponing an event

COMPARATIVE APPROACH

Le Royaume-Uni dispose de trois types de protection pour les réfugiés : asile conventionnel garanti par la Convention de Genève de 1951, asile pour motifs humanitaires basé sur la loi sur l'immigration de 1971 (complétée et modifiée presque chaque année depuis) et le permis de séjour discrétionnaire (*discretionary leave to remain*) si un demandeur d'asile ne remplit pas les conditions du statut de réfugié conventionnel ou pour motifs humanitaires).

En France, il existe aussi trois formes de protection : le statut de réfugié garanti par la Convention de Genève de 1951, la protection subsidiaire et le statut d'apatride. Le statut de réfugié est accordé par l'Office français de protection des réfugiés et apatrides (OFPRA) si une personne ne remplit pas les conditions d'octroi du statut. Le statut d'apatride est basé sur la Convention de New York de 1954 si aucun État ne considère le réfugié comme son ressortissant.

□ 124 BORDER CONTROLS

Asylum and border control policy and operations of the UK are managed by the UK Border Agency, which is an executive agency of the Home Office. It is responsible for managing immigration in the interests of the UK's security, social stability and economic growth. It considers applications from people who want to work and study in the country, deals with asylum and citizenship applications and facilitates the arrival of passengers to the UK. Of course, applications which are turned down may give rise to litigation.

The first stage of immigration control is the entry clearance operation managed overseas by UK visas which implements UK's immigration policy by facilitating legitimate entry and preventing entry for those who do not qualify under the Immigration Rules. There are different types of entry clearance that can grant permission to travel or enter the UK : visa, entry certificate, EEA family permit and exempt vignette.

The second stage which takes place at the borders (including ports or airports) involves Immigration Officers who check passports and examine arrivals to determine if people have the right of abode or the required leave to enter. These checks when performed before the person arrives in the UK are known as "exporting the border" as asylum seekers are checked before arrival. Recent initiatives include required carriers to check passengers' documents, using Airline Liaison Officers to carry out visa checks, and operating juxtaposed controls where Immigration Officers operate UK immigration controls at Eurostar check points and French ferry ports. The systems used for immigration controls are the Iris Recognition Immigration System (IRIS), biometric chipped passports and fingerprint checks.

In the final stage of immigration control, people who have been allowed to enter into the country can apply to the Home Office for permission to extend their existing leave to remain on the same conditions, switch to a different category or apply to settle in the UK.

GLOSSARY

- airline liaison officer : airline staff who have been trained to identify passengers who are not in possession of the appropriate documents to travel abroad; they have an awareness of UK passport and visa requirements; *fr. : officier de liaison aérienne*
- bio-metric chipped passport : e-passport with an additional security feature which contains a chip with the holder's facial biometric; *fr. : passeport biométrique*
- carrier (n.) : aircraft that transports passengers; *fr. : transporteur aérien*
- check point : pre-embarkation immigration posts where travel documents are verified before embarkation at a port or airport; *fr. : point de contrôle aux frontières*
- entry certificate : document authorising entry into the UK of non-visa nationals belonging to any other country outside the European Economic Area (EEA) and Switzerland; *fr. : certificat d'admission*
- entry clearance operation : process of authorising legitimate entry into the UK after verification of travel documents and authorisation to enter; *fr. : point d'autorisation d'entrée*

- EEA family permit : document granting family members of EEA nationals autorisation to enter into the UK; *fr. : ≈ titre de séjour délivré aux familles de l'EEE*
- exempt vignette : document authorising diplomats who are exempt from the requirements of the Immigration Act 1971 to enter into the UK; *fr. : vignette-visa/passeport diplomatique*
- fingerprint check : process of verifying finger prints with the relevant database before authorising someone to enter into the UK; *fr. : vérification des empreintes digitales*
- Iris recognition : automated method of biometric recognition that compares the patterns of the eye iris of an entrant with others stored in the relevant database to verify legal entry into the UK; *fr. : reconnaissance de l'iris*
- juxtaposed (adj.) controls (n.) : border clearance operations carried out at border crossings by two neighbouring customs administrations sharing physical and technical infrastructures; *fr. : postes de contrôle juxtaposés*
- switch (v. or n.) : change or move from one category to another; *fr. : changer/changement de catégorie*
- visa (n.) : document authorising entry into the UK to nationals of countries or territories listed in the Immigration Rules of the UK; *fr. : visa*

USEFUL EXPRESSIONS

- to check someone's travel documents; *fr. : vérifier les documents de voyage de quelqu'un*
- to extend someone's leave to remain; *fr. : prolonger le permis de séjour de quelqu'un*
- to go through border controls; *fr. : être contrôlé à la frontière*
- to obtain leave to enter; *fr. : obtenir une autorisation d'entrée*
- to qualify for immigration clearance; *fr. : recevoir l'autorisation d'immigrer*
- to require clearance; *fr. : nécessiter une autorisation*

FURTHER INFORMATION

- the word control (*contrôle ou vérification*) refers to clearance operations in both French and English and must not be confused with the other French meanings of tests, supervision and continuous assessment

COMPARATIVE APPROACH

Le Royaume-Uni n'a pas signé l'accord Schengen permettant la libre circulation des ressortissants et conserve donc le droit de contrôler les personnes à ses frontières. Il participe seulement à la coopération judiciaire et policière en droit pénal, et au *Schengen Information System* (Système d'information Schengen) (SIS) en menant une lutte contre les stupéfiants.

En tant qu'un des pays fondateurs qui a signé les premiers accords de l'espace Schengen en 1985, la France autorise la libre circulation des ressortissants des États signataires et pays associés qui sont dispensés de présenter un visa pour entrer en France. Le fichier européen du SIS, un réseau informatique composé d'une section centrale (C. SIS) située à Strasbourg et de sections nationales dans chacun des pays Schengen, permet aux autorités françaises (police, garde-frontières, ambassades) de disposer de données sur les personnes, les véhicules à surveiller et les objets volés ou disparus.

□ 125 DEPRIVATION OF NATIONALITY

According to the Immigration Asylum and Nationality Act 2006, the Secretary of State may deprive a dual national British citizen of his citizenship if it is considered conducive to the public good, if he is found guilty of having obtained registration or naturalisation by fraud or of disloyalty or disaffection to Her Majesty, of helping an enemy in time of war, or of having committed a criminal offence within five years of obtaining citizenship. This power of deprivation may apply to those who are citizens by birth provided they have another nationality (and not rendered stateless), to naturalised or registered citizens but also to people of migrant descent. It is a way of not testing allegiance to Britain by bloodline, but by laying emphasis on a judgement that is based on loyalty to the country.

The Secretary of State issues a deprivation order. The person concerned will cease to hold a British passport. Appeal rights have to be exercised (within 28 days) from outside the UK in these circumstances. In most cases, these appeals involve security issues in the UK and are heard by the Special Immigration Appeals Commission in secret.

GLOSSARY

- allegiance (n.) : obligation of loyalty to one's country; *fr. : allégeance*
- bloodline (n.) : direct descent or act of tracing ancestry; *fr. : lignée*
- cease (v.) : to stop or discontinue; *fr. : cesser*
- citizenship (n.) : see 61
- conducive (adj.) : favourable to or contributing to; *fr. : favorable à/propice à*
- deprive (v.) : to remove, withdraw or take away; *fr. : priver de*
- deprivation order : here, decision taken by the Home Secretary removing someone's British nationality; *fr. : acte de déchéance de nationalité*

- disaffection (n.) : here, state of losing affection, respect or love for one's country; *fr. : désaffection*
- disloyalty (n.) : act of not being faithful and loyal to someone or to one's country; *fr. : déloyauté*
- dual national British citizen : person who possesses two nationalities and pledges allegiance to both countries; *fr. : citoyen britannique ayant une double nationalité*
- fraud (n.) : act of being deceptive and falsely representing facts by words or by actions; *fr. : fraude*
- lack (n.) : state of falling short of the required criterion; *fr. : manque*
- naturalisation (n.) : see 61
- public (adj.) good (n.) : act or commodity that contributes to the general welfare and wellbeing of society at large; *fr. : bien public*
- registration (n.) : see 61
- stateless (adj.) : here, relating to a situation where an asylum seeker has no nationality and no state to find refuge; *fr. : apatride*

USEFUL EXPRESSIONS

- to appeal to the Home Secretary; *fr. : relever appel auprès du Ministre de l'Intérieur*
- to be protected against arbitrary deprivation of nationality; *fr. : être protégé contre la déchéance arbitraire de la nationalité*
- to conceal facts from immigration authorities; *fr. : dissimuler des faits aux services d'immigration*
- to deprive someone of his nationality; *fr. : priver quelqu'un de sa nationalité*
- to exercise one's right to appeal; *fr. : exercer son droit de recours*
- to hold a passport; *fr. : être muni/être titulaire d'un passeport*

FURTHER INFORMATION

- the word offence (*infraction*) must not be confused with the French word *offense* referring to the action of insulting someone

Comparative approach

Au Royaume-Uni la procédure de déchéance de nationalité est appliquée systématiquement en cas de préjudice sérieux aux intérêts vitaux du pays (haute trahison ou *high treason*, espionnage or *spying* ou terrorisme ou *terrorism*). En revanche, en France, cette procédure est très rarement appliquée. Seuls les citoyens naturalisés condamnés à certaines infractions précises considérées comme des actes préjudiciables aux intérêts de la France (comme le terrorisme) risquent d'être déchus.

☐ 126 IMMIGRATION ENFORCEMENT

Power to detain

It is a statutory power found in the Immigration Act 1971 and in the Nationality, Immigration and Asylum Act 2002. This power is vested in Home Office officials and Immigration Officers (IOs) although in the latter case it is usually exercised by a Chief Immigration Officer. IOs' detention powers derive from their border control functions. Detention takes place in a detention centre also called Immigration Removal Centre. Unauthorised or illegal migrants (such as overstayers or asylum seekers whose application was turned down) cannot be detained in prisons with convicted prisoners. Immigration detainees have a right to apply for bail, but do not have a right to bail as in criminal cases.

Removal power and deportation

The Crown has the power to control the entry of aliens in the UK. The Immigration Act 1971, the Asylum and Immigration Act 1996, the Immigration and Asylum Act 1999 and the Nationality Immigration and Asylum Act 2002 have set the statutory limits for that removal power. Illegal or unauthorised immigrants in the UK who do not opt for a voluntary or assisted return, are liable to be arrested, detained and their departure from the UK can be enforced. The basic enforcement procedures are administrative removal and deportation. Extradition can be carried out after a Deportation Order is issued by the Home Secretary.

Litigation

Upon receiving a decision ordering him to be detained, deported, removed or extradited, the person concerned can dispute the relevant decision before the two-tier tribunal structure introduced by the Tribunals, Courts and Enforcement Act 2007.

GLOSSARY

- administrative (adj.) removal (n.) : removal on the same grounds as in cases of deportation, but is classified as "administrative" to distinguish it from deportation which has an enduring legal effect, as appeals in this case can be made again from a country outside the UK; *fr. : ≈ arrêté de reconduite à la frontière*
- bail (n.) : sum of money given to secure the release of a detainee provided that he promises to appear before the immigration services on the set date; *fr. : libération sous caution*
- convicted (adj.) prisoner (n.) : person found guilty of a criminal offence; *fr. : détenu condamné*
- deportation (n.) : act of removing an illegal alien from a country; *fr. : expulsion*

- deportation order : order requiring an illegal or unauthorised alien to leave the country and authorising his detention until his removal; *fr. : ordonnance d'expulsion*
- detention (n.) : act of restricting the freedom of movement of refugees whose application for leave to remain in the UK is being processed or has been denied pending removal; *fr. : rétention administrative*
- enforcement (n.) : here, act of regulating the entry of unauthorised aliens by taking the necessary administrative steps such as removal, deportation or extradition; *fr. : exécution (d'une mesure ou disposition)*
- extradition (n.) : process of transferring an illegal alien to his country of origin or to another country which agrees to offer him refuge; *fr. : extradition*
- Immigration Removal Centre/detention centre : area containing accommodation and medical facilities to house unauthorised aliens awaiting deportation orders or whilst their application for a visa is in process; *fr. : centre de rétention administrative*
- invalidate (v.) : to nullify or make invalid a decision; *fr. : invalider*
- statutory (adj.) : relating to a statute or drawing legislative value; *fr. : législatif*

USEFUL EXPRESSIONS

- to deport illegal migrants; *fr. : expulser des immigrants clandestins*
- to enforce a deportation order; *fr. : exécuter une ordonnance d'expulsion*
- the removal of an illegal immigrant; *fr. : mesure d'éloignement/expulsion d'un immigré clandestin*
- to exercise a right; *fr. : exercer un droit*
- to opt for assisted voluntary return; *fr. : opter pour l'assistance au retour volontaire*

FURTHER INFORMATION

- the word bail (*liberté sous caution*) must not be confused with the French word *bail* referring to a lease
- the word prohibition (*interdiction*) meaning an act of forbidding someone from doing something, must not be confused with the French word *prohibition* referring only to the prohibition of drugs and alcohol

COMPARATIVE APPROACH

La durée de rétention administrative (*detention*) des migrants en instance d'éloignement (*pending deportation*) varie dans les pays de l'Union européenne. Avec seulement trente-deux jours, la durée maximale de privation de liberté en France est la plus courte en Europe. Quant au Royaume-Uni, aucune durée maximale n'a été fixée à la date de mise sous presse du présent ouvrage.

12

Family litigation

□ 127 DIVORCE AND DISSOLUTION

A marriage or a civil partnership can be ended in several ways – upon the death of one of the spouses or partners, when a decree of divorce is issued or a civil partnership is terminated, or when a marriage is held to be void or voidable by a court of law.

Ending a marriage or a civil partnership

In some cases when a marriage is not valid, courts can annul a marriage which can be held to be either void or voidable, or considered as non-marriage. A decree of nullity can be issued.

A petition for divorce can be filed only after one year of marriage. When filing the petition or applying for the termination of a civil partnership, the petitioner has to prove that there is an irretrievable breakdown of the marriage or partnership by choosing one of five grounds : adultery, unreasonable behaviour, desertion, two years' or five years' separation. In England and Wales, pleading irreconcilable differences is not ground for divorce. If the respondent disagrees with the facts alleged by the petitioner, he can defend the divorce. Since this kind of proceedings can be time consuming, very expensive and uncertain, 99 % of divorcing couples opt for an undefended divorce. The special procedure for undefended divorce enables the parties not to attend the hearing; their case is decided on a piece of paper.

Civil partnerships are dissolved the same way as marriages, except that adultery is not part of the grounds to prove that the relationship has irretrievably broken down. The Marriage (Same-Sex Couples) Act 2013 did not extend adultery as a ground for the divorce of same-sex couples.

Court procedure

In case of a marriage breakdown and further to the petition of one of the spouses, Family courts (county courts or the Family Division of the High Court) can either issue an order of judicial separation, decide the dissolution of a civil partnership or put an end to a marriage by delivering first a decree nisi, and then a decree absolute of divorce. The court is entitled to refuse to grant a divorce if the two parties failed to agree on matters related to the children, such as rights of contact, residence or shared parenting. In case of disagreement over financial issues, the divorce process will be slowed down but not stopped. The judge will then decide about the financial arrangements (such as the distribution of assets and the possible payment of (spousal) maintenance – formerly called alimony – by one spouse to the other one). The formal divorce can be finalised before the completion of the financial arrangement.

GLOSSARY

- adultery (n.) : when one of the spouses has had sexual intercourse with a third party of the opposite sex during marriage; *fr. : adultère*
- annulment (n.) : the court has the power to annul a marriage when it has been proved that it was void or voidable; *fr. : annulation d'un mariage*
- assets (n.) : see 62
- decree absolute : document that legally ends a marriage; *fr. : jugement de prononcé du divorce*
- decree of nullity : order issued by a judge stating that the marriage was not valid in the first place; *fr. : ≈ ordonnance de nullité*
- decree nisi : legal document stating that the court sees no reason why the couple cannot divorce; *fr. : ordonnance de non-conciliation*
- desertion (n.) : the respondent has left the matrimonial residence for a minimum of two years immediately preceding the filing of the petition for divorce; *fr. : désertion du domicile conjugal*
- dissolution of a civil partnership : legal termination of the civil partnership entered into by same-sex partners; *fr. : ≈ rupture de la convention de Pacs*
- divorce (n.) : legal termination of a marital union; *fr. : divorce*
- divorce settlement : legal agreement reached by a divorcing couple, describing how the assets will be divided and providing for the custody of the child(ren); *fr. : convention de divorce*
- irreconcilable (adj.) differences (n.) : serious conflicts that a married couple cannot overcome, inevitably leading to a separation; *fr. : incompatibilité d'humeur*
- irretrievable (adj.) breakdown (n.) : the legal separation of the married couple cannot be avoided despite all the efforts of conciliation; *fr. : altération définitive du lien conjugal*
- judicial (adj.) separation (n.) : court order which does not terminate the marriage, but enables the spouses to live separately; *fr. : séparation de corps*
- maintenance (n.)/spousal (adj.) maintenance (n.) : formerly called alimony, amount of money given to the former spouse to compensate the financial loss incurred by the divorce; *fr. : prestation compensatoire*
- marital (adj.) breakdown (n.) : when the marital union is over and the two parties cannot be reconciled; *fr. : rupture des liens du mariage*

- non-marriage (n.) : legal concept developed by the courts to annul a marriage where parties have failed to comply with the formalities such as notice of marriage, which is different from a voidable marriage; *fr. : ≈ mariage putatif*
- order for financial provision : if one of the spouses fails to support the other financially or fails to comply with a court order, he can make an application to the court for an order obliging the other party to comply with his matrimonial duty; *fr. : ordonnance d'exécution* (or) *de recouvrement public de la pension alimentaire*
- petitioner (n.) : when applied to divorce proceedings, spouse who issues a petition with the court, seeking a divorce order; *fr. : époux demandeur*
- residence (n.) : home where the child of divorced parents live on a permanent basis with his primary carer; *résidence habituelle de l'enfant*
- respondent (n.) : when applied to divorce proceedings, spouse who defends the divorce petition; *fr. : époux défendeur*
- right of contact : right granted to the parent who is not the primary carer of the child and who has the right to spend time with him; *fr. : droit de visite*
- shared (adj.) parenting (n.)/residency (n.) : court decision whereby each parent has equal right regarding the child's residence; usually, the child lives with one of his parents every other week; *fr. : garde alternée*
- undefended (adj.) divorce (n.) : divorce in which the respondent is not opposed to the grounds on which the petition is based; *fr. : divorce par consentement mutuel*
- termination (n.) : when applied to civil partnership, the legal ending of the partnership; *fr. : ≈ rupture de la convention de Pacs*
- unreasonable (adj.) behaviour (n.) : when the respondent has behaved or is behaving in such a way that the petitioner cannot live with his spouse/partner any more; *fr. : ≈ incompatibilité d'humeur*
- void (adj.) marriage (n.) : a marriage will be considered as void if the parties lack capacity to enter into such a union, for instance, if one of the spouses is under the age of sixteen or is already legally married to someone else at the time of the celebration; *fr. : mariage nul (nullité absolue)*
- voidable (adj.) marriage (n.) : a marriage can be deemed voidable when it has not been consummated or when one of the spouses did not validly consent to the marriage, or when one of the parties suffers from a mental disorder making him or her unfit for marriage; *fr. : mariage nul (nullité relative)*

USEFUL EXPRESSIONS

- to apply to court for a divorce; *fr. : déposer au tribunal une demande de divorce*
- to break up a marriage; *fr. : détruire un mariage*
- to file a divorce petition with the court; *fr. : déposer une demande de divorce auprès du tribunal*
- to grant judicial separation; *fr. : ordonner la séparation légale*

- to get a divorce; *fr. : divorcer*
- the marriage has irretrievably broken down; *fr. : le mariage est irrévocablement terminé*

FURTHER INFORMATION

- custody/access : even though custody is still used today in everyday life, in legal texts, this term was replaced by residence; access has also become contact
- contrary to England and Wales, irreconcilable differences can be pleaded in most states of the United States as valid grounds for divorce
- contrary to the French system of legal aid (*aide juridictionnelle*) in which the French state actually funds the legal action or defence of a litigant subject to complying with a means and merits test, the legal aid system applicable in England and Wales is similar to a loan of public funds; a clawback applies which means that the loan will be reimbursed by the litigant if he benefits from it, in the event of (for example) financial compensation being awarded; in the context of a divorce, many legally aided spouses who recovered assets saw these assets used by the state to reimburse the loan of public funds made by way of legal aid

COMPARATIVE APPROACH

Les procédures de divorce anglaise et française reposent sur une différence fondamentale : les motifs du divorce (*grounds for divorce*). En Angleterre et au Pays de Galles, même lorsque les époux se séparent d'un commun accord, ils doivent donner une raison pour que le juge accorde le divorce. Sans motif, le juge ne peut pas prononcer la fin du mariage ou de l'union entre homosexuels.

En France, le divorce par consentement mutuel est un divorce consensuel, qui n'est soumis à aucune durée minimale du mariage et repose sur l'accord des parties. Les parties soumettent au juge aux affaires matrimoniales une convention réglant toutes les conséquences pratiques du divorce pour eux (telles que le paiement d'une éventuelle prestation compensatoire) et leurs enfants (paiement d'une pension alimentaire). Outre-Manche, la procédure de *undefended divorce* est ce qui s'apparente le plus au divorce par consentement mutuel avec la procédure française de divorce pour acceptation du principe de la rupture du mariage, dit divorce demandé/accepté.

En France, le divorce pour faute, telle que l'adultère (*adultery*) est en voie de disparition, tout comme la procédure de divorce pour adultère Outre-Manche, du fait de son extrême complexité qui fait durer la procédure. Le divorce pour altération définitive du lien conjugal (*irretrievable breakdown*), possible après 2 ans de vie commune, se rapproche autant que possible des procédures applicables Outre-Manche après une séparation de fait de 2 ou 5 ans, ou encore, éventuellement, de la procédure pour *unreasonable behaviour*.

□ 128 DIVORCE AND CHILDREN

While most divorcing couples manage to reach an agreement over contact arrangements and financial issues, the animosity between parents can give rise to complex cases in court. The issue of child maintenance will be discussed in a chapter below.

Section 8 orders

In the event of a dispute over children, the parents can apply for a section 8 order under the Children Act 1989. A judge can issue different kinds of orders which are primarily related to residence, contact, order of specific issue or prohibited steps. A residence order determines where the child is to live and who the resident and non-resident parents are. It is now possible to apply for a joint residence order which grants residence to both parents every other week provided the parents live in the same area and the child can go to the same school. A contact order allows the non-resident parent to have contact with his child, usually every other week-end. Specific issue orders are granted in particular cases, such as when a child needs some medical treatment. Prohibited steps orders are applied for when one parent wants to prevent the other from performing a certain action, such as circumcision or removing the child from the country.

Welfare of the child

When an application for a section 8 order is made to the court, the welfare of the child is invariably the paramount consideration for judges. They take into account the child's age, sex, background, his ascertainable wishes and feelings, his physical and emotional needs. They can give weight to the child's views.

Enforcement

Enforcing orders may be more complex than issuing them. Many resident parents refuse to follow the court's decision and breach the order, usually because they fear that the non-resident parent will be violent towards the child. The court can issue orders to oblige the resident parent to allow contact with the other parent. Contact activity directions or conditions can be added to the contact order. They aim at encouraging communication and agreement between the parents through counselling or parenting classes. A judge can ask the Children and Family Court Advisory and Support Service (Cafcass) to supervise the parent's compliance with the order. Money can be used as a way of punishing the parents such as requiring unpaid work or ordering compensation for financial loss.

GLOSSARY

- ascertainable (adj.) wish (n.) : wish that can be expressed by a child who has reached a certain level of maturity to understand the consequences of his choices; *fr. : ≈ capacité de discernement*

- child (adj.) maintenance (n.)/maintenance (n.) : amount of money paid by the non-resident parent to the primary carer of the child to meet with the expenses related to the child; *fr. : pension alimentaire*
- compensation (n.) : here and in the case of breach of a contact order, a judge can oblige the resident parent to pay a sum of money to the other parent to cover any costs incurred by planned activities with the child that could not take place because of the resident parent's failure to allow contact; *fr. : compensation financière*
- contact activity condition : mandatory requirement added to the contact order by the judge; it can include attendance at parenting classes or anger management courses; *fr. : ≈ obligation afférante au droit de visite*
- contact activity direction : recommendation added to the contact order by the judge; it aims at improving contact with the child through counselling or parenting classes; *fr. : ≈ médiation familiale*
- contact arrangement : agreement reached by the divorcing parents over the child's residence and contact with the non-resident parent; *fr. : ≈ convention fixant les conditions du droit de visite et d'hébergement*
- contact order : court decision whereby the residential parent has to allow contact between the child and the other parent (or grand-parent); *fr. : droit de visite*
- enforcement (n.) : here, ways of executing a particular order; *fr. : exécution*
- joint residence order : court decision allowing divorcing parents to live with their child half of the time; *fr. : ordonnance autorisant la garde alternée*
- non-resident (adj.) parent (n.) : parent who does not live with the child on a permanent basis; *fr. : parent qui n'a pas la garde*
- prohibited steps order : court decision preventing one parent from doing something to a child; e. g circumcising a child while the other parent is opposed to it, or removing the child from the country; *fr. : ≈ ordonnance faisant interdiction au titulaire de la responsabilité parentale de prendre certaines mesures*
- residence order : court decision defining who will be the primary carer of the child and where he or she will live; *fr. : ordonnance fixant la résidence habituelle de l'enfant*
- resident (adj.) parent (n.) : parent who is the primary carer of the child and lives with him on a permanent basis; *fr. : parent qui a la garde principale*
- specific issue order : court decision requiring that a particular action be carried out in relation to the child (e.g., going to a specific school); *fr. : ≈ ordonnance relative à l'éducation de l'enfant*
- unpaid work requirement : here and in case of a breach of a contact order, court order requiring the resident parent to carry out unpaid work so as to punish him; *fr. : ≈ obligation de faire des travaux d'intérêt général*
- welfare (n.) : well-being; *fr. : bien-être/intérêt*

USEFUL EXPRESSIONS

- removal of children from jurisdiction; *fr. : ≈ sortie des enfants du territoire*

FURTHER INFORMATION

- over the past few years, groups such as Fathers 4 Justice have defended fathers' rights of contact and residence over their children in spectacular and publicity-seeking ways

COMPARATIVE APPROACH

La garde des enfants (*access*) peut toujours devenir une question épineuse lors des divorces dans les deux pays. La solution de la garde alternée, longtemps rejetée par la Cour de cassation, mais désormais largement ordonnée, est davantage adoptée en France qu'Outre-Manche où les juges anglais demeurent réticents à accorder ce mode de garde. En France, en cas de non présentation de l'enfant, l'un des parents peut porter plainte. La loi française considère la non présentation d'enfant comme un délit passible d'une peine d'emprisonnement ou d'une amende. En Angleterre et au Pays de Galles, le non respect d'une ordonnance peut également être sanctionné par une peine d'emprisonnement. Cependant, étant donné que les juges estiment que l'emprisonnement du parent fautif serait contre-productif, des mesures intermédiaires d'ordre financier (*unpaid work requirement* ou *compensation for financial loss*) ou de conciliation (*contact activity direction or condition*) ont été créées.

□ 129 DIVORCE AND FINANCIAL ISSUES

Agreement and mediation

When separating, parents usually try to reach an agreement over finances and child maintenance. They may apply to the Child Maintenance Service for a calculation of the financial support the non-resident parent (or the paying parent) has to pay each month to the primary carer (the receiving parent) to meet with the child(ren)'s upkeep. These services are also responsible for collecting unpaid child maintenance. They are allowed to take a number of steps such as taking money from the paying parent's income, benefits or bank account, and can even issue proceedings against them. Once an agreement has been reached, the divorcing couple usually apply for a consent order from the court. They both submit their agreement to the judge who checks its contents and if satisfied, ratifies the consent order by signing it. In case of disagreement between the former spouses, it is necessary to go through a family mediation with a mediator to solve any outstanding problem.

Court proceedings

When the mediation has failed, the divorcing couple can apply for a financial order (previously known as ancillary relief order). The claimant can seek a court order that his former spouse be ordered to make a lump sum payment, grant him ownership of a property, pay him maintenance or give him a share on a pension payment.

The courts have discretionary powers to redistribute property and to order financial support for the spouse and the children. Before issuing a financial order, the judge considers various factors. The age of the spouses and the years they remained married can have a great impact on how the marital assets are divided. When a couple remained married for a long time, all the assets will be divided. The standard of living, the financial needs, the income and even the future earning capacity of one of the spouses can lead judges to redistribute property and assets in very different ways. They do not distinguish between the money earner and the child-carer or home-maker.

A court can order one of the former spouses to make a periodic payment to the other one (usually monthly instalments) or a lump sum order or a property adjustment order for the financial support of a child whether the parents were married or not. Judges can also alter the ownership of property in the case of separation of a cohabiting couple. Although judges always try to be as fair as possible, their priority is always the welfare of children and maintenance payment.

GLOSSARY

- ancillary relief order : name formerly given to a court's financial order which is ancillary to the actual divorce order; the court determines the financial compensation which one of the former spouses may have to pay to the other former spouse and/or towards the upkeep of the former couple's children; *fr. : ≈ ordonnance statuant sur les mesures financières dans le cadre d'un divorce/≈ liquidation du régime matrimonial*
- child-carer (n.) : here, parent looking after the child on a daily basis during marriage; *fr. : ≈ époux au foyer*
- child maintenance : financial compensation given to the spouse who is the primary carer of the child(ren); *fr. : pension alimentaire*
- consent order : here, document agreed upon by the parties which becomes binding when signed by the court (to which it is submitted) once the divorcing couple has agreed over a number of issues (e.g. financial issues); *fr. : ≈ homologation de la convention entre époux*
- earning capacity : individual's power to earn money according to his skills and/or experience; *fr. : capacité à gagner*
- financial (adj.) order (n.) : see ancillary relief order; *fr. : ≈ ordonnance statuant sur les mesures financières dans le cadre d'un divorce/≈ liquidation de la communauté*

- home-maker (n.) : spouse in charge of the upkeep of the house; *fr. : ≈ ménagère/époux au foyer*
- income (n.) : money earned by one of the parties through work, investments, rent, etc.; *fr. : revenu*
- instalments (n.) : amount of money paid on a regular basis (usually weekly or monthly); *fr. : rente*
- lump (adj.) sum (n.) : once and for all payment; *fr. : capital*
- marital (adj.) assets (n.) : any property acquired during marriage, such as house, bonds, goods or insurance; *fr. : biens du ménage*
- money earner : spouse providing for the main part or the whole of the family's income; *fr. : soutien de famille*
- periodic payments order (PPO) : here, court decision fixing the amount of money that must be paid, usually on a monthly basis, to the other spouse; *fr. : ordonnance fixant le paiement d'une rente*
- primary (adj.) carer (n.) : parent who lives with the child(ren) on a permanent basis; *fr. : parent qui a la garde*
- property adjustment order : court decision requiring the transfer of one or all property from one spouse to the other; for example, the matrimonial home can be given to the wife so that she and the children can live there; *fr. : ≈ attribution d'un bien dans le cadre de la liquidation de la communauté*
- redistribute (v.) : divide up assets; *fr. : liquider*
- standard of living : level of lifestyle calculated by wealth, material comfort; *fr. : niveau de vie*
- upkeep (n.) : everything related to the education of a child; *fr. : éducation*

USEFUL EXPRESSIONS

- to pay alimony to a former spouse; *fr. : être redevable d'une prestation compensatoire au bénéfice de son ancien époux*
- to be the breadwinner of the family; *fr. : être le soutien de famille*

FURTHER INFORMATION

- "clean-break" order : when applying for a consent order in a divorce action, it implies that the financial issues are definitely settled and that both ex-spouses waive their right to make any further claim on each other

COMPARATIVE APPROACH

Contrairement à la France, le droit applicable en Angleterre et au Pays de Galles ne connaît pas l'existence de régimes matrimoniaux. Dès lors, les règles de liquidation du mariage seront différentes. En France, les questions telles que la liquidation du régime matrimonial, l'autorité parentale, l'entretien, l'éducation et l'hébergement des enfants, font en général l'objet d'un seul et même jugement. En revanche, Outre-Manche, le prononcé du divorce et les questions dites accessoires sont traitées successivement.

□ 130 GUARDIANSHIP

Guardianship is the general term referring to any situations when it is necessary to appoint a person – a guardian – to take care of a child or a person whose mental capacities have been altered.

Deputyship is related to adults who lack the mental capacity to manage their assets, property or even their health because of health impairment for example. An adult can anticipate the moment when his mental capacities will be affected by legally appointing a Lasting Power of Attorney – the donor gives authority to a donee to take care of his assets and his health in the future. When the person's mental capacities are diminished, the Court of Protection appoints a deputy to manage the person's assets and/or health for a limited period and under strict conditions described in the deputy order. The deputy's actions are then supervised by the Office of the Public Guardian. When the adult depends on state benefits, the Department of Work and Pensions chooses an appointee. When no relative is available or willing to become a deputy, the Court of Protection appoints a panel deputy. Standard authorisations are usually issued by the court, but a judge can deliver an urgent authorisation in the case of an accident.

GLOSSARY

- appointee (n) : here, person who is given the authority by the Department of Work and Pensions to manage the state benefits of mentally incapable adults; *fr. : ≈ mandataire judiciaire (protégeant l'incapable majeur)*
- Court of Protection : specialist court hearing cases related to the protection of people lacking mental capacity. It is a superior court with the same authority as the High Court. Appeals to this court's decisions lie in the Court of Appeal; *fr. : ≈ juge des tutelles près le tribunal d'instance*
- deputy (n.) : here, person – either a member of the family or a friend – appointed by the Court of Protection to manage the assets, savings, property or the welfare of adults lacking mental capacity; *fr. : ≈ curateur & tuteur*
- deputy order : here, legal document issued by a judge sitting in the Court of Protection, describing the powers of the deputy; *fr. : ≈ ordonnance du juge des tutelles*
- deputyship (n.) : legal system authorising someone to act on someone's behalf; *fr. : ≈ curatelle & tutelle*

- donee (n.) : in the case of an LPA, person receiving the authority to act on a person's behalf in the future; *fr. : mandataire*
- donor (n.) : in the case of an LPA, person giving the authority to someone else to act on his behalf in the future; *fr. : mandant*
- guardian (n.) : person who is given legal responsibility for a child whose parents are both deceased or when the legal responsibility of the parent(s) has been suspended; *fr. : tuteur*
- guardianship (n.) : general term to define the jurisdiction regulating guardians and deputies; *fr. : protection juridique des incapables (majeurs ou mineurs)*
- Lasting Power of Attorney (LPA) : legal document in which an individual – the donor – gives authority to someone – the donee – to act on his behalf when his mental capacity is altered, whether it be for his property and affairs or/and his personal welfare; *fr. : mandat de protection future*
- Local Social Services Authority (LSSA) : local body managing guardianship applications among other things; *fr. : ≈ direction départemantale de la cohésion sociale (DDCS)*
- Office of the Public Guardian : state service supervising and supporting court-appointed deputies; *fr. : ≈ greffier du juge des tutelles près le tribunal d'instance*
- panel deputy : approved professional deputy who can be referred to by the Court of Protection when no relative or friends were found to act as a deputy; *fr. : ≈ mandataire judiciaire à la protection des incapables majeurs*
- standard (adj.) authorisation (n.) : here, order whereby the adult lacking capacity is deprived of some of his liberties for a limited period; *fr. : ≈ mise sous curatelle ou tutelle*
- urgent (adj.) authorisation (n.) : here, order whereby the adult lacking capacity is deprived of some of his liberties in cases of emergency; *fr. : ≈ sauvegarde de justice*

USEFUL EXPRESSIONS

- to act on someone's behalf; *fr. : agir au nom de quelqu'un*
- to apply to the Court of Protection; *fr. : déposer une demande auprès du juge des tutelles*
- a ward of the state; *fr. : un pupille de l'État*

FURTHER INFORMATION

- the word guardian should not be confused with the French *gardien*
- tutor and the French *tuteur* (guardian) are not synonyms; in British universities, a tutor is someone who teaches students during face-to-face sessions (≈ *professeur particulier*)

COMPARATIVE APPROACH

Il y a une différence primordiale entre les systèmes de protection des incapables majeurs applicables en France et Outre-Manche. S'il y a trois modes de protection en France (sauvegarde de justice, curatelle et tutelle), il n'y en a vraiment qu'un en Angleterre et au Pays de Galles (procédure de *guardianship*). Dans les deux pays, l'idée est de sauvegarder la liberté de l'individu et de faire en sorte que la mesure de protection juridique soit la moins contraignante possible. Outre-Manche et afin d'éviter tout abus, un organisme indépendant (*Office of the Public Guardian*) a été créé afin de surveiller les actes des curateurs/tuteurs, mais aussi de les conseiller. Il n'existe pas d'équivalent direct de ce service en France où cependant, le tuteur doit remettre un rapport de ses activités au greffier du juge des tutelles.

□ 131 PROTECTING CHILDREN

The United Nations Convention on the Rights of the Child and the European Convention on Human Rights (ECHR) indicate that all the states have a duty to protect children from violence and abuse and should take all the necessary steps to meet this target. However, removing a child from his family is always a very delicate issue and courts have to take into account the welfare of the child and assess the impact of any order on his life. The role of the local authorities is of paramount importance. Before making any order, judges have to assess if the child is suffering or likely to suffer any harm, ill-treatment or any sexual abuse, and whether his emotional or physical development is not impaired. A local authority can apply for four types of order. In court, the council social worker presents a report while a guardian appointed by the Children and Family Court Advisory and Support Service (Cafcass) can represent the child's interests. Some parents might opt for a voluntary placement avoiding any court proceedings.

Care order

When a local council suspects that a child is not receiving proper care or is in serious danger, it can apply for a care order so as to place the child in foster care or in a children's home when no relative is available. The parents' parental responsibility is not extinguished as social services are expected to maintain contact between the child and his parents. Care proceedings are usually carried out in the long term starting with an interim care order. Nevertheless, the local authority is not obliged to remove the child from his family straightaway, but can do so at any time without applying for a new order.

Supervision order

This type of order aims at appointing a supervisor to advise and help the child who is not removed from his family. Should the family fail to comply with this order, the local authority can apply for a care order.

Emergency protection order

In some exceptional circumstances, a judge can deliver an emergency protection order when the child's safety is at stake. This is a last resort option. Notice of application is not compulsory. The order is limited to an eight-day period which can be extended to a further seven days. In emergency cases, the police also have the authority to remove any child from his home for a maximum period of 72 hours.

Child assessment order

While a local authority can provide support and accommodation to children in need, it can sometimes apply for a child assessment order to carry out a medical and/or psychiatric assessment of a child.

GLOSSARY

- care order : court decision whereby parental responsibility is transferred to a local authority without putting an end to the parental rights of the parents; *fr. : ≈ placement d'un enfant (sur décision judiciaire)*
- child assesment order : court decision requiring that the child be assessed by a doctor and/or a psychiatrist; *fr. : ≈ ordonnance de suivi médical de l'enfant*
- council social worker : official representative working for the Social Services; *fr. : assistante sociale*
- children's home : home administered by the local council or a private institution or a charitable organisation; *fr. : ≈ établissement habilité par le Conseil général pour l'accueil temporaire ou permanent d'enfants*
- emergency protection order : court decision whereby parental responsibility is transferred to the applicant for a limited period of time, usually fifteen days; *fr. : ≈ ordonnance de protection d'urgence*
- foster carer : here, family where the child will live for a certain period of time before a judge decides where his permanent residence will be; *fr. : famille d'accueil*
- interim care order : court decision issued at the outset of care proceedings lasting up to eight weeks, and which can be renewed for one year; *fr. : ≈ ordonnance de placement temporaire*
- placement (n.) : here, court decision consisting in removing a child from his family so as to allow him to stay with a foster carer for a fixed period of time; *fr. : placement*
- Social Services : body run by local councils to advise, help and supervise families in need; *fr. : ≈ services sociaux*
- supervision order : court decision whereby a social worker is in charge of supervising a child for up to one year; *fr. : ≈ mesure d'assistance éducative*
- voluntary (adj.) placement (n.) : when parents are temporarily unable to raise their children, they can agree to place their children in foster care; *fr. : ≈ placement volontaire d'un enfant*
- welfare (n.) : see 128

USEFUL EXPRESSIONS

- to live with foster parents; *fr. : vivre avec une famille d'accueil*
- to be put up in a home; *fr. : être hébergé dans une maison d'accueil*

FURTHER INFORMATION

- there should be no confusion between children's homes and borstal homes which used to be a type of youth detention centre (where children were usually ordered to go as punishment for an offence); the borstals homes would have been the equivalent of the former French *maisons de correction*

COMPARATIVE APPROACH

Les services de l'aide à l'enfance sont gérés localement dans les trois pays, par le Conseil général en France et par le *local council* en Angleterre et au Pays de Galles. Les procédures de placement se ressemblent. Cependant, en France, il n'existe pas d'organisme indépendant comme le *Cafcass* (*Children and Family Court Advisory and Support Service*) pour évaluer le travail des assistantes sociales et pour représenter les droits de l'enfant. Seule l'IGAS (Inspection générale des affaires sociales), service interministériel, rend des rapports annuels sur les activités des services à l'enfance, mais elle n'agit pas localement ni de façon directe. Outre-Manche, les établissements accueillant des enfants en placement peuvent être gérés par les autorités publiques que sont les *local councils* ou par des instituts privés ou organismes caritatifs (*charities*). En France, ces établissements sont sous la responsabilités des Conseils généraux.

13

Probate litigation

☐ 132 GENERAL RULES

Dispute concerning the personal representative (PR)

In case of dispute arising between potential or existing heirs or beneficiaries with a PR (executor or administrator), an application can be made to the Chancery Division of the High Court to have the PR removed and another one appointed in his place.

Dispute over the will

There are different reasons to contest a will. A beneficiary can challenge a will in court if he believes that the testator was not *compos mentis* when he drew up the will. Suspicion of undue influence or duress can also lead to invalidate a will. The existence of an old will which was not revoked by the deceased in his lifetime can also lead to litigation. Any claim disputing a will must be made within six months running from the start of probate.

Claims are lodged either in a county court or in the Chancery Division of the High Court by a surviving spouse, a child or even a former spouse or civil partner. If not remarried, a former spouse is entitled to make a claim on the will if the death occurs less than one year after legal separation and maintenance may be granted by the court. The judge can rectify a will even if the gifts are already distributed. A probate settlement is also possible pending the outcome of the litigation.

GLOSSARY

- administrator (n.) : see 65
- *compos mentis :* of sound mind; *fr. : sain d'esprit*
- civil (adj.) partner (n.) : relationship similar to marriage exclusively for same-sex couples before the Marriage (Same Sex Couples) Act 2013; *fr. : ≈ pacsé*
- contest (v.) : when applied to a will, dispute its provisions, usually by bringing a claim in court; *fr. : contester (un testament)*
- duress (n.) : see 80

- executor (n.) : see 64
- maintenance (n.) : see 127
- personal (adj.) representative (n.) (PR) : individual acting on behalf of the deceased to administer his will; he pays off the debts from the deceased's estate and distributes the residue to the beneficiaries according to the deceased's wishes; *fr. : ≈ exécuteur testamentaire/liquidateur de la succession*
- probate (n.) : legal document allowing the executor to distribute the estate of the deceased according to his wishes; *fr. : ≈ action successorale*
- rectify (v.) : when applied to a will, alter its provisions; this is done by a judge; *fr. : changer (les dispositions testamentaires)*
- settlement (n.) : agreement between the parties to a civil trial, signed before the end of the litigation; *fr. : accord*
- undue (adj.) influence (n.) : see 80

USEFUL EXPRESSIONS

- to challenge a will; *fr. : contester un testament*
- to seek the invalidation of testamentary provisions by the court; *fr. : solliciter du tribunal l'annulation de dispositions testamentaires*

FURTHER INFORMATION

- two divisions of the High Court have (different) jurisdiction to deal with probate cases; while the Family Division is in charge of non-contentious issues such as grants of representation or letters of administration, the Chancery Division hears cases related to contentious probate

COMPARATIVE APPROACH

En France comme Outre-Manche, un testament peut être annulé si le testateur n'était pas sain d'esprit au moment de la rédaction du testament ou s'il a subi des pressions (voir C. civ., art. 901). À l'inverse de l'Angleterre où il est possible de déshériter ses enfants, un enfant du défunt peut, en France, saisir le tribunal de grande instance en cas de non respect de la clause réservataire.

14

Property litigation

☐ 133 INTRODUCTION

Many disputes over land arise over proof of good title, as the records showing the chain of ownership in land may be broken or incomplete. Disputes may also arise from the difficulty in determining exactly what interests (leases, licences, easements, etc.), whether legal or equitable, may affect a piece of land. The land registration scheme was introduced to try to address some of these problems. The land register serves two main purposes : to show all the interests and charges that may affect a particular parcel of land, and to prove the title of the registered owner. However, not all land, and not all interests and charges are registered.

Land that has not changed ownership for a long time may remain unregistered. Certain proprietary interests (e.g., equitable easements, mortgages, and restrictive covenants) in unregistered land must be entered in the land charges register to be protected. If such interests are not entered in the register, they risk being void against purchasers of the land, even in cases where the purchasers were aware of their existence.

Some interests in land – including short leases, easements, and *profits à prendre* – are not subject to compulsory registration. Disputes can arise when these unregistered encumbrances conflict with the rights of a registered landowner. A purchaser who acquires freehold title in a property that is subject to a three-year lease may be bound by the terms of the leasehold interest, even though it was not registered and the purchaser was not even aware of its existence. These are known as overriding interests. These interests are binding both on the registered proprietor and on any person who acquires an interest in the property. The purpose of the Land Registration Act 2002 is to reduce the number of overriding interests and thereby limit potential litigation over conflicting interests.

There is a range of remedies available to a person whose property rights have been violated. As the transfer of any interest in land is effected through a contract, courts may award damages for any breach of its terms. Equitable remedies, which may be granted separately or concurrently to financial compensation, are also available. Thus, a court may make an order for specific performance compelling an owner to transfer title to a purchaser of the land, or an injunction restraining a person from any further breaches of a restrictive covenant.

Although a licence does not bind third parties, equity may protect a licensee against third parties through the doctrine of proprietary estoppel. If a person (B) spends money on land following a landowner's assertion that he will acquire an interest in that land, equity will prevent (or "estop") the landowner from later denying that B had any interest at all in the land. In certain cases this will give rise to a licence by estoppel; in other cases, the court may award B a proprietary interest in the land.

GLOSSARY

- charge (n.) : here, interest in unregistered land imposing an obligation on the landowner in favour of another person; charges entered in the land charges register will be binding on future purchasers of the land; *fr. : charge*
- damages (n.) : financial compensation awarded by a court to compensate the loss sustained by someone; *fr. : dommages et intérêts*
- easement (n.) : see 67
- encumbrance (n.) : proprietary right or interest belonging to someone other than the owner of the property; *fr. : charge*
- estop (v.) : bar or prohibit by estoppel; *fr. : ≈ empêcher*
- freehold title : right to possession of land in fee simple; *fr. : ≈ pleine propriété*
- good (adj.) title (n.) : adequate evidence to establish a person's right to ownership of property; *fr. : ≈ titre de propriété faisant foi*
- injunction (n.) : equitable remedy (as opposed to a common law remedy) awarded by a court whereby someone must do or refrain to do an act; *fr. : injonction*
- land charges register : register recording certain interests affecting owners of unregistered land; *fr. : ≈ service de publicité foncière* (formerly known as *conservation des hypothèques)*
- land registry : government agency in charge of registering the ownership of property; *fr. : service du cadastre*
- lease (n.) : agreement by which a property owner (landlord or lessor) grants another person (tenant or lessee) the right to exclusive possession of the property for an agreed period, usually in exchange for the regular payment of rent; *fr. : bail*
- licence (n.) : here, informal right over land granted by the landowner to someone else (e.g. a licence to enter property to fish in a stream, to collect firewood, etc.); *fr. : ≈ autorisation/permission informelle relative à un terrain*
- licensee (n.) : person to whom a licence is granted; *fr. : ≈ personne titulaire d'une autorisation/permission informelle relative à un terrain*
- licence by estoppel : form of proprietary estoppel preventing a licensor from revoking a licence; *fr. : ≈ permission par préclusion*

- mortgage (n.) : see 67
- overriding (adj.) interest (n.) : right or interest in registered land which is not protected by registration but is still capable of binding the registered proprietor and future purchasers (e.g., legal easements and *profits à prendre*); *fr. : ≈ droit non enregistré au cadastre mais opposable*
- *profits à prendre :* see 67
- proprietary (adj.) estoppel (n.) : equitable doctrine by which a court may exercise its discretionary power and grant relief to someone who spent money on a property, or incurred some other detriment, in reliance on a landowner's assertions that he would acquire rights in the land; *fr. : ≈ acquisition d'un droit par estoppel*
- restrictive (adj.) covenant (n.) : here, an obligation imposing some kind of restriction on the rights of a landowner (e.g., a covenant not to build on the land); such covenants may attach to the land and bind third parties; *fr. : clause restrictive*
- specific (adj.) performance (n.) : equitable remedy (as opposed to a common law remedy) awarded by a court whereby someone is required to do something; *fr. : obligation de faire*
- void (v.) : see 77

USEFUL EXPRESSIONS

- to be bound by the terms of the lease; *fr. : être lié par les conditions du bail*
- a charge is registered on the property; *fr. : la propriété est grevée d'une charge*
- to register the transfer of title in the property; *fr. : enregistrer le transfert de titre de propriété*

FURTHER INFORMATION

- the noun charge, in the context of property law, can refer to an encumbrance over land (such as a mortgage) or to amounts paid by a tenant to a landlord to cover certain service-related costs (such as insurance or management fees)

COMPARATIVE APPROACH

En Angleterre et au Pays de Galles, le régime de transcription immobilière a une valeur juridique plus grande qu'en France. En effet, Outre-Manche, l'enregistrement vaut preuve de la propriété. En revanche, en France, le plan cadastral est un document administratif qui permet d'établir les bases des impôts locaux. Il ne constitue qu'une présomption (simple) de preuve de propriété.

□ 134 DISPUTES CONCERNING LEASES

A lease is a special type of contract. It creates proprietary rights capable of binding third parties. For example, a person who buys a house which is occupied by a tenant will be bound by the existing lease, even though the buyer was not a party to the original lease and may not even have been aware of its existence.

The most common disputes arise out of the breach of the terms of a lease. For example, the tenant in a tenancy agreement is in rent arrears or fails to comply with some other term of the lease agreement. Sometimes the landlord will take the steps necessary to forfeit a lease. Detailed information on the landlord's and tenant's respective liabilities is given in chapter 71. Chapter 136 sets out the procedure which a landlord must follow to evict a tenant.

GLOSSARY

- arrears (n.) : here, money for rent which should have been paid earlier and is now overdue; *fr. : arriérés*
- evict (v.)/eviction (n.) : expel a tenant; the expulsion of a tenant or other occupier from property; *fr. : expulser (v.)/expulsion (n.)*
- forfeiture (n.) : here, loss of tenant's right to occupy property following a breach of the lease agreement; *fr. : ≈ résiliation (d'un bail)*
- landlord (n.) : property owner who leases his property to a tenant; *fr. : propriétaire-bailleur*
- rent (n. and v.) : here, regular payment of money by a tenant to a landlord; *fr. : loyer*
- tenancy (n.) : person's proprietary interest in land; often used as a synonym for lease; *fr. : location/bail*

USEFUL EXPRESSIONS

- to be in rent arrears; *fr. : avoir un arriéré de paiement sur son loyer*

FURTHER INFORMATION

- landlady is the corresponding feminine form of landlord
- the English noun location refers to place or position (*emplacement*)

COMPARATIVE APPROACH

En France, la majorité des baux d'habitation prévoit une clause résolutoire en cas de non présentation d'une attestation d'assurance. En revanche, en Angleterre et au Pays de Galles, les locataires (*tenants*) n'ont pas l'obligation d'assurer un bien immobilier. C'est en général le propriétaire-bailleur (*landlord*) qui souscrit les polices habituelles.

□ 135 DISPUTES CONCERNING FREEHOLD LAND

Disputes about boundaries

When property is registered, a title plan showing the general boundaries of the property will be created. However, disputes may arise about the exact boundaries of a property. In such cases the parties can apply to Land Registry to determine the exact line of a boundary. A surveyor will draw up a detailed plan. If the neighbours agree with the proposed boundary it will be registered; otherwise the parties will seek to resolve the dispute either before the independent Adjudicator to HM Land Registry or in court.

Repossession

A mortgage lender (e.g. a bank) is the legal owner of a property until such time as the loan is repaid by the landowner/mortgagor. If a landowner defaults on his mortgage payments, the mortgage lender may agree to vary the way in which repayments are made. Alternatively, the mortgage lender may exercise his right of foreclosure : forcing the sale of the property in order to recuperate any outstanding debt. An application to the court is made for a repossession order. If the order is made, the landowner is usually required to surrender possession of the property within 28 days. If the landowner fails to vacate the premises by then, the mortgage lender can apply to the court for an eviction order.

Adverse possession

Squatting consists of knowingly entering a residential building as a trespasser in order to live there. In some rare cases, adverse possession over a long period of time can result in rights over that land for the squatter (often referred to as squatters' rights). In extreme cases, an adverse possessor may, after a long period of occupation, even become the legal owner of the land. Adverse possession does not pose any real threat to owners of registered land under the current statutory scheme.

Restrictive covenants

A restrictive covenant is a promise not to do certain things with land or property. For example, a buyer may promise the seller not to run a business from the property, or not to keep non-domestic animals. Certain restrictive covenants are attached to the land (they run with the land), and continue to have effect even after the land is sold. However, a covenant created after 1925 will usually only bind purchasers of the legal estate if it has been registered. The courts may also refuse to enforce a restrictive covenant if the person benefitting from it has remained inactive despite repeated breaches, or if the character of the neighbourhood has changed significantly.

Co-ownership

Co-ownership arises where two or more parties share an undivided interest in land. Co-owners may be joint tenants or tenants in common. Joint tenancy means that the owners all share an identical and undivided entitlement to the entire property. If one of the joint tenants dies, his interest will pass to the surviving joint tenants. In the case of a tenancy in common, which is the equitable ownership of land in undivided shares, each of the co-owners is entitled to sell his share in the land and this interest will not automatically pass to surviving co-owners.

GLOSSARY

- Adjudicator to HM Land Registry : independent office created to resolve disputed applications to the Land Registry; *fr. : ≈ médiateur du bureau du cadastre*
- adverse (adj.) possession (n.) : occupying land to which another person has title with the intention of living there; *fr. : prescription acquisitive*
- boundary (n.) : here, limits or borders of a property; *fr. : limite cadastrale*
- charge (n.) : legal or equitable interest in land which secures the payment of a debt owed to the chargee; *fr. : sûreté réelle/droit de gage immobilier*
- co-ownership (n.) : possession by two or more parties of an undivided interest in the same land; *fr. : propriété indivise*
- estop (v.) : see 9
- eviction order : court order expelling a tenant or other occupier from land; *fr. : ordonnance d'expulsion*
- foreclosure (n.) : action taken by the mortgage lender (mortgagee) to force the sale of a property and recover any debt secured under the mortgage; *fr. : saisie hypothécaire*
- joint (adj.) tenancy (n.) : form of co-ownership of land whereby each of the joint tenants has identical interests in the whole of the land; *fr. : propriété indivise*
- mortgage lender : entity that lends money to a property owner under the terms of a mortgage; *fr. : prêteur hypothécaire*
- mortgagor (n.) : person who borrows money and pledges his property as security for the mortgage lender (or mortgagee); *fr. : débiteur hypothécaire*
- override (v.) : be more important than; assume superior authority over; *fr. : prévaloir*
- proprietary (adj.) estoppel (n.) : see 133
- repossession (n.) : mortgage lender's right to vacant possession of a property occupied by the mortgagor; usually exercised following the mortgagor's failure to make payments under the mortgage agreement; *fr. : reprise de possession des biens*
- restrictive (adj.) covenant (n.) : see 133
- squatting (n.) : common name given to practice of adverse possession; *fr. : squat/occupation sans droit ni titre*

- surveyor (n.) : professional who establishes boundary locations and land parcel corners; *fr. : géomètre*
- tenancy in common : equitable co-ownership of land allowing each of the tenants in common to sell off his undivided share in the land; *fr. : ≈ propriété divise*
- title plan : graphic representation of a registered property, showing its location, boundaries and buildings; *fr. : plan cadastral*
- trespass (n. and v.) : see 91

USEFUL EXPRESSIONS

- to grant an eviction order; *fr. : rendre une ordonnance d'expulsion*
- the surveyor delimits the boundaries of the property; *fr. : le géomètre définit le bornage de la propriété*

FURTHER INFORMATION

- the land charges register should not be confused with the land register; the former records certain interests affecting unregistered land, whereas the latter records title to registered land
- although tenancy usually refers to a leasehold interest, the expressions "joint tenancy" and "tenancy in common" designate forms of co-ownership rather than types of leases

COMPARATIVE APPROACH

En France, le Code civil définit clairement les délais de prescription acquisitive. En revanche, en Angleterre et au Pays de Galles, les tribunaux anglais ne confèrent une prescription acquisitive que dans de rares cas.

□ 136 SPECIFIC CASE : LANDLORD'S EVICTION OF A TENANT

This chapter exclusively refers to the eviction of a private tenant (i.e. someone who pays rent with his own money) as opposed to a council tenant or a housing association tenant, with specific rules applying in the last two cases. Eviction is usually sought when the tenant owes rent arrears, in breach of other terms of the tenancy agreement, caused nuisance or deteriorated the property. Eviction is possible throughout the whole year : unlike some continental legal systems, there is no winter period during which a tenant is protected from eviction.

Possession claim procedure

The procedure applicable when the landlord seeks repossession of his property depends on the nature of the tenancy agreement. Non-compliance with the rules may result in the landlord being prosecuted for illegally evicting or harassing his tenant. Harassment may consist of withholding or changing keys to the property, cutting services (like electricity) or anti-social behaviour on the landlord's part. Illegal eviction may result from the grant of an insufficient period to quit the premises, as stated in the notice, or the fact of repossessing without complying with the procedure required.

Assured Shorthold Tenancy (AST)

Different rules apply depending on whether the AST is a fixed-term one or a periodic one.

A periodic AST runs on a weekly or monthly basis and has no fixed end date. The landlord must give his tenant a written notice to quit at the end of a period. Should the tenant fail to leave on that date, the landlord sends him a notice of intention to seek possession by which he informs the tenant that he will apply to the court for a possession order unless the tenant leaves the premises on his own accord. If necessary, the relevant application is lodged with the court which may hand down a possession order, thus giving the landlord the right to evict his tenant and take possession of his property. If the tenant does not leave the property, the landlord can apply for an eviction warrant, which gives the bailiff/sheriff the right to remove the tenant from the property.

A fixed-term AST runs on a set period of time. The notice period should be set out in the tenancy agreement and the landlord must comply with it when sending his written notice to quit. Should the tenant refuse to leave at the end of the notice period, the procedure applicable is similar to the periodic AST one.

Assured or regulated tenancy

Tenants who have an assured or regulated tenancy, i.e. who moved into the property before 27th February 1997, benefit from an increased protection from eviction. There are not many assured or regulated tenancies still in effect these days.

Licence or non-regulated (excluded) tenancy

If the tenant benefits from a licence or a non-regulated (excluded) tenancy or, in other words, if he is the landlord's lodger, renting a room in his house, the landlord just needs to give his tenant/lodger reasonable notice to quit, which does not have to be in writing. It usually means the length of the rental payment period. If the lodger does not leave at the end of the notice period, the landlord can change the key to his room, even if the tenant still has belongings in it. However, those belongings must be returned to the former tenant in due course.

Special accelerated procedure

If certain conditions are fulfilled, the landlord can obtain accelerated possession to evict his tenant. In such circumstances, eviction is obtained more quickly and normally, no court hearing is necessary. However, this is only possible if the tenancy agreement is a written AST and if the landlord gives his tenant at least 2 months' notice to quit. For a fixed-term tenancy, the notice period must correspond to the end of a tenancy period.

The landlord must lodge an application for accelerated possession with the court. Upon receipt, the court serves a copy on the tenant. If the tenant wants to dispute the application, he has 14 days from the date of service of the application to do so. The judge will then decide whether a possession order should be issued forthwith (thus allowing the landlord to evict the tenant and take possession of his property) or fix a court hearing. A court hearing will only be held if the paperwork in unclear in which case any outstanding issues will be clarified at the hearing. The judge will then decide whether to order possession or not.

When a possession order is made, the tenant has 14 or 28 days to leave the property. This may be extended to 42 days if the enforcement of the order is likely to cause the tenant exceptional hardship. The landlord may instruct a bailiff/sheriff if necessary to execute the order.

Possession hearing

The possession order is not made as of right. Alternatively the judge can dismiss the application if it does not rely on solid legal grounds (e.g. the procedure was not complied with or the rent is not due or was paid before the hearing), or adjourn it i.e. postpone it to a later date (e.g. if there are issues to clarify). There are different categories of possession orders.

There may be an ordinary or outright possession order : the tenant must leave the property by the date (usually 14 to 28 days after the hearing) given in the order. Should the tenant refuse to leave once more, the landlord can apply to the court for a warrant for possession. If the warrant is granted, an eviction notice is served by the court on the tenant, setting a date when he must leave the property.

The possession order can be suspended : for instance, if the tenant has settled part of the rent arrears due, the court may suspend the order to give the tenant a chance to pay the outstanding sums by a set date. If the tenant fails to comply with the conditions set by the court, the landlord may apply for eviction.

The court can also make a money order, ordering the tenant to pay the amount set out in the order. Should the tenant fail to comply with the order, the court may, at the landlord's request, send the bailiff to seize some of the tenant's possessions or alternatively, order that monies be seized from his bank account. If further rent arrears are due, the landlord can go back to court again to apply for a possession order. It is also common for a possession order to contain a money judgment as well.

Whatever order is made by the court in favour of the landlord, the tenant will usually be ordered to pay the landlord's costs i.e. the sums which he had to incur to recover payment of the rent arrears and/or possession.

Appeal against the court's first instance decision

The dissatisfied party may wish to appeal in which case he must obtain prior leave from the first instance judge before doing so.

GLOSSARY

- anti-social (adj.) behaviour (n.) : behaviour or attitude which goes against the well-being of society such as playing loud music at night, being drunk on the street, threatening other people, vandalising public or private property; such behaviour may give rise to an anti-social behaviour order (ASBO) which can be made against anyone above 10 years of age; *fr. : ≈ comportement antisocial*
- arrears (n.) : see 72
- Assured Shorthold Tenancy (AST) : see 70
- assured (adj.) tenancy (n.) : see 70
- bailiff (n.) : see 4
- costs (n.) : here, sums which the landlord had to incur (e.g. issue fee for a court claim, fees to be incurred by a bailiff/sheriff to enforce an order) to recover payment of the rent arrears and/or possession; *fr. : dépens*
- council tenant : person who rents a property through the local council; the protection given to a council tenant is better than that granted to a private tenant; *fr. : ≈ locataire d'un HLM*
- dismiss (v.) : reject; *fr. : débouter*
- enforcement (n.) : here, execution of a court order; *fr. : exécution*
- eviction order : court order by which a tenant is ordered to vacate a leased property within a specified period of time; *fr. : ordonnance d'expulsion*
- excluded (adj.) tenancy (n.) : see non-regulated tenancy
- grounds (n.) : in a legal context, reasons on which a claim is based or a court order is rendered; *fr. : motifs (de droit)*
- harassment (n.) : systematic, annoying or threatening pressure or action from a particular individual or a group of people against someone that is aimed at causing alarm and distress; the Protection from Harassment Act 1997 was passed to punish this criminal offence; *fr. : harcèlement*
- hardship (n.) : cause of privation, pain or suffering; *fr. : privation/≈ préjudice*
- hearing (n.) : in a legal context, formal adversarial meeting before a judge, to deal with a specific issue (as opposed to a trial); *fr. : audience*
- housing association tenant : person who rents a property through a housing association; the protection given to a housing association tenant is better than that granted to a private tenant; *fr. : ≈ locataire d'une association d'aide au logement*

- licence (n.) : see 70
- lodge (with) (v.) : here, file a document with the court; *fr. : enrôler*
- money order : court's financial order; *fr. : ≈ jugement de condamnation à payer une somme d'argent*
- non-regulated (adj.) tenancy (n.) : see 70
- notice to quit : landlord's request to his tenant asking him to leave the property rented out before a specific deadline; *fr. : ≈ avis de congé (du bail)*
- notice period : see 71
- possession order : court order whereby possession of a property should be returned to the owner or another claimant; *fr. : ordonnance de restitution*
- regulated (adj.) tenancy (n.) : see 70
- serve (on) (v.) : bring a document (like a claim, a court decision, etc.) to someone's attention in an official way; *fr. : notifier/signifier*
- sheriff (n.) : see 4
- suspend (v.) : stay; *fr. : surseoir*
- tenancy agreement : see 70
- warrant (n.) : document which a landlord can obtain from the court if a tenant refuses to leave his property after a possession order, allowing a bailiff to take the necessary steps to evict a tenant and return possession to the landlord; *fr. : ≈ ordonnance*

USEFUL EXPRESSIONS

- to apply to the judge for leave to appeal; *fr. : demander au juge l'autorisation de relever/interjeter appel*
- to serve a document on someone; *fr. : notifier/signifier un document à quelqu'un*
- the court hands down an order; *fr. : le tribunal rend un jugement*
- to instruct a bailiff; *fr. : mandater un huissier*
- to give one's tenant notice to quit premises; *fr. : donner à son locataire congé de quitter les lieux*

FURTHER INFORMATION

- anti-social behaviour orders (ASBO) are civil orders, as opposed to criminal ones, which were introduced by the Crime and Disorder Act 1998 to fight against minor incidents not requiring criminal prosecution
- the term costs used in a legal context (*dépens*) should always be plural
- a court hearing (*audience*) is different from a court trial (*procès*)

Comparative approach

Tout comme Outre-Manche, il existe en France un régime d'expulsion spécifique pour les locataires d'habitations à loyer modéré (HLM). En ce qui concerne l'expulsion de logements vides (c'est-à-dire, non meublés) dans le secteur privé, les locataires en France bénéficient d'une trêve hivernale de plusieurs mois, pendant laquelle aucune expulsion n'est possible. Cela rend l'éviction du locataire, pour impayés de loyers (*arrears of rent*) ou pour toute autre cause, tout aussi complexe qu'en Angleterre et au Pays de Galles, voire davantage.

Avant d'engager une quelconque action en résiliation du bail, et si le locataire perçoit une aide au logement, le propriétaire-bailleur peut s'adresser à la caisse d'allocations familiales pour que ladite aide lui soit versée à lui, et non au locataire. Si le locataire ne perçoit pas d'aide au logement, deux types de résiliation existent.

Si une clause de résiliation de plein droit (*termination as of right*) en cas d'impayés de loyers figure au contrat de bail, le propriétaire-bailleur doit envoyer au locataire un commandement de payer. À défaut de paiement dans un délai de 2 mois, ou de tout autre délai qu'un juge pourrait déterminer (sur saisine du locataire), le propriétaire-bailleur saisit le Tribunal d'instance, statuant en référé (≈ *summary judgment*), pour lui demander de constater que le bail est résilié et ordonner l'expulsion.

En l'absence de clause de résiliation, le propriétaire-bailleur peut requérir la résiliation judiciaire du contrat de bail. Il doit pour cela assigner le locataire (*lodge a claim against the tenant*) devant le Tribunal d'instance aux fins de voir prononcer la résiliation du contrat et l'expulsion. Il est conseillé, mais pas obligatoire (*not mandatory*), d'envoyer préalablement une mise en demeure (*letter before claim*) au locataire.

Le juge use de son pouvoir discrétionnaire (*he exercises his discretionary power*) pour accorder éventuellement au locataire des délais de paiement. À défaut, il peur ordonner la résiliation. Le propriétaire-bailleur doit alors faire adresser au locataire, par voie d'huissier (*bailiff/sheriff*), un commandement l'invitant à quitter les lieux (≈ *notice to quit after judgment*) dans un délai de 2 mois.

Index

The numbers below refer to card numbers (*numéros de fiches*).

A

abandoned 118
abatement 90
abet 111
abode 61
absolute 57, 89, 108, 111
– absolute assignment 11
– absolute discharge 108
– absolute privilege 89
– absolute right 57
abstract 38, 50
abuse 122
acceptance 7, **8**, 22, 48
– acceptance by conduct 8
– acceptance of (construction) works 48
– acceptor 22
accessorial infringement 111
accommodation party 22
accomplice 27, 104
according to a law 92
accords 50
account 15, 23, 110
– account (of profits) 110
– account party 23
– accounts 15
accrue (interest) 18
accumulated losses 14
achievable 52
acknowledgment 74
acquit 108, 109
act of God 12, 90
action 1, 84
– action for an agreed sum 84
– action for annulment 1
– action for failure to act 1
actionable **79**, 89
– actionable *per se* 89
active euthanasia 60
actuary 40
actus reus 27
adaptation right 36
adduce (evidence) 85, 105
adjourn 106
Adjudicator to HM Land Registry 135
administration 65, **96**, **98**, 126, 132
– administration 96, 98
– administrative receivership 98
– administrative removal 126
– administrator 65, 132, 98
admissibility 34
admission to the Roll 5
adopt 3, 56, 63
– adoptee 63
– adopter 3, 63
– adoption 56, 63
adultery 127
adversarial 59, 75, 102, 136
– adversarial 102, 136
– adversarial principle 59
– adversarial system 75
adverse possession 135
affirm 105, 83
affirmation 83
agency 11, 13, 19, 40, 53, 60
– agency agreement 19
– agency worker 53, 60
– agent 11, 13, 19, 40
• commercial agent 18
• commission agent 19
• *del credere* agent 19
• general agent 19
• managing agent 69
• patent agent 38
• self-employed agent 19
• special agent 19
– disclosed agency 19
– undisclosed agency 19
aggravating 108
– aggravating circumstances 108
– aggravating factor 108

aggressive practices 18
aggrieved party 73
agnosticism 58
agreement 8, 18, 49, 50
– agreement to agree 18
air quality standard 51
airline liaison officer 124
alibi 34
alien 122
all-encompassing right 58
alleged **27**, 85
– alleged wrong 85
allegiance 61,125
allot 14
allowance 25
amends 89
ancillary order 108, 128
annual aggregate excess 41
Annual General Meeting (AGM) **16**
– convene (AGM) 16
– summon up (AGM) 16
annuity 43
annulment 127
anti-social behaviour 118, 136
anticipatory breach 83
appeal 3, 75, 103, 109, **122**
– appellant 75, 109
– appellate committee of the House of Lords 2
– appellate jurisdiction 3, 103
– lodge (appeal) 3, 75
appellations (of origin) 39
applicant 38, 75
application for registration 15
appointee 130
apprentice 53
appropriation 21
approved repairer 45
arbitrary 59
arbitration 74, 120
arise 76
arraignment 103, 104
arrears 4, 72, 101, 134
arrest **33**
– arrest warrant 33
– arrestee 33
– arrestor 33
arson 29
articles of association 15
artistic work 36
ascertain 20, **38**, 128
– ascertainable wish 128
– ascertained goods 20
assassination 28
assault 28, 91
assembly 58
asset 14, 30, **62**, 64, **94**, 127, 129
– asset stripping 30
– dissipate (assets) 14
assign 11, **123**
– assignee 11
– assignment 11
– assignor 11
assistant 5, 32
– assistant chief constable 32
– assistant solicitor 5
assisted 60, 63, 123
– assisted reproduction 63
– assisted suicide 60
– assisted voluntary return 123
assisting the enemy 31
association 58
assured tenancy 70
– assured shorthold tenancy 70
asylum **61**, 122, 123
– asylum claim 123
– asylum qualification 61
– asylum seeker 122
atheism 58
atmospheric pollution 49
attainable 52
attempted murder 28
attribution 36
auction 8
auction without reserve 8
author 36
– authorial 36
– authorship right 36
authorisation right 36
authority 11, 19, 57, 58
– actual authority 19
– apparent authority 11, 19
– authority by necessity 19
– authority by ratification 19
– express authority 11
– implied authority 11
– public authority 57, 58
– usual authority 19
automatism 104
average consumer 17

avoid 1, 77
- avoid (claims) 1
- avoid (contract) 77, 84

B

back-up copy 111
bail 24, 33, **126**
- bail sheet 33
- bailee 24

bailiff 4
bailment 20
ban 60
bank 1, 17, 23
- correspondent bank 17, 23
- European Central Bank (ECB) 1
- issuing bank 17, 23

bank holiday 54
bankruptcy 94
Bar Council 5
bare licence 68
bare ownership 64
bargain 7
barrister 4
barter 20
battery 28, 91
battle of forms 18
beneficiary 19, 23, 64, 68
beyond reasonable doubt 102
bid 8
bilateral contract 7
bill 21, 22
- bearer bill (of lading) 21
- bill of exchange 22
- bill of lading (BOL) 21
- foul bill 21
- inland bill of exchange 22
- order bill (of lading) 21
- received for shipment bill (of lading) 21
- sea waybill 21
- straight (consigned) bills (of lading) 21

bind 2, 10
- binding 7, 49, 50, 59, 63, 95
- binding agreement 7
- non-binding 50

bio-metric chipped passport 124
biotechnological invention 113
birth certificate 63
blackmail 29
blanket protection 89
bloodline 125
board 16, **107**
- board of directors 16

body corporate 13
bona fide 16
bonus 55
border 122, 135
- border control 122
- border frontier 122
- boundary 135

brand 35, 114
breach 20, 77, 86, 100
- breach (duty) 86, 92
- breach of trust 100
- in breach (duty) 86

break into 29
bribery 30
bridging loan 69
brief 6
bring (action) 87
British person 61, 125
- British citizen 61
- British nationality citizenship 61
- British national residing overseas 61
- British overseas citizen 61
- British overseas territory citizen 61
- British protected person 61
- British subject 61
- citizenship 61, 125
- dual national British citizen 61, 125

British Army 31
British Transport Police 32
broadcasts 36
broker 6, 19, 40
bulk 20
burden 85, 86
- burden of proof 85, 102

burglary 29, 47
business rates 26
buyer 19

C

c.i.f. contract 21
- cost, insurance and freight 21

call to the Bar 5
cap 120
capacity to contract 10

capital 13, 14, 26, 101
– capital gain 26
– capital gains tax 101
– capital maintenance 14
– debt capital 15
– loan capital 14
– minimum capital requirement 13
– paid-up share capital 14
– raise (capital) 14
care order 131
carrier 17, 21, 124
case 2, 3, 74, 75, 94
– case law 2
– case management 74, 75
casual worker 53
cause 85, 86, 111, 112
– causal link 111, 112
– causation 86
– cause (damage) 85, 86
– cause (loss) 85
caveat emptor 41, 69
cease 125
certification 21, 39, 121
– certification officer 121
– certification trademark 39
– certify (BOL) 21
chain 69
challenge 76
Chambers (set of) 5
charge 14, 33, 96, 133, 135
charging scheme 52
chartered accountant 6
chattels 64, 91
check point 124
cheque 23
chief 32
– chief constable 32
– chief inspector 32
– chief superintendent 32
child 25, 129, 131
– child assessment order 131
– child benefit 25
– child-carer 129
– child maintenance 129
– child tax credit 25
– children's home 131
circumstantial evidence 34
citizen-led network 52
citizenship 61, 125
City of London Police 32
civil 2, 53, 60, 62, 94, 117, 132
– civil ceremony 62
– civil law 2
– Civil Nuclear Constabulary 32
– civil partner(ship) 62, 132
– civil right 60
– civil sanction 117
– civil servant 53, 94
claim 38, 45, 61, 74, 75, 85, 86, **89**, 90, 100, 136
– claim (tort) 86
– claim letter 74
– claimant 74, 85
– common law derivative claim 100
– counterclaim 74
– dismiss (claim) 89
– fast-track claims 75
– functional claim 38
– human rights claim 61
– lodge (claim) 90
– no-claims bonus (NCB) 45
– particulars of claim 75
– personal injury claim 74
– process claim 38
– product-by process claim 38
– product claim 38
– small claims 75
– statutory derivative claim 100
– *sur place* claim 61
clause 12, 16, 18, 72, 81, 83, 84, 92
– break clause 72
– entire agreement clause 12
– exclusion clause 18, 81
– exemption clause 81, 92
– force majeure clause 12, 18
– hardship clause 18
– honour clause 10
– indemnity clause 81
– objects clause 16
– onerous clause 92
– penalty clause 84
– restraint of trade clause 81
– severability clause 81
– time clause 83
– variation clause 12
clean 21
clerk 103
clinical dispute 74
closing speech 105
co-accused 104
co-defendant 104

co-ownership 135
coassurance 40
– coassure 40
codicil 64
coercion 80
– coerce 80
cohabitation contract 64
– cohabiting couple 64
collateral contract 11
collective 39, 54, 57, 121
– collective agreement 54, 121
– collective bargaining 121
– collective grievance 121
– collective right 57
– collective trademark 39
College of Law 5
Commanding Officer (CO) 107
comment 89
commercial 19, 35, 42, 112
– commercial dealing 112
– commercial name 35
Commission 1
commit 103, **116**
– committal proceedings 103
commitment 50
committee 96
common law 2, 17, 73, 100
– common law implied term 17
Common Travel Area 122
commonhold estate 67
communication 8, 36
– communication right 36
Community environmental legislation 50
community of risks 40
community sentence 108
– community service order 108
company 3, **13**, 15, 53, 97, 100, 114
– Companies House 15
– company search 15
– company voluntary arrangement (CVA) 97
– comparative advertising 114
– limited 13
– limited by guarantee 13
– limited by shares 13
– limited company 13, 53
– limited partnership 13
– public limited company 13
– private company 13
– register (company) 13
– registered company 13, 15
– restore (company) 100
– set up (company) 13, 15
– simple contract 10
– unlimited 13
– unlimited company 13
compel 34, **80**, 106, 109
– compellable witness 106
– compelling evidence 109
– compelling interest 34
compensation 108, **128**
– compensation order 108
competition 35
completion 69, 95
– complete 95
compliance 57, 69
– comply with 69
compos mentis 10, 132
composition 98
compromise agreement 119
compulsion 80, 94
– compulsory liquidation 94
computer-generated work 36
conciliation 74, 120
condition 17, 83
condition precedent 8
conditional 24, 33, 75, 108
– conditional caution 33
– conditional discharge 108
– conditional fee agreement (CFA) 75
– conditional guarantee 24
conducive 125
confess 34
confidence 56, 58
– confidential information 58
– confidentiality 56
confirming house 19
confiscation order 108
conflicting 116
conform 50
conscience 58
consent 33, 88, 113, 129
– consent order 129
conservation 52
consideration 9
consignee 21
conspiracy 27
construction 2, 115
– construe 2, 115
constructive 80, 120
– constructive dismissal 120
– constructive notice 80

consultation 46, 119
consumer 81, 92
contact 128
– contact activity condition 128
– contact activity direction 128
– contact arrangement 128
– contact order 128
contempt of court 105
contest 132
contingency risk 42
***contra proferem* rule** 18
contract 3, 7, 17, 18, 19, 21, 54, 68, 79
– avoid (contract) 18
– conform (contract) 21
– contract of employment 54
– contract of service 54
– contract of utmost good faith 79
– contracting party 7
– contractual capacity 15
– contractual licence 68
– informal agreement 19
– invalidate (contract) 18
– rescind (contract) 17
– rescission (contract) 17
– vary (contract) 18, 19
contractor 53
contributory negligence 88
control test 54
conversely 73
conveyancing 66, 69
conviction 38, **59**, 60, 104, **105**, 108
– convict 104, 108
– convicted prisoner 60, 126
copying 111
copyright **35**, 36, 37, 38
– copyright protection 36
– crown copyright 36
– parliamentary copyright 36
core provisions 18
coroner 34, 103
corporate 15, 26, 28, 30, 101, 116, 118
– corporate crime 30
– corporate espionage 30
– corporate manslaughter 15, 28, 30
– corporate personality 15
– corporate promoter 15
– corporation tax 26, 101
– corporate veil 15
• lift the corporate veil 15
• pierce the corporate veil 15
• corporate world, 116
corporeal hereditament 66
correspondence 58
corroborating evidence 34
corruption 30
costs 74, 95, 136
Council/Council of Ministers 1
council 25, 71, 131, 139
– council social worker 131
– council tax 25, 71
– council tenant 136
counsel 4, 104
count 106
counter-offer 8
counterfeiting 29, 110
countermand 23
course of 18, 92, 114
– course (of trade) 114
– course of dealing 18
– course of their employment 92
– outside the course of their employment 92
court 1, 2, 3, 4, 50, 64, 73, 75, 85, 94, 103, 105, 107, 130, 136
– apply (court) 85
– contempt of court 105
– county court 3
– court clerk 4
– Court Martial 107
– Court Martial Appeal Court 107
– Court of Appeal 3
– Court of Auditors 1
– Court of Justice of the European Union (CJEU) 1
– Court of Protection 130
– court officer 94
– court usher 4
– Crown Court 3, 103
– High Court of Justice 3
– international court
– lodge (with) 136
– Magistrates' court 3, 4, 103
– payment into court (Part 36 payment) 75
– Principal Registry of the Family Division of the High Court 64
– Service Civilian Court (SCC) 107
– Supreme Court of the United Kingdom (UKSC) 2, 3, 73, 103
– youth court 103
courtesy car 45
covenant 10

cover 41
- cover note 41
- coverage 41

credit 17, 23, **24**, 25, 42, 94, 95, 96, 99
- credit insurance 42
- creditor 94
- creditors' meeting 95
- creditors' voluntary liquidation (CVL) 99
- documentary credit 17, 23
- fixed-term credit 24
- loan credit 24
- preferential creditor 96
- revolving credit 24
- sales credit 24
- secured creditor 96
- tax credit 25
- unsecured creditor 96

crime 15, 27, 32, 60, 103, 105, 118
- Crime and Disorder Committee (CDC) 32
- crime-specific policy 60
- criminal cases review 103
- Criminal Investigation Department (CID) 32
- criminal offence 27
- criminal record 105
- National Crime Agency 32
- white-collar crime 15

criteria 37
cross-examination **75**, 102, 106
- cross-examine 102, 106

cross-purposes mistake 78
crossed cheque 23
Crown Prosecution Service (CPS) 27, 104
crystallisation 14
culprit 109
curfew orders 108
custody 33, 108
- custodial sentence 108
- custody officer 33

customer 92

D

damage 1, **85**, 86, 87, 93, 118,
- criminal damage 118
- heads of damage 93
- inflict (damage) 86
- psychiatric damage 87
- remote damage 86
- suffer (damage) 1

damages 84, 88, 91, 93, **133**
- aesthetic damages 93
- aggravated damages 93
- apply for payment 93
- assess (damages) 88, 93
- award (damages) 93
- consequential damages 93
- cosmetic damages 93
- damages "at large" 93
- damages in lieu 93
- exemplary damages 93
- general damages 93
- grant (damages) 93
- liquidated damages 84, 93
- nominal damages 84, 91, 93
- recover (damages) 86
- special damages 93
- statutory damages 93
- unliquidated damages 84, 93

debate 60
- debatable issue 60

debenture 14, **96**
- debenture stock 14
- unsecured debenture 14

debt 4, 14, 18, **94**, 95
- debt capital 14
- debt recovery 4
- debtor 94
- incur (debts) 14
- proof of debt 95
- set off (debt) 18

deceased 64
deceive 39
- deceptive 39

decision **1**, 50
- decision-making 50

decree 127
- decree absolute 127
- decree nisi 127
- decree of nullity 127

deductible 41
- deduction 54

deed **9**, 65
- deed of variation 65

defamation 58
default 97, 100
default judgment 75

defect 77, 92
– defective 92
– defective goods 92
– defective performance 77
defendant 27, 74, 102, 104
defraud 81
degrading 59
delay 76
delegation of interpretation 50
deliberation 105
deliver 105
delivery **20**, 21, **23**
– delivery (goods) 21
– delivery order 21
demand guarantee 24
demise 64
demonstrate 121
deport **122**, 126
– deportation 126
– deportation order 126
deposit 18, 69, 70
deposition 34
deprivation 122, 125, **126**
– deprivation order 125
– deprive 125
deputy 32, 130
– deputy chief constable 32
– deputy order 130
– deputyship 130
derivation 111, 114
derogable right 57
descent 61
description 38
desertion 31, 127
design **35**, 37, 110, 112, 114
– community design 37
– costume design 37
– design infringement 110
– design right 37, 112
– fashion design 37
– graphic design 37
– industrial design 35
– packaging design 37
– product design 37
– registered community design 37
– registered design 37, 114
– stage design 37
– unregistered community design 37, 112
– unregistered design 37
designation 35
detain 33, **60**, **122**
– detainee 33
detective 32
– detective chief inspector 32
– detective chief superintendent 32
detention 33, **126**
– detention warrant 33
– detention without charge 33
deterrence 27
detrimental 114
devolution 51, 116
– devolved administration 51, 116
direct 37, 101, 111
– direct evidence 111
– direct protection 37
– direct tax 101
directive 1
director 16, 53
– *de facto* director 16
– *de jure* director 16
– shadow director 16
director general of fair trading 18
Director of Public Prosecutions (DPP) 104
disability 59
disaffection 125
discharge **77**, **82**, 86, **95**, **105**
– discharge (duty) 86
disciplinary hearing 119, 121
disclaim 65
disclose 38, 56, 79, **106**
– disclosure 75, 79
discontinue 104
discount 25
discretionary remedy 93
discrimination **56**, 59, 123
– direct discrimination 59
– indirect discrimination 59
– racial discrimination 123
discussion-governance forum 51
disinherit 64
disloyalty 125
dismiss 89, 109, **136**
– dismissal 107, 119
dispense with 73
disposal of assets 65
dispute **2**, 3, 50, 73, 132
– dispute-settlement 50
– disputed will 3, 132

disqualification 16, 95
dissemination 58
dissolution 127
distinctive 114
distinguish 39
distress 91
distribution 19, 36
  – distribution right 36
  – distributor 19
  – distributorship agreement 19
district judge 103
dividend 14
division 3
divorce 127
  – divorce settlement 127
DNA 34
dock 106
document of title 21
domestic agreement 10
domestic violence 3
dominant tenement 67
donate 130
  – donee 130
  – donor 130
double-barrelled name 62
draft 7, 15, 97
  – draft (articles) 15
dramatic 36
draw 22
  – drawee 22
  – drawer 22
drawing 38
due 94
due process right 59
duress 80, 104, 132
duty of care 30, 55, **86**
  – duty of care (to someone) 86
  – owe (duty of care) 86
duty of household expense 62
duty solicitor 33
duty-interest test 89
dwelling 25

E

early 38
earnings 25
  – earning capacity 129
easement 67
eco-auditing tool 51
economic 36, 52, 54, 80
  – economic development 52
  – economic duress 80
  – economic reality 54
  – economic right 36
educational programme 118
EEA family permit 124
effect 1
  – directly effective 1
  – effective 1
  – have (effect) 1
  – horizontal direct effect 1
  – vertical direct effect 1
egg-shell skull principle 88
elect 99
embezzlement 29
emergency 46, 131
  – emergency protection order 131
  – emergency treatment 46
emission standard 51
empanel 105
employment 4, 47, 53, 119, 120
  – employer 53
  – employers' liability 47
  – Employment Appeal Tribunal (EAT) 120
  – Employment Tribunal (ET) 4, 120
  – unemployment benefit 119
  – voluntary redundancy 119
enactment 92
encumbrance 133
endeavour 116
endorsement **21**, 41, 97
  – endorse 41, 97
  – endorser 22
  – general endorsement 22
endowment policy 43
enforce 1, 4, 7, 9, 23, 50, 71, **122**, 123, 126, 128
  – enforceable 7, 9, 23, 50
  – enforced removal 123
  – enforcement 4, 126, 128, 136
  – enforcement mechanism 50
  – enforcement notice 71
  – enforcement order 4
ensue 118
entail 83
entitlement 37, **57**
  – entitlement right 37
entrepreneur 36

entry 122, 124
- entry certificate 124
- entry clearance officer 122
- entry clearance operation 124

environment 49, 50, 51, 52, 116, 117, 118
- environment tribunal 117
- environmental auditing 51
- environmental campaign 118
- environmental crime 116
- environmental development 52
- environmental domain-based workshop 51
- environmental education 52
- environmental footprint 51
- environmental governance 50
- environmental issues 49
- environmental management standard 51
- environmental offender 118
- environmental policy 116
- environmental quality 50
- environmental regulation 52, 116, 117, 118
- environmental standard 51

equal pay 56
equity **2**, 24, 68, **73**
- equitable charge 24
- equitable interest in land 68

escape route 55
escrow agreement 10
establish (elements of negligence) 86
estate 62, 64, 65, 67, 95
- estate accounts 65

estoppel 9, **20**, **133**
- estop 9, 20, 133
- promissory estoppel 9

European 1, 38
- European Central Bank (ECB) 1
- European Coal and Steel Community (ECSC) 1
- European Community (EC) 1
- European Council 1
- European Parliament (EP) 1
- European patent 38
- European Union (EU) 1

euthanasia 60
eviction **70**, 134, 135, 136
- evict 134
- eviction order 135, 136

evidence 21, 34, 74
examination-in-chief 75, 106
excess 41
exchange 69
excluded tenancy 136
exclusion order 108
exclusive 19, 38, 110, 112
- exclusive distributorship 19
- exclusive right 18, 38, 110, 112

exculpatory evidence 34
execute **7**, 9, 10
- executed consideration 9
- executed contract 7
- executory consideration 9
- executory contract 7

executor 64, 132
exemption **25**, **113**, 124
- exempt vignette 124

exert 80
exhibit 106
expectation losses 84
expense **55**, 84, 100
- expenditure 84
- expenses incurred in the litigation 100

experimental purpose 113
expression 58
- expressive medium 58

extenuating circumstances 108
extortion 29, 30
extradition 126
extrinsic evidence 12

F

free on board (f.o.b.) 21
- classic f.o.b. contract 21
- f.o.b. contract 21
- f.o.b. contract with additional duties 21
- modern f.o.b. contract 21

fail (establish) 86
fair 59, 82, 89, 111
- fair comment 89
- fair dealing defence 111
- fair procedure 59
- fair solution theory 82
- fair trial 59, 102

faith 20, **59**
- good faith 20

false 36, 79, 89, 91
– false attribution 36
– false imprisonment 91
– false representation 79, 89
– false statement 89
farmer's privilege 113
fast-track application 123
fees 5, 67, **95**
– fee earner 5
– fee simple absolute in possession 67
fiduciary 15, **19**, 79
– fiduciary duty 15
– fiduciary relationship 79
file 15, 38, **99**
– file (accounts) 15
– filing 38
financial 14, 22, 25, 129
– financial assistance 14
– financial instrument 22
– financial order 129
– financial year 25
fine 107, 108
fingerprint 34, 124
– fingerprint check 124
fire 55
– fire extinguisher 55
– fire regulation 55
firm 5, 13
first instance 103
first reporting event 123
first to file 38
first-tier 117
fiscal instrument 52
fisheries 52
fixed charge 14, 96
fixed penalty notice 118
fixed-term contract 54, 119
fixtures and fittings 44, 69
flexible working 56
floating charge 14, 96
flood 52
– flood defence 52
– flood defence levy 52
fly posting 118
food packaging industry 51
forbearance 9
force majeure 12, **18**, 41
– force majeure insurance 41
foreclosure 24, 135
foreman 105
forensic pathologist 34
foreseeability 86
– foreseeable 86
forfeiture 97, 134
– forfeit 97
forgery 22, **29**
– forge 22
– forger 22
formal agreement 10
foster parents 63, 131
fraud 30, 79, 100, 125
– fraudster 30
– fraudulent misrepresentation 79
– fraudulent trading 30, 100
freedom 57, 89
– freedom of contract 7
– freedom of speech 89
– fundamental freedom 57
– universal freedom 57
freehold 67, **69**, 133
– freehold estate 67
– freehold title 133
frustration 82
– frustrate 82
– frustrating event 82
fuel duty 26
fulfil (criteria) 1
full age 61
full capacity 61
full application 38
full-time hours 53
fundamental mistake 78
furnished 70

G

gazumping 69
gender reassignment 59
general conditions 41
general practitioner (GP) 46
generic use 39
genetic 51, 63, 117
– genetic mother 63
– genetic parentage 63
– genetically modified crops 117
– genetically modified organisms 51, 117
geographical indication 35, 39
gestational mother 63
gift 20
gift with reservation of benefit 64
give (evidence) 24, 106

global endeavour 51
go back on 9
go-slow 60
– go-slow action 121
going concern 98
golden parachute 119
good 9, 16, 39, 61, 89, 91, **133**
– good character 61
– good consideration 9
– good faith 16, 91
– good name 89
– goodwill 39
goods 20, **91**
– existing goods 20
– future goods 20
– goods defined 20
– goods unascertained 20
– intangible goods 24
– specific goods 20
graffiti 118
grant **35**, 52, **65**, 85
– government grant 52
– grant (redress) 85
– lending grant 111
grassroots 52
gratuitous 7
green 49, 52, 117
– green deal 117
– green growth 49, 52
grievance 54, 120
grievous bodily harm 28
gross (economics) 47, 54
– gross profit 47
– gross wage 54
gross (law) 28, 119
– gross misconduct 119
– gross negligence manslaughter 28
ground 60
grounds 87, 136
Group Litigation Order (GLO) 75
guarantee 24
guardian 63, 130
guideline 38, 50

H

habitat 49
handling (stolen goods) 29
harassment 28, 136
hard law 49, 50
hardship 18, **136**
harm 55, 89, **116**
– harm (reputation) 89
hazard 49, 51, **55**
– hazardous 51
– hazardous waste management 49
head office 15
health **46**, 55
– health and safety policy 55
hearing **5**, 136
– hear 5
hearsay 34
heir 64, 66
Her Majesty's Armed Forces 31
Her Majesty's Revenue and Customs (HMRC, HM Revenue & Customs) 13, 25, 53
hereditament 66
high treason 59
highway 90
hire 20
– hire purchase 20
hold 88
– hold (liable) 88
– hold (negligent) 88
holder 21, **22**
– holder (of the BOL) 21
holographic will 64
Home Office 122
homicide 28
house/home 25, 53, 62, 70, 71, 129, 136
– home-maker 129
– homeworker 53
– household 62
– household allowance 62
– housing association 70
– housing association tenant 136
– housing benefit 25, 71
human endeavour 35
human rights 57, 61

I

illegal 30, 81, **90**
– illegal contract 81
– illegal gratuity 30
illegitimate 80
immigration 61, **122**, 124, 126
– immigration law 61, 122, 123, 124, 126
– Immigration Officer 122
– Immigration Removal Centre 126

immunity 121
implement 1, **74**, **97**, 51
– fail (implement) 1
– implementation 74, 97
– implementation method 51
– incorrectly (implement) 1
impose 59
impropriety 80
in-house 5, 40
inception date 41
inchoate offence 27
incidental use 111
incite 27
income 25, 101, **129**
– income tax 25, 101
incorporate 13, **92**
– incorporated business structure 13
– incorporation 92
incorporeal hereditament 66
INCOTERMS 21
inculpatory evidence 34
incur 82
indemnity **24**, 47, 55, 81
– indemnify 55
– indemnity clause 81
– indemnity period 47
independent contractor 53
indict 27, **103**, 106
– indictable offence 27, 103
– indictment 106
indirect protection 37
individual right 57
individual character 37
individual voluntary arrangement (IVA) 97
indoctrination 58
induce 11, 77, 79
– inducement 79
industrial 29, 35, 47, 55, 121
– industrial accident 55
– industrial action 121
– industrial espionage 29
– Industrial Injuries Disablement Benefit 55
– industrial property 35
– industrial risks 47
inequality 59
infanticide 28
inference 111
informed user 37
infringe 1, **110**, 111, 112, 113, 114
– infringement 110, 111, 112, 113, 114
– infringement proceeding 1
– infringer 110, 111, 113, 114
– infringing material 110
inheritance 62, 64, **65**, 101
– inherit 62, 64, 65
– inheritance law 64
– inheritance tax 101
inhumane 59
injunction 85, 93, 117, **133**
– injunction order 110
– interim injunction 93
– interlocutory injunction 93
– final injunction 93
– grant (injunction) 93
– mandatory injunction 93
– perpetual injunction 93
– prohibitory injunction 93
– seek (injunction) 93
injury 28, 55
innocent 79, 102
– innocent misrepresentation 79
– innocent until proven guilty 102
Inns of court 5
inquisitorial system 102
insanity 104
insolvency 3, **94**
– Individual Insolvency Register (IIR) 94
– insolvency law 94
– insolvency practitioner (IP) 94
– insolvency procedures 94
– insolvent 94
inspector 32
instalment 93, 129
instructions 6
insurance 21, 25, 40, 41, 42, 43, 44, 45, 46, 47, 48, 75
– after the event insurance (AEI) 75
– agricultural risk insurance 42
– aviation insurance 42
– bedroom-rated home insurance 44
– buildings insurance 44
– business interruption insurance 47
– commercial and industrial risk insurance 42
– comprehensive car insurance 45
– contents insurance 44
– contractors' all risks insurance 48
– convertible insurance 43

– credit insurance 42
– decreasing-term life insurance policy 43
– force majeure insurance 41
– general insurance 42
– group insurance 42
– health insurance 42
– home insurance 44
– insurance certificate 21
– insured 40
– joint life insurance 43
– legal expenses insurance (LEI) 42, 75
– level premium insurance 43
– level-term insurance 43
– liability insurance 42
– life-related insurance 42
– long-term insurance 42
– machinery breakdown insurance 48
– marine insurance 42
– National Insurance contributions (NIC) 25
– non-life insurance 42
– non-marine insurance 42
– personal lines insurance 44
– personal (lines) risk insurance 42
– private medical insurance (PMI) 46
– property insurance 42
– reinsurance 40
– reinsure 40
– special risk insurance 42
– sum-insured buildings insurance 44
– term insurance 43
– third party car insurance 45
– third party, fire and theft car insurance 45
– unit-linked insurance 43
– universal life insurance 43
– whole-of-life insurance 43
– without profit insurance policy 43

integrated management 52
integration test 54
integrity right 36
intellectual property 3, **35**
intended purpose114
intention 10, **27**, 91
– intentional tort 91
– oblique intention 27
interim 93, 131
– interim care order 131
– interim payment 93
international 21, 38, 49, 51
– international environmental law 49
– international framework 51
– international patent classification 38
– international principle 49
– international sale 21
international law 49
– private international law 49
– public international law 49
interpretation 18
intestate 62, 64, 65
intimate search 33
intoxication 104
invalidate 126
invention **35**, 38, 113
– inventive step 38
invitation 8
– invitation to tender 8
– invitation to treat 8
invoice 21
Iris recognition 124
irrebuttable 10, **80**
– irrebuttable presumption 10
irreconcilable differences 127
irretrievable breakdown 127
island status 122
ISO 51
issue **2**, 3, 14, **55**, **74**, **105**
– issue (legal proceedings) 85
– issuing bank 17
item 35

J

job 54, 119
– job insecurity 54
– Job Seeker Allowance (JSA) 119
joint liability 13, 88
– joint and several liability 13, 88
joint residence order 128
joint tenancy 135
judge **4**, 107
– Judge Advocate 107
judicial 3, 76, 127
– Judicial Committee of the Privy Council 3
– judicial review 76
– Judicial separation 127
– judiciary 2
jurisdiction 2, 3, 115, 117

jury 105
- juror 105
- jury box 105
- jury room 105
- jury tampering 105
- swear in a jury 105

Justice of the Peace 103
justification 89
juxtaposed controls 124

K

key contract 54
kickback 30
kidnapping 28
kinship 63
knowledge 35, 52
- knowledge hub 52

Kyoto Protocol 51

L

labelling 51
labour 35, 53
- labour market 53

lack 125
laissez-faire (doctrine of) 7
land 49, **66**, 69, 101, 117, 133
- land charges register 133
- land management process 49
- land register 66
- land registry 133
- land registry search 69
- landfill tax 101, 117

landlord 70, 90, 91, 134
landowner 91
lapse of offer 8
Lasting Power of Attorney (LPA) 130
launch 51
Law Lords 2
Law School 5
Law Society 5
lawfulness 76
lay 119
layout 35
leapfrog 3
lease 67, 69, **133**
- leasehold 69
- leasehold estate 67
- lessee 67
- lessor 67

leave 3, 75, 95, 109
legal aid 75, 102
legal costs 93, 102
legal default rule 18
legal entity 8, 13
legal estate 68
legal field 2
legal obligation 50, 85, 106
legal professional privilege 75
legal regime 39
legal relations 10
legal sanction 50, 58, 59, 74, 75, 116
legal title 68
legalese 73
legality 49
legislator 2
lending right 36
letter 18, 24, 74, 110
- letter before action 110
- letter of claim 74
- letter of comfort 24
- letter of credit 24
- letter of intent 18
- letter of pledge 24

liability 1, **18**, 27, 47, 55, 62, 64, 85, 86, 88, 92, 94, 118, 121
- corporate liability 118
- liabilities 62, 64, 94
- liable (tort) 86
- products liability 47
- public liability 47
- secondary liability 88
- several liability 88
- state liability 1
- strict liability 27
- tortious liability 121
- vicarious liability 9, 55, 88, 118

libel 58, 89
library use defence 111
licence 3, 4, **68**, 69, **70**, **91**, **110**, 133
- licence by estoppel 133
- licensed conveyancer 4, 69
- licensee 133
- licensing 3

lien 20, **24**
- general lien 24
- special lien 24
- right of lien 20

life imprisonment 108
life interest 64
likelihood 114, 123
limitation period 74, 90

limited right 57
liquidation **94**, 95
– liquidator 95
list 13, 69, 95, 121
– listed 69
– listed company 13
– listing 121
– priority list 95
– waiting list 46
– white list 123
literary work 36
litigation **2**, 6, **73**, 75, **76**
– litigant 6, 73
– litigant in person 75
– litigator 73
littering 29, 118
Lloyd's Name 40
loan 14, **24**
– loan capital 14
– loan credit 24
local authority search 69
local custom 12
Local Social Services Authority (LSSA) 130
lock-out agreement 18
lodger 70, 72
long-term contract 54
looting 31
Lord Chancellor 2
loss **84**, 93
– loss of amenity 84, 93
– loss of earning capacity 93
loyalty 56
lump sum 43, 93, 129

M

magistrate 3, 4, **103**
– magistrates' court 3, 4, 103
maintenance 48, **71**, **127**, 132
– maintenance period 48
maker 23
malice 27, 89, 90
malicious falsehood 89
maliciousness 27
managed migration 122
mandate 23, 116
mandatory 59
mandatory **93**, 108
– mandatory sentence 108
manslaughter **28**
– involuntary manslaughter 28
– voluntary manslaughter 28
marine pollution control 49
marital 62, 104, 127
– marital breakdown 127
– marital coercion 104
– marital property 62
market value 45
marriage 62, 127
– marriage breakdown 62
– marriage certificate 62
– marriage register 62
– non-marriage 127
– wedlock 62
married couple's allowance 25
mate's receipt 21
material **36**, 79
– material fact 79
materialise 123
maternity leave 56
matrimonial home 62
means 113
mediation 74, 120
meeting of the minds 8
members' voluntary liquidation (MVL) 99
membership 16, **121**
– membership right 16
memorandum of association 15
mental 27, 87, 93
– *mens rea* 27
– mental anguish 93
– mental condition 87
merchandise 20, 112
– merchantability 20
merge **2**
– merger 2
merits 76, 93
– unmeritorious 76
– upon the merits 93
Metropolitan Police Service 32
MI5 (Military Intelligence section 5) 32
MI6 (Military Intelligence section 6) 32
military law 27, 31
minimum right 59
Ministry of Defense Police (MDP) 32
mirror-image rule 8
miscarriage of justice 103, 109
misconception 78

misconduct 31, **56**, **119**
- misconduct of operations 31
mislead 39
misrepresentation 39, 79, 84
- misrepresent 79
mistake 78, 104
common mistake 78
- mistake as to quality 78
- mistake as to the existence of the subject matter 78
- mistake as to the identity (of the other party) 78
misunderstanding 78
- misunderstand 78
misuse (assets) 16
mitigating factor 108
money 129
- money earner 129
- money laundering 29
- money order 136
monopoly 38
moral rights 36
mortgage 3, 14, **24**, **67**, **69**, 135
- mortgage lender 135
- mortgagee 14, 67, 69
- mortgager 3, 67
- mortgagor 14, 67, 69, 135
murder 28
musical work 36
mutiny 31

N

named driver 45
national 61
naturalisation 61
national minimum wage 53
nature 49, 52, 90
- natural hasards 90
- natural resource 49
- natural resource base 52
Naval Service 31
necessity 88, 104
negative obligation 58, 59
negligence 6, 55, 56, 85, **86**, 79
- negligent 6
- negligent misrepresentation 79
negotiable 22
neighbouring right 36
net wage 54
new-for-old replacement value 44
no-reflective loss principle 100
noise 49, 51
- noise control 49
- noise level 51
non est factum 84
non-departmental public body 52
non-derogable right 57
non-governmental organisation 50
non-indictable offence 27, 103
non-molestation order 62
non-regulated tenancy 70
non-resident parent 128
norm 38, 111
- relevancy norm 111
notice 21, 41, 54, 62, 71, 106, 136
- notice of appropriation 21
- notice of marriage 62
- notice of opposition 106
- notice period 41, 54, 71
- notice to quit 136
novation 11, 15
novelty 37, 38
nuclear family 63
nuisance 58, 90
- private nuisance 90
- public nuisance 90
null and void 10
nursing 46

O

oath 61
obiter dicta 2
objective test 8
obligate 57
obstruct 106
- obstructing operations 31
occupational sick pay 56
occupier 90, 91
occurrence 41
offence 3, 27, 28, 29, 103
- offence against property 27, 29
- offence against the person 27, 28
- offence triable either-way 27, 103
- offences against the state 27
- offender 27
offer 8
- offeree 8
- offeror 8

office 16, 53
- office (of a director) 16
- office holder 53
- office of fair trading 18
- Office of the Public Guardian 130
- officer 16

official receiver 94
ombudsman 74, 76, 115
omission 27, 59
on the merits 76
on-going 60
one-off guarantee 24
onerous **81**, **82**, 92
- onerous clause 92

onus 85
opening speech 106
operative 78
opinion 1
order 21, 22, 24, 75, 127
- order bill (of lading) 21
- order for costs 75
- order for financial provision 127
- order of sale 24
- order to pay 22

ordinary resolution 16
ordinary trademark 39
original 36, 111
- original creation 36
- originality criterion 111

outsourced 60
outstanding **18**, 95
- outstanding monies 95

overdraft 14
override 73, 133, **135**
- overriding 133
- overriding objective 73

overseas 122
overstaying 122
own 20, 35, 38, **66**, 91
- owner 91
- ownership 20, 35, 38, 66
- rightful owner 84, 91

P

pact 50
paid holiday 54
pain and suffering 93
panel deputy 130
paralegal 4
parent 56, 62, 63
- parentage 63
- parental leave 56
- parental order 63
- parental responsibility 62, 63
- parenthood 63

parliamentary 36, 58
- parliamentary copyright 36
- parliamentary privilege 58

parol 10, 12
- parol contract 10
- parol evidence rule 12

parole 108
part payment 20
part-time 53
partnership 3, 5, **13**, **51**
- partner 5, 13

pass **5**, 16, 21
- pass (property) 21
- pass (resolution) 16

passing off 39
passive euthanasia 60
past consideration 9
patent **35**, 38, 110, 113
- British patent 38
- cooperative patent classification 38
- patent agent 38
- patent infringement 110, 113
- patent specification 110
- patentable subject matter 38
- patented 113
- patented invention 38
- patentee 38, 113

paternity 36, 56
- paternity leave 56
- paternity right 36

pay/payment 22, 24, 26, 54, 75, 93, 129
- Pay As You Earn (PAYE) 26, 54
- pay slip 54
- payee 22
- payment default 24
- payment into court (Part 36 payment) 75
- payment on account 93
- periodic payment 129
- periodical payment order 93

pecuniary 64, 84
- pecuniary legacy 64
- pecuniary loss 84

pedagogical purposes 111
pension scheme 54

performance 18, 23, 36, 77, 82, 84, 119, 133
– part-performance 77, 82
– partial performance 77
– performance bond 23
– performance guarantees 23
– poor performance 119
– public performance right 36
– specific performance 73, 84, 133
personal data protection 58
personal injury 92
personal representative 64, 132
pet 70
petitioner 75, 127
physician 46
picketing 60
piracy 110
placement 131
plaintiff 40
planning 76
plea 104, 106
– plea in mitigation 106
plead 6, 75, **104**
pleadings 6, 75
pledge 24, 61
pointless 82
police 32, 33
– Police Community Support Officer (PCSO) 32
– police constable 32
– police interview 33
– police officer 32
– police station 33
policy 40, **50**, 51
– policy coordination 51
policyholder 41
political scientist 116
political right 60
pollution 51, 116
– polluter pays principle 51, 116
– pollution-reducing technology 51, 116
positive obligation 58, 59
possession order 136
post-nuptial contract 62
post-traumatic stress disorder (**PTSD**) 87
postal acceptance rule 8
practice direction 73
practising certificate 4, 5
pre-action protocol 74
pre-emption right 14
pre-nuptial contract 62
pre-strike ballot 60
precautionary principle 116
– precautionary measure 51
precede 78
precedent 2
precise wording 50
predecessor in title 90
pregnancy 60
preliminary enquiries 69
preliminary reference 1
– give (preliminary ruling) 1
– preliminary ruling 1
– reference (preliminary ruling) 1
premises 70, 91
premium 40
preparatory hearing 106
prepayments 18
prerequisite 98
prescribed disease 55
prescribed method of acceptance 8
prescription 90
press bench 106
presumption 10, 80
– presume 80
prima facie 34, 100
– *prima facie* evidence 34
– *prima facie* test 100
primary infringement 111
– primary infringer 111
primary carer 129
primary legislation 1
primary rights 36
primary victim 87
principal 11, 19, 48
priority 51, 95
– prioritise 51
privacy 58
privileged 89
privity (doctrine of) 11
– privity of contract 11
pro-life advocate 60
proactive regulation 51, 117
probate 65, 132
probation 54, **108**
– probationary period 54
procedural right 57, 59
– procedural guarantee 59
process standard 51
procure 60

product 37, 47, 51, **92**
 – producer 92
 – product standard 51
professional 19, 74
 – professional negligence 74
profits *à prendre* 67, 133
prohibited steps order 128
promise 7
 – promisee 7
 – promisor 7
promissory note 23
property 3, **20**, 36, 47, **58**, **66**, 129, 133
 – property adjustment order 129
 – property law 3, 66
 – property rights 36
 – proprietary 133
 – proprietary rights 66
 – real property 47, 66
proponent 60
proposal form 41
prosecution 55, **59**, **102**, 104
 – prosecutor 104
protected 39, 59, 111
 – protected characteristic 59
 – protected designation (of origin) 39
 – protected geographical indication 39
 – protected parts 111
protocol 50, 58, 59, 60
provision 12, 54, 56, 116
proximity 87
proxy 16
public 27, 36, 47, 51, 81, 89, 116, 125
 – public domain 36
 – public figure 89
 – public funding 51
 – public good 125
 – public order 27
 – public participation principle 51, 116
 – public performance right 36
 – public policy 36, 81
publication 36, 38, **89**
 – publication stage 38
 – publication right 36
 – published edition 36
 – unpublished 36
pull out 69
pupil 5
purchaser 69
pure economic loss 87
purpose 74
pursuant to 2
 – pursuant to a law 92

Q

qualified 1, 5, 57, **89**
 – qualified majority voting 1
 – qualified privilege 89
 – qualified right 57
quality standard 51
quantum meruit 84
quash 109
Queen's Counsel (QC) 5
quiet enjoyment (land) 90
quorum 16

R

rape 28
ratio decidendi 2, 47
re-engagement 120
re-examination 75, 106
realise 14, **95**, 96
 – realised profits 14
reasonable 18, **81**, 86
 – reasonable man 86
 – reasonableness 18
rebut 10
 – rebuttable presumption 10
receipt for the goods 21
receiver 95
recipient 82
recklessness 27
recommendation 1
reconcile 116
recoverable 82
rectification 78, 132
 – rectify 132
red-handed 33
redistribute 129
redress 85
 – seek (redress) 85
reduction 107
redundancy 119
 – redundancy package 119
refrain 57
refugee 122, 123
registration 13, **15**, 37, **38**, **61**, 112
 – register of charges 14
 – register office 62
 – registered owner 66

– registered trademark 35, 114
– Registrar of Marriages 62
regulate 35
regulated tenancy 70
regulation 1
regulatory standards 116
rehabilitation 27
reinstatement 120
reject 20
relapse 108
relationship of trust 80
release 33, 96
reliability of evidence 34
relief 25
religious ceremony 62
rely (provision) 1
remand 60, 106
remedial expenditure 90
remedy 1, 2, **85**
– apply (remedy) 85
– award (remedy) 85
– entitle (remedy) 85
– get (remedy) 1
– grant (remedy) 85
– have (remedy) 1
– offer (remedy) 85
– seek (remedy) 1
removal 16, 61
remuneration 54
render 78
renewal notice 41
rent 36, **134**
– rental right 36
replacement-as-new value 44
repossession 135
representation **12**, **79**
– representation by conduct 79
– representation of fact 79
– representation of law 79
– representee 79
– representor 79
reprimand 33
reproduction **111**, 36
– reproduction right 36
repudiation **83**
– repudiatory breach 83
reputation 114
requirement 35, 36, 59, 113, 114
requisition 102
rescission **84**
– rescind 84
reserved 75
residence **61**, 63, **127**, 128
– residence order 63, 128
– resident parent 128
residue 64
resignation **16**, 119
– resign 119
resolution 16, 99
resource management 116
respondent 75, 109, 127
restitution **84**, 93
– *restitutio in integrum* 93
restrictive 69, 71, 111, **133**
– restricted act 111
– restrictive covenant 69, 71
retailer 19
retirement 16
retraining program 119
retribution 27
retrospective law 59
revenue 3, 25
reverse 109
revoke 8, **64**
– revocation of offer 8
right 6, 24, 67, 69, 84, 90, 127
– right of contact 127
– right of subrogation 24
– right of way 67, 69, 90
– rightful 84
– rights of audience 6
Rio Declaration 51
risk 40, 55
robbery 29
Royal Air Force 31
Royal Marines 31
Royal Navy 31
ruling 2

S

safe country 123
safeguard 59
salary 54
sales 24, 79
– sales credit 24
– sales talk 79
sanctions-based approach 118
scepticism 58
schedule 41
Schengen zone 122

scope 116
screening interview 123
seal 10
search 33
– search warrant 33
seasonal worker 53
secondary infringement 111
secondary legislation 1
secondary victim 87
Secretary of State for Justice 104
security 14, 24, **33**, 70, **96**
– consensual real security 24
– non-possessory real security 24
– personal security 24
– possessory real security 24
– real security 24
– secured 24
– secured creditor 96
– secured debenture 14
– security of tenure 70
seizure 24, **3333**
selective distributorship 19
self-assessment 26
self-defence 104
self-employed 19, 53
– self-employed worker 53
self-help 18
seller 19
sentence 27, 59, 104, 105
sergeant 32
Serious Fraud Office (SFO) 32
serve 4, 75, **95**, 136
– serve on 75, 136
service 4, 31, 35, 69, 95, 107
– service charges 69
– service discipline 31
– service marks 35
– service offence 31
– service person 31
– serviceman 31
servient tenement 67
set aside (a contract) 77
settle 18, **44**, **64**, **74**
– settle (dispute) 18
settlement 44, 74, 132
sever 81, 118
– severability clause 81
– severance 81
– severance payment 119
sexual assault 28
share 14, 16
– preference shares 14
– share capital 14
– shareholder 16
shared parenting 127
sheriff 4
ship 21
– on board a ship 21
– received for shipment bill (of lading) 21
– ship's rail 21
– shipped 21
– shipped on board 21
shoplifting 29
shortfall 46
sibling 64
sign 39
skeleton argument 75
skill 56
slander 58, 89
smoothly 2
Social Services 131
soft law 49
sole 5, 13, 19
– sole distributorship 19
– sole practitioner 5, 13
– sole proprietor 13
– sole trader 13
solicitor 4, 6
– solicitor-advocate 6
solvency 94, **99**
– solvent 94, 99
sound 36, **51**
– sound recording 36
span 36
Special branch 32
special constable 32
special endorsement 22
special relationship 87
special resolution 16
specialty agreement 10
specific issue order 128
speech 58
spouse 62
squatting 135
staff 53
stamp duty 26, **69**, 101
– stamp duty land tax 101
– stamp duty land tax (SDLT) 26
– stamp duty reserve tax (SDRT) 26
standard authorisation 130

standard of living 129
standing 76
stare decisis 2
state 25, 58, 125
- state pension 25
- state surveillance 58
- stateless 125
statement 15, 51, 75, **79**
- statement of compliance 15
- statement of need 51
- statement of truth 75
statute **2**, 17, 53, 54, 56, 92, 93, **95**, 100, 126
- statutory 2, 92, 95, 126
- statutory damages 93
- statutory demand 95
- statutory derivative claim 100
- statutory implied term 17
- Statutory Maternity Pay 56
- Statutory Paternity Pay 56
- statutory protection 54
- statutory provisions 92
- statutory sick pay 53, 54
stenographer 106
stepfamily 63
stop 23, 33
- stop (cheque) 23
- stop and search 33
strand 59
strict settlement 68
strike (n.) 58, 60, 121
strike (v.) 81, 99
- strike off 99
- strike out 81
sub-contractor 48, 53
subject matter 81
submissions 75
subrogation 115
subside 44
subsidence 44
substantiality question 111
substantive 38, 57, 73, 112, 123
- substantive examination 38
- substantive infringement 112
- substantive interview 123
- substantive law 73
- substantive rights 57
succeed 85, 86
- succeed (defendant) 85
- succeed (negligence suit) 86
suicide pact 27
summary 27, 75, 103, 107, 119
- summary dismissal 119
- summary hearing 107
- summary judgment 75
- summary offence 27, 103
summing up 105
summon up 95
summons 102, 105
superintendent 32, 62
- Superintendent registrar 62
supervision order 108, 131
supplier 19
Supreme Court of the United Kingdom (UKSC) 2, 3, 73, 103
surety 24
surgery 46
surrogacy 63
- surrogacy arrangement 63
- surrogate mother 63
surveyor 135
surviving spouse 64
suspect 33
suspend 108, **136**
- suspended prison sentence 108
sustainable development 49, 51, 116
switch 124

T

tackle 51
take the oath 105, 106
tangible 35
tarnish (reputation) 89
tax **3**, **25**, 26, 52, 69, 71, 101, 117
- annual tax on enveloped dwellings (ATED) 26
- capital gains tax 101
- child tax credit 25
- corporation tax 26, 101
- council tax 25, 71
- direct tax 101
- income tax 25, 101
- indirect tax 101
- inheritance tax 101
- landfill tax 101, 117
- personal tax year 25
- poll tax 25
- stamp duty 26, **69**, 101
- tax avoidance 101
- tax credit 4, 25
- tax evasion 101

– tax planning 101
– tax relief 101
– tax return form 26
– taxation of pollution 52
– taxman 25
– taxpayer 25
– Value Added Tax (VAT) 26
– working tax credit 26
telecommuting 53
temporary work agency 53
tenancy **5**, **67**, **70**, 72, 134, 135
– tenancy deposit protection (TDP) 72
– tenancy in common 135
– tenant 5, 67, 70
– tenement 67
tender 8
term **12**, 17, 18, 21, 67, 83
– common law implied term 17
– express term 12, 17
– implied term 12
– INCOTERMS 21
– innominate term 83
– minimum terms 18
– standard terms of business 18
– statutory implied term 17
– term implied by usage 12
– term implied in fact 12
– term implied in law 12
– term of years absolute 67
– Unfair Contract Terms Unit (UCTU) 18
– unfair standard term 18
termination 83, 54, **127**
– terminate 83
– termination of contract 54
testator 64
testify 34, 106
theft 29
– thief 29
thing in action 14
third party 11, 19, 38, 118
thought 58
threat 80
threshold 25, 26
time-barred 74, 76, 90
title **20**, 66, 69, 91, 135
– title plan 135
– title to goods
– title to land 66, 67, 91
– title to property 69
tort 3, **85**, 118, 121
– tortfeasor 85
track 3
trade **24**, 39, 54, 60, **99**, 121
– trade dispute 60
– trade symbols 39
– trader 39
trade union 54, 121
trademark 35, 39, 110, 114
– trademark infringement 110
traditional speciality guaranteed 39
trainee 5, **53**, 55
– training 55
trans-boundary harm 51
transfer document 69
transferable 21, 22
– transferor 22
transmission 61
transport document 21
treason 31
treaty 1, 49, 50
trespass **58**, 90, 91
– trespass to goods 91
– trespass to land 91
– trespass to the person 91
– trespasser 90
trial 75, 106
trial period 54
trivial 83
trust **19**, 68, 95
– trust of land 68
– trustee 68, 95
try 103
turnover 47
TV licence 71

U

uberrimae fidei 41
ultra vires 16
unaided senses 87
unauthorised migrant 122
unborn 60
undefended divorce 127
undertake 9, 23
– undertaking 23
underwrite 40
– underwriter 40
undischarged 95
undue influence 80, 132

unfair 81, 100, 119, 120
- unfair dismissal 119, 120
- unfair prejudicial conduct 100

unilateral 7, 8, 78
- unilateral contract 7
- unilateral mistake 78
- unilateral offer 8

United Kingdom classification 38
unjust enrichment 84
unpaid work requirement 128
unreasonable behaviour 127
update 73
uphold 109
upkeep 129
urban planning 37
urgent authorisation 130
usher 105, 106
utilities 47, 69

V

vandalism 29
vendor 69
venire 105
verdict 105
vest (power) 16
visa 124
visibility 37
visitor 91
vitiating factor 77
void 14, 77, 81, 127
- void *ab initio* 81
- void marriage 127
- voidable 77
- voidable marriage 127

voluntary bankruptcy 99
voluntary group 51
voluntary liquidation 99
voluntary placement 131
voluntary return 123, 126

W

wage 54
waiting period 61
waive 8
- waiver 8

warning 33, 119
warrant 33, 136
warranty 83
waste disposal 117, 118
water 49, 52
- water regulation 49
- water resources 52

wear and tear 44, 72
welfare 128, 131
wildlife conservation 49
win (case) 85
wind up 65, 95, 98
- winding up order 95
- winding up petition 98

withdraw 8
- withdrawal 8

witness 10, 34, 75, 87, 106
- witness (incident) 87
- witness box 106
- witness statement 75
- witness summons 106

work 26, 53, 54, 55, 60, 121
- work-to-rule 60, 121
- worker 53
- working hours 54
- working tax credit 26
- workplace 55

write off 45
written statement of particulars 54
wrongdoing 56
wronged party 83
wrongful 100, **111**, 120
- wrongful dismissal 120
- wrongful trading 100

Y

yield 14
youth court 103

Z

zero-hour contract 54

PHOTOCOMPOSITION
SCM • Toulouse

713727 - (II) - OSB-A 80 g - SCM - HCH

Achevé d'imprimer sur les presses de Snel
Z.I. des Hauts-Sarts - Zone 3
Rue Fond des Fourches 21 – B-4041 Vottem (Herstal)
Tél +32(0)4 344 65 60 - Fax +32(0)4 286 99 61
Réimpression en décembre 2014 – 68008

Dépôt légal : avril 2014

Imprimé en Belgique